"Something Urgent
I Have to Say to You"

"Something Urgent I Have to Say to You"

THE LIFE AND WORKS OF
WILLIAM CARLOS WILLIAMS

Herbert Leibowitz

FARRAR, STRAUS AND GIROUX   NEW YORK

Farrar, Straus and Giroux
18 West 18th Street, New York 10011

Grateful acknowledgment is made to New Directions Publishing Corp. and Carcanet
Press Ltd. for permission to reprint excerpts from the following previously published
works by William Carlos Williams: *Autobiography*, copyright © 1948, 1951 by William
Carlos Williams. *Collected Poems Volume I* and *Volume II*, copyright © 1938 by New
Directions Publishing Corp., copyright © 1944, 1953, 1962 by William Carlos Williams,
copyright © 1982, 1986, 1988 by Paul H. Williams and William Eric Williams. *Imagi-
nations*, copyright © 1974 by Florence H. Williams. *Paterson*, copyright © 1946, 1948,
1949, 1958 by William Carlos Williams. *In the American Grain*, copyright © 1933 by
William Carlos Williams. *Pictures from Brueghel*, copyright © 1954, 1955, 1962 by William
Carlos Williams. *Pound/Williams Letters*, copyright © 1957 by William Carlos Williams.
A Voyage to Pagany, copyright © 1970 by New Directions Publishing Corp. *White Mule*,
copyright © 1937 by New Directions Publishing Corp. *Yes, Mrs. Williams*, copyright © 1959
by William Carlos Williams. All works by William Carlos Williams used by permission
of New Directions Publishing Corp. and Carcanet Press Ltd.

Unless otherwise indicated, all photographs are used with the permission of
New Directions Publishing Corp.

Library of Congress Cataloging-in-Publication Data
Leibowitz, Herbert
    "Something urgent I have to say to you" : the life and works of William Carlos
Williams / Herbert Leibowitz. — 1st ed.
        p.   cm.
    Includes bibliographical references and index.
    ISBN 978-0-374-11329-2 (alk. paper)
    1. Williams, William Carlos, 1883–1963.   2. Poets, American—20th
century—Biography.   I. Title.

PS3545.1544 Z619 2011
811'.52—dc22
[B]
                                                                    2010046548

Designed by Jonathan D. Lippincott

www.fsgbooks.com

1   3   5   7   9   10   8   6   4   2

For Gabe, Francesca, and Julian
and
In memory of James Laughlin

Contents

Overture to William Carlos Williams's
Danse Américaine

I.

Randall Jarrell, a notoriously hard-to-please critic, called William Carlos Williams the "America of Poets," an extravagant compliment usually reserved exclusively for Walt Whitman. Despite his many-sided and contradictory nature, Williams lacked Whitman's ebullient self-approbation; and while he shared his predecessor's openness to experience, he would never have boasted, "I contain multitudes." If Williams sometimes protested being glibly paired with Whitman as a practitioner of free verse, he fully grasped the radical importance of the older poet's "language experiments" in *Leaves of Grass*; he just wanted to get out from under the long shadow Godfather Walt cast. Whitman's poetic rhetoric, derived in part from the Bible, the Psalms in particular, appropriately represented nineteenth-century American democracy in all its gritty and lyrical oppositions. "*Leaves of Grass*," Williams wrote, "was a challenge to the entire concept of the poetic idea and from a new viewpoint, a rebel viewpoint, an American viewpoint. In a word and at the beginning it enunciated a shocking truth, that the common ground is of itself a poetic source to be dealt with, if a man were able, fundamentally from a democratic viewpoint." So Whitman's voice ranges from celebratory chants, "buzz'd whispers," and "barbaric yawps" to historical elegy (the Alamo, "the horrors of fratricidal war," and the "hounded slave") and the breaking of taboos about sex. Williams's goal was to make significant twentieth-century stylistic innovations, to pioneer a distinctively American poetic based on speech rhythms. The Irish playwright John Millington Synge had put his ears to the floorboards of a room in the Aran Islands in order to transcribe the lilt and gravity of the neighbors' folk speech and move them into the mouths of his characters.

Williams was equally alert to the varieties of demotic he overheard as he went about visiting patients or stopping for a brief chat with an elderly black man who took pride in keeping the sidewalk in front of his house neat; the razor-sharp cadences of the town pharmacist as he entertained his friends in a Rutherford, New Jersey, luncheonette with an anecdote about a blushing teenager trying to screw up his courage to ask for condoms; an Italian immigrant woman's anxiety about her husband's pneumonia, expressed in halting pidgin English; or the cultivated talk at Alfred Stieglitz's An American Place gallery in Manhattan, where artists gathered to debate Cubism or John Marin's paintings. All found their way into Williams's poems and stories. The question Williams repeatedly turned over in his mind was, How can I represent the diverse realities that surround me in America?

The story of Williams's ambitious desire and long, circuitous struggle to resolve that conundrum and to gain the recognition and respect he craved is a major theme of this biography. He started at a disadvantage that might have scared off poets of a less tenacious will than his: his early efforts were derivative, mawkish, and written as a retrograde Victorian lyric that would have fit snugly into *Palgrave's Golden Treasury,* the anthology from which his father read poems to the family in the parlor of their house at 131 Passaic Avenue in Rutherford. Ezra Pound presciently noted that Williams's "slower mental processes" meant that his poetry would develop erratically and that his influence would be felt in the future. Pound's timeline was correct. As the critic R. W. Flint remarked about Williams's career,

> Consistency in the short run he may have lacked, but stamina and consistency in the long run he surely possessed. Raffish on occasion, unpredictably rebellious in everything, an Aeolian harp to the breezes of modernism, he was also endowed with the same patient watchfulness, tempered with self-distrust, that marked the great Victorians.

The wildly fluctuating opinions of that "unpredictable rebelliousness" were why Williams's reputation as a poet was then and remains today controversial. It irked his detractors, who viewed him as a banal and technically flawed versifier, a monstrous Pied Piper leading countless young poets astray, or an ignorant vandal trashing the glory of English lyric poetry: the iambic pentameter line. (Ironically, it is Pound who recalls in canto 81, "To break the pentameter, that was the first heave.") Blaming Williams is arrant nonsense. He did not regard himself as a Moses leading American poetry out of bondage to the iambic pharaohs and through the wilderness to the borders of a vernacular Promised Land. He used iambic pentameter when it suited him, especially in his three late books of poetry—*The Desert Music, Journey to Love,* and *Pictures from Brueghel*—which John Berryman praised as "the mysterious late excellence which is the crown / of our trials & our last bride." Williams mistrusted systems and doctrinaire rules, including his own makeshift ones, and dissected them with what Robert Lowell called a "hard nervous secular knowingness." What his critics see, however, is not "knowingness" but intellectual muddle, foolish slogans ("no ideas but in things" being labeled the worst offender), and an infatuation with new-fangled forms that expose him as a poet who flunked Basic Prosody.

The most savage attack on Williams's poetry came from England. In a famous—or infamous—review in 1986 of the first volume of *The Collected Poems,* the poet Donald Davie hurled brickbat after brickbat at Williams: he was "the most embarrassing poet in the language," a "dumb ox," "anti-intellectual," "incapable of consecutive thought." His "practice [of poetry] and his belated reputation have debased the dignity of the poetic calling." Davie consigns all but three poems to the rubbish heap. There is something almost phobic in the violence of Davie's ex cathedra judgments. In a humorless misreading of the bagatelle "This Is Just to Say," a favorite of poetry anthologists but hardly a representative example of Williams's art, Davie claims that Williams is unconsciously underwriting "the suburban life style," whatever that may be. Kenneth Koch twitted its ingenuous apology for stealing the plums in the refrigerator:

> I chopped down the house that you had
>   Been saving to live in next summer.
> I am sorry, but it was morning, and I had
>   Nothing to do
> And its wooden beams were inviting.

Had Davie done his homework, he'd have known that Williams was acutely conscious and critical of the stodgy parochialism that suburbs such as Rutherford were capable of. (The town was not without cultured people Davie might have enjoyed talking with.)

Davie did not always loathe Williams's poetry so absolutely. In the essay

"Two Ways Out of Whitman," Williams is not a deplorable "simple-minded," provincial poet guilty of "lax and lawless versification" (one of Dr. Johnson's criticisms of Abraham Cowley's verse) but a cosmopolitan, an "elaborate and sophisticated theorist of poetry," though still rated by Davie a flawed minor poet. It is often asserted that the insular British ear finds it difficult to pick up American rhythms and thus finds Williams's verse "anathema." Charles Tomlinson, who came to Williams's work through D. H. Lawrence's 1925 review of *In the American Grain* reprinted in *Phoenix*, expressed the hope that he'd "be the second Englishman to get you aright." He admitted that "your three-decker cadences are your own and in using them one rapidly discovers one's technical incompetence." Tomlinson had no problem in adjusting to Williams's freewheeling phrasing, which did not scan according to traditional measures, or in hearing his inimitable music.

In every decade, Williams's perfectionist streak left him so dissatisfied with poems that misfired or stammered that he was tougher on himself than his critics were. So he tore up failed designs and started over, looking for ways to push his art in new directions (his preferred term for the process was "improvisation"): playing with the arrangement of words on a line to break open calcified forms; deploying typography and white space to give the page a fresh look; elongating or compressing syntax to avoid verbosity; and using line breaks, enjambment, and punctuation, especially dashes, to syncopate rhythms and avoid monotony. If a poem wheezed, Williams would try to open its airways; if the sounds were too loud or too soft, he'd tinker with the acoustics or remove clumsy repetition. (Seamus Heaney remarked in an interview that Williams had "a very delicate ear," and so he did.) Williams's hard-earned technical advances account for the mercurial range of styles in his poetry. Some poets and readers on both sides of the Atlantic have been confounded by this heterogeneity. Others, such as Jarrell, marveled, *"Why, he'd say anything!"* so long as he believed it was true; after reflection Williams might decide that what he had written was unwieldy or feeble and scrap the poem. (This is standard practice for most poets.) For Jarrell, Williams was a pragmatist in the mold of William James. Facts, not metaphysics, were the foundation of their beliefs. Jarrell did not blind himself to poems that were mediocre or incomplete; they were worth reading because they offered clues to the way Williams's imagination went about its business, just as a scientist's initial notes in his laboratory investigation of brain abnormalities may show the obstacles that must be overcome before a new method of treatment can be approved or deemed unworkable.

Davie claimed that Williams ad-libbed too much, a sign he had no idea where the poem was heading. The reader can indeed sometimes watch Williams groping in the dark for the organization that will weld together words and feelings in a shapely form. (Most poets go through this struggle.) What separates him from other poets is that he was uncommonly frank in acknowledging his failures. In 1925 he was in the grip of one of his periodic funks. It was caused by his friend Kenneth Burke praising T. S. Eliot's poetry and, to rub vinegar into that wound, reviewing *In the American Grain* in the *New York Herald Tribune* coolly. Burke scolded Williams for writing "subjective history," the very charge Williams had labored hard to avoid by inserting pertinent historical documents. (Burke did not single out the prose for commendation either.) Feeling morose and unappreciated, Williams perked up when he opened a letter from a young engineer named John Riordan, who had read Williams's poems with care and who harbored literary ambitions himself. Riordan asked Williams to define modernism, which Williams did by taking a swipe at what it wasn't: the poems of his old bugaboo, T. S. Eliot, "a romantic philotaster" whose "brand of despair" he abhorred. Burke had advised his friend to articulate a poetics, but for Williams the made poem was the articulation. "The actual getting of work upon the page is a very complex mechanism," he explained to Riordan, which required sidestepping stale formulas. In a letter to the young man, he outlined his quandary: "As I exist, omniverous [*sic*], everything I touch seems incomplete until I can swallow digest and make it part of myself . . . But my failure to work inside a pattern—a positive sin—is the cause of my virtues. I cannot work inside a pattern because I can't find a pattern that will have me." Despite his wry confession of "a positive sin," his "failure to work inside a pattern," Williams is not boasting that his talent and ambition are so large that his poems cannot be judged by codified rules; rather, because his poetic goals are fluid and mutable—he shares the modernist's antic pleasure in transgressing against decorum, caution, and received opinion. Experimenting with new forms breeds freedom and intoxicates Williams, like driving down the open road with abandon in his Ford or Buick. Yet pattern, he came to realize, need not stifle the imagination.

2.

Williams's life as a writer was inextricably linked, in concentric circles, to his lifelong residence in Rutherford, where his immigrant parents put down roots in 1882 and he was born the next year; to his immediate family; to his long, successful career practicing medicine, mainly as an obstetrician and pediatrician; and most complex of all, to the seismic events that shook and transformed America: two world wars, a flu pandemic, the fizzy 1920s and the Great Depression that followed it, the Red scares after each war, the oppression of minorities, Prohibition, and women gaining the vote. Williams was the only modernist poet whose politics were of the left. No dandies sporting a monocle or high-toned old Christian women populate his poems and stories. His portraits are of ordinary people: Paterson hat workers walking a picket line, nurses and prostitutes, policemen and religious fanatics, farmers and fish peddlers, drunkards, grifters, and murderers, blues singers and barbers, mothers, fathers, and children. He seldom romanticized those considered marginal in American society; he knew their strengths and weaknesses from intimate contact with their woes, physical and emotional, as he knew the inequities of an unacknowledged class system that left the poor living in squalid slums and scrambling to survive, and as he knew every corner of the ugly industrial landscape in Passaic and Paterson, which spewed black soot from smokestacks and slag from factories into the polluted Passaic River. He diagnosed the diseases of the lungs and heart and liver that poisoned the bodies and mauled the spirit of the common people, whom he seldom referred to as "the masses."

Throughout his adult life Williams was obsessed with defining what it meant to be an American. (He agreed with Henry James that it was "a complex fate.") It fueled his many efforts to discover an American language supple and rugged enough to express the messy, dysfunctional, boastful, contradictory, and incomparable textures and flavors of a country he often despaired of and yet stubbornly believed, against all odds, could produce great art. *Paterson*, the long poem Williams toiled over for thirty years, attempted to compile an encyclopedia of local (New Jersey) history, geology, economics, and folklore. The poet in *Paterson* is a forensic anthropologist who sifts diverse material—city records, geological surveys, old newspapers—to learn how Americans lived and thought, worshipped and loafed, earned a livelihood, wrangled over religion and public morality, sought thrills and instant riches, courted and married. But he is also a strolling troubadour mingling with and aloof from the crowds in a park, transcribing their dreams and superstitions and sexual fumbling. Although Williams admired America's democratic pluralism, he was alarmed by the country's sordid violence and rudderless drift. America is the overt and covert subject of nearly all the experimental works of the 1920s, and the crisis precipitated by the Great Depression is consciously addressed in the poems and stories of the 1930s; it is also a nagging theme of Williams's correspondence.

Williams was born in Rutherford, New Jersey, on September 17, 1883, and died in his bed at 9 Ridge Road on March 4, 1963. We cannot understand the unfolding of his complicated nature or the gradual efflorescence of his poetry or the kind of doctor he became without assessing what Rutherford meant to him as daily reality and metaphor. When his parents moved from Brooklyn to the small suburb the year before Williams was born, the population in the town numbered five thousand; Rutherford was conservative in its politics (predominantly Republican) and in its mores. Over the years, it prospered as a middle-class enclave, attractive to families as a healthy place to raise young children; and because of its proximity to New York City, it was easy for the husbands, the breadwinners, to commute to their offices and get home in time for supper. In 1883, Rutherford was more rustic village than suburban town; the idea of putting down roots in its tranquil village atmosphere may have appealed to William George Williams, because, from the age of five, he had wandered with his mother from London to Puerto Plata in the Caribbean. Traveling often as a salesman for a New York perfume maker, he made Rutherford his safe haven.

In his 1951 *Autobiography*, Williams remembers the town affectionately as a very primitive place:

> No sewers, no water supply, no gas, even. Certainly no electricity; no telephone, not even a trolley car. The sidewalks were of wood, cross-pieces nailed to two-by-fours laid on the ground; cracks between the boards in which yellow jackets nested to swarm out as we walked over them. It is astonishing how the sting of those insects hurt. The streets were not paved at all in most places; a macadam road was a novelty.

> Indoor plumbing did not exist; everybody used outhouses. Because there was no running water, rainwater had to be pumped by hand, collected,

and stored. This strenuous process could last an hour. Bill and his brother, Ed, were given a dime each for taking on this chore once a week, so that the family had water for washing and cooking. These conditions did not bother or confine the young Bill Williams. He lived as much as possible outdoors. Farmland began at the outskirts of town and fanned out in every direction. Nearby, the Meadowlands, a series of marshes fed by the Passaic and Hackensack Rivers, was the major hub of the region's ecosystem. Egrets nested in the cattails, and migratory geese from Canada found the reeds that grew in abundance a desirable nesting and feeding spot. Stands of cedars dotted the swampy area. Gradually, industries encroached on the terrain and ate away large chunks of land, destroying the cedars and cattails and fouling the rivers. This landscape became a permanent setting for Williams's poems and stories, just as windmills, churches, and peasants appeared in seventeenth-century Dutch painting.

In Rutherford, ruinous change came more slowly. Kipp's Woods, "just over the back fence, was our wilderness," Williams recalled. It was consecrated turf for him, Ed, and Bill's friend Jim Hyslop, an Arcadian playground where the boys could run, roughhouse, fish, shoot squirrels with a slingshot, or torment old man Kipp—not viciously, Williams asserts. It was in Kipp's Woods that Williams came into the rich inheritance he husbanded his entire life: his "unbounded" curiosity about and love for nature and the physical world. From an early age he treasured flowers, trees, animals, and birds and trained his eye to describe them with exacting precision. He drew "half-ashamed" pleasure from these unsystematic encounters; they were as much a part of his moral and poetic education as the boyhood experiences described in "Nutting" and *The Prelude* were critical in forming Wordsworth's sensibility, vocation, and moral fiber:

> What I learned was the way the moss climbed about a tree's roots, what growing dogwood and iron wood looked like; the way rotten leaves will mat down a hole—and their smell when turned over— every patch among those trees had its character, moist or dry. I got to know the box turtle and the salamander and their spots and how the former hisses when annoyed.

When Williams noses about in flowerbeds and shrubs with his "bugologist" friend Jim Hyslop, he learns and caresses the names of flowers: "stars of Bethlehem, wild geranium, hepatica." In hundreds of nature poems,

Williams sublimated his dream of being a forester; one can see how his early schooling for ear and eye later paid literary dividends.

Williams called his boyhood his "lyrical years," and in most respects it was typical: he attended school, read books, played games and sports, and performed pranks. But some adventures, like Huck Finn's, were often darkened and menaced by exposure to death and insanity: he saw a lamb's throat cut, a rabbit skinned with sadistic cruelty by a hunter, a squirrel knocked out of a tree and immediately killed by a dog. Although sickened by what he witnessed, he characteristically refused to avert his eyes. This mixture of sensitivity and observation would serve him well as doctor and poet.

Williams's family and its history, the subject of my second chapter, were anything but conventional. The strain of insanity that ran in his family, embodied in his half-uncle Godwin, disquieted Williams; he worried it was genetic and might be transmitted to him. Godwin was prone to sudden paranoid rages that might escalate into a violent attack on Bill and Ed; once, he threatened Mrs. Dodd, an unsuspecting friend of their mother, Elena, for allegedly staring at him as at a crazy man. Edgar cocked a pistol in case Godwin tried to push his way in the door, but he backed off. Eventually, after his mental state worsened, Godwin was locked up in the Morris Plains insane asylum, where he died. Such episodes haunted the young Bill. That he took a bottle until the age of six bespeaks a deep-seated emotional insecurity. He weaned himself of that habit while traveling on a boat with his grandmother to West Haven, Connecticut, only because he feared being publicly humiliated as an overgrown baby.

Williams also fondly salutes Godwin as a "grand rouser of the imagination" and a repository of quaint morsels of ersatz folklore, doggerel poems, and pranks that he played on the credulous Bill, who, again like Huck Finn, earnestly tested their veracity:

> In the barnyard Godwin put a needle in a fresh laid egg and made me suck out the contents. It was also he who told me that if I put a horsehair in the water trough by the well in the barnyard it would turn to an eel by morning. I went to look and did see some slender black worms wriggling at the bottom . . .

Williams took pains in his *Autobiography* to depict his childhood as normal: the young squirt delighting in athletics and games to the point of "wild abandon," even frenzy; the brat occasionally lying or stealing fruit from a pushcart; the athlete playing baseball on the sandlot with his brother; and the shy boy aching to know girls but awkward in their company, withdrawing into "sorrowful isolation." That didn't stop him from bringing pictures of half-naked women into his fourth-grade class. (Where he obtained them he never said; the principal suspended him for a day.)

The house at 131 Passaic Avenue in which Bill and Ed grew up was not a hideaway for the mentally ill sealed off from the boisterous world outside its walls. Aunts, uncles, cousins, and friends of both their parents and grandmother visited often, and sometimes overstayed their welcome. It was a lively, noisy social scene, as family gatherings can be, the air echoing with laughter, shrill arguments, and resentments flaring up and subsiding. At communal meals, children competed for the grown-ups' attention with memories of ancestors from Puerto Rico, Martinique, London, and Puerto Plata. A charivari of languages rang out, though Spanish dominated. Williams's house was a stage on which spectacle, chitchat, family tensions, jokes, monologues, dialogues, and a buzz generated by the news of the day were all on display. It is possible that in those exciting scenes Williams first fell in love with theater.

3.

Williams served two apprenticeships in the years 1902–1920: the first was to the profession of medicine, the second to poetry. Despite spotty grades, he passed a difficult entrance exam and went directly from Horace Mann secondary school to the University of Pennsylvania School of Medicine, from which he graduated in 1906. The second youngest student in a class of 120, he applied himself diligently to his studies and did reasonably well; he knew his parents back in Rutherford were monitoring his progress and were afraid that, on his own, he would succumb to temptations, not go to church on Sunday, abuse his freedom, and become a backslider. Williams was annoyed at the nagging sermons and directives on how to conduct himself that arrived in letter after letter from Rutherford. This correspondence makes clear just how rough Williams's coming-of-age was. A prim, earnest, self-righteous twenty-one-year-old Williams slips into the tone of an aggrieved and misunderstood adolescent (his angst is not shammed). He adopts the passive-aggressive's tactic of defending his behavior, losing his temper, then apologizing abjectly in the next sentence, or admitting his guilt and denying it in the next breath. He is grateful that his parents were willing to pay for his education and he doesn't want to disappoint them; yet equally compelling is his wish to cut the apron strings tying him to Elena. Caught in a bind, he squirms, promises to be a paragon of virtue, and squelches his desire to taste the forbidden fruit of freedom from parental rules. So well had he internalized Pop and Elena's moral imperatives that even when he achieved independence he could never lull or suppress his hyperactive conscience.

Nonetheless, Williams's gregarious self, hiding in its cave and cautious about showing itself, soon emerged. He was not a grind. Philadelphia was hardly Vanity Fair, but it was a bustling, cultured city that allowed him room to breathe. Though circumspect, Williams gladly sampled the pleasures the place offered. He sneaked into an outdoor performance of *As You Like It* and watched as a new friend, a poet named Ezra Pound, in a fright wig and emoting in a hilariously posturing way as a member of the Chorus in Euripides's *Iphigenia in Aulis* (performed in the original Greek, no less), wildly flailed his arms and "heaved his massive breasts." Despite his naïveté and inexperience, and dazzled by his new friend's brilliant talk, Williams assessed Pound's character shrewdly. In a letter to Elena from his dorm room, Williams remarked on Pound's "cast-iron" assurance that he would achieve literary eminence, and on his unmistakable "false pride" and artificial manners; he was "full of conceits and affectations." Most people detested Pound as "a laughing boor," but for Williams those faults counted little against the Hailey, Idaho, comet's spectacular ability to open Williams's eyes to literary marvels. His rarefied conversations with Pound were not his steady diet. He enjoyed the usual college pastimes—football and baseball games, parties, band concerts—while indulging his budding passion for grand opera (Caruso and Scotto in *Aida*). Williams's letters to his brother Ed (nicknamed Bo) in Rutherford and then in Boston are chronicles of larks and truancies from his medical school homework memorizing the names of muscles—he fenced, sang in a chorus, wrestled, and acted in plays. Occasionally he'd slip in a comment on his medical courses (bacteriology was "interesting but tedious"). His epistolary style is rather stilted, especially when he dishes out advice to Ed on how to handle Pop, who hates to be crossed and resists change: "give into him always." Playing Mr. Worldly-Wise brings out the didactic adage-maker in Williams. To his extroverted younger brother, who was a successful ladies' man in the making and a favorite of his professors, he confides, "I'd rather risk being thought conceited than foolish." To attain his dream of "becoming a great doctor, the best in the world," he declares: "Stick to your ideals, even if you get contradictory advice and everybody says you are crazy." That maxim helped Williams stick to his poetic principles and ride out storms of mockery from debunking critics.

On the topic of girls, who aroused his nervous curiosity and fantasies, the inexperienced Williams pontificated—it's perfectly normal to pursue girls, he assures Ed, because even General Grant did it—or sounded like a cynical lady-killer: don't "get mixed up seriously with any girl yet. Just play. If you find yourself getting into trouble think of your ideal and then pick the girl apart. It is mean but it is necessary. It always cures me for you will always find defects." One should not judge Williams harshly. As innocent as a lamb, he was beginning the transition from what Keats called "the infant or thoughtless Chamber" to the "Chamber of Maiden-Thought," which at first is irradiated by a dazzling light that makes one see nothing but "pleasant wonders," but soon leads the neophyte thinker to discover "the World is full of Misery and Heartbreak, Pain, Sickness and oppression," which Williams took as his life's mission to treat. That world and its vicissitudes were a crucible for Williams's maturation.

At Penn the impressionable Williams had a series of crushes on young ladies he met at teas and dances or rehearsals of plays. Pound introduced him to H.D., a student at Bryn Mawr College, who intrigued and mystified him. The first woman poet he'd ever met, she seemed to live mostly in a state of aesthetic transport—her toes never grazed the grass, Williams recalled—gazing at elusive nebulae. (Her father was a renowned astronomer and head of the observatory at the University of Pennsylvania.) Williams fondly remembered taking long walks into the countryside with her; it was like escorting a nymph of the woods. H.D. was also the first woman outside his family he associated with mystery and creativity, with what Dr. Johnson called "the fertility of invention." In the *Autobiography*, his thumbnail sketch of her highlights her aesthete side. "She fascinated me, not for her beauty, which was unquestioned if bizarre to my sense, but for a provocative indifference to rule and order which I liked."

He was more mesmerized by her than he says, briefly hoping to supplant Pound as her beau, even though she had the knack of making him feel uncomfortable, uncouth, and uneducated in her presence.

When in 1906 he began his internship at French Hospital, situated in a high-crime area of New York City, Williams was by his own admission mostly ignorant about women, but he soon received a crash course, not just in diseases singular to female anatomy or in crises that put a pregnancy or birth at risk, but also in the social pathologies of children born out of wedlock, of women viciously beaten by their pimps or husbands, of mothers addicted to drugs or to alcohol, of women and children malnourished and vulnerable to cholera, typhus, or diphtheria. He even had to break up catfights between feral women whose talons could draw blood or gouge out an eye. Williams worked long hours, rotating from cardiology to pediatrics. Some nights he was so tired he fell asleep on his feet, only to be jolted awake to treat a woman in labor or a man with a gunshot wound demanding his attention. The daily testing of his skills in emergencies was exhilarating, but watching a woman die of postnatal septicemia or pulling from the womb a baby with spinal bifida could not but disconcert him: death was tireless, and doctors, not being miracle workers, had to cope with failures, all the more chastening when he lost a child he felt attached to. Yet French and Children's Hospitals were the sites where his lifelong empathy for women and respect for the working poor were planted. In the hospital wards, remote from H.D.'s ethereal womanliness, he shed a good portion of the innocence that had sheltered him from the brutish injustices of life. The lessons he received there were engraved on his mind and eventually imprinted on what he wrote.

Even with his medical degree, Williams did not immediately strike out on a straight path to success. He chose not to join a Park Avenue practice, the stink of filthy lucre nauseating him, but instead to return to Rutherford, which did not greet his arrival with cheers or a steady traffic of patients choosing him as their doctor. He had to make do with being appointed school physician, which was the lowest rung of the profession. Several years passed before the town relaxed its suspicions of Williams and began trusting his acumen, and even then he was rarely picked by the wealthier, prominent families in town to minister to their pains and ailments. He shrugged off their snobbery and attended to the immigrant families in the towns around Rutherford. The "best doctor in the world" had a hunger for experience and for the perfecting of his medical skills, which he satisfied by ministering to the Italian, Greek, and Polish new-comers in Lyndhurst and Garfield, who were crushed by poverty and bigotry. It didn't matter to him that in these neighborhoods English was a foreign tongue. Most important of all, from being admitted into their lives he acquired an in-depth education in the traumas of everyday American life and in the self-sacrificing generosity of immigrant women and decent, striving men. Although Williams's middle-class parents chose not to become American citizens, they had no trouble participating in the life of Rutherford: they helped found the Unitarian Church, for example. Working-class immigrants faced barriers to assimilating fully into a baffling American society that often vilified them and their children as the undesirable, alien "other," deemed unworthy of entering the company of the "elect." Williams never stopped appreciating the courage of these common folk and the old-world courtesies they carried with them from Sicily or Poland to the new world. During Prohibition, an Italian man brought grapes he had grown to 9 Ridge Road, trampled them in the basement, bottled the wine, and with natural grace bestowed it on Williams as payment for the house calls the doctor had made to take care of the man's sick kin. It was all he could afford. Such incidents inform and enrich Williams's poems and prose.

4.

In 1909, Williams's apprenticeship to poetry was still in an embryonic state; he was more poetaster than journeyman poet. *Poems*—the generic title of his debut collection—was Pop's indulgent gift to his son's ambition; he paid the printer's bill out of his own pocket, despite having severely criticized Bill's lame, old-fashioned versification. (His editing could not hide the amateurishness of Bill's performance.) That the book sold only a few copies was an augury, though Williams could not know it then, of the tiny readership he would attract for the next thirty years. He was not surprised or defensive or discouraged by this fiasco. He realized that the task of transforming himself into a respectable poet would take years. During the decade 1910–1920, he completely overhauled his style, sometimes aided by Pound's practical advice and disparaging comments, and even more by his encounters with modernist painting and sculpture, most dramatically at the 1913 Armory Show, where the radical innovations of

Picasso, Braque, Klee, Matisse, Duchamp, Kandinsky, and Brancusi were like a hard slap to Williams's face, awakening him to the ways an artist—and, by extension, a composer, novelist, or poet—could blithely shatter cherished pieties. The names of the movements—Futurism, Cubism, Fauvism—mattered less than the audacity of the makers of the bold paintings. Williams returned to the Armory Show several times, as if to inhale draughts of life-giving oxygen in its rooms. What he experienced was a series of epiphanies during which, for the first time, he felt the godlike power of the imagination and saw the "Beautiful Thing" appear to him, as in an Annunciation he could not ignore.

Williams could take in at a glance the gulf between the brazen artistry of a Picasso or Braque still life and the timid, torpid, diffuse, and mostly second-rate poems of *The Tempers* (1913), which Pound had been instrumental in getting published in London. Williams could not repair all the tears in the frayed fabric at once. Progress would come slowly but steadily, and so it did. *Al Que Quiere!*, his 1917 book of poems, showed promise that he would eventually find his own voice. He was not too proud to seek tutors who might hasten his acquisition of a flexible technique. Luckily, across the Hudson River, the New York art scene was fermenting, and the headquarters for the avant-garde was Alfred Stieglitz's 291 gallery, whose influential magazine *Camera Works* was the photographer's sounding board for publicizing the new art before the Armory Show. Stieglitz's expert eye reconnoitered the European skies like a powerful telescope to discover the newest stars, such as Juan Gris, or a movement, such as prankish, subversive Dadaism, but also swept the horizon for emerging American artists such as Charles Demuth and Marsden Hartley. On the walls of his gallery hung paintings and photographs that deliberately set out to shake up the complacent traditions and premises of what art could and should do. Nothing was sacred or impervious to the breakthroughs the new art trumpeted. All the time Williams could spare from his medical rounds and office hours he spent staring at a Kandinsky abstraction or a Brancusi sculpture, which both elated and puzzled him. Probably his ambition to remake American poetry with a similar astounding modernist invention was kindled in these hours spent with the works of art imported from Paris. To meet the challenge, he would have to play catch-up and reinvent himself as a poet. As he recalled in his *Autobiography*, "Here was my chance; that is all I knew. There had been a break somewhere, we were streaming through, each thinking his own thoughts, driving his own designs toward his self's objective." Fortunately, the little magazines were teeming with big ideas, and a nonstop conversation and debate about art, change, and the new moved from art exhibits to gatherings in restaurants to the drawing rooms of rich patrons such as Walter Arensberg and Mabel Dodge Luhan. Williams found himself part of a literary community in a state of flux, at times torn apart by feuds and jealous rivalry, but also intellectually agile and supportive of innovation. His decadelong effort to master the craft of poetry, by trial and error, bore its first fruits in the improvisations of *Kora in Hell*. Williams couldn't say if he was halfway to hell or riding a moonbeam to modernist heaven. Either direction, he figured, would rocket him into a new orbit. This pivotal work brought Williams in 1920 to the brink of his most prolific and experimental decade.

5.

In his personal life, the decade of the 1910s was equally a story of momentous changes, many linked to his complicated relations with women. On this subject he was both voluble and secretive. Writing about women, he could be romantic, crude, admiring, bawdy, protective, insolent, or ambivalent, depending on which whims ruled his moods. Women gravitated to him: he had a matinee idol's handsome face, dashing manners, and charisma, along with a humane doctor's focused and frank interest in what the woman seated opposite him was saying about her decision not to bear any more children, her grandfather's fanatical loathing of Jews and blacks, her plan to become a scientist in anatomy, or her low opinion of Dr. X's churlish treatment of patients. But he also had a furtive side that is exposed, consciously or unconsciously, in dozens of his poems, in fictional guise, and in offhand comments scattered throughout his letters and memoirs; more often than not, the subject was his marriage and, obliquely, his extramarital affairs. At the center of Williams's conflicted, torturous views of women was his wife, Floss (Florence Herman). Their marriage endured many shocks, but lasted fifty-one years. Williams portrayed Floss as helpmate, devoted wife, and exemplary mother to their two sons; he admired her competence in crises; because she was often the intelligent first reader of his poems and stories, he trusted her assessment of a new poem. This privileged access to his creative life pleased her. However, whenever she alighted on stanzas in which her husband painted her as an unexciting sexual partner, or himself as trapped in his marriage, like Gulliver trussed up by the Lilliputians and yearning for freedom, or as straying from the matrimonial bed to seek a hoped-for electrifying passion with another woman, what did Floss feel? A reserved woman, she mostly stifled her fury, though when he touched the raw nerve of his disaffection and demeaned her, Williams sometimes let the Floss character spew molten disdain at her philandering husband. Still, she knew that most of the time he loved her in his awkward fashion. He always returned to her, and this fact allayed any anxiety that their marriage would end in an acrimonious divorce that would harm their sons and banish her to that ignominious state of permanent exile, the rejected woman. In the early 1950s, after two strokes convinced Williams he might die, he confessed his infidelities to Floss in detail; he had an overwhelming need to shrive his conscience. But he had given no thought to the crippling effects this explicit knowledge might have on her. He had counted on her forgiveness almost automatically before; why would she react differently now? But he miscalculated: this time she was shocked, mortified, and depressed. Eventually, she rallied from this nadir of their life together and provided a steady hand on the tiller as Williams's health deteriorated in the dozen years left to him. Berryman's lines in his "Elegy for W.C.W., the lovely man," in *The Dream Songs*, "you had so many girls your life was a triumph and you loved your one wife," is a facile judgment. If their *Scenes from a Marriage* lacked the spiritual agony and defoliated emotional landscape of Ingmar Bergman's film, its episodes let us watch the tangled ways Williams's life and poetry intersected.

6.

In Williams's long life in poetry he met nearly all of the players, major and minor, who contributed significantly to the history of modernism in the arts. Literary friendships and enmities are built into the very infrastructure of creative endeavors. Poets and painters are not immune from spite and envy or from backbiting and slander, if they think it will advance their careers. What is in vogue may generate principled dissent from poets of another aesthetic persuasion or, like political alignments, abruptly turn antagonistic and cause irreconcilable rifts. It is no accident that in the polemical debates about Futurism, Dadaism, and surrealism, opposing factions resorted to metaphors of war: one hears of skirmishes and battles, heavy ordnance and casualties, allies and traitors. Williams was no exception. In his *Autobiography*, he likens the effect of T. S. Eliot's *The Waste Land* on his poetry to the dropping of the atomic bomb on Hiroshima. That was not meant as hyperbole.

Soon after his arrival at the University of Pennsylvania, Williams met Ezra Pound, who became a lifelong friend. Pound is a biographer's prize. How could he not be? He was an amazing personality. He appears in every phase of Williams's life from 1902 on, playing an infinite number of roles: scourge, mentor, vaudeville top banana, avant-garde scout, magazine editor, patron, grouch, and hanging judge. He did impressions of the police in a hundred voices and several languages and dialects; he was eminently quotable, funny, and preposterous, like all four Elizabethan humor characters rolled into one eccentric monologist. Williams found "Ezry" irresistible and insufferable, but he could tolerate only small doses of the man and poet who consumed 90 percent of the oxygen in any room he entered. However shrill and autocratic Pound was in his pronouncements from the throne, though, he could not be ignored. He got angry with Williams hundreds of times for being stubborn as "six oxen" (in letters, his salutation often began "Dear Bull"). When Williams refused to embrace Pound's latest poetic enthusiasm, he felt the lash of Pound's insults and his assumption of superiority. Pound mocked Williams for his "cockeyed" notion that he could find pure water in the American Deserta or fashion a world-class poetry out of the materials in his own backyard. To Pound, that was chasing an illusion—a colossal waste of time and creative energy. When he couldn't take Pound's guff anymore, Williams blew up at his rambunctious pal. Still, though he never matriculated in the Ezuversity, as James Laughlin had, he gained much from their transatlantic correspondence course: he would think through even Pound's battiest theories, so that when he matched wits with his adversary, the blade of his intellect would be sharp and draw blood. There are moments when Pound tries to upstage Williams, and endless times when he is a nuisance. Williams learned when to ignore Pound's fulminations and when to go on the offensive and rail at his friend's presumptions. Through Pound and on his own initiative, as we shall see, he became friends with Mina Loy, Marianne Moore, Wallace Stevens, Louis Zukofsky, George Oppen, Charles Reznikoff, Charles Olson, and countless other poets.

7.

Williams's last fifteen years were burdened by frequent health crises. He suffered a heart attack, several strokes, a nervous breakdown, and an operation for colorectal cancer, and in his last years he became seriously aphasic. People who knew him when he was as vigorous as an oak were taken aback when they saw his stooped body and heard his broken speech. (He was often too embarrassed to say anything.) He survived all these blows, but at a high cost to his sense of self. He leaned on Floss for comfort, which she gave freely. Yet miraculously his imagination remained intact and gave off new green leaves. As the advancing seasons came and went, he somehow managed to write splendid new poems. The step-down tercets of "The Desert Music" and *Journey to Love* may have been dictated by necessity—his hunt-and-peck typing with one finger—but they were ingenious innovations that paradoxically imbued his poems with space, not contraction. My chapter "The Lion in Winter" explores this harsh last period of physical decline and late flowering.

During his lifetime Williams had the pleasure of becoming a beloved figure. His generosity to young poets was legendary. After his death, an outpouring of elegies and prose reminiscences, some like religious benedictions, attested to the affection in which Williams the man and Williams the poet were held. Naturally voices of dissent rang out from the choir loft, basically rehearsing the accusations that he lacked the rudiments of technique or an understanding of form, that he was a sentimentalist and a shallow thinker, and, most damaging of all, that his quest for a uniquely American poem grounded in speech was a foolish enterprise, doomed to fail: he had reached for a holy grail that was a forgery or an ignis fatuus. These accusations still resonate in formalist circles and in academic departments. Writing to Williams in 1958, the year *Paterson V* was published, Robert Lowell remarked, "You're very famous now, but I have been thinking a lot about how bone-headed most of the popular and even good critics have been about you most of your lifetime. It must be fearful to have done something with deadly originality and lucidity and beauty, and then be ignored, scolded, patronized!" Williams shrugged off the negative verdicts. It is undeniable that he exerted an influence on poets of diverse tastes and practices, both during his lifetime and posthumously. A short list would include Robert Duncan, Robert Creeley, Denise Levertov, James Wright, Robert Lowell, Allen Ginsberg, Frank

O'Hara, Jonathan Williams, A. R. Ammons, Theodore Weiss, and Robert Pinsky. Richard Wilbur joked that Williams believed that any American poet who wrote a sonnet was curtseying to Queen Elizabeth I, but Wilbur, as if determined to rebut the charges that Williams was a chaotic poet, observed that Williams viewed the world with "a describing eye and interrogatory mind and a personality eager for coherence." He noted that in "The Yachts" Williams stayed close to standard meters, but elsewhere was more concerned with stresses than with meters. A final sign of Wilbur's esteem for Williams is in his comparing him to Cézanne: "a practicing master too deep in his own work to think like a critic."

When poets praise Williams, they admire different qualities. For Berryman, it is the older man's ear: "Rest well, who worked so hard, who made a good sound / constantly, for so many years: / your high-jinks delighted the continents & our ears." Lowell singles out Williams's "short lines, often in quatrains, sure in their line divisions, though these divisions might be hard to guess if we first saw his poems in prose." American poets do not panic when a poem does not scan easily; it is not necessarily a sign of ineptitude or tone deafness or sacrilege. "Few poets can come near to his wide clarity and dashing rightness with words and almost Alexandrian modulations of voice," Lowell wrote of Williams in 1964. Williams would have been especially pleased that Lowell discerned in his poems the clarity of the words as well as his ability to capture the full range of American voices. For Louis Zukofsky, Williams is a sharpshooting outlaw like Billy the Kid, but what he most fondly remembers is "The expanse / of his / *mind.*" Kenneth Rexroth has a field day matching Williams to the gentle, loving St. Francis and to Brother Juniper, "who suffered / All indignities and glories / Laughing like a gentle fool." If he is a fool, he is one who stands for "All wisdom and beauty." Rexroth singled out the wonderful stillness in Williams and the "Sacramental relationships" he creates in his poetry. Octavio Paz, moved by Williams's "magnificent" translation of his "Hymn Among the Ruins," visited 9 Ridge Road in 1955 and commented, "I have never met a man less affected. Just the opposite of an oracle. Possessed by poetry, not by his role as a poet." These estimates, a sampling of many, are not insincere eulogies but, rather, tributes from one practitioner to another.

A biographer sometimes succumbs to the hubristic belief that he knows his subject better than the subject knew him- or herself. Having lived a long time with William Carlos Williams and his multitudinous works, I have tried to quash such dangerous impulses; they can lead to unfair moralistic judgments or to hagiography. Williams was neither a saint nor a satanic figure. He was a likable, empathic doctor, poet, and friend who in certain moods could be icily detached and cruel: he writes of Marsden Hartley, whose paintings he admired, "He was one of the most frustrated men I knew . . . A tragic figure. I really loved the man, but we didn't always get along together, except at a distance." What most distinguished Williams was his drive to turn himself into a masterful *American* poet. He brought the same intellectual focus to that Herculean task as he did to deciding what sickness lay beneath a patient's recital of symptoms. "Something urgent I have to say to you," Williams addressed Floss at the beginning of "Asphodel, That Greeny Flower." He brought that same urgency—and an uncommon faith in the imagination—to everything he touched. There are flaws of character I dislike, as there are poems whose obscurity I have not cracked and others whose forms, even after several readings, appear diffuse and incomplete. None of this has diminished my affection for Williams or tarnished my esteem for his works. Like many of his contemporaries, I felt it a delight and a privilege to spend time in his company, even those interludes when he became violently combustible. His voice is permanently lodged in my head. Williams's development as a poet, its peaks and troughs, and his discovery of an American idiom did not unfold in a neat, straight line. He took wrong turns that required a correction of course, and like most poets he suffered through periods of drought and agonizing self-mistrust, but he took to heart as his guiding principle Pound's best advice: "And remember a mans [sic] real work is *what he's going to do* not what is behind him. Avanti e coraggio" (forward and courage!). Williams's life was interwoven with his literary aspirations and achievements. We cannot understand one without reference to the other.

"Something Urgent I Have to Say to You"

ONE

Poetry as Biographical Evidence

I.

The high priests of the New Criticism schooled their acolytes in an art of reading poems that elevated technique—modulations of meter, subtle shifts in tone, adroit maneuvers with syntax, ironies planted in dramatic monologues to detonate later—to an unaccustomed sovereignty. The critic explained how a poem worked, much as a chemist explained the elements of the periodic table: which words caused catalytic change and which entropy, which mixtures were volatile and which inert. According to this view, a poem chartered its own laws, which were often proudly tortuous, even baffling. Nothing was what it appeared to be: the most innocent line might shelter a furtive renegade who aimed to overturn conventional order and install ambiguity in its place. The job of the critic was to ferret out linguistic clues scattered on and below the poem's surface and, through patient analysis, put the circuitry back together. For this task, a poet's biography—his idyllic childhood or poisoned upbringing, his strivings to escape the yoke of poverty, racial bigotry, religious strictness, or even gentility—was deemed either irrelevant or mere raw material to be stored away or disposed of like slag, a by-product of the poetic process.

Under New Critical rules, all poets were not created equal. John Donne and Richard Crashaw prospered because they brandished witty paradox like expert swordsmen. Their poems demanded the close scrutiny and concentration of solving a chess problem. Romantic poets such as Shelley and Wordsworth, allegedly guilty of talking too much or too emotionally, were often disparaged as clumsy versifiers and bombastic idealists who clung to literalism, and therefore were assigned nosebleed seats in the bleachers at Elysian Fields.

Although the New Critics undeniably taught two generations to read poems more alertly and to respect their intricately spun webs, forms, and textures, the poet in their scheme mostly was seen as creating the verbal artifact in the manner of a demiurge, then withdrawing to the sidelines, becoming a spectator as the critics dissected—or scavenged—his creation. The poet's intentions, motives, if not his experience, counted for little compared to the striations and glazes of, or cracks in, his well-wrought urn. Biography could only distract the reader from his duty as inspector of a poem's structural soundness or fault lines; dwelling on incidents from the poet's life would lead to sentimentality or a sloppy impressionism that corrupted and trivialized the work itself. Interpreting Donne's "The Flea," New Critics might mention in passing the youthful sexual escapades that landed Donne in prison, but even such pivotal events inspired little commentary. A peculiar bias blinded them to the fact that *discordia concors*, what Dr. Johnson defined as "a combination of dissimilar images, or discovery of occult resemblances in things apparently unlike," might reside in the metaphysical poet's character as well as in his style, that hyperbole and poetic conceits are a psychological thumbprint left on a poem and worthy of study and speculation. Curiously, the ironies and puns that the New Critics reveled in analyzing often resemble the slips of the tongue and dreams Freud interpreted so methodically as clues to unconscious motives, conflicts, character flaws, and erratic patterns of development.

Strong hostility was generated in many quarters to biographers who ventured to investigate just such constellations and their relation to poems and novels. If the individual begins, the psychotherapist and literary critic Adam Phillips asks, with an "always recondite sense of himself," how can the biographer "penetrate the inner life" of a Hemingway or an Ezra Pound? Leslie Stephen's answer, "with a great deal of guesswork," could only galvanize the skeptics among the historians and theorists who scoffed at the very idea of seeking the sources of creativity and identity crises in "unconscious mental processes." They dismissed it as mystical mumbo jumbo or an illicit method that substituted unverifiable suppositions about a poet's erotic fantasies, say, for precise documentary proof. In a *New York Review of Books* essay several years ago, Joyce Carol Oates excoriated biographers for their Wal-Mart version of psychoanalysis that she labeled "pathography," a term of opprobrium that gained wide circulation. Oates viewed the biographers' efforts as tawdry and exploitative, the

projection of their own neuroses and unconscious agendas on their helpless subjects' lives. Putting Hemingway and Pound retroactively on an
analyst's couch *is* futile and hubristic, since no biographer can ever know
exactly what his subject was thinking. No wonder Dr. Johnson observed
in his *Life of Cowley*, "Actions are visible though motives are secret," and
Emily Dickinson remarked acerbically to Thomas Wentworth Higginson
that "biography first convinces us of the fleeing of the biographied." It's
true that dead artists cannot refute the calumnies that sometimes mar
the interpretations of their behavior.* Nonetheless, biography is not a
branch of pathography or fantasy that specializes in reductive psycho-
babble.

Unlike Oates, John Updike is not ready to preside over a requiem mass
for biography, but all he can muster in appreciation of the genre is one
and a half cheers. Biographers are trapped in Plato's cave, he contends,
twice removed from reality, so they can offer readers little more than a
blurred facsimile of a writer's life. Occasionally biography performs a useful if derivative job, like Piero della Francesca's assistants filling in patches
of a fresco's background against which the master's evocative figures stand
out. Mostly it behaves like a loutish Lytton Strachey in *Eminent Victori-
ans*, "ridiculing and denigrating his subjects."†

After treating biography as if he were a bouncer tossing a boorish
drunk from a classy tavern, Updike decides to sing another tune. He is
pleased when biography, excavating an archaeological site, turns up a glittering shard of fact—that Nabokov wrote on three-by-five cards, for example. Although he worries that a gang of vulgar biographers is snooping
around his house and writing desk, casing the joint and biding their time
before invading his privacy and stealing his treasures, including his good
name, he makes several handsome if grudging concessions. Psychoana-
lytical theories of compensation and Edmund Wilson's moving essay
"[Philoctetes:] The Wound and the Bow" have "alerted biographers to the
relation of creative drive to a human insufficiency elsewhere," or "the mysteries of [artists'] affective lives." Implying that a biographer can be an

---

*Oates conveniently forgot that her novels often indulged in the very practices she condemned in
biographies. *Black Water*, a thinly veiled retelling of the Chappaquiddick incident and Mary Jo
Kopechne's horrific drowning, resembles a *National Inquirer* story that revels in a celebrity's
sleazy conduct in which we learn virtually nothing about Ted Kennedy's character: *Black Water*
is soft-core pathography.
†This is an odd judgment, since Strachey admired Cardinal Newman and Florence Nightingale
and painted vivid, complex, and balanced portraits of them.

indefatigable lover and seeker of truths, Updike restores biography to its place in literature's household. "Viewing the intimate underside of writers we have read is fascinating," Updike declares, and near the end of his essay he notes, "The life of a writer, which spins outside of itself a secondary life, offers an opportunity to study mind and body, or inside and outside, or dream and reality, together, as one."

Because he is an artist, Updike can distinguish between a literary biography of superb quality, like Boswell's *Life of Johnson* or George D. Painter's *Marcel Proust*, and a biography that piles up facts, bales them, stores them, then recounts them in the droning voice of an inventory clerk. We've all read and deplored obese biographies that cram facts into their narrative maws as if suffering from a compulsive eating disorder. Thoroughness is commendable, shapelessness deplorable. Herschel Parker's massive two-volume biography of Melville, however useful as reference, fails as portraiture and interpretation. The artist is suffocated by the weight of facts. Do we need to know how many bottles of bourbon Faulkner, John Berryman, and James Dickey drank? Not really, though how their alcoholism affected their personality, their relationships, and, above all, their work is germane to the biographer's task. If William Carlos Williams was a sometime womanizer, does it matter how many women he took to bed? No, but how his philandering affected his marriage and his poetry is crucially important to assess. In the foreword to his *Autobiography*, Williams cagily warns biographers, "We always try to hide the secret of our lives from the general stare. What I believe to be the hidden core of my life will not easily be deciphered, even when I tell, as here, the outer circumstances." Therein lies the biographer's challenge: to cross the minefield to the site of "the hidden core" and, once arrived safely there, to refuse to adopt reductive or formulaic explanations of the subject's behavior.

It's a commonplace that biographers cannot be indifferent to facts beyond the personal lives of their subjects. Individual lives, after all, are inescapably entangled in the events of their times. Yeats's poetry is inconceivable apart from the painful, fractious political history of Ireland, as Guillaume Apollinaire's, Isaac Rosenberg's, and Wilfred Owen's are inextricably associated with the slaughter of the Great War. In a presidential address to the American Historical Association, William Langer set forth his misgivings about psychobiography, reminding his audience that if biography neglects to locate its protagonist in a historical context and lacks a convincing theory that explains the interplay between large groups and institutions—reformers, armies, corporations, state legislators, anarchists—and aspiring or crushed men and women, the biography leaves a gaping hole in its narrative fabric. Langer's worry is legitimate and applies to poets such as Anna Akhmatova, Bertolt Brecht, and Yusef Komunyakaa, who, caught in the cogs of history's machinery and suffering grievous wounds, bear witness to, respectively, the murder of a husband and the imprisonment of a beloved son, the wrenching limbo of exile, and the atrocities of war (the napalming of innocent peasants in Vietnam and the death of a buddy in his battalion). A few poets seek to escape the historical furies by retreating into a pursuit of their art, but there's no hiding from the juggernaut of tyranny: a writer such as Primo Levi is driven out of his chemistry laboratory and sent to a concentration camp, where he survives by a mixture of luck and ingenuity, whereas the Hungarian poet Miklós Radnóti is executed along with a large group of ordinary citizens. A poet such as William Carlos Williams lives through the disasters of world wars, economic depressions, genocides, and strikes physically unscathed, but with heightened social consciousness, he sometimes highlights these "outer circumstances" in his poems and at other times drops them suggestively into the background, like a church seen in the distance in a Constable landscape.

Despite these caveats, the New Critics' insistence on a poem's autonomy is a useful shot across the biographer's bow. Though a sonnet may present self-communing on a stock theme—carpe diem, for instance—it's not necessarily a coded autobiographical statement. Shakespeare's sonnet cycle has resisted innumerable attempts to probe for evidence of his sexual preferences or partners. Other poems, such as *Paradise Lost*, also stymie the biographer poised to search its heroic verse for self-disclosures. The sectarian schisms and political tumult that tore England apart in the seventeenth century—regicide, civil war, exile, religious persecution—infiltrate the majestic theological drama of the Fall of Man in subtle ways. Since an epic poem is not a roman à clef or a disguised allegory, we can't compile a list of glib correspondences—God equals Oliver Cromwell, Belial stands for Charles II—however tantalizing it may be to do so.

Blake famously claimed that Milton was a member of the Devil's Party without knowing it. Satan's charismatic oratory, cool leadership, love of adventure, and wily, fearless nature, which in the epic's kinship system make him a first cousin to Odysseus, tempt us to think so. But those dramatic traits don't entirely suit Milton's bookish nature. When Satan first glimpses Adam and Eve, whom he has sworn to destroy for revenge, Milton memorably sketches an Iago figure, who "saw / Undelighted all delight." Is this an unconscious self-portrait? A gibe at sexual repression? A condemnation of jealousy? A voyeur's stance? How much did Milton identify with rebellion? Milton's biographer must wrestle with these questions; they don't yield easy answers. Yet because the poet's prodigious learning colors the dramatic narrative of *Paradise Lost* on every page, the biographer can pick up valuable data on many topics: Milton's championing of freedom of expression, his misogyny, his positions on theological controversy, his relish of slashing polemics. Tracing these sources, a biographer will gain a fuller knowledge of Milton's formidable mind and the doctrinal soil out of which *Paradise Lost* sprang, but a limited connection between Satan's psychology and Milton's.

There is a second hurdle. At some basic level—call it the poem's genetic makeup—Milton goes about his artistic business without regard to his unkempt life or the political circumstances that hem him in. As the self-styled heir and rival of Homer and Virgil, he clearly flaunts his mastery of epic conventions and his ambition to produce a Christian *Iliad*. With its strategically deployed battalions of commas, semicolons, and colons, Milton's thorny Latinate syntax drives the familiar biblical plot at a leisurely pace. In the sonorities and cadences of his blank verse, Milton's virtuosity dazzles, as even those detractors who found it cold and pompous conceded. Virile, impersonal, haughty, convoluted, Milton's sentences coil and spring, halt, contemplate, digress, and advance like a serpent. But it's nearly impossible to parse Milton's character or erotic nature from his labyrinthine grammar. Though he lingers over Eve's languid voluptuousness, she remains embalmed in the amber of women's submissive role as sanctioned by Christian dogma ("Hee for God only, Shee for God in him"). Because *Paradise Lost* is an escape from personality into epic style, Milton's biographer must warily account for the myriad ways the epic's rules and restrictions modify our sense of who the poet was.

2.

Are biography and poetry, then, continents linked only by a narrow isthmus often flooded and impassable? Yes and no. Take the twentieth century's most famous poem, *The Waste Land*. Even though Eliot called the poem "a personal and wholly insignificant grouse against life," its exegetes ignored his remark and, like a pack of beagles, fanned out to uncover and pounce on every allusion, from *The Golden Bough*, Dante, Vedic scripture, Spenser, and Jacobean drama to Wagner's *Tristan and Isolde*. (Eliot's notes made the job simpler.) Critics tended to shy away from commenting on how the misery of his failed marriage to Vivienne Haigh-Wood seeped into the refined ennui of "A Game of Chess" and the tawdry coupling between the carbuncular clerk and the typist in "The Fire Sermon." By marshaling facts and ideas from the poet's letters, anecdotes in friends' memoirs, and interviews, Eliot's biographer can document the poet's despair as his marriage crumbled and he suffered a nervous breakdown that required treatment in a Swiss sanatorium. Despite *The Waste Land*'s ritualistic tone, thematic ambitions, and numerous allusions, it confirms our suspicions that sexual disgust and fear were rooted in the poet's psyche. The clipped dialogue and flurry of questions in "A Game of Chess," like the expensive rococo stage set, highlight the emotional estrangements of a marriage on the verge of dissolution. There is nothing euphemistic about the wife's agony. Rattled by her husband's stony politeness, she succumbs to hysteria; her impoverished vocabulary, broken rhythms, and flurry of beseeching questions are revelatory:

"My nerves are bad tonight. Yes, bad. Stay with me.
"Speak to me. Why do you never speak. Speak.
"What are you thinking of? What thinking? What?
"I never know what you are thinking. Think."

The relationship between life and art here serves the biographer's purposes well.

Poets often admonish their readers not to identify them with their personae: Browning isn't Andrea del Sarto or Bishop Bloughram; Eliot's not Prufrock, and John Berryman's not Henry, the educated clown of *The Dream Songs*. Henry is "an imaginary character (not the poet, not me)," Berryman declares irately in a prefatory note. There's some truth in this warning. But while there's no simple psychological connection between the poet and his fictional creation, the biographer can't overlook the examples, sometimes blatant and sometimes disguised, of poets projecting their unconscious feelings on personae. It's legitimate, I believe, to read in the bloodthirsty shrillness of Bertrans de Born, the mad cocksure speaker of an early Pound poem "Sestina: Altaforte," symptoms of the pathology that erupted in Pound's 1930s Fascist broadcasts with their racial slurs and ranting crackpot pedagogy. But the biographer must also analyze Pound's perfect musical pitch, which manages the sestina's repetitions and formal constraints to mimic and expose Bertrans's elated warmongering and dissonant martial airs.

How should Pound's biographer, picking his way slowly through *The Cantos*, judge its design, forty years in the making? He might be forgiven for thinking he'd stumbled on a strange Paleolithic site. Excavating it, he'd find wondrous ruins, scraps of papyrus that seem to be official documents, coins, baubles, ideograms inscribed in exquisite calligraphy, Pound's favorite quotations (the poem's a global commonplace book); whole sections devoted to sketches of Confucius, Malatesta, Jefferson, and humble artisans; quotes from manuals on statesmanship; and accounts of church councils. This potpourri of lovely yet fragmented images evokes civilizations at their acme and in their decline. In the poem, the polymath scholar-poet compulsively retrieves slivers from these disparate cultures, which he then shapes into collages that a reader might at times be persuaded is the work of a creative, demented personality. (There's method and some pedantry in Pound's madness.)

Yet except for *The Pisan Cantos*, which record obliquely Pound's incarceration in a cage at the close of World War II and his first small steps toward acknowledging guilt for his anti-Semitic screeds and his propaganda broadcasts on behalf of Mussolini's Fascist government, this miscellaneous long poem discloses precious little of his messy, busy daily life—his ménage à trois with Dorothy Shakespeare and Olga Ridge, for instance—over several decades. If *The Cantos* promises to lure the biographer into constructing theories about Pound's impulsive acts, he had better remember that poems are often wiser than the poet who writes them. Pound's megalomania was tempered by an imagination that could enter into the mind and emotions of, among many, a rich middle-aged London dilettante, a shy Chinese wife of seventeen, and an old weatherbeaten Anglo-Saxon seafarer. His repertoire of voices was astonishing: sarcastic in one poem, tender in the next, and ruggedly eloquent in the third. In its delicate understatement, "The River-Merchant's Wife: A Letter," a version of a Li Po poem, is one of the most beautiful love poems of any period, and such is the self-discipline of Pound's art that he never once whispers the word "love." In canto 116, the valedictory poem, Pound, not a man given to humility, confesses that his "palimpsest" is a botched attempt to "make a Cosmos." "I cannot make it cohere." Yet his pride does not permit him to accept this judgment outright. Immediately, he challenges the reader with a wistful self-justification:

> I have brought the great ball of crystal;
>   who can lift it?
> Can you enter the great acorn of light?
>   But the beauty is not the madness
> Tho' my errors and wrecks lie about me.
> And I am not a demigod.

Several lines later, he changes his mind, drawing a strained distinction: "it coheres all right. Even if my notes do not cohere."

This disjunction between life and work complicates the biographer's task; the two don't run on parallel tracks—they cross over or switchback at many places—but there is a vast difference between using the poem as a chronicle of events and using it as a seismograph of sensibility and character traits. Like a painter, the biographer must choose the right perspective. Listen to the opening lines of canto 1:

> And then went down to the ship,
> Set keel to breakers, forth on the godly sea, and
> We set up mast and sail on that swart ship,
> Bore sheep aboard her, and our bodies also
> Heavy with weeping, and winds from sternward
> Bore us onward with bellying canvas,
> Circe's this craft, the trim-coifed goddess.

This ravishing passage goes beyond epic imitation; it's a tribute to Pound's superb command of rhythm and momentum and acoustics; the four strategically placed "and"s, along with the brisk "winds from sternward," swell the lines, as they do the sails. Circe ably taught him her sorcery. The swinishness came later, when he glorified Mussolini and applauded the rise of Hitler to power. The decorum and harmony that mark the surefooted melodies from canto 1 deserted Pound when his ideological theories became pathological obsessions. To scant either is to distort a crucial half of Pound's being.

The confessional poem, which poses tricky problems for the biographer, at first glance seems to satisfy his wildest fantasy. After all, his subject—be it Robert Lowell, Sylvia Plath, or Anne Sexton—appears to blurt out everything, often with childish glee: adulteries, suicide attempts, hatred of parents and spouses, sibling rivalry, impotence, and drunkenness—all the dirty laundry of boudoir and psychiatric sessions hung out for public view. Nothing new under the sun, you might say, except a tacit assumption that there's no shame—indeed, there's relief or pride—in exhibiting scars and tallying callow, self-destructive behavior. Yet Plath's biographers so far scarcely give her enough credit for developing a brilliant technique that liberated her verse from stale conventions. *Ariel* is not an archive of theatrical gestures to be ransacked for symptoms of rage against father and husband, or suicidal impulses, though all are present in "Medusa" and "Daddy." Plath's besieged self often transcended its desperation by discovering moral order in audacious experiments with poetic forms. If a biographer neglects these literary inventions, he is likely to diminish Plath to a mere clinical specimen of mental illness.

On the other hand, there are poets such as Elizabeth Bishop who struggle to guard their privacy, secrets, and passions, even from beyond the grave. That Bishop chose perfection of the work, not of the life, and thought of biographers as paparazzi, hasn't scared off the throngs who comb through her poems looking for signs of her lesbianism, alcoholism, and any emotional damage stemming from her mother's madness and her Brazilian lover's suicide. And while Bishop's frugal similes and reserved tone don't quite function as a barbed wire fence enclosing her feelings, neither do they court an intimacy with the reader. Sublimation, for Bishop, made an art of loss. Not surprisingly, she detested confessional poems. When Robert Lowell pillaged his wife Elizabeth Hardwick's letters and, without asking permission, incorporated her words into his poems, Bishop was shocked and embarrassed by her friend's deeds. She considered this violation a moral felony, protesting that the end of producing a memorable poem didn't justify employing base means.

By admitting his own weaknesses and throwing himself on the mercy of the court of literary opinion, the authority he chiefly cared about, Lowell hoped to disarm his demons, to be forgiven—and to enjoy the thrill of breaking a taboo. Typically, he couched his private ordeals—and found a measure of comfort—in grandiose terms, as if he were a modern Job or Agamemnon:

> The gods, employed to haunt and punish husbands,
> have no hand for trigger-fine distinctions,
> their myopia makes all error mortal.

Blessed with the gift of tongues (sometimes that gift's a curse, a verbal hullabaloo kicked up to avoid sitting silently with himself), he could in his best poems look unflinchingly or wryly at his manic flights and the plunges into depression that often landed him in mental hospitals: imagination alone rescued him from himself.

Lowell's sonnet "'To Speak of Woe That Is in Marriage,'" from *Life Studies*, illustrates his mingling of art and life. The poem begins with an epigraph from Schopenhauer:

"It is the future generation that presses into being by means of these exuberant feelings and supersensible soap bubbles of ours."

> The hot night makes us keep our bedroom windows open.
> Our magnolia blossoms. Life begins to happen.
> My hopped up husband drops his home disputes,
> and hits the streets to cruise for prostitutes,
> free-lancing out along the razor's edge.
> This screwball might kill his wife, then take the pledge.
> Oh the monotonous meanness of his lust . . .
> It's the injustice . . . he is so unjust—
> whiskey-blind, swaggering home at five.
> My only thought is how to keep alive.
> What makes him tick? Each night now I tie
> ten dollars and his car key to my thigh . . .
> Gored by the climacteric of his want,
> he stalls above me like an elephant.

How does Lowell the poet depict Lowell the man? Ingeniously. The reader must cross two barriers before reaching the sonnet. First is the poem's title, a line from "The Wife of Bath's Prologue" in *The Canterbury Tales*. That connoisseur of marriage—she's been to the altar five times, twice more than Lowell—does indeed speak of the woe that can destroy a marriage, but in her good-humored, racy, well-traveled, garrulous way she also dwells on the pleasures marriage can give (three of her five mates were stellar—a Hall of Fame batting average). The Wife of Bath's not diffident about taking on and rebutting St. Paul either, so there's precedent for mixing narrative and quotation.

The Schopenhauer maxim shifts our attention from woe to exuberance, as if Lowell's defense lawyer (or conscience) recommended he plead no fault. If sexual desire springs from both natural and supernatural forces, by inference that compulsion mitigates Lowell's responsibility for his conduct. But the bubble bursts: when he's cruising for prostitutes, he's not thinking of "future generations," just immediate gratification.

By pretending that in the sonnet the reader is overhearing Elizabeth Hardwick's soliloquy—is she talking to herself or confiding in a friend?—Lowell indirectly concedes that she has earned a Croix de Guerre for surviving his loopy behavior. But even though a sonnet leaves little space for an extended indictment, Lowell turns its limits into assets, snapping a dual psychological mug shot of himself and his long-suffering wife.

The poem starts casually. Out of a hothouse erotic atmosphere that recalls *A Streetcar Named Desire*, "Life begins to happen." The rush of alliteration and plosives, in lines 2–4, cleverly conveys the husband's impulsivity; like a Hessian or a gang member, he looks to mix it up "out along the razor's edge," which shopworn phrase describes both Boston's seedy East End and Lowell's reckless state of mind. The rueful yet affectionate humor of line 6 siphons off the menace of Lowell's madcap behavior. But exasperation returns. Like the Wife of Bath, the speaker runs "out of alle charitee." The ellipses heighten her sputtering indignation and she switches from the excusing pronoun "it" to the incriminating "he". The "swaggering" soldier of sexual fortune comes back not only drunk but blind to the pain his careless meanness causes. As if exhausted by her self-protective mothering of this adult baby, she asks, in banal terms, "What makes him tick?" (her pun suggests a time bomb). Rather than answering the question, she shares her strategy for coping with his erratic behavior: by tying ten dollars (mad money) and the car keys (not a garter!) to her thigh, she hopes either to keep him from tomcatting or to prepare her getaway. With the final couplet our view of Lowell and this peculiar marriage is rounded off in a grotesque image that makes the reader wince; victimized by his waning sexual powers, the once cruising poet, likened to a bull, an elephant, and, implicitly, an old car, stalls. There's something ignominious and poignant in this failure, especially because we expect the participle "Gored" to be modified by "I," not "he." Lowell doesn't gild his flaws.

If Lowell's lust is monotonous, the sonnet in which he dramatizes its waywardness is not. The language moves easily from the colloquial "hopped up" to the clinical "climacteric"; the couplets avoid obvious, chiming rhymes, while the cadences rise and fall as the syntax expands and contracts. Here's a paradox worth pondering: even as Lowell willingly exposes his character to a harsh public glare, the poet, by virtue of his literary art, salvages a modicum of self-respect. "'To Speak of Woe That Is in Marriage'" must complicate Lowell's biographer's judgment of the poet's marriage and of the feckless man who fails to heed the consequences of his hurtful acts for himself and others.

3.

In "The Pink Locust," a poem from his 1955 volume *Journey to Love*, the septuagenarian William Carlos Williams offered this mild warning to prospective biographers:

It would be
too much

if the public
    pried among the minutiae
        of our private affairs.
Not
    that we have anything to hide
        but could *they*
stand it? Of course
    the world would be gratified
        to find out
what fools we have made of ourselves.
    The question is,
        would they
be generous with us—
    as we have been
        with others?

Throughout most of his career Williams kept close tabs on his reputation among his peers (the public that loved Frost's verse ignored Williams's). Though unhappy about his lack of popularity, he persisted. He had been a long-distance runner in high school, so he had the stamina to be a survivor. Still, in the twilight of his life, even though he had won some prizes and was esteemed by young poets as a bighearted paterfamilias and model, he turned over in his mind his place in the pantheon and speculated about his posthumous reputation. About the first he adopts an almost defensive modesty:

> I am not,
>   I know,
> in the galaxy of poets
>   a rose
>   but *who*, among the rest,
> will deny me
>   my place.

His fierce ambition to be a peer of the poetry realm like Shakespeare, which consumed him in the 1923 *Spring and All*, has abated; he's content now to be considered a minor star: an honorable status. But he worries that a biographer, or a prurient public, will snoop into "the minutiae" of his private affairs and attack both his character and his art. This is not a symptom of crippling insecurity. Williams knows that salacious gossip is a blood sport for some readers, who enjoy seeing a poet exposed as a fool, ridiculed and unhorsed. Hence he doubts that his mistakes will be treated with charity. But when, in a throwaway line, Williams claims "Not / that we have anything to hide," the biographer smiles warily. Not one to deny himself over the course of a long marriage the occasional duplicity to conceal his adulteries from his wife's or townsmen's scrutiny, Williams knew that biographers might unearth a few skeletons rattling around in his closet. Yet his will left no instructions to the executors of his estate that his wife or friends must burn "incriminating" letters about love affairs or destroy manuscripts that might embarrass his family. (Some letters and a diary were declared off-bounds for two decades after his death, out of solicitude for Floss and his son William Eric's feelings; but once the moratorium was lifted, those who read these works found no damaging new revelations about his conduct.) Williams did not try to control opinion from beyond the grave. He would depend on the goodwill of those chronicling his life to place it in the context of his life as a poet.

His faith was not misplaced. To be sure, formalists have denounced or looked askance at Williams's experiments with American speech patterns as ignorant, uncouth, or simply misguided, as if he was stone-deaf to the music of the English lyric tradition: what Stanley Plumly wittily calls "American speech barking at song." Countering the detractors are enthusiasts and acolytes for whom Williams is a saintly icon.

Neither of these camps pays sufficient attention to the links between Williams's work and his life. Because he lived until the age of eighty and wrote prolifically, the task of gathering evidence from his poems to illuminate the life, and vice versa, is exhausting. Indeed, the poems are not simple, single-celled organisms. Obviously, not every poem is so freighted with biographical fact that it needs to be collated, dissected, and analyzed. But some poems are highly revelatory, often in ways not intended by the poet. Take the popular "Asphodel, That Greeny Flower," a poem from *Journey to Love*, which poets as different in style and taste as W. H. Auden, Adrienne Rich, Robert Duncan, and James Laughlin have adored. In his 1951 *Autobiography*, Williams quipped that every husband needs a confessional the size of Pennsylvania Station. When it came time for him to build his own confessional, "Asphodel," the result was neither imposing nor monumental. "Asphodel" sprawled and skittered, as if having to apologize to his wife, Floss, for his infidelities gave Williams a bad case of the jitters—and impaired his poetic control.

First some background. What motivated Williams's disclosures were two circumstances, one private, one public, that converged to assault his well-being. In the summer of 1952, while vacationing in upstate New York, Williams suffered a second stroke that left his speech severely curtailed and his right side and arm paralyzed. (For a long time, he couldn't even write out or type his poems, except with one finger of his left hand.) Death, he feared, ticked like the bomb that had exploded inside his head; that's probably the psychic origin of the atomic bomb motif, that destructive flower of evil in "Asphodel" that everybody, Williams feared, was worshipping.

In addition, the hysteria of the McCarthy witch hunts had reached Rutherford: Williams came under fire for disloyalty. His crimes? He had written a poem in the 1920s praising the young Bolshevik regime and had signed leftist petitions. This uproar blocked his appointment as

Poetry Consultant to the Library of Congress; he never served a day. (More about this later.) He was disappointed that this public honor that he had coveted had slipped away, but he didn't have the strength to fight back. Devastated by these two blows, Williams plunged into a depression in 1953 that caused him to enter Hillside Hospital in Queens for eight weeks of treatment, a descent into hell that fortunately ended in a gradual, if subdued, renewal.

During this crisis the balance of power in the Williams marriage shifted: Bill now depended on Floss to nurse him back to health and to superintend his literary business. Perhaps his brush with death and his gratitude for his wife's care induced him to want to clear his conscience and make amends—and to write "Asphodel." But confession was a treacherous rock face to scale. As a doctor, Williams was accustomed to honesty: breaking the news of a fatal cancer or a Down syndrome baby to a patient, he could be gentle, direct, and compassionate. But in emotional and sexual matters, though he praised frankness, he often waffled, as his works from *Kora in Hell* (1917–1920) to "Asphodel" and the plays *Many Loves* and *A Dream of Love* confirm.

How aware was Floss of his extramarital affairs? That she lacked all sibylline powers about them, or willfully repressed the evidence of them, strains credulity. As Rodney Jones wisely notes in his poem "Plea for Forgiveness," the "chronicle / Of his peccadilloes, an unforgivable thing, a mistake / Like all pleas for forgiveness," which Williams forced, out of guilt, on Floss, and a belief that "It would relieve her to know the particulars / Of affairs she must have guessed and tacitly permitted," is etched in many of his works. Williams may have been enamored of secrets, but the guile of a practiced dissembler would have taxed his acting skills. And since Floss read all of her husband's work, she knew he habitually portrayed her as a frump while lauding the Mina Loys of his circle as Aphrodites. Take this passage from *Kora in Hell*, eight years after their wedding in 1912: "The time never was when he could play more than mattress to the pretty feet of this woman who had been twice a mother without touching the meager pollen of their marriage intimacy." Such contemptuous words could only wither Floss's spirit—and such put-downs outnumbered the affectionate poems about her.

Was Floss merely a drab, if competent, suburban wife and mother? H.D., who came to dislike both Williamses, drew a snide sketch of the couple as country bumpkins making fools of themselves in the gaudy bohemian salons of Paris. In a letter of January 10, 1924, to Viola Baxter Jordan, an old flame of Bill's before he married Floss, H.D. remarks cattily:

> By the way, I thought Williams most banal. Don't tell him so, and Florence we all thought was too silly. She tried to carry on like a movie vamp and it didn't become her and it was so futile with a husband in the background. They both wanted "relationships" we all thought. But nobody was having any from either of them. I thought Williams commonplace, common and banal. Don't say so to anyone. I can't afford to make enemies. But really, really there are limits.

De haut en bas, H.D., as hostile and hypocritical witness, spews out Parisian gossip that, even if only partly true, compels us to rethink and revise our estimate of Floss: in H.D.'s version, Floss is not a mousy, provincial wife but an aspiring Theda Bara. Watching the Williamses playing at dangerous liaisons, H.D. dismisses them as inept amateurs, not adept schemers, and hisses them off the stage. There's something smarmy in H.D.'s wish to peddle her slander and not be caught making snide comments. But if she's right that both Floss and Bill were looking for "relationships" in Paris, she has exposed a deep strain in their marriage. Did Floss refuse to sit passively, suffering, while Dr. Bill flirted and enjoyed the easy sexual morality of Paris? There is no corroborating testimony from any of the many friends and gossipmongers in Paris who spent time in their company that she did.

From "Asphodel" we can learn much about the Williamses' marriage and the poet's equivocal responses to it. A reader first notices the stepdown tercets, a grid Williams follows in every poem of *Journey to Love*. The appeal of this form lies in its fluency and speed, its spaciousness; its sturdy roadbed can handle all kinds of verbal traffic, from the colloquial to the elevated (poets in their old age often feel the freedom to mix seemingly incompatible modes); it permits, democratically, narrative, anecdote, rumination, summing up, aesthetic speculation, epigrams, views of nature and politics (the execution of Ethel and Julius Rosenberg, for example), even near hallucinations (a stark imagined encounter on the subway with his dead father). While periods and commas lightly dot the highway, Williams frequently runs stop signs. Whenever he decides to exit a topic because he can't bear the humiliation of his mea culpa, he slams on the brakes and veers off-ramp to a public reference, a historical citation, an aphorism about poetry, a remark about art, a hodgepodge of memories: the Rosenbergs, Columbus, Darwin, Chaucer, Verrocchio, Cézanne, and his father all make brief appearances, as if actors in a pageant. The scraps of vignettes tossed up, like sea wrack, by the flow of speech are mainly social, not personal; more understanding and camaraderie flow between Williams and other artists—Marsden Hartley, for example—than between Williams and Floss.

There is scarcely a moment in "Asphodel" that confirms his contention that love for Floss "might / send [him] hurtling to the moon." Even in memory no erotic pulse beats. When he addresses her as "your dear self," "my sweet," and "my Queen of love / forever more," these honeyed terms sound hollow, not deeply felt. Williams did not follow the sound advice and praise he gave Louis Zukofsky for love poems written in 1943: "They don't try to SAY anything where nothing can be said. They seek to embody love in the words. To make love." The failures of language in "Asphodel" undermine the credibility of Williams's apology. One needn't be an American vernacular vigilante to find fault with Williams's stiff usage of archaic words like "lief" and "guerdon." Minor lapses, they nonetheless help to brand "Asphodel" as a false lyric that strays far from the vigorous speech melodies he pioneered.

Williams's diction, in fact, repeatedly forces us to question the sincerity of his declarations of love. Let me illustrate:

> It was the love of love,
> the love that swallows up all else,
>   a grateful love,
> a love of nature, of people,
> animals,
> a love engendering
> gentleness and goodness
> that moved me
>   and that I saw in you.

"Love" appears six times in nine lines, as if he were mechanically reciting his vows or protesting too much. These sentiments lack presence, conviction, spontaneity, and music ("a love engendering / gentleness and goodness" is so clumsy that one wonders what was blocking his ear and his critical faculty, and "a love of nature, of people, / animals," is so vague as to render the list virtually generic). Or consider the end of Book 3:

Are facts not flowers
      and flowers facts
or poems flowers
or all works of the imagination,
interchangeable?
Which proves
that love
rules them all, for then
you will be my queen,
      my queen of love
      forever more.

As poetry, this passage reads like a treacly pop lyric without rhyme. These flowers are not objects of beauty or spiritual facts, as Emerson might have argued, and they give off no perfume. (Since Williams wrote hundreds of poems carpeted with fragrant flowers, he knew how to braid a garland of sweet-smelling blossoms.) Instead, in "Asphodel," rhetorical constructs and clichés, pledges of love "forever," are like an adolescent's awkwardly phrased feelings. What should be a modernist madrigal, in homage to Thomas Campion, an Elizabethan doctor poet Williams admired, turns into doggerel and a specious Q.E.D.

Why did Williams's imagination, so tender, lithe, and graceful in "The Ivy Crown," "The Sparrow," "The King!" and "Tribute to the Painters," other poems in *Journey to Love*, falter in "Asphodel"? The verbal surface and the psychological subtext scatter many clues: Williams finds it excruciatingly hard, despite virtuous intentions, to apologize. He cannot, as he does in "The Ivy Crown," admit that "love is cruel / and selfish / and totally obtuse—." Tongue-tied, he stalls for time. He blusters. He free-associates. He hastily changes the subject or invokes a shared past that's like the logo for an insurance company: "We have stood / from year to year / before the spectacle of our lives / with joined hands. / The storm unfolds." Catching at any straw, the magpie poet recalls that he and his beloved read a serious book together, caught a glimpse of the Jungfrau. Such hackneyed verse matches the insipid content.

Williams understandably doesn't relish crawling before his wife like a beggar. His pride balks. Sometimes he pretends that they are equals, and sometimes he plays the humble petitioner, only to speak to her as all-knowing god to mere mortal: "Love / to which you too shall bow / along with me," lines that mix prophecy, command, and beseeching. In rare moments of candor, he'll acknowledge the fissure between them: "my very bones sweated / that I could not cry to you / in the act." But mostly Williams lectures and maunders along, fumbling for the word that will let him, the eelish man, wiggle off the hook.

Williams's timing is even more gauche in Book 3. After the "lean-cheeked" penitent watches his wife, a devoted gardener, watering the parched roots of flowers, he imagines her treating him as tenderly. Cozily, he invites her, "Sweet, creep into my arms." But immediately he adds, "I call on you / as I do on myself the same / to forgive all women / who have offended you." It is illogical and naïve to expect a wounded Floss to munificently forgive all the women he slept or dallied with, while he shrinks from asking her directly to forgive him. He seems oblivious that his request might be tearing open scar tissue.

Williams unconsciously sabotages his avowed wish for atonement and a reconciliation that would enable him to "die at peace in his bed." At the end of Book 2 occurs a brusque put-down of Floss, all the more insulting for being so careless: "With your smiles / and other trivia of the sort / my secret life / has been made up." The word "trivia" jumps out at the reader, expressing a cruelty that Williams seldom could entirely suppress when portraying Floss. In a curious plea bargain, he again fails to show contrition: "Imagine you saw / a field made up of women / all silver-white. / What should you do / but love them. / The storm [of recriminations] bursts / or fades! It is not / the end of the world." This shrug of the shoulders could hardly be what Floss longed to hear from her apologizing husband.

Does "Asphodel" appease Floss? Despite a belated, patronizing compliment that Floss belonged with those women who "have Helen in their hearts"—in truth, Williams was the Helen in their marriage—the poet is forced to exculpate himself. Just before the poem's coda, Floss remains obstinately silent, reproachfully shutting "the valves of her attention, like stone," to borrow Emily Dickinson's grim line. Williams rushes to fill the emptiness, declaring "you have forgiven me / making me new again." But the bald pseudo-poetic statements and unconnected fragments of

"Asphodel" do not inspire any more trust in the reader than they apparently did in Floss. Williams seems to be trotting out any line that might persuade her to absolve him—or let him absolve himself. A slightly rank odor of the disingenuous rises from the page.

The compulsion to confess his infidelities to Floss was not new. In 1948, Williams wrote a play, *A Dream of Love*, that examined his marriage with a frank thoroughness and honesty that is missing in "Asphodel." The play depicts a chasm between a husband and wife, at times with bantering humor and affection and at other times with a violent bluntness that borders on misogyny on his part and masochism (made up of gloom and genteel sarcasm) on hers. The plot is simple: Doc Thurber, the Williams surrogate (he quotes several of Williams's poems), goes into New York for an assignation with his mistress and dies of a heart attack after sex, as if Nemesis struck him down for his infidelity. That is the formal cause. In a bizarre twist, Dan, a most robust ghost, comes back to justify his adultery *and* to profess his love for Myra, the Floss character, who is convulsed by contradictory emotions: distraught at and outraged by the betrayal, and descending into a near-comatose state of inconsolable depression, yet clinging to her love for him. Williams's portrait of the fictional yet transparently autobiographical Floss is his most psychologically acute, balanced, and genuine limning of her. She is extremely conscious of her husband's flawed character, particularly his womanizing, likening him to an infant and a boy. When she asks him, "What would you do without all your women, darling?," he replies, "I'd find one up a tree somewhere." To which she comments with droll forbearance, "You sure would. And drag her down by the hair [like a caveman]—if she didn't drop down on you first from a low branch. I don't care—so long as I have my garden. Really, Dan. I'm getting awfully fed up with this routine. The same thing, the same thing, over and over and over and over."

Elsewhere she flares up with resentment, sure that he was itching to be rid of her, to be free to do as he pleases; "I've never had you," she says dolefully. She may "stupidly" love and admire him despite his serial unfaithfulness, but she cannot trust him. Ruefully, she recalls his answer when, before their marriage, she asked him if he loved her: "Love you? Hell no. I want to marry you." (Almost the same phrasing recurs in Williams's *Autobiography*.) To the husband, "love is a matter of the will pure and simple"; to the wife, his withholding of commitment rankles, leaving her insecure, "lonely, neglected." Her children grown, she is "of no use" to herself. As a middle-aged housewife and mother, she is remarkably free of illusions: "Who wants a woman like me?"

Compulsive erotic desire, a will to power, and unyielding gender roles can maim or destroy a marriage. Feeling trapped and restless, the bored doctor yearns to escape the bourgeois chains and live free, yet he does not wish to end their long relationship. When he describes Myra as "an amazing woman whom I sometimes greatly admire, frequently count on in emergencies and always love—and protect," even though she calls him a liar, he's not being hypocritical: there is truth in his claim. When she hears that he died in one of "the priceless dry / rooms / of illicit love," however, she is almost insanely driven to wring from the mistress all the offensive details. Thwarted in this, she retreats to her room, as if repudiating the world.

In the last scene, Doc speaks like a silver-tongued orator, mesmerizing Myra as he had Dotty, his mistress. "Anything you say—just so that you keep talking so beautifully," she says sleepily. The text upon which he sermonizes is in Williams's self-justifying sophistry: "to renew our love, burn the old nest and emerge transcendent, a flame for you!" he had to take advantage of his sexual opportunities. In his later works, Williams frequently claims, "That's one thing about sex—you're never so happy as when you're rid of it." But in speech after speech, Doc dredges up memories of a tormented self-consciousness; he justifies his affairs as a form of compensation for years of deprivation; fulfilling his need was "none of your business": "She [Dotty] was good-looking, hot as a hound and practically asking me to love her. I'd be mad to pass up a chance like that. Naturally, I took her up." Doc argues that his straying made him love Myra even more, but when she poses the hypothetical question "Suppose you had found me in such a position," he mocks her with smug machismo: "You couldn't be in such a position. You've got *me!*" She slaps him and later calls him a "dirty, lying, cheap guy." At the final curtain, after a scene reenacting the seduction and death in the hotel room and an explosion that fills the stage like a battlefield, Myra recovers her equanimity and returns, a widow, to her former competent self.

Three years separate *A Dream of Love* from "Asphodel," but they are worlds apart in giving us a convincing picture of Floss and the Williams marriage. The hit-or-miss rhetorical gambits in "Asphodel" lay bare for the biographer the unconscious self-deceits and lame defenses that sometimes came into play when Williams's conflicts about women, and Floss in particular, assailed him. If the sick mind is to be cured, Williams assures us in "Asphodel," one's will can turn an ailing marriage into a blooming garden. In his letters from medical school at the University of Pennsylvania (1903–1905) to his brother Edgar, Williams asserts again and again that the will plays the key role in the fashioning of character in doctor and poet, and in "Asphodel" the will is elevated to a place above imagination in an enduring marriage. But when the will buckles, the physician cannot heal himself, nor can poetry, a usually effective elixir, bring the desired peace of mind. So in the end, "Asphodel" resembles a landscape of patchy beauty overrun by weeds, tended by a distracted gardener. This messiness, however, recalls Yeats's wise maxim that "rhetoric is the will doing the work of the imagination." It is ironic that two lines by Auden (an avowed fan of "Asphodel"!)—"Lay your sleeping head / Human on my faithless arm"—distill all that the prolix Williams attempts to say in his poem's ill-managed petition for absolution.

Freud remarked in 1930, "Once, in discussing the difficulty of psychoanalyzing Goethe, you observed, 'This is because Goethe was not only as a poet, a great self-revealer, but also, in spite of the abundance of autobiographical records, a careful concealer.'" In writing the life of Williams, I have relied heavily on the poems. But as rich as this hoard is, it had to be supplemented by all the other available records in library archives and people's memories of their encounters with him: letters, memoirs, interviews, stories, and plays perforce correct or modify what the poems say explicitly or equivocally. Throughout his long career, Williams was prodigal in setting down his opinions, and like Goethe he revealed and concealed his "inner life." The biographer must sift the paper trail, compare versions, and decide which words express Williams's deepest feelings and which are self-serving or cursory. The task is further complicated by the fact that Williams often changed his mind. Take his courtship of Floss, which I shall examine in a later chapter. He portrayed her in poems, in plays, in a trilogy of novels, and in his *Autobiography*—all valuable bits and pieces of evidence. But the letters he and Floss exchanged before and during his trip to Leipzig in 1909, right after he proposed marriage to her and she accepted, are fascinating for their changeable moods: in one letter, he sounds like a suitor trying to persuade his lady that he is in earnest and will prove a desirable husband; in the next, he sounds nervous, wondering if he should bolt; and in a third letter, he veers from hurtful put-downs to arch teasing to promises of unshakable loyalty. Floss, too, is overwhelmed and unsure of her feelings. Her cheeks flush with anger at his gibes and she leaves the door open for him to break off their engagement; then she relents and starts dreaming of their life together. Both are caught up in a whirligig of emotions that seems likely at any moment to rage out of control and lead to a breakup.

4.

Biographers often worry that when they halt the narrative of a poet's life in order to discuss his poems, they are tampering dangerously with chronology and breaking the guild's solemn vow to revere objective fact. Some biographers, such as Clive Fisher in *Hart Crane: A Life*, abstain from literary analysis of the poems. This is a strategic mistake, I believe. Without his poems and letters, Crane is just another tormented alcoholic who ended his own life. Literary criticism is an indispensable stethoscope in the biographer's bag. William Carlos Williams wrote poems for sixty of his eighty years. That exacting art commanded his most profound loyalty. His life was not filled with events of high-pitched intensity, as Marina Tsvetayeva's was; history was not his chronic bane. Having chosen medicine as a profession, he inevitably lived by its rhythms and bowed to its pressures, all of which he described eloquently in story and memoir and poem. The biographer doesn't have to follow Williams year after year on his medical rounds so as to gain a full understanding of what his practice meant for him—by all accounts, he was a highly able doctor—since he provided a running commentary on its rewards and satisfactions and strains (and the physical and mental toll it exacted) and, above all, on how it shaped his art. Medicine seldom aroused emotional turmoil in him.

Women did. And so Williams's poems about women and desire are an incalculable trove for the biographer, not as transcripts in cipher of his fantasy life or diaries that confess adulteries, struggles, conquests, and disappointments, but as episodes in a cumulative bildungsroman. We gain glimpses of the "unfettered leewardings" (to use Hart Crane's suggestive phrase) during which Williams fashioned his complex identity and his poetic style. From 1903 to 1963, the year of his death, major themes; psychological issues of great, unsettling import; hasty and recurrent trial-and-error methods of solving problems imprint themselves, like DNA, on Williams's poems.

If God is in the details, the poet's life and character are emblazoned on his changeable art. It is therefore incumbent on the biographer to be as familiar with Williams's rhythmic quirks and line breaks, his experiments with vernacular and typography, as he is with the friends Williams most cherished and the inescapable humdrum of the doctor's rounds. By patiently examining this massive, crucial poetic evidence, which is in its own way as telling as external fact, the biographer may find that the disjointed parts eventually cohere into a multilayered portrait of the artist.

TWO

Roots and Branches of the Family Tree

I. Grandmother Wellcome

Like many children whose parents migrated to America from older cultures, William Carlos Williams brooded over his family's origins and his parents' reluctance to embrace new-world customs. Although his father lived in the United States for over thirty-five years, he never bothered to take out American citizenship, claiming that it was easier to carry a British passport on his business travels through Central America. Coming from a man of impeccable rationality, this explanation could not have been the entire truth; Williams correctly saw that while Pop did not object to his sons being raised as Americans, he withheld his own commitment to the brash young republic in whose precincts he had settled.

The three adults who made up Williams's family constellation—his Cockney grandmother Emily Dickinson Wellcome, whose name seemed an augury of his vocation; his father, William George Williams, as respectable and balanced as his signature; and his mother, Raquel Hélène Rose Hoheb Williams, whose florid run of melodious names suited her mixed ancestry and theatrical personality—led nomadic lives before they even reached America. For each, Rutherford, New Jersey, was never a satisfactory Ithaca. To the impressionable young Williams, there was poetic magic and mystery—and danger—in these family journeys, heirloom stories he often rummaged through looking for clues to his fractured identity.

Williams eventually chose a different path: apart from a couple of Wanderjahre in Europe, he put his roots down in the soil of his birthplace in suburban New Jersey, even though his circle of artist friends sometimes razzed him for fearing New York's gaudy cosmopolitanism. When Pound cuttingly mocked Williams as a hick ignorant of the "real" America,

Williams bore his friend's gibes with restive dignity, but they did rankle, and he swore an oath that he would eventually prove Pound wrong. (He did.) For Williams, who sometimes played the rube, it was crucial to be counted in the census of American artists, and so he sublimated his family's vagabondage into a restless search for a poetic idiom that would signal that he belonged to the company of democratic polemicists and innovators who, like Whitman and H. L. Mencken, relished the swagger and singular cadences of the American language. Growing up, he mostly heard Spanish spoken at home—Grandma Wellcome spoke "pig Spanish"; his mother French, Spanish, and a halting English; and his father both the King's English and Spanish—so he had to consciously train his ear in American English. His poems often include snippets of conversation he overheard in the streets or the hospital wards.

Because origins fascinated Williams, he kept returning, in poems, memoirs, and letters, to the lives and characters of his parents and grandmother. (*In the American Grain*, a gallery of Plutarchan portraits of the founding figures from Leif Eriksson and Columbus to Lincoln and Poe, extended that interest into the sphere of the country's historical and spiritual origins.) His parents' estrangement from their adopted country embarrassed and irked him: most children desire conventional behavior from the older generation, reasoning that it will shield them from being branded as "different."

Williams especially yearned for the normal because both his mother and grandmother were spiritualists. He recalls Elena falling into a trance during a séance and appearing "insane, failing to recognize him"; even his rationalist father "believed literally . . . that the spirits of the dead did materialize through her and did try to reach us." As his grandmother grew older, she became increasingly cranky and erratic. Moreover, Godwin, her oldest son, was mentally unhinged and probably schizophrenic. He claimed to hear "evil spirits" and was prone to paroxysms of violence.

Williams's family could never have posed for a Norman Rockwell magazine cover. Until the end of his days, his accounts of them, in all genres, bristle with moody contradictions, as if, caught in powerful emotional undertows, he had had to thrash about to survive. With such forebears, it is not surprising that he chose the safety of a bourgeois life, leaving the door ajar just enough for him to play the thrill-seeking sexual rebel and maverick poet. This conflict, which erupts in all phases of his life, never got fully resolved.

Consider Williams's shifting attitudes to his grandmother Wellcome. Echoing Henry Adams, he declares portentously in the introduction to *Yes, Mrs. Williams* (1959), an informal archive of his mother's memories, "Determined women have governed my fate." Among the spunkiest and most strong-willed of these women was his grandmother. With her five-year-old son from a failed marriage to the mysterious George Williams, she had braved the Atlantic crossing and survived the ship's running aground on Fire Island. In New York she met and soon married an itinerant photographer from St. Thomas and moved with him to that Virgin Island and later to Puerto Plata, where William George grew up and where she gave birth to three more children: Godwin, Irving, and Rosita, an epileptic who died young. (Puerto Plata is the tropical setting of "Adam," a 1936 poem in which Williams caustically demolishes his father's character.) Seizing on the tight-lipped Mrs. Wellcome's cryptic hint that she was raised in the "Godwin" home—on her deathbed, she forced her son to swear he would never reveal the secret of his paternity (he kept that vow)—Williams speculated in his *Autobiography* that it was perhaps the family of the famous radical William Godwin who sheltered her.

Williams was in the habit of saying that his grandmother, not his mother, had brought him up: an implicit criticism of Elena's care. The idea of these two willful women battling over Williams appealed to him. As he gleefully recalls, "Grandma took me over or tried to. But once Mother lost her temper and laid the old gal out with a smack across the puss."

When it came to rousing his imagination, Grandma Wellcome won hands down, at least until her death in 1920. The key poem in Williams's artistic coming-of-age is "The Wanderer: A Rococo Study." (An early version appeared in the March 1914 issue of the literary magazine *The Egoist*; a revised one in *Al Que Quiere!* in 1917.) Strands of aesthetic religiosity run through this odd sequence, expressed in pseudo-biblical rhetoric. The first section, "Advent," describes not the coming of Christ but Williams's poetic "novitiate." His "semimythical" grandmother takes on several roles: a mother bird teaching her fledgling how to fly; a sphinx posing enigmatic questions (Williams wonders, "How shall I be a mirror to this modernity?"); a "high-wanderer of by-ways" who is "imperious in beggary" yet also reveals to him the beauty of the world as it looked at the end of creation's first day. In her final guise as a "marvelous old queen," she changes into a crone muse who, like a rouged courtesan dressed in rags, tries to recover her youth.

Grandmother Wellcome inspires the eager recruit to marvel at and observe nature and to learn how social injustice and economic exploitation brutalize the lives of the poor. So he portrays the striking Paterson silk workers waiting patiently on bread lines as proletarian Herculeses who lift "beeves" and barrels with ease. Stirred by what he sees, Williams experiments with a coarse, realistic style, much like the cartoons that appeared in *The Masses* during the 1930s:

> The flat skulls with the unkempt black or blond hair
> The ugly legs of the young girls, pistons
> Too powerful for delicacy!
> The women's wrists, the men's arms red
> Used to heat and cold, to toss quartered beeves
> And barrels, and milk-cans, and crates of fruit!
>
> Faces all knotted up like burls on oaks,
> Grasping, fox-snouted, thick-lipped,
> Sagging breasts and protruding stomachs,
> Rasping voices, filthy habits with the hands.

"The Wanderer" is in fact a laboratory of styles. Williams alternates between comic bombast (marked by a torrent of exclamation points), earnest prophecy (usually in earthbound diction), and hortatory romantic sentiments that can make the reader squirm:

> "Waken! my people, to the boughs green
> with ripening fruit within you!
> Waken to the myriad cinquefoil
> In the waving grass of your minds!
> Waken to the silent phoebe nest
> Under the eaves of your spirit!"

As the two excerpts show, except for a handful of linguistic arabesques, the poem hardly seems rococo, as its subtitle advertises; even its flights of fancy are lumbering. Many of Williams's flower poems—"Blueflags,"

"Daisy," "Queen-Anne's Lace"—could be classified as rococo, but there's nothing polished or ironical in "The Wanderer." Grandmother Well-come as a blend of Calliope and hag dressed in tatters—"Ominous, old, painted— / With bright lips and lewd Jew's eyes / Her might strapped in a corset / To give her age youth"—is hardly a figure in a Fragonard painting. If Williams was temperamentally unable to overcome his fond-ness for Romantic diction—it was lodged in his limbic brain—he could, aided by his medical training, look fearlessly at horrific facts, thus travel-ing a back road to a more tough-minded realism.

The climax of this peculiar poem is the poet's baptismal immersion in the filthy waters of the Passaic River. Mrs. Wellcome plays many parts in this ritual: the "personification of poetry," a wizened priestess initiat-ing the acolyte poet, a divinity turning the riverbank into a sacred grove and bird refuge. All of these underscore the close bond between grand-mother and votary-grandson. Mrs. Wellcome consecrates Williams as a sacrificial offering to the river god, in exchange for the return of an un-named "old friend of my revels." She acts and speaks and chants like a daft nanny urging her ward to essay a bizarre ceremony: "'Enter, youth, into this bulk! / Enter, river, into this young man!'" Williams's chronicle of his initiation resembles a perplexing dream in which elemental forces buffet and nearly kill him. As in the story of Abraham and Isaac, the sacrificial beloved is not allowed to perish, rescue arriving in the nick of time:

> Then the river began to enter my heart,
> Eddying back cool and limpid
> Into the crystal beginning of the days.
> But with the rebound it leaped forward:
> Muddy, then black and shrunken
> Till I felt the utter depth of its rottenness
> The vile breadth of its degradation
> And drooped down knowing this was me now.
> But she lifted me and the water took a new tide
> Again into the older experiences,
> And so, backward and forward,
> It tortured itself within me
> Until time had been washed finally under,

And the river had found its level
And its last motion had ceased
And I knew all—it became me.
And I knew this for double certain
For there, whitely, I saw myself
Being borne off under the water!
I could have shouted out in my agony
At the sight of myself departing
Forever—but I bit back my despair
For she had averted her eyes
By which I knew well what she was thinking—
And so the last of me was taken.

For his art to be of any value, his wily grandmother teaches him, he must plumb both the depths of degradation, even at the risk of drowning, and the pristine ideal, however muddied it eventually may become. Internalizing both aspects of the river god tortures Williams, but the struggle is presumably worth the prize, a knowledge that confers power: "And I knew all—it became me."

As Williams admitted, "The Wanderer" was a failure. The flow of its quasi-mystical experience is sluggish; the seven lines that begin with "And" tie up the narrative in a pedestrian knot; and its language lacks the allure, flair, and exaltation of, say, Elizabeth Bishop's folkloric poem "The Riverman." In hindsight, Williams noted that "The Wanderer" was "a disappointed, a defeated person—myself." Nonetheless, in this disheveled poem he finishes, at the late age of thirty-four, serving his long apprenticeship. Stability, for the driven Williams, is stultifying; change, a wilderness of desires and possibilities. The virtue of the new is that it rouses his senses, stamina, and imagination, thereby permitting him to reinvent himself and his poetry.

Seven years after "The Wanderer," Williams wrote the first of two versions of a poem titled "The Last Words of My Grandmother." In the 1939 revision, he added the adjective "English" to the title and lopped off the poem's initial ten stanzas, which make up a cheeky portrait of a pimply, self-involved nineteen-year-old. Although ostensibly of his cousin, it seems to be a covert autobiographical sketch:

She stayed over after
the summer people had gone
at her little shack
on the shore, an old woman

impossible to get on with
unless you left her alone
with her things—among them
the young grandson, nineteen

whom she had raised.
He endured her because
he was too lazy to work
too lazy to think and

had a soft spot for her
in his bright heart, also a
moustache, a girl, bed
and board out of the old lady

the sea before him
and a ukelele—The two
had remained on and on
into the cold weather

Thanksgiving day
after the heavy dinner
At a good neighbor's table
Death touched the old lady

in her head—Home she must
go leaning heavily on the
boy who put her to bed and
gave her what she wanted—

water and Mother Eddy's
Science and Health and

forgot her for other things.
But she began to rave in the night.

In the morning after frying
an egg for her
he combed his whiskers
picked his pimples

and got busy with
a telegram for help—
Gimme something to eat
Gimme something to eat

I'm starving
they're starving me
was all I got out of
the dazed old woman

Williams's narrative crackles with sarcasm directed against this fop-pish beach bum. The gulf between him and the old lady who raised him seems immense. She is ending her days as a dotty recluse living in a shack on Long Island Sound, surrounded by her Christian Science tracts, scraps of precious memories, and hoard of curios. Part aspiring Casanova, part uncrowned prince, part vain moocher, the youth "loafes and invites his soul," to borrow Whitman's words. When he does notice his grandmother, it's through peripheral vision, as an afterthought. Yet he's a kindly narcis-sist, redeemed by his "bright heart."

His complacency splinters when "Death touched the old lady / in her head"—the change announced in that spare sentence. It takes him time to grasp the fact that the disaster that has struck his grandmother will also sweep away those sentimental dreams he strummed on the ukulele, the poor youth's blue guitar. Like a Beau Brummel, he carefully prepares his morning toilette and composes "a telegram for help" as if sitting down to write a billet-doux.

But fact often blows through a Williams poem to dispel the murk of illusions. In "The Last Words of My English Grandmother," it is Emily's raving voice, couched in a demotic that has no room for niceties and that conveys her nervous breakdown, hysterical commands, and the "scrimmage of appetite" still strong in her, that effortlessly dominates the second half of the poem; Williams's role shrinks to interjection, remonstrance, or the reading of stage directions:

> There were some dirty plates
> and a glass of milk
> beside her on a small table
> near her stinking bed
>
> Wrinkled and nearly blind
> she lay and snored
> rousing to cry
> with anger in her tones
>
> They're starving me—
> You won't move me
> I'm all right—I won't go
> to the hospital. No, no, no
>
> Give me something to eat!—
> Let me take you
> to the hospital, I said,
> and after you are well
>
> you can do as you please—
> She smiled her old smile:
> Yes, you do what you please
> first then I can do what I please—
>
> Oh, oh, oh, she cried
> as the ambulance men lifted her
> to their stretcher on the floor—
> Is that what you call
>
> making me comfortable?—
> Now her mind was clear
> Oh you think you're awfully
> smart, you young people,

she said to us, but I'll tell
you you don't know
anything—Then we started.
On the way

we passed a long row
of elms, she looked
a long while out of the
ambulance window and said—

What are all those
fuzzy looking things out there?
Trees? Well, I'm
tired of them.

As she's carted off to the hospital, her dazed mind clearing for a moment, Grandma Wellcome, memorably, stays true to her querulous self:
the triple "oh"s poignantly echo the earlier flurry of "no"s that protested
against being uprooted from her home. In a last hurrah, she lashes out
impotently at the youngsters with her customary scorn, then lapses into
an apathy broken only by her question about the elms—"fuzzy looking"
because of her near-blindness and dwindling consciousness—and her
petulant valedictory, "Trees? Well, I'm / tired of them."

Why did the fifty-nine-year-old Williams cut the first ten stanzas of
this poem? Perhaps like the stodgy Wordsworth of the 1850 edition of
The Prelude, he wished to distance himself from his early impudence.
Perhaps he realized that by upstaging his dying grandmother in the 1924
version he had distracted the reader. As a doctor, he had witnessed many
such death scenes and had been forced to order patients hospitalized
against their will. This enabled him to portray his aged grandmother's noble weariness with accuracy and compassion.

Williams often dropped autobiographical materials into the oddest
contexts—he routinely played slyboots with the reader or squirreled away
embarrassing items about his conduct in obscure hiding places. Though
he often shows himself in an unflattering light, as if following the doctor's
method of recording a patient's symptoms, confusion and deception came
upon him suddenly like a tic.

The third extended portrait of Grandmother Wellcome is a prose cadenza that Williams inserted as the second movement of a 1927 com-position in four parts, "From: A Folded Skyscraper." (The sequence origi-nally appeared in Paul Rosenfeld's *American Caravan* anthology.) Section 1 is a poem piquantly titled "Hemmed-in Males," which Williams glossed for John Thirlwall this way: "I was making fun of anyone who objected to the dirty images. I'll make a poem out of anything. I was trying to defy woman." "Dirty images"? *The Police Gazette* would have rejected them for not being lurid or defiant enough; the only coded sexual reference is to "black sand," which, Williams says, stands for pubic hair; as innuendo, this doesn't fly. The "hemmed-in male" is one "poor George," a janitor at the local school who has lost his pituitary gland and vas deferens to sur-gery and whose favorite saloon has shut down. The most visible women in the poem are WCTU members knitting, like the three Fates, "elastic stockings / for varicose veins." The river of life having drowned poor George and his masculine world, the poet mockingly bids farewell to po-etry and returns to his home, that limbo for "hemmed-in males" like him. The brief third section, "The Winds," evokes hurricane-force gales that strip "the bark from the trees, . . . scales from / the mind and husbands from wives."

These poems frame an unorthodox prose tribute to Emily Wellcome, a eulogy that in its catalogue of her quicksilver traits shuns pieties and lovingly paints her eccentricities: serving food with dirty utensils; riding a bicycle at sixty, even if injury resulted; and, at eighty, lying in the surf so long she had to struggle to stand up. Though Williams doesn't highlight the quirks of character and taste she bequeathed him, when he writes that "the city stifled her, she could not wait for the spring," he could just as well be describing himself. The same goes for her contradictions: "She liked no society, no gadding," yet "talk was her best weapon, she could lay you an argument like a steel fence and you might try to get through it for a day or a week or till doomsday and there she'd be still back of it laughing at you." Or "the only fault she confessed to was a lack of self-assertion," although "when she moved into a neighborhood she'd go out and clean it up, tonguewise. She'd lay 'em out, male and female— . . ." Williams often careens between these poles, too. He might argue with her in a tone of cheerful combativeness about such hygienic issues as the need for "clean dish rags," but from *Kora in Hell* onward, filth exerted an appeal to his imagination; in "the ischial-rectal grottoes" of the human body, the doctor poet discovered valuable truths that the pure, averting their eyes, repressed.

"When I think how my grandmother flirted with me I often wonder why I have not been attracted by women of her type. She was a devil if ever there was one," Williams begins section 2. In fact, he was drawn to, or at least titillated by, "devilish" women. But Emily Wellcome, whatever her insecurities and disappointments, nurtured him reliably; she didn't raise the demons sleeping in his mind. Grateful, he loved her unstintingly, blemishes and all.

2.

In Book 3 of "Asphodel, That Greeny Flower," a poem that moves by abrupt jump cuts according to some internal law of associations, Williams rides the subway, on his way to a medical meeting. His attention is arrested by a bearded man sitting across from him: "For some reason / which I could not fathom / I was unable / to keep my eyes off him." Williams inspects the stranger from head to toe, as in a medical exam, jotting down such details as "a worn knobbed stick / between his knees / suitable / to keep off dogs," "a brown felt hat / lighter than his skin," intelligent eyes "wide open / but evasive, mild," and the shabby gentility of his attire. Suddenly, in the panicky cadence of a dream, Williams realizes that the man reminds him of his father—"Some surface / of some advertising sign / is acting / as a reflector. It is / my own"—and admonishes himself to speak to the man because "He / will know the secret." But Williams hesitates, and the man disappears into the crowd, leaving the poet to regret the missed opportunity. He then veers off to comment on a sexual orchid that Melville had admired in Hawaii, not remarking on the curious link between the depiction of his father's shriveled sexuality (that "worn knobby stick / Between his knees" and his own similar plight (he had been felled by strokes).

William George had kept the secret of his own paternity, as Grandmother Wellcome had demanded. But this encounter with a chimera on the subway implies that at age sixty-eight, William Carlos Williams, still haunted by his father, couldn't pluck out the heart of William George's mystery; perhaps some important word of approval or love never passed between them, so they failed to build a bridge that would draw them close to each other.

In a late interview with Walter Sutton, Williams equates William

George's refusal to become an American citizen with T. S. Eliot's apostasy in abandoning the country of his birth. It is a classic case of displacement:

> I was insanely jealous of [Eliot], who was much more cultured than I was, and I didn't know anything about English Literature at all. But when I recognized what he was doing, I didn't like it at all. He was giving up America. And maybe my attachment to my father, who was English and who had never become an American citizen influenced me because I was— You know, the Oedipus complex between father and son—I resented him being English and not being American.

Forty years had passed since his father's death from cancer in 1918. If it seems grotesque for the son to harbor such a tenacious animosity toward his father, those complex, roiled emotions confirm how deeply Pop's character imprinted itself on Bill, who feared that Pop disdained his poetry as much as T. S. Eliot did.

Who was William George Williams? His son made many stabs at solving this riddle, sifting a sparse set of clues. One was Pop's last gift to Williams: a figurine of Confucius, a revered sage, august and dignified, who taught self-command and the promotion of virtue. Pop's conservative rules of conduct, which might be summed up in the Confucian maxim "The cautious seldom err," influenced Bill throughout his life, though not without inciting sporadic rebellions. A man of sedate temperament and settled habits, the very model of a bourgeois gentleman, William George worked as an advertising manager and traveling salesman for the New York firm of Lanman and Kemp, peddling Florida Water (a popular scent) in Central and Latin America, often for months at a time. In 1897, for example, when Bill was fourteen, William George was asked to spend a full year supervising the building of a Florida Water factory in Buenos Aires.

During the year William George was in Argentina, Elena deposited Bill and Edgar at the Château de Lancy, an international school near Geneva, Switzerland. This plan did not shock or faze Bill. It had two clever advantages: it allowed Elena to enjoy a nostalgic last fling in Paris, the scene of her indelible three-year taste of bohemian liberty, yet remain close enough to her sons to monitor their well-being; and it would rescue them, at the start of puberty, from the parochialism of Rutherford, a desirable loss of innocence. "We were mere infants, hundreds of years younger than most of the sixty-two other boys there," Williams recalled in his *Autobiography*. The school, populated by students from twelve countries, proved to be an idyll for Bill (he fails to mention Edgar by name, possibly because his younger brother was more nuisance than sidekick or had his own circle of friends). If not quite a Prince of Misrule, Bill led the merry life of a mischievous schoolboy, playing pranks such as "dropping a paper water-bomb on the head" of a British boy, shinnying up trees to steal magpie nests, and tunneling into the gymnasium for the sheer joy of tweaking authority; he even warded off an elegant old pederast who twice tried to molest him. At the same time, he stored up memories of asphodels and "the odor of violets." What's striking in Williams's retelling of this year and a half in his *Autobiography* is his pleasure in dwelling on how, far from his father's monitoring eye, his conscience could relax; there are no moments of terror like those in Wordsworth's *The Prelude* when the young poet steals a rowboat and the mountains loom like avenging gods. Rather, like Benjamin Franklin, Williams lingers contentedly on his blithe younger self, approving his "general deviltry." His memories of the school were so positive that he sent his own boys there when they were thirteen.

Propriety, order, discipline, and moderation were the Lares and Penates of the Williams household, and Pop their staunch priest. In the family, he decided most crucial matters of education and child rearing, such as sending Bill and Edgar to Horace Mann for high school. From Rutherford to Morningside Heights and back was a commute of three hours by ferry and trolley, which meant their getting up at the crack of dawn. Bill and Edgar did not balk at this daily Spartan regimen. The boys knew that Pop expected his sons to set high goals for themselves and to excel in their studies. (Edgar was the star pupil, not Bill.) Williams internalized his father's precepts as a drive for perfection, but this striving also aroused an instinct to choose imperfection so as to escape the burden of ethical imperatives. His poems, which often flaunt their ragged edges, mirror this suspicion of excessive order.

Pop was literate, even bookish. Culture, for William George, was an integral part of a balanced education. "He loved to read before anything else, even before working in his garden," Williams remembers. "He invariably spoke with a distinguished choice of words." The family would gather in the parlor as William George read from Shakespeare's plays or Palgrave's *Golden Treasury*, an anthology as Victorian as antimacassars and beloved as a reliquary of English poetic jewels. It was doubtless during these readings that Williams first fell under the spell of lyric poetry, especially Keats's; throughout his career he both honored and cheekily professed to dislike and subvert the dominant English poetic tradition.

During his final illness in 1918, William George and son Bill collaborated on a translation of the Guatemalan writer Rafael Arévalo Martínez's story "The Man Who Resembled a Horse." In these hours, grappling with a knotty text, father and son regarded each other with mutual respect, and Bill could temporarily distract his father from his pain. Pop had never been timid about expressing his judgments of poems or prose. When Ezra Pound, on a visit to Rutherford, read aloud one of his own poems, Pop pounced on it for not saying precisely what Ezra avowed he meant it to say, a lesson, Williams remarks, that Pound took to heart. But it is much touchier for a father to criticize his child's work. Here, too, Pop did not hesitate. In 1909, he facilitated the publication of Williams's "disastrous" first book (actually a pamphlet), which "bears the marks of Pop's corrections and suggestions all over it—changes most of which I adopted. Poor Pop, how he must have suffered."

That the poet was sensitive to, even unnerved by, his father's comments is evident in a nightmare Williams had a few days after Pop died:

> I saw him coming down a peculiar flight of exposed steps, steps I have since identified as those before the dais of Pontius Pilate in some well-known painting. But this was in a New York office building, Pop's office. He was bare-headed and had some business letters in his hand on which he was concentrating as he descended. I noticed him and with joy cried out, "Pop! So, you're not dead!" But he only looked up at me over his right shoulder and commented severely, "You know all that poetry you're writing. Well, it's no good." I was left speechless and woke trembling. I have never dreamed of him since.

This is a harrowing encounter between father and son, their exchange amplified from a private flaying to a public humiliation. Pop takes on the dual roles of Pontius Pilate, a figure of Roman authority reviled for his part in Jesus's crucifixion, and preoccupied businessman. From these four monosyllabic words there can be no appeal. In this brief primordial scene,

Williams is crushed and rendered nearly speechless. His curt statement "I have never dreamed of him since" is feeble, even as symbolic patricide, though it conveys his devastation.

The wound obviously never healed, since Williams recounted that dream in his *Autobiography* of 1951, thirty-five years after Pop's death. In that memoir, William George's portrait is like an incomplete collage, the artist pasting on the canvas scraps of fact, anecdote, and gossip. From these details, the reader can discern in outline the figure of a paterfamilias who was openhanded—he never stinted on his boys' education—but obstinate; when, for example, Pop refused to let Bill open an office at 131 Passaic Avenue, Williams was so incensed he walked several miles into the country and back to quell his violent anger. No single chapter, however, exhaustively fathoms his father's character.

His most ambitious attempt occurred in 1936 in the poem "Adam," paired with "Eve," which dissects his relationship with his mother. ("Eve" was written first.) Both poems appear in one of Williams's most cohesive books, *Adam & Eve & the City*. A scattering of short poems and five translations of Spanish *canciones* serve as ornamental borders around four longish poems: the aforementioned "Adam" and "Eve," "The Crimson Cyclamen" (a rapturous elegy for his friend Charles Demuth, the noted painter), and "Perpetuum Mobile: The City," an allegretto finale in which motifs of love and desire, art and dalliance, separation and fusion, fall into a skittish but discernible pattern and Williams takes stock of his marriage.

In "Adam," he appraises his father's past and speculates on how his youth in the tropics shaped and warped him. The poem is nearly barren of mercy and affection. Alternately clinical and satirical, it is also at times quasi-biblical:

> Thence he was driven—
> out of Paradise—to taste
> the death that duty brings
> so daintily, so mincingly,
> with such a noble air—
> that enslaved him all his life
> thereafter—

A drop of venom seeps into Williams's brush. The dash after "driven" forces the reader to dwell on Pop's obsessed personality and to savor the expulsion; the alliterative *d*'s and the perfectly balanced fourth line add to the taunting delight in his father's punishment. William George's original sin was not eating of the Tree of Knowledge but shrinking from the carnal sensuality and beauty of the tropics. He was never a natural man. Duty is thus a contemptible form of slavery dressed in the garments of noble self-sacrifice.

Throughout "Adam," Williams speaks of his father in the third person, establishing a formal distance. The abridged version of Pop's coming-of-age begins in a straightforward way:

> He grew up by the sea
> on a hot island
> inhabited by negroes—mostly.
> There he built himself
> a boat and a separate room
> close to the water
> for a piano on which he practiced—
> by sheer doggedness
> and strength of purpose
> striving
> like an Englishman
> to emulate his Spanish friend
> and idol—the weather!
> And there he learned
> to play the flute—not very well—

Eden's locale and the drama of the Fall are shifted to a "hot" island in the Caribbean, where the "torrid" Latin ladies and black women play the serpent, sexual temptresses ready to ensnare the handsome young Englishman, as the northern Venuses of New York later beckoned to Williams. Williams concedes that his father is drawn to the "darker whisperings" of tropic nights, the roar of the ocean in shells, "the smells / and sounds and glancing looks," and the sultry, unpredictable stormy weather. Against all but Elena, Adam's dogged will, an armor of "roseate steel," shields him from the Sirens' wiles.

According to his son, William George is stove in by his stolid nature. He is no satyr like Pan, no ravishing musician like Orpheus, not even a skillful flute player like his friend Carlos, Elena's beloved brother.

Marooned on an isolated island, he reconstructs English culture on alien ground, playing the piano and flute "not very well." Eros is locked in his mind as a liberating idea, but he has lost the key.

In "Adam," Williams takes on dual roles: that of a prosecutor building his case against Pop by an accumulation of circumstantial details, and that of defense attorney speaking across the barrier of cultural misunderstanding that separates the "Latin" and the Englishman (these passages can usually be spotted by their lines beginning "But"). Williams hands down three related indictments of his father. He is a deformed voluptuary whom

> duty has marked
> for special mention—with
> a tropic of its own
> and its own heavy-winged fowl
> and flowers that vomit beauty
> at midnight—

The startling verb "vomit," the adjective "heavy-winged," and the pun of "fowl" (foul) suggest an unnatural beauty, a bogus sensuality. The defense is allotted seven lines to rebut the charge:

> But the Latin has turned romance
> to a purpose cold as ice.
> He never sees
> or seldom
> what melted Adam's knees
> to jelly and despair—and
> held them up pontifically.

Williams contends that the Latin's knowledge of the senses is corrupt at the core. Because he exploits sexuality in a calculated fashion, as in a heartless seduction, romance vanishes, to be replaced by ennui. His knees never buckle from self-doubt, as Adam's do. Adam is not without some sexual fervor, since desire "melts" him, albeit into fear and despair. But this defense turns into a second felonious count: Adam is like Prufrock, yearning to assert himself but paralyzed by timidity. "Pontifically," which unexpectedly rhymes with "sees" and "knees," implies both celibacy and a strict set of rules that must be obeyed, lest one lose control.

Williams's third count, more a statement than an accusation, drives a stake through Pop's self-esteem:

> Naked on a raft
> he could see the barracudas
> waiting to castrate him
> so the saying went—
> Circumstances take longer—

Even when Pop takes off his armor and lies naked, a gesture of bodily freedom that for a moment allies him with the black boys who swim in the menacing waters, his manhood is threatened ("so the saying went" elevates these lines from a personal opinion into the island's judgment). But though Pop dodged castration in Puerto Plata, Williams alleges, he succumbed to a slow, horrific emasculation, day by ordinary day. These severe lines seem to reflect an Oedipal wish to castrate his father.

The evidence is laid out in the next stanza, Williams's summing-up of the case. He keeps his tone flat so as to persuade the jury that the facts are irrefutable, not tainted by subjective biases. He feels no scruples, no shame, in exposing his father to the gaze of strangers. Nor does he hide his contempt for his father's even temperament (in all his writing, he recalls Pop getting angry only once). What might be construed as a strong will he views as a chilly negation of self:

> But being an Englishman
> though he had not lived in England
> *desde que tenia cinco años*
> he never turned back
> but kept a cold eye always
> on the inevitable end
> never wincing—never to unbend—
> God's handyman
> going quietly into hell's mouth
> for a paper of reference—

fetching water to posterity
a British passport
always in his pocket—
muleback over Costa Rica
eating pates of black ants . . .

An antihero, William George descends into hell neither to bring back Eurydice nor to commune with the dead as Odysseus and Aeneas had, but to find "a paper of reference"; a factotum, he fetches "water to posterity"— a pinched, menial destiny.

Pop's exotic adventure in Costa Rica, "eating pates of black ants," enthralled Bill, but fails to soften this caustic portrait. "Adam" also vents Williams's spleen on the colonial Englishman with his stiff upper lip and the northern man's implied poverty of imagination. Williams frequently scapegoats the British when he feels their insular sense of superiority is blocking his own advance to full recognition as an important American poet.

The last stanza ends this extended trial on a bleak, solemn note:

He never had but the one home
Staring Him in the eye
coldly
and with patience—
without a murmur, silently
a desperate, unvarying silence
to the unhurried last.

Patience is here a depressing virtue. The last two lines, with their polysyllabic adjectives—"desperate," "unvarying," "unhurried"—toll like funeral bells, sealing Pop's doom as he marches silently to his servitude, his death-in-life.

Williams defines his father in "Adam" almost entirely through clusters of negatives—the word "never" recurs eight times. The fact that Pop never knew his own father, which charity might cite to mitigate his silences and paternal mistakes, Bill ignores. In "Adam," the poet is icily unforgiving. And he forgets that when he became a father, though he was far more of a daily presence in his sons' lives than William George was in his own, his medical practice and poetry took precedence over fatherhood.

Why such a flood tide of animosity? Did Williams need to suppress his unease at having inherited many of his father's traits—"sheer doggedness" and a belief in iron self-control, for instance? The latter troubled Williams's peace of mind, particularly when it clashed with importunate sexual desires. And while Williams took risks and acted out those desires in romantic affairs from time to time, he was no carefree Don Juan. The evidence is strong that the prospect of letting go caused emotional strife: Pop's caution might rise up in him without warning.

What nettles Williams most about his father in "Adam" is his self-denial, his embrace of "Duty / the angel [Michael] / which with whip in hand" expelled Adam and Eve from Eden. Yet the doctor felt that same lash of obligation on his back nearly every day: he seldom questioned that his devotion to his patients must be paramount—an annoyance of course, especially when it took him away from his writing, but never a martyrdom.

In 1959, four years before his death, Williams published *Yes, Mrs. Williams*, subtitled *A Personal Record of My Mother*, a charming, informal appendix to the *Autobiography*. In it, Williams, mellowed by time and illness, sketches his father in a kindlier light, rather as he appears in a family photo of 1899: with his affable smile and rambling shrub of a moustache, he seems a man comfortable in his parental role. Though something of an outsider in both memoirs, Pop is a pillar of respectability in the Rutherford community. "A stickler for principles," he "was not one to keep anything from me if he thought I could understand," Williams recalls. There was a freethinking, heterodox streak in him, too: he was a follower of Henry George's single-tax movement and a Darwinist who offered Bill "a dollar . . . if [he] would read *The Origin of Species* and *The Descent of Man*, which he did." Alone among the great modernist poets—Yeats, Frost, Pound, Eliot, Moore, Stevens—Williams was in politics an unrepentant liberal. Doubtless Pop's mild, undoctrinaire socialism influenced his political leanings.

How, then, could the superintendent of the Unitarian Sunday school, an eminently sane man, believe in séances, "that the spirits of the dead did materialize through [Elena's seizures] and did try to reach us"? Was it an unconscious relief from his lifelong habit of self-repression? Uxoriousness? Intellectual curiosity? Whatever the explanation for them, these trances scarred Bill, and while William George tried to allay his son's anxieties, they never disappeared. Williams craved abandonment as a form of emotional release, but also came to abhor any state that meant surrendering control, because it brought back the trauma those trances set off and the "monster insanity" that ran in his family: against the mortal danger of losing his self, he waged a mostly successful series of campaigns.

Williams's depiction of his father's death on Christmas Day 1918 is a poignant vignette. Emaciated by a spreading cancer, Pop remains faithful to his ingrained orderly nature, laying out his Christmas presents (all labeled) and enduring without complaint a painful enema in which Williams forces a tube into his rectum "by unjustifiable pushing." Remorsefully, Williams wonders if this procedure verged on sadism and provoked the fatal cerebral accident. His last time at his father's bedside is symbolic of the mishaps that made their relationship so fraught: "'He's gone,' I said. But he shook his head slowly from side to side. It was the last thing I could ever say in my father's presence and it was disastrous."

Called away to deliver a baby, he is absent when Pop does pass on.

Williams wrote about his father most tenderly and with quizzical humor in the lovely 1955 lyric "The Sparrow," which he dedicated to Pop. The phrases that depict the sparrow—who "carries on / unaffectedly / his amours," whose cheep is "insistent," and who displays a "general truculence"—only half fit the reticent William George. Sparrow and father are, however, allied poetical truths. Standing over the mutilated body of the sparrow, Williams half sings, half speaks an eloquent homily, as if to a congregation of mourners:

> Practical to the end,
>   it is the poem
>   of his existence
> that triumphed
>   finally;
>   a wisp of feathers
> flattened to the pavement,
>   wings spread symmetrically
>   as if in flight,
> the head gone,
>   the black escutcheon of the breast
>   undecipherable,
> an effigy of a sparrow,
>   a dried wafer only,

> left to say
>
> and it says it
>
> without offense
>
> beautifully;
>
> This was I,
>
> a sparrow.
>
> I did my best;
>
> Farewell.

To the end, Pop remains an "undecipherable" mystery, but in this conciliatory poem Williams draws nearer to his spirit.

3.

Before he died, Pop told Williams, "The one thing I regret in going is that I have to leave her to you. You'll find her difficult." Bill already knew that his mother was an unusually demanding woman; he could testify to her baroque, willful temperament. One can liken Elena to a grande dame, a Gypsy medium, an Eleonora Duse, a deposed queen banished to a provincial suburb where she languishes, performing throughout the rest of her long life (she died in 1949 at 102) before a tiny audience. By turns withdrawn, imperious, melancholy, and captious, she exasperated her son. But he also understood that her husband's death left her totally unprepared for life on her own.

Three years after Pop's death, Elena was still in deep mourning, unable to reconcile herself to her loss. In "The Widow's Lament in Springtime," one of Williams's most psychologically acute and plangent lyrics, he lets his mother speak her sorrow in a voice of quiet, controlled desperation. Through most of the soliloquy, she shuns any histrionics. "Thirtyfive years / I lived with my husband," she confides; that number suffices to explain her inconsolable grief. Her loneliness is heightened by the burgeoning life around her. She can't help noticing the "new grasses" flaming with a familiar brilliance or the plum tree and cherry branches "loaded down" by masses of white flowers. Ever since William George's death, she feels a "cold fire . . . close round" her; she cannot be warmed by nature's display of color. Her spirit wearing funereal widow's weeds, she turns away from the profligate scene of beauty. That she can recall a past when she joyously greeted the advent of spring serves only to taunt her current despair and emptiness.

Williams appears in the poem briefly as a devoted son who informs Elena that he had espied in the distant woods "trees of white flowers." He cannot know that reporting this fact, which normally would please her, instead unhinges her:

I feel that I would like
To go there
And fall into those flowers
And sink into the marsh near them.

Elena's wish can be construed as a yearning for annihilation. She is "half in love with easeful death" as a method of ending the pain that she can bear no longer. The emotional logic and spare language that come before these lines draw the reader into feeling that her misery, the grim consequence of what seems to her a cruel blow delivered by fate, is hopeless. The linked verbs, however, tell a slightly different story: she is not, like Ophelia, grieving over the death of her father, a "document in madness"; Elena has taken a sequence of steps, a purposeful, if faltering, action to end her isolation. She did not die; indeed, she lived on for almost three more decades. Her will to live was indestructible.

Elena's chronic touchiness may in large part have been the product of failed ambitions. Dreaming of a glamorous career as a painter, she had studied in Paris at the École des Beaux-Arts. But with two boys to raise, often on her own, and foreign ways to adjust to, she was forced to set aside her art. For American women, too, who aspired to an artistic career, the road was filled with potholes and obstructions. Besides talent, they needed drive, a thick skin, and a fearless will to repel the barrage of prejudice and ridicule they faced. Elena was not cut from such pioneer cloth. After her death, Williams unearthed several of her paintings, rolled up raggedly in a closet; she didn't have the heart either to hang them on the walls of her home or to throw them in the trash.

"Men! men that accomplish great things are her ideal," Williams notes in an insightful passage at the end of *Yes, Mrs. Williams*. Her father, Solomon, a busy merchant who imported food and clothes from Europe and resold them in the West Indies, personified discipline and mild authority: he might slap her hands with a bunched-up napkin if irked by her manners at the dinner table, but he was mainly a gentle patriarch. The Hoheb home was not a haven for philistines or frivolous gossips. Louis Moreau Gottschalk played the family's upright piano there, and Solomon was renowned for his dancing skills. But because her father died when she was only eight years old, her model for a man of accomplishment was her brother, Carlos, a surgeon and fine musician who served in loco parentis after their mother died (Elena had just turned fifteen) and indulgently raised her. She gave her son her brother's name in loving gratitude.

Elena remembered her mother fondly, not as a pretty woman content with her position as wife and mother and enjoying a large circle of friends, but as a scrappy battler. Left a widow with two children to feed and cheated by her husband's German partner, Krug, who claimed the deceased owed him money, the naïve Meline Hurrard sold a hacienda to discharge the fabricated debt, then valiantly started a small business that held the family together and let her send money to Carlos, her son, in Paris so that he could continue studying medicine.

Surprisingly, Elena, so Williams explains, "despised women and especially the modern emancipated woman. She would never understand her brazeness [sic], her pretense of being equal with man and militantly asserting that equality. Look at what men can do! she would say. 'A woman can't do that.'" Elena's attitude reflects what Williams calls her "rancors of regret" for not having "lived as [she] desires." She could and did live vicariously through her sons' achievements, but that did not restore her amour propre.

Elena believed that the artistic calling was noble and that she was ready to answer it, but that she'd foundered on the rocks of inopportunity; all her adult life she brooded over what she considered a "spoiled" chance to prove her mettle. For the proud, defensive Elena, Rutherford and, by extension, America were to blame; had she remained in Paris she might, in her view, have become a peer of Berthe Morisot and Mary Cassatt. As Williams puts it, she could not "exhale her fragrance—or lack of it—into the surrounding air." It didn't matter that her training in Paris (1876–1879) was purely academic, that she was totally unaware that Cézanne, Manet, and Degas were painting in radically original styles. The grand prix and gold medals she had won at the Beaux-Arts testified to her unused talent, so she buried them in an attic trunk: tarnished emblems of her yearning. In Rutherford, Elena pulled her head into a shell like a turtle. She did not avail herself of the lively American art scene, even as an expedient surrogate for that of Paris. Perhaps she suffered a failure of nerve or simply could not come to terms with her resentment at having to jettison a precious fantasy and function mainly as wife and mother. Playing the piano at family soirées had to be a poor substitute for an artistic métier, and presiding as hostess over the busy social life in the house on Passaic Avenue, crowded with relatives and guests, could not compare to sipping wine and arguing aesthetic ideas at a café on the Boulevard St.-Germain. And yet Elena wins accolades from Williams for disdaining passivity and marshaling the energy to "break life between her fingers": at some interior altar, a crust of bread is sustenance and communion. If the son found her irritating, the poet considered her fascinating and wrote many more poems about her than about Pop, sometimes pugnacious and sometimes tender.

Near the end of her life, when she was a housebound invalid, he took on the job of interviewer-scribe to record Elena's reminiscences and sayings and to annotate them. These tête-à-têtes became a means to rouse her from torpor and depression: he would coax, from her large storehouse, memories of vivid West Indies personages, African dancers, swarms of gallant Spanish soldiers courting the señoritas—and herself as a girl, gorging on guavas and mangoes, her whole face "yellow with the juice up to [her] eyes." The result was *Yes, Mrs. Williams*, a book whose form is rumpled biography-cum–table talk. "I don't want you to write my biography," she said. "My life is too mixed up." Williams simply overrode her objection. He needed to decant the wine of her past and sniff the sediments, he said, in order to find what was good in his own life—and to entertain her.

Elena's mixed ancestry symbolized the bold initiatives that stirred her son's imagination. Her French maternal grandfather prospered as an *armateur*, that is, a merchant who outfitted ships for seagoing trade. Her mother, Meline Hurrard (her surname is Basque), came from Martinique, the youngest of three daughters, and her father, Solomon Hoheb, from Holland, though before his family settled in Amsterdam they lived in Spain—his ancestry was partly Sephardic. Hoheb was born poor but rose in the world as an import-export businessman who amassed moderate wealth. Elena remembers oil portraits of burghers in Dutch costume in her parents' house. Solomon's half brothers, from his mother's second marriage to a man called both Enriquez and Henriquez, play a mysterious role in the family history as pests and parasites. "How many generations there had been of them in Puerto Rico and how they had mixed with the Spanish there is completely lost," Williams says, but Elena believed that she was the last of three generations.

"All the races of the earth mingled in the West Indies," Williams noted approvingly, and "intermarried, . . . imparting their traits one to another and forgetting the orthodoxy of their ancient and medieval views." Though Elena's family owned slaves, what Williams calls a "revolution of sentiment and intelligence" began softening "the old rigidities" and traditions of prejudice, and in this atmosphere of enlightened tolerance, "too lovely to last long," Elena was born and grew up. The product of one melting pot, Elena was to resist a second one in North America.

At times, Elena dominates like an aged star in a retirement home, happily leafing through photo albums and identifying faces; she especially likes to linger over her years growing up in Mayaguez, Puerto Rico, where she was born on Christmas Eve 1847. "The vortex of her childlike imagination" dances before her dim eyes and delights her, only to subside into querulous self-pity. Aware of the hasty nature of their sessions, Williams concocts a harmless ruse, persuading her to tell him about her life "while we were working over the translation" of Francisco de Quevedo's picaresque novella *El Perro y La Caliente* (*The Dog and the Fever*), then abruptly drops it. A few entries are dated, but when Elena talks, nothing is consecutive: what comes out may be a ribald account of an old woman farting or a memory of being frightened as a little girl and curling up next to her mother for comfort, only to be "cruelly" sent back to her own bed.

Yes, Mrs. Williams ably evokes the texture of life under Spanish colonial rule in mid-nineteenth-century Puerto Rico: secluded spots where ladies went to bathe; the tremors of an earthquake and her mother's pleas to God to save them; songs and poems, folk proverbs—for instance, *El que se hace de mile, se lo comen las hormigas*: "He who makes himself honey will be eaten by the ants"; an inventory of the succulent fruits that grow in Puerto Rico; the ancient echo of children's laughter as the seven-year-old Elena made monkey faces; and the reportage of customs a cultural anthropologist would gather in the field: "In Puerto Rico, in the country, they put the white of egg in a glass of water and next morning—if it form a ship or a coffin—they believe in such things. (The day of the dead)."

Williams often sits, rapt, as Elena spins her yarns; when she falters, he enters the narrative to ask questions or carry it forward with colorful bits of local or family history, to correct the record, or to savor and analyze some revelatory incident, like Elena's performance at a meeting of the Polytopic Club, a group formed by Williams and friends—the Rutherford superintendent of schools was a member—"to relieve the occasional monotony of our [suburban] lives." Dramatic readings from poems in many languages were a highlight: Ed, for instance, memorably delivered a passage from Dante's *Inferno*. Elena was mostly a spectator, but one evening, at 9 Ridge Road, she walked onstage from the wings, like an amateur diva seizing the spotlight she had always craved. Here is Williams's review:

> She was almost blind with cataracts, but when I called on her, the room anticipating what was to take place, was intently listening. We could have heard ourselves breathe. Taking her time she delivered, in French, a speech from Corneille ending in the famous curse, Rome *enfin que je hais!* [,] which left us speechless. All her contempt and even hatred that we had earned in this country through the years was contained in that anathema. She finished and from the depth of her soul it came out, but good. She sat back, her cheeks were aflame, her audience was spellbound.

The Corneille speech is the match that lights her stored-up hatred of America, which she deemed a "gross" and "dreadful" culture. She felt, Williams says, like Gulliver among the Brobdingnagians: puny, nervous, and scorned. Hence her nostalgia for Puerto Rico and Paris. (One cannot imagine Pop, ever self-contained, baring his prejudices so nakedly.)

During such hours of cherished intimacy, Williams forgets his mother's vanity and obstinacy; she ceases being the crone—"a small woman with straggling white hair, clumsy hands, lame, extremely deaf and only recently recovered from the removal of cataracts from both eyes"—and turns into Scheherazade. No wonder she eclipses Flossie, the other Mrs. Williams, who is reduced to a walk-on role. Elena, not Flossie, came closest to being the muse of 9 Ridge Road, because she possessed an imagination, even if one caged and beating violently against the bars of its prison. To explain his mother's extravagant character, Williams often has recourse to oxymorons. In the prologue to *Kora in Hell*, he pays her a moving homage: "She is [living in] an impoverished, ravished Eden but one indestructible as the imagination itself." In a tableau vivant, she could pose as a witch encircled by a halo. There is nothing commonplace about her. Her imagination is her redeeming grace.

Elena bequeathed many traits to her poet son—impatience, instability, fiery passion, confused idealism—but her gift of imagination was of inestimable value. He needed it for his art, but also, as he came to understand, because "her romantic ideas had deceived her and me in the modern world which we in our turn had to push behind us to come up fighting or smiling." Orthodoxies, Williams ardently contended, blocked the path to an indigenous poetry. Adapting Whitman's manifesto for American poetry, he strove to break down the traditions that inhibit "the spirit of the New World" from putting forth new shoots. The imagination became his weapon of choice for change in this sphere.

In her late years, Elena's broken hip hampered her mobility, and deafness and blindness left her isolated in the brittle shell of her body. Floss, Bill, and hired caretakers tried to shake her out of her lethargy and gloom. An example of their efforts can be seen in "The Artist," from *The Desert Music* (1954):

Mr. T.
           bareheaded
                      in a soiled undershirt
his hair standing out
           on all sides
                      stood on his toes
heels together
           arms gracefully
                      for the moment
curled above his head.
           Then he whirled about
                      bounded
into the air
           and with an entrechat
                      perfectly achieved
completed the figure.
           My mother
                      taken by surprise
where she sat
           in her invalid's chair
                      was left speechless.
Bravo! she cried at last

and clapped her hands.
The man's wife
came from the kitchen:
What goes on here? she said.
But the show was over.

This poem takes place at a nursing home run by a British couple, Harry and Anne Taylor. The son of a wealthy banker, Harry had chafed under the yoke of being an apprentice banker; he wanted to dance onstage and so studied ballet in secret. After a stint in the British Navy during World War I, he ran off to the American West, where he met his future wife, a nurse, married her, and rambled east.

As an artist manqué (Williams's term for him), Mr. T. cuts an unprepossessing figure. His very name sounds as if borrowed from a circus poster touting a freak in the sideshow. His scruffy uniform and sloppy hair calls up the image of a sweaty laborer, not a soloist in velvet suit and leotards. But unself-consciously, the often tipsy Mr. T. takes up the ballet dancer's first position, and the poem's first section closes with him in a state of poised flight.

Whirling about to gain momentum for the liftoff, Mr. T. "bounded" into the air, the trochaic verb miming the leap; "into the air" is so gossamer-like that the reader feels the dancer suspended in a weightless state. But unless he perfectly executes the entrechat, a jump in which he must cross his feet a number of times, the effect will be ruined. Mr. T. "completed the figure" beautifully, rounding off what he began in seamless fashion. His entrechat—the technical French term is the only unusual word in the poem, a touch of refinement that sets off the plain diction of the rest—is flawless art. Mr. T's performance is spontaneous, offering a tonic freshness and surprise that would be impossible without his formal training.

Mr. T.'s disheveled appearance, which promised a travesty, was deceiving: he upheld the highest standards of his art. Williams's voice-over records an aficionado's admiring remarks, but he is not the intended audience for Mr. T's performance. Elena is. So the poem pans in for a close-up of her sitting immobile in her "invalid's chair." Though unable to walk, let alone dance, she is indispensable to "completing the figure." Elena is mesmerized and left speechless by Mr. T's mastery: before she can react, her imagination must transform his down-at-the-heels clothing and his familiar role as male nurse into the costume and bearing of Prince Sieg-fried in *Swan Lake*. As an invalid, she cannot give Mr. T. a standing ova-tion, but she can cry, "Bravo!" and clap her hands. The poetry of motion is echoed in her wholehearted attention. (Carried away by enthusiasm, she later urged Williams to beg Mr. T. for another performance. He demurred.)

Williams could have ended "The Artist" with the third and fourth sentences. But he shrewdly adds a terse epilogue. Mrs. Taylor, playing the bit part of "the man's wife," has been lured by the applause to see what was going on. Nobody answers her question because the curtain has rung down and she has missed out on the magic. The performance cannot be duplicated. Williams choreographs this poem artfully, using words, rhythms, line breaks, and long and short sentences—the step-down tercets soar and descend, glide and stop, as in a dance piece—to captivate his readers.

"The Artist" exudes benevolence, but Williams cannot sustain this light mood for long. Like a pendulum, he swings back and forth, ticking off Elena's shortcomings and then, as if overpowered by remorse at such filial impiety, singing her praises. First, the deficits. "She has always been incapable of learning from benefit or disaster . . . She loses her bearings or associates with a disreputable person." She is subject to "dark, grotesque turns"—her soul uncouth, her stance pugnacious, her voice a whiny lament, she asks, "Why am I alive? No one can realize what I have de-sired. I succeeded in nothing. I have kept nothing. I am nothing." Then the positives: Williams sees through Elena's maudlin outburst to its hidden message. Here is his decoding:

> That is the defeated romantic. It is not by any means a true pic-ture. Despondency, discouragement, despair were violent periodic factors in her life. Under it lies the true life, undefeated if embit-tered, hard as nails, little loving, easily mistaken for animal selfish-ness. Unexcavated from her own consciousness, the good that is in her—crying for release, release from herself, a most difficult animal. I never knew her to succumb long to her most profound depressions, but would see her come up again finally stronger than ever— . . . She remains unbroken.

Williams lauds his mother's mental toughness, her resiliency, and her tri-umph over adversity. In this passage, neither riled up nor in an exculpatory humor, he ignores Elena's stingy mothering, which caused him emotional damage. (Her derelictions contrast with Pop's faithful discharge of duty.) Williams focuses instead on her lack of his father's righteous Puritanism: she can understand imperfection, which licenses Williams to prescribe it for himself, too, as a remedy for a lacerated conscience when he falls short of achieving his goals. She earns further praise "for living intensely in the present moment and for exercising keen powers of perception." "Whatever is before her is sufficient to itself and so to be valued," he comments approvingly, whether a Spanish poem or the town's lowlife characters. These are all bonds with Elena—and the linchpins of his poetic.

In an 1895 cameo of her, she looks like a suffragette or a Roman empress of indomitable will and hauteur who has survived countless setbacks. She bravely fronts the world with a wintry mien, her large antenna-like ears and scrutinizing eyes warning, "Don't cross me. I'm nobody's fool. I have tasted the ashes of exile and felt betrayal's poisonous sting. So keep your distance. I will not be easily taken in by your politic flattery and broken promises." Time did not soften her features or sweeten her disposition. How could it? Her lack of fulfillment distressed her continually, so it is no surprise that she did not age gracefully. After Pop's death, she lived for another eight years in her own home, remaining fairly self-sufficient. But that soon changed. Obstinately ignoring Williams's warning not to venture outside and cross the icy street, she slipped and broke her hip. Hobbled by this infirmity, she sank into apathy and became more and more grouchy, infantile in her demands, literally a burden: Williams sometimes had to carry her down the stairs for meals. The responsibility for her welfare fell entirely on him and Floss; Edgar, who seems to have been exempt, was rarely called on, except in emergencies. It would have been reasonable for Floss to protest her mother-in-law's moving in as an intrusion on their marriage, and for her to lobby Bill to send Elena to a nursing home, but with self-effacing grace she ministered to her despite receiving little or no thanks for small kindnesses, such as bringing in flowers from the garden to cheer her up. As with Pop, duty was second nature to Floss.

By 1936, when Williams wrote "Eve," Elena was nearing ninety, her body a husk yet her will to live still strong. "Willie" (her pet name for her son) and Floss could no longer keep her in their home, so she went for a while to live with the Taylors, who treated her, despite her constant grumbling, with compassion and patience, as if she had been their mother.

This arrangement was ideal for Bill and Floss. But "Eve," the second panel of a diptych painted in wildly discrepant styles, shows Williams at the end of his tether: the methodical tone of "Adam" is gone; emotion recollected in agitation governs. Williams reviews his battles with Elena, tallying every casualty, every fiasco, every episode of insubordination. He cannot get the reek of a long, exhausting war out of his nostrils. Old combatants, they know each other's feints and lunges and stratagems by heart. But Williams does all the talking, because Elena's sclerosis from a stroke left her with "a typical expressionless face": "Eve" is an abrasive soliloquy.

To his credit, Williams tries to be impartial, to see their relationship through her eyes. There's no question that his expressions of guilt are sincere, his contrition unfeigned. When he slips on his hair shirt, the material, as it is meant to do, makes him squirm. The next moment, though, unable to bear the discomfort, like a quick-change artist, he sheds it and rages like a bull sighting a red cape and rushing headlong to gore it. Williams's resolution to be calm and deliberate crumbles; insults slip past his guard; an almost oceanic anger foams, crests, ebbs, and surges again. Inside of the opening eleven lines, he is so worked up that he doesn't seem to notice his almost comical zigzagging:

> Pardon my injuries
> now that you are old—
> Forgive me my awkwardnesses
> my impatience
> and short replies—
> I sometimes detect in your face
> a puzzled pity for me
> your son—
> I have never been close to you
> mostly your own fault;
> in that I am like you.

What starts out as a son beseeching his mother, in measured tones, to pardon his offenses breaks off immediately, as he is disturbed and distracted by her look of "puzzled pity" for him. The very idea so incenses him that he reverses roles, becoming the aggrieved party. Yet Williams's poetic art in "Eve" loudly proclaims his immutable closeness to her: the tricky rhythms, never smoothly linear, that modulate every few phrases

from confession to analysis, that brake suddenly and create rough cadences; the plain syntax that strains to keep his emotions from erupting,
the spasmodic placement of dashes, as if he desperately needs to catch
his breath before finishing a sentence or completing a thought, and the
curt diction that relentlessly drills into the carapaces of their psyches and
shuns subtlety as lying.

This identification with his mother scares Williams because it is a
threat to his separate identity. Yet he cannot shake off his sense of her as
a goddess, a superior being who "looked down from above / at me—not /
with what they would describe / as pride but the same / that is in me: a
sort / of shame that the world / should see you as I see you, a somewhat
infantile creature—." This passage, which links Williams and Elena in
shame and childishness, forces us to consider a crux of Williams's nature.

His detractors often argue that because of his immaturity his poems
lack music and complexity; they sprawl; they show little evidence of
thought or deep feeling; their homemade forms are poorly constructed or,
as in the many short-lined poems scrolling down the page, trivial; his
pursuit of an American poetic vernacular is self-deluding humbug. There
are some grams of truth in the accusation. As "Adam" and "Eve" demonstrate, at age fifty-three Williams had not resolved his conflicts about Pop
and Elena. In his medical practice, he was always a self-possessed adult
who inspired confidence with his skills and coolness in emergencies. But
in emotional and sexual matters, as in poetry, he seemed to depend on
friction and conflict for igniting his creative energies. At some unconscious level, he came to believe that not becoming a well-developed self
enabled him to function as a poet; his anguished feelings could be put at
the service of his imagination.

One can understand why Williams cringes at his mother's "infantil-
ism," her cries for attention, her egotism, her vulnerability: where Pop
bristled with defenses, Elena is "defenseless," taken advantage of, not
least by her son, who, in the name of protection, is her jailer. As such, he
controls her, a wild animal "kicking blindly" against the metal frame of a
hospital bed, until exhausted, "a demon, fighting for the fire / it needed to
breathe / to live again" and to reclaim her freedom. His guilt stems from
his sympathy for her frantic rebellion: he, too, wishes "to escape and leap
into chaos / (where Time has / not yet begun"). In these arresting lines—
chaos is the *tohu bohu* of Genesis 1:1, the undifferentiated matter from

which God formed the universe—Williams comes close to losing control and buoyantly leaping into the freedom that precedes an act of creation.

He returns to an old irritant and a familiar resentment in a later stanza when he revisits Elena's attempts to "communicate with the dead." As we have seen, the doctor and rationalist is skeptical of mediums and occult experiments. With disgust he sketches her deranged gestures as, lost in a trance, she reaches out "to self-inflicted emptiness":

> Trembling, sobbing
> and grabbing at the futile hands
> till a mind goes sour
> watching you—and flies off
> sick at the mumbling
> from which nothing clearly
> is ever spoken—

What fuels his disgust is that he cannot stop her from making a fool of herself: the "natural faces" stare at her body's contortions. As a boy, he could rely on Pop to intervene and console him and guide the blinded spiritualist back to reality; she, however, is impotent to protect herself— "and me too," Williams slips in parenthetically. In 1936, the son and doctor trained to identify and treat the diseases that can ravage the body knows that he is the sole "bridge between herself and a vacancy as of the sky at night, the terrifying emptiness of non-entity." But as a man, no longer frightened by her antics, Williams cannot stop her from twitching and talking to ghosts. She inhabits a realm of unreality he resists. Yet despite his scorn for her mutterings and spells—the fruit on that tree does not tempt him—he senses that women have powers that he and most men lack access to.

Yet Williams exchanges roles with his mother, and this time, swallowing humble pie, he abases himself as the greater fool of the two and asks her to forgive him. In four short lines, however, the supplicant vanishes into a poet with godlike powers to immortalize her and to shape her confusion into art: "I will write a book about you— / making you live (in a book!) / . . . unforgiving." Given his earlier anger, it is a handsome gesture— poets rarely write their mothers' biographies—meant to bring about a truce, though he knows that in her nearly comatose condition she cannot negotiate terms. As her physician, he promises to give her brandy or wine because alcohol "whips up / your mind and your senses / and brings color to your face." The drink, like a magic potion, sets off a chain of powerful effects, whipping up Williams's verse, too:

> —to enkindle that life
> too coarse for the usual,
> that sly obscenity
> that fertile darkness
> in which passion mates—
> reflecting
> the lightnings of creation—
> and the moon—
> "C'est la vieillesse
> inexorable qu'arrive!"

Elena still represents for her son a kind of Ceres, a goddess of fecundity. He explicitly equates sex and creativity as "sly obscenity" and "fertile darkness." Passion is a dangerous yet exhilarating natural force, like lightning and the changeable moon, traditionally linked with women. A poet who ignores passion or who dismisses it as "coarse" puts his art at risk. The French maxim about the inexorable arrival of old age confirms Williams's acceptance of a biological law. Elena, however, cannot reconcile herself to Time and instead claws at it like a cornered cat, "terrified / in the night— screaming out / unwilling, unappeased / and without shame—." (Arthritis had gnarled her hands so badly that they looked like claws, Williams reports.) This caterwauling amazes him.

The last stanza of "Eve" is its finest. As Williams sits by her bedside and studies her broken-down body and "ruined face," he lapses into reverie, wondering yet again about her unconquerable spirit. He addresses a question to either God or Time:

> Might He not take
> that wasted carcass, crippled
> and deformed, that ruined face
> sightless, deafened—
> the color gone—that seems
> always listening, watching, waiting

ashamed only
of that single and last
degradation—

Time's answer he already knows: "No. Never." It's pointless to contest the matter further. So the poem switches to the second person:

> Defenseless
> still you would keep
> every accoutrement
> which He has loaned
> till it shall be torn from
> your grasp, a final grip
> from those fingers
> which cannot hold a knife
> to cut the meat but which
> in a hypnotic ecstasy
> can so wrench a hand held out
> to you that our bones
> crack under the unwonted pressure—

To her last breath, Elena remains a paradox: defenseless, yet an old woman with such preternatural strength that she can wrench a person's hand and crack its bones. Unlike Pop, she can be swept away by a "hypnotic ecstasy" that, for a brief time, transports her to the paradise she dreamed, lived, lost, and lamented.

These final thirteen lines, one sentence uninterrupted by dashes or doubts, parentheses or sniping, build in lyric intensity to a climax that bestows a long-sought-for blessing: forgiveness of Elena and himself. In her last theatrical role, Elena performs the deathbed scene with astonishing virtuosity: prostrate, she clutches her accoutrements to her as death tears them from her grasp, and in a final sensational gesture, the poor, ravaged soul nearly breaks the outstretched hand of her son—and the audience's heart. "Bravo!" we shout, and clap our hands. And so does Williams.

If Pop and Elena take after Adam and Eve, as these two jagged, exhausting poems insist, then they were as opposite in emotional makeup as it is possible to be. Williams never says outright that the marriage of his patient, sober father and impetuous, romantic mother was a misalliance;

perhaps he could never decide. Certainly the Williams household was no armed camp. "We have always been a closely knit family, relying on each other when the chips were down," Williams states matter-of-factly, and he harbors no doubts that his mother loved her children. He usually wrote about his childhood and boyhood years warmly, insisting they were normal, his days crammed with playing games, pranks, and sports (baseball and track); attending school; reading books; roughhousing; and satisfying his shy curiosity about nature and girls.

Candor will not allow Williams to conceal family secrets—for example, Godwin's erratic behavior, his own murderous impulses toward his mother: "There is an incentive arising from the weak and defenseless that drives us devilishly to want to insult and even to kill them." There is nothing uncommon in children chanting a litany of complaints against their parents or seeking space for their own evolving identities. In this Williams was normal. But as many of his poems and memories attest, his disaffection from both parents also grew, although never to the point of his breaking off relations. After his marriage in December 1912, he and Floss, having little capital to set up their own household, moved into the big house on Passaic Avenue. This was like sitting on a powder keg. For the sake of everybody's domestic peace, Floss and Bill had to move out.

In a weird, hybrid way, Williams, the result of his parents' mating in the "fertile darkness," combined attributes of Cain and Abel: aggressive and obedient, afraid of telling the truth and afraid of not doing so. As a young man, he was tugged in two directions at once: he wished to establish his independence from his parents yet also to please them; he had tried on his father's attitudes "facing life" and they did not fit him, so he fumbled to cobble together his own set; he wanted to work out a mode of conduct that appeased his sexual desires but could not shed his parents' moral code. In late 1904, at age twenty-one, he wrote to his mother from the University of Pennsylvania a polite, reproachful letter that illustrates his turmoil and annoyance:

> It seems to me that you and Papa need advice, not me. This sounds funny but still judge it coldly. You have told me lots of things that made me feel awfully bad and taken lots of things for granted that I never dreamed of till you spoke to me of them . . . I know I am almost always wrong, but still, Mama, give me credit for just a

little judgment. You and Papa seem to think that I am always doing just what I shouldn't do.

Williams clearly feels that his parents are treating him as a naughty child and he resents it. Since this is not the first time they have accused him of straying from the Golden Rule, he wearily rehearses a fruitless conflict he has often had with them:

First, that I never did and never will do a premeditated bad deed in my life. Also that I never have had and never will have anything but the purest and highest and best thoughts about you and Papa, and that if anybody ever says a word contrary to your wishes or high ideals I never fail to fight them to a standstill . . . I have always tried to do all that you and Papa wished me to do and many times I have done things against my own feelings and convictions because you wanted me to . . . Still, Mama dear, I know you are right and I am wrong. Don't think I blame you, for a second; I don't, but feelings will come . . .

Williams sounds here like a schoolboy chalking "I promise to be good" on the blackboard a hundred times. Even if tactically prudent, the act of capitulating to his mother leaves him unhappy and irked. Betraying his "feelings and convictions" is a high price to pay. Little did he know in 1904 that those feelings of blame he squelched would come back, unbidden, for the rest of his life. Like his father, he would "work, work, work." Like his mother, he would struggle to "beat the game and be free." Their joint influence is stamped on his character and everything he wrote.

THREE

"Halfway to Hell"

I. Transplanting American Myths in American Soil

The three years during which Williams composed *Kora in Hell*, his "unhappiness book," yet also his favorite child, were crowded with events, both familial and public, that pushed him to the brink. In rapid sequence, America declared war on Germany in 1917; his father-in-law, Pa Herman, was accused of pro-German sympathies and Williams sprang to his defense, thereby inciting some townspeople in Rutherford to urge a boycott of Williams's budding medical practice; the influenza epidemic broke out; Williams's father died on Christmas Day 1918; Paul, Floss's young brother, was killed in a gun accident; and Grandma Wellcome died. With two young sons and a strained marriage as further burdens, Williams recalled in his *Autobiography* that he felt like "Persephone gone into Hades, into hell. Kora was the springtime of the year; my year, my self, was being slaughtered."

Appropriate to the carnage of a world war, "slaughtered" sounds histrionic when applied to personal circumstances, but since Williams was no more hysterical than he was stoical, the word clearly signals that he was floundering in a rising tide of defeats. All the same, it is puzzling that the weary doctor identified with Kora (also known as Persephone), a maiden innocently gathering flowers in a meadow when the god of the underworld spirits her away to be his queen. In the most common version of the myth, Kora's outraged and grief-stricken mother, Demeter, appeals to Zeus to secure the return of her daughter. Sent by Zeus, Hermes retrieves Kora, but not before Hades tricks her into eating a number of pomegranate seeds, which force her to return to Hell each fall and winter.

Why did this myth appeal so powerfully to Williams? After all, he could have chosen Hercules, Odysseus, Aeneas, or other classical figures as models: militant or wily heroes on noble missions who defied the odds and descended into hell as part of their probation. Instead, when he transplants the Greek gods and heroes to American soil, he subjects them to democratic parody (levity being his peculiar tone of respect). They are "fallen gods," "smothered in filth and ignorance." In the improvisations of section 16 of *Kora in Hell*, Williams transforms himself first into a satyr chasing a wood nymph and then into Zeus, "a country doctor without a taste for coin jingling," while Floss plays "Hebe with a slack jaw and a cruel husband—her mother left no place for a brain to grow" (a gibe that might whet any wife's appetite for vengeance). Hercules appears twice: as a muscular farm boy in Hackettstown and rowing boats on Berry's Creek. The dance of wayward libidos in this section—Venus is a "weak-minded," promiscuous girl, an early version of Elsie in "The pure products of America," who is arrested by the "Chief of Police our Pluto"—matches Williams's moods as they shift from gaiety to derision to farce to pity; he can't decide if lust is a sin, a lark, a "bastard nectar," a violation of innocence, or a betrayal that induces guilt.

Williams was restless in his domestic life. Like Odysseus, he'd have jumped at the chance for a fling with Circe or at least a tryst with Calypso. In *Kora in Hell*, he describes a dance with a flirtatious woman; he's aroused by the "twang and twitter to the gentle rocking of a high-laced boot and the silk above it" and the woman's "glossy leg." But the dance that promises a racy adventure ends with a thump: out of sync with each other, three times they "come down flatfooted." Grace and joy yield to boredom "and the play's ended." The tone of bilious disappointment at the end of section 13 modulates in section 18 to a measured assessment of the status of his marriage after six or seven years. This extended soliloquy could have taken place in the kitchen of 9 Ridge Road, with Floss his captive listener. Williams lays out his position candidly:

> How deftly we keep love from each other. It is no trick at all: the movement of a cat that leaps a low barrier. You have—if the truth be known—loved only one man and that was before my time. Past him you have never thought nor desired to think. In his perfections you are perfect. You are likewise perfect in other things. You present to me the surface of a marble. And I, we will say, loved also

before your time. Put it quite obscenely / And I have my perfections. So here we present ourselves to each other naked. What have we effected? Say we have aged a little together and have borne children. We have in short thriven as the world goes. We have proved fertile. The children are apparently healthy. One of them is even whimsical and one has an unusual memory and a keen eye. But—it is not that we haven't felt a certain rumbling, a certain stirring of the earth, but what has it amounted to? Your first love and mine were of different species. There is only one way out. It is for me to take up my basket of words and for you to sit at your piano, each his own way, until I have, if it so be that good fortune smile my way, made a shrewd bargain at some fair and so by dint of heavy straining supplanted in your memory the brilliance of the old firmhold. Which is impossible. Ergo, I am a blackguard.

In the first half of his brief, Williams explains why the distance between him and Floss has widened. "How deftly we keep love from each other" is delivered in a bemused tone, as if it were an incontrovertible fact. His analysis sounds surprisingly Freudian: Floss so idealized and adored her father, Williams argues, that this attachment prevented an intimate relationship with her husband from taking root. He could never compete with Pa Herman. By comparing her to a marble, shiny and opaque, her inner life eluding him, Williams seems to blame her for the fault line in their life together. He sums up their marriage in withering terms: after an initial period of sexual excitement, soon extinguished, the two slowly drifted apart, and theirs became a marriage lacking passion. By his calculation he can travel one of two routes: become a successful poet so that Floss will be impressed by his brilliance knitting together the material in his "basket of words," thereby displacing her father's preeminence ("firmhold") in her memory; or justify to her his need to search for love elsewhere on the grounds that he, like Kora, is an inmate in hell, unfulfilled. This improvisation proceeds with the grim logic of Hades, not the swerves and leaps of the satyr he sometimes wished to be, until in the last clause he concludes he's a "blackguard."

It was never easy for him to break the rules; he was brought up to be Dr. Virtue, as his straitlaced letters from medical school to his brother and parents demonstrate. Mr. Williams's wanderings and long absences took on the character of fitful desertions. That left Williams, a suburban Telemachus, to figure out how to manage the competing claims of desire and duty. He could not mine this emotional and poetic material until he devised a rough map in *Kora*.

Duty ruled Williams as it did Aeneas; the poet would have torn himself from Dido's arms in order to bring a baby into the world or treat a patient felled by a heart attack. But he would have balked at the gods' command to found a city. If such a glorious destiny ever appealed to his fantasy, Williams's practical self scotched it. He chose to live in leafy Rutherford, not in New York, "the lurid red city" that looms in the distance in *Kora*, a stage set for a melodrama—or, more accurately, a psychodrama—that might have been called *The Fleshpots of Babylon*, in which a modernist Siren beckons him to embrace her, and Williams, sorely tempted, flirts, hangs fire, succumbs, regrets, and covers the tracks of his infidelities. That temptress had a real-life counterpart, as we shall see: the Baroness Elsa von Freytag-Loringhoven. But his imagination couldn't turn her into a goddess of love.

As for Orpheus, that consummate lyric poet, Williams seldom invokes him at this stage of his career. Where marriage and poetry produced no discordant music for Orpheus, Williams was not so enamored of his Eurydice that he would bargain with the gods to let him fetch her back from hell. Not until "Asphodel, That Greeny Flower" would Williams tune his lyre and declare halfheartedly:

> I cannot say
> that I have gone to hell
> for your love
> but often
> found myself there
> in your pursuit

Artistically, Williams was adrift on a choppy sea. After the Armory Show and much prodding from Ezra Pound, he had tossed overboard most of the Romantic baggage that made his early verse as anachronistic as a galleon. Here is a brief sample of Williams's youthful effusions:

> Love is twain, it is not single,
> Gold and silver mixed in one,

Passion 'tis and pain which mingle
Glistering then for aye undone.

This Keats imitation, with its singsong and trite rhyming, would have
been outmoded in 1809. Although Imagism taught him a valuable lesson
in poetic concision, he was still using defective compasses to guide him
to unknown destinations—and possible shipwreck.

Medicine, though, anchored Williams in objective reality. In the early
years of his practice, no position, however humble, was beneath him: he
worked, for example, in the Rutherford schools as a part-time physician.
Attending to his patients, many of them from poor Italian and other immigrant families, he realized that they were a source of rich poetic material. *Al
Que Quiere!* is filled with ribald or sympathetic portraits of a young man
with a bad heart, a little girl brought to his office for a vaccination, a querulous whore. The poems' content was mostly superior to their language,
Williams knew, but "January Morning" pointed to a new kind of poem.

This lovely 1917 suite of poems is in its visual immediacy like a set
of impromptu photographs, and in its musical deftness like the dance
movements of a Bach or Couperin suite for harpsichord. In the fifteen
short movements of the poem, Williams registers the details of his local
world in rapid but telling strokes. The Church of the Paulist Fathers in
Weehawken is no St. Peter's in Rome, but "seen against a smoky dawn,"
its domes inspire a frisson of pleasure and spiritual anticipation. In "January Morning," it's as if Williams on his rounds, carrying a handheld camera, pans in on the wintry sights and sites as he travels around Rutherford
and its vicinity "at strange hours" and prints them out, one to a stanza,
some spliced together by the conjunction "and." There is logic in this
structure: "the tall probationers [interns at the hospital] / in their tan
uniforms / hurrying to breakfast" contrast with the doctors emerging "from
basement entries / neatly coiffed, middle aged gentlemen / with orderly
moustaches and / well-brushed coats." The glancing images of sections
5 and 6 would fit neatly into a print by an American Brueghel, if one
existed:

V

—and a young horse with a green bed-quilt
on his withers shaking his head:
bared teeth and nozzle high in the air!

VI
—and a semi-circle of dirt-colored men
about a fire bursting from an old,
ash can,

The images suffice. The objects are clearly presented. There is no need
for the poet to comment.

The exuberance of "January Morning" is that of a gifted young poet
melding acute perceptions of objects with accurate analogies. Despite
the use of third-person narrative and offbeat adjective-noun combinations ("curdy barnacles," for instance), Williams's subjectivity breaks in
irresistibly:

The young doctor is dancing with happiness
In the sparkling wind, alone
At the prow of the ferry! He notices
The curdy barnacles and broken ice crust
Left at the slip's base by the low tide
And thinks of summer and green
shell-crusted ledges among
          the emerald eel-grass!

He will, again like a photographer, crouch in an awkward position in
order to look at an object from a fresh angle—for example, "staring up
under / your chiffonier at its warped / bass-wood bottom." Even a "rickety
ferry-boat," called "Arden," sets his imagination free to invent, as he likes
it, a whimsical voyage in which Shakespeare's clown pilots Henry Hudson's ship:

          "Put me a Touchstone
     at the wheel, white gulls, and we'll
     follow the ghost of the *Half Moon*
     to the North West Passage—and through!
(at Albany) for all that!"

"January Morning" ends on a surprise note. When Williams returns
to 9 Ridge Road and tells his mother that he "wanted to write a poem"
she'd understand, he admonishes her that as part of the contract between

poet and reader "you got to try hard." But the boyish glee he feels has not dissipated: he compares his giddy mood to young girls who "run giggling" on Rutherford's Park Avenue when "they ought to be in bed." Breaking rules is pleasurable, though "January Morning" violates no Imagistic tenets.

Along with self-discipline, Williams acquired a respect for innovation. In 1917, medicine was in a state of flux, much like the poetry scene, and though he wasn't, like Lydgate in *Middlemarch*, ambitious to be a physician overturning obsolete ideas, Williams scanned the medical journals for the latest strides in research and drugs, and for epidemiological statistics. There was no magic bullet, he concluded, just careful observation, dogged accumulation of facts, guesswork, hands-on knowledge of the human body—and the imagination, which sometimes pulled everything together.

These were Williams's methods of gauging the changes in art, too. He did not dismiss Duchamp's urinal as an impish hoax, nor was he outraged by Cubism; Picasso and Braque intrigued him because they were subverting received ideas coolly and authoritatively. Their experiments encouraged him to believe that he could push the frontiers of American poetry. His unpredictable mix of patience and volatility stains the prose on every page of *Kora in Hell*.

Why, then, at this crossroads in his art and life did Williams choose the myth of Kora? He never explicitly says. Instead he scatters contradictory clues. Probably at the instigation of Pound, he had read Ovid and Bulfinch. Poetic interest in myths and *The Golden Bough* wafted in the air like a heavy scent. But that just accounts for atmosphere. More to the point, like Kora, Williams was callow, awakened from perilous innocence and a false sense of security by Death, a force of sudden and implacable aggression that left him reeling. Yet he also took comfort in the myth's depiction of the rotating seasons. If Kora mirrored his divided self, she also affirmed his faith that after winter's desolation came spring's fecundity: his fortunes would revive. That is why hundreds of pastoral poems in Williams's *Collected Poems* record with botanical precision trees budding or bending from an ice storm, branches, leaves, flowers in bloom or wilted; his fluctuating moods follow nature. Or as he put it in section 15 of *Kora*: "Often when the descent seems well marked there will be a subtle ascent over-ruling it so that in the end when the degradation is fully anticipated the person will be found to have emerged upon a hilltop."

Kora ("maiden" in Greek), more frequently known as Persephone, was the daughter of the goddess Demeter (the goddess of fertility). One day while she was picking flowers, Hades, the god of the underworld, spied her and, with the connivance of Zeus, abducted her to the underworld to become his queen. When she ate a pomegranate seed she became inexorably tied to Hades. Her mother, mourning for her daughter's disappearance, searched in vain for her. Demeter brought famine on the land and, as a result, Zeus worked out a compromise whereby Kora would be allowed to come up to earth in the spring and summer and spend the fall and winter in the darkness below. This myth raises tricky questions about sexuality, a force that engrossed Williams the doctor and that sometimes rattled Williams the man. Was Kora an innocent victim of Hades's brutal masculinity or did she unwittingly conspire in her own imprisonment? Eating pomegranate seeds suggests that she may, like Eve, have been tempted by that which she rejected. As a doctor who delivered babies, Williams knew women intimately and was not conflicted by notions of purity and filth; in that professional setting he was sure of his authority. In his emotional life, though, women confused him. About the mercurial relations between the sexes he was no young master. He was repeatedly attracted to bohemian or artistic women such as Viola Baxter Jordan, Mina Loy, and even the ravaged Baroness. Decidedly not Kora types, they were fashioned in the mold of his exotic, artistic mother. In the prologue to *Kora in Hell*, he pays tribute to her scorn for conventions:

> Thus, seeing the thing itself without forethought or afterthought but with great intensity of perception, my mother loses her bearings or associates with some disreputable person or translates a dark mood. She is a creature of great imagination. I might say this is her sole remaining quality. She is a despoiled, molted castaway but by this power she still breaks life between her fingers.

Williams coveted her attributes: intensity, imagination, and, most acutely, wanton surrender of rational control—she was an artiste resembling his touchy, raffish ethnic patients more than the pillars of Rutherford society he saw in church. Even as an old woman she sometimes exerted the force of a Demeter.

But with women of opulent sexuality, Williams either did not pick up their cues or acted timid, as if afraid he'd be caught in their webs. In the case of Viola Baxter Jordan, he brooded over his hesitation to commit himself to her. He was an odd mixture of the passive and the assertive, who, one sometimes thinks, would have waited for Helen of Troy to abduct him! I don't want to portray Williams as a bumbling Casanova, since he was actually a bit of a fox.

But he married Flossie, a Kora figure, on the rebound. Given to subterfuges on many subjects, he's brutally frank about her in *Kora* and the 1951 *Autobiography*: "Her pretty, pinched face is a very simple tune but it carries now a certain quasi-maidenly distinction," he remarks patronizingly in section 15 of *Kora*. Though he lambastes "Richard [Wagner, who] worked years to conquer the descending cadence" as an "idiotic sentimentalist," Williams, like Tannhäuser, preferred the sensuous music of Venusberg to the chaste prayers of Elizabeth. It's as though Hades, finding Kora's "perfections" boring, quickly tired of her and was glad to return her to his mother-in-law for six months every year, leaving him free to "dance," to philander.

A few months after his wedding in 1912, Williams wrote a letter to Viola seeking a sexual liaison. The shocked Jordan sharply rebuked him for unethical conduct; feeling like a rogue, he retreated to the higher ground of literary friendship. In the many crevices of *Kora in Hell*, Williams hides such illicit desires and takes stock of his trove, though that may be too orderly an image for a process that's often charged and helter-skelter.

2. Prospecting for a Poetic

Williams was an active participant in, and observer of, the New York cultural scene between 1910 and 1920. The Armory Show in 1913, which he remembered as "a fabulous moment," gave a bracing shock to his artistic consciousness. In this period he began experimenting with the poetic line and how "the image was to lie on the page, jettisoning rhyme and omitting capital letters at the beginning of a line." He backed the little magazine *Others*, founded by Walter Arensberg and Alfred Kreymborg, contributing cash, time, poems, and advice. There is a famous photo of the *Others* brain trust gathered in the yard of 9 Ridge Road, including Man Ray and a smiling Marcel Duchamp, his arm hooked through that of his patron Arensberg. Williams sits in the front row, his ears like a troll's, holding a cat and staring guardedly into the camera. All the men wear suits and ties, as if at their college reunion. (In a parallel photograph, the wives stand, like members of the ladies auxiliary. Hands in her cardigan pockets, Floss, clearly a *jeune fille*, gazes, unintimidatedly, at the camera.) Williams's friendship and collaboration with Kreymborg lasted half a dozen years, until, in 1919, Kreymborg accused Williams of sabotaging *Others*.

That charge was patently false. But Williams increasingly felt he had outgrown the somewhat tepid Imagistic verse the magazine featured. Still, he tried to cover his defection by finding innovative music in this Kreymborg poem, "Goober Peas":

> We have no dishes
> to eat our meals from.
> We have no dishes
> to eat our meals from
> because we have no dishes
> to eat our meals from.
>
> We need no dishes
> to eat our meals from,
> we have fingers
> to eat our meals from.

There's meager nourishment in these puerile, monotonous lines; even a dish of goober peas would satisfy the hungry reader more. It's hard to believe that Williams could stomach the bland singsong of Kreymborg's poem. He knew that the modernist uprising—and he counted himself a foot soldier in its ranks—had bypassed Kreymborg. Williams had thrilled to the raucous freshness of Mina Loy's "Poems to Joannes," which broke taboos and mixed sexual candor ("Pig Cupid his rosy snout / Rooting erotic garbage") with an exotic vocabulary of abstractions ("infructuous impulses," "pubescent consummations"). When Loy wrote,

> We might have coupled
> In the bed-ridden monopoly of a moment
> Or broken flesh with one another

> At the profane communion table
> Where wine is spill'd on promiscuous lips

she sounded like a mischievous priestess expropriating the language of religion for sensual purposes. Such bold riffs—the mistress of two Italian Futurist poets, Loy absorbed their lessons in dissonance—heralded the electrifying shocks that the Dadaist and surrealist poets would soon administer. These influences were crucial to liberating Williams's verse from stale rhythms and prudery.

At Pound's urging, Williams submitted poems to Harriet Monroe's *Poetry*. But if by nature he was generous and by medical training empathetic and methodical, in matters of poetry and commitment he was slow to make up his mind. The question of whether he should wholeheartedly join the modernist ranks incited a zany, pugnacious debate with himself and others in the prologue to *Kora in Hell*. Written in 1920, after he had finished editing the improvisations, the prologue consists of a series of comic vaudeville skits that take as their theme how to respond to the roiling new but also to the "old" poems of *Al Que Quiere!*

Like a wary newspaper journalist, a poker-faced Williams quizzes Arensberg about what makes the Cubists modern. Arensberg replies: "The only way man differed from every other creature was in his ability to improvise novelty." With just the hint of a smile breaking through his studied neutrality, Williams recalls Arensberg's enthusiasm for an "old Boston hermit who, watched over by a forbidding landlady (evidently in his pay), paints the cigar-box-cover-like nudes upon whose fingers he presses actual rings with glass jewels from the five-and-ten store." Does Williams approve the crumbling of distinctions between high art and mass-produced artifacts? One would expect so, since this is "improvised novelty," the very sort of iconoclastic gesture Williams cherishes, and tries his hand at, in *Kora*. In the atelier Arensberg sponsored, the manufacture of art verges on a hoax that Duchamp might have, with a sharpie's wink, designed. Arensberg's lesson was not lost on Williams; its whimsy clearly appealed to him, for, seized by a weird curatorial idea, he proposes a mom-and-pop *salon des refusés*, which would exhibit "the abortive paintings of those men and women who without master or method have evolved perhaps two or three unusual creations in their early years." Such a painting, a still life by an Englishwoman, A. E. Kerr, hung in Williams's parents' house and

later at 9 Ridge Road. If these Sunday painters, as Williams argues, descended from prehistoric rock pictographers (an astonishing provenance),
their work could not be derided as thrift-shop discards, what we would
call kitsch. It's as if, owing to some unconscious, self-protective scruple,
Williams was reluctant to give up his amateur standing and plunge into
the maelstrom of stylistic experiment.

But his immersion in modernism tells a different story. One of the
paintings that Williams saw at the Armory Show was Wassily Kandinsky's *Improvisation 27: The Garden of Love*, which Stieglitz bought and
hung in his 291 gallery. This painting and some of Kandinsky's statements and prose poems made a deep impression on Williams. It was
probably Marsden Hartley who recommended Kandinsky's books *On the
Spiritual in Art* (1911) and *Reminiscences* (1913) to him and discussed
them with Williams. The Russian painter, who had moved to Germany
and was an important member of the Blue Rider circle, had written to
Arnold Schoenberg in 1911 applauding the composer's "rupture of conventional compositional structure." This was the goal Williams was reaching for in his poetry. Reading Kandinsky's grandiose credo in *Reminiscences*
could only embolden Williams to start liberating his poetry from mori-
bund forms: "Every work comes into being in the same way as the cosmos
by means of catastrophe . . . The creation of the work of art is the creation of the world." Williams was not yet ready to view himself or the poet
in such a Promethean way—that would have to wait until the opening
pages of *Spring and All* in 1923—but Kandinsky's insistence that the artist created out of an "Inner Necessity" struck a resonant chord in Williams. He could see in *Improvisation 27* that Kandinsky had fearlessly
overthrown, albeit in stages, traditional representation and naturalistic
subject matter. As he moved closer to embracing abstraction, Kandinsky
let color dissolve form. In *Improvisation 6*, the figures are recognizably
African by their hats and clothes, but they are missing facial features; in
Improvisation 14 (1910), Kandinsky adopted an extreme stylization of
trees and the people sitting on a bench. It is possible that Hartley showed
Williams Kandinsky's *Klange*, prose poems that aimed to create a new
musical, artistic, and poetic language.

Williams could delight in Kandinsky's freedom without following him
into radical abstraction. Poetry, Williams believed, could not do without a
recognizable subject. But it is clear from his prologue to *Kora in Hell: Improvisations* that he was familiar with Kandinsky's definition of improvisa-

tion as "a largely unconscious, spontaneous expression of inner character, non-material in nature." As the art historian Gail Levin pointed out, "Williams later paraphrased Kandinsky's 'axioms for the artist':"

> Every artist has to express himself.
> Every artist has to express his epoch.
> Every artist has to express the pure and eternal
> qualities for the art of all men.

Williams then commented on the above: "So we have the fish and the bait, but the last rule holds three hooks at once—not for the fish, however." Kandinsky's ideas, which also had Pound's imprimatur, gave Williams the permission he needed to experiment with language in *Kora in Hell*: structure didn't have to be premeditated; it could be improvised on the fly.

This pattern of rising to the modernist bait and then cautiously paddling away from it is repeated in the prologue when he lays his poetic credentials on the table to compete with, and be judged by, Marianne Moore, Pound, H.D., and Wallace Stevens. While Williams struggled to acquire a poetic voice that wasn't derivative, they had all settled on a satisfactory creative method and begun to earn a reputation for poetic mastery. Remarkably, Williams is willing to expose his poems publicly to his peers' sarcasm, abuse, and misinterpretation, to be treated as a novice by them. In the dock, he frankly admits that his poems are marred by verbal infelicities and that his ideas are not yet fully crystallized. Yet he is not a martyr to others' opinions. Alternately amused and infuriated by these prosecutors, he goes on the offensive, striking back with vitriolic wit at the "subtle conformists" (T. S. Eliot is his main target), "content with the connotations of their masters" and an "attenuated intellectuality." No fool, Williams salutes Eliot's exquisite workmanship, but swats it aside as "rehash." Employing a medical term, Williams concludes: "confine them [Eliot and his admirers] in hell for their paretic [paralyzed] assumption that there is no alternative but their own groove."

So he scouts the poetry scene for potential allies. Toward Marianne Moore, Williams bears the utmost respect. He praises her (and Mina Loy; the two were often paired) for "freshness of presentation, novelty, freedom, [and] break with banality": the very goals he was striving to reach. But Moore was too much the hedgehog for Williams. Her poetic ideal demanded a puritanical exclusivity neither the doctor nor the poet in Williams could accept. He quotes her as saying, in the voice of the Book of Leviticus, "My work has come to have just one quality of value in it: I will not touch or have to do with those things which I detest." Enamored of the discursive and the miscellaneous, he could never choose one quality and stick with it.

By contrast, Pound—centaur, harpy, erudite snob (despite hailing from Idaho), and demotic farceur opening doors and slamming them shut, all rolled into one able propagandist—delivers a crushing put-down of Williams's ignorance and ambition to fashion an original American poetic idiom. A few key passages from Pound's hilarious long letter, laid out in prose tercets, give a taste of its peppery flavor:

> And America? What the h—l do you a blooming foreigner know about the place. Your père only penetrated the edge, and you've never been west of Upper Darby, or the Maunchunk switchback.
>
> Would H., with the swirl of the prairie wind in her underwear, or the Virile Sandburg recognize you, an effete easterner as a REAL American? Inconceivable!!!!!
>
> My dear boy you have never felt the woop of the PEEraries. You have never seen the projecting and protuberant Mts. of the Sierra Nevada. WOT can you know of the country?
>
> You have the naive credulity of a Co. Clare emigrant. But I (*der grosse Ich*) have the virus, the bacillus of the land in my blood, for nearly three bleating centuries. (Bloody snob, 'eave a brick at 'im!!!).
>
> You thank your bloomin gawd you've got enough Spanish blood to muddy up your mind, and prevent the current American ideation from going through it like a blighted colander.
>
> The thing that saves your work is opacity, and don't you forget it. Opacity is NOT an American quality. Fizz, swish, gabble, and verbiage, these are echt americanisch . . .

This is a shrewd appraisal. Williams *was* "naively credulous"; he had seen nothing of the United States west of Kenneth Burke's farm near the Delaware Water Gap. But Pound's ancestral one-upmanship misses the point. Like a benevolent autocrat sitting on his throne in Kensington, Pound viewed America as a barbarian colony in the vast poetic empire he controlled through his connections in publishing. He sent directives, heckled the "rude mechanicals," and laughed at their gaffes as if they were performing the absurd comedy of Pyramis and Thisbe with solemn ignorance, and offered free advice to civilize them. For Pound, it was an irksome if necessary task, tutoring these mostly untalented provincials. The future of the American language didn't interest or concern him as it did Williams; Pound's attention was turned toward ransacking cultural treasures from China to Provence. Europe was the epicenter of modernism.

Yet Williams doesn't collapse under Pound's barrages. (They squabbled for nearly sixty years.) Fenollosa is of less importance to Williams than fennel. I suppose he envied his friend's cocky freedom of opinion, exclamation points hurled like Zeus's thunderbolts, oracular pronouncements, and patter in three languages and Cockney dialect ("fizz, swish, gabble, and verbiage!"). Because he was not sure how much study and muddying of the mind were good for his poems, Williams tolerated Pound's gibes; they set him thinking about limits, traditions, standards—and resistance. Wasn't Pound's endorsement of opacity hollow, since in another letter he beseeched Williams to disclose his intentions in *Kora* more clearly? An intellectual flâneur, Pound had the luxury of visiting libraries, of reading and writing anytime; the young doctor could barely snatch an hour to scribble down lines for a new poem.

About H.D.'s criticisms of his poems, Williams was less gracious. In her pursuit of beauty, "the desolation of a flat Hellenic perfection of style," she represented an aesthete's preciosity that made him feel like an oaf in comparison: "When I was with her," he tells us, "my feet always seemed to be sticking to the ground while she would be walking on the tips of the grass stems." Any whiff of incense from the Temple of Art sickened Williams, arousing his desire to blaspheme. Having edited his poem "March," H.D. defends her action on the grounds that "the beautiful lines are so very beautiful—so in the tone and spirit of your Postlude—(which to me stands, a Nike, supreme among your poems). I think there is real beauty—and real beauty is a rare and sacred thing in this generation—in all the pyramid, Ashur-ban-i-pal bits and in the Fiesole and in the wind at the very last." After this pompous dithyramb, she aims her barb at his weak spot: "I feel in the hey-ding-ding-touch running through your poem a derivative tendency which, to me, is not you—not your very self. It is as if you were ashamed of your Spirit, ashamed of your inspiration!—as if you mocked at your own song. It's very well to mock at yourself—it is a spiritual sin to mock at your inspiration."

Since Williams barely knew that "very self," it was surely presumptuous and glib of H.D. to chastise him. Naturally he bristled. "There is nothing sacred about literature," he retorted in his best François Villon manner, "it is damned from one end to the other. There is nothing in literature but change and change is mockery. I'll write whatever I damn please and as I damn please and it'll be good if the authentic spirit of change is on it." H.D.'s idea of the "real"—an Assyrian king, Nike, pyramids, Fiesole—seems remote, like a historical pageant acted out behind a scrim, as if she could not bear to confront the recently ended World War I, whose killing fields made her versions of art for art's sake look escapist to Williams. On poetry's battlefield, imagination was a casualty of "false values": the neoclassicism H.D. championed and the romanticism he had repudiated. Still, typically, Williams accepted several of her editorial changes.

Williams hated "fixity" because he equated it with "finality" ("the walking devil," he called it in the prologue). Since his poetic identity remained fluid, he worried that fixity would lock him into a style before he had a chance to survey the coordinates and test the power of his imagination. When he reprints Wallace Stevens's letter commenting on the poems of *Al Que Quiere!* Williams annotates it with polite irony, out of deference to Stevens's genteel authority and acknowledges that Stevens concedes that his quarrels with Williams's miscellany spring from a personal taste for order:

> Given a fixed point of view, realistic, imagistic or what you will, everything adjusts itself to that point of view; and the process of adjustment is a world in flux, as it should be for a poet. But to fidget with points of view leads always to new beginnings and incessant new beginnings lead to sterility.
>   (This sounds like Sir Roger de Coverley)
>   A single manner
>   or mood thoroughly matured and exploited is that fresh thing . . .
> etc.

All the evidence suggests that as a doctor Williams was lynx-eyed and disciplined. As a poet, however, he fidgeted and fiddled with his style his entire career, and his frequent recourse to "new beginnings" did not lead, pace Stevens's schoolmaster's lecture, to sterility.

3. Improvisation

"Carelessness of heart is a virtue akin to the small lights of the stars," Williams announces in section 24 of *Kora*. This is less an aphorism about the emotions than a stab at a poetic he could believe in. Since he had no reliable road maps to reach that goal, he decided to travel "some back road of the intention." This meant, as he confesses, that he might take the wrong turn, lose his way, ask directions, yet like his mother in Rome, "extricate [himself] from the strangeness of every vista and find a landmark by which to steer." What Williams was hunting for was a key that would release his imagination from the shackles of rusted forms. What he chanced upon was the art of improvisation, a flexible technique that could help him sidestep the "malignant rigidities" blocking his path. All his life Williams loved theater. At medical school, he relished amateur revues; he acted with Mina Loy at the Provincetown Playhouse; he built a stage in the backyard at 9 Ridge Road; he wrote plays and libretti. Improvisation offered him the chance to try on roles without committing himself to them.

In improvisation, an actor starts with the barest germ of an idea or situation, a rhythm, a word, or a person's gesture, riskily inventing a character and structure from whatever is cast off and drifts by, as Huck Finn and Jim built their raft. "Improvisation always requires a plan," Octavio Paz said in *The Double Flame*. "It may have been worked out only a minute before, or be vague and schematic: it is still a plan." Paz's statement is that of a subtle, orderly intellect, but for Williams, the crux and appeal of improvisation is precisely its lack of forethought, the surprises that free association confers. The actor can let her mind follow its impulses. She is not bound by predetermined rules of form: if she wishes to conduct a dialogue between the two sides of a murderer's mind, she can; if she chooses five minutes of silence, that, too, is permissible. Improvisation is a means to an end, not an end in itself; the actor searches for a technique rather than for an answer. A feint at the truth may fall flat and leave the actor in danger of making a fool of herself: "Fools have big wombs" is *Kora*'s opening gambit. Nonetheless, she immerses herself in this scary and exhilarating process, hoping to crystallize a moment, clarify a feeling, or break through an internal barrier into new terrain.

For the stymied Williams, this procedure was a windfall. After a long night of visiting patients, he would return home, fatigued and agitated but with his mind in a state of eerie receptivity, and go up to his attic studio and write. The censor asleep, he would dive into his unconscious and come up with seaweed, junk, and pearls. The uncertainty of what he'd retrieve was part of the game's pleasure. It was a relief to escape for a few hours from his identity. Improvising opened up new pathways for his imagination to explore.

Yet the process was not random. He developed ad hoc signposts that he could follow or abandon halfway. Words or sounds that sprang up from the unconscious could be shaped consciously. Improvisation eventually demanded hard choices: eliminate these words; string together those. At least half of the improvisations in *Kora* therefore read like purposeful free association. Here is Williams noodling about remorse:

> Marry in middle life and take the young thing home. Later in the year let the worst out. It's odd how little the tune changes. Do worse—till your mind's turning, then rush into repentance and the lady grown a hero while the clock strikes.
>
> Here the harps have a short cadenza. It's sunset back of the new cathedral and the purple river scum has set seaward. The car's at the door. I'd not like to go alone tonight. I'll pay you well. It's the king's evil. Speed! Speed! The sun's self's a chancre low in the west. Ha, how the great houses shine—for old time's sake! For sale! For Sale! The town's gone another way. But I'm not fooled that easily. *Fort Sale!! Fort Sale!* if you read it aright. And beauty's own head on the pillow, *a la Maja Desnuda! O Duquesa de Alba! Duquesa de Alba!* Never was there such a lewd wonder in the streets of Newark! Open the windows—but all's boarded up here. Out with you, you sleepy doctors and lawyers you,—the sky's afire and Calvary Church with its snail's horns up, sniffing the dawn—o' the wrong side. Let the trumpets blare! *Tutti i strumenti!* The world's bound homeward.

This passage resembles a linguistic flea market in which everything is for sale. Williams peddles high art (Goya and Shakespeare) and speaks four languages, as if competing with—or parodying—Pound's pedagogy and fondness for cultural polyphony. The narrator begins the second paragraph with a "short cadenza" on the harp and ends with trumpets blaring and the orchestra going full blast. You'd think he was announcing the Dies Irae, but it's just his townsmen going home at the end of a day. Visually, Williams brackets his gnomic utterances with two samples of postcard art. The first is almost picture-perfect souvenir shop kitsch: the sun setting behind the new cathedral with a purple river running to the sea (the scum is a trademark Williams curlicue). The second, a depiction of dawn, employs the same palette but is saved from cloying prettiness by the lovely image likening the church spire to a snail's horn sniffing the dawn. In the midst of this artistic mélange, a mysterious car appears and a few short bursts of cryptic pleading are overheard at the door. We soon learn that this is an old friend "whose brain is slowly curdling due to a syphilitic infection" and who wants Williams to accompany him to New York City, which Bill agrees to do. This night out on the town produces a curious yet typical defensiveness in Williams: he rants about "the city's prone stupidity" and "make[s] light of his friend's misfortune." Perhaps the practical lesson he drew from this "journey" was that the wages of "lewd wonder" is syphilis: *Fort Sale!* Poetic wonder, however, pays dividends in beauty. Syphilis as the "king's evil" and the chancre projected as the sun's rays might have been lifted from *Measure for Measure*. But several sections later, the doctor and poet cooperate in defining syphilis and showing that it yields a floral beauty worthy of Baudelaire—and of reflection: "Pathology literally speaking is a flower garden. Syphilis covers the body with salmon-red petals. The study of medicine is an inverted sort of horticulture. Over and above all this floats the philosophy of disease which is a stern dance." If Williams doesn't bother to analyze that philosophy, it's because in 1917 he's more comfortable talking about anesthetics than about aesthetics.

In its self-conscious sporting with words, this passage contrasts Williams's "broken style" with the perfections attained by Goya or Rembrandt. Williams's sentences careen wildly, as if obeying the command "Speed! Speed!" and suddenly jam on the brakes, then lurch forward again. He'll try anything to keep the vehicle on the road. If a pun on "For sale!" doesn't work, he throws in a Ha! or a growl (Haagh!), or sprinkles the page with exclamation points. When he comes to a dead end of inspiration, often marked by a dash, he pauses, then swerves in a new direction, reverses, or executes a U-turn. Curiously, when he feels unsure what he's driving at, he switches to the imperative mode. We can imagine him shrugging when an improvisation flops: it's not an ignominious failure that should make him blush, for he's gained dexterity and valuable experience.

Kora in Hell is a prompt book for two other kinds of improvisation. When Mozart the child prodigy played in the palaces of Europe's nobility, the court composer would normally set him the task of improvising on a theme from a finished work. In the variations that followed, the theme would undergo dazzling transformations and embellishments, sometimes disappearing for long stretches, at other times surviving by an audible thread. That is approximately Williams's compositional method in several sections of *Kora*. Key words and images—dance, perfection, tunes, caresses, for example—sometimes stand for a lucid whole whose pattern will emerge, if at all, at the end. That is why transitions are abrupt or dropped altogether. But though Williams is fumbling for solid poetic footing, *Kora in Hell* is not a display of automatic writing. As proof, take this reverie from section 5:

> Beautiful white corpse of night actually! So the northwest winds of death are mountain sweet after all! All the troubled stars are put to bed now: three bullets from wife's hand none kindlier: in the crown, in the nape and one lower: three starlike holes among a million pocky pores and the moon of your mouth: Venus, Jupiter, and Mars, and all stars melted forthwith into this one good light over the inquest table,—the traditional moth beating its wings against it— except there are two here. But sweetest are the caresses of the county physician, a little clumsy perhaps—mais!—and the Prosecuting Attorney, Peter Valuzzi and the others, waving green arms of maples to the tinkling of the ragpicker's bells. Otherwise—: kindly stupid hands, kindly coarse voices, infinitely soothing, infinitely detached, infinitely beside the question, restfully babbling of how, where, why and night is done and the green edge of yesterday has said all it could.

Williams's presence at an autopsy makes him pensive. Mostly, as we would expect of a doctor, he looks at death unflinchingly. Here, bored by the routine business of affixing causes and time of death, he falls into a trance in which the corpse, whether boor or dedicated teacher, becomes a romantic image, the stench of death is cleansed by a wind, and the bullet holes are "starlike." Williams may be fantasizing that he is the victim of the wife's murderous wrath, the third bullet to the groin hinting that retribution is justified for the county physician's ladykilling (those sweet if clumsy caresses). The French word "mais" breaks his train of thought, just as the cosmic light from the planets and the stars dissolves into "the good white light over the inquest table." Although this improvisation has an uncharacteristic closure, its motifs are echoed elsewhere in *Kora*.

There's a third kind that also pertains to *Kora in Hell*. When we find ourselves in an emergency and without our usual resources, we have to ad-lib a solution. On a battlefield, the surgeon amputating a soldier's leg without anesthesia must come up with a substitute on the spur of the moment. A party of hikers lost in the higher elevations of the Rockies during a blizzard must rig up some form of shelter. Desperation is the mother of invention. It is not far-fetched to say that Williams, who in *Kora* ruefully called himself a "half-poet," took that aphorism to heart. It's one of his most endearing traits that he can laugh at his own "stupid" blunders, or play the Shakespearean fool, clowning seriously.

Renouncing most of his poetic inheritance—"Confute the sages," he exhorts himself—Williams started over with huge ambition but no plan and only the scraps of a new faith to sustain him: "A poem can be made of anything." "There is nothing that with a twist of the imagination cannot be something else." He possessed "that elasticity of the attention which frees the mind for the enjoyment of its special prerogatives." Dissatisfied with the immature work he'd written, he clutched at this straw: "Often a poem will have merit because of some one line or even one meritorious word. So it hangs heavily on its stem but still secure, the tree unwilling to release it." *Kora in Hell* is thus a blotted transcript of Williams arguing with himself and poetic tradition, often in elliptical terms; he's frustrated that his words only fitfully "pirouette with the music" he hears, though sometimes he's jaunty about the split and his chances of overcoming it: "And imagining himself to be two persons he eases his own mind by putting his burdens upon one while the other takes what pleasure there is before him."

If there is a heroic savior in all these improvisations, it is the imagination, to which *Kora in Hell* is an extended, broken hymn. Doubtless Williams first learned to exalt this term, the key word in Romantic poetics, from Keats. Among modern poets, only Stevens rivals Williams in rever-. ing the imagination and talking about it so obsessively. It is one thing to sense and invoke its powers, as Williams does in *Kora* on every page; it is another, tougher matter to harness it in a poem. How to reconcile a poetics of inclusion with "a kind of alchemy of form, a deft bottling of a fermenting language," as Williams puts it in section 23, posed a conundrum that he puzzled over his entire career. In *Kora*, the poetic imagination, like Columbus, embarks on its discovery of a New World, overcoming mutiny, despair, and ignorance of where it was sailing.

Williams comes closest to formulating a tentative poetic creed in a charming, self-effacing passage near the end of *Kora*:

> My little son's improvisations exceed mine; a round stone to him's a loaf of bread or "this hen could lay a dozen golden eggs." Birds fly about his bedstead; giants lean over him with hungry jaws; bears roam the farm by summer and are killed and quartered at a thought. There are interminable stories at eating time full of bizarre imagery, true grotesques, pigs that change to dogs in the telling, cows that sing, roosters that become mountains and oceans that fill a soup plate. There are groans and growls, dun clouds and sunshine mixed in a huge phantasmagoria that never rests, never ceases to unfold into—the day's poor little happenings. Not that alone. He has music which I have not. His tunes follow no scale, no rhythm— alone the mood in ramblings up and down, over and over with a rigor of invention that rises beyond the power to follow except in some more obvious flight. Never have I heard so crushing a critique as those desolate inventions, involved half-hymns, after his first visit to a Christian Sunday school.

We are back with the Romantic poets' myth of the child's incandescent imagination. "Shades of the prison-house" have not closed around the poet's son; "the light of common day," what Williams calls "the day's poor little happenings," is rich in metaphors and metamorphoses: there's a peculiar sense of scale, a natural ease as the child moves from the menacing to the gleeful, from the oceanic to the local, that borders on the miraculous (the three-year-old William Eric can turn stones into bread). "The little Actor cons" many parts, as does Williams in *Kora in Hell*, the difference being that the poet looks askance at the "odd ramblings up and down" as sometimes lacking "rigor of invention." (Typically, Williams turns sour the next moment: "The screaming brat's a sheep bleating"! Not all metamorphoses are equal—and later, as a poet in whom the child is alive, he whips up some concupiscent nonsense rhymes: "When beldams dig clams their fat hams . . .")

What Williams claimed he most loathed was the idée fixe. His prescription for avoiding it, the piecemeal, was criticized by the patrician Wallace Stevens as too casual. "Personally," Stevens told his friend in the letter that Williams quotes in the prologue, "I have a distaste for miscellany." But for Williams in this period, the miscellany, the piecemeal, that improvisations allowed was a saving grace. It gave him the freedom to choose which paths he'd amble down, to discover which led to dead ends and which to the open road. But first he would attempt to impose at least a temporary grid. His method, borrowed from Metastasio, the great eighteenth-century librettist for Gluck and Mozart, was as follows: he divided each section into three asymmetrical parts, allowing paragraphs to run short or long, to be linked or autonomous, depending on how much interest he sustained in his theme. Sometimes Williams peters out or grumpily shifts gears, and the sentences jostle each other violently, breaking down and stranding the reader in a no-man's-land. At other times, when his imagination is fully in charge, the paragraphs "remain of a piece from one end to the other," crossing the bar line, as in medieval music. Interspersed among these paragraphs are commentaries in italics— baffling and lucid, whimsical and epigrammatic—that parse the episode in the numbered unit that precede them or state contrary aesthetic intentions, often falling into platitude or deepening the mystery. In these commentaries, Williams plays the high-strung theater director who interrupts the actors to suggest a more nuanced line reading or to interpret the subtext of the playwright's words.

Pound complained to Williams that the improvisations were "wholly incoherent unamerican poems." Pound was wrong. Opaque, uneven, disheveled, jagged, and, in spots, sophomoric *Kora in Hell* may be, but incoherent it is not. I'd propose two entranceways into the slippery art of *Kora*. The first again leans on a theatrical metaphor: the twenty-seven sections constitute an audition of poetic voices and a repertoire of assorted genres, heard solo, in unison, and in bizarre combinations. So a delicate lyrical sentence—"See, there it [the city] rises out of the swamp and the mists already blowing their sleepy bagpipes"—can follow a passage of almost demented sarcasm: "Something to get used to; a stone too big for ox haul, too near for blasting. Take the road round it or—scrape away, scrape away: a mountain's buried in the dirt! Marry a gopher to help you! Drive her in! Go yourself down along the lit pastures. Down, down! Here's Tenochtitlan! here's a strange Darien where worms are princes." Williams tries almost everything: comedy, prayer, burlesque, soliloquies out of Browning, dialogues, lampoons, fairy tales, even an autodidact's homilies. One minute he's a Maenad drunk on literary experiments; the next he's impersonating a bookish poet quoting his favorite lines or sending up the great tradition from Dante, Shakespeare, and Villon to Whitman, Eliot, H.D., and Pound. Then he reverts to the nature lover bird-watching or sketching cloud formations. In such a theater of the mind, the forms inevitably sprawl and "there is neither beginning nor end," but he doesn't lose his bearings. The original Stuart Davis frontispiece for *Kora* featured "a human ovum surrounded by spermatozoa black and white," and this seems an apt image for the hit-or-miss, high-stakes goal Williams was rolling the dice for: a wholly new poem, albeit in a sort of musical prose.

Early in *Kora*, Williams tells a brief anecdote about Roald Amundsen, the explorer of the South Pole, a restless, taciturn man once jilted by a village girl. "One knew why the poles attracted him," Williams comments. Because polarity ruled Williams's mind and behavior, it churns up every page of *Kora*. Take this passage from section 28:

> After thirty years staring at one true phrase he discovered that its opposite was true also. For weeks he laughed in the grip of a fierce self-derision. Having lost the falsehood to which he'd fixed his hawser he rolled drunkenly about the field of his environment before the new direction began to dawn upon his cracked mind. What a fool ever to be tricked into seriousness. Soft hearted, hard hearted.

Kora's governing polarities include heaven and hell, purity and filth, perfect and imperfect (or broken), pastoral and urban, sublime and gross, fixity and motion (or, in its most obsessive guise, dance), up and down. Despite its flaws—maddening obscurities, clumsy dances, vague tunes, badly camouflaged autobiography—it is a singular work of the imagination. By descending "Halfway to Hell" and no farther, Williams fulfilled his goal of traveling the back roads like an itinerant actor, touching the world, then recoiling from it. *Kora in Hell* is a surly, rowdy rehearsal for future great poems—and "the recognition of the world."

FOUR

Youthful Fumblings

In *The Education of Henry Adams*, with a flourish of dandified chivalry, Henry Adams declared his debt to the women who licked an uncouth Brahmin cub into civilized shape. His frequent tributes to the superiority of women were a blend of debater's trick, emotional belief, uxorious habit, and feline flirting. But in his teasing manner, Adams posed a serious question: Why was the sphere of action for American women so limited? Why were their energies mainly dissipated on cultural consumerism, and how did American men abet this waste? (To prove his theories, alas, Adams restricted his evidence to upper-class females, such as his wife, Clover, and his Platonic paramour Elizabeth Cameron; not a peep about Jane Addams, Alice Hamilton, Elizabeth Blackwell, Mother Jones, or any of the fearless women who refused to accept this gilded life and, against long odds, took up arms against the forces of social inequity.)

Drawing on his acute skills as a historian, Adams exhumed sex from its burial place in the national psyche and proceeded to analyze it with shrewd gusto. "In America," he asserted, "neither Venus nor Virgin ever had value as force—at most as sentiment. No American had ever been truly afraid of either." Certainly the men who ran the machinery of moneymaking after the Civil War cared little for Venus or Virgin; their imaginations were captivated by the Sirens of the marketplace, by the "materialistic scramble," upon which they lavished their talents and drive. "The typical American man," Adams observed a little enviously, "had his hand on a lever and his eye on a curve in his road [,] . . . and he could not admit emotions or anxieties or subconscious distractions, more than he could admit whiskey or drugs, without breaking his neck. He could not run his machine and a woman too; he must leave her, even though his wife, to find her own way." Perfunctory churchgoers, men consigned religion to their women. Culture, too: when they escorted their wives and daughters to a performance of *Tristan* or *Tannhäuser*, it was the women mostly who thrilled to the sensual music. These bankers and industrialists married, of course, and sometimes took mistresses, but for them, with few exceptions, sex was a distraction or anodyne, like European Old Masters a trophy of economic success, the spoils of buccaneering power.

From a census of American literature, Adams counted only one writer for whom sex was a force and vibrant presence: Walt Whitman. (In the novels of Adams's friend Henry James, sex was an unsettling, covert drive, but cloaked in decorous or subtle euphemisms.) Adams himself, as Thomas Beer pointed out with malicious glee in *The Mauve Decade*, was a puritan aristocrat who became an effete votary of the Virgin Mary, thereby indirectly promoting the goals of the "Titanesses," Beer's term for the prudish sentinels who guarded society against such licentious scoundrels as Whitman.

Adams, who acknowledged Venus's force in the abstract, not in his life, realized that this fear of sex threatened to sanitize American art and literature. Anthony Comstock's loud crusades against vice, nude paintings, Native American fertility dances, and "salacious" novels attracted many zealous followers—priests, temperance advocates, club ladies, expedient politicians—who skillfully browbeat public officials, harassed newspaper editors, called for censorship of "immoral" books, and propagandized from the pulpit. Like other cultural skirmishes about values throughout American history, this one was fought in the courts of both law and public opinion, with mixed results. A throwback to the most bigoted strain of Puritanism, Comstockery claimed the high ground of defending the soul from defilement and society from wanton impulsivity. Despite this campaign, brothels drew throngs of men, and readers snapped up copies of tabloids detailing sex scandals such as the murder of Stanford White by Harry Thaw, the jealous husband of Evelyn Nesbit, or Victoria Woodhull's sensational charges that the famed Brooklyn minister Henry Ward Beecher had committed adultery with several female congregants.

In 1900, eight years after Whitman's death and nearly half a century since he proclaimed boldly, in "Song of Myself," the end of "ducking and deprecating" about sex, the "poet of the Body" and the "poet of the Soul" was virtually ignored by his countrymen. "Hankering, gross, mystical, nude," Whitman had strutted in "Song of Myself," but the public, abashed or bored or puzzled, looked away. As self-styled conduit of "forbidden voices," Whitman enjoyed tweaking middle-class opinion and breaking rules; "mad for contact," he provocatively hugged and caressed men, women, himself, anybody he could get his hands on—at least in imagination. Above all, in frank, carnal language Whitman attributed to sex an almost supernatural force:

> Something I cannot see puts upward libidinous prongs,
> Seas of bright juice suffuse heaven.

At age seventeen, in the throes of a normal suburban adolescence, William Carlos Williams knew little about Whitman, sex, or women, all of which would profoundly affect him and his poetry. As Adams had, Williams asserted often that women had shaped his destiny. In letters, poems, stories, essays, and memoirs, Williams left a voluminous record of that influence and his fumbling attempts to understand their complex natures and to abandon the conventional male view of women as either virgins or whores. In "Portrait of a Woman in Bed" (1917), trying on a female persona, he both leans on that outmoded prop and bends it into a new shape, drawing an admiring portrait of the slatternly Polish peasant, Mrs. Robitza, a querulous, defiant cook willing to cast her children off to fend for themselves or to let society take care of them. Williams's purpose in the poem, he remarked to John Thirlwall, was "to throw her in the face of the town. The whores are better than my townspeople." Beneath this cliché of the idealized whore versus the hypocritical citizens lurks a fondness for misfits and rousers of scandal. Though Williams doesn't whitewash the unfeeling mother, he identifies with the provoking nuisance who speaks her mind bluntly and five times hurls the word "trouble" at the "county physician" and at the town "overseer of the poor" seeking to evict her—"I won't work / and I've got no cash. What are you going to do / about it?" In an act of homage, Williams salutes the defiant Robitza for being so natural, a state that eludes him. Though the poem is neither lyrical nor subtle—it is rough speech from the mouth of one Polish mother—Mrs. Robitza, a first sketch for the Baroness Elsa von Freytag-Loringhoven, another flouter of propriety who amused and shocked him, lives memorably on the page.

Depending on his mood and situation, Williams attaches the words "clean" and "filth" to women's sexuality—and to his own desires. He longed to surrender himself to passionate intimacy (or libertinism), yet feared either would result in the erasure of his identity. As a way out of this psychological dilemma, he acted no differently from most writers: he sublimated his libido and emotional confusions in poetry. But escape them he could not; they shadowed his poems and his often belligerent efforts to define a poetics he could embrace, live with, and not be unfaithful to. Just as Williams sometimes dreamed of overthrowing the inherited order of poetic tradition, so he wished to rebel against his cautious self. That was not an easy undertaking, since his parents had instilled in him a strong respect for virtue. When the word "perfect" chimes in his poems and prose, it's usually a muezzin's summons to ideal, or self-suppressing, behavior. By contrast, the word "imperfect" serves as a potion to lull the censor asleep so that Williams can then enjoy—or explore, if only in fantasy—forbidden pleasures: sexual revels with the glamorous Mina Loy, say, or other Venuses of casual morality beckoning from New York.

These idylls of freedom, however, even when merely yearned for, brought in their wake attacks of guilt. Williams turns prickly, defensive, blames his lax conscience for succumbing to temptation, imagines extreme punishments for himself, then puts the brakes on any indiscretions that might jeopardize his medical practice and his marriage. Then an opposite reaction sets in: feeling like a "Hemmed-in Male," he starts plotting to break out of prison again. This pattern was not confined to his youth. It lasted his entire life. The doctor in Williams's late play *A Dream of Love*, as we've seen, comes to New York for a tryst and suffers a fatal heart attack in his mistress's room, then after his death returns to his wife in order to apologize for and rationalize his conduct.

From a study of the clues to his feelings about women that Williams scatters everywhere, it's clear that he often taints the evidence and obscures its implications from himself (and his readers) or is genuinely unsure how to master his fractious desires. Looking back in the *Autobiography*, he portrays himself as a Penrod romping mischievously through an average boy's wholesome childhood, which means failing to notice girls or being awkward around them. The next moment, with a conspiratorial wink he spins harmless fictions about his sexual prowess, as when he boasts of his "madcap erotic adventures" with the girls in his seventh-grade class. Or he adopts the grim tone of a Sisyphus forever rolling the stone of virginity up a hill. If none of these accounts is trustworthy—self-disclosure was not Williams's strong suit—they show that he never satisfactorily settled his inner debate as to what was or was not permissible behavior with women.

Nevertheless, all of the record is not smudged with fairy dust or deliberate obfuscation. In the tangled skeins of metaphors, the jittery rhythms of poems, and the wayward confessions of letters, we can appraise Williams as he explains (or blurts out) his views and justifies his behavior and attitude toward women, be they his female patients or those with whom he had long-term, peculiar, stymied, or casual relations: his wife, Floss, his friend Viola Baxter Jordan, and the Baroness Elsa von Freytag-Loringhoven most prominently.

How did Williams's attitudes toward women, in life and in art, evolve? Circuitously but in traceable patterns. To the young Williams, as we saw, the two most powerful women were his mother, Elena, and his grandmother Wellcome, both strong-willed survivors of cultural uprootings and romantic unhappiness. An adventuress and painter stranded in a suburban backwater, Elena was something of a misfit who schooled herself to adapt to diminished expectations. Outwardly, she might have conformed to the small-town ethos—going to church and keeping house, for example—but she pursued a dark, clandestine life, too; on occasions, her care could be as unreliable as Robitza's. Williams inherited enough of his father's rationality not to let Elena's traits cripple him; his behavior with women, though, suggests that he was, given a mix of volatile amorous provocations, ready to blaze up at any time, like Mount Pelée or his mother, and cause emotional havoc. Luckily for Williams, as he often conceded, Floss's temperament resembled William George's more than Elena's; he respected Floss's steady intelligence and coolness in crises. But he couldn't escape viewing her as a prosaic wife who would tolerate her husband's womanizing. Only gradually did he grow aware that in their marriage he was the fickle partner, whose infidelities were wrenching and damaging to Floss.

At twenty-two, however, Williams was a likable, conventional young man. He had jumped directly from high school to medical school, a fairly common occurrence in the early twentieth century. Apart from bouts of homesickness, he had no difficulties handling the transition. By his own account, he "work[ed] his head off," though he was no Gradgrind.

Williams's 1905–1906 chatty letters to his "little" brother Edgar, who was studying architecture at MIT, chronicle a typical college student's activities: "pluggin' away" at his studies like a "blooming truckhorse," cheering at the Penn-Harvard football game, fencing, dancing, attending Mask and Wig plays, and of course rating the girls. (H.D. "certainly is a fine girl even if she isn't a quintessence of grace," he confides to Ed.) Williams's epistolary style at this stage favors gee-whiz, rah-rah locutions ("By gosh") and fraternal chaffing; like the James Stewart character in a Frank Capra movie, he's given to "nebulous but high-minded" exhortations. Imbued with a hyperactive will and a moralistic streak, "ambitious Bill," as he signs one letter, urges Ed to honor the manly ideal of striving for perfection, disparages reason as useless, while commending patience, grit, faith, and truth for their rewards: "We must therefore do things that will last forever." "Truth and never fail. They will always bring forth their fruit in due season." "How ridiculous it is for us to sit down on Sunday with folded hands and loaf yes loaf and loose [sic] one day in which we might be working at some beautiful secret of nature. Our work is the man himself in a tangible form so that our senses can grasp him." Like Poor Richard, Williams cranks out platitudes about pursuing the grail of success. (This habit persisted in "Tract" and other poems in which he harangues Rutherford's citizens for their failings. "I wanted to tell people, to tell 'em off plenty," Williams noted in his *Autobiography*. "There would be a bitter pleasure in that, bitter because I instinctively knew no one would much listen." What saves him from the charge of fatuity and bullying is that he usually puts himself in the docket alongside those he chastised.)

When the yoke of his medical school tasks galled him and the "blues" overtook him, he sought diversion in romantic fantasies. In a letter of January 14, 1906, he tells Ed of meeting a French girl, the first "into whose eyes I have looked & forgotten everything around me." From these "Dissipated" moments, Porphyro in Philadelphia composes bland poems, such as the "Eve of St. Agnes" imitation he encloses for Ed's approval:

> Last night I sat within a
> blazing hall
> and drank of bliss from out
> a maiden's eyes
> The jewelled guests passed by
> as forms that rise

The charm in dreams the
sleepy night for all
   Sped nameless on no face can
I recall
   Those eyes those eyes my
love lies
in their deep dephths [*sic*] beyond
recalling cries
as lost as rings adorn as
well that fall cold unawed
I go, such pulseless healthy love
forbids.

With one glance the poet succumbs to the maiden's charms, but the state of bliss doesn't last; as in Keats's poem, cold numbs the flushed senses, isolating the speaker in a state of edgy reverie. The lover cannot awaken the sleeping beauty and learn his fate from her eyes because her lids are closed. What the Frenchwoman would have made of this lovesick swain had she woken up and read his poem we can only guess, because she disappears like a phantom. In a companion poem, he moans of "shrouds," "sable fringed / clouds," and "degrading dust," perhaps examples of his purgatorial, "turgid obsessions." It's easy to poke fun at Williams's apprentice work about love and women, since he's so oblivious to the jingling rhymes ("rise," "eyes," "lies," "cries"), the lachrymose rhythms (only one comma interrupts the melodious wave), the tautological "deep depths," and the amusing oxymoron "pulseless healthy." Poets in their youth begin, notoriously, in imitation, clearing their throats and searching for a singular voice. This quest can last a long time—witness Roethke and Berryman, who until well past their fortieth year could not get rid of the stylistic mannerisms they'd picked up from Yeats, Eliot, and Auden. It took Williams years of sweat and bumbling experiments to outgrow his adolescent poetic infatuations, his Keatsean "delirium," and like most American men, he matured slowly.

Williams's first two books, *Poems* (1909) and *The Tempers* (1913), bear the watermark of a poetic greenhorn: pastiche. Predominantly love lyrics sung by a miscast Feste, they are, predictably, confected out of other poets' work and worship Beauty with all the ardor of Keats and the pre-Raphaelites or sing in a faux Shakespeare style: "Sing merrily, Truth: I tried to put / Truth in a cage! / Heigh-ho! Truth in a cage!" With its stilted voice "First Praise," a lame pastoral, could easily be mistaken for a Tennyson poem (if the bumpy lines were smoothed out):

> Lady of dusk-wood fastnesses,
>   Thou art my lady.
> have known the crisp, splintering leaf-tread with thee on before,
> White, slender through green saplings;
> I have lain by thee on the brown forest floor
>   Beside thee, my Lady.
>
> Lady of rivers strewn with stones,
>   Only thou art my Lady.
> Where thousand the freshets are crowded like peasants to a fair.
> Clear-skinned, wild from seclusion
> They jostle white-armed down the tent-bordered thoroughfare
>   Praising my Lady.

The peasant's homage to Floss is standard romantic twaddle, as implausible as a medieval tournament in the Catskills, where "First Praise" is set. (America lacked even the flimsiest of peasant traditions, Williams would note in "The pure products of America.") It is not wildness that he is striving for, but command of syntax and stanzaic pattern. Hence the stiff lyric formality and an "I" that lacks a body. In his *Autobiography*, Williams charitably forgives the young poet for rushing into print with *Poems 1909*: "There is not one thing of the slightest value in the whole thin booklet—except the intent."

There's little visibly or audibly American in language or scenery, heroes or flora and fauna. "Thee"s and "thou"s abound, as at a Quaker meetinghouse. What's conspicuously missing is Williams's own experience, as if he mistrusted it or muzzled it because he knew how shallow it was (about love he was a novice). Bookish sentiments rule. Williams writes watery, sincere verse like thousands of aspiring poets. In the sonnet "The Uses of Poetry," he and his lady drift in an enchanted boat "glid[ing]" by many a leafy bay, / Hid deep in rushes, where at random play / The glossy black winged May-flies . . ." These lines derive their images from Keats, not Rimbaud, whom he had not yet read; several years would pass before

Williams scrapped these stage sets and replaced them with the swampy Hackensack meadows, whose gunmetal gray skies and foliage and bird-calls he knew intimately. The finale of "The Uses of Poetry" follows Romantic writ: "We'll draw the light latch-string / And close the door of sense; then satiate wend, / On poesy's transforming giant wing, / To worlds afar whose fruits all anguish mend." These lines are the kind of poesy Pound was crusading to sweep away.

There's nothing surprising in this backwardness. Williams, after all, was no Stendhalian adept or disciple of Whitman's "amativeness." Except for what he learned in anatomy classes or from his desultory courtship of H.D., women were remote goddesses whose altars he was prepared to garland with flowery tributes.

In the summer of 1906, Williams began an internship at the French Hospital, run by the Catholic Sisters of Charity, on West Thirty-fourth Street between Ninth and Tenth Avenues. When he reaches this crossroads in his *Autobiography*, Williams presents himself as a sexual innocent:

> Twenty-three or -four before I became fully aware of what had been a mystery theretofore called "love." No wonder I thought to myself when I remembered Doc Martin's lecture on the subject, "Everyone in this class has committed masturbation including your present instructor—don't let's be overimpressed by its importance." I hadn't known what he meant.

Is this just an old man's faulty memory rubbing away all traces of his youthful escapades? A cagey fabrication? A chance to poke good-natured fun at his naïveté? Probably a bit of each. But he was mostly in earnest. Four months after he had taken up his duties at the hospital, Williams wrote a tense letter to his brother trying to explain why he practiced a kind of voluntary celibacy:

> To do what I mean to do and to be what I must be in order to satisfy my own self I must discipline my affections, and until a fit opportunity affords, like no one in particular except you, Ed, and my nearest family. From nature, Ed, I have a weakness wherever passion is concerned. No matter how well I reason and no matter how clearly I can see the terrible results of yielding to desire, if certain

conditions are present I might as well never have arrived at a consecutive conclusion for good in all my life, for I cannot control myself. As a result, in order to preserve myself as I must, girls cannot be my friends.

Despite these caveats, Williams's libido was as healthy as any twenty-five-year-old man's; at the hospital, he is susceptible to the allure of the Irish maid "who inhabited a skin . . . tightly packed with goodies," and he mentions a caper in which he and a friend sneaked into the nurses' dormitory, "they in their nightgowns and we in pajamas," but left before their raid was discovered. "[My] life was too fixed for much gaiety of that sort," he remarks, as if his lofty career goals didn't allow time for randy pranks. Yet he enjoyed the camaraderie with the nurses, who were looking for husbands, the spirited exchanges and rivalry with the other interns, and above all, the endless theater provided by the patients under his care. Still, he confides to Ed that the fear of losing control is surprisingly strong, like an alcoholic alarmed that his feeble will cannot withstand the urge for another drink, yet he downplays it by vowing to aspire to greatness (he even invokes Napoleon!).

The young Williams of 1907, seen through the roseate lens of his 1951 *Autobiography*, is a charming neophyte who, by his own account, "hardly knew women and felt tender to them all." Even though both hospitals he interned at were situated in high-crime neighborhoods, he was ill prepared for, and appalled by, the wanton cruelty inflicted on female victims brought to the emergency room for treatment. Of a young whore beaten by a pimp or a john, he notes, "her breasts were especially lacerated and on one could be seen the deeply imbedded marks of teeth, as if some animal had attempted to tear the tissues away." His gallantry toward the poor and the abused is genuine, chaste altruism. In the hospital, despite long hours and unrelenting pressure, he saw his imagination thrive on the teeming life that the city of the hospital staged: from huddled masses to illegitimate babies to the discovery during a medical exam that a construction worker injured in an accident was wearing women's undergarments. The hidden life always fascinated him.

Poem 9 of *Spring and All* (1923), taking a long look back at a romantic episode with a nurse at French Hospital in 1907, paints a peculiar self-portrait. As the poet drops his guard, broken, vivid memories of passion and its soured aftermath spill out. Slowly, Williams's voice, that of an irascible tribune scrutinizing the facts, unwittingly censures his own behavior as loutish. There's not a scintilla of pleasure in his recollections. Indeed, they reenact the conflict that repeatedly buffeted him: strong sexual cravings (*le médecin* as satyr *malgré lui*) prompting him to dodge the repressive Puritan installed in his head. At some flashpoint, a red light goes on and he turns on himself or flees.

Williams clearly did not share Eliot's sexual revulsion, as expressed in *The Waste Land*; the numbed coupling of the typist and carbuncular clerk and the glum, agonized estrangement of the wealthy married pair in "A Game of Chess" suggest a profound mistrust of, and disgust at, the body. Sex, for Eliot, is little more than lust and violation, a mechanistic act; sex, for Williams, is a tempting feast, the forbidden fruit he yearns for but fears to pluck from the tree. As he thinks aloud, his internal struggle gets imprinted on the jumpy rhythms of the poem.

Poem 9 is organized around three questions. The first, "What about all this writing?" launches his playlet with mock apostrophes and a somersault: "O Kiki! / O Miss Margaret Jarvis / the backhandspring." Linking Kiki, the notorious model-whore of Montparnasse, and Margaret Jarvis (Purvis), the virginal nurse he romanced fifteen years earlier, suggests that Williams hasn't shaken his Madonna/whore complex. He then turns his mockery against the memory of himself as an unsullied naif (the triple "clean"s stress that he's no rake) come to the exotic mix of fantasy and self-invention that's New York, where there's something for every taste: art, vanguard architecture, medicine, ads, amorous dalliances:

I: clean
clean
clean: yes . . . New-York

Wrigley's, appendicitis, John Marin:
skyscraper soup—

Either that or a bullet!

Who speaks that last line, both a histrionic threat of murder or suicide and a sexual innuendo, remains tantalizingly unclear, because Williams rushes the Dadaistic list and the antic punctuation—colons, ellipses, dash, exclamation point—off the stage:

> Once
> anything might have happened
> You lay relaxed on my knees—
> the starry night
> spread out warm and blind
> above the hospital—
>
> Pah!

The fairy-tale setting seems cozy and cosmic, as if Cupid protects the lovers and their limitless dreams, but the word "Pah!" like a drop of acid banishes the romantic mood: "It is unclean / which is not straight to the mark." Then, in a short surrealistic passage, Williams lapses into passivity—instead of chewing up the scenery, it devours him. Appetite is dangerous; he pretends to be blameless:

> In my life the furniture eats me
>
> the chairs, the floor
> the walls
> which heard your sobs
> drank up my emotion—
> they which alone know everything
>
> and snitched on us in the morning—

Williams's tone is playful—the lovers' secret is betrayed by the gossipy furniture—but he cannot hide his offhand indifference to Miss Margaret Jarvis's sobs; he ignores her cri de coeur.

The humble question "What to want?" which begins the second section, haunted Williams his entire life. Blake's answer, "Less than all cannot satisfy mankind," might have appealed to the incorrigible romantic in Williams, but one day spent with patients doubtless cured him of that illusion. If he had given musical markings to his poems, this movement would have been a scherzo agitato:

Drunk we go forward surely
Not I

beds, beds, beds
elevators, fruit, night-tables
breast to see, white and blue—
to hold in the hand, to nozzle

It is not onion soup
Your sobs soaked through the walls
breaking the hospital to pieces

Everything
—windows, chairs
obscenely drunk, spinning—
white, blue, orange
—hot with our passion

wild tears, desperate rejoinders
my legs, turning slowly
end over end in the air!

Though not a teetotaler—he enjoyed a highball before dinner and a glass of wine—Williams would never join the ranks of Dionysus's bacchants. In this scene, though, he's tipsy, which gait the syntax mimics. Perhaps the couple was emboldened by drink to take their sexual passion further than they had anticipated; Williams remembers himself, even as he made his rounds in the hospital wards, in a state of arousal. To the young, inexperienced intern, the line between holding a woman's breast during an examination ("to nozzle" may refer to a new mother whose breasts spurt milk) and nuzzling a breast during lovemaking is blurred. Clearly he can't exorcise the vivid memory of a passion that left the lovers and the room in "a fine frenzy rolling." Williams is turned upside down. And in a horrific image out of Poe, her sobs are like a murderous wound whose blood soaks through a wall, and her shrieks so violent they could break the hospital (and Williams?) to pieces.

Fifteen years later, when Williams reruns this incident in his mind, the sluice gates of blame and self-justification are flung open by the third question—half-bewildered, half-exasperated—"But what would you have?":

> All I said was:
> there, you see, it is broken
> stockings, shoes, hairpins
> your bed, I wrapped myself round you—
>
> I watched.
>
> You sobbed, you beat your pillow
> you tore your hair
> you dug your nails into your sides
>
> I was your nightgown
>   I watched!
>
> Clean is he alone
> after whom stream
> the broken pieces of the city—
> flying apart at his approaches
>
> but I merely
> caress you curiously
>
> fifteen years ago and you still
> go about the city, they say
> patching up school children

Defending himself against Jarvis's unspecified accusations, Williams adopts an aloof tone at odds with her hysterical sobs. His cool, almost clinical admission "I watched" would likely infuriate her. To her storms of tears and self-abuse, his retort "I was your nightgown" could mean "I was intimate with you, not detached," or "I covered your nakedness when we were found out." The repetition of "I watched," shifted five lines later to the right as Williams tries to find a new perch for viewing the past, could reinforce his voyeurism or his amazement that he'd acted so icily (the exclamation point favors the second reading).

Yet the pompous, inverted construction that follows exonerates Williams of guilt; he returns from the fractured city to the safety of the suburbs. (Normally, women's instinct for wholeness ignites praise and envy in Williams; in poem 9 it's missing entirely.) Before tying up the frayed threads, he can't resist one last cruel remark: "but I merely / caress you curiously." This emotional removal occurs frequently in Williams's poems; it allows him to escape intact. Jarvis has also survived: by performing acts of mercy, fixing what's broken, she patches up herself as well as the schoolchildren—which soothes the poet's bruised memory. Taken all in all, poem 9 is a Portrait of the Artist as a Confused Young Blackguard.

The years 1908 and 1909 were filled with crises and dashed hopes. Although Williams hugely enjoyed his residency in pediatrics at Nursery and Child's Hospital, he resigned his post because of a run-in with the administration over ethics. Despite the coaxing of senior doctors and his mentor Dr. Kerley's dangling of a lucrative job in his office, which would have ensured a well-oiled career as a "New York specialist," Williams refused to sign papers that falsified the hospital's monthly report to the state government spelling out admissions, discharges, births, and deaths. (As a result, Albany withheld financial aid calculated by these data.) There was no question of waffling; on this moral issue, Williams behaved admirably. He had been taught by his parents to be "a stickler for his principles"; "I had no choice in the matter," he recalled modestly.

Discovering that the chairman of the board of trustees had been conducting a furtive affair with the hospital administrator, Miss Malzacher, and that the tainted money had gone to her, did not sway Williams's decision. When none of the senior doctors backed him up, he returned to his parents' home in Rutherford to salve his wounded pride, to sort out the meaning of a corrupt link between sex and ethics, and to mull over his future in medicine.

Bad luck dogged him, however, for he was unsuccessful in his courtship of Rutherford's most eligible beauty, Charlotte Herman. A cultivated pianist who had studied at the Leipzig Conservatory, this bewitching woman turned heads; suitors thronged her doorstep. In a photograph taken around 1908, when the Williams brothers were wooing her, Charlotte poses like a statuesque lady in a George Romney painting, conscious of her beauty and the elegance of her fashionable dress; a flowered hat shades her brow and leaves her slightly abstracted eyes staring confidently and a touch disdainfully from underneath its penumbra; she looks ready to stroll the pathways of Rotten Row in Hyde Park, to conquer the demi-monde and enjoy the spectacle of rich aristocratic beaux throwing themselves at her feet.

Rutherford offered her no such social and marital opportunities, but Charlotte inhabited a more refined realm than the nurses Williams had chummed with; her artistic temperament intrigued him, perhaps reminding him of his mother's. Nor was he frightened off by the awkward fact that his chief rival was his own brother. Smitten, he read his poems to Charlotte, played piano duets with her in *soirées musicales*, escorted her to concerts, and gave her a tour of the hospital, as if auditioning his artistic and practical sides. The courtship could have been lifted from Orson Welles's film *The Magnificent Ambersons*: the young couple sitting on a porch swing on a humid summer night sipping lemonade and chatting idly. Unfortunately for Bill, Charlotte's mother frowned on the match, apparently viewing him as a dreamer whose prospects for supporting a wife in the affluent style to which she was accustomed were slim; his diffidence might also have raised doubts in Charlotte's mind.

Whatever the cause, Williams lost the role of husband in this drama: she spurned his proposal of marriage and, to make matters worse, accepted Ed's. We have little trustworthy information about this pivotal moment in Williams's life: scrappy inferences from letters, clues in *The Build-up*, the third novel of his Stecher trilogy, but no poem in which he laid bare and analyzed his distress at being rejected by Charlotte. (He lacked the requisite technique and detachment at the time to manage that heroic labor anyway.) At age ninety-one, when Paul Mariani interviewed her and asked whether she had ever loved Bill, Charlotte replied, coyly, "Perhaps." What she chose to remember was a "self-absorbed" young man with a "very big ego." This judgment doesn't square with Bill's unformed character and insecurities: a young man of twenty-five who could not ask the lady directly which brother she preferred suffered, at least in matters of love, from a low opinion of himself or crippling shyness. Thirty-five years later in *The Build-up*, Williams calmly gazed at "the sweep of his emotional reaction and the wreckage it would cause." When Ed broke the bad news to his brother, Bill, dreading and foreseeing the handwriting on the wall, "flung his arms about his brother's neck and went mad," "sobbed and sobbed, uncontrollably. He ground his teeth, he fought back his unreasoning tears," then retreated to his room, as to a monastic cell, for three days of fasting, self-flagellation, and brooding. "I myself am hell," he might have said. The novelist, who cannot fault his brother's behavior, adopts a tone verging on portentous self-pity: "And yet something had come to an end. It was a deeper wound than he should thereafter in his life be able to sound. It was bottomless."

In these circumstances, some cooling was inevitable, and indeed a subtle decline in his closeness with Edgar took place, though not a rift. As boys only one year apart in age, the brothers had been inseparable partners in everything. Starting with adolescence, Ed outstripped Bill in size, grades, sports, and success with girls. Women found him manly and self-assured, and his professors at Boston Tech (MIT) were impressed by his intellectual acuity. It was no surprise to anybody in the Williams family that after graduation Edgar won the coveted and highly competitive Prix de Rome in architecture. (He later designed the Donnell Library across the street from the Museum of Modern Art.) Defeat was galling for Bill, but it roused his determination not to resign himself to being second best.

FIVE

Many Loves

I. An Embattled Courtship

Charlotte's rebuff precipitated a far-reaching decision: to propose marriage to her sister Florence, whom he scarcely knew or had even much noticed. It was in keeping with Williams's needy character that, despite his vows of self-control, he engineered an emergence from his misery with a heedless surprise twist: to woo Floss as a substitute wife (no Shakespearean bed trick here). This abrupt idea, bordering on the bizarre, was a blatant example of "marrying on the rebound." It indicates how desperate Williams was. In the flurry of actions that followed, an almost unhinged resolve, "the stuff of blind / emotions," possessed him. Cornering the "kid" Floss, he made it clear that though he wanted her as his wife, he did not love her. Love would come, if at all, after they lived together. The absence of any romantic fervor or idealization is striking—Flossie is no Fanny Brawne; the poet's will silences any misgivings his imagination might have raised. Indeed, it is hard to conceive of a more inauspicious beginning to a relationship. His amour propre wounded, Williams had first to confront and overcome his defeat at the hands of Charlotte and Ed. (The word "defeat" always carries a special resonance for Williams and prompts a quest for compensatory action.) Any rope that might pull him out of the trough of his misery was worth trying: hence the proposal to Floss.

The gamble in choosing her for his wife faced long odds. Like Hawthorne, Williams preferred the voluptuous Zenobias with begonias in their hair to the prim Priscillas and Phoebes. But in the company of confidently sexual women, he often felt maladroit, not suave. In 1958 he recalled his youthful self as a sexual simpleton: "The real thing is I didn't know anything about life. I was completely ignorant." This is not glib self-abasement or hyperbole. In relations with women, as in his poetic fumblings, he started behind others and had to play catch-up. Charlotte's rejection could only confirm any anxieties he harbored about being an attractive male.* By choosing as his wife the inexperienced Floss, who presumably would not make scary demands on his masculinity, Williams could protect himself, for stretches, from his erotic demons.

Can we plumb Floss's motives in conditionally accepting his proposal? For the gawky eighteen-year-old girl, Bill's attention was both flattering and confusing. She could not compete with her sister in artistic flair or beauty. In a family photograph taken in 1907, Floss smiles shyly at the camera, looking like the studious, dependable Beth in *Little Women*—not pretty or sexy, but with a pleasant plain face. Unlike her sophisticated sister, Floss had led a fairly sheltered life. Did she feel sheepish gleaning her sister's discarded harvest? Did being Williams's second choice rankle? It's hard to believe that that cold fact wouldn't have troubled her as she made up her mind whether to accept his proposal. Did she have a secret crush on her sister's suitor, a feeling common in teenagers, and therefore take pride in having snared a fine prize: a handsome doctor who was, besides, that exotic beast, a poet? Did she calculate that this marriage offered her her best chance to venture out of the family cocoon? Because Floss did not record her struggles in a diary or to a friend in letters, we can only speculate as to what made her accept Williams's suit. Flustered by the swift march of events, perhaps feeling somewhat browbeaten, she was relieved when he left for a working holiday in Europe in July 1909. Pop's gift to Bill for his ethical conduct during the brouhaha at the Nursery and Child's Hospital allowed Floss time to sort out the tangled skeins of what promised to be a complicated relationship. Not having to see Bill every day for a while was a reprieve; she could defer a final decision about marrying him.

Floss's tentative acceptance in his pocket—their engagement was kept secret so as not to arouse Mrs. Herman's suspicion and opposition, though she soon ferreted it out—Williams also welcomed the separation.

---

*After their friendship faded and their literary partnership terminated, the poet and novelist Robert McAlmon, sounding like a macho Hemingway character, cast baseless aspersions on Williams's virility.

He was no Achilles prepared to sulk in his tent for a prolonged period. Having taken the plunge somewhat eased his mind of despair about Charlotte, but his letters to Floss and his behavior prior to sailing to Antwerp were so brusque and careless that they sound like a lover regretting his commitment and looking for pretexts to jilt the young lady. At twenty-six, not particularly mature or introspective, Williams by his own admission needed space to examine his offer of marriage and the messy emotions that surfaced in its wake. His barely repressed disquiet returned with a vengeance. His letters to Floss were filled with cutting and reproachful words. Since he was primarily concerned with his own feelings, he pulled out the knife only when the wounded Floss cried out in pain and threatened to break their betrothal.

Williams's first letter to her informed her that, under the influence of a fickle summer moon, he had necked with a girl named Kate, for which he begged Floss's forgiveness. What explains so blatant a bolting the moment he was out of Floss's sight? In part, a desire to test and prove how sexually irresistible he was to other women; in part, a worry that he had chosen unwisely and an ensuing panic that he would be trapped in a loveless marriage. This early, he established a pattern alternating malice and (tactical) contrition, one that endured, on and off, throughout their married life: in the guise of truth telling, he would confess an unfaithful act and wait patiently for Floss's response, almost certain that, though bitter at being humiliated, she would forgive him.

If Williams had transcribed all his remarks about Floss, both calculated and impromptu, from his letters, poems, plays, and fiction into a diary, he would have required an oversize folio to hold them. The majority consisted of bellicose, patronizing insults. Floss often recoiled in horror and dismay reading them, as Williams himself noted, so that she could hardly avoid wondering what kind of man she had pledged herself to. Even forty years after their marriage, Williams's caustic tone when speaking of her slips by his lax censor, as in the following passage from the *Autobiography*: "My mind was always rebellious and uneasy. This was my wife-to-be, excluding all the rest. How could one stand or understand it? And yet, there was Flossie, no Venus de Milo, surely—Flossie, in some ways hard as nails, thank heaven. She had to be." How did he quell a mind in rebellion? One way was leaving the exit doors wide open. Another was becoming adept at vacillation, passing a compliment with one hand and yanking it back with the other, or, in what became second nature to him, indulging in tortuous rationalizations and amorous subterfuges during which he hoped to improvise a strategy that would leave him free to philander yet remain tied to Floss.

Following his upsetting initial confession of knight-errantry, Williams sketched his speckled character in detail for his fiancée, warning her that he would be an unreliable, emotionally destitute husband: "Sometimes I will appear childish, sometimes weak and impotent, often I will come to you for sympathy when I am hurt with what you believe is a foolish thing. I will put all faith in you. Sometimes I will rave you may think and go off in vain dreams." He subsequently tenders her an offer to bow out of the relationship if she meets a more desirable young man at the seashore, where the Hermans were summering. (This would have allowed him to bail out, too.) Yet when she mentions that several young men were pursuing her, Williams grows jealous and miserable; he is in no mood for a rejection by another Herman sister. Yet for all his highfalutin talk of faith and truth, he would not bind himself to any strict monogamous code. His warning to Floss exposes a streak of sly weakness in his character. Even for a neophyte lover, his cavalier, even harsh style of wooing reflects egotism coexisting with self-doubt.

Williams hoped that Leipzig, his destination, would distract him from the conflicts his engagement had set in motion; the Judgment Day when Mendelssohn's wedding march would sound in his ears lay in the future; much could happen to change his fate. Europe's complex glamour beckoned as a potential idyll of romance, though not as a place for advancing his literary career. Williams's choice of Leipzig for home base irked Pound, who sneered at it as a cultural backwater. Why not set up shop in London, the center of ferment in the English-speaking poetry world? Pound protested. But the truth was that, still mostly clueless about the direction his poetry should take, Williams shrank from the prospect of tagging along as a minor equerry in King Ezra's court. His entire life, Williams looked askance at and harshly condemned literary expatriates; he was bent on rooting his poems in American ground.

Leipzig was provincial. In August 1909, soon after his arrival, Williams sent Ed a letter detailing his impressions of the city. "The whole life here is a picture of economy, specialization, long, hard systematized work and a quiet perseverance . . . The people are plodders and house lovers and beer lovers . . . [T]hey lack spontaneity or something akin to innocence and joyousness." He shrewdly detected "how identical is the East Rutherford spirit with the sub-middle-class German spirit." The women were broad in the beam and plodding, while the burghers were prosaic and unattractive, targets for the kind of barbed poetic sermons he could not resist delivering to his townspeople in New Jersey. Still, ending up in a larger version of Rutherford did not faze him. He knew he was not ready to test himself in a metropolitan center.

Despite acute loneliness—he knew virtually nobody—bouts of homesickness, and his stammering German, Williams did not feel Leipzig was a grim prison. By temperament reserved with strangers, he did not rush to join the students banging their tankards on the tables of a beer garden and singing loud, maudlin ditties about *Blutbruderschaft.* Germany had the reputation of being a major center in pediatric research, so it made sense to enroll in science courses at Leipzig University. But like the young Henry Adams before him, Williams found German society airless and its pedagogy, dependent on rote learning, monotonous: though he dutifully attended classes, the science curriculum could not inspire the dreamy poet, newly engaged and erotically adrift. Nobody, including Bill himself, would think of him as a restless Faust haunting the taverns and ready to accept Mephistopheles's offer of unrivaled knowledge of nature and metaphysics in exchange for the proud intellectual's soul—at most, he might have been fleetingly tempted by a fling with Margarethe. His own sparse sexual adventures in Leipzig could have been lifted out of an opera buffa: he once tried to pick up a prostitute, who soon deserted him for a table of wealthy South American businessmen, thus preserving this American Candide's virtue. (He had a knack for bumbling into such situations and being rescued by the angel whose task was to protect naifs.)

In matters of culture, conservative Leipzig was not parochial. During his months in the city, he attended productions of Ibsen's *A Doll's House* and *The Wild Duck*, and heard Wagner's *Götterdämmerung* and Richard Strauss's opera *Elektra*, which must have sounded daringly modern to a budding poet still intoxicated by the fragrances in romantic poems. And there were sentimental reasons for sojourning in the city of Bach. Because Charlotte had studied there, he was like a pilgrim eager to lay a bouquet at the shrine of his lost love. Germany was also a prudent choice, since his residence there would likely endear him to his future father-in-law, who was a staunch partisan of his old homeland.

However tedious his studies, Williams eventually adjusted to Leipzig's drabness—he was ambitious to succeed and had been raised not to squander any favorable chance of getting ahead in the world—made a few friends, and even relaxed enough to sample the city's night life. But when March rolled around, he was glad to escape to more dynamic urban centers. Crossing the English Channel, he arrived in London to spend a week with Pound (he stayed at Pound's cramped lodgings in Church Walk, Kensington). Ezra shepherded his friend to readings, lectures, and galleries, introducing him to his intimates Olivia Shakespeare and her daughter, Dorothy, Pound's future wife, and his prize trophy, William Butler Yeats. Williams heard the Irish poet read before a tiny circle of aesthetes and lecture on the Celtic Twilight at the Adelphi Club. In his *Autobiography*, Williams draws a wonderful Daumier-like picture of the scene: the conservative Edmund Gosse, chairing the evening, rudely interrupted Yeats as he was explaining why the neglected 1890s poets—Dowson, Wilde, Lionel Johnson, whom Pound was to elegize in "Hugh Selwyn Mauberley"—turned to "drunkenness, lechery or immorality":

> He got no further, for Sir Edmund, to everyone's consternation, at that point banged the palm of his right hand on the table beside him. Yeats was taken aback, but after a moment's hesitation went on or tried to go on with what he was saying. Again Sir Edmund rudely whammed his bell—and again Yeats tried to continue. But when it happened the third time, Gosse, red in the face and Yeats equally so, the poet was forced to sit down and the lecture came to an end. My own face was crimson and my temples near to bursting but I had not been able to get to my feet and protest.

Williams wanted to leap to Yeats's defense against the slate-thumping of this benighted Beckmesser—Pound, who loved mixing it up, remained uncharacteristically silent, to the dismay of some lady friends in the audience—not because he particularly admired the British "decadents" but because Gosse's crude philistinism resembled the artistic prudery in America. Lacking confidence, he stifled his impulse to speak out and "sank back once more into anonymity." However intense and thrilling the literary gladiatorial combats were in London, they disturbed Williams; he didn't want to be eaten by the lions. He realized how far from a bona fide cosmopolite he was; he could not begin to compete with Pound's erudition and snappy pronouncements. Williams felt like an unbeliever in the Temple of Art, the panoply of high priests, acolytes, blazing candles, incense, and chanting "completely foreign to anything I desired." He "was glad to get away."

After a brief stop in Paris, Williams traveled to Milan, where he met Ed to begin a seven-week tour of Italy's museums and antiquities, first Venice and Florence, then an exhilarating week in Rome, and finally south to Paestum, Pompeii, and Naples. With his training in art and architecture, Ed made an ideal cicerone; he had adapted easily to European cultural life, as Pound had—Ed's manners were more polished than the strutting Pound's or the bumptious Bill's—and could hold forth authoritatively about Brunelleschi's Duomo, Michelangelo's design for the Laurentian Library, or the history of the Roman catacombs. In Ed's presence, Bill again felt like an apprentice. The tension between the brothers had subsided but not evaporated. That Ed fully expected to return to Rutherford at the end of his fellowship and marry Charlotte, whereas Bill faced a problematic marriage to Floss, his second choice, galled Williams. He would be sailing back to uncertainty. And so it transpired.

Landing in Hoboken on June 4, 1910, the Wanderer was miffed that Floss had not come to the pier to greet him. Distance had lent their relationship not even a patina of enchantment. Since they were virtual strangers, they had little material out of which to spin affecting fantasies; they were not deliriously in love. Quite the contrary. They had exchanged acrimonious letters. Bill was extremely critical of what Floss wrote; what epistolary marvels he expected from a timid ingénue is unclear. When her letters were slow reaching him, he scolded her for the lapse. And when she tried to satisfy his request for a photograph of her he could place on his dresser, he peevishly criticized her pose, accusing her of impersonating a fashionable belle like Charlotte instead of presenting the spindly gamin she was. Resenting her wish to appear winsome and sophisticated, he even went so far as to scrape off the photo's offending artificial look. Floss, bitterly nonplussed by his barrage of rebukes, was again prepared to break off their engagement.

Soon after his sabbatical in Europe, Williams hung out a shingle advertising his medical practice; business was slow despite his being a local son, because the townspeople viewed him as a young unknown, therefore a perhaps untrustworthy doctor, because his office was not in a fashionable part of town and, most of all, because he lacked confidence in himself "and my mind was wild—as anyone, I thought, must have seen." He was patient about building up trust in his competence. (To make ends meet, he accepted a part-time job as school physician, looking into children's mouths for cavities or signs of tonsillitis.) It would have been folly to put off his reunion with Floss. He hastened to win himself back in her good graces, which after a renewed courtship he managed to accomplish. Two and a half years were to elapse before he and Floss married (on 12/12/12, he noted bemusedly). Although the couple's long engagement, not unusual for the period, was an ordeal for Williams because it deferred sexual gratification, it allowed him to spend ample time with Floss so that they would not sleep in the nuptial bed as complete strangers. In his *Autobiography*, he confesses, "I had to do a lot to come out softened down for marriage. Floss and I wandered about fumbling with our emotions. I think that long period of breaking in was all that made our later marriage bearable."

2. The Good Grey Wife

Williams's poems furnish abundant evidence of his wavering emotions toward Floss. Sporadically, he conjures charming moments in a contented marriage. In "Idyl," it's the joy of parenthood—William Eric was born on January 7, 1914, and Paul Herman on September 13, 1916—not avid passion, that brings the couple together. Only in "A Coronal" does Williams sing out like an adoring lover: "Anemones sprang where she pressed / and cresses / stood green in the slender source—." In the three "Love Song" poems, he invites Floss to savor a delicious spring day and his expansive mood:

> Sweep the house clean,
> hang fresh curtains
> in the windows
> put on a new dress
> and come with me!
> The elm is scattering
> its little loaves
> of sweet smells
> from a white sky!

Who shall hear of us
in the time to come?
Let him say there was
a burst of fragrance
from black branches.

Floss is personified as a cheerful spirit of bustling domesticity; invited
outside, she shares a moment of rare communion with him. ("Loaves"
looks like an intentional misspelling of "leaves" and a shy nod toward
"loves.") Williams avoids the grand rhetorical gesture of Marlowe's "Come
live with me, and be my Love; / And we will all the pleasures prove."
Such an unabashed declaration would have made him nervous, endanger-
ing a relationship that was not firmly fixed in either love or habit. Besides,
Williams was hardly the Passionate Shepherd wooing his love. The "burst
of fragrance / from black branches" is a modest remembrance. Williams
dryly annotated this poem years later, saying only that he was "conscious
of Floss, my girl."

The first "Love Song" in the collection is more ambiguous:

Daisies are broken
petals are news of the day
stems lift to the grass tops
they catch on shoes
part in the middle
leave roots and leaves secure.

Black branches
carry square leaves
to the wood's top.
they hold firm
break with a roar
show the white!

Your moods are slow
the shedding of leaves
and sure
the return in May!

We walked
in your father's grove
and saw the great oaks
lying with roots
ripped from the ground.

Williams does not mention love, except in the title. Walking in a grove
after a storm, the young couple inspect the damage that high winds have
inflicted: when the daisies break, they leave the roots and leaves secure;
when the black branches break, it is the culmination of a wonderful
upward thrust, like a sexual push, that carries the leaves "to the wood's
top," where "they hold firm" for part of the season, then break dramatically with a "roar" (a startling orgasmic noise in an otherwise quiet poem),
exfoliating white blossoms. The burgeoning life force just shown is only a
part of nature; the roots of majestic great oaks ripped out by a destructive
gale expose its dark underside. The one stanza directly about Floss calls
attention to the slowness of her moods (this appears to be a neutral comment), but the shedding of leaves in autumn is not final, since they will
return in spring. Five years married, Williams muses in this "Love Song"
on the feelings of security and breakage that contend within him.

As early as 1917, however, Williams colored Floss in shades of "grey
over and over." The most striking is "A Portrait in Greys":

Will it never be possible
to separate you from your greyness?
Must you be always sinking backward
into your grey-brown landscapes—and trees
always in the distance, always against
a grey sky?

   Must I be always
moving counter to you? Is there no place
where we can be at peace together
and the motion of our drawing apart
be altogether taken up?

I see myself
standing upon your shoulders touching

a grey, broken sky—
but you, weighted down with me,
yet gripping my ankles,—move
    laboriously on,
where it is level and undisturbed by colors.

With its four testy questions—angry reprimands, really—and its abso-
lutes ("never," "always" repeated four times, "altogether") this glum poem
gives off a rancid smell of marital misery. Williams's palette for Floss is
uniformly dreary; the landscape and the sky, oppressively grey, aptly depict the atmosphere of a couple "drawing apart." Williams gives no direct
answers to his own questions. Instead, in seemingly the only form of contact with her, he mounts Floss like a rider on a beast of burden, or a master
on his servant (there is nothing sexual about the position); on her shoulders
he reaches for transcendence, but all he can touch is the "grey, broken
sky." Earthbound, she, by contrast, grips his ankles so as to anchor him to
her and prevent him from straying, then plods on, the word "laboriously"
imitating her slow pace: their relationship is a grim burlesque of marital
joy or sexual fulfillment. "Bed's at fault," Williams grumbles in *Kora in
Hell*, hinting broadly that it's unlikely Dr. Orpheus, a bored husband dol-
ing out caresses, would descend to hell to fetch his Eurydice, yet he remains attached to, and dependent on, Floss, as he would through fifty-one
years of marriage. Williams's sketches of his feelings are often unreliable,
yet one grows accustomed to the skittish pulse of his desires and his fear
of withering without ever achieving full enjoyment. In *Kora*, he invites
the reader to follow along as the satyr "goes in pursuit of a white-skinned
dryad" in the underbrush, or to watch as "the gaiety of his mood full of
lustihood, even so, turns black with a mocking jibe," or to commiserate
as, stung by remorse, he retreats to his burrow, excuses himself or apolo-
gizes for his conduct, and ponders his next moves. In his unsettled emotional life, "violence has begotten peace, peace has fluttered away in
agitation."

3. "Caviar of Caviar": Viola Baxter Jordan

There were early premonitory signs of this pattern in Williams's relations
with H.D. and Viola Baxter Jordan, both friends of Ezra Pound, but he

was not equipped to decode them. When his enthusiasm for poetic ideas
and experiments waned, Pound would sometimes palm them off on Williams. Awed by Pound's cocksureness, Williams took most of his friend's
obiter dicta (and largesse) seriously and examined them methodically, but
until the mid-1930s he always lagged two or three steps behind his pal
and rival. Bill stuck with Imagism long after Ezra had converted to Vorti-
cism. In truth, he also envied the swashbuckling Pound, who boasted a
lot about his attractiveness to women, though neither qualified as a libertine in training. At the University of Pennsylvania, Pound was H.D.'s
beau, squiring her to theatrical performances and passing on his poetic
theories to her as to a disciple. In 1903, Pound introduced her to Bill, who
found her recherché looks and verbal sallies intriguing; he had never met
a young woman like her. In his walks with her into the countryside around
Upper Darby, he listened to her slightly dotty ideas and measured her as
a potential girlfriend should Pound drop her. Tall and with an androgynous face that was neither beautiful nor ordinary, she was a headstrong,
sometimes affected young woman often swept away by aesthetic ardors
and ecstasies. At a beach party at Point Pleasant, New Jersey, she rushed
into the choppy surf like a Nereid and would have drowned had not
her host, Bob Lamberton, pulled her out of the surf unconscious. Such
erratic behavior disturbed Williams; it could only have reminded him of
his mother's. H.D. might be piquant, but her ethereal nature and her
poetic predilections—she was a nascent aesthete—he came to see were
unsuited for him. In any case, if Williams cherished any notion of courting H.D., Pound quickly scotched that idea. He didn't quite accuse Bill of
trying to steal his girl, but he was tetchy and territorial. Pound got engaged
to H.D. for a time, but a marriage between the pair would have been as
much of a fiasco as one between her and Williams. Bill backed off, and
over the years his friendship with her soured into a strong mutual antipathy.

He felt no such negative feelings about Viola Baxter, a nineteen-year-
old friend of Pound's from his Hamilton College days who was living in
New York. In 1907, playing matchmaker, Pound pressed Bill to call on her,
assuring him that she was beautiful, spirited, and artistic; at the least, her
company would divert him from his exhausting hospital rounds. A year
before his first meeting with Viola, in a November 12, 1906, letter to Ed
from French Hospital, Williams analyzed his dangerous susceptibility to

passion—dangerous because it could interfere with his goal of "daring to follow his dreams," accomplish great things, and "satisfy my own self."

Solemnly, Williams confesses his fear that his sex drive could destroy his ambitious plans. On the great stage where he will compete for success with others, he is confident he won't be a "whimpering weakling who is frightened away by obstacles," but about sex he sounds like a Puritan minister warning his congregants that if they cannot restrain their desires, their sins will damn them to eternal hellfire. Yet Williams's admonishment holds a clue to his image of himself: because sexual urges can rob him of self-control, the beast must be tamed. Best to proceed cautiously.

Which is what he did with Viola Baxter. His failed first meeting with her is vintage Williams. Nervous and curious, he took the El to her East Side address. Let in by the German landlady and signaled up the stairs to the third-floor front apartment, he knocked timorously. The door was flung open, he reported to Ed in a letter, by a "big woman [who] started talking to me very familiarly while behind her back I saw a beautiful maiden in decided negligée on a sofa." This tantalizing glimpse of a Keatsian houri vanished as the chaperone slammed the door in Williams's face. Embarrassed, he retraced his steps and, back in his room at the hospital, sent a note apologizing for his gaucherie in arriving at an inappropriate hour; he invited Viola to the Penn-Columbia basketball game the next night (a safe, neutral venue), where he began a long, vacillating courtship punctuated by periods of silence. Williams could never decide whether he wanted an intimacy with Viola; for years he would draw close, then back off and straddle the fence.

The poems and letters he addressed to Viola range from awkward confessions of psychic impasse—"It is the impossibility of being what I must be which is so trying"—to such chivalric bagatelles as "For Viola: De Gustibus":

Beloved you are
Caviar of Caviar
Of all I love you best
O my Japanese bird nest

No herring from Norway
Can touch you for flavor. Nay

Pimento itself
Is flat as an empty shelf
When compared to your piquancy
O quince of my dependency.

Williams never strikes this jocular tone and breezy rhyming with Floss, never calls her *"Geliebste* Hedda" in mock horror at her haughty, elusive ways. Viola, with "the most delightful touch of the devil," inspires him to put together a savory menu-poem of exotic dishes. From Leipzig he mused, "There is something magical about you and yet not entirely fairy-like. It riles me and, frankly, makes me think more of imps than angels, but even here you have no counterpart."

On the verge of marrying Floss, Williams cannot drive the imp out of his mind. He pines for Viola "with ever increasing tenderness and appreciation"; she is a "most delightful woman." Yet any exile from her favors has all along been self-imposed, not due to an unattainable queen's curt dismissal. Nine months before his wedding, Williams had similarly engaged in romantic badinage with Viola about the pleasure-pain she'd feel if they "spoused." He talks as if she were desperately in love with him, apostrophizes her as "a charming creature of transparent contradictions" ("Let us fly away and be united in impossibilities"), and confides that his father, "being asked directly whether or not in his estimation I was a simple jassack [*sic*]," replied drily "that I am tardy in development." Williams seems to have agreed with his father's judgment, but he shows no interest in examining what caused that "tardy development." In "a merry mood," he encloses a piece of awful doggerel about her brushing her teeth and, playing the clown, a mock-Shakespearean song about the "charming spring." Williams presents himself to Viola as a man trapped in suburbia with "the intellectually unborn" for company from sunup to sunset, his hot passions allowed no outlet. Floss is merely a supernumerary.

Less than two months after his marriage, he gingerly stokes the embers of their romance: "Not to be a liar here, to be near you; to be true here yet to be comforted by you—*lâche!*" This wish goes beyond flirtation. Williams knows these equations cannot work, as his use of the French word "*lâche*" (base) shows. Viola immediately rebuked him for his mental infidelity. Her letter contains several deletions, as if she had had a hard time finding the right words, but Williams got the message. Three days later he humbly begs her pardon for his louche insinuations. She and his "saving conscience" extricate him from a potential moral smashup.

But Williams's apology did not quite appease his ache. When he made his debut in the June 1913 issue of *Poetry* with four Imagist poems— "Peace on Earth," "Sicilian Emigrant's Song," "Postlude," which had appeared in Pound's *Des Imagistes* anthology, and "Proof of Immortality"—he wanted to share this breakthrough with Viola, so he sent her a copy, dated June 12, 1913. The inscription running on a diagonal, like a step-down tercet, reads, "Viola from Billie." In the upper right-hand corner of the page, Williams drew a picture of himself as an angel, naked, haloed, bald, with wings that look more batlike than cherubic, and a left foot that reminds one of a centaur's hoof. His hands clasped as if in prayer, he beseeches heaven to grant his wish or forgive his trespass. On the lower left-hand side of the page, he sketched Viola as a distraught and grimly unhappy woman—she is wearing a dress that falls to her shins—her halo consisting of arrows, her head tilted, her eyes dark with fear, her jaw obdurately set, her mouth a slash of disapproval. In her left hand, she clutches a flower. The figure is not in repose. Her left foot is fully extended, while her right foot, tucked behind her, catapults her forward, as if she is fleeing from an assailant. Neither figure looks at the other, which suggests that Williams viewed them as profoundly incompatible.

Williams soon learns that Viola is to marry Virgil Jordan, a businessman, in the spring of 1914, thus dashing any lingering fantasies of an affair with her. In a letter dated "March the Snows!" Williams tries to strike a note of levity, quoting Jean-Jacques Trousseau and ruing that she will no longer be free to adore him, but when he admits he's jealous of her soon-to-be husband—he can't bear to mention his rival's name—his syntax crumbles, and a slip of the tongue measures his dismay: "It is plain that he is—this, that and the other—nonsense. He speaks with distinction—I almost said extinction, but if I thought that I was thinking of his virtues only. He evidently knows how to posess [sic] Do you know how? It is to kill—you then have the thing, the idea, the joke—all to yourself." That Virgil "knows how to possess" is a bitter potion for Bill to swallow, and he even feels a murderous impulse toward Viola's beau. Williams rallies from his disappointment, coining the arresting image of love as "a net of filmy wires" made of "spun steel" from which "nothing escapes." Love is a trap, he concludes. His inchoate feelings, he vows yet again, will be mastered in the poems of his next volume.

On June 7, 1914, Williams wrote a long, thoughtful letter to Viola, attempting to answer frankly and finally, as at a psychological inquest, why he could neither marry her nor stay away from her. Although he takes a roundabout path to this topic, because circumstances had changed their relationship—he was no longer a petitioner for her favors—he feels less defensive and judged. Williams dispenses homespun advice like a concerned country doctor to a shy patient. He compares Viola to a butterfly emerged from a chrysalis, but fearful of unfurling her wings and flying. "Trust your wings," he assures her. (His struggles to grow and fly were far from over.)

The letter shifts gears, with Williams impersonating an aesthetic sage correcting the tyro's mistakes. Viola rather priggishly had been shocked by the "filthiness" of *The Egoist*, a British literary magazine founded by Dora Marsden, an iconoclastic feminist, and later edited by Richard Aldington and H.D. Williams published poems in the magazine, but more important, he responded like a psychiatrist to her prim aversion to ribald writing. First he gently chides her:

> You are wrong to overlook the worth of the "Egoist" in a fit of temper against the filthiness you may find there. You might as well detest your own hands because your nails do on occasion get muck under them. I know of no one who has yet advocated pulling out the nails to prevent this annoying accident. Hands are to use (So is the Egoist. [sic]) for free carrying out of the will (So is the Egoist.) Use them and learn to keep clean—this is the moral O Vanessa J Album (a rare butterfly).

Then he teaches her an elementary lesson: be wary of art that's finicky and sterile. Frankly conceding that he has "no satisfactory definition of beauty" to offer, he ventures three tentative images: "a kind of defiance to passion—the tea-pot in which passion is the tempest—the sky that feels the pin prick of lightening [sic] and laughs back—the real that defies sex (that damnable sex, there it is again)." It's amusing to remark Williams genteelly rebutting her "lie" that sex is all-important and prevents men and women from "seeing the same thing in the same way."

An old obsession, the struggle between dirt and cleanliness for control of his will, informs this letter. He professes to "love pleasure," which means sometimes wallowing in filth or succumbing with abandon to sex and drunkenness. It's clear to him that he must do so if he is to become "a person who owns himself to bestow himself perfectly." Despite his brave words and the adverb "perfectly," between desire and act falls a shadowy restraint. Yet Williams challenges Viola, "how can you say you own yourself if you are not free to be touched filthily (slapped on the one cheek [?]) . . . Simply because you soil your skirt edge on the street is no reason for keeping always to the house—though it is one excellent reason for going naked."

His folksy advice is sound, but Williams can't act as his reason dictates. He forces himself to admire cleanliness because he thinks he should. His wily superego promises him that a Platonic friendship will keep him from being constantly plagued by sexual desire; a sort of expedient cowardice will, at least temporarily, push his conflict out of sight. To save face, he puts a positive spin on this retreat: "Any woman who can look me in the eye—I mean not glance but look—and still leave me, clean, free and happy, yes happy, to her I have applied myself for love . . . Thus much for my Frenchiness." (With heavy whimsy he calls this his "stomachic test.") But he cannot patrol the vast domain of his unconscious and keep out all erotic thoughts. Unbidden, they break into his sober analysis: "I dreamt of a beautiful young high school graduate last night— she leaned on the door of my Ford car—silently and surrepticiously [sic] stroking my hand—and her soul came up out of her eyes. I awoke exquisitely unhappy." Although Williams changed "happy" to "unhappy," the dream depicts a state of bliss that is the fulfillment of a long-delayed if standard male fantasy: a nubile young woman leans on the car door and strokes his hand; he thrills at the female's absolute receptivity to him: "her soul came up out of her eyes." Sex and soul merge. This is as close as Williams gets to mystic rapture. Is this high school graduate a screen for Viola or another out-of-reach, unsuitable Venus? I suppose a little of both. Williams's euphoria peters out and he once more diagnoses, in a clinical tone, his on-again, off-again relations with Viola: "We are alike—and tortured. Far enough apart from each other we are companionship and peace but if we should strike against each other in our contortions we would hate and claw without end." For them, therefore, he concludes, it was best that they remained cordial friends, meeting for dinner with their spouses—Floss and Viola got on well. In the 1920s and '30s, Viola became the unofficial New York bureau chief for Pound, H.D., and the poet and novelist Bryher, sending them news and gossip of the American gang's doings in boudoir and gallery; in turn, she listened to H.D. revile Williams's character and verse, but she neither remonstrated with her nor disloyally nettled Bill by divulging H.D.'s hostility.

In memory, Williams associated Viola with his seven crucial years of erratic growth between 1907 and 1914. She loomed as an important figure in his pursuit of a "complete self." He would tear down and remake that self, and his poems, many times, but he kept an affectionate place for her in his heart as a sometime muse and the wife who got away. They remained friends for the rest of their lives.

In *Kora in Hell*, Williams experimented with Dadaism in diary entries that weaned his poetry from moldy romantic habits and searched for substitute styles in "the dark void coaxing him whither he has no knowledge." He also appraised his conjugal disappointments in glancing or cryptic ways—as a dance in which the partners are rhythmically out of sync with each other, and "boredom takes a hand." With such discord he can only withdraw into an erotic dream of deliverance from "misery and brokenness": dancing a "tarantelle that wears flesh from bones."

Kora took three years to germinate. Williams could not rush it. He was enormously busy: a new practice to tend, a growing family to provide for, America on the brink of war, deaths in his and Floss's families, an influenza epidemic that left him alternately exhausted and furious at having to fight death without any remotely effective weapons. No wonder he shrugged his shoulders and declared that "it's hard to tell loss from gain anyway." Yet, amazingly, while disease and war decimated populations indiscriminately, Williams thrived, found a Sea of Tranquility near the dark side of the moon. He carved out time to play with his children; he looked after his ailing father, kept regular office hours, drove from house call to hospital; he even managed to snatch a few hours of leisure to scan the avant-garde magazines and browse the art galleries. Routine was a saving grace, a palisade of sanity. Above all, after a debilitating night of ministering to the sick and the dying, he returned to his attic and typed out poem after poem. He was inconsolable at the losses that piled up—the influenza epidemic took a huge physical and mental toll, rampaging death viciously parodying his creative surge, but like Dr. Rieux in Camus's novel *The Plague*, he acted with clearheaded sympathy and waited for the slaughter of innocents to ebb.

The poems of *Al Que Quiere!* surpassed the verse of *The Tempers* in originality, even if they didn't match the capering wit of *Kora*'s improvisations. They reflected, as he confided to Edith Heal in 1958, "things around me. I was finding out about life. Rather late, I imagine. This was a quiet period, a pre-sex period, although I was married." In this chrysalis stage, he slips into a kind of autoerotic solitude or into fantasies about other women. Take "Danse Russe," a likable piece of make-believe in which he stars as the Nijinsky of Rutherford:

> If I when my wife is sleeping
> and the baby and Kathleen
>   are sleeping
> and the sun is a flame-white disc
>   in silken mists
> above shining trees,—
> if I in my north room
>   dance naked, grotesquely
> before my mirror—
> waving my shirt round my head
> and singing softly to myself
> "I am lonely, lonely,
> I am best so!"
> If I admire my arms, my face,
> my shoulders, flanks, buttocks
>   against the yellow drawn shades,—
>
> Who shall say I am not
> the happy genius of my household?

The audience of potential carpers slumbering, Williams contemplates dancing his own hymn to the uninhibited human body, like a Russian pagan in *Sacre du printemps*. Although the stage is his own bedroom at dawn, he supplies the romantic magic in the minimalist scrim evoking sensuality and erotic heat. (Diaghilev's company was notable for commissioning great artists such as Picasso to design its sets.) Williams dances naked before his mirror, waving his shirt like a Cossack: virile, grotesque (a key word), and abandoned to the pleasures of exhibitionism. The physical energy dissipates, however, replaced by a surprisingly effete music, as Williams declares that he is condemned to loneliness. There's a grain of truth in this good-humored torment, but Williams relishes playing this role to the hilt. (Frank O'Hara's poem "Autobiographia Literaria" owes much to "Danse Russe.") In the brief third movement, Williams inspects his body with the hedonism of self-love, then, with an actor's split-second timing, delays a moment before asking the question, at once challenging, complacent, and defensive, "Who shall say I am not / the happy genius of my household?" that the poem intentionally lets hang in the air, like the "silken mists." He can be happy, he seems to imply, as the guardian angel of [his] "household"—an honorific title—but the amiable bravado of his question hints that he expects somebody to step forth and clip his wings. Nonetheless, "Danse Russe" slides from primitivism to domesticity, like the Eumenides transformed into the watchdogs of Athens's hearths. This modulation is built into the poem's choreography: the three syntactic movements all begin with the conditional "if" and end with a question. Yet Williams is not as bold as he wishes to be; his solo dance takes place against the backdrop of "yellow drawn shades," so the neighbors cannot witness him cavorting nakedly in his north room.

It's virtually impossible to find a jubilant love poem by Williams in his vast corpus. Melancholy seizes him at the outset or gradually seeps into his reveries. Consider "Love Song," here quoted in its revised version:

I lie here thinking of you:—

the stain of love
is upon the world!
Yellow, yellow, yellow
it eats into the leaves,
smears with saffron
the horned branches that lean
heavily
against a smooth purple sky!
There is no light
only a honey-thick stain
that drips from leaf to leaf
and limb to limb
spoiling the colors
of the whole world—

you far off there under
the wine-red selvage of the west!

If Solomon had wanted to compose The Song of Songs but a duende had mysteriously dictated Ecclesiastes instead, "Love Song" might have been one of its strophes. What lies on the other side of the white space between lines 1 and 2 is a vision of onanism and infidelity that induces guilt. The word "stain," repeated twice, spoils "the colors / of the whole world"; until the last two lines, the speaker tracks the progress of an emotion that spreads like an infectious disease: "eats," "smears," "drips," "spoiling." Yet the poem is, paradoxically, suffused with painterly beauty (purples, reds, yellows) and with an incantatory music. At the climax, he yearns for the distant lover, identified only as "you," whom he imagines in some woods ablaze with wine-red foliage. (The addressee is clearly not Floss.) Significantly, what Williams cut from the first version of the poem were his expansive feelings of delight at love's bond: "The weight of love / Has buoyed me up / Till my head / Knocks against the sky," and "My hair is dripping with nectar." (His internal critic doubtless deleted the last line.)

When Williams lets his roaming eyes and imagination free, he often notices and is aroused by women, from a woman draping a foot over a second-story railing, which he fancies is a come-hither gesture, to slatterns. Desire is promiscuous, even if it is not acted on. Williams's choice of profession brought him into close contact with women's bodies. Practicing obstetrics meant seeing women as mothers, whose courage as they give birth he deeply admires—for example, in "Complaint," called out on a freezing night to attend a woman in labor, he observes, "Here is a great woman / on her side in the bed. / She is sick, / perhaps vomiting, / perhaps laboring / to give birth to / a tenth child. Joy! Joy!" Night may be, as he says, a "room / darkened for lovers," but his role is different: "I pick the hair from her eyes / and watch her misery / with compassion." His intense focus is on urgent medical procedures, but out of the corner of an eye, he may see "the round and perfect thighs of the Police Sergeant's wife." The fever of his sexual desires can be measured in the diverse portraits of women that hang on the walls of Al Que Quiere!: Mrs. Robitza, a farmer's daughter, three teenage girls "in crimson satin," even two little girls. In fact, Al Que Quiere!, besides being the first volume in which

Williams's voice sounds unlike that of other poets, is a kind of Hubble telescope orbiting the earth and sending back crucial data about him and women from every conceivable angle: aerial views, close-ups, through a car's windshield, etc. He had been married long enough to know that while he sometimes enjoyed being a husband, matrimony, especially its finality, often stifled him and made him restive, as the poems corroborate.

Domesticity is not without its mild satisfactions. In the amusing poem "Good Night," Williams stands at the kitchen sink drinking a glass of water and looking round at the immaculately polished room. A bunch of parsley sits in a glass and "a pair of rubber sandals / lie side by side / under the wall-table / all is in order for the night." Floss's sandals are not exactly an exciting sex toy. At this commonplace moment, three "vague, meaningless girls" pass by "full of smells and / the rustling sound of / cloth rubbing on cloth and / little slippers on carpet— / high school French / spoken in a loud voice!" Though Williams dismisses his amorous twinges as "memory playing the clown," "the murmurous background of / the crowded opera" captures his fancy. In this droll poem, he shuns the role of small-town lothario. Rather, he bids good night to adolescent maunderings, finding compensatory pleasure in the parsley, "still and shining," in its glass. He "yawns deliciously" and heads for bed.

When monogamy vexed him, however, Williams's fantasies sometimes crossed the border of what society decreed as permissible sexual thoughts into a no-man's-land lined with booby traps he managed not to trip off. Two thirds of the way through *Al Que Quiere!*, Williams inserts a pair of poems about little girls, patients of his. "Sympathetic Portrait of a Child" has often correctly been singled out for its audacity in picking a "murderer's little daughter" as its subject, and for its naturalistic touches that announce a break from plush romantic diction. Far more intriguing are Williams's views of childhood sexuality and his responses to a young girl's body and movements. Those stirrings shed light on his own nature; they're not inherent in the situation. Here is the first short poem:

The murderer's little daughter
who is barely ten years old
jerks her shoulders
right and left
so as to catch a glimpse of me
without turning round

Her skinny little arms
wrap themselves
this way then that
reversely about her body!
Nervously
she crushes her straw hat
about her eyes
and tilts her head
to deepen the shadow—
smiling excitedly!

As best she can
she hides herself
in the full sunlight
her cordy legs writhing
beneath the little flowered dress
that leaves them bare
from mid-thigh to ankle—

Why has she chosen me
for the knife
that darts along her smile?

Williams's medical training schooled him to notice gestures that signal obliquely what the patient wishes to conceal. Sometimes this mutual looking over leads to a cat-and-mouse game, as here; at other times it erupts into warfare, as in the story "The Uses of Force," where Williams must pry open a girl's mouth to confirm his suspicion that she had contracted diphtheria; the use of force is justified because it is crucial to saving her life. Nonetheless, Williams is aware that he is violating her body; it is not rape, but he employs physical force to get his way. Typically, Williams admires the young girl's violent resistance.

In "Sympathetic Portrait of a Child," from the moment his eye alights on the nearly ten-year-old girl, Williams registers so many salient details about her that we trust his authority and competence: her anxieties at being in a doctor's office (natural to children), her nervous mannerisms and stratagems, all expressed in strong physical verbs both awkward and beautiful. By jerking her head right and left, she hopes to spy out who this stranger is without his catching on so that she can decide if he's friend or foe; she hugs herself and frantically searches for a safe way to ward him off; she crushes her hat about her eyes to block the doctor's view of her face; and her legs writhe. But she cannot conceal herself in the "full sunlight." There's something seductive to the doctor in the child's twitching, bare legs, and excited smile, which make her, in his mind, a coconspirator. Williams's manner is gentle and professional, but he's jittery, too, as the question he poses in the final three lines shows: "Why has she chosen me / for the knife / that darts along her smile?" Common sense might reply that the child did not choose him, her mother did, perhaps because of his low fees and high reputation as a pediatrician. But that would not account for Williams's pleasurable unease or explain the poem's chief ambiguity: Who wields the knife? If it is Williams, then he seems to wonder: Why is it that girls look at me and see a menacing weapon? If it is the girl, there is something dangerous in her smile that turns him into the victim, as if she, though little and frail (those matchstick arms), inherited her father's murderous character. The verb "darts" conveys the slashing motion of a knife. "I was sympathetic with her but had to be careful," Williams remarked about this poem. Through fantasy, the poem allows him to entertain and deflect feelings that the respectable would have condemned as perverse.

"The Ogre," the companion poem to "Sympathetic Portrait of a Child," further explores prohibited sexual feelings:

> Sweet child,
> little girl with well-shaped legs
> you cannot touch the thoughts
> I put over and under and around you.
> This is fortunate for they would
> burn you to an ash otherwise.
> Your petals would be quite curled up.
>
> This is all beyond you—no doubt,
> yet you do feel the brushings
> of the fine needles;
> the tentative lines of your whole body
> prove it to me;
> so does your fear of me,
> your shyness;

likewise the toy baby cart
that you are pushing—
and besides, mother has begun
to dress your hair in a knot.
These are my excuses.

Williams plays a neurotic fairy-tale monster whose prey are innocent chil-dren. He speaks to the sweet child as to an adult (she pushes the baby carriage like a mother, but she cannot be more than three or four years old). Of course, she cannot grasp his deception or tear the web he spins to entrap her or extinguish the blaze of his lust, which would incinerate her. The factual tone of "Your petals would be quite curled up" cannot dis-guise the ogre's gloating that his power over his victim is so total—and inappropriate. If all this was "beyond you," his satisfaction would be di-luted, so he attributes to her a precocious intuition of his sensual interest in her. She cannot "touch his thoughts," but she can feel the "fine needles" that he uses to give her a vaccination. Still, his excuses take a weird and irrational twist: the evidence he adduces of her awareness is simply not plausible. That her mother has put her hair up in a knot is hardly a sign of female coquettishness. Since his feelings, however unseemly, cannot harm the little girl, he can indulge them: the poem and words serve as a shield against any accusations that he was a closet pedophile. In fact, it is the imagination that stamps his passport, so that he can enter the orchard of forbidden fruits and freely taste illicit feelings without any worries about punishment. That he's not afraid of publishing the two poems is proof that he is not conscious of their subtext.

For the first dozen years or so of his medical practice, the working poor of Lyndhurst, Passaic, and Paterson made up the bulk of Williams's patients. He understood the vicissitudes of poverty, the difficult pregnan-cies and frequent childbirths, the husbands' toil (long hours at low pay) and alcoholism, the physical and mental abuse that were all too often the hard lot of working-class women—they ignited a tender solicitude and sexual interest. In "Woman Walking," a young rustic woman, who might have posed for an advertisement extolling the benefits of milk, strides down the street. She appeals to Williams because she seems "kind and natural," but he scales down his fantasy and hedges about arranging a sexual meeting with her. His tone is tinged with boastful condescension: there is little challenge in such a conquest.

In the well-known 1916 poem "The Young Housewife," Williams takes another tack:

> At ten A.M. the young housewife
> moves about in negligee behind
> the wooden walls of her husband's house.
> I pass solitary in my car.
>
> Then again she comes to the curb
> to call the ice-man, fish-man, and stands
> shy, uncorseted, tucking in
> stray ends of hair, and I compare her
> to a fallen leaf.
>
> The noiseless wheels of my car
> rush with a crackling sound over
> dried leaves as I bow and pass smiling.

In a car cruising to or from a house call, Williams sits in the driver's seat, his eye roaming like a movie camera or a voyeur's, observing the passing townscape and editing it as a drama in three brief scenes. In each stanza, the poet lingers over the young housewife who has aroused his sexual and poetic interest, then closes with a final directorial flourish or comment. He first catches a glimpse of the indolent woman—at 10:00 a.m. she's still wearing a negligee—and thinks of her as a lounging prisoner in her husband's house. But despite her being solitary, Williams makes no move; he goes about his business; the distance fuels his fantasy. A second time, when she ventures out to the curb to buy ice and fish from itinerant peddlers, he gets to study her up close. What he notices are her innocent shyness and her slightly tousled appearance; just as "uncorseted" hints at a fetching lack of constraint, so "tucking in / stray ends of hair" is both lyrical and coquettish, like some eternal feminine guile. Williams's response, however, is curiously deadpan and unexpected: he compares her to a "fallen leaf." The autumnal tenderness in this image is inapt: a young blooming woman is anything but a sere leaf. Perhaps this poetic trick distracts him from his own desire; if she resembles a fallen or unobtainable woman, then he can blithely move on; the metaphor aids by drastically aging her: she becomes an out-of-reach or undesirable matron.

Where the first two stanzas beat time slowly, the last stanza rushes away from the crimeless scene (this is not a suburban version of Leda and the Swan), but the figure that the poet cuts is disquieting. Like a gallant courtier, the smiling Williams bows to the young housewife in homage to her beauty, yet when the car's "noiseless wheels" make a "crackling sound over / dried leaves," the oxymoron seems to bring a heartless impulse out of hiding: he tramples, in imagination, the object of a foiled sexual triumph.

SIX

A Risqué Liaison
with the Fabulous Baroness

In a catalogue of Williams's sexual fantasies and escapades, the young housewife would barely count as a footnote. His fitful relations with the Baroness Elsa von Freytag-Loringhoven, however, deserve several chapters. He never got embroiled in a more peculiar or farcical folie à deux. One could call it, after *Don Giovanni*'s subtitle, a *dramma giocoso*. As a theatrical genre, farce cruelly exposes the follies of sexual desire gone awry. When the curtain falls, an ambiguous cackle rises from the embarrassed characters who discover that they were exposed as victims wriggling before the audience's pitiless gaze. This public humiliation Williams feared, but for the Baroness he laid it aside, like a medical researcher studying a dangerous strain of virus.

Williams remembered being introduced to the "fabulous creature" by Margaret Anderson and Jane Heap, the editors of the literary magazine *The Little Review*, to which the Baroness contributed Dadaist poems and dithyrambic reviews. Before she emigrated to America, the Baroness had been married for a brief period to a minor German baron ten years her junior—hence her title—who returned to Germany and killed himself. She quickly became a colorful supporting actor in New York's avant-garde circles, modeling for Duchamp, turning up at Walter Arensberg's parties and at gallery openings, and starring in an avant-garde movie directed by Man Ray in which she unself-consciously cavorted naked. Her appearance was more bizarre than one of Picasso's Demoiselles d'Avignon. She would carry a dominatrix's whip or dangle from her hip a plaster-cast penis, which she wielded on the sidewalk to shock spinsters and "signal her . . . claim to traditionally male rights." Her body was tomboyish, her hair shaved, shellacked, and dyed blue, perhaps to combat ringworm. Her costumes, flamboyant even by Greenwich Village bohemian standards in the 1910s, were a patchwork of materials, colors, and textures; nobody ever forgot the Baroness's coal scuttle hat. She also scavenged odds and ends from trash cans and discards on the street, weaving them into artful Dadaist collages. In her autobiography, Margaret Anderson described the Baroness's grand entrance into *The Little Review* office:

> She wore a red Scotch plaid suit with a kilt hanging just below the knees, a bolero jacket with sleeves to the elbows and arms covered with a quantity of ten-cent-store bracelets—silver, gilt, bronze, green, and yellow. She wore high white spats with a band of decorative furniture braid around the top. Hanging from her bust were two tea-balls . . . On her head was a black velvet tam o'shanter with a feather and several spoons—long ice-cream-soda spoons. She had enormous earrings of tarnished silver and on her hands were many rings, on the little finger high peasant buttons filled with shot. Her hair was the color of a bay horse . . .

Such *bas couture* chic on a woman part starving waif and part vamp brought her, for a few years, a kind of minor celebrity—and Williams's equivocal courtship.

The Baroness's notoriety also sprang from the way she garishly flaunted her sexuality. "I radiated sex attraction," she fondly recalls in her 1925 memoir. As a cultured adventuress, she piqued the interest of men, but also repelled and scared them. Timid suitors, unworthy of "a woman of my far-flung spacious simple grandeur," earned her contempt. In his *Autobiography*, Williams teases Wallace Stevens for fearing to walk below Fourteenth Street, lest he run into the Baroness. Williams, by contrast, was intrigued by this outlandish figure, who lived in abysmal poverty, cadged off friends when she couldn't find modeling jobs, and was an occasional kleptomaniac. He implied that he enjoyed the challenge of a risqué (and risky) liaison with an outlaw who seemed to promise nights of electrifying lovemaking. Yet the Baroness was a strange choice for a sexual partner. She had a sexual dossier unrivaled in its variety: serial monogamy; love affairs galore with heterosexuals, lesbians, and gay men; an elopement; bouts of syphilis and gonorrhea. The respectably brought-up Williams was not at first put off by her flea-market outfits or by her combative moves on him. Smitten by the handsome doctor poet, the Baroness cockily promised Anderson and Heap that "I will get this man." (She could not foresee Williams's evasive maneuvers.) For him, this Lorelei was a spectacular blend of the civilized and the uncouth, oblivious to rules and limits, even rapacious. She could, he believed, "crack open [his] defended self." When Anderson and Heap reported that the Baroness admired his poetry, he was hooked.

Williams wrote about her three times: first in a fictionalized account of his relations with her in "The Three Letters," printed in *Contact* (1921); then in a 1931 unpublished meditation titled simply "The Baroness Elsa von Freytag-Loringhoven," and finally in the 1951 *Autobiography*, where she appears, incongruously, in a dramatic chapter in which his father and grandmother die. Such attention argues that the Baroness played a prominent role in the theater of Williams's psyche, like a messenger in Greek tragedy bearing important news, though vilified for doing so.

Williams was thirty-seven when he wrote "The Three Letters," and a squalid little fable it is. The first letter describes the callow hero, Evan Dionysus Evans, who, the poet remarks in *I Wanted to Write a Poem*, "was, of course, myself; his experiences, in a measure, mine." Meeting the Baroness on the morning she leaves prison after being acquitted of the charge of petty larceny, Evans accompanies her to her slum apartment, a cluttered museum of *objets trouvés* and *objets réfusés*. In that setting, the Baroness is a gross, sexually voracious Siren with broken front teeth. Williams romanticizes the foul odors rising from her armpits and her room as a rebuke to "the spoiling grey bath of Methodist-Episcopalian sunlight." The Baroness both mesmerizes and disgusts the puritan in Evans. He's not sure he wants to be her man on the dump, but he doesn't flee.

Henry James would have recognized in Williams's brief epistolary scenes the basic plotline of his novels and been shocked by the tawdry atmosphere, as if he had stumbled into an unsavory bordello. America is virginal, naive, clean, and fearful of sex; Europe is pagan, dirty, sinful, and deadly. In search of experience, the New World woos the Old, declares its love, and submits to a kiss—whether foreplay to a consummated act, one can't say for sure—in which her "broken incisor," like a fang, "presses hard into his lip." At first, the Dionysus in Evans revels in her touch, like a decadent thrilling to the whiff of a decomposing corpse. Accustomed to the rank smells associated with the body, doctors nonetheless are high priests of the goddess Hygeia. But a writer cannot find his material in "the

clean muslin souls of Yankeedom," Williams contends. He must gourman-
dize on the rancid. Ben Hecht wrote of the Baroness in a similar rhapsodic vein: "She is a dis-ease. Her flesh is insane. She is the secret of
ecstasy and of gods and of all things that are beautiful."

Williams portrays the Baroness as a fantastical muse, indifferent to
conventional morality, yet intransigently herself. She teaches the novice a
valuable lesson: that the artist must live on the edge. With whimsical humor Williams even reports that she offered to make him a man and a better
artist by giving him syphilis, an offer he politely spurned, though in *Kora
in Hell* he points out that syphilitic lesions look like gorgeous salmon-pink
flowers. Williams has a frisky time praising the Baroness's charms and
"religious fervors of soul." Her romanticism far outstrips his.

Evans rashly declares his love in a letter. Why? His explanation is plausible up to a point: the barren environment of a New Jersey suburb and
"holy matrimony" were not conducive to poetic creativity; from the Baroness he could acquire knowledge of the forbidden, soiled, or fallen woman,
the precious, if perilous, gift of excess that would aid him in breaking the
shackles that limited his poetry. (She also reminds him of his "wolfish"
grandmother.) In extravagant language he remarks, gratefully, "Against so
many he would rub his match without lighting it that at the unexpected
flare he would cry out when he did. To her kind only could his mind go
and be kindled." Is Williams being honest or peddling a line of balderdash?
Either, depending on his mood. That she violated moral codes in pursuit
of gratifying her desires is part of her attraction—and of his sentimental
education.

When Evans abruptly loses his appetite for the Baroness, Williams
sketches her as graphically as Hogarth drew the prostitutes of Covent Garden. A mood of savage malice seizes him, as in this noisome misogynistic
passage: "the old sloop [she was in her forties] leaned far over once again
until her scuppers [an opening cut through the bulwarks of a ship so that
the water on deck can pour out into the sea] were awash and began to
regain headway, first paralleling the sand, then jibbing with a crash out to
sea." When the Baroness discovers that Evans has been toying with her,
she grows maddened, writhing naked on the bed, "bumping against the
walls, mocking the dull Americans," then taking a swing at him that he
ducks. (In a reversal of roles, she is the Dionysian, not Evans.) Although
this is a clear case of "American unresponded love emotions," she bom-
bards him with poems and letters that reach him "on phallus wings"; she

denounces him as a scoundrel one minute and in a flurry of tears the next begs him not to cut off their relations. Evans tosses her communiqués aside, unopened, except for a "full length portrait of herself" as a wrinkled Venus "in moth-eaten furs" that he keeps as a souvenir. Evans watches the Baroness's tantrums with a cool insolence and jaded eye, dismissing them as a meretricious trick.

In the second letter, the Baroness requests Evans's aid in translating a Latin proverb about love and a cow, *Quod licet Jovi non licet bovi* ("What is permitted to Jove is not possible to a cow"). He complies, but this brief truce is quickly shattered. The American Jove and Europa go their separate ways, though not before a no-holds-barred skirmish. Still in the throes of a violent passion for Evans, the Baroness sends a third letter many months later, declaring her desire for him. He fends off her protestations of love, as if swatting a fly, with sarcastic one-liners: "What a good memory you have." Indeed, they act like a pair of shrill music-hall clowns or an old bickering married couple. He affects a smug, weary worldliness—"But it's always well to find out what the women want, he chewed, at no matter what cost"—though he cannot help admiring her fecund imagination. "She knows what art means," he concedes.

Although Williams had doubtless scrutinized the Baroness's poetry in *The Little Review*, he never passed judgment on it in any formal way. Today, it often seems both a kind of automatic writing and a mélange of pretty sounds confected from a dog-eared Romantic lexicon. Consider "Appalling Heart":

City stir—wind on eardrum—
dancewind : herbstained—
flowerstained—silken—rustling—
tripping—swishing—frolicking—
courtesing [curtseying?]—careening—brushing—
flowing—lying down—bending—
teasing—kissing : treearms—grass—
limbs—lips.
City stir on eardrum—.
In night lonely
peers— :
moon—riding !
pale—with beauty aghast—

too exalted to share !
in space blue—rides she away from mine chest—
illumined strangely—
appalling sister !
Herbstained—flowerstained—
shellscented—seafaring—
foresthunting—junglewise—
desert gazing—
rides heart from chest—
lashing with beauty—
afleet—
across chimney—
tinfoil river—
to meet—
another's dark heart—
Bless mine feet !

What could Williams take from this highly mannered poem, this avant-garde period piece? Joycean portmanteau words ("shellscented," "herb-stained," "foresthunting") and strings of participles, in the absence of verbs, that give the poem its faint motion; rhythm chopped into small units by a profusion of dashes; single lines almost weightless; initial words of a line typed in lowercase letters; extra space allotted to exclamation points and colons, as in a long breath; a preponderance of short lines. Though coin of the Dada realm, these stylistic models he could and did adapt to his own purposes. Of no use were the awkward inversions ("in space blue") and Germanic constructions ("Bless mine feet !"), signs of the Baroness's halting English, or the hothouse atmosphere of "Appalling Heart," its fondness for self-hypnotic lyricism, whose effect is like a heavy dose of aromatherapy: he had already passed through this phase of verbal preciosity.

In reality, as in the third letter, the Baroness, stung by his loss of interest, threatens to blackmail Evans by publishing their correspondence. Unperturbed, he hurls a merciless barrage of invective at her, likening her first to a hissing snake, then to a cow whose lust "mooed up out of her soul" (Jove's looking for a younger wench now), to shit flowing "from a broken sewer main" and finally to "a roundshell clam in the mud, throbbing, quivering, protruding and withdrawing its obscene neck." The woman who earlier "filled his soul with a strange rest" is reduced to an inedible mollusk.

The Baroness did not take Williams's scabrous change of heart lightly. Like a general, she went on the offensive, twice boldly taking her campaign to Rutherford. Although he claimed in 1931 that had the Baroness knocked on the door Floss would have invited her into the house, the truth is that because she had invaded his sacred space, he grew incensed, absorbing a punch from her the first time and "flattening her with a stiff punch to the mouth" and having her arrested the second time (he claims in his *Autobiography* to have feared "she was going to stick a knife in me"). Dismayed by what she called his petty, dictatorial ways, she retreated across the Hudson and attacked him on another front: in a review of *Kora in Hell*, "Thee I call 'Hamlet of Wedding-Ring,'" she launched a fusillade of name-calling: "Agh——pah! Carlos Williams—you wobbly-legged business satchel-carrying little louse!" The Baroness was right on one point: he was a Hamlet; his soliloquy might have run, "To be married or not to be married / That is the question."

Williams directs virtually no irony at his alter ego in "Three Letters." He probably did not care that his portrait degraded the Baroness or that his conduct was vindictive; he makes no effort to disguise—or excuse—how fatuous he has been. "The great light that had broken in Evan's turgid soul" consists of a puerile rant: "You damned stinking old woman . . . you old dirty bitch." As far as Williams was concerned, the curtain had rung down on the long farce. He took pity on her pauperism and "gave her two hundred dollars to get out of the country," money "stolen by the go-between." That was a huge sum for a doctor of modest income to pay out; it smacks of allaying a guilty conscience.

In April 1923, the Baroness set sail for Berlin, a city in economic ruin after the Treaty of Versailles. Extreme poverty was everywhere and the Baroness had few resources to combat it. So she scrounged for pfennigs to keep a roof overhead and put food on her table just to stay alive. Still a romantic peacock, she wrote ornate letters to cousins, ex-lovers, acquaintances, explaining her literary plans—and seeking a handout. After two years, she entered a poorhouse, from which she was expelled, and even sought a haven in an insane asylum, but her ruse was uncovered and she had to leave.

Elsa's chief benefactor in these harrowing years was Djuna Barnes, who sent money when she could and urged her friend to write her autobiography, as much for Elsa's sanity as for documenting her eccentric personality. (The Baroness fancied that posterity would judge her to be a gilt-edge literary bond.) Easily persuaded, she composed her *Apologia Pro Vita Sua*, tormented confessions that Rousseau might have commended for their rhapsodic candor, if not their coherence. Diligently penning draft after draft in the purple style that was second nature to her, she chronicled her quest for an ideal romantic love and her numerous defeats at the hands of men who either failed to care for her material and emotional needs or were sexually cold or impotent. The self-portrait that she draws in her memoir is an odd blend of feminist *avant la lettre* and "mansick" woman. She seldom blames herself for choosing men, including Williams, the last of her American beaux, who disappointed her. In *Holy Skirts*, her perceptive and poignant novel about the Baroness, René Steinke convincingly shows that Marcel Duchamp was the object of the Baroness's grandest passion, but despite her ardent courtship of the mysterious Frenchman, the Baroness could not crack the opaque glass of his demeanor. His imperturbability only provoked her to increased efforts to seduce him, which he repelled: he seemed indifferent to sex, or at least to sex with her. Her defeat amounted to a textbook example of unrequited love.

In May 1926, the Baroness arrived in Paris, a depressed, forlorn woman, hoping to resume a modeling career or, more grandiosely, to start a modeling agency, but indigence continued to stalk her. In December 1927, as she slept in a dreary rooming house, someone—a "French Jokester," Williams guesses—entered her room and turned on the gas jets, asphyxiating her. The murder (or accident) was never solved. News of her death eventually reached Williams. "I was really crazy about the woman," he notes in 1951, in his final tribute to her. He knew that he infuriated her, and he doubtless had read her verdict of his character which tumbled out in the coda to "Thee I Call 'Hamlet of the Wedding-Ring.'" The Baroness pricks Williams at his most vulnerable spot: his masculinity. Where a European gentleman "never loses balance—in deepest abandon of gayety—numbed senses—subconsciously breeding tells how far to go—when to retire[,]" and "Thus carries artist intoxication of feeling," Williams, she implies, is haunted by fears and inhibitions and so is "unfit to indulge!" Like a victim supplicating the gods for revenge, she prays: "pour [anathema] upon those jabbering uncreative joyless sincere nobodys [sic] that write, potter, live, are uninteresting for force of honesty!" In the unkindest cut of all, she calls Williams a "tortured child." It stung him that friends and critics, like the Baroness, viewed him as an unformed, pusillanimous juvenile. The gist of their condemnation was that he did not want to go "the limit as they thought I should." By holing up in a suburban bunker instead of going out and facing "a dangerous and rewarding world," he doomed himself in their eyes to be a lightweight. The Baroness had sneered at his address, 9 Ridge Road, calling it 9 Rich Road and him a complacent bourgeois.

In 1931, Williams set out to refute these charges, penning a meditation on the Baroness notable for its lack of vitriol. With the composure of hindsight he attempts a balanced assessment of her—and women's— importance to him. He labels the Baroness a "clandestine faker" who was "like a Cortez coming to Montezuma and she wanted to do the same stupid thing he did. Destroy. They imagine somehow that clarity and delight are to be gained by shedding the blood of someone." Williams doesn't apologize for his harsh tactics in warding off the Baroness's siege; indeed he concedes that he was "helpless to end it," perhaps in part because he was "not the bravest or the most honorable in the world"—men, he adds, not exempting himself, are "selfish liars," "insignificant to me, interested in fire engines"; "women I have found tremendous, absorbed in the body of their opponent, real." Throughout this essay, Williams renounces the meanly sarcastic tone of "Three Letters" and speaks of the Baroness with sympathy and a tinge of shame at not being able to lift her from poverty or relieve her unhappiness. He touches delicately on her pathology, as if he were palpating a tumor: "The Baroness to me was a great field of cultured bounty in spite of her psychosis, her insanity. She was right. She was courageous to an insane degree. I found myself drinking . . . pure water from her spirit. I found it so that is all. I could not go to bed with her. Disease has no attraction for me. I couldn't. But I did feel a shame."

Williams here has defected to the camp of Apollo. One would need a god's potion to drink "pure water from the spirit" of a mind deranged by passion, a woman he earlier ridiculed for her filthy body; but it is not the "sexual tropic" that rivets him, he insists. Rather, now the philosopher of Eros, he argues that sex is a useful means to a transcendent end, the "corridor to a clarity." This is neither an ascetic's nor a sybarite's creed. Williams lingers, with a sensualist's memory and a doctor's lingo, on "the odors, the lights, the filamentous [sic] stimulae of the sexual contact, the languorous delights . . . the building up of the constriction in every phase from the first electric shock to the fainter, refused parries." He claims dual citizenship: in the country of Eros and on the planet Urania. Once the body's fevers have subsided, "the mind afterward is my field. Coming to that with the satisfaction of performance ensanguined in me the mind is lit, serene, the eyes are as if released from cages, the breath comes unobstructed and the mind rushes to its inventions." In this passage, Williams gives himself a clean bill of bodily and mental health. Postcoitally, he is left in a state of bliss, at ease in the Zion of his imagination. But conflict, like a disease in remission, lurks ready to strike.

SEVEN

Adventures in the Skin Trade

I.

Although it began with uncertainties about his marriage and his poetry, for the most part the 1920s were a liberating decade for Williams. His practice, always an anchor of his stability, began to prosper. The hysteria of the Palmer Red Scare, which resulted in the deportation of people accused of Communist or anarchist affiliations (Emma Goldman and Alexander Berkman were prominent casualties of the xenophobic mindset), lingered for a while, then spent itself, as did the influenza pandemic. Similarly, the horrific carnage of the Great War and its aftermath soon gave way to an economic boom that lasted until the stock market crash of 1929 ushered in the Great Depression. Given these historical events, it's not surprising that a devil-may-care hedonism and more permissive morality took hold of the country. Flouting convention while pursuing pleasure and wealth was the menu du jour. The flappers; the corporate criminals jailed in the Teapot Dome Scandal; the petty bootleggers; even the stolid presidents Calvin Coolidge and Warren Harding, who ran a sort of laissez-faire government in which corruption flourished; the cynical manipulators; the dreamers and addicts hungry for sensation, the Gatsbys and Lady Bretts—all have entered our folklore about the twenties. America seemed to crave change, which meant rebelling once more against Puritanism, but as always in such transitions, many were left behind or forgotten or clung to familiar traditions. A few of Williams's patients may have worn short skirts and bobbed their hair or drunk under-the-counter gin, but most struggled to eke out a livelihood, pay the rent, put food on the table, and raise their children. Nor should we neglect the conservative backlash to this new freedom, which culminated in the Scopes trial. The teaching of evolution alarmed large numbers of people across the country, who regarded it as undermining fundamental Christian beliefs. And racial prejudice continued to be an ugly blemish on American life: blacks were disenfranchised, mired in poverty, given inferior educations, ghettoized, lynched with chronic regularity in the South, and discriminated against in the North. Conflict, not consensus, ruled the American psyche—and Williams's.

Williams's innate caution and self-interest kept him from surrendering wholly to the euphoria and license of the twenties. He did not dance the night away and tipple in speakeasies, seek nirvana in brothels, or jump into the fountain of the Plaza Hotel. His artist friends in New York, as disdainful of sexual constraints as their bohemian counterparts in Paris or London, were puzzled by his decision to live in Rutherford and by his apparent diffidence. They teased him that lovely women were available for the asking, and yet he chose to be uxorious, nervous about a frolic in bed, earnest and tied to bourgeois habits. For Williams this accusation was a sore point. He reacted to their sarcasm by defending himself with peevish ripostes: he would do as he pleased when it pleased him. The twenties was, in fact, a decade of sexual exploration for him, and his extramarital affairs put severe strains on his marriage. Unlike Henry Miller, though, he did not brag about his conquests; he could not ignore, bribe, or lull his conscience. The tug-of-war between desire and duty, freedom and respectability, played itself out in nearly everything he wrote, and particularly in his poems.

Take the epistolary "To a Friend Concerning Several Ladies" in *Sour Grapes* (1921). Williams convenes a sort of psychological tribunal to test the truth or falsity of the allegations that he's a milquetoast. In the course of the poem, he raises and explores indirectly the relation between sex and creativity, both crucial to his quest for the freedom to break rules. Here's Williams's brief:

> You know there's not much
> That I desire, a few chrysanthemums
> Half lying on the grass, yellow
> And brown and white, the
> talk of a few people, the trees,

an expanse of dried leaves perhaps
with ditches among them.

But there comes
between me and these things
a letter
or even a look—well placed,
you understand,
so that I am confused, twisted
four ways and—left flat,
unable to lift the foot to
my own mouth:
Here is what they say: Come!
and come! And come! And if
I do not go I remain stale to
myself and if I go—
        I have watched
the city from a distance at night
and wondered why I wrote no poem.
Come! Yes,
the city is ablaze for you
and you stand and look at it.

And they are right. There is
No good in the world except out of
a woman and certain women alone
for certain things. But what if
I arrive like a turtle
with my house on my back or
a fish ogling from under water?
It will not do. I must be
steaming with love, colored
like a flamingo. For what?
To have legs and a silly head
and to smell, pah! like a flamingo
that soils its own feathers behind.
Must I go home filled

with a bad poem?
And they say:
Who can answer these things
till he has tried? Your eyes
are half closed, you are a child,
oh, a sweet one, ready to play
but I will make a man of you and
with love on his shoulder—!

And in the marshes
the crickets run
on the sunny dike's top and
make burrows there, the water
reflects the reeds and the reeds
move on their stalks and rattle drily.

The frame of this poem is da capo: recitative, aria with chorus, recitative. Williams depicts himself as a man of modest, not "unfading" desires. The landscape of the Meadowlands surrounding Rutherford that begins and ends the poem is far from gorgeous; its deciduous trees suggest a drab autumn, an emotional aridity, which he implicitly blames on the predictable routines of domestic life in the suburbs. One might expect the restless poet to be as susceptible to a new wish list for sexual partners as he has been to changing his poetry.

On cue, a letter comes from across the Hudson River, attempting to coax him out of his shell. A flirtatious look is enough to arouse and discompose him, so that he literally doesn't know if he's coming or going. Williams mocks his confusion: why, he wonders, is he unable to feed himself the (spicy) dish that tempts him? The ladies are brazen in their sexual invitation, promising in the triple repetition of "Come!" fantastic orgasms. "To know the profundities of life, at some point in one's career," Williams exhorts himself in *The Build-up*, "one must abandon oneself completely to the full range of emotional shock." Abandonment was easy to tout on paper but difficult to achieve, which is why he breaks off the thought "if I go": he has already calculated the threat to his marriage that straying poses. Not to take up the thrill of the hunt, however, means "I [will] remain stale to myself," stuck in an unexciting marriage and doomed like Kora to the "hell of repression." When Williams resumes his meditation, he links women with writing poetry. The seductive city promises ambrosia for the imagination—play, novelty, pleasurable sensations—but he gazes at the glittering lights from a distance, like a spectator, not an actor. Internalizing the ladies' bewitchments, he caresses the magical word "Come!" and rebukes himself for his fear. Perplexed as to why, with the prospect of such stimuli, he has written no poem, he intimates that sex may interfere with his creativity. He's leery of losing control. The next stanza begins with a large concession to the ladies' argument: "And they are right," then states Williams's irrefutable belief that "[t]here is / no good in the world except out of / a woman and certain women alone / for certain things." The first half of this proposition he knows from his experiences as an obstetrician; the second half is a rationale for sexual infidelity if he cares to endorse it. In the debate between "And" and "But," the attorney for the defense steps in to submit his what-if rebuttal, ticking off three images. If Williams is a turtle dragging his house with him, that means he's too armored, slow, and hesitant for a casual romance; if "a fish ogling from under water," he's a cold-blooded voyeur. These attitudes, he wryly notes, won't do for the role of ladies' man. The third and most elaborate image is the most ludicrous: Williams as a flamingo "steaming with love" and colorful (the bird's wings and quills are scarlet and black). "For what?" The flamingo has legs and "a silly head" (probably a sexual innuendo), and "soils itself" (is a shit and maybe infantile). So Williams rejects "empty decadence." (In 1938, he insisted, "I was not a roué.") The clinching reason for his aversion is that from this encounter he returns with "a bad poem." Either way—no poem or bad poem—the doctor's dilemma is a losing proposition.

Because prosecutors have the last word, the chorus of ladies mocks his qualms by likening him once more to a child eager for play and transport, yet afraid of the consequences. Their promise, an echo of the Baroness's boast that "I will make a man of you," irks Williams. Yet when they bait the hook cleverly—with "love on his shoulder!" (arm candy for a sweet tooth?), who knows what Turkish delights will come his way?—he's sorely tempted. But again the sentence dangles, incomplete: Williams can't refute or answer their argument. Instead, he returns the poem to the marshes, a habitat with its own logic and protection (the "dike"), where the reeds, though dry, make a rattling music. The result? A hung jury.

No such conflict perturbed Williams when he observed the boisterous new spirit afoot in the country—and its potential beneficent effect on his search for a poetic style he could call his own. He was encouraged

by the propulsive energy of jazz, a popular art form grown in our backyard, and by the fact that Comstockery had suffered a severe if not fatal
wound. Poets and novelists began writing frankly and graphically about
sex. Although James Joyce's *Ulysses* was still labeled obscene and could
not legally be published in America until after Judge John M. Woolsey's
landmark decision on December 6, 1933, overturned the ban, writers and
artists returning from Europe considered it a badge of honor to smuggle
in a contraband copy of the novel, an early example of samizdat, and
circulate it widely. Williams had read portions of *Ulysses* in *The Little
Review*, where it ran serially and concurrently with *Kora in Hell*. (Margaret Anderson and Jane Heap defied and outwitted the postal authorities'
campaign of censorship and confiscation.) Joyce's verbal daring and
imaginative plenitude had impressed Williams as a brilliant assault on
sclerotic literary conventions, on the "malignant rigidities" he wished to
smash also, though he readily conceded that his poems were not good
enough to bear comparison with the Irishman's tour de force of a modernist novel. The figures most like Molly Bloom were Mrs. Robitza and
the Baroness, but he didn't wholly approve of them.

Still, intense ambition drove Williams's work of the 1920s, and to fulfill it, he wrote prolifically in a variety of styles and experiments: short
lyrics; hundreds of nature poems; torsos of novels (the whimsical *The Great
American Novel*, 1923); heady mixtures of poetry and prose, sometimes
beautiful, sometimes obscure (*Spring and All*, 1923, and *The Descent of
Winter*, 1928); short stories drawn from his observations of patients and
doctors; historical portraiture (*In the American Grain*, 1925); and his account of his travels in Europe, disguised thinly as a novel (*A Voyage to
Pagany*, 1928). In all these books, even when his subject is historical,
women and sex are a major preoccupation. In July 1920, Marsden Hartley, "an eagle without a cliff," in McAlmon's witty image, took the twenty-
year-old Robert McAlmon to a party at Lola Ridge's apartment at 7 East
Fourteenth Street, where he met Williams. McAlmon grew up in a small
town in South Dakota, the son of a Presbyterian minister who had graduated from Princeton Divinity School and who barely scraped together
enough money to feed his family of ten children (two died), but he and his
wife, Bess, preached the gospel of education. Nearly all excelled: on the
football field, as successful businessmen, teachers, and a nurse. Bob enrolled at the University of Minnesota and later at USC, but bored by the
classes, he dropped out and took off for the open road, eventually landing

in New York. Unfazed by the fast-paced city, he supported himself, like the Baroness, by posing in the nude for artists, and not the least bit embarrassed, he lived on a garbage scow in the harbor; he cared little for middle-class comforts. What drove him was a love for literature and a towering ambition to become a writer. Precocious and arrogant, he had already published a poem in *Poetry* in 1919. But that credit he deemed not worth boasting about.

At Lola Ridge's gathering, the handsome, charismatic young man sitting next to Williams and pouring out cocksure literary opinions like Pound redux dazzled the older, more insecure poet. Theirs was an immediate meeting of minds and matching of sensibilities. A few conversations confirmed that McAlmon shared Williams's heady—or obstinate—belief that American writers did not have to kowtow to European models. That McAlmon regarded Eliot's poetry as "mouldy" and "the perfect expression of a clerkly and liverish man's apprehension of life" could only endear this "upstart crow" to Williams.* McAlmon liked the roughhousing of literary controversy and never muzzled his irreverent ideas or impatience with cant about "morals," "soul," and "conscience." Kay Boyle remarked the pair's "violent dissatisfaction with themselves." McAlmon was one of the first readers of Williams's poems and stories to notice their originality and force. Eight years after McAlmon's death in 1956, Kay Boyle wrote, "Bill Williams was a soil, a core, a homeland to which McAlmon always returned, and to which he gave a total loyalty." McAlmon the porcupine was capable of hero worship. That Williams idealized him was no secret to the New York literati. In *Being Geniuses Together*, McAlmon, with self-irony and searing honesty, attempts to remove himself from the pedestal without appearing ungrateful for their friendship:

> Williams has often said that I have a "genius for life," while in the same breath he bemoans his own New England soul and the fact that he has not ventured far from the town of his birth, where he practices medicine. He may be right about me. If absolute despair, a capacity for reckless abandon and drink, long and heavy spells of ennui which require bottles of strong drink to cure, and a gregarious but not altogether loving nature is a "genius for life," then I have it. But with Bill I always feel more or less gay, and he is one of

*When McAlmon met Eliot, he was surprised to find him charming and likable.

the few who can talk of his soul problems and probe the deeper darknesses of life without irritating or boring me.

Of the items on McAlmon's list Williams would have coveted just one: "a capacity for reckless abandon," but only in relations with women; he would never have been so reckless as to ruin his medical skills and standing.

Because Williams had soured on Kreymborg and the stale poems he believed *Others* was settling for, he was not eager to start up yet another literary magazine. But McAlmon's enthusiasm, his willingness to invest his own money, however limited, to fund such a venture, and his cheerful indifference to the prospect of failure overrode most of Williams's hesitancy. The two men launched *Contact* with the proverbial wing and a prayer into a literary marketplace dominated by two avant-garde magazines: Scofield Thayer and Sibley Watson's *The Dial*, and *The Little Review*, edited by Margaret Anderson and Jane Heap. Both adopted an editorial policy that was eclectic and heavily represented by English and continental writers. In a bold move, Thayer hired Ezra Pound to be his literary scout and foreign agent. Pound took his responsibility seriously, drawing up lists of people to seek out. No mere factotum, he negotiated ground rules to ensure his advice would not be shunted aside. He worried about two issues in particular. American postal authorities and leaders of church and social organizations, viewing themselves as guardians of public morals, were quick to brand French novels (and Joyce's *Ulysses*) as obscene and to call for their censorship. Anderson and Heap bravely defied the thought police campaign of harassment and continued serializing Joyce's experimental novel. Censorship was a threat from outside, not to be taken lightly. A more dangerous threat, Pound warned Thayer and Watson, came from inside the literary community itself: "You and W[atson] are learning lesson A: you can't publish *anything* of the slightest interest without rousing hate. The vendetta of imbeciles is endless, swine once headed in stampede, no *possible* access to non extant intelligence, no chance of any indication reason for going [in the] other direction *can* reach them."

Thayer and Watson did not meddle with Pound's literary choices, nor did they abdicate their editorial power to him. Letters flew back and forth between Europe and New York as the three men hammered out editorial policies each could accept. From 1920 to 1923, when Thayer fired him, Pound assembled a glittering constellation of modernist stars, from de

Gourmont, Joyce, and Yeats to Ford Madox Ford and Unamuno. (Pound did not exclude American writers. Williams published regularly in *The Dial* and in *The Little Review*, too.)

McAlmon and Williams lacked the financial means and glamour to compete with their rivals or recruit the best writers to submit major work to *Contact* for a relatively small readership. Novelists and poets understandably would choose a magazine with some cachet over one that was stapled together like a school principal's flyer to be brought home to parents. Furthermore, McAlmon and Williams's conscious decision to exclude international writers cut their legs out from under them. Pound could skim the cream of European letters, export their experimental fictions and poems to New York, where Thayer and Watson bound them artfully inside the pages of *The Dial*. McAlmon and Williams's idea to take up the cudgels for talented American poets and novelists and showcase their pioneering attempts to fashion a style that could have sprung only from native grounds was well intentioned but doomed to fail. They ran work by Pound, H.D., Ford, all living abroad, and Marianne Moore, and filled out an issue with middling writers. In a rueful postmortem, Williams confessed to Kenneth Burke, "Bob and I thought that geniuses would rush forward and fling masterpieces at us"—all literary editors dream of that bounty—but any illusion they harbored that the American public or even their literary colleagues would pay attention soon evaporated; many were cultivating Dadaistic gardens, using French grafts. *Contact*'s circulation never rose above two hundred copies, and after five issues Bob and Bill closed it down. McAlmon, more resilient than Williams, took the setback with equanimity; Williams needed more time to lick his wounds and recover his optimism. Feeling embattled and blue, he turned to metaphors of war; even if he could not yet outline a convincing strategy to free American poetry from "the bondage of banality" and decorum, as he put it to Marianne Moore, he enjoyed the smell of gunpowder. Although he couldn't depend on a battalion of like-minded poets to rally to his cause, he dreamed of inspiring more than a solitary disciple. At least his friendship with McAlmon remained intact.

The pugnacious editorials and manifestos he and McAlmon wrote for *Contact* were meant to clear room for the planting of an indigenous poetic, but the poet-farmer, "composing-antagonist," as he phrased it in the third poem of *Spring and All*, wasn't sure if the seeds he collected and cultivated would take root and flower. In 1913 he had confessed to Harriet

Monroe with a kind of bearish humility, "To tell the truth, I myself never quite feel that I know what I am talking about—if I did, and when I do, the thing written seems nothing to me." Eight years later, recognizing that some of his enthusiasms and plans still lacked staying power or were "completely incomplete," as he put it to Monroe, he shrugged his shoulders and gardened on. It was the effort that counted because it was his way of thinking through and testing, affirming and weeding, both the ideas that teemed in his mind and those that crowded the pages of the little magazines he read assiduously. These rough drafts are often memoranda to himself, or just lists of unconnected facts and images to be appraised and edited at a later time, like the lines he jotted down on prescription blanks and later transferred to paper, scrapping those that were lame and saving and revising those that showed promise. (You could never tell when an ingenious homegrown solution would work—Pa Herman had fished successfully for trout using cigar butts as bait.) If Williams changed direction abruptly or contradicted himself, sounded fuzzy or tentative, that was better, he believed, than clinging to outmoded principles. (He never bragged of his infinite variety.) His medical schooling had trained him not to hang on to a theory indefinitely. Make a diagnosis based on empirical evidence, trust your knowledge and instincts, and if you do not attain the results you expected, search for a better alternative, which may or not be there.

In 1921, however, the year he published *Sour Grapes*, Williams could be excused for feeling unsure of the aesthetic ground he stood on. The center of poetic gravity, one of Pound's dispatches from the front announced, had shifted from London to Paris. Even McAlmon, exasperated by the cultural yahooism in America, had defected to the expatriate camp. This loss of his chief ally was a stinging blow to Williams. "I wish I had the boy back with me and not lost there, abroad, to no good purpose," he confided to Amy Lowell. Nine months later, with his usual hardheaded accuracy, McAlmon explained to Wallace Stevens that Bill was "upset and churning about in realms of misery, doubts, timid and reckless moments of emotion and ideation." During their collaboration on *Contact*, McAlmon listened many times to Williams's "violent appeal for 'faith' of some sort in the value of life, or literature." How he might transform faith into good works was the challenge. Periodically, Williams fell into troughs of despair from which he slowly clawed his way back to hope. With so many of his artist friends in Europe, who was left to join him in his pioneering plans? By her discerning praise of *Kora in Hell*, Marianne Moore, a trenchant poet-critic, had made the blood "flow in my smallest capillaries again" and fed his "brain, somewhat dull of late, as amply as my skin." But though he admired her nimble and quirky mind, she was not a person to invite intimacy. (Sex did not appear to be a factor in her creativity.) Williams occasionally exchanged letters and poems with Stevens, but in Hartford, where he had taken up a position as an insurance executive, the frosty Stevens was not available for the freewheeling colloquies between equals that Williams craved. (On a visit to Hartford, Williams stayed at a hotel, not Stevens's home.) This left Kenneth Burke, a stimulating talker and correspondent about everything and a specialist in rhetoric, as his chief interlocutor. Burke, who read poetry avidly and wrote some, which he wryly admitted was unlikely to go into a second edition, was unafraid to express his opinions. Secure in their mutual respect, the two men swapped ideas and good-humored insults, gossip, and news of their families.

So Williams felt trapped in a familiar cul-de-sac, as if time had stood still. Where was the exit door? In Paris, as McAlmon and Pound said? Or in America? (Williams did not get to Paris until 1924, when the fevers of Dadaism and surrealism had begun to subside.) Was Pound reading the bones correctly or was he, ever the crack salesman, peddling an old nostrum in a new patter? When Harriet Monroe had begun setting down the ground rules for *Poetry* in 1913, she appointed Pound in London as her unofficial troubleshooter and arbiter of the new, despite his derisive view that America lacked the cultural credentials for poetry. Pound's early clarion call for an "American Risorgimento" that would "make the Italian Renaissance look like a tempest in a teapot!" would have been stirring martial music to Williams's ears if he, rather than Monroe, had read the Pound missive. Pound's agenda for poetic reform echoed Williams's own: "no Tennysonianness of speech—nothing, nothing, that you could in some circumstance, in the stress of some emotion, actually say. Every literary-ism, every book word fritters away a scrap of the reader's patience, a scrap of his sense of your sincerity. When one really feels and thinks, one stammers with a simple speech."

But Pound the sage, the scribe, the shaman, and lawgiver was a changeling. In the robes of Czar Ezra, he decreed that only by following his ukases, his "guiding sense" and "discrimination," might bumpkin Williams avoid sinking into the morass of American philistinism. Championing Eliot, the darling of modernism, and editing *The Waste Land*, Pound dismissed Williams's search for an American vernacular as sophomoric rumblings of sedition from a distant colony. Offended by his old friend's condescension, Williams asked sarcastically in a letter to Amy Lowell, "My God, have we not had enough Pounds and Eliots? The Sacred Wood is full of them and their air rifles."

Williams, of course, was not the yokel or literary chauvinist Pound enjoyed chiding. Like Mencken, he railed at the parochialism of the American booboisie—in the poem "Tract," he pompously lectures his Rutherford neighbors for the vulgarity of their funerals. While he didn't spend time in libraries boning up on Provençal or Chinese art, poetry, and politics, he was a cultivated man who didn't need Pound's pedagogy to appreciate Cavalcanti and Li Po, Dante and Laforgue. In fact, he possessed his own brand of cosmopolitanism: he spoke Spanish fluently (it was his first language) and translated Spanish poems, stories, and novels his entire adult life. (Pound was mostly indifferent to Iberian literature.) Since it would have been foolish to ignore Pound's obiter dicta altogether, Williams patiently mulled them over, but as a sign of independence, he took seriously the linguistic games of Gertrude Stein, a self-styled literary renegade anathema to Pound and Eliot. (Pound did not appreciate his friend's apostasy.) As Harriet Monroe shrewdly observed, Williams was at most an auxiliary of his "militant friend . . . No group could hold him." (As no woman could, save Floss.) Still, nettled by Pound's nasty put-downs and Eliot's treatment of him as a poet who didn't matter—Eliot never published a Williams poem in *The Criterion*—he vowed, and it's a constant refrain across the decades, that he would defeat the expatriate gang by invigorating American poetry, as Whitman had. How was yet to be determined.

If that meant being a workhorse, so be it. Williams was accustomed to a doctor's long, backbreaking hours and could draw on astonishing reservoirs of energy—he would not pay the price physically for his strenuous schedule until he reached his sixties, when his health began to fail. Most of his spare time he devoted to poetry, but he managed to find some hours to play with William Eric and Paul, or visit New York for a poetry reading, an hour at Demuth's studio to inspect a new painting, a concert, a party. Floss sometimes accompanied him, but with two young children to care for, she usually stayed home. Though he was a sociable man, not a recluse who craved "sweet loneliness," Williams claimed that for the sake of perfecting his writing he had intentionally striven to be "free of the world," thereby sacrificing many chances to burnish his reputation. This was a partial truth he probably didn't take seriously, since a doctor was immersed in the world up to his ears.

Searching through *Sour Grapes* for clues to Williams's state of mind, the reader encounters a man sending a drumbeat of mixed signals, the captive of what he called "impromptu" moods. Williams jeered at the book just before and after publication, as though his artistry lagged in development, just as life irksomely fell short of his expectations. "I am late at my singing," he declares in the first lines of the first poem; that admission, he knew, wouldn't stop the critics from heaping scorn on the book. But why should he care what they said any more than he should heed the circle of artists who found fault with his sexual wariness? Still, *Sour Grapes* roused more self-contempt than most of Williams's other work. In a letter to Burke in the fall of 1921, after promising to send a copy of the book, he grumbled about the quality and staying power of the vintage:

> Of the few books I have spewed, this is the one in which I have been least interested. For this reason, perhaps, it will turn out to be one of the best, though I think not. It has been more "composed" than any so far, which, if it is discoverable, should please you. The fact of its appearance is due more to the pressure of ordinary circumstances, such as having a lot of stuff around, than to anything else. Yet, one hopes—proof that I am not yet an artist. An artist is always beyond hope—please do not remind me of it.

In being unable to decide whether *Sour Grapes* was "composed," thrown together carelessly, or vomited out, Williams is not warding off his friend's criticism in advance or soliciting praise so much as simply being downcast, as many poets are, about work that seems, in hindsight, not original enough. His breakthrough book, *Spring and All*, his wished-for quantum leap into unmapped terrain, was not far off, but it required *The Waste Land* and the accolades with which that poem was greeted to catalyze him.

He did not soften his negative judgment of *Sour Grapes* with the passage of time, however. His account of its miscellaneous contents in the 1958 *I Wanted to Write a Poem* makes for a surprisingly detailed self-portrait of a tentative and ornery artist "sticking my fingers up my nose at the world" that rejected him. "All the poems," he claimed, "are poems of disappointment, sorrow." (This is not so.) "What is it that is dragging at my heart?" Williams asks in "The Late Singer." He does not answer his own question, which is not perplexity so much as a reluctance to admit his marriage was often not a happy one; undeniably, his mood in *Sour Grapes* is often like the raw weather of "March": woebegone snowy fields, stripped trees, and "[c]ounter-cutting winds" that shrivel his hopes and bring out a slightly posturing humor. "I deride with all the ridicule / of misery / —my own starved misery." Williams was seeking some warmth that would thaw his frozen spirit.

Spring eventually arrives, dispelling his wintry moroseness, followed by summer, with its profligate benison of flowers that Williams culls in a series of lovely botanical poems. In short bursts, he's even amused or happy. In "Light Hearted William," he twirls his moustaches, pops his head out the window to drink in delicious draughts of a spring day in Rutherford; in "The Gentle Man," he mocks himself as a would-be lothario:

> I feel the caress of my own fingers
> on my own neck as I place my collar
> and think pityingly
> of the kind women I have known.

But his encounters with women, even when wished for, trouble him. Sex is seldom casual for him. Consider the ten lines of "Arrival":

> And yet one arrives somehow,
> finds himself loosening the hooks of
> her dress
> in a strange bedroom—
> feels the autumn
> dropping its silk and linen leaves
> about her ankles.
> The tawdry veined body emerges
> twisted upon itself
> like a winter wind . . .

The impersonal "one" and the vague "somehow" permit Williams to distance himself from the scene, as if he hadn't come to this tryst by his own volition and some other Bill was loosening the hooks of the woman's dress. The description of the dress rustling to the floor like leaves is sensuous enough, but the silky image of autumn is trumped by the grotesque image that reveals the lady's body as tawdry and twisted "like a winter wind," or the veins of an old woman. The poet is not overjoyed by the sight of the lover or driven by "stiff lusts" as in "Cicerone." Instead, guilt and disappointment chill his heart, and he behaves like a censorious moralist. His sexual partner is apparently one of those kind women he pities for his ungallant behavior.

On a trip to Chicago in March 1919, to deliver a lecture (later titled "Notes from a Talk on Poetry" and printed in the July 1919 issue of *Poetry*) under the aegis of *Others*, Williams spent a week with Marian Strobel, an attractive assistant editor of *Poetry* magazine. In the blustery Second City, he satisfied his hunger for a brief romance and descanted on a favorite theme, change—the poet as saboteur of entrenched orthodoxies—or in Mariani's astute phrase, as "New World Jacobin." In the first stage, the poet would clear the field by dismantling outmoded traditions and stodgy emotions (the easy part, dramatized in the early prose passages of *Spring and All* with such apocalyptic vigor that the Book of Revelation seems to depict a wan Judgment Day); in the second stage (the hard part), he would build poems according to a blueprint that emphasized American materials and virile, improvised rhythms.

The freedom to fashion poems that flouted or tinkered with accepted traditions elated Williams; no guilt was involved, though he could be as severe a critic of his efforts as any of his detractors. But being an occasional libertine meant he had to contend with some pesky demons. "A Goodnight," which he wrote for and about Marian Strobel, is an anomalous nocturne, so tense and overwrought that it stifles directness and even the simplest expression of joy or furtive pleasure. Williams later characterized his behavior that week as "insane," and he wasn't referring to the appointments he broke with Harriet Monroe, whose company he might have been expected to seek out and whose goodwill it would have been prudent for the aspiring poet to cultivate. (She did not take umbrage.) In "A Goodnight," he's spooked by the noises of the city—"wildfowl police whistles, / the enraged roar of traffic, machine shrieks"—and a landscape decidedly wintry: blizzards, howling winds, "gulls' cries," Lake Michigan's "thundering waves" and "half-stripped trees." Williams stands guard over Strobel's bed to protect her from "The Night," which he personifies variously as a "black fungus" and a "crackbrained messenger" who sings a jabbering lullaby and storms menacingly at her window like a demon lover seeking to break into her sanctuary with "cooings, gesticulations, curses!" "You will not let him in," Williams commands her portentously. The poem's cacophonies seem to murder sleep like the stabbings of remorse that afflicted the Macbeths (a dagger is a prop in "A Goodnight," at the ready for defense or suicide). Yet in a fit of remorse, Williams repents and caresses the word "sleep" with an almost crazed urgency, like a man saying farewell, not good night, to Strobel, and reluctant to admit that their encounter was gratifying: "the night passes—and never passes," he concludes wistfully. Yet twenty years on, he looked back at this week as an idyllic turning point, not an insane escapade.

Another intriguing specimen of Williams's gyrations about women and marriage in *Sour Grapes* is "Romance Moderne," written when Williams was thirty-eight, married for nine years, and the father of two young sons. If the Gallic title hints at a Flaubertian sentimental education, the scene reminds one of an Updike novel: as two married couples drive along a mountain road, Williams and the driver's wife sit in the back and flirt with each other. In a French novel, the hero would bed the lady and deal with any awkward consequences later. (Williams admired the French for their candor and nonchalance about sexual matters.) In "Romance Moderne," the speaker's inner thoughts reveal a man in turmoil. "I wanted to be free and attached at the same time," Williams remarked tersely to John Thirlwall about this poem many years later. The poem is an ode grown agitated and rudderless because Williams is buffeted by contrary impulses. Mentally rehearsing the perils of illicit sex, the poet worries that the car will careen into a ditch, killing him.

Who the woman in the back was doesn't matter; that desire churned him up does. The temptation to "fling" himself into a dance of delirious liberation with another partner, to sway to a forbidden music, excites him, but he worries that Floss has monitoring eyes in the back of her head. (She does.) He detects danger in the erotic web being spun in the back of the car and is flustered.

The "first desire" barely lasts a nanosecond, stamped out by the dissonant triad that opens stanza 4: "Peer Gynt. Rip Van Winkle. Diana." Peer Gynt, a satyr, loved women and then abandoned them. Even though he's a rascal, he's saved by a woman's love and forgiveness. Playing with ideas of infidelity in the car inspires this identification with Ibsen's charming, destructive lover. Williams also relies on Floss's ultimate forbearance. From Peer Gynt to Washington Irving's slovenly hero represents a precipitous drop in romantic fever. Married to a notorious shrew, Rip drinks himself into a stupor and sleeps away a century. Diana, the virgin goddess, embodies a principle that is the antithesis of Peer Gynt's; Williams holds his wayward desires in check, however temporarily. It might be simple for a young man to "try a new alignment," Williams reasons, but burdened by responsibilities, he cannot walk cavalierly away from his marriage.

"Romance Moderne" is not the first time Williams examined the fault lines in his marriage. In June and December 1918, he published two short essays in *The Little Review* in which he wrestled with the stark choices available to a husband and wife when one is in the wrong (Williams "telling bold lies") and the other (Floss) in the right: "It [means] dissolution ending in a complete separation, involving a rebeginning or it means a reunion between the severing parts," he writes in "The Ideal Quarrel." He continues in terms that foreshadow "Romance Moderne": "For to break and begin a new alignment is recapitulation but to recement an old and dissolving union is without precedent, a totally new thing." This tortured, grandiose language indicates the abyss Williams felt himself staring into and the difficulty he would face climbing out of it. If, as he asserts in "Prose About Love," the companion piece to "The Ideal Quarrel," "marriage is permanent" and "love is changing," the danger is that cement cracks and the foundation can crumble, bringing down the conjugal house.

A poetic psychodrama, "Romance Moderne" pushes this welter of conflicting feelings to the surface:

> I would sit separate weighing a
> small red handful: the dirt of these parts,
> sliding mists sheeting the alders
> against the touch of fingers creeping
> to mine. All stuff of the blind emotions.
> But—stirred, the eye seizes
> for the first time—The eye awake!—
> anything, a dirt bank with green stars
> of scrawny weed flattened upon it under
> a weight of air—for the first time!—
> or a yawning depth: Big!
> Swim around in it, through it—
> all directions and find

vitreous seawater stuff—
God how I love you!—or, as I say,
a plunge into the ditch. The end. I sit
examining my red handful. Balancing
—this—in and out—agh.

Despite his antipathy to Eliot as both man and poet, there's a Prufrock chromosome in Williams's makeup. Thus an onerous question hangs in the air: dare he or daren't he? The "dirt of these parts" suggests the woman's appealing earthy nature—"Imagination has as much to do with dirt as with whatever other fiber," Williams noted—but what's carnal may be unclean and therefore disgusting. Williams balances the lovely image of "sliding mists sheeting the alders" with "the touch of fingers creeping / to mine"; the woman is both Eve and the serpent in the garden. These sexual games, "all stuff of the blind emotions," are to be avoided.

This dismissal of what he cannot control is not the final word. Indeed, the staccato rhythms, interrupted by a profusion of dashes, signal how disturbed he is. He shifts to the compensations of aesthetic arousal, gazing with lyrical wonder on "a dirt bank with green stars / of scrawny weed flattened upon it under / a weight of air." There's momentary relief in focusing on nature, but the dangerous chasm he hoped to skirt looms anyway. This time Williams urges himself to swim in and through "the vitreous seaweed stuff," transparent like glass. For a moment he's rid of "the stuff" of opaque emotions, but with the dejected reprise of the phrase "a plunge into the ditch" and its foreboding of retributive death, the stanza fizzles out in self-mockery, sex reduced to a mere "in and out," for which he utters the Bronx cheer "Agh."

By 1921, Williams had slept with enough women to know the "fire in the blood" whose heat scorches and consumes, like "the rising sun," as he put it in "Romance Moderne." Adultery is a scary, delicious, titillating novelty, an experience that can make him feel good about his masculinity. But when he returns home from an assignation, he must face the reality of living with a wife he finds, some of the time, unexciting. In the poem, the lackluster image of Floss as "the grey moon" flickers on his mental screen and puts out the sexual fires. Yet despite his tepid feeling, he's not ready to seek a divorce. In "Prose on Love," sounding like a Calvinist preacher, he denounces concupiscence as "the imbecile side of love attractions." For years he tried to solve a problem as intractable as Fermat's theorem.

Williams's honesty or stabs of conscience force him to acknowledge the marital friction in "Romance Moderne." Floss, the aggrieved wife, finally speaks out. Since Williams supplies no quotation marks, the speech may be all in his head, but he pointedly gives space to her bruised feelings:

Oh get a flannel shirt, white flannel
Or pongée. You'd look so well!
I married you because I liked your nose.
I wanted you! I wanted you
In spite of all they'd say—

Floss begins her reproach with a tinge of sarcasm, advising Bill that if he's planning to go philandering, he should buy a silk shirt and dress for the part. (Elena owned a dress made with pongée.) But she is quickly overwhelmed by distress. In the doubling of "I wanted you" can be heard a touching reminder, amid the humiliation she feels at his affairs, that she had defied her mother's disapproval of a Williams-Herman match. That she married him because she liked his nose seems like such a bizarre claim that he ignores it, as if he has heard it too often. (In the pivotal courtship scene of *The Build-up*, Floss uses those exact words.)

The tension from their argument hovers in the air. In the last stanza, where one might expect a reconciliation or at least a patched-up truce, Floss administers a tongue-lashing (or Williams imagines one) beyond anything Katrina Van Winkle gave her husband: "You are sold cheap everywhere in town!" she jeers. Then she savagely declares that she wishes Bill dead so that she might sit gloatingly over him: revenge is sweet. Sunk in meditation, the poet hears her taunts just enough to record them, but he remains aloof, watching the "myriads of counter processions" (his jumble of thoughts and feelings) cross and recross his mind like a slow caravan. The last weary lines, "it's the grey moon—over and over. / It's the clay of these parts," voice Williams's glum resignation: there's no escape from his psychic and sexual impasse, or from Floss.

In its alternately madcap and stiff structure, verbal parries and thrusts, and rendering of Williams's chaotic feelings, "Romance Moderne" has assimilated the lessons of modernism, to which Williams has added his own nervous calligraphy. Poet Yvor Winters called the poem one of the worst he'd ever read, trashing its form as anarchic and its prosody as incompetent, ridiculing it as an act of premeditated vandalism.

(Poet William Logan recently echoed Winters's judgment.) Their opinion misreads Williams's intentions, and is blind to what is good in the poem. Its title reflects the romance of modernism for a poet not yet in possession of a singular or varied style and uncertain how to obtain one. Everywhere he looked, painters, poets, novelists, and composers were overthrowing tradition, which surely sanctioned his own experiments, however ragged they might be. So he flirted with Imagism, Dadaism, and surrealism, as in matters of the heart he dallied with women from different classes if the opportunity presented itself. He did not rush headlong into affairs and he did not commit himself to one school of poetry. He mixes a plain style with passages of lyric self-communing, a dash of caustic humor, and sudden modulations of tone. Even if Williams's voice cracks now and then or he flattens notes, the performance is not generic.

Williams never claimed "Romance Moderne" was anything but a flawed means to better-written poems. For his biographer, however, it contains seams of valuable ore along with some dross. Sifting them, we can shed light on Williams's inner debate. Though he might dream of joining the company of Duchamp's "rapacious" bachelors, he cannot act like them. Nor does a relaxed sensuality come naturally to him or his poems. All angles, knots, and tangents, "Romance Moderne" shows a man floundering in the labyrinth of sexual desire and succumbing to an ailing conscience. Guilt takes a heavy toll: the poem crushes any trace of romantic hope.

To his credit, Williams faces the crisis in his marriage. He had clinically diagnosed the symptoms of disenchantment in *Kora in Hell*, grousing that his marriage was a product of his will. In "Romance Moderne," as in his improvisations, he borrowed from the Cubists' sense of form and portraiture; wearing his heart on a geometrical sleeve and venting his anger and disappointment through disjointed argument and sullen humor, he might call on "the unseen power of words" to console him and transform the "blind emotions" into radical if imperfect art. In 1921 he couldn't know that task would be a lifelong project successfully realized.

2.

It is highly unlikely that Williams confessed his serial unfaithfulness to Floss; nevertheless she clearly was Argus-eyed about his affairs. The furious wronged wife in "Romance Moderne" is not erupting in simulated anger. Although she lacked any literary training and often felt shy around her husband's voluble, self-possessed friends, Floss loved books and read nearly everything Williams wrote, so she could not help registering his discontent with her and their marriage and feeling cast-off; Bill lacked a baccalaureate degree in dissembling. Yet he strategically places "The Desolate Field," a tribute to, or acknowledgment of, Floss's love for him immediately after "Romance Moderne":

> And amazed my heart leaps
> at the thought of love
> vast and grey
> yearning over me.

It's doubtful that his amazement could mollify Floss, since it is not a surge of love for her he expresses; "leaps" is merely one or two skipped heartbeats. He recognizes that despite the rifts in their marriage, she yearned for him and loomed over him like a dark cloud. He could not ignore her presence or her determination to keep their marriage from disintegrating, but she's still colored grey.

In *Sour Grapes*, there are a few moments of respite in the conjugal wars. "The Delicacies," a prose poem, is one such. It reads like a small-town newspaper's report of a soirée at the mayor's house: paragraphs devoted to the food and wine served (caviar sandwiches, Rhine wine); chitchat about the new car the councilman has bought or the pharmacist's habit of not answering the telephone in the middle of the night until he first lit a cigarette. With a connoisseur's eye Williams appraises the women, and acerbically notes the husbands and wives mismatched by age or temperament. At the center is a sketch of Floss, "young and pretty when she cares to be" in animated discussion with the mayor's wife about the Day Nursery across the tracks in run-down East Rutherford. "The Day Nursery had sixty-five babies the week before last, so my wife's eyes shine and her cheeks are pink and I cannot see a blemish," an affectionate Williams notes. She's no New Jersey Emma Bovary bored with her neighbors and driven to seek a lover.

There's even a brief sexual frisson in the bagatelle "The Thinker," in which the poet talks "in [his] secret mind" to his wife's pink slippers with gay pom-poms "out of pure happiness" as they, not a nude, descend the stairs. It's a small sip of contentment. A more erotically charged poem is

"Queen-Anne's Lace," which Williams laconically told John Thirlwall was about "Flossie again," although, given its clinical language, the reader might be excused for thinking that Williams the doctor-botanist rather than Williams the lover had written the poem:

> Her body is not so white as
> Anemone petals nor so smooth—nor
> so remote a thing. It is a field
> of the wild carrot taking
> the field by force; the grass
> does not raise above it.
> Here is no question of whiteness,
> white as can be, with a purple mole
> at the center of each flower.
> Each flower is a hand's span
> of her whiteness. Wherever
> his hand has lain there is
> a tiny purple blemish. Each part
> is a blossom under his touch
> to which the fibres of her being
> stem one by one, each to its end,
> until the whole field is a
> white desire, empty, a single stem,
> a cluster, flower by flower,
> pious wish to whiteness gone over—
> or nothing.

Though technically a weed, Queen Anne's lace is a common variety of wild carrot that grows riotously, "taking / the field by force" in summer. Williams's examination of Floss's body proceeds in small steps. In the terse first eleven lines, Williams sounds like a medical school lecturer on female anatomy, explaining what it resembles and what it does not, lingering briefly over imperfections (the bruise of the "purple mole," either a woman's nipple or a mark left by sexual passion) and beauties (the distinctions of whiteness). Williams's syntax employs several copulatives, but in a curiously schematic way: the first eleven lines are crisply objective (the couple are labeled his and her), as in a scientific study; the last ten lines retain this controlled sobriety, but give prominence to his skill in bringing her body to a pitch of ecstasy. The syntax builds in rhythmic waves with few interruptions by punctuation, as husband and wife, empty of self, are joined together in desire, and she blossoms under his touch like the Queen Anne's lace in the Hackensack meadows. After orgasm comes disappointment verging on hopelessness, like the mystic's difficulty in adjusting to ordinary life after his union with God. The poem ends in lines of somber alternatives, like an ultimatum: "A pious wish to whiteness gone over—/ or nothing." The word "pious" is a surprising choice, since Williams borrows the sacred, which he was not normally interested in, to describe the sex act, as John Donne did, and "gone over" is vague and ambiguous. Does he mean mowed, scrutinized, edited, defected? The dash seems to pose, bluntly, limited alternatives (the reader expects "then nothing"): either surrender consciousness or face the prospect of an inconsolable nihilism. All the energy leaches out of "Queen-Anne's Lace" in that ominous last line, but it doesn't spoil a beautiful erotic poem.

The couple's oneness does not survive the short time it takes to cross over to the next poem, "Great Mullen." (Mullen is the herb of the snapdragon family that Whitman celebrated in "Song of Myself" and that was a favorite flower in the Williams garden.) The poem, Williams commented to Thirlwall, was about a marital spat with Floss. That is the subject, but Williams gives no indication of its caustic subtext:

One leaves his leaves at home
being a mullen and sends up a lighthouse
to peer from: I will have my way,
yellow—A man with a lantern, ten
fifty, a hundred, smaller and smaller
as they grow more—

The jaunty, surreal opening—a flower sending up a lighthouse—betrays the speaker's conceit. He struts like an important personage, the Great Mullen, who "leaves his leaves at home" in order to climb to the heights from which he will scan the horizon for danger (the lighthouse becomes a ship's mast on which hangs a lantern). From this perch he peers down at his lowly wife, whose image diminishes, and in safety he waits out her storm of invective and recriminations.

That storm strikes with violent force. Floss's tirade is the most explicit proof that she knew that her husband was cheating on her, and that he was aware of how combustible her rage would be. There's no dodging the barrage of abuse that, at the end of her tether, she hurls at him ("djer-kiss," Williams glossed in a letter to Robert Wallace, was "the name of [a] very popular perfume with which ladies used to scent their lingerie"; "your kiss" and the word "jerk" lurk mockingly in "djer-kiss"):

> Liar, liar, liar!
> You come from her! I can smell djer-kiss
> on your clothes . . .
>   You are cowdung, a
> dead stick with the bark off. She is
> squirting on us both. She has had her
> hand on you!—well?—[he baits her] She has defiled
> ME.— . . . Every hair on my body will
> hold you off from me. You are a
> dungcake, birdlime on a fencerail.— . . .

Williams not only relishes her insults—he doesn't deny her charges—he delights in goading her on. In this marital altercation, he jokes: "I love you, straight, yellow / finger of God pointing to—her!" and adds his own unpleasant name-calling: "Your leaves are dull, thick / and hairy." Yet he himself condemned such conduct in "Prose About Love": "[T]o deride a wife who is disarmed because of her affection is the pastime of a numbskull." "Love," he adds, "does not seek to calumnise anyone nor to injure any." Williams doesn't bother to square these statements with his observation that "fully roused men in every age have had all the lovers they wanted, but usually one wife—imagined or real." Does he count himself among the "strong men" who vaunt their boldness or the weaklings who keep their mistresses secret? Williams vacillates between the two positions. If the long-suffering wife vents her hate, well, "flame will be tied to the heels of love in no other way." It's a healthy sign of "sturdiness holding its own." In "Great Mullen," however, an unrepentant Williams makes clear that he will not change his ways. (Calling her "yellow," like a nickname, squeezes an extra drop of gall on her wound.) Williams gets the last, gloating laugh in the poem: in a reversal of the initial image, he pretends that he's a lowly "cricket waving his antennae" and she's "high, grey, and straight." Once again the devious poet paints her a humorless grey. In the letter to Wallace, Williams further explicates the poem: "The dialogue is correctly assumed to be between a young poet and his wife, with whome [sic] he is deeply in love but to who he has been unfaithful—in the way a man and a woman in the modern world often are. The reference to ejecta, 'burd [sic] lime' etc, is disgust with himself—but he will not evade speaking of it. God be my witness."

The extent of the malaise that hounds Williams can be measured by his short poem "Waiting." Greeted by "the happy shrieks" of his children, his "heart sinks. / I am crushed." "It seems much as if Sorrow / had tripped up my heels," and he is not sure what words he should address to Floss, contrition or terms of divorce. In "Portrait of the Author," despair engulfs him. He gazes coldly at a cold world at home, while around him birch leaves open in spring; he is maddened by the burning and seething exfoliation of leaves obeying natural law:

> My rooms will receive me. But my rooms
> are no longer sweet spaces where comfort
> is ready to wait on me with its crumbs.
> A darkness has brushed them. The mass
> of yellow tulips in the bowl is shrunken.
> Every familiar object is changed and dwarfed.
> I am shaken, broken against a might
> that splits comfort, blows apart
> my careful partitions, crushes my house
> and leaves me—with shrinking heart
> and startled, empty eyes—peering out
> into a cold world.

Any magic charm that protected the couple's domestic tranquillity is helpless against the implacable force that "blows apart / [his] careful partitions" and leaves him in misery. The verbs and adjectives brilliantly communicate Williams's dread that his house, his marriage, is in ruins; he faces doom. "Mad with terror" and envious, he watches the fury of nature unfolding before him; humbled, he wishes for the oblivion drink can provide and waits for the end. "And it ends." But he couldn't put the lid back on Pandora's box. Uncertainty ruled and roiled his love life and his poems; the frigid blasts of winter would return. But crises also brought out resilience and resoluteness in Williams. "New thresholds, new anatomies," Hart Crane would write in "Voyages," a motto fit for the doctor poet to engrave above the lintel of 9 Ridge Road.

<h1 style="text-align:center">3.</h1>

In 1922, Williams withdrew for a year into virtual poetic hibernation. He published only a handful of poems, all of which steered clear of his messy home relations. Instead, they described, with the precision and detail of an artist painting a still life, a wild orchard, a bull, fish, and a performance by the Bat Theatre of Russia. The language and forms are restrained, effective, but unexceptional. That Williams stopped writing poems about Floss or other women does not mean the couple's problems had been smoothed out. Rather, they lived together, on and off, in purgatory. Their children were not oblivious to the discord. In an interview a few years ago, his son Paul recalled William Eric telling him that he had overheard their father pleading with Floss for sexual favors, only to be curtly rejected. Although this memory was seventy years old and based on hearsay, Floss's angry obduracy seemed plausible: the poems corroborate it. At eighty-seven and suffering from Parkinson's, Paul Williams, the younger son, spoke straightforwardly about his father's adulteries. He was sure they deeply hurt Floss, but he did not think them a cosmic betrayal, as William Eric did. Bill, Jr., agreed to talk to me and invited me to 9 Ridge Road, but he was so protective of his mother, even many years after her death, that when he opened the door he glared at me, growing beet red in the face, and in a preemptive strike exclaimed, "If you're a bloodhound come to sniff out my father's affairs, well, there weren't any." I was taken aback and puzzled by this vehement greeting. Surely he knew that based on the evidence laid out in the poems and the *Autobiography*, this denial was not plausible. As I had come with the blessing of James Laughlin, his father's former publisher, William Eric had no reason to believe I had prurient designs for the interview. I reasoned that his filial attachment to Floss had led to this irascible outburst, a theory later confirmed by Laughlin.

Adducing further proof of his father's unfaithfulness, Paul Williams recalled being taken two or three times to a hospital to visit a woman who had given birth to a baby girl. Paul broadly hinted that this might have been his father's love child: the hospital, at a considerable distance from Rutherford, was not one his father was affiliated with. Paul spoke of an electric current passing between the woman and Bill—and lodging in the boy's mind. I have not been able to verify this startling allegation in any official records, like a birth certificate. But this skeleton summoned from the family closet danced before us in the room. Why, I wondered, would Paul, in a Machiavellian ploy, fabricate a tall tale about his father once siring an illegitimate child, guard the secret for decades, only to blurt it out before a stranger? (Paul's wife, Betty, scowled when she realized that he had confided a memory she considered either unreliable or best kept from the public's gaze.) From our conversation it was clear that Paul admired his father greatly for his many accomplishments, and harbored no covert desire to besmirch his character.

But there is one tantalizing clue, one piece of internal evidence in a passage of Williams's 1927 journal, which might corroborate his son's memory. Williams wrote down the name of a girl child with the meticulous care required of doctors when they sign birth certificates: an identity and parentage are at stake. In his journal entry, Williams insists that she is "real." Then he concludes, with defiant elation, "The thought of her illegitimate conception fills me with joy. I conceived her. I begat her—under the powdery light in the falling leaves—the day I coughed and spat at the telephone and nearly choked when the liquor went down my windpipe."

This is no drunkard's hallucination: Williams remembers the romantic al fresco scene of the conception fondly, proudly. Nor is it a dramatic confession of a long-repressed sin, like Hester Prynne and Dimmesdale's in *The Scarlet Letter*, though a spasm of panic and guilt may be inferred from the three verbs, "coughed," "spat," and "choked," that rack his body. However, Williams scrupulously refrains from revealing who the mother of the child was, as his father had withheld the name of *his* putative father, and with good reason: if Floss read the journal, the odds of an emotional cataclysm destroying his marriage and his career would be vastly increased. No apology would win Floss's forgiveness. Williams knew he was playing with dynamite, so he made sure the incriminating paragraph never fell into her hands. The journal was sealed and locked away, but not, significantly, destroyed.

EIGHT

Experimental Breakthroughs

In the 1920s, Williams worked to develop a voice that would be personally unique and recognizably American. Immature and insecure in art as in life, angry at both the New World and the Old, he longed to establish himself as an important literary figure. In this period, his artistic coming-of-age paralleled America's emergence as a world power, and his search for an American language—even his relationships with American and European artists—was part of the larger history of American culture.

In pursuing a sound and style that would be unmistakably his, and unmistakably American, Williams struggled to define his identity. He believed that America's lack of cultural traditions and social texture made it a hard place to create art. Yet in his personal demonology, Europe was assigned the role of villain, the capital of empire and cultural superiority, and America its colony in shackles. Williams felt patronized and inadequate, and resented it. He'd learn from Europe's excellences when he was damn well ready. Still, his anger did not blind him to the painfully obvious limitations he would have to overcome on native grounds.

Williams was of course aware of his literary forebears. He knew he was echoing the complaints of Nathaniel Hawthorne and Henry James (though he irascibly and unfairly dismissed Emerson and Thoreau as imitators). He acknowledged Edgar Allan Poe as an antecedent who made art despite the deficiencies of his environment. He felt himself particularly aligned with Walt Whitman's "liberty of choice," inclusiveness, quickening of the senses, and colloquialism. Nevertheless, he didn't want people to think of him as Whitman diluted.

He knew that in his own time, too, he did not labor entirely in isolation.

There were other homegrown rebels working with native materials. Marianne Moore, for instance, he praised as a pioneer who had skillfully planted modernism in American soil and harvested a crop of poems with a rugged style distinctively her own. In an essay on Moore, he wrote:

> Miss Moore, using the same material as all others before her, comes at it so effectively at a new angle as to throw out of fashion the classical conventional poetry to which one is used and puts her own and that about her in its place. The old stops are discarded. This must antagonize many. Furthermore, there is a multiplication, a quickening, a burrowing through, a blasting, a flight over—it is modern . . . with superlative effect.

American efforts in other arts paralleled the literary struggle. Among composers, for example, Charles Ives and Aaron Copland were committed to establishing an American musical identity. Copland drew on jazz and the blues. At its premiere his composition called *Ukelele Serenade* elicited guffaws and jeers from the cultural elite who looked to Europe for direction in matters of musical taste, but Copland ignored them and persevered, as did Williams, in his quest for a bold, essentially American synthesis of high and popular arts.

The first project that emerged from Williams's decision to experiment with long forms was a mongrel he titled *The Great American Novel*. It is neither great nor a novel, but it is indisputably American in its ambition and its mockery of that ambition. Williams claimed facetiously in his *Autobiography* that the book was about a love affair between a comely red Ford roundabout and a sleek, virile Mack truck—hardly an epic theme. Two coy passages about cars, even allowing for Williams's passion for driving them—he was "no milquetoast on the road," William Eric recalls, and even gave in on occasions to road rage—fail to qualify as satisfactory plot or pattern of motifs. In truth, Williams lacked any idea what he wanted to say, so once again he improvised.

It's not easy to classify *The Great American Novel*. In its sixty-odd pages, it most resembles a journal into which Williams crammed whatever was pressing on his mind: notes about medical cases, snatches of dialogue with a Russian émigré who criticizes the poet's vehement attacks on Europe as childish jingoism, a memory of meeting Charles Demuth at a Philadelphia boardinghouse in 1903, a brief lecture on how mercury is inserted in thermometers, and, above all, assorted episodes from the violent history of the New World, from De Soto's burial in the Mississippi River to the Burr-Hamilton duel to the Mormons' westward trek and the massacre at Mountain Meadow. These are like outtakes from *In the American Grain*, which would appear three years later.

The Great American Novel is divided into chapters, but that's Williams's only concession to convention. He has erased the lines that separated the episodic entries in *Kora* from the italicized commentaries and that gave that book a semblance of coherence, and he refuses to furnish logical transitions. Yet the reader seldom gets lost in the narrative as it shifts gears and motors to a new topic. In one paragraph, for example, Williams describes how for a lark one night he drove on the sidewalk for several yards, then careened back on the road. Nobody saw or was harmed by this daredevil impulse. It was satisfying to break the law, and not be caught, and then go on his merry way. That pretty much describes the zany structure he devised for *The Great American Novel*. One might call it a loose collage.

Again and again the book denounces Europe: "Europe is nothing to us. Simply nothing. Their music is death to us. We are starving—not dying—not dying mind you—but lean-bellied for words." Even Joyce, whom he normally lauded for his revolutionary art, is assailed as "a priest, a roisterer of the spirit, . . . an epicurean of romance," whose "real, if hidden, service" was to be the Simón Bolívar of words, freeing them "for their proper uses." Whenever he damns Europe and its "complicated consciousness," his voice grows strident and he emulates Apollo, that godly sore loser, flaying his rival Marsyas. He does not spare America his contempt either. In overheated rhetoric he belittles the country as Yahoos and know-nothings: "America is a mass of pulp, a jelly, a sensitive plate ready to take whatever print you want to put on it—We have no art, no manners, no intellect—we have nothing. We water at the eyes of our own stupidity. We have only mass movement like a sea. But we are not a sea."

When a sudden rush of pride in his iconoclasm makes Williams feel euphoric, he wakes Floss to announce, "I have added a new chapter to the art of writing. I feel sincerely that all they say of me is true, that I am truly a great man and a great poet." With droll wit, she deflates his tongue-in-cheek pomposity and elation: "What did you say, dear, I have been asleep?" Boasting, even in jest, brings Williams no closer to finding a solution to his dilemma: even if he succeeds in sundering America from its European models, where can he find homegrown examples that would make Europe sit up and take notice? He doesn't know. Pumping himself up, releasing a shower of words to help himself think, he romances "dear Miss Word" as if she were his "poetic sweetheart." Faithful to his mantra "The words must become real," he prospects for words as a forty-niner panned for gold in the High Sierras and itemizes the life cycle of words: "Words are the flesh of yesterday. Words roll, spin, flare up, rumble, trickle, foam— Slowly they lose momentum. Slowly they cease to stir. At last they break up into their letters." Williams appears to be signing a death certificate for the American linguistic corpse. "America is lost," he cries. But no, it can be saved through "suffering recorded in palpitating syllables." How? Williams climbs into his pulpit to explain:

> The imagination will not down. If it is not a dance, a song, it becomes an outcry, a protest. If it is not flamboyance it becomes deformity; if it is not art, it becomes crime. Men and women cannot be content, any more than children, with the mere facts of a humdrum life—the imagination must adorn and exaggerate life, must give a splendor and grotesqueness, beauty and infinite depth. And the mere acceptance of these things from without is not enough—it is not enough to agree and assert when the imagination demands for satisfaction creative energy. Flamboyance presses faith in that energy—it is a shout of delight, a declaration of richness. It is at least the beginning of art.

The afflatus upon him, Williams exhorts us to find the grace that imagination's holy powers alone bestow. If in the beginning were the American Words, where can he find them incarnated? One place is in the speech of Appalachian mountain women and men who can get "plumb crazy over the yaller lady slippers up that-a-way," or in the natural homilies of Ma Duncan, an itinerant midwife and healer who, like Williams, went out at all times on "errands of mercy." Her natural piety awes the poet. She explains why she stretches out on the grass: "So as I can hear what the old earth has to say me . . . Reckon it says, 'Quit your fussin' you old fool. Ain't God kept your gang a young uns all straight so fur? He ain't a-going back on you now, just because they're growd.'" She also displays the gift of tongues of an eco-evangelist preacher: "I wish you could have seen the great old trees that used to be here and a preachin' the gospel of beauty.

But folks is all for money and all for self. Some-day when they've cut off all the beauty that God planted to point us to him, folks will look round and wonder what us human bein's is here fur—"

Ma Duncan is a surrogate for Williams here. Paul Mariani has objected that because Williams had never been to Appalachia, his transcription of the mountain folks' speech is secondhand and contrived. Williams's retort, one suspects, would be to warn against prohibiting the imagination from flinging open the doors of consciousness and entering into the treasury where stories and language and figures from the past and regions he hadn't visited were—as he did on a grand scale when he wrote *In the American Grain*. The fact that the speeches he put into the mouths of Eric the Red, Cortés and Montezuma, and Père Sébastien Rasles were culled from books, diaries, and letters doesn't discredit them. Ma Duncan and Lory's modest "shouts of delight" and "declarations of richness" are akin to Daniel Boone's hymn to the beauty of the New World wilderness.

In *The Great American Novel*, Williams teaches us "the essentials of the American situation." The crass young nation might not value its poets, but they can be original. In poetry as in other crafts, it takes time and seasoning to progress from apprentice to journeyman to master. Williams's own progress was marked by the publication of this modest book, through Pound's good offices, in Bill Bird's Three Mountains Press series, in the distinguished company of Hemingway's *In Our Time* and Pound's *Indiscretions*.

Poetically, 1922 was a landmark year for Williams. When *The Dial* published *The Waste Land*, Williams felt that his dream of "a new art form rooted in the locality which should give it fruit" had been as blighted as the landscape Eliot evoked so memorably. For the rest of his life he demonized Eliot's poem, often in extreme language. In the *Autobiography*, he called it "the great catastrophe to our letters" that had "wiped out our world as if an atomic bomb had been dropped upon it and our brave sallies into the unknown were turned to dust." (The first person plural means to show that the damage was not just to his personal ambitions.) Williams conceded Eliot's vast erudition and technical prowess—"metrical construction," he called it—while deploring the ease with which Eliot "gave the poem back to the academics." "I had to watch him carry my world off with him, the fool, to the enemy."

The extreme language shows how intensely personal his response was, as if his best friend had run off with his wife. Class antipathy played a role, too: Williams made no bones about loathing Eliot as a snob and a reptilian man. Knowing he had not yet developed a mature style, Williams felt at a disadvantage taking on Eliot—he was a guerrilla with limited weapons battling a general leading a large, confident army—and was afraid that, overshadowed by Eliot, nobody would notice him. From 1922 on, resentment of and competition with Eliot cast a dark shadow over much that he wrote for the rest of the decade.

That Pound was godfather and editor of, and zealous pitchman for, Eliot's poem upset and enraged Williams. In his sibling rivalry with Eliot, he lost the battle for Pound's approval. So deeply did this affect Williams that in 1939, a full seventeen years later, he wrote a letter to Pound, still vigorously setting out his dissent:

> I'm glad you like Eliot's verse, but I'm warning you, the only reason it doesn't smell is that it's synthetic. Maybe I'm wrong, but I distrust that bastard more than any writer I know in the world today. He can write, granted, but it's like walking into a church to me. I can't do it without a bad feeling at the pit of the stomach. Nothing has been learned there since the simplicities were prevented from becoming multiform by arrested growth. Bird's-eye foods, suddenly frozen at fifty degrees below zero, under pressure, at perfect maturity, immediately after being picked from [for?] the can. It's pathological with me perhaps. I hope not, but I am infuriated by such things. I am infuriated because the arrest has taken place, just at the point of risk, just at the point where the magnificence might possibly have happened, just when the danger threatened, when the tradition might have led to the difficult new things. But the God damn liars prefer popes, prefer freezing, prefer if you use the image, "the sterilization of the Christ they profess." And the result is canned to make literature, with all the flavor, with all the pomp, while the real thing rots under their noses and they duck to the other side of the street. I despise and detest them. They are moles on a pig's belly instead of tits. Christ, how I hate their guts and the more so because Eliot, like his monumental wooden throne on wheels, that he carries around with him to worship, Eliot takes the place of the realizable actual, which is that much held back from realization precisely, of existence.

It would be a mistake to read this letter as merely the ravings of a envious poet. Williams's hilarious invective aside, his diagnosis has a shrewd logic: if Eliot's poetic is diseased and repulsive like the moles on a pig's belly, it can't nurture the art because it has no "tits." Eliot's poems are a symbol of a tradition that might have led to "new difficult things," but instead suffered from "arrested development" and religious sterility. By 1939, time has made Williams confident of the artistic ground he's standing on, though "the realizable actual" is a vague slogan with which to win converts to his cause.

In 1922, however, Eliot's conquest of the English-speaking world resembled a juggernaut, leaving Williams trapped in poetic hell with all the exits sealed. Struck by Eliot's "sardonic bullet," Williams claimed it would take him twenty years to recover the poetic line from "stodginess." In fact, he refused to take defeat quietly and began plotting his counterattack on two fronts: *Spring and All,* an odd mix of poetry and prose published in 1923, and *In the American Grain,* a sweeping and eclectic study of the origins of the American character through historical portraiture, published in 1925.

In 1922, still searching for a sturdy yet pliant set of poetic principles, Williams consoled himself with the belief that frequent raids on the luxuriant storehouse of the imagination would yield plentiful American themes, as they had for Whitman. *Spring and All* would be Williams's experiment to see what a world kindled by the imagination would look like. Reading this remarkable, if uneven, work is like walking through an artist's studio where paintings hang on the walls, some in a complete and polished state, others in a rough and sketchy one. The restless eye lingers on objects strewn about the room: driftwood, an African mask, a child's photograph, a recipe clipped from a glossy magazine, a friend's novel half read. The atmosphere hums with intense activity and high purpose; people gather to drink, smoke, flirt, gossip, debate the merits of Cubism, read poems from a crinkled manuscript. The imagination visits, hovers, and departs. The second half of Williams's title, *and All,* is apt: everything, except the kitchen sink, is allowed into this sprawling work.

Williams never disputed the fact that his slingshot of a poem couldn't knock down Eliot's Goliath. As he admitted, "Nobody ever saw it—it had no circulation at all." McAlmon printed 324 copies of *Spring and All,* most of which went unsold. (Not wanting another bawling out from abroad,

Williams never showed it to Pound for comment and editing.) The prose, a wild throwback to the improvisations of *Kora in Hell*, trots out every Dada trick in the repertoire: typographical mayhem—"Chapter headings . . . printed upside down on purpose, the chapters . . . numbered all out of order, sometimes with a Roman numeral, sometimes with an Arabic, anything that came in handy"—and an antic blend of "philosophy and nonsense."

Most tellingly, Williams added, "It made sense to me, at least to my disturbed mind—because it was disturbed at that time—but I doubt if it made any sense to anyone else." That "disturbed mind" is manifest in the opening pages, and though Williams doesn't name "the Traditionalists of Plagiarism," it's clear that his incendiary proposals for a cleansing apocalypse, which at moments sound like a Futurist manifesto advocating the necessary hygiene of violence, are aimed at Eliot and his legions of admirers. The prose snarls melodramatically—it is cranky, sportive, vacillating, vituperative—as if Williams, in permanent opposition to the prevailing taste, expected any readers who picked up his book to ridicule him and his ideas. This venting of anger was therapeutic for him. Ironically, he was not afraid to pilfer from Eliot from time to time—for example, in "The Descent."

Williams knew he had no ripened alternate model to Eliot's vision and method in *The Waste Land* to propose, so *Spring and All* does not attempt, poem by poem, to emulate Eliot's erudition or counter *The Waste Land*'s pessimistic view of European civilization's decline. Williams lacks a unifying vision or narrative strategy to do so. In the very first sentence of *Spring and All*, he crouches in a defensive posture: "If anything of moment results—so much the better. And so much the more likely will it be that no one will want to see it." He then quotes a pillorying of his own poems as shallow, pagan, ignorant of suffering, "positively repellent . . . heartless, cruel, make fun of humanity . . . Rhyme you may perhaps take away but rhythm! Why there is none in your work whatever. Is this what you call poetry? It is the very antithesis of poetry. It is antipoetry. It is the annihilation of life upon which you are bent." If these accusations were true, Williams deserved to lose both his poetic and medical licenses, and the public was right to blackball his experimental work! That Williams is willing to air such charges—he took umbrage whenever a critic or poet called his work "anti-poetry," as Wallace Stevens did in his 1934 introduction to Williams's *Collected Poems, 1921–1931*—shows again his unique blend of recklessness and moral courage flecked with grim humor.

This opening gambit soon proves a sly debater's trick. The critic follows his diatribe with a litany of traditional formulas for poetic greatness that are nothing but middlebrow banalities: "[p]oetry that used to go hand in hand with life, poetry that interpreted our deepest promptings, poetry that inspired, that led us forward to new discoveries, new depths of tolerance, new heights of exaltation." When his accuser assails modernism as a fiendish art that will cause "the death of poetry," Williams is acquitted of being the sole murderer; he belongs to an international gang of literary assassins!

Though it won't curry favor with the old guard, Williams consecrates himself to serving the imagination, which is a force worshipped throughout *Spring and All*, "To refine, to clarify, to intensify that eternal moment in which we alone live." Indeed, that marriage of poet and imagination is a happy one, without incidents of disloyalty, though not free of stress. In Book 3 of *Paterson* (1949), Williams admits that "to find one phrase that will / lie married beside another for delight? / —seems beyond attainment." Nonetheless, he trusts that through patience and passion the inevitable dry spells will pass; the imagination keeps its seasons as nature does. "The riddle of a man and a woman," by contrast, is not easily solved. "Love is no comforter rather a nail in the skull," Williams declares. Within a marriage both partners can hide and plot to destroy each other. If it is perilous for a poet to "*divorce* [himself; my italics] from life," as he says in *Spring and All*, so is it folly to escape a troubled marriage through divorce. Postponing any decision, he brazenly steals Whitman's rhetoric of camaraderie and amativeness, which gilds the opening stanza of "Song of Myself": "In the imagination, we are from henceforth (so long as you read) locked in a fraternal embrace, the classic caress of author and reader. We are one. Whenever I say 'I' I mean also 'you.'" The "caress of author and reader" is welcome; the embrace of husband and wife is fraught. The imagination is androgynous. Curiously, Williams here fails to give sufficient credit to Whitman as a bold innovating forerunner. He seems to need to shove old Walt out of the way so that he has room to upstage the wily old master.

In the next chapter, labeled chapter 19, Williams dons prophetic robes and in the name of his god pours out his wrath upon the human race. Williams foresees a holocaust that eclipses anything Eliot dreamed up in *The Waste Land*. A carnivalesque literalism takes over the prose, relieved by gestures of Dadaistic clowning. "Intoxicated by prohibitions," the imagination goes on a rampage to annihilate "every human creature on the face of the earth"; only the lowest organisms on the evolutionary scale survive to inherit the earth. Williams's vision in *Spring and All* differs from Eliot's in this: there's no Fisher King with a mysterious wound sitting mournfully and passively on the banks of a river; symbols of cultural ruin are invoked rarely (the one notable exception is "The pure products of America"); no scraps of Christian or Sanskrit liturgy, so integral to Eliot's scheme of redemption, are chanted. As proselytizer and henchman for the imagination, Williams levels the world in order to remake it in his own image. On his banner is stamped a half-mocking, half-bombastic creed: "I speak for the integrity of the soul and the greatness of life's inanity; the formality of its boredom; the orthodoxy of its stupidity." (One would expect Williams to proclaim "the boredom of its formality" and "the stupidity of its orthodoxy," qualities he despised in Eliot, but he's spoofing Eliot's solemnity.) Curiously, the imagination repeats evolution exactly as it had previously unfolded, yet "everything IS new." Novelty, beloved by American poets since Emerson and Whitman, may appeal to Williams as a key to secure escape from his "mind-forged manacles," but it looks at first suspiciously like the old faith. Williams repeats his creed that the imagination is "undeceived," but it's also aggressively capricious. In short, it's a composite of many of Williams's own character traits.

For Eliot, the land is sterile and "April is the cruelest month"; for Williams, spring is a harbinger of nature's fecundity. For Eliot, the crowds streaming across London Bridge are a procession of the living dead; for Williams, the crowds at a baseball game are beautiful, fickle, rowdy, "alive, venomous"; but in a democracy, this sleeping giant, he feared, could turn into an ugly mob. In the prose of *Spring and All*, Williams succumbs to few illusions: nature blossoms in an industrial slag heap, beautifying the ugly. He tests different styles: "It is spring by Stinking River where a magnolia tree, without leaves, before what was once a farmhouse, now a ramshackle home for millworkers, raises its straggling branches of ivorywhite flowers." These straightforward sentences hew closely to Williams's binary patterns in the prose of this period—"stinking," "ramshackle," and "straggling" played off against "magnolia" and "ivorywhite flowers."

More problematic are those passages in which Williams employs a heightened, dense syntax to announce spring's approach:

> In that huge and microscopic career of time, as it were a wild horse racing in an illimitable pampa under the stars, describing immense

and microscopic circles with his hoofs on the solid turf, running
without a stop for the millionth part of a second until he is aged
and worn to a heap of skins, bones and ragged hoofs—In that majestic progress of life, that gives the exact impression of Phidias'
frieze, the men and beast of which, though they seem of the rigidity
of marble are not so but move, with blinding rapidity, though we do
not have the time to notice it, their legs advancing a millionth part
of an inch every thousand years—In that progress of life which
seems stillness itself in the mass of its movements—at last SPRING
is approaching.

This passage is a hodgepodge of Imagism, echoes of Keats ("Phidias'
frieze"), grandiose measurements of time and progress, ostentatious flour-
ishes of syntax (for instance, the parallel openings of sentences that mimic
chant, one of Whitman's rhetorical trademarks). Perhaps Williams refers
to Phidias in order to refute the view of him as a semiliterate versifier,
which he suspected was the literary community's verdict whispered behind his back. One hears Williams straining to impress in this elliptical
paragraph; modernist experimentalism runs to seed. Still, it attests to
Williams's dogged eagerness to explore new combinations, even if the results expose glaring faults. Improvisation had served him well in *Kora in
Hell*, so he turned to it again when temporarily blocked, as he would un-
pack his troubles to an old reliable friend.

Several poems come apart at the seams, as if from a structural tear he
can't detect or sew up. Others are brilliant, original, and coherent, as recognizably American as Charles Ives's spiky rhythms and mixture of high
cultural dissonance and village green band marches. The first poem to
emerge from the topsy-turvy prose sounds nothing like Eliot's voice:

By the road to the contagious hospital
under the surge of the blue
mottled clouds driven from the
northeast—a cold wind. Beyond, the
waste of broad, muddied fields
brown with dried weeds, standing and fallen

patches of standing water
the scattering of tall trees

All along the road the reddish
purplish, forked, upstanding, twiggy
stuff of bushes and small trees
with dead, brown leaves under them
leafless vines—

lifeless in appearance, sluggish
dazed spring approaches—

They enter the new world naked,
cold, uncertain of all
save that they enter. All about them
the cold, familiar wind—
Now the grass, tomorrow
the stiff curl of wildcarrot leaf

One by one objects are defined—
it quickens: clarity, outline of leaf

But now the stark dignity of
entrance—Still, the profound change
has come upon them: rooted, they
grip down and begin to awaken

"By the road to the contagious hospital" describes three kinds of par-turition: the process by which spring emerges out of sere winter, aware-ness out of confusion, and a poem's form out of a welter of details. The poem opens with an array of prepositions that coerce the eye to shift perspec-tive, to look up and down, to search for relation and pattern. Appropri-ately, because the freezing nor'easter grips the earth like a contagious disease and only the clouds move swiftly—the word "surge" sets them in motion—the stanza omits predication. When Williams takes a second, more careful look around him, however, he sees that the mulch of dead leaves serves as a placenta for new life: spring is ready to burst into bloom, as a baby is ready for its journey down the birth canal.

In stanza three, adjectives cluster like buds on the tree and bushes; "standing" changes, subtly, into "upstanding" and brown into red and purple. The "leafless vines" chime with "lifeless" across white space until "sluggish / dazed spring" approaches. Williams's pronouns act dazed and elliptical, too, as though uncertain of the things they should stand for, entering without fanfare, like the naked plants and, by extension, the words the poet brings with stark dignity into the American world. There is nothing routine or hyperbolic about any new birth. Anything can go wrong, including a poem with defects.

Williams's heavy enjambment controls the tempo of each stanza; birth moves forward implacably, in spasms or evenly spaced contractions. Whereas the first stanza scuds along like the mottled clouds, the third stanza slows down because the piling up of adjectives acts as a brake. To avoid full end stops and to emphasize transitions and hesitancies, Williams substitutes dashes for periods. Change is irresistible, as the verbs "quicken" and "awaken" underscore, but it can't be rushed.

"By the road to the contagious hospital" offers solid proof of Williams's mastery of the basic elements of poetic style: line breaks, tonal shadings, stanzaic integrity, increments of repetition that function like crescendos and diminuendos. He listened to the acoustic properties of words with the same care and skill he devoted to the beating of a patient's heart. In a letter to Denise Levertov in 1961, Robert Duncan remarked: "We do not believe that Williams imagined the road to the contagious hospital . . . —in the sense that he made [it] up—but he followed the melody in which the . . . poem set into movement his form."

Poem 2 moves indoors, the cold winds giving way to the hothouse atmosphere of a Charles Demuth watercolor, *Tuberoses* (1922), which renders a flowerpot set on a table near a lamp. (Bill and Floss bought this work from Demuth and hung it in their dining room next to Demuth's watercolor *Pink Lady Slippers,* a gift "in appreciation for food, lodging, and medical care in the early stages of his diabetes.") Initially, the flowerpot, table, and lamp seem standard Victorian props; indeed, except for the loose typography, the poem reads like one of Ernest Dowson's enervated lyrics tinged with eroticism. But Williams and Demuth sketch branch, leaf, petals, and moss with the practiced eye of a modernist who deliberately breaks up the surface into whirling planes of light and dark. In 2, the purplish and reddish buds near the contagious hospital burst into flame and the "transpiercing light" floods both watercolor and poem. For Williams, a kind of romantic ecstasy is manifested in a jubilant riot of color and vigorous words: "spill," "darting," "lays," "transpiercing," "contending," and "reaching." The dark pit of the pot and the "petals darkened with mauve" only underscore the revelry of light, the gaiety of life, both of which have no counterpart in Eliot's long poem.

That gaiety virtually disappears in the prose passages that Williams interleaves with his poems in *Spring and All*. The prose can be exasperatingly slapdash, hackneyed, cloudy, and didactic. *Spring and All*, Donald Davie remarks, with some justice, "had the format of many pages of hectic, discontinuous, and obscurely polemical prose, out of which the poems rose at irregular intervals like so many knobby outcrops from a sea of lava." Davie fails to see that Williams's method aims, worthily enough, at getting rid of "crude symbolism," "strained associations, complicated ritualistic forms designed to separate the work from 'reality'—such as rhyme, meter as meter and not as the essential of the work, one of its words." Williams insists, rightly, that he is the sworn enemy not of meter and rhyme but of "layers of demoded words and shapes."

The poems of *Spring and All* realize Williams's sizable ambitions roughly half of the time. When inspiration deserts him, he resorts, like any stymied poet, to "demoded words" and such questionable gimmicks as lines that trail off into the void, as if he gave up on a metaphor and forgot to delete it. Some poems protrude awkwardly rather than being artfully laid into the sequence to form an elegant mosaic. Poem 4, for example, titled "Flight into the City" in the 1934 *Collected Poems*, sketches a thirteen-year-old Rutherford schoolgirl, probably a patient, whom Williams described to Thirlwall as "fresh, and rough, and tough" (he had a soft spot for spunky adolescent girls):

The Easter stars are shining
above lights that are flashing—
coronal of the black—

                              Nobody
to say it—
            Nobody to say: pinholes

Thither I would carry her

among the lights—

Burst it asunder
break through to the fifty words
necessary—

a crown for her head with

castles upon it, skyscrapers
Filled with nut-chocolates—

dovetame winds—
tars of tinsel

In the spirit of the season, the Easter stars are lauded as "coronal of the black," but that's nature's one triumph over art. Unexpectedly, Williams casts himself as the magus who must utter the taboo word "pinholes." Why would the aperture through which children love to squint at swirling patterns of stars be the password, unless to establish poetic artifice as a rival to nature? "The man of imagination who turns to art for release and fulfillment of his baby promises contends with the sky," he declares in a prose passage. This "seeking to invent and design," he implies, is a heroic labor. "Pinholes" would seem a trivial image, yet it mysteriously releases some inhibition, since Williams next turns, in fantasy, into a Hades who abducts the nymphet Persephone from the streets of Rutherford and transports her not to the underworld but to New York, the city of light. (Where whimsy is needed, Williams musters the trite line "Thither I would carry her.")

What does Williams mean by "Burst it asunder / break through"? Duncan called it "a programmatic sensationalism." Is he dreaming of bursting the girl's hymen or simply empowering the imagination to purge poems of "strained associations"? Presumably those fifty breakthrough words he mentions are necessary to forge a style that will catapult him into the front ranks of modernism. The vehicle for his display of gallantry in the last two stanzas is troubling: is he bribing the teenager with an Easter gift of chocolates in a glass jar festooned in tinsel? Her "coronal" is a horned hat of plenty decorated with skyscrapers (contemporary castles) such as dot the Manhattan skyline. If a poem demonstrates personality, as Williams asserts in the prose, what does this poem, in which he takes an imagined joyride with a suburban Lolita to the wicked city, tell us about him? Since there's not a shred of evidence that he ever acted out any pedophiliac fantasies, such a poem must fulfill a hidden need to dabble in forbidden realms, like Elena, and to defy social and artistic rules. In poem 4, Williams's typography revels in thumbing its nose at barriers. Words, clauses, sentences, and stanzas begin or end at will, run for one, two, or three lines, luxuriate in white space, skittishly disregard authority; only the occasional dash reminds one of institutional order. Williams has imbibed the Dadaesque liqueurs: "arabesques, skips and jumps about the room with a lamp on one's head—for a crown," as Robert Duncan put it. This play is harmless artifice to set the imagination and libido free. The Baroness would have been amused, surprised, and pleased at Williams's headgear.

Foul weather—a "black wind"—and a murderous mood blow through poem 5. Humanity is "beastly," voices are "strident," "men knock blindly together / splitting their heads open." However accurate his diagnosis, he is not referring to Oswald Spengler's warning that Western civilization was in irreversible decline, a motif crucial to *The Waste Land*. To subscribe to such a view of history would be tantamount to betraying his faith in the American future, its robust youth condemned to premature senescence. The source of Williams's pessimism is personal: his frustrated striving to achieve in verse the equivalent exquisite rhythms and sensuous plasticity of May Wirth, a circus rider whose body, as his friend Marsden Hartley had written, is "harmonically arranged for personal delight."

Williams splashes "cold rain" on the prospect of erotic pleasure. His dejected playfulness is a symptom of Poem 5's blatant feeling and scrappy form; the imagination falters and slips, as he recognizes in the last lines, "into the old mode, how hard to / cling firmly to the advance—". Thus when Williams echoes Whitman or alludes to Pound's bowmen of Shu, for whom time passes slowly, frozen in a "winter casing of grief," he's not mimicking Eliot's penchant in *The Waste Land* for weaving together lines and snippets culled from his reading. He just can't write himself out of a rut. (Throughout *Spring and All* he's fitfully at the mercy of what he calls "emotional complexes.")

Poem 6 finds Williams absorbed in deep thought like the farmer in poem 3, toying with abstractions in order to examine his own contradictions:

No that is not it
nothing that I have done
nothing
I have done

is made up of
nothing
and the diphthong

ae

together with
the first person

singular
indicative

of the auxiliary
verb
to have

everything
I have done
is the same

if to do
is capable
of an
infinity of
combinations

involving the
moral
physical
religious

codes

for everything
and nothing
are synonymous
when

energy in vacuo
has the power
of confusion

which only to
have done nothing
can make
perfect

At first reading, this poem looks like a series of exercises in which logical propositions are broken down into their smallest units. We're not sure of Williams's intention: to parody the codes of "deep thought" or to beguile and scare us by stringing paradoxes like a high wire over the abyss of nothingness and surviving the perilous walk across it? The first line slyly refers to "Prufrock" (the reader automatically adds "at all"), as if in taking stock of his accomplishments, Williams shared that flâneur's habit of self-abasement. He is haunted by a sense of nullity. Yet ex nihilo comes the diphthong *ae*, isolated on its own line, the linguistic cell out of which he can construct an "I" and a poem. Like a genetic building block, he hazards, the auxiliary verb "to have" can bond with "everything" as easily as with "nothing." Perhaps uneasy with both slippery proposition and syntax, he subjects them to Talmudic reasoning. If "everything / I have done / is the same," then his imagination hasn't managed to reconstitute the world; it's derivative, mired in repetition. But if his lines and actions ("to do") are governed by the imagination, he can knit together bits of nothing into multiple meanings, because the possible combinations are infinite.

Typically, Williams qualifies these three possibilities at once, limiting them to sanctioned moral, physical, and religious codes; this last, surprising word occupies a line by itself, the diphthong *ae* apparently having evolved into "codes." Groping for the term he wants, he lands in the arms of the very conventional opinion he has set out to overturn. Or does he?

His meaning is tantalizingly elusive. When energy is not in a vacuum, are everything and nothing synonymous? The poem's intricate reasoning unravels before it reaches its end: there's no main clause to anchor and clinch the idea. Through a slight shift in tense, "to do" returns as "to / have done." An implied comma after "have done" would argue that the emptiness can never be filled or made perfect, but by omitting the comma Williams seems to be advocating Wordsworth's "wise passiveness," so that only to "have done nothing" can make error perfect. The last stanza echoes Stevens's "The Snow Man," where the poet listener, "nothing himself, beholds / Nothing that is not there and the nothing that is." But whereas Stevens coolly melds everything and nothing, Williams is stumped by his riddle: whether the poet fashions his verse from everything or nothing, what he creates must bear the stamp of the imperfect. This uncertainty does not panic Williams. The poem ends without a period, keeping the investigation open-ended: words are separated from references; the discourses of "deep thought" can be slothful and empty (nothing) or provocative (a road to everything). Since he hasn't quite broken away from the old sanctioned codes of what poetry is and can do, he can't decide whether what he has done in poetry has any merit.

To answer that question, he turned to the painters he admired. Foremost among them was Juan Gris, whose exacting geometric art moved Williams and reinforced his own attempts to use "the forms common to experience so as not to frighten the onlooker away but to invite him." Gris had accomplished the feat of making "familiar, simple things . . . touched by the hands during the day" appear sensuous, bewitching, and detached. Though Williams saw only a black-and-white reproduction of Gris's collage *Roses*, he lauds it in poem 7, which is as close to an ars poetica as Williams gets in *Spring and All*:

> The rose is obsolete
> but each petal ends in
> an edge, the double facet
> cementing the grooved
> columns of air—The edge
> cuts without cutting
> meets—nothing—renews
> itself in metal or porcelain—

whither? It ends—
But if it ends
the start is begun
so that to engage roses
becomes a geometry—

Sharper, neater, more cutting
figured on majolica—
the broken plate
glazed with a rose

Somewhere the sense
makes copper roses
steel roses—
The rose carried weight of love
but love is at an end—of roses

It is at the edge of the
petal that love waits

Crisp, worked to defeat
laboredness—fragile
plucked, moist, half-raised
cold, precise, touching

The place between the petal's
edge and the

From the petal's edge a line starts
that being of steel
infinitely fine, infinitely
rigid penetrates
the Milky Way

The fragility of the flower
unbruised
penetrates space

Unceremoniously, Williams announces that the rose as symbol is obsolete—long live the rose as "made object." Like a docent in an art gallery, he explains Gris's precise design as an industrial process that doesn't lose any of its power to delight the eye; indeed, its geometry engages the spectator's mind and sensibility. Two problems that vexed Williams in poem 6—"nothing" and the imperfect—hold no fear for Gris, because his collage is grounded in the "real": the "nothing" renews itself in the metal or porcelain, while the "broken plate / glazed with a rose" is still beautiful despite its flaw.

Gertrude Stein, another admirer of Gris, would have applauded his solution of making exquisite copper or steel roses that strip the painting (or poem) of sentimental associations. Gris's roses replace the "crude symbolism" of Robert Burns's famous line "My love is like a red red rose." In his early work, Williams had been susceptible to such lyric hyperbole. Now he wants verse that, when it speaks of love, is edgy. Hence, of the seven adjectives he clusters together, only "touching" recalls the vocabulary of feeling, and in this adjectival company it's technical. Because Gris "worked to defeat / laboredness," he's an excellent modernist model for Williams to emulate. In working the process out in his head, Williams is aware that it's not easy to write a Cubist poem. As such lines as "The place between the petal's / edge and the" indicate, he is unsure how to complete the measure; one thought ousts another; he continually corrects himself, reopening a question he hoped he had answered. Gris's paintbrush, by contrast, Williams likens to a telescope that penetrates space: as the metaphor exfoliates, the rose is kept alive and elicits awe. The doubling of the word "infinitely" subtly reinforces this freedom. The made rose is its own reality.

Success in one poem, however, does not guarantee success in another. There's no denying a miscellaneous quality to many of the poems in *Spring and All*, which comes of Williams's method of casually writing down "that which happens." Poem 11 is an amiable trifle. While driving, Williams notices in passing—his eyeglasses are not folded as they were at the end of the previous poem, but perched on his nose ready "to see everything"—three figures posed in a painterly composition. "The supreme importance / of this nameless spectacle / sped me by them / without a word—" Despite the "supreme importance," he doesn't have the time or inclination to stop and watch the spectacle unfold, or it requires no comment from him. He also notably declines to tell us where he's going. He just barrels along the wet road until he's arrested by the sight of "a girl with one leg / over the rail of a balcony," which makes him step on the brake. Williams typically records the scene rather than moralizing on it. The images' transient satisfactions suffice, so the poem yields modest pleasure.

The poems grouped in the middle of *Spring and All* are, like Juan Gris's copper rose, constructed out of odds and ends, utilitarian or industrial products—paper clips, glue, a spool of thread, a trunk, and motorcars. In their materiality, they are as much a part of the texture of his poems as the Queen Anne's lace and dahlias that grow in profusion there. Because things without people would be boring, Williams also takes snapshots of crowds and ordinary people. These poems in *Spring and All* constitute an informal group portrait of democratic America, circa 1923, its citizens at work and play, the young in each other's arms. From the start of his professional career, Williams had privileged access to the lives of average Americans. The cast of characters in his poems, his comédie humaine, were drawn from all walks of life: "colored women / day laborers," the town drunk, the young man with a bad heart, a "neatly coiffed, middle aged gentleman / with orderly moustaches and / well-brushed coats." A sociologist studying Rutherford and Paterson could draw on Williams's observations of these people for detailed anecdotal evidence and analysis of suburban mores and daily life.

Thus, in poem 15, Williams dispassionately examines "the dynamic mob" sitting in movie houses (the new cathedrals), enthralled by the illusions, the "selfspittle," projected on the screen—for him, this merely substitutes a secular opiate for the incense and liturgical chants by which the Catholic Church, over two millennia, won and held the allegiance of the masses. Williams does not underestimate the seductive "moral force" of movies or simply deplore it. In *The Great American Novel*, he shrewdly observes how movies "are gaudy in the imaginations of the people who watch them; gaudy with exaggerated romance, exaggerated comedy, exaggerated splendor of grotesqueness or romance . . . Such people wistfully try to find these things outside themselves; a futile, often a destructive quest." Williams published one of the early pieces of film criticism by a poet, yet he adapted more forms and techniques from art than from cinema.

In poem 16, he sketches in grisly brushstrokes an old woman, a patient in the hospital who, much like Grandmother Wellcome, fights to prevent the "old barber" Death from cutting off her life. Williams does not spare the reader from looking at the graphic images of her "jaundiced" body—a sore netherlip, toppled belly, matted hair, slobber on her handkerchief—or hearing her moan three times "I can't die." Yet by means of empathy and unusual adjective-noun pairs such as "elysian slobber" and "saffron eyeballs," Williams transfigures the old woman into an unforgettable figure of distress and pathos.

The aged woman on the verge of death is a universal icon; only the cadences of the poem imbue her with an American identity. In its racy patter and bouncy sounds, poem 17 is a set of hot licks with an unmistakably American intonation:

Our orchestra
is the cat's nuts—

Banjo jazz
with a nickelplated

amplifier to
soothe

Nobody else

but me—
They can't copy it
the savage beast—
Get the rhythm

That sheet stuff
's a lot of cheese.

Man
gimme the key

and lemme loose—
I make 'em crazy

with my harmonies—
Shoot it Jimmy

Nobody
Nobody else

but me—
They can't copy it

Williams's ear has expertly captured the jaunty rhythms, both verbal and musical, of a pickup orchestra and the American language in its popular song mode. ("Nobody else // but me" could be the refrain of a lyric in a Broadway musical.) A good-humored braggart, the speaker knows he is good at improvisation: "the cat's nuts," the "sheet stuff / 's a lot of cheese," and "gimme" and "lemme" amuse and wow audiences until they're literally out of their mind. The bandleader earns Williams's highest praise: "They can't copy it."

In an effort to free the word from "the fixities which destroy it" and let it "move independently, which distinguishes the language of poetry from the language of prose which is concerned with 'emotional implications,'" Williams contrived short-lined stanzas, mainly couplets, though sometimes he expanded them into tercets, quatrains, or sestets, as in poem 13:

Crustaceous
wedge
of sweaty kitchens
on rock
overtopping
thrusts of the sea

Waves of steel
from swarming backstreets
shell
of coral
inventing
Electricity

Lights
speckle

El Greco
lakes
in renaissance
twilight
with triphammers

which pulverize
nitrogen
of old pastures
to dodge
motorcars
with arms and legs—

Into the crucible of this poem Williams pours words drawn from the vocabulary of modern industrial processes: "electricity," "triphammers," "motorcars," "bridge stanchions" (Hart Crane's cityscape), then adds a dash of older pictorial elements—El Greco and "renaissance / twilight"—as if to temper the aggressive rawness and energy of New York City. The poem's original title, "The Agonized Spires," refers to the skyscrapers rising out of Manhattan's bedrock, a force to rival the coral reef that like a horizontal tower generates light and awesome power. In the poem, Williams records the cacophony of jackhammers at construction sites pulverizing eardrums as the "old pastures" are covered over by new buildings. (In the 1930 poem "The Flower," he would watch the girders of the George Washington Bridge being put into place and write: "For years I've been tormented by / that miracle, the buildings lit up— / / unable to say anything much to the point / though it is the major sight / / of this region. But foolish to rhapsodize over / strings of lights, the blaze of a power / / in which I have not the least part.") As the imagery and stuttering steps of the last two stanzas of poem 13 tell us, Williams finds New York an environment both magnificent and "pulverizing."

Not only poetry but also the visual arts and music add to the effect of poem 13. In his 1920 photographs of New York skyscrapers and, later in the decade, his photographs of the Ford River Rouge Complex, Williams's friend Charles Sheeler had grasped the prodigious fecundity of American technology. Sheeler neither celebrated it unconditionally nor deplored it as commercial degradation of the cityscape. In his precisionist photographs of skyscrapers in Park Row, the buildings, even when seen in shadow and smoke, rise and cluster together with a dignified sublimity and abstract beauty. The eye climbs the tiers of windows but cannot look inside at whatever human business is being transacted; nobody looks out, either. In this dense architectural milieu, emotion is beside the point. Similarly, the factories and steel foundries Sheeler depicted in 1927 are not "dark satanic mills" or symbols of oppressive materiality or capitalist aggrandizement but "totems in steel." (Joseph Stella incorporated "stanchions" and steel into his paintings of the Brooklyn Bridge.)

Perhaps because Williams's roots were in the suburbs, he felt ambivalent, like Henry Adams and Henry James, about the dynamic energy unleashed by cities. In poem 13 he highlights urban perils, agonies, and irritants: the stanchions threaten to pierce the heart; crossing a street, pedestrians take their lives into their hands; the drilling triphammers are deafening. He examines the skyscrapers and infrastructure of New York City with the methodical detachment of a civil engineer or a medical researcher. His tone is clinical, not romantic or kinetic like Hart Crane's.

Culture, as represented by El Greco and Renaissance painters, seems in this context an elitist pursuit likely to be crushed by the vortex of commerce. The kaleidoscopic effects of poem 13 put one in mind of scattered atoms waiting to be fused. It's as if Williams jotted down notes on a pad, then rushed out to a sick patient's house on an emergency call, only to find when he returned to the poem that his inspiration had flagged. Short lines can speed a poem along. The short lines of 13, however, are unwieldy, the words stacked on top of each other, then tossed about, as if by the "thrusts of the sea." The poem lacks the quality Williams himself said rhythm needed: "rapidity of motion and quality of motion."

The poem also evokes modernist music, which was sometimes made out of such noise and power. Williams never claimed more than an amateur's love and comprehension of music, and his tastes were fairly traditional, but he did venture occasionally to avant-garde concerts, guided by Paul Rosenfeld, the music reviewer for *The Dial*. When he wrote *Spring and All*, Williams had not yet heard George Antheil's *Ballet Mécanique*, which cut loose with a battery of gongs, sirens, electric bells, and even airplane propellers. (Pound had helped launch Antheil's career in Paris, and the Frenchman had reciprocated by aiding Pound with the composition of his opera *Testament*, based on the life of Villon.) But when he heard Antheil's tour de force performed at Carnegie Hall in 1927, even without the sixteen player pianos the score called for, Williams became its champion.

The event aroused controversy and bewilderment in equal measures. American audiences were shocked by Antheil's sonic boom—some walked noisily out in protest—but Williams enjoyed it, as he had Duchamp's *Urinal*. When the music critics attacked Antheil personally, instead of explaining why they thought *Ballet Mécanique* failed musically, they fell back on empty phrases such as "childish rhythms" or blamed him for not using "cantilene" when that bore no relation to what his imagination had actually created. Williams was so appalled that he wrote a short essay defending Antheil's art. The poet's wise conclusion applied equally to all unfamiliar art: "Everything new must be wrong at first since there is always a moment when the living new supplants that which has been and still is right and is thus sure to be wrong in transition until it's seen that that which was right is dead."

Another composer whose music is akin to what Williams was doing was Edgard Varèse. There is no evidence that Williams heard Varèse's music at this time, but he could not have missed reading about it in the newspapers and literary reviews. Dubbed by Henry Miller "The Stratospheric Colossus of Sound," Varèse was inspired by the noises of the city to compose *Amériques*, a piece of radically abstract program music, during the same period that Williams was working on *Kora in Hell*. An elegant, somewhat aloof theorist of modernism, Varèse was particularly fascinated by the promise of the new electronic technology to generate daring sounds.*

Poem 14, by contrast, demonstrates how effectively short lines could be fit into a spare, shapely narrative. The poem begins

Of death
the barber
the barber
talked to me

then segues into a conversation between the barber cutting hair and the man in the chair about to be trimmed. The short lines enable the reader

---

*Judging Americans more likely to welcome his avant-garde compositions, Varèse left Paris and became an American citizen in 1926.

to follow the rapid volleys of talk down the page. The tone could be lifted from a folk parable; the rhythm is sprightly. The idiom, though speckled with elements of American humor and tall tales—the old man who grows a third set of teeth, for example—is common to folklore worldwide.

Williams's most ambitious and successful poem in *Spring and All*, "The pure products of America," employs a modified version of these short-lined stanzas: every second line consists of one or two words, ranging from one to four syllables. Nothing he had written to this point came close to this stunning dissection of what he considered the breakdown in American values. Here is the poem in its entirety:

> The pure products of America
> go crazy—
> mountain folk from Kentucky
>
> or the ribbed north end of
> Jersey
> with its isolate lakes and
>
> valleys, its deaf-mutes, thieves
> old names
> and promiscuity between
>
> devil-may-care men who have taken
> to railroading
> out of sheer lust of adventure—
>
> and young slatterns, bathed
> in filth
> from Monday to Saturday
>
> to be tricked out that night
> with gauds
> from imaginations which have no
>
> peasant traditions to give them
> character
> but flutter and flaunt

sheer rags—succumbing without
emotion
save numbed terror

under some hedge of choke-cherry
or viburnum—
which they cannot express—

Unless it be that marriage
perhaps
with a dash of Indian blood

will throw up a girl so desolate
so hemmed round
with disease or murder

that she'll be rescued by an
agent—
reared by the state and

sent out to work in
some hard-pressed
house in the suburbs—

some doctor's family, some Elsie—
voluptuous water
expressing with broken

brain the truth about us—
her great
ungainly hips and flopping breasts

addressed to cheap
jewelry
and rich young men with fine eyes

as if the earth under our feet
were
excrement of some sky

and we degraded prisoners
destined
to hunger until we eat filth

while the imagination strains
after deer
going by fields of goldenrod in

the stifling heat of September
Somehow
it seems to destroy us

It is only in isolate flecks that
something
is given off

No one
to witness
and adjust, no one to drive the car

A sense of urgency drives the first nine stanzas. Like an epidemiologist sounding the alarm, Williams reports the anecdotal data of a psychosexual plague and lays bare its etiology. Although he gathers evidence mainly from New Jersey, his findings apply equally to the hillbillies of Kentucky and to all regions of the country. The disease cuts across all classes, but as the pun on "pure" makes clear, it hits the poor the hardest. Innocence is tainted, preyed on. Williams's census takes in lowlifes and deaf-mutes, those pariahs on the margins—he probably treated them when they fell sick—and the swashbuckling Whiskey Irish railroad roués who copy the dress and gestures of movie villains and tabloid celebrities. Their partners in and victims of promiscuity, the slatterns "bathed in filth," lack even a rudimentary sense of self. Because they are not guided or protected by peasant traditions, they are particularly vulnerable to the sweet talk of the lusty adventurers. The young women dress up on Saturday nights in flashy trinkets and "sheer rags," and like coquettes "flutter and flaunt" their bodies before succumbing to the "devil-may-care" men under a hedge of honeysuckle, their only emotion terror. Williams's imagination and artistry allow him to speak for the brutalized mute victims (the triad "succumbing," "numbed," and "viburnum" is an especially lovely set of rhymes for a loveless act).

The next section of the poem moves from social types to a specific person: a young woman who is rescued by the state from a New Jersey orphanage and placed in a "hard-pressed" house in the suburbs, namely the Williamses'. Elsie (her real name was Kathleen) was a slightly retarded fifteen-year-old hired as a nanny to take care of William Eric and Paul. As Williams tells the story in his *Autobiography*, to gain attention she concocted a hoax that she had been tied up by burglars come to steal the family silver. Elsie is bovine—her name would remind readers of the Borden cow—and like the slatterns in the first part of the poem, she decks herself out in "cheap jewelry" in the hope of attracting one of the "rich young men with fine eyes." Her voluptuousness, however, is grotesque, a symptom of her "broken / brain," as the line break emphasizes. But Williams does not exempt himself or us from complicity in the tawdry lives of the many Elsies America has mass-produced. A Swiftian disgust plunges him into despair, "as if the earth under our feet / were / excrement of some sky / / and we degraded prisoners / destined / to hunger until we eat filth." The switch to the first-person plural permits no facile comfort. We cannot look down our noses at the slatterns and working-class Don Juans: we, too, are "degraded prisoners." The goldenrod shimmering in the late summer heat is no symbol of hope.

In the poem's last eight lines, Williams fumbles for a solution but cannot find one. Against a spreading cancer that "seems to destroy us," what can the doctor propose? "Isolate flecks" that give off a vague "something" provide neither cure nor palliative. The last stanza ends with a bleak vision:

> No one
> To witness
> And adjust, no one to drive the car

Just as there are no verbs in the sentence and "no one to drive the car," so there are no rules of conduct to stave off the collision and wreckage ahead. At the onset of the roaring twenties, Williams foresees American society, like the car, hurtling toward disaster. There is no period to bring the poem to a close. The stock market crash of October 1929 fulfilled his nightmarish prophecy.

In "The pure products of America," Williams found the distinctive voice he was searching for; it enabled him to negotiate "the jump between fact and imaginative reality" with near-perfect art. The remaining poems of *Spring and All*, except in flashes, mostly fall off in quality from this summit. In the prose, Williams continues to obsess about the imagination, but in the poems it appears fitfully or not at all. Poem 19 observes the adolescent rites of spring: two boys wearing two stolen "horned lilac blossoms / in their caps—or over one ear" swagger like young lords of Rutherford. Irked and affronted by their vulgarity, Williams labels them "Dirty satyrs," suspecting perhaps that they will grow up to be the ne'er-do-wells of "The pure products of America," though he tempers his hostility a bit at the end.

Poem 20 is pastiche: a cross between a song from a Shakespearean play and a spoof of the "Shakespeherian rag" in *The Waste Land*. Onomatopoeic sounds like "Oom barroom," "ula lu la lu," and "marruu" blend with echoes of Poe's "Ulalume" and the mermaids in "Prufrock" who beckon J. Alfred with their Siren songs to drown in the cold sea. "An awkward thing. I never tried it again," Williams confided to Thirlwall about this poem. He was right—its lullabies don't rise above a jingling formula.

"The Red Wheelbarrow," Williams's most frequently anthologized work, has become his signature poem. It's not hard to account for the poem's immense popularity: its images are simple and accessible, posing no bristling challenges to the reader, as a modernist poem might. A wheelbarrow is a useful object that Williams might have noticed in the yard of the Hermans' farmhouse in Monroe, New York, or picked up in a garden supply store. But in fact, he explains in a note in *Fifty Poets: An American Auto-Anthology*, "the wheelbarrow in question stood outside the window of an old negro's house on a back street in the suburb where I live. It was pouring rain and there were white chickens walking about in it." The rain accounts for the glaze on the wheelbarrow. Williams liked to say jocularly that anything can be material for a poem, a proposition that this particular poem (it has no title, just the Roman numeral XXII) tests:

so much depends
upon

a red wheel
barrow

glazed with rain
water

beside the white
chickens

At first glance, poem 22 is an American variant of the haiku, the outer couplets using four and two syllables and the inner couplets three and two. Indeed, one feels that Williams, who was a deft carpenter, has taken his tape measure out of his overalls pocket and measured the lines carefully. He's equally precise in where he breaks lines; he wants to foil our conventional expectation that wheelbarrow and rainwater should be one word. By breaking them where he does, he demands that we pay close attention to the discrete elements that make up the words. His subject is a kind of interplay of hardware and nature, but the poem is also a painterly composition, the red of the utilitarian wheelbarrow played off against the white of the chickens, and the glaze both natural and artful. But what of the first two lines, where Williams asserts that "so much depends / upon" this accidental configuration of ordinary objects? Williams must be fooling with us. Couldn't he have substituted "so little depends" without disturbing the poem's balance and meaning?

In part, Williams may want us to read "depends" in the sense of "hangs down." The objects in the barnyard and the poem itself literally depend from his initial statement, and the unity of the poem depends upon this arrangement of syntax. Since "depends" also suggests contingency, Williams introduces a tiny ambiguity into the poem: is "so much" a McGuffin or a mystery? Whatever the answer, for Williams "The Red Wheelbarrow" was a personal favorite:

The sight impressed me somehow as about the most important, the most integral that it had ever been my pleasure to gaze upon.

And the meter though no more than a fragment succeeds in portraying this pleasure flawlessly, even it succeeds in denoting a certain unquenchable exaltation—in fact I find the poem quite perfect.

As *Spring and All* winds down, Williams juxtaposes two poems that use the living American language in peculiarly diverse ways. Poem 25 weaves a tapestry out of statistics ("Somebody dies every four minutes / in New York State"); an angry curse (from Floss?), "To hell with you and your poetry— / You will rot and be blown / through the next solar system / with the rest of the gases—"; typographical oddities (the word "axioms" in large caps, adjectives separated by an ampersand, a stanza shifted several spaces from the left margin); advertising copy from a brochure touting Long Island Sound as a resort; a hyper-alliterative public service sign, "Careful Crossing Campaign / Cross Crossings Cautiously"; a subway clerk's brisk directions to a lost passenger; and a doctor's advice that his patient exercise outdoors: "Ho for the open country / / Don't stay shut up in hot rooms." A mild swipe at the overregulated poem and a patchwork of American idioms, poem 23 tests how many different kinds of fact and useful knowledge can be irradiated by the imagination. Fact, however, checkmates imagination here.

Following one tenet of modernist scripture, Williams argues that it is words that must be "civilized." But which basic words are unmistakably American? And how are they to be tamed and welded into a harmonious whole? Intellectually honest, Williams admits he is not sure. This uncertainty is reflected everywhere in the prose of *Spring and All*. Nearing forty, Williams was an impatient reformer with high-minded goals. What he said to Thirlwall is true of many of his poems from the 1920s: "I was writing in my own language, and whatever the language suggested I wrote. I was following the beat in my own mind, of the American idiom." Though he didn't entirely suppress the lyric impulse, he kept circling back to a poetry based on American speech rhythms, which meant rationing the use of iambic pentameter.

Without idealizing the "people" as Whitman had, Williams in poem 26 probes their role in a raucous democracy. The setting for his study is a ball park where a crowd has gathered in "a spirit of uselessness" to watch "all the exciting detail / of the chase / / and the escape, the error / the flash of genius." (He had taken William Eric and Paul to the Polo Grounds to watch the New York Giants play.) His first (rather high-flown) conclusion is that the baseball game represents "beauty the eternal," the very cliché he had earlier disowned. But although the crowd is cheering and laughing, Williams detects something ominous: if incited, it can turn into a dangerous mob that "without thought" hurls "deadly, terrifying" abuse on, and brutally victimizes, the objects of its wrath—Williams's example is the Jews, who for two millennia were persecuted by the rabble, often at the instigation of tsars and popes and demagogues. Hence the crowd must be "warned against / / saluted and defied." Williams's conclusion seems to be: the people, *maybe*.

The last prose passages of *Spring and All* laud the imagination for making words radioactive. Williams's own words attain this state only intermittently. His best poems are "liberated to pirouette with the words which have sprung from the old facts of history, reunited in present passion." But Williams's imagination is not yet commanding enough to prevent *Spring and All* from morphing at times into a loose and baggy monster. The final poem, though, is so quiet and terse that it seems to fade away like a movie dissolve or a dying cadence. Marjorie Perloff correctly notes that each word of poem 27, except "Susan," subtly brings back words from earlier poems, including "By the road to the contagious hospital." But are these echoes enough to hold together the disparate parts of the sequence? I think not. The "rich savagery" of America is unexpectedly personified by the poem's last three lines: the "Arab / Indian / dark woman," all outsiders looked down on by the majority and put in purdah, so to speak, reflect Williams's strong solidarity with harassed minorities and immigrants. America is not the Promised Land of their dreams; it remains a country of cultural and racial divisions. What is broken is not mended. But despite its shortcomings, *Spring and All* was, for Williams, an invaluable experiment. The sequence laid the foundation for a home-grown style that he hoped would make even Pound cry Uncle Sam.

Finding a publisher for *Spring and All*, however, proved a challenge. Williams was reluctant to approach Edmund Brown of the Boston-based Four Seas Company, who had brought out *Al Que Quiere!*, *Kora in Hell*, and *Sour Grapes*, because each book had lost money. He tried Monroe Wheeler, who had invited him to submit poems for a pamphlet series called *Manikin*. (Marianne Moore was its debut poet.) A small press publisher on a skimpy budget, Wheeler offered to print nine of the poems from *Spring and All*, but Williams's heart was set on an unabridged edition. He courted Wheeler by asking him to dinner at 9 Ridge Road, but the publisher explained that he lacked the resources to take on the complete collection. After some soul-searching, Williams grudgingly agreed to let Wheeler publish the nine poems along with "The Hermaphroditic Telephone" in a chapbook Williams curiously titled *Go-Go*. The book received little notice (the fate of most chapbooks), though Marian Strobel, Williams's old Chicago flame, savaged it in *Poetry*, calling it the work of a "middle-aged adolescent."

Still, Williams longed to publish the full text of *Spring and All*. Learning of his plight, McAlmon rode to the rescue. Flush with money settled on him by Bryher for their divorce (and in accordance with their prenuptial agreement), McAlmon founded Contact Editions and published books he admired, such as Hemingway's *Three Stories and Ten Poems*, Mina Loy's *Lunar Baedeker*, and Gertrude Stein's massive experimental novel *The Making of Americans*. Hemingway rewarded McAlmon with a punch in the face, and Stein treated him with her customary hauteur. Williams, by contrast, was grateful for his friend's intercession. But *Spring and All* met the same ignominious fate as Williams's other books. Few of the less than four hundred plus copies reached American bookstores. With a shrug, McAlmon explained to Williams that customs officials in the States had probably confiscated most of the copies, their French origin suggesting salaciousness. The near impossibility of finding a first edition today proves how thoroughly those officials did their job.

Williams might have been pardoned if he'd withdrawn from the poetry battlefield at this point. Reed Whittemore, in *Poet from Jersey*, argues that Williams's feeling of being "isolated, ignored, rejected" bordered on a martyr's complex and was tinged with paranoia. This is partly true. Williams did imagine himself persecuted, or at least unfairly undervalued, by the poetry establishment. But it was not in his nature to succumb to a prolonged paralysis of the will. Defeat invariably galvanized him to throw himself once more into the fray. Even at the nadir of his despair, he expected, like the phoenix, to rise from the ashes of failure—and so he did, most of the time.

NINE

The "Strange Phosphorus" of American History

In 1923, Williams was preparing to write *In the American Grain*, the book that is his masterpiece and that expressed his thinking about a central concern: America's position in the world. In order to accomplish this, he needed an extended break from his daily routine and his life in Rutherford. He first moved the few miles to New York City, where he completed more than half the book, then took his big trip to Europe, and finally returned to America, where he finished the writing. Although *In the American Grain* dealt with America, it was inextricable from Williams's feelings about, and experiences in, Europe.

In 1921 and 1922, Ezra Pound had kept trying to entice Williams to Paris for a lengthy stay. Only the French metropolis, he argued, could save Williams's provincial artistic soul. There he'd rub shoulders with avant-garde poets, novelists, painters, sculptors, and composers of every stripe, ready to drink the night away and debate the future of art. Pound dropped the names James Joyce and Ford Madox Ford as stars of the expatriate scene Williams would want to meet. In another skein of argument, Pound asserted that because aristocracy was dead, the future of "better art" rested with the cognoscenti. Williams was tempted to join that junta, headquartered in Paris. But he had qualms, which he outlined in a letter to Pound dated March 29, 1922:

> I'd enjoy a trip to Paris. But I don't care much to trade my own illusions for yours. By unfortunate circumstance I have stumbled on a few particles of truth about writing that I know, things which you

might have pointed out to me in three words if you had the skill
or understanding.

What I see before me in my work needs no special companionship or food other than that which is before it. I long for intelligence and good will, as I detest as the essence of stupidity all of
your assumptions referable to what I am and what I need.

While he envied Pound the luxury of unencumbered hours to write
poems or pore over books in the library, he declared that he couldn't "leave
his medical practice and keep it . . . Romantic starvation for the one thing
that deeply concerns me in life—composition, does not appeal to me."

In 1923, however, Williams reversed himself. The prospect of a sabbatical year and a change of scenery seemed irresistible. Floss proposed
that their leave run from late summer 1923 to late summer 1924 and be
divided between several months in New York, during which Williams
would conduct research on *In the American Grain* at the New York Public
Library's Reading Room, and the rest of the time in Europe, their itinerary geared mostly for pleasure but also to include a stint in Vienna, then a
center for vanguard medicine, where Williams would take courses in pediatrics. (He never could justify to himself playing the tourist exclusively;
he needed to improve his medical skills as well.)

The first task was to arrange the complicated logistics. During the
school year, William Eric and Paul would live at 9 Ridge Road with Lucy,
the family's reliable longtime black maid. "Razor" Watkins, the Rutherford
High School football coach, would keep an eye on the boys, and Ed would
look in periodically to make sure the household was functioning smoothly.
As long as their parents remained in New York, the boys would visit them
on the weekends. One last piece of the puzzle remained: finding a doctor
to take care of Williams's patients during his absence. By a stroke of good
fortune, his cousin Albert Hoheb and his wife, Kathleen, had just completed residencies at Passaic General Hospital, and volunteered to tend to
the practice in exchange for room and board at 9 Ridge Road. In the summer of 1923, thus freed, Bill and Floss settled into a brownstone on Manhattan's Upper East Side that they shared with their friend Louise Bloecher,
and Bill buckled down to writing *In the American Grain*.

Williams conceived *In the American Grain* as half of a diptych, *Spring
and All* being the other panel. *Spring and All* takes a panoramic view of
the polyglot American populace he knew so well in the towns around

Rutherford, highlighting their fears, hopes, speech, rituals, courtships, bigotries, and distractions (movies, baseball games, dance halls); it is a kind of episodic local history. *In the American Grain*, by contrast, takes a long view: covering almost nine hundred years, it examines the origins and consequences of the discovery and settlement of the Americas, and tracks the many tributaries forming the country's identity. With few exceptions, the historical figures Williams focuses on were familiar to anybody with a high school education, including Christopher Columbus, Daniel Boone, and Edgar Allan Poe.

Because Williams's immigrant parents never assimilated, he thought long and hard about the nature of citizenship. It was a logical next step to consider the antecedents of American identity and democracy. Although he never mentions de Tocqueville, if he had read *Democracy in America*, he would have recognized in this passage the American incomprehension of history:

The American lives in a land of wonders; everything around him is in constant movement, and every movement seems an advance. Consequently, in his mind the idea of newness is closely linked with that of improvement. Nowhere does he see any limit placed by nature to human endeavor; in his eyes something which does not exist is just something that has not been tried yet.

This was exactly the limitation Williams was reacting against. He wanted Americans to understand how the past burdens the present: that America's history was the source of many of its contemporaneous problems. In the process, he would reflect on such major themes as puritanism, materialism, and the vast unruly contributions of immigrants, especially those from Europe.

The time was ripe. Van Wyck Brooks's *America's Coming of Age* (1915) was only the first in a series of books—others included Waldo Frank's *Our America* (1919), D. H. Lawrence's *Studies in Classic American Literature* (1924), and Paul Rosenfeld's *Port of New York* (1925)—that stringently reassessed a variety of influences on American values. For example, starting from different perspectives, these commentators all agreed that the puritan mentality stunted the development of creativity in the arts and inhibited a healthy attitude to sex. Williams's goal was to place all these influences in a larger context.

Although Williams did not know Henry Adams's *History of the United States During the Administrations of Thomas Jefferson and James Madison*—it was not until 1927 that Louis Zukofsky introduced him to *The Education of Henry Adams* and *Mont-Saint-Michel and Chartres*—what he came up with has affinities with Adams's brilliant overview of America in 1800, albeit on a more modest scale, and with vastly fewer hours of library research behind it. Williams strove, like Adams, to strike a balance between the details of local history—the innocent bystanders slain by invaders or the tattoos on a young Indian's body—and the big picture. Yet *In the American Grain* is defiantly and explicitly not a history as Adams understood the term; it represents, rather, a highly unorthodox, hybrid approach to historical narrative.

To this day, American historians usually ignore *In the American Grain* altogether or, baffled by its eccentric vision of the American past, regard it as little more than an impressionistic sketchbook. Williams, the charge runs, substitutes poetic fables and biographical sketches for detailed, sober analysis and conscripts historical narrative for purely aesthetic purposes. Alan Trachtenberg puts the case succinctly in his essay "Mumford in the Twenties":

> The motive . . . toward a "usable past" discloses itself as much in the form as in the content, as much in the invention as in the excavation. For in the form, or let us say in the very concern with form, with presentation, lies the implication that "history" itself demands a creative response, that the past can become "present" only through a kind of personal encounter. This, of course, is the extreme aesthetic view of Williams and [Hart] Crane, for whom "past" is constantly in the process of realization through fresh encounters, and history nothing if not realizable as personal experience.

Admittedly, Williams does not always handle documents as a traditional historian would. He often employs the collagist's art, deftly making the part stand for the whole (though it should be pointed out that for centuries historians have quoted selectively and used ellipses to indicate omissions). Sometimes, as with Columbus's journals and Cortés's letters, Williams will rearrange the order of sentences or even paragraphs in order to stress a theme he deems crucial. Or else he will tactically leave out parts of, say, Cotton Mather's *Wonders of the Invisible World* because they don't jibe with the points he's making. Yet he never abandons objective assessment in favor of wildly subjective judgments ("personal experience"). And while he *is* fascinated by form, it is largely as an expression of content, of spiritual blindness or amplitude, of wise governance or abusive power. Each chapter of *In the American Grain* takes on a different shape or mode of "presentation," suggested by the stories that Williams or a surrogate narrates: the foiled plot to assassinate Samuel Champlain, the Salem witch trials, the war between the French and the English for control of Quebec, and the frequent bloody clashes with Native American tribes. Williams cites documents as evidence of the kind of men America produced—for example, John Paul Jones's letter to Benjamin Franklin describing the "Battle Between the *Bonhomme Richard* and the *Serapis*." Jones's letter, like Whitman's account in *Song of Myself*, mixes official dispatch and short story, but does not dress up the facts in ornate myths.

What's unconventional and audacious about Williams's treatment of history is the major role he assigns to style, which shifts like the flow of history itself, now cascading, now meandering, now violent, now placid. One is struck by the quantum leap forward in prose styles between *Spring and All* and *In the American Grain*. Gone are the bombastic sentences that embody Williams's struggles to shape imprecise and tortuous ideas into a coherent manifesto. The poetic prose of *In the American Grain* is remarkably poised, idiomatic, piercing, and protean.

If Williams's initial impulse was, as he put it in the *Autobiography*, "to find out for myself what the land of my more or less accidental birth might signify," he soon dropped this aim as too vague. Instead "the plan was to try to get inside the heads of some of the founders or 'heroes,' if you will, by examining their original records. I wanted nothing to get between me and what they had recorded."

Williams espoused no theory of history; he steered clear of such sweeping generalities as Emerson's "It is the universal nature which gives worth to particular men and things." Nor did he agree with the Concord sage's contention that "we are always coming up with the emphatic facts of history in our private experience, and verifying them here. All history becomes subjective; in other words there is properly no History; only biography." This radical claim, encapsulated in Emerson's famous statement "All history is the shadow of one man," is not how Williams viewed human agency working out its destiny in historical time. Emerson also blithely skated over the intransigence of essential facts about human nature: our outsize appetite for power, the stubborn persistence of evil, the indifferent trampling on the rights of the least fortunate. Williams was no closet transcendentalist; the healthy respect for facts he had acquired in medical school was reinforced every day in his interactions with patients. Therefore, the representative men he sketched in *In the American Grain* were sometimes heroic but more often victims of an overweening confidence that they controlled events, when in actuality they were swept up in a maelstrom of contradictory forces—economic, spiritual, military, and psychological—for which their traditions and teachings did not prepare them.

There are no portraits of women hanging on the walls of *In the American Grain*'s gallery, yet women play a central role in the book, because Williams personifies America as a ravishing woman violated again and again by men so ravenous for material gain, fame, and the wielding of absolute power that, showing no restraint, they drove out, enslaved, or slaughtered the indigenous residents. Throughout *In the American Grain*, how men treat women and the Native American tribes living in ecological harmony with and on the land, or how, like the Puritans, the colonizers fail to see the majestic nature around them, are, for Williams, two major touchstones for understanding the formation and contradictions of America's national identity.

The opening chapter, "Red Eric," takes the form of a dramatic soliloquy. Eric is both a real historical protagonist and a bard in the king's hall, enthralling his listeners with a tale out of the Norse sagas. Though tersely told, his story has an almost Wagnerian grandiosity to it, weaving together treachery, lust for power, curses, and murders galore, as if the characters, including Eric's daughter Freydis, a blend of Amazon and Valkyrie, are angling to obtain the Rheingold and become master of the world. Eric's voice is rugged and free of abstractions, his rhythms harsh and elemental, his syntax quick and true as the thrust of a sword, his rough eloquence and virile music hewn of "the single strength" of his character and expressed in the rush of active verbs:

> Eric loves his friends, loves bed, loves food, loves the hunt, loves his sons. He is a man that can throw a spear, take a girl, steer a ship, till the soil, plant, care for the cattle, skin a fox, sing, dance, run, wrestle, climb, swim like a seal . . . through a fog, a snowstorm, read a reckoning by the stars, live in a stench, drink foul

water, withstand the fierce cold, the black of winter and come to a new country with a hundred men and found them there.

Williams lovingly catalogues Eric's versatility and heroic feats. But despite his oaklike stature, Eric is caught in the *retiarius* that the Church throws over him. He strives to fathom the Christian mission and ethic, which according to his pagan logic he interprets as weak foxes harrying their individualist prey by "the crookedness of their law." Branding him a Cain, the bishops connive to drive Eric into exile from Iceland to Greenland. His own sons and the king of Norway join the Church that regards Eric as an outlaw and servant, and his wife, Thorhild, "bars" him, "godless," from her bed. Even as he tries to cut the netting of hypocrisies and stratagems that have ensnared him, his moral code will not let him capitulate or lie to himself. His brusque physical prose embodies the essence of the man: "Outlaws have no friends. Murderers are run down like rabbits among the stones . . . Pestilence struck us. The cattle sickened . . . Hardship lives in me. What I suffer is myself that outraces the water or the wind."

Despite being a pariah, when his son Leif leads an expedition to storied Vinland (North America), Eric is on board the ship sailing south: "Fate has pulled him out at the holes of his eyes and flung him again to sea," Williams writes. In the prehistory of America, nearly five centuries before Columbus's voyage of discovery, the bounty of this new, unmapped continent unleashes slaughters as cold-blooded as the North Atlantic is numbingly frigid. Despite the Christianity that the quarreling brothers and Freydis have sworn fealty to, a primordial violence and greed grip them: Freydis shows no mercy toward her own clan, butchering women and children. And in the settlement, battles break out between the Skrellings, the native tribe, and the foreigners come to colonize their land. Out of the chronicle of *The Long Island Book*, his primary source, Williams has composed a premonitory overture that introduces the motifs he will explore and develop in subsequent chapters.

In conducting his historical inquiry, Williams proceeds by juxtaposition. The second chapter, "The Discovery of the Indies," draws on Columbus's journals, each daily entry recording aspects of his voyage: latitude and longitude; the number of miles covered each day; scrapes with disaster as storms threaten to wreck the ships; hours of ineffable loveliness— sunshine on the tropic sea, a tern spotted flying overhead, and the sun, "a marvelous flame of fire," falling into the ocean, "temperate breezes" that remind Columbus of "April in Andalusia." These benign moments are transient. Columbus chronically worries that the crew is planning to mutiny because they fear they'll never see Spain again; and an inner crisis brews, provoked by his wavering faith in a capricious "Divine Will." Is it guiding him to achieve an unprecedented glory or to endure a cosmic defeat? The orderly ship log acts as a temporary barrier against his fears.

For Williams, history abounds with many such ironies and uncertainties, as if some demonic force delights in toying with men, filling their minds with self-deceptions, dangling immense wealth and power just out of their reach, then crushing their hopes with implacable cruelty. America is Circe, voluptuous, intoxicating as perfume, enslaving most of the men who seek to ravish her and turning them into beasts. (The more austere Daniel Boone is at home in the silent forests; the wilderness is his chaste paramour.) America is also, in Williams's metaphor, the Garden of Eden before and after the Fall: the Europeans eat "a predestined and bitter fruit existing perversely, before the white flower of its birth, it was laid bare by the miraculous first voyage. For it is as the achievement of a flower, pure, white, waxlike and fragrant, that Columbus' infatuated course must be depicted, especially when compared with the acrid and poisonous apple which was later by him to be proved." Retribution is as swift for the Spaniard's trespass as it was for Adam and Eve.

In a peculiar narrative reversal, Williams's terse commentary about Columbus's later defeat by plotters back in Madrid precedes and is interleaved with the eight or so pages of extracts from his journals. Williams is appalled by the ingratitude, insults, and broken promises that Columbus endures. Where before the first voyage, Ferdinand and Isabella had smiled on his expedition, helping him raise the money to outfit the ships and enlisting the blessings of the Holy Church, they and their successors later breached their contract with Columbus, robbing him and his sons and brothers of their rightful share of the gold and jewels they brought back, so plentiful that Croesus would have gasped in envy; pauperized, they are thrown in prison, and Columbus is pilloried and humiliated, his service forgotten. "The Discovery of the Indies" is thus a cautionary tale. The moral comes before the discovery:

With its archaic smile, America found Columbus its first victim. This was well, even merciful. As for the others, who shall say?—

when riding a gigantic Nature and when through her heat they could arrogate to themselves a pin's worth of that massive strength, to turn it against another of their own kind to his undoing—even they are natural and as much a part of the scheme as any other.

Williams admires Columbus's contemplative nature—the antithesis of Cortés's haughty aggressiveness—and his calm assessment of the pitfalls of his voyage. Columbus concedes his friend Peter Gutierrez's point that he has staked his life and the lives of his companions "upon the foundation of a mere speculative opinion." Yet Columbus was no feverish gambler; he had astutely calculated the odds of success and the perils of failure. In writing this chapter, Williams sweated over the problem of how to circumvent chronology. "I had a devil of a job making the chapter end with the discovery," he noted. But his solution worked.

Stumbling on an earthly paradise, Columbus marvels at the fruitfulness of the land and, like a bewitched naturalist, records "the branches growing in different ways and all from one trunk; . . . thus one branch has leaves like those of a cane, and others like those of a mastic tree; and on a single tree there are five different kinds." He gazes at the welcoming party of Indians with curiosity, not hostility; he is not shocked by the coarse hair and painted bodies of the handsome young men or by the sight of unabashedly naked women. Columbus is not a predator but the first poet the New World has produced.

The "Letters of Hernando Cortés to Philip of Spain and Charles V," supplemented by other sources, served Williams when he came to meet his third and most difficult challenge, constructing a chapter that would do justice to Cortés's toppling of Montezuma, the emperor of the Aztecs, from his throne. In Williams's telling, it is a spellbinding drama in which a civilization of great sophistication and beauty is utterly destroyed. He does not scapegoat Cortés, who "was neither malicious, stupid, nor blind, but a conqueror like other conquerors. Courageous almost beyond precedent, tactful, resourceful in misfortune, he was a man of genius superbly suited to his task." Though a military man to his roots, even Cortés is "overcome with wonder" at his first glimpse of Tenochtitlán. But for Williams, the mettlesome Spanish hidalgo is eclipsed by the figure of Montezuma, a sun god whom Velázquez might have painted.

Playing the role of historian as cicerone—he seems imbued with the spirit of curiosity Herodotus brought to his sojourn among the

Persians—Williams walks the reader around the extraordinary city the Aztecs had built, pointing out their highly evolved world with its exotic codes and customs and its architectural wonders: spacious palaces, temples, pleasure halls, markets, houses, and gardens. His eyes dazzled, Williams composes opulent catalogues of the crafts, books, and clothing, all of an exquisite workmanship—the only possible response to the sensuality of Tenochtitlán:

> Scarcely an element in the city's incredible organization but evidenced an intellectual vigor full of resource and delicacy which had given it distinction. Half land and half water the streets were navigated by canoes and bridge at the intersections by structures of great timbers over which ten horses could go abreast . . . There were public squares, and one of great size surrounded by porticoes where daily sixty thousand souls engaged in buying and selling under the supervision of twelve central magistrates and numbers of inspectors. Here "everything which the world affords" was offered for purchase, from the personal services of laborers and porters to the last refinements of bijouterie; gold, silver, lead, brass, copper, tin; wrought and unwrought stone, bricks burnt and unburnt, timber hewn and unhewn, of different sorts; game of every variety, fowls, quails, partridges, wild ducks, parrots, pigeons, reed-birds, sparrows, eagles, hawks, owls, likewise the skins of some birds of prey with their feathers, head, beak and claws, . . . : a fabulous cornucopia of fruits, vegetables, grains, fish, and pottery.

But it is not the cornucopia that turns Williams's head; it is the Aztecs' "sensitivity to the richest beauty" of the soil into which they sank their roots and "a spirit mysterious, constructive, independent, puissant with natural wealth."

In *I Wanted to Write a Poem*, Williams told Edith Heal, "The Tenochtitlán chapter was written in big square paragraphs like Inca masonry. I admired the massive walls of fitted masonry—no plaster—just fitted boulders. I took that to be a wonderful example of what I wanted to do with my prose; no patchwork." He did lay down the prose with the ingenious skill and sumptuous invitation to the senses that the astonishing Aztec urban planners and engineers used in designing their city. For a world so luxuriant, Williams finds words as colorful as the plumage of the birds in the royal aviary.

The "orchidean" beauty and plenitude of the New World is memorably on display in Tenochtitlán. For Williams, this fabulous city eclipses Winthrop's vision of "a city on a hill" and throws into relief the profound poverty of imagination the Puritans brought with them to the New World. Yet, for all its magnificence, Aztec civilization crumbles under the Spanish onslaught. Williams understands Cortés's motives and justifications: he does not blame him in hindsight for coveting vast quantities of gold and land. The Spaniard's destruction of the causeway, the royal route into Tenochtitlán, was a clever military stratagem, Williams recognizes, but it also symbolized Cortés's myopic belief that Aztec civilization was merely "the evil of the whole world," fit for extirpation. The Spanish conqueror exemplified "the spirit of malice which underlies men's lives and against which nothing offers resistance," Williams bleakly concludes. (Emerson could never have written this fatalistic sentence.)

At the same time Williams mourns, in magnificent baroque prose, the razing of a spectacular culture. Williams is cognizant of the flaws in Aztec civilization—their barbaric practice of human sacrifice in particular— that contributed to their extinction. The chapels and halls that held the "principal idols" were a sanctuary for darkness:

> Decorated with curious imagery in stone, the woodwork carved in relief and painted with figures and monsters and other things, unpaved, darkened and bloodstained, it was in these chapels that the religious practices which so shocked the Christian were performed. Here it was that the tribe's deep feeling for a reality that stems back into the permanence of remote origins had its firm hold. It was the earthward thrust of their logic; blood and earth; the realization of their primal and continuous identity with the ground itself, where everything is fixed in darkness; . . . it was a ceremonial acknowledgment of the deep sexless urge, the hungry animal, underlying all other power; the mysterious secret of existence whose cruel beauty they, the living, inherited from the dead.

Williams's grim analysis leaves no possibility for redemption except through art: "The earth is black and it is there; only art advances." But art is as vulnerable to extinction as the dinosaurs.

The "unfathomable" mystery for Williams is why Montezuma, with the means to crush the outnumbered Cortés, turned his cheek to the Spaniard's insults and provocative acts, such as his pulling down of the pagan idols in the chapel and his replacing them with effigies of the Madonna and Jesus. It was as if Montezuma switched sides with his Spanish adversary, Cortés becoming the barbarian and Montezuma the Catholic. Montezuma's behavior was an anomaly, because it radically broke with centuries of Aztec dynastic principles and military policy: it was imperative to refuse to surrender to the enemy and, if necessary, to die bravely.

The consensus of historians today is that Montezuma must have believed that the coming of the Spanish fulfilled an ancient prophecy that required him to propitiate the strangers. This is close to Williams's conjecture: Montezuma acted as though history did not favor his cause, and so it was futile to rally his people, however ready they were to defend their emperor and way of life. When his subjects "laid siege to the intolerable intruders, determined to have done with them," Montezuma, imprisoned by Cortés, tried to persuade them to put down their arms. Their reply was to hurl a stone that struck him in the head and killed him. After a pitched battle from which Cortés narrowly escaped, he regrouped the Spanish forces and suppressed the belated rebellion led by Montezuma's nephew Guatimotzin. Cortés judged correctly that burning the aviaries would demoralize his adversaries. His triumph? A great civilization lay in ruins about him. Cortés later tried to rebuild the city: Williams wisely refrains from commenting on this irony. He lets a Spanish proverb serve as epitaph: *Viva quien vince!* "Long live he who conquers."

The Spanish could not see the other, except through the lens of their unexamined prejudices. For Williams, whose mother grew up in Puerto Rico, Ponce de León, its governor, was a classic example of this benightedness: a vain, bloodthirsty, greedy aristocrat who "killed [the Indians'] kings, betrayed, raped, murdered their women and children; hounded them into the mountains" and then systematically enslaved the people, turning paradise into a killing field.

The question implicitly posed by Williams's scathing and graphic account in this chapter is: Who is the real savage, de León or the Caribs, condemned by the haughty governor as "heathen" deserving to be annihilated? Williams's short sentences slash at the Spaniard's delusions like the machete used to mutilate a Carib woman's breasts. America creates and destroys illusions, he seems to say, as he shows the ironic twists by which history exacts revenge: an old crone dupes the avaricious Ponce de León into believing there are mountains of gold in Bimini, and later he is tricked into seeking a Fountain of Youth in Florida: "But this time the Yamasses put an arrow into his thigh at the first landing—and let out his fountain. They flocked to the beach and jeered him as he was lifted to the shoulders of his men and carried away. Dead."

There is nothing romantic, credulous, or evasive about Williams's depiction and analysis of evil: murder, betrayal, cruelty, jealousy, avarice, and expropriation of land are constants from Leif Eriksson's voyage to Long Island to Cortés's sacking of Tenochtitlán and the depredations of Ponce de León and de Soto. All nations, Williams remarks, share "a wolfish ferocity." In this chapter, he comes close to matching the gorgeous pageantry, political machinations, and poetic eloquence of Shakespeare's history plays.

Williams enjoys breaking conventional protocols in *In the American Grain*. Once past the early conquerors, he allots pages to his subjects in a ratio that cannot but set a professional historian's teeth on edge: George Washington gets five pages; slavery, four; Lincoln, five paragraphs; and Jefferson, Adams, and Madison are omitted altogether; Hamilton is assigned a minor role as a foil to the commanding figure of Aaron Burr, whereas Edgar Allan Poe is awarded twenty pages. But these choices are not as perverse or ill proportioned as they may seem at first blush: Williams thematically links these men—active during the first seventy-five years of the republic, by which point the American character was already fashioned—to the country's prehistory and to colonial America.

This explains why he devotes three chapters to an appraisal of the Puritan mentality and morality: "Voyage of the Mayflower," "The MayPole at Merry Mount," and "Cotton Mather's Wonders of the Invisible World" all describe the Puritan ethos that over time came to permeate all strata of institutional and social life. Another reason is that of all the constricting influences of the past, puritanism was the one Williams was most vividly aware of, sensing in its effects an analogy with those of his own personal past—social, parental, and temperamental—on his imagination.

If Williams quotes sparingly from the sermons John Winthrop delivered on the *Mayflower*, it is because he is not interested in the fierce polemical debates about theology, the religious schisms, or the "metaphysical subtleties" that agitated the New England mind. Rather, in "Voyage of the Mayflower" he dissects with surgical precision the blighted psychology of

the Pilgrim fathers; "stripped and little," they are unprepared for what
awaits them on the new continent: fear, cold, starvation, and Indian tribes
dwelling on a land disappointingly unlike the Promised Land of their vision and hope. Taking refuge in "the jargon of God," Williams contends,
the Pilgrims lost a magnificent opportunity to achieve a peerless individuality. Ironically, he adopts the scathing style of denunciation with which
the preachers castigated the so-called sinners in their midst. The Puritans' sin, according to Williams, was their lack of imagination, their doctrinaire rigidity, which left them spiritual husks, unable to flower. The
chapter is rife with metaphors of stunted growth: "Their religious zeal,
mistaken for a thrust up toward the sun, was a stroke in, in, in—not toward germination but the confinement of a tomb." "The Pilgrims, they, the
seed, instead of growing, looked black at the world and damning its perfections praised a zero in themselves."

The last three paragraphs of "Voyage of the Mayflower" read like a
cross between an autopsy report and an Old Testament jeremiad. The
spirit of seventeenth-century Puritanism has, for Williams, been transmitted like a deformed gene across three centuries:

> The result of that brave setting out of the Pilgrims has been an
> atavism that thwarts and destroys. The agonized spirit[,] that has
> followed like an idiot with undeveloped brain, governs with its
> great muscles, babbling in a text of the dead years. Here souls per-
> ish miserably, or, escaping, are bent into grotesque designs of vio-
> lence and despair.

Taking stock of America in 1923, and echoing the cadences of "The pure
products of America," Williams is so swept away by anger that he sometimes overstates his case, excoriating America like an infuriated prophet
and attributing to it a kind of savagery that, like a "malfeasant ghost,"
haunts and befouls the present:

> [America] has become "the most lawless country in the civilized
> world," a panorama of murders, perversions, a terrific ungoverned
> strength, excusable only because of the horrid beauty of the great
> machines. Today it is a generation of gross know-nothingism, of
> blackened churches where hymns groan like chants from stupefied
> jungles, a generation universally eager to barter permanent values

(the hope of all aristocracy) in return for opportunist material advantages, a generation hating those whom it obeys.

Williams's peroration, in the vein of Jonathan Edwards or Timon of Athens, condemns the aggressive self-interest that he sees as ruling the body politic; he commandeers the language of the Puritans to call our attention to what he considered a national crisis: "souls perish miserably." Williams's revulsion sounds extreme, as does his invective. What are their sources?

Williams regarded America as a fractured society. In 1919–20, the Palmer Raids exhibited an intolerance of dissenting views, whether anarchism, socialism, or pacifism, that was reminiscent of the seventeenth century. The year 1920 also saw the beginning of Prohibition. Fundamentalist evangelism—deeply hostile to science and modernity, as the Scopes trial of 1925 proved—swept the land. In such an America, Williams worried over the fate of the country and of his still-gestating verse.

His next essay, "The May-Pole at Merry Mount," examines the conflict between Thomas Morton and the Puritan community over Morton's pagan revels. Williams analyzes this odd, pivotal episode mainly by comparing historians' accounts and finding them all deficient. Curiously, he ignores Hawthorne's short story of virtually the same title ("The Maypole of Merry Mount"), which traced the origins of the Merry Mount colonists' celebration of pleasure and sexual license back to English fairs, masques, theaters, and the raucous street life and alehouses of London—all of which the Puritans saw as abominations. For the Puritans of nearby Plymouth, the residents of Merry Mount were dangerous Lords of Misrule, who might ally themselves with the dreaded savages. (Williams notes that the Puritans' animus against Morton was not due solely to his lewd behavior; they were also angling to control the lucrative fur trade and were afraid he'd sign a pact with the Indians and shut them out.) Sympathetic to the party of Eros, though sure it would lose its struggle with the Puritans, Hawthorne acutely sums up, in an image of flowering so pervasive in Williams's work, the high stakes that this incident symbolizes:

The future complexion of New England was involved in this important quarrel. Should the grizzly saints establish their jurisdiction over the gay sinners, then would their spirits darken all the clime, and make it a land of clouded visages, of hard toil, of sermon and psalm forever. But should the banner staff of Merry Mount be fortunate, sunshine would break upon the hills, and flowers would beautify the forest, and late posterity do homage to the Maypole.

For Williams, who shares Hawthorne's point of view, historians had failed to grasp the Puritans' true motive for the destruction of Merry Mount: to root out Eros from their midst. They countered "Morton's peccadillo with fantastic violence," Williams remarks. "Trustless of humane experience, not knowing what to think, they went mad, lost all direction. Mather defends the witchcraft persecutions."

This is an elegant transition to the long chapter on the Salem witch trials, which consists entirely of long quotations from Cotton Mather's *Wonders of the Invisible World*. We listen like spectators in the courtroom, mesmerized as judges and prosecutors interrogate witnesses and accused alike. Williams withholds all interpretation, letting Mather's vivid words suffice to indict the irrationality of the Puritan beliefs that unleashed mass hysteria in Salem and led inexorably to the burning of innocent people for the alleged crime of witchcraft. The draconian orderliness of the court proceedings contrasts starkly with the chimerical testimonies of ordinary citizens, who charge their neighbors with the crime of doing the Devil's bidding. The fabricated accounts of these witnesses—women assuming the shapes of malevolent cats and so forth—travesty the workings of Williams's cherished imagination. For Mather, these narratives carry incontrovertible proof of guilt. It never occurs to him that there might be more worldly reasons for these accusations: a long-simmering feud over the boundaries of a farm, say, or an unpaid loan. Mather's chronicle, delivered in vigorous, hypnotic prose, represents his belief in demonic possession as fact. Williams rests his case without summing up the issues or his argument. For the poet, Mather has convicted Puritanism by his own words.

From Cotton Mather, *In the Grain* moves on to his antithesis, the Jesuit missionary Père Sebastien Rasles, representing an alternative vision of religious faith on the new continent. When the time came to leave for Paris, Williams had made little headway writing this chapter. (He was also fiddling with the ending to the Columbus chapter and revising the de Soto, Boone, and Burr essays.) He was forced to lug the manuscript to Paris, where an encounter with the poet Valéry Larbaud so inspired him that he wove an account of it into his chapter on Rasles.

Adrienne Monnier, proprietor of La Maison des Amis des Livres and partner of Sylvia Beach, had insisted on bringing the two men together. Originally Williams balked: "Who is this man Larbaud who has so little pride that he wishes to talk with me?" he asked with disingenuous humility. But eventually he gave in to courtesy. His first impression of Larbaud was not encouraging: "He is a student, I am a block, I thought. I could see it at once: he knows far more of what is written of my world than I. But he is a student while I am—the brutal thing itself." That phrase "brutal thing itself" exhibits Williams in his foxiest role: a primitive American ignoramus, a tongue-tied, unprepared novice, sure to fail the professor's cross-examination—a bogus ploy, for as their conversation unfolded it was obvious that he was not overmatched by the learned "hippopotamus" slouching in his chair across from him.

The Frenchman was a nimble dialectician with a well-stocked mind, a poet and a translator of Coleridge's "Rime of the Ancient Mariner," Whitman, and Joyce's *Ulysses*. But it was the fact that Larbaud had written a biography of Simón Bolívar that most interested Williams—here was someone with an informed take on Spanish colonialism and the New World. Larbaud shared Williams's disapproval of the Puritans' parsimonious, "mean" appraisal of the New World—"Larbaud seemed cultivating my intimate earth with his skillful hands," the American visitor noted approvingly—though Williams dissented from the Frenchman's praise of Spanish "nobility, learning, refinement." The mere mention of the Puritans triggered in Williams a vitriolic attack on America as a degraded country with no books—Larbaud remonstrated with him about this wild charge—and a vast ignorance of its own past; its citizens' failure to recognize that "there is a source in [contemporary] America for everything we think and do" threatened, Williams felt, the growth of a mature democracy that can nurture the arts.

In Larbaud's civilized parlor, Williams unexpectedly found release. He roared like a lion—his tirade against the Puritans recalls his indictment in "Voyage of the Mayflower"—while his host interjected mild questions and proposed subtle modifications of Williams's thesis that his guest would have none of. When Larbaud called the Puritans giants, Williams scowled; he was, as Larbaud wryly noted, St. George on a mission to slay the Puritan dragon. Williams's rebuttal was eloquent:

No, no. True they had their magnificent logic, but it was microscopic in dimensions—against the flamboyant mass of savagery.

This disproportion has no representation in the contemporary Puritan imagination. The Puritan, finding one thing like another in a world destined for blossom only in "Eternity," all soul, all "emptiness" then here, was precluded from SEEING the Indian. They never realized the Indian in the least save as an unformed PURITAN. The *immorality* of such a concept, the inhumanity, the brutalizing effect upon their own minds, on their SPIRITS—they never suspected.

Larbaud was taken aback by the vehemence of Williams's disgust at the pernicious influence of puritanism, which the American poet likened first to a "ghostly miasma," then to a "mermaid with a corpse for [a] tail," and finally to "a relic of some died out tribe whose practices were revolting." When Williams called puritanism "an immorality that IS America" and must be annihilated, the more cautious Larbaud protested that it could not be done, but Williams, annoyed at this "cultivated tolerance," held his ground: "I wish only to disentangle the obscurities that oppress me, to track them to the root and to uproot them." His new "friend" was skeptical that one can "uproot history," but Williams declared that he only sought "the support of history," the better "to understand it aright, to make it show itself." Larbaud reminded him that to "disentangle obscurities" is as hard as to extract ore from the earth, and acutely observed that Williams was brimming "with those three things of which you speak: a puritanical sense of order, a practical mysticism as of the Jesuits, and the sum of all those qualities defeated in the savage men of your country by the first two." But Williams was so absorbed in expounding his thesis that either the comment passed him by or he refused to answer it.

Larbaud shrewdly put his finger on a tendency of Williams to become belligerent and polemical whenever he fancied himself under attack from his literary foes. Yet in the middle of his colloquy with Larbaud, another Williams makes a dramatic entrance, pulling two surprises from his sleeve that belie his earlier claim to ignorance: first, he demonstrates his knowledge of King Philip's War and then his fluency in French—the main source for his portrait of Père Sebastien Rasles was the Jesuit priest's *Lettres Édifiantes*, from which Williams quoted a paragraph in the original.

In the last several pages of the chapter, Williams's voice, like a charismatic actor's, dominates the Parisian salon. Larbaud sits mesmerized, unwilling to break the spell as Williams describes this "gentle, earthy man"

"with a fresh mind [that] could open eyes and heart to the New World."
The model of the "anti-Puritan," Rasles, "blossoming, thriving, opening,
reviving," is a "river bringing sweet water to us." Living among the Abenaki tribe of southern Maine for thirty-four years (1689–1723), Rasles
struggled, to the amusement of the tribe, to learn their guttural tongue
and eventually succeeded, to the point that he compiled a dictionary of
Abenaki and translated the Bible into it. He shared the tribe's privations,
fished and hunted and planted corn, fought alongside the warriors, whom
he greatly admired for their courage and ingenious military tactics, "settled disputes," and took his "altar of a pine board with him" on the trail
and tended their souls like a kindly shepherd: he is unafraid "TO MARRY,
to *touch*—to *give* because one HAS, not because one has nothing." This
is the highest accolade Williams can bestow. It explains Rasles's open-
hearted, *maternal* love for the Indians, his rare ability to understand, without censure or fear, their point of view.

Rasles's death was of a piece with his life: after several attempts to kill
him, the British finally cornered and slew him "at the foot of his rude
cross which he had erected in the center of his village—seeking to draw
the fire of the enemy upon himself in order that the women and the children might escape—and they mangled him besides, leaving him disfig-
ured and with his bones all crushed within him." The English army's
sadism allies them with the Puritans. Williams intends Rasles's altruism
and death to instruct his ignorant countrymen in 1924 that the origins of
their suffering dwell in the Puritans' emotional remoteness and spiritual
emptiness. In this chapter, partly set in contemporary Paris, Williams
lifts Rasles out of obscurity and elevates him to a prominent place in the
American pantheon, without lapsing into hagiography.

After Daniel Boone and George Washington, the reader next encounters Benjamin Franklin. Williams's dissenting opinion of Franklin is not a
case of personal bias run amok. It springs from his analysis of Franklin's
pamphlet *Information to Those Who Would Remove to America* (which
Williams reprints whole), in which Franklin dangles before prospective
immigrants the opportunity for artisans to thrive and for farmers to own
land and pass it on to their children—if, that is, they live by the gospel
Franklin preaches: hard work and thrift. To land-starved Europeans,
their advancement blocked by a hierarchical class system, even though
Franklin cautions that in colonial America "it is a general happy mediocrity that prevails," the incentive to own land could only cause a rush to

book passage on an Atlantic steamer. Franklin is far from puritan; indeed, he subverts puritanism not only in his own jovial nature but in his concentration on this world rather than the next.

Poor Richard's Almanac, though not quoted from, is obviously another source for Williams's shrewd appraisal of Franklin. Like D. H. Lawrence, he mocks the Philadelphian go-getter as "sly, covert, almost cringing." "He is our wise prophet of chicanery, the great buffoon, the face on the penny stamp." Williams does not downplay the obstacles that the New World posed for Franklin, or demean his astonishing energy, practical ingenuity, and many benefactions to the commonweal, from the invention of the lightning rod to the founding of the University of Pennsylvania, from whose medical school Williams graduated. But he is caustic about Franklin's complacent hypocrisies and popular maxims for getting ahead (Williams calls Franklin "the biggest winner" of eighteenth-century America): *Poor Richard's Almanac* was a self-help manual "as important in founding the nation as Paine's *Age of Reason*—he adaged them into a kind of pride in possession," Williams notes. Even in the wilderness of frontier Pennsylvania, Franklin barely notices the beauty surrounding him; if he does take it in, it's only to imagine how to pave it for the sake of civic utility and commerce.

By contrast, William lauds Aaron Burr, a man vilified in his day as power-hungry, untrustworthy, and morally shady, as frank and free-spirited. If there was a figure Williams identified with, it was Burr, the hero of a chapter mischievously titled "The Virtue of History" (for which Floss did much of the research). Williams frames his assessment of the dashing soldier-politician as a dialogue between an ardent partisan (Williams) and an unidentified skeptic (an anonymous historian). Williams argues that Burr was defamed in his own time by enemies and rivals as an unscrupulous politician who committed treason against the young republic by fomenting a rebellion to advance his own quest for power. For Williams, this is a grotesque misreading. He lauds Burr for three qualities: he is a brave soldier, he is a flower of American chivalry with a rare appreciation of women (who returned his affectionate regard), and above all, he is an exponent of freedom who "lived in unconstraint." The second and third attributes are the ones Williams dwells on.

That Burr defies conventional moral codes endears him to Williams. Burr could have married into an aristocratic family and exploited the connection for political gain. Instead, he married an older widow with two sons, "unbeautiful, a scar on her face—but the most refined, courteous, gracious creature he had ever laid his eyes upon. He loved these things, as in all he does, openly—in the teeth of the world." His cultivated wife gave him his daughter, Theodosia, with whom he forged an intimate relationship: she was both companion and disciple of unconstraint. Newspapers and political enemies traduced him as a satyr who sired a hundred bastards. Williams cares little for the truth or falsity of the charge, because Burr showed "disrespect for the applause"—and brickbats—"of the world." Even the twin blows of Theodosia's death at sea and his grandson's death at an early age did not break Burr's spirit. Williams's near idolatry of Burr is logical, because it mirrors his own admixture of womanizer and courtly gallant sensitive and sympathetic to the plight of women.

Burr lived out Williams's impassioned dream in another way, too: he embodied "freedom of conscience, a new start, and to be quit of Europe." Whereas the cautious, manipulative Hamilton, cast in *In the American Grain* (and later in *Paterson*) as a slippery villain who served the interests of the moneyed classes, Burr stood for "a yeast in the sap, an untracked force that might lead anywhere; it was springtime in a new world when all things were possible." Williams might have written that sentence about himself, since his faith in change runs deep and is the foundation on which he built his poetic. His interlocutor is amused by the poet's enthusiasm for Burr, implying that it is like a schoolgirl's crush, but he does not push back hard enough against Williams's panegyric. Williams's rhetoric is so charged and he repeats the word "freedom" so often that he transforms Burr into the statue of an idealized hero on horseback, say, in the park under the Great Falls in Paterson, where Hamilton established his industrial complex. But as D. H. Lawrence perceptively noted in his review of *In the American Grain*, Williams "sees the genius of the continent as a woman with exquisite, super-subtle tenderness and recoiling cruelty. It is a myth-woman who will demand of me a sensitive awareness, a supreme sensuous delicacy, and at the same time an infinitely tempered resistance, a power of endurance and resistance." In his resistance to and rebellion against received opinion, Burr is, for Williams, the template of the American hero.

Edgar Allan Poe, the subject of the long penultimate essay of *In the American Grain*, is a surprising choice and a more problematic model. Curiously, Williams extols Poe as "a genius intimately shaped by his locality and time." A poet who wrote verse in a singsong meter that was remote from the American vernacular, and whose lurid main subject was the death of women, is a peculiar candidate to be lauded as "the first great burst through to expression of a re-awakened genius of *place*." But for Williams, Poe is the first American man of letters to "clear the ground" of "colonial imitation." (Pound grudgingly conceded in "A Pact" that Whitman had done the same by swinging his free-verse axe that "broke the new wood," thus paving the way for Pound's carving skills.) Poe's *Philosophy of Composition* is not a prosodic manual Williams kept on his desk, nor was Williams's "imaginative intellect" "preeminently mathematical" as Poe's was. What the two shared was a fervent belief that "either the New World must be mine as I will have it, or it is a worthless bog. There can be no concession." Poe's originality lay in his use of language:

> With Poe, words were not hung by usage with associations, the pleasing wraiths of former masteries, this is the sentimental trap-door to beginnings. With Poe words were figures; an old language truly, but one from which he carried over only the most elemental qualities to his new purpose; which was, to find a way to tell his soul. Sometimes he used words so playfully his sentences seem to fly away from sense, the destructive! With the conserving abandon, foreshadowed, of a Gertrude Stein. The particles of language must be clear as sand.

Poe is at once Founding Literary Father, trailblazer like Eric the Red (Williams repeats the Viking's defiant "Rather the ice than their way"), and visionary modernist who anticipated Stein's experiments with abstract language and Williams's unsystematic ideas in *Spring and All*. The cost of Poe's originality, of being "a light in the morass," was an extreme isolation that drove him to drink and an ignominious death on a Baltimore street. Although Poe's emphasis on method and ratiocination is 180 degrees away from Williams's practice, Poe is Williams's comrade in arms, "*surrounded* by his time, tearing at it, ever with more rancor, but always at battle, taking hold." Williams does not blame the Puritans in this chapter for the poverty of means available to Poe, but they lurk in the shadows as a banal, inert mass to be resisted with all the force at a writer's disposal.

Williams does not ignore Poe's limitations. Indeed, he brilliantly analyzes them, but they carry the seed that would produce the modernist revolt against tradition, Cubism, and abstract expressionism:

> The language of his essays is a remarkable HISTORY of the local-
> ity he springs from. There is no aroma to his words, rather a lumi-
> nosity, that comes of a dissociation from anything else than thought
> and ideals; a coldly nebulous side to side juxtaposition of the words
> as the ideas—It seems to fall back continuously to a bare surface
> exhausted by having no perch in tradition. Seldom a long sensuous
> sentence, but with frequent reduplication upon itself as if holding
> itself up to itself.

And no one has described the atmosphere of Poe's poems as pithily as Williams:

> It is especially in the poetry where "death looked gigantically
> down" that the horror of the formless resistance which opposed,
> maddened, destroyed him has forced its character into the air, the
> wind, the blessed galleries, above a morose, dead world, peopled by
> shadows and silence and despair—it is the compelling force of his
> isolation.

If at irregular intervals Williams suffered the terrors of isolation, his profession shielded him from the extremes of "unreality" that Poe suc-cumbed to. Poe valiantly tried to be an independent man of letters in an environment both indifferent and antagonistic, but scraping out a living as a journalist condemned him to chronic privation. A writer who attempts to live by uncompromising aesthetic principles can end up a pariah like Poe or confined like Pound in a solipsistic and real jail. Williams avoided these fates.

In the course of writing *In the American Grain*, Williams and Floss took a trip to Farmville, Virginia, to visit Wallace Gould, a poet whose work Bill had taken a fancy to. Floss and the boys were very fond of Gould. Once, when Gould had run out of money in New York, he became a sort of non-paying boarder in the Williams household for several months. To reciprocate, he cooked meals, taught William Eric the piano, helped out with chores, and spun yarns like a professional storyteller. When Gould, who was born in Maine, decided to go south, he ended up in Farmville, a town not far from Appomattox and Monticello, where he eked out a living selling cakes by mail and playing the piano in the town movie theater. Eventually, he moved in with Mary Jackson, the retired principal of the local high school and a member of the FFV (First Families of Virginia). For Williams, Gould represented a small but authentic voice of the local. Williams liked to soak in the atmosphere of historical places, and on this visit he found himself intrigued by Virginia's mix of the old and the new, of rednecks and presidents, slavery and freedom.

He walked the battlefields where the Confederate army had camped, picking up Indian arrowheads and rusted cannonballs. It had been at the nearby courthouse in Appomattox that General Robert E. Lee had surrendered with noble gravitas to General Ulysses S. Grant, a scene that haunted Williams—not so much Grant as Lee, a man of dignity and exquisite manners, mounted on his horse and drinking a cup of tea before ceremoniously signing the official papers bringing the internecine bloodshed to an end. But though he penned a brief essay on Virginia, published in *A Novelette and Other Prose*, Williams did not explore the Civil War as a coda to the fuguelike themes of violence that *In the American Grain* weaves together. Instead, he composed a five-paragraph prose elegy to Abraham Lincoln, in the mysterious tone of Charles Ives's *The Unanswered Question*, the flags lowered to half-mast. Williams audaciously sketches Lincoln as a woman "with a great bearded face and a towering black hat above it, to give unearthly reality." It is an apt metaphor, mixing maternal comfort with a pietà, bleak proof of "the brutalizing desolation of life in America up to that time; yet perversely flowering."

This was the final chapter of *In the American Grain*. As he prepared to show the manuscript to Charles and Albert Boni, who had expressed interest in reading it, Williams felt he had avoided turning it into a reductive, tendentious chronicle of state-sponsored villainy. He had made it clear that even among the first wave of conquistadores there were some exceptional souls so fascinated by the cultures of the New World that they sympathetically set down the language, dress, architecture, food, religious rituals, and mores of the tribes in whose midst they lived. Williams had portrayed humble figures such as Père Sebastien Rasles and men of exquisite civility, equipoise, and practicality such as Samuel de Champlain, who embodied "the perfection of what we lack here": wholeness and "almost a woman's tenderness." A third hero is Daniel Boone, an ascetic rhapsode and hunter who breathed freely in the vast, nearly secret valleys and forests of Appalachia. Aaron Burr, whose love of women mirrors Williams's own, rounds out the small roster of men who serve for Williams as models of New World sprezzatura. Beyond these heroes, he had conveyed the New World's sense of wonder, its invitation to make something new, which was what he was trying to do in his own poetry.

Charles Boni not only agreed to publish *In the American Grain* but he also came up with its title. However, although the book received mainly favorable reviews, Boni's enthusiasm waned quickly. He refused to launch an advertising campaign. Sales were anemic, and the book virtually disappeared from view. A few critics such as Waldo Frank and D. H. Lawrence appreciated what Williams had achieved; Yvor Winters, a caustic detractor of Williams's poetry, extravagantly praised the prose of "The Destruction of Tenochtitlan"; and Hart Crane's long poem *The Bridge* was strongly influenced by the book. Still, Williams could not help being discouraged by its reception. It seemed as though his best work was doomed to reach only a tiny cadre of discerning readers.

TEN

Revisiting the Seductions of Europe

In the first week of 1924, with *In the American Grain* mostly completed, Floss and Bill busied themselves with last-minute arrangements for their departure to Europe. They looked forward to the trip with mounting excitement. Williams had booked tickets on the SS *Rochambeau*, sailing from New York on January 9, 1924, to Le Havre. The crossing would take nine days. The luggage packed, what remained was saying their last goodbyes to friends and family. Never having been away from the boys for any long period, Bill came down with a bad case of separation anxiety (neither Floss nor William Eric and Paul seem to have shared it); he moped and sighed and felt pangs of guilt, though he never considered canceling the trip.

The night before the ship sailed, several friends fêted Williams at the Columbia University Club, perhaps thinking to prepare him for the heavy tippling he'd face in sybaritic Europe. In the morning, in a mandatory party for Americans going abroad, relatives and "the gang" (several friends), bringing flowers and baskets of fruit as tokens of their affection, crowded into the Williamses' stateroom to wish them well.

The Atlantic crossing proved rough: a violent storm shook the old ship and made walking on deck treacherous. But Williams did not like being cooped up belowdecks, preferring to stand at the railing and gaze down at the sea, "home of the wild gods in exile," or up at the clouds, driven by gale winds, changing shapes and colors. He watched whales spouting and birds hovering above the ship, as they had over the *Niña*, or else simply gave in to the luxury of uninterrupted daydreaming. Floss, for her part, enjoyed being pampered by the ship's crew. The voyage was uneventful.

After passing through customs, Floss and Bill met Kay Boyle at the Le Havre train station; she tried to persuade them to stay overnight in the port city—she was leading a lonely, monastic life and craved company—but they were eager to hurry on to Paris, where Bob McAlmon had booked a room for them at the Hotel Lutétia, and was ready to initiate them into the bohemian life of Left Bank Paris.

Throughout their stay, when the spirit moved him, Williams would record events and people that he could deposit in his memory bank for future reference. Later he drew on this free-form journal for his novel *Voyage to Pagany* (1932) and his *Autobiography* (1951). The beauty and enchantments of Paris overwhelmed him and Floss, as they had visitors for centuries. To Marianne Moore he confided that in Paris "the European virus was injected into Floss and me," not to immunize them from delirium, but to help them gorge on the city's cultural riches, its serious frivolities "that release what there is in men" and "that mean a knife cut through self-deception." Paris licensed them to indulge in the pleasure principle. Paris was, as Hemingway later named it, a "moveable feast." Nearly every day was crammed with visits to museums and bookstores and galleries; to the Tuileries Gardens and Notre Dame; to bars, cafés, and restaurants; to hear Sidney Bechet and Josephine Baker perform; to the premiere of a Jean Cocteau play; and to an adaptation of Jules Romains's droll hit *Dr. Knock*, "the success story of a young physician in a small French village where, through his zeal for cures, he all but ruined the health of the entire community." And courtesy of Robert McAlmon, who seemed to know everybody, Bill and Floss were swept up in a whirlwind of social engagements.

McAlmon moved among the large expatriate colony like a prince bestowing largesse on his subjects—the divorce settlement conferred on him by Sir John Ellerman, Bryher's immensely rich father, had enabled him to be a patron to Joyce, to George Antheil, and, as we've seen, to avant-garde writing—but he also had entrée into French artistic circles. Despite his newly acquired suavity, McAlmon remained the melancholy, pugnacious young rebel who had edited *Contact* with Williams. Bill marveled at how his protégé and friend drove himself—"he knew no limits, physical or for intellectual honesty"—and he worried that this madcap drive would lead eventually to a breakdown (as it did).

McAlmon was a heavy drinker who grew surly or gauche when in his cups—proposing a toast to sin, for example, which offended Joyce—and insulted people who could have flattened him with one punch. "Whisky," Williams observed, "was to the imagination of the Paris of that time like milk to a baby"; it broke down inhibitions and inspired gaiety, flirtations, maudlin praise, savage debunking, and witty bons mots that would circulate rapidly like *pneumatiques* through all twenty arrondissements. With so much alcohol fueling passions, an offhand put-down at an art exhibit might easily escalate to a confrontation in a café, and from there spread to newspapers, which stoked the fires to sell copies. Parisians seemed to enjoy reports of this verbal swordplay.

In Brancusi's workshop, to which McAlmon escorted Bill and Floss, uninvited, one afternoon, Williams was drawn to *Socrates*, a sculpture the artist had recently finished. Williams had admired Brancusi's airy sculpture *Bird in Flight* at the Armory Show. Now, as he took a fancy to the unaffected Romanian peasant, he immediately grasped the meaning of this new work: "a big hole through the center of the block showing Socrates the talker, his mouth (and mind) wide open expounding his theses." That spacious, receptive mind was exemplary of more than the great Greek philosopher-soldier; it symbolized the richly textured, sometimes incestuous Parisian art world, where poets, painters, composers, dealers, critics, and hangers-on, whatever their jealousies and petty biases and enthusiasms, commingled: the stream of chatter, polemic, and commentary, by turns strident, fulsome, merry, and contemplative, was seldom dammed up. Nearly everybody kept track of the shifting status of poets' and painters' reputations, which could degenerate into the blood sport of character assassination or become a source of comic banter. So when the mild-mannered Brancusi denounced Pound's opera *Villon* as little more than a dilettante's conceit, Williams was pleased and joined in the trouncing. "'Pound writing an opera?' I said. 'Why, he doesn't know one note from another.'" Williams remarked in the *Autobiography*: "It must infuriate Ezra that there is *something* in the world of which he is not the supreme master." Having received many a tongue-lashing from Pound for amateurish verse and ignorance, Williams enjoyed the taste of vicarious revenge.

Sylvia Beach's bookstore, Shakespeare and Company, functioned informally as an information bazaar: tips on agents, editors, restaurants, lodgings, and parties; gossip about trysts and marriages coming apart. La Maison des Amis des Livres, the French bookshop of her partner,

Adrienne Monnier, stood across the rue de l'Odéon from Shakespeare and Company, and there was easy commerce between the two. Indeed, the Beach-Monnier love affair was a triumph of Franco-American amity.

Williams liked the hospitable Sylvia Beach, but he fell hard for Adrienne Monnier, a stout French Gaia of "unflinching kindness" and frank appetites—"the senses were her meat," Williams remarks of her—determined "to conserve and to enrich the literary life of her time." A minor poet, Monnier translated Whitman and Hemingway, among others, and later would edit a magazine that devoted an entire issue to Williams. Like a fairy godmother doubling as cultural attaché, she served as an informal matchmaker, intuitively sensing compatible tastes and interests. Williams's fruitful meeting with Valéry Larbaud was but one of her engineered triumphs.

On one occasion, Monnier pulled Williams out of a funk by spending an hour with him looking at Brueghel prints, both relishing the image of a great fish cut open only to find in its belly a smaller fish, which, cut open, "discharges" smaller ones: an unforced symbol of the power and instinctual laws of appetite in nature—and of their consequences—that Williams explored in all his work and Monnier benignly embodied.

When McAlmon introduced him to Bill and Sally Bird, Williams took an immediate shine to them. He and the affable Bill Bird, a businessman turned publisher, became good friends. Williams liked Bird's modest, lively presence and civility. Bird was the prototype of the adventurous publisher willing to take a chance on avant-garde writing, and he didn't stint on using fine paper and bindings. His exquisite taste extended to wine, about which Bird was an authority; in 1924, French oenophiles would have scoffed at the idea of an American expert on French wines, but Bird's connoisseurship, put to the test in Dijon and Beaune, provided rare pleasures for Bill's and Floss's palates.

Since James Joyce was the reigning literary potentate, a meeting with him was as mandatory for literary pilgrims to Paris as one with Gertrude Stein. Williams was pleased to make the gregarious Irishman's acquaintance. Evenings spent in Joyce's company proved memorable. His eyesight was poor, but his conversation was voluble and eccentric. One night Joyce, who was writing *Finnegans Wake* at the time, grilled Floss because he heard she came of Norse stock, hoping to glean a few facts or words to flavor his linguistic stew. After drinking a certain amount he would sing Irish ballads with quivering earnestness. At the end of many evenings, his long-suffering wife, Nora, would, with the help of friends, dump Joyce in a cab and take him home for a sobering up.

Though Williams loved Paris enough to briefly toy with the idea of opening an office and practicing pediatrics in the French metropolis, this was a whimsical fantasy, since it would have been as impossible for an American doctor to attract Parisian patients as it was for Christopher Newman, Henry James's wealthy hero in *The American*, to conquer the social fortress of the aristocratic Bellegarde family and marry their beautiful daughter, Claire. Since half the time Williams expected the Parisians to patronize or reject him as an American rube, why would he think they would abandon their cherished prejudices and accept him as their family doctor? He would be shunned as too exotic, too risky, just as Sally Bird, who had a lovely operatic voice, could not get past the sentinels protecting the Paris Opéra's roster from outsiders. Talent was no guarantee of success.

Nine days of nonstop activity had taken a toll, and Bill and Floss were relieved to set out on the itinerary they had mapped in Rutherford. A brief stop at Carcassonne in cold, damp weather to look at the monumental medieval fortress left Williams feeling oppressed. In Marseilles, they ordered the customary bouillabaisse and strolled around the port before moving on to Villefranche, where they stayed for a full month in the Pension Donat, accompanied for part of the time by McAlmon. Perched on a cliff commanding a dramatic view of the harbor and the Mediterranean, the inn was comfortable, though the food was ordinary. Bill and Floss were free to pursue their interests at their own pace. They hiked on the upper Corniche on Valentine's Day, the Alpes Maritimes rising above them majestically, walked all the way to Monaco, admired the flowering mimosa and lemon trees, and played roulette in Monte Carlo (and won). In rainy or cold weather, they huddled in their room before a fire and read, Williams taking the measure of E. E. Cummings's *Tulips and Chimneys* and McAlmon's latest fiction. They even got to play host to Bill Bird, down from Paris, and to Lady Emerald Cunard, who came to inspect the American couple and, pleased with what she found, returned several times to sit on their veranda and talk books or anything that occupied her "courteous, cultivated, and fearless mind."

Nancy Cunard, her beautiful daughter, also visited. Born into an enormously rich English family that made its fortune carrying passengers across the Atlantic on sleek ocean liners, Nancy had developed a renegade mind that often put her at odds with her American mother, who disapproved of her daughter's friends, love life, Negro husband (the poet Henry Crowder), and flouting of social propriety. Nonetheless, they shared a love of the arts, and Lady Cunard encouraged her daughter to write. Nancy had both captivated and puzzled Williams when they met in Paris, where she was the belle of literary and artistic society. Man Ray and Cecil Beaton photographed her, Oskar Kokoschka painted her portrait, Wyndham Lewis sketched his impression of her, and Brancusi paid homage in two abstract sculptures, *Jeune Fille Sophistiquée* and *The White Negress*. She collected African art and amassed an idiosyncratic collection of paintings by de Chirico, Tanguy, and Picabia, among others. She was the quintessence of glamour and chic. Each portrait captures a different quality. In Beaton's and Man Ray's photographs, she is posed artificially against striped, dotted, and floral wallpapers, wearing bracelets and bangles (her trademark ornament) that run up her arms from her wrists to her elbows—yet she stares at the world out of large piercing eyes, seeming to search for some elusive truth. She is still, but her identity changes, from a model in a gorgeous coat topped by a helmet-like cloche, to a Joan of Arc or aviatrix, an ingenue like Natasha in *War and Peace*, or a matron weary of her manic social life yet unable to break with it. No wonder Williams, a votary of change, hung a picture of Nancy Cunard in his attic studio where he wrote his poems. Yet despite his fascination with her, she was an odd choice to cast as his muse, unless as an admonition to himself to question authority and live, as much as possible, according to his own lights.

During Floss and Bill's sojourn in Villefranche, Nancy stayed with her mother in Monte Carlo, so Williams had several opportunities to study her character. He likens Nancy, this "tall, blond spike of a woman," to a martyr "burned to the bone" by her passionate intensity. She was a voluptuary who acted "without restraints"; her legendary promiscuity—she had had affairs with Pound, Tristan Tzara, and Louis Aragon—paradoxically conferred on her a "depraved saintliness." She and her friend Iris Tree "denied sin by making it hackneyed in their own bodies, shucking it away to come out not dirtied but pure." Williams could never regard his own sexual profligacy as spiritual purity, because unlike these *jeunes filles* who never seemed inhibited by guilt, he had to wrestle with his conscience. In a throwaway sentence, he tantalizingly remarks that Nancy "was very fond of Floss and later protected her on more than one wild occasion," but he never spells out what "wild occasions" required Nancy's intervention.

Nonetheless, her unbridled pursuit of erotic pleasure seems to have sparked and spiced up his and Floss's sexual relations.

Nancy's appetite for the arts was as huge as her appetite for sex; they were interlocked. She had fallen in love with Pound's Adonis-like looks, but even more with his capacious mind. (It's not clear if Williams knew of their liaison, though likely the gossip mills put the news in his ear.) Pound took her on as a pupil and encouraged her to write poems. Like him, she was a deracinated free spirit, though he had only a mild interest in the Dada and surrealist circles she frequented and did not suffer from her compulsive restlessness, which drove her from European city to city, apparently in search of relief from an inner core of loneliness. But she had her own moral compass. When Pound married Olga Rudge and became a father, she broke off relations with him, though in 1930 her Hours Press published *A Draft of XXX Cantos*. But when later in the decade Pound championed fascism and made racist and anti-Semitic comments, a disgusted Cunard severed all contact with him. Williams's left-liberal politics was more congenial to her, and she admired his altruistic medical care of workers and the poor.

The next leg of the Williamses' trip took them to Rome. Williams had spent time in the city in 1910 with Ed, who had won a Prix de Rome in architecture. On this trip, he and Floss stayed for three weeks, interrupted only by a brief excursion to Pompeii and the Amalfi coast. Like Gibbon, Goethe, Hawthorne, and countless other writers before him, Williams walked the streets of the city that, in a letter to Kenneth Burke, he called "this ripe center of everything." Yet Rome was no longer a hub of American artists, and Williams could safely lower his guard and not worry that he might be making a bad impression on some expatriate. Thus meeting Norman Douglas, the author of the novel *South Wind* and admired travel books, roused no anxieties. What he remembered most were the Englishman's irreverent maxims, in particular a comment about child rearing: "the best thing a father can do for his son after he conceives him is to die when he is born." This facetious counsel, based on Douglas's long separation from his son, was not something Williams as father, obstetrician, and pediatrician could ever subscribe to.

Rome made such a profound impression on Williams that he started composing a piece in several parts titled simply "Rome." He jotted down notes for the work in the Italian capital, added sections during his month in Vienna, and then tinkered with it on and off back in Rutherford. Perhaps not satisfied that "Rome" went much beyond a series of memos to himself about themes that obsessed him—art, sex, medicine, and history—he put it back in his drawer. (It was not published until 1978.) Yet it deserves more than passing notice, since it belongs with his other experimental work of the 1920s, all to greater and lesser degrees some form of improvisation.

The challenge for Williams was to explore how slavery and freedom tensely coexisted in Rome's history. "The monuments of Rome," he remarks, "are the monuments of enslavement—attacked by a freedom of the arts." He draws no facile parallels to American life, but in "Rome" he stresses once again that in the United States freedom is both feared and abridged—a frank sculpture like the Capitoline Venus would never get past the censors back home. Curiously, throughout the early draft of "Rome," Williams, sounding like a stevedore, scatters words like "cunt," "cock," "fucking," and "shitting," but in later drafts he crosses most of them out or replaces them with a euphemism: "phallus" for "stiff prick," for example. He cannot unequivocally practice the candor he swears by. He wants to break free of the habits that have impeded his efforts to write poetry and prose that cuts close to the bone, but as he says, "There is escape only by moments of easy walking out from a self and in saying it was."

In "Rome," Williams keeps circling back to the words "pleasure" and "clarity." Later, in *A Voyage to Pagany*, he would return to this dichotomy, explicitly connecting pleasure with Rome. His alter ego in the novel, Dr. Dev Evans, admires and envies Nero, Caligula, and the "other reckless Roman emperors" for their "fullness of abandon," equating "their unchecked voluptuousness [and] headlong humor" with "the fullness of life." To reach this state of intense pleasure, the Roman emperors stopped at nothing, including extreme violence. Williams was not seduced by, nor did he countenance, such horrific immorality. But as Steven Ross Loevy points out, "Williams thought of Rome as a center of dangerous but fertile chaos, where one might as easily be lost as dazzled, [but] where one might shed 'staid and tired acceptances and moralities' and emerge changed, refreshed, in repossession of one's self." To shed those "acceptances and moralities" is a goal Williams voices throughout the twenties. That dream of "fertile chaos," the womb of the unconscious out of which change is born, preoccupied him in *Kora in Hell*, but though he had made remarkable progress toward incorporating change in the experimental works that followed, he was still not satisfied. His stated wish to repossess his self suggests he fretted that he had lost or misplaced it along the way. In Rome, he felt the thrill of the hunt for its recovery. The process was a form of sublimated pleasure.

Pleasure's sibling, clarity, though insisted upon as an ideal, is only fitfully present in "Rome." The most lucid passages relate to medical topics—tuberculins, syphilis, malaria—because these are an integral part of the whole body of knowledge he has mastered; they open wide the "poor human rose windows of learning." Sometimes Williams plays the clever aphorist—"The sum of knowledge is the destruction of stupidity," "We mutilate and call it wisdom to maim our bodies to be little"—or arranges paragraphs, in anaphoric patterns, to look like a prose poem, as he does in a dithyrambic musing about violence. But elsewhere the prose resembles a diary whose entries have a tendency to ramble on and to be disconnected from one another.

In a seeming paradox, "unity" is the antithesis of clarity. Unity, Williams contends, asphyxiates the intelligence. In his essay on Virginia, he asserts that unity "is the shallowest, the cheapest deception of all composition. In nothing is the banality of the intelligence more clearly manifest." Clarity, by contrast, is like a penetrating solar ray that irradiates details. "Intelligence is a motion through multiplicity but its result is not unity but clarity, release of many diverse things." That fracture and "the intercrossing of opposed forces" are the by-product of composition does not disturb Williams; thoughts and grumpy feelings may tumble pell-mell onto the page, because "clarity is movement and stasis kills it at once." What frees movement in speech rhythm? Williams debated this in his own mind as early as 1913. In one formulation he observes, "Each piece of work, rhythmic in whole, is then in essence an assembly of tides, waves, ripples—in short, of greater and lesser rhythmic particles regularly repeated or destroyed."

This makes elegant sense as far as it goes. But in practice how does any poet, Williams included, "assemble" tides, waves, and ripples? Rhythmic particles, like debris carried by ocean currents, can clog movement; "regularly repeated and destroyed," they bring about the very killing stasis Williams wishes to avoid. Hence Williams experimented with ways of controlling motion: speeding up a line and breaking it at unexpected places, letting syntax expand and contract as the feeling or subject dictates, and varying rhythm to defeat monotony.

Thus in "Rome," wishing to convey the lawless, violent nature of

American life, Williams lets his rhythms career wildly and derail into linguistic fragments. Mike Weaver glosses the text this way:

> Williams poured out his radical thoughts on the value of the murderous and perverted element in American life. He suggested to himself that it was the degenerate element, the pure products of a country gone inane or syphilitic, which was the remnant of a heroic pioneer society. The wild, decayed, and doomed represented an aristocracy of the mind whose bodies obeyed impulses which if not socially beneficent showed a wholly admirable independence of conservative thought. No perversion, no matter how shocking, was worse than inversion. Inversion stemmed from an exaggerated respect for given form; whether for woman, which resulted in homosexuality in men; or for the line in poetry, which resulted in the inversion of the phrase. It was encouraged by the absurd prohibitions, by the forces opposed to change. An eruption like that of Mount Pelée was inevitable since "the pleasure of motion to relief," whether in sex or poetry, was something which could not be averted, but only perverted in its outlet.

In Rome, where debauchery had once been rampant, almost commonplace, Williams might have been tempted to see in such behavior "a wholly admirable independence of conservative thought" and "given form" and an overthrow of "forces opposed to change." But it's unlikely that he would have idealized "the "wild, decayed, and doomed" in America as representing an "aristocracy of mind." Quite the opposite, to judge from "The pure products of America": degeneracy as a "motion to relief" is a deadly caricature of mind and intelligence in a decidedly *unheroic* society that is heading for a smash-up.

Williams's prose in "Rome" crackles with energy. Its sentences illustrate the openness to experience he advocates: "Art from everything [is] what is wanted—from between Venus' thighs or the mathematic of Jewish writing—from the Bible or the quality of Alabaster—a Saracen column of green porph[y]ry, Greek relic, or the arch of a bath." Williams admonishes himself to be inclusive. This program is not new—it's part of his inheritance from Whitman—but in "Rome" Williams imbued it with a fresh urgency; it was a rallying cry for him and for America to "crack the seed" and create a poetics that would bear ripened fruit equal or superior to what Europe produced.

In "Rome," with his imagination in overdrive, the piecemeal once again takes charge. Even a patient reader who loves diversity and enjoys Williams's restless pursuit of it may feel that the poet overstates the lethal effects of unity and wish to find in "Rome" more consistency in fusing clarity and pleasure. And indeed Williams himself apparently judged the piece broken, since in his lifetime he never revised it for publication.

On the way back to Paris from Vienna, Williams made a sentimental stopover at the Château de Lancy, on whose grounds he had romped as an adolescent. In Paris, Bill and Floss once more plunged into a nonstop round of dinners, concerts, outings to museums, and endless socializing. The unexpected always seemed to happen: at a supper in a Montmartre bistro, Sally Bird spotted the leading tenor of the Opéra Comique. When she began singing Mimi's duet with Rodolfo from *La Bohème,* the tenor joined in on cue; the performance was incandescent, the seedy joint magically turned into the Café Momus. As the last notes faded away, Sally swooned with ecstasy and had to be carried out, but despite her fine display of musicianship and vocalism, the tenor did not think to use his influence to win her a contract to sing on the Paris opera stage. Singers needed sponsors, which often meant a letter or a tumble on the casting couch, as in Hollywood, which Sally was unwilling to do.

Williams retells the amusing (apocryphal?) story of a brief encounter between Joyce and Proust. Expecting verbal fireworks from the meeting of the Titans of modern fiction, the two entourages leaned in to catch an elegant exchange of lacquered aperçus. What they heard were Proust and Joyce groaning like old men about their respective ailments and then slinking off into the Paris night.

Although Paris brought out the bon vivant in Williams's nature, it also highlighted its opposite, the bilious malcontent. In his diary and *Autobiography,* Williams did not hide how thin-skinned he was, taking umbrage at slights real and imagined. The waiter serving him and Floss Chateaubriand on their first night in Paris filched half of it, Williams claimed. Another time, when he ordered a bottle of Meursault with dinner, he thought he noticed the sommelier sneering, as if Americans couldn't possibly appreciate such a fine wine. Incidents involving people he knew sparked a deeper resentment. Agreeing to be photographed by Man Ray,

Williams dressed elegantly, with a cravat neatly tucked into his vest and a scarf draped around his shoulders. In Man Ray's portrait, his handsome face is unsmiling and quizzical. His high forehead hints at a strong intelligence, but his gaze is sphinx-like. When Man Ray submitted his bill, Williams was outraged and felt taken advantage of. There was nothing to do but swallow his ire and pay it. He wanted the photograph, which he thought a poor likeness, destroyed, but fortunately it wasn't.

A particularly curious and revelatory episode took place a few days after Floss and Bill's arrival. McAlmon arranged a lavish and expensive supper at the Trianon in their honor. Williams knew many of the thirty guests from parties and gallery openings in New York—Man Ray, Duchamp, Mina Loy—and from Paris's bohemians Joyce, Ford Madox Ford, and Louis Aragon. Although by 1924 improvisation came easily to Williams, the prospect of speaking extemporaneously to this group daunted him. Etiquette, however, dictated that he deliver a short speech or a toast. His account twenty-seven years later in his *Autobiography* still startles with its ill-humored tone:

> What had I to say with all eyes, especially those of the Frenchmen, gimleted upon me to see what this American could possibly signify, if anything? I had nothing in common with them.
>
> I said thank you, naturally, to Bob, thanked them all for their kindness and then told them that in Paris I had observed that when a corpse, in its hearse, plain or ornate, was passing in the streets, the women stopped, bowed their heads and that men generally stood at attention with their hats in their hands. What I meant was my own business. I did not explain, but sat down feeling like a fool.

What devil possessed Williams to deliver such a cryptic speech? Had too much wine addled his brain? Even if he drank too much, that's still not an adequate explanation: his peevishness seems totally out of proportion to the occasion, since he had much in common with this diverse company of writers and artists. Williams twitches at being cast in the role of "this American"; it robs him of his individuality—and his poise and wits. He turns a tense moment into a mortifying faux pas: first, like a callow American innocent abroad Mark Twain might have lampooned, he belittles the French for their custom of stopping what they are doing and doffing their hats when a hearse drives by, out of respect for the dead; then he withdraws into embarrassed silence, compounding his gaffe. He has rigged the situation so that he'll offend the assembled guests. This is a blatant case of self-sabotage.

The next day, while a chastened Williams is walking off his hangover and boorish behavior, he stumbles on the "medieval Place François Ier, as French in its way as anything I have ever known, of that French austerity of design, gray stone clearly cut and put together in complementary masses, like the Alexandrines of Racine." He finds solace for an hour in the classicism his brother, Edgar, extolled in the buildings he designed; classicism offered a temporary holiday from the jarring dramas of modernism and his own as-yet-undefined part in them.

Another spasm of paranoia occurred at a gala social event of the haut monde, a benefit performance of *Salade* (a spoof of Satie's ballet *Parade*). Williams had chosen to wear a ratty tuxedo, and in consequence felt self-conscious and inadequate. "It was intended as a gesture of contempt," he reports, "and received just that." In a surly mood, he gives vent to vituperation that would have won him the blue ribbon in a contest with Thersites. The objects of his venom included not only the French upper crust, the consumers and patrons of high culture, but also familiar faces such as H.D. and Bryher, who were also in the audience that night; he railed against nearly everybody's "cupidity," "bitchery," and "half-screaming hysteria . . . It [the coterie] was a gelatinous mass, squatting over a treasure; a *Rheingold-musik*." This venal elite group is willing to sell themselves to the highest bidder. What fuels Williams's rage is in part the audience's materialism and air of invincible superiority, expressed in its supposed indifference to him—with one sneering remark, H.D. vaporizes him as an American nobody with feeble tastes. (Her malice may have been partly motivated by his closeness to McAlmon, who, she imagined, posed a threat to her relationship with Bryher.)

Williams makes a show of being "a rustic in my own eyes, uninitiated," but adds, "It is certain that though I was in no way affected by the well-dressed crowd[.] . . . I ground my teeth out of resentment, though I acknowledge their privilege to step on my face if they could." One minute he's humiliated and galled that he cannot crack the glassy surface of the "social automatons" in the theater and discover what they really feel about him or the ballerina onstage he professes to admire; the next minute, he's certain that his judgment of them as cosmopolitan sharks waiting to feed is correct. That the fashionable spectators can be both alert *and* indifferent irks Williams. He tries in vain to frame his own conflict as a pitched battle between society and art, in which art is trounced. How can new works find purchase, he asks, if sophisticated audiences only glance at the performance? Williams's internal monologue, hilarious and splenetic in its contradictions, sounds suspiciously like his displeasure at the cool reception to his poems in America.

Despite contact with the most brilliant group of creators anywhere in the world, Williams could not shake off a sense of disappointment; driven back on his "resistant core," he felt himself "with ardors not released but beaten back, in this center of old-world culture where everyone was tearing his own meat, *warily* conscious of a newcomer, but wholly without inquisitiveness—No wish to know . . ." This bitter self-accounting, this yearning for release, recurs frequently in Williams's letters, poems, and hybrid works. Only the setting changes.

Although he did succumb to what he called the "infuriating meanness" of others at times, he did not try to hide the root cause of his behavior: his insecurities. Yet despite the rant of his set piece, he did not sulk or brood over the made-up slight of being regarded as a lightweight. He rushed around Paris, sampling all its hedonistic wares: food, wine, poetry, galleries, ballets, and stimulating conversations with many of the gods and demigods of modernism. Moreover, his ability to make new friends—the Birds, Philippe and Madame Soupault, Ford Madox Ford—is a sign of psychological health and proof that many writers did wish to know him.

Introduced to Philippe Soupault, thirteen years his junior, Williams warmed to him immediately, though they spent relatively little time together: a few dinners and conversations at parties or cafés. Soupault was good company, an amusing raconteur who could talk "about Picasso, his poor beginnings, his profusion, one of the greatest reasons for his success, the women who had walked into and out of his life, his single-mindedness." Soupault's modernist credentials were impeccable. He began his career as an acolyte of Apollinaire, converted to Dadaism, and soon after, together with André Breton, founded surrealism. The two men cowrote *The Magnetic Fields*, the *ur*-text of surrealist automatic writing. Although Williams never enlisted in the ranks of the surrealists, he was sympathetic to their deliberate overturning of conventional rules.

Perhaps Soupault's surrealist verse, with its indifference to method—he seldom bothered to revise—snared Williams's attention. In 1926, Soupault was expelled from the surrealist movement and took up journalism, becoming a newspaper correspondent. When he published his novel *Les Dernières Nuits de Paris* (*Last Nights of Paris*) in 1928, Williams got hold of a copy and decided to translate it.

The prototype of *Last Nights of Paris* is Restif de la Bretonne's 1793 novel *Les Nuits de Paris*, which the surrealists rescued from neglect. Restif prowled the streets of Paris during the five days of the September Massacre (September 2–7, 1792), witnessing mob atrocities against clergymen and prisoners, dragged out of the Bastille, who were deemed to be counterrevolutionaries. In Soupault's novel, however, politics is replaced by a kind of surrealist detective story: a murder is committed, and there is a circuitous attempt by the police to solve it. If the plot is often skimpy, and the motives of the characters as unfathomable to themselves as they are to the reader, Soupault ably furnishes an extended nocturnal tour of the Parisian underworld, populated by petty criminals and prostitutes, vagrants and runaways and drunkards, and sailors on shore leave.

In Soupault's novel, Chance, beloved of the surrealists, rules a capricious, violent universe, reducing people to slaves "subject to the grievous visitations of its harsh and malicious power." Chance also governs the novel's form, the pieces of the puzzle, as in nightmares, never quite fitting together. The narrator, a transparent stand-in for Soupault, restlessly walks the sinister streets of Paris, sometimes stalking Georgette, a prostitute of unknown origins whom he once slept with, but he is more muted observer and reluctant amanuensis of what he sees than actor; a man afflicted with ennui, like a relic of Baudelaire's urban hell, he is besieged by phantoms. He is not a rebellious or perverse kin of Dostoyevsky's Underground Man, challenging society and the status quo: his enigmatic quest, what he desires, lacks discipline. Indeed, the narrator is most of all a surrealist poet, his tone detached and factual, like the newspapers he reads every morning, yet recording on every page odd turns of phrase—"the hygiene of fear," for example, or "the tempest of silence"—that are both provocative and empty. Without warning, an unhinged image or a portentous aphorism springs from the page and arrests the reader's attention: "A passerby dragged his cane against the railings, the strollers' imbecilic xylophone," or "A corpse confronts us with eternity." The bizarre or fantastical is commonplace: seventeen clocks stop at 11:35; Paris becomes a woman and Georgette a city: "She was the night itself and her beauty was nocturnal." The narrator and other characters are not so much lost souls as literary wraiths. Fires burn and corpses rot, and the narrator gourmandizes on repulsive images—"slimy gigantic lepers," "pustules," and a "sunless forest." Paris, we're told, was "merciless at night," and an air of menacing unreality does hang above the city: "Already the districts we were traversing had lost their Parisian color, just as the polar regions are shown faded out on geographic maps."

In *I Wanted to Write a Poem*, Williams calls Georgette "a very wonderful little whore, very intellectual, exotic, strange—one couldn't capture her mood in any way at all—contradictory, amusing." Memory must have played a trick on Williams, since she's more dated, bloodless cardboard figure than "intellectual" whore. Possibly his praise derives from the fact that living "without restraint," yet "regular of habits," she manages a synthesis that eluded him. But her strongest attachment, as well as that of other characters, is to Paris itself, which enslaves and cradles them. Soupault is an expert cartographer of his own city.

As a *coup de dés*, however, *Last Nights of Paris* does not add up to a satisfying work of art. What drew Williams to it can only be conjectured. The translation offered an opportunity to draw his mother, Elena, into a project that, despite a seamy milieu that might have shocked her prudish nature, could stimulate her mind and distract her from the ailments that made her a cranky burden to her son. Her fluency in French, he hoped, would ensure that the translation would be idiomatic and accurate.

Williams's translation is crisp and deft at rendering the unnerving shadows, irrational violence, and temptations of a world with murky boundaries. *Last Nights of Paris* is an extended footnote to his Paris adventure and experimental works of the 1920s, but it also reflects his growing interest in surrealism and in how he might incorporate it into his poems.

With the days of his sabbatical dwindling, Williams stepped up the tempo of his social visits. He was in perpetual motion, slowed only momentarily by Floss coming down with a fever that for a day or so he worried might be diphtheria. (He also was summoned to the bedside of Hemingway's infant son, who was fine, if underweight.) But she soon recovered and joined the farewell lunches, suppers, teas, and parties. Mina Loy came and sketched Williams as a "wild Indian," and drew Floss rather too "delicately," he thought. The journal entries for these frenetic last days are a jumble of names, like the dance card of a popular belle of the ball. Every so often Williams broke away for a solitary walk in the Bois de

Boulogne. He was, in his deepest self, more *homme sérieux* than playboy of the Left Bank. It was typical that at a reception for Cocteau, he "soured on the scene" of "drunken hilarity" and sought the evening air to restore his equanimity.

He and Floss and the Birds went to Rheims, where, unlike the rest of the party, Williams was content to walk around the outside of the Gothic cathedral, admiring its soaring grandeur, and not to inspect the equally impressive interior. They then took a tour of the Veuve Clicquot winery, where they learned how champagne is made and happily guzzled the fizzy brew. And in a more solemn detour, the four visited the battlefield of the Marne, where trench warfare had taken an astonishingly high toll of French, German, and British soldiers. Both Bills felt melancholy at Williams's impending departure; their friendship had brought them as close together as brothers.

Finally, shortly before it was time to return to Rutherford, Williams snatched a few hours of conversation with Pound. His relationship with Pound had continued to be a tense match of wills and ideas. When Pound adopted a tone of irksome condescension, Williams would erupt like Vesuvius and scorch his friend with invective or joke teasingly, "Ezra has always been thoughtfulness itself in his efforts to bridge the gap between my academic lacks and his superior learning." (Williams was probably unaware that Pound referred to him as "lil Bill," Yeats being "big Bill.") Nonetheless, Williams tried to crowd in as much time with Pound as possible. Their shoptalk was stimulating. Discussing musical "time," Williams readily conceded that Pound had an exceptional ear, "attuned to the metrical subtleties of the best in verse." Yet Williams couldn't resist letting in a note of sarcasm to his evaluation of Pound and his circle. When Pound takes him to the long-running salon of the openly lesbian writer Natalie Barney, Williams feels sure that he's been allowed entry only because Ezra promised to exhibit him as a specimen of the American "primitive." After admiring Barney's garden and Japanese servants, and staring uneasily at lesbian couples dancing closely, he acts the part of vulgar American primitive to perfection: "I went out and stood up to take a good piss." Williams's crude shower of contempt, intended for Pound as well as for his hostess, cheers him up, even if it doesn't resolve his queasy feelings about homosexuals and lesbians. Much as he admired Pound, however, he could not stand being constantly in his company. Pound could not resist playing the superior learned professor to Williams's bumbling pupil. Leaving Paris, Williams realized it might be far better for the friends to joust and banter and debate through the mails.

At the station where they waited to board a train for Cherbourg, the only people there to see them off were Bill's elderly cousins Alice and Marguerite Trufly. On the SS *Zeeland*, an exhausted reveler, Williams went to bed early. But a couple of days later, caught up on sleep, he started revising the Boone chapter of *In the American Grain*. The trip home was blessedly routine, the seas calm. Back in Rutherford, he and Floss were relieved to discover that the boys had fared well during their absence.

To Williams's surprise, it was relatively easy to resume his medical practice. Although he did not abandon either his general or his obstetrical practices, he decided to focus on pediatric care. Keen on joining the staff of Passaic General Hospital, he opened an office in Passaic, thus doubling the number of patients he would see most days—and further reducing the time left for writing. But it was a necessary step in the development of his medical skills, which he took as seriously as he did the poetry world. Furthermore, the sabbatical had eaten into the family's cash reserves, and Williams knew he could never earn more than a pittance from stories and poems. Appointed to the staff, he would devote nearly thirty years of service to the hospital and head the Doctors' Association and the Medical Board.

Europe had sharpened Williams's perceptions that America remained a mass of contradictions, half pagan and half Puritan. With Prohibition now the law of the land, bootleggers made a fortune supplying gin and other liquors to lovers of Bacchus in speakeasies and other clandestine . clubs and even in respectable homes like Bill and Floss's. "Roy, the bootlegger, was a regular caller at Ridge Road," William Eric recalls, "bringing everything from scotch to applejack," and "Patients from the Italian colony in Lyndhurst would settle an old account by bringing crates of grapes and crushing them in a huge hogshead in the basement." Williams was no alcoholic.* But as the 1924 and 1927 journals attest, he could and did drink to excess occasionally, and not just to break down inhibitions.

If America was not much different from the country he had left six months before, Williams himself was in a different place artistically and

*William Eric's claim never to have seen his father drunk or incapacitated by alcohol while practicing medicine takes a too rosy and protective view.

William Carlos Williams's mother, Hélène
(Elena) Hoheb Williams, c. 1895

William Carlos William's father,
William George Williams, 1898

William Carlos Williams in 1885, age two

William Carlos Williams as an infant

Edgar Williams and William Carlos
Williams as young boys

Studio portrait of William Carlos
and Edgar Williams

William Carlos Williams
with a Van Dyke beard, 1918

William Carlos Williams with sons Paul and William
Eric, and his grandmother Emily Dickinson Wellcome

Back row, from left: Jean Crotti, Marcel Duchamp, Walter Arensberg, Man Ray, R. A. Sanborn, Maxwell Bodenheim. *Front row, from left:* Alanson Hartpence, Alfred Kreymborg, William Carlos Williams, Skipwith Cannell (Courtesy of the State University of New York at Buffalo)

From left: Helen Slade, Mary Caroline Davis, Yvonne Crotti, Floss Williams, Kitty Cannell, Mrs. Davis (Kitty Cannell's mother), Gertrude Kreymborg, Mrs. Walter Arensberg (Courtesy of the State University of New York at Buffalo)

Drawing and dedication by William Carlos Williams on frontispiece in presentation copy to Viola Baxter on the occasion of his debut in the pages of *Poetry*

Ezra Pound and William Carlos Williams: lifelong friends and dueling poetic antagonists, June 30, 1958

William Carlos Williams with his mother, Elena, the formidable family matriarch

William Carlos
Williams in his study

William Carlos Williams talking with his old loyal friend Louis Zukofsky,
along with Celia Zukofsky, who set Williams's poems to music, and Floss

A subdued William Carlos Williams in his study, where his creative fires blazed before his strokes broke his health

spiritually because of the experiences and ideas he had acquired abroad, so plentiful they would take years to sort out and meditate and act on. The cream of cultured Europe had mostly treated him as an intellectual equal, a poet and man of qualities whose opinions were worth listening to. The trip was an invaluable immersion experience, a chance to sound the depths of Pagany and to compare it with the America that he knew was in many respects a shallow and unripened culture and that often made him despair of its "granite changelessness."

Taking stock of America in 1924, he could not but see that the struggle between repressive morality and sexual freedom at Merry Mount was being reenacted nearly three hundred years later. America in the 1920s may not have offered a haven for relaxed sexual mores as Europe did, but there were plenty of individual pagans pushing against the restraints and codes of church and state. With his highly developed social conscience, Williams closely followed the stories of spectacular corruption—the Teapot Dome scandal, for instance—that made headlines. Coolidge and Harding, in cahoots with a Republican-controlled Congress, winked at the unregulated economy. It seemed that Hamilton's economic policies had triumphed, spawning a new class of robber barons. American democracy worked for the benefit of the plutocracy, not the people. American life was acting out the themes Williams had examined in *In the American Grain*.

Just before Christmas 1924, Williams wrote a moping letter to Pound, who had moved to Rapallo, near Genoa: "Europe seems closer since we have been there but—again—it seems infinitely further off: so great has my wish to be there become intensified by the recent trip." This nostalgia for Europe was Williams's attempt to ward off his anxiety that America might not, after all, open up new directions for his poems to take. He poses his dilemma in stark terms: "Either I must be a tragic ass or, nothing—or an American—I scarcely know which is the worst." This statement seems to have reignited the old quarrel over Williams's alleged inauthentic Americanness. Pound flaunted his status as a genuine American blueblood who, by a twist of fate, resided in Europe, and he heckled Williams as a European impersonating an American: "you are a foreigner, and that America interests you as something EXOTIC (damned but exotic)." Both inhabited the wrong continent! When Pound repeated his familiar advice that Williams should steep himself in world poetry, Williams replied, "I need something else, an adequate electrical connection that I can't manage to fix up." If he died before he found that vital current, so be it; at least he would not succumb to pursuing a "false replica" of European traditions. "You talk [like] a crow with cleft palate," Williams shot back, "when you repeat your old gag of heredity, where you come from or where I come from."

In a more hopeful mood, Williams decided that the expatriates did not hold all the aces in the deck. There were pockets of excellence in homegrown American art, poetry, fiction, and criticism—Charles Sheeler, Charles Demuth, Marianne Moore, Wallace Stevens, F. Scott Fitzgerald, Nathanael West, and Kenneth Burke. In time Williams would add his name to this impressive roster. Between 1924 and 1928, he wrote fewer poems, mainly because the long works he concentrated on siphoned off most of whatever creative energy remained after office hours and house calls.

The poems he did write are notable for their dissimilarity: the brisk, heartfelt "The Last Words of My Grandmother"; a tour of the sculpture in the Capitol rotunda ("It Is a Living Coral"); a prose poem ("Poem") listing the names of scouts, generals, Indian fighters, pioneers, and patriots that reads like a series of plaques in a war museum; a 1927 poem titled "Paterson" that is the nucleus from which his American epic evolved; an exceptional nature poem, "Young Sycamore," hewn out of one sentence that, like the tree, vigorously thrusts upward from a "round and firm trunk" until it sends out "young branches" and "two / eccentric knotted / twigs / bending forward / hornlike at the top"; "Impromptu: The Suckers," a rant against the railroading of Sacco and Vanzetti; and two slight poems about his mother.

In 1925, asked by *New Masses* for a contribution, Williams rummaged in his drawer and pulled out a story, "The Five Dollar Guy," based on an anecdote he had heard. Instead of rereading it, he put it in an envelope and mailed it. This carelessness nearly cost him dearly. Because he had used the real name of the person in the story, he was sued for libel and $15,000, a sum that threatened bankruptcy. Luckily he was able to settle out of court: Williams was assessed $5,000 in damages, a stiff but not a ruinous amount. The $2,000 that came with his award from *The Dial* was a godsend; he managed to scrape together the rest of the money, though not before Floss berated him for his foolish mistake in an effort to prevent future follies.

In 1927, Floss proposed that William Eric and Paul should follow in the footsteps of their father and uncle Edgar and spend a school year at the Château de Lancy, housed in new quarters in Coppet, outside of Geneva. Williams liked the idea and the symmetry. According to their plan, after both parents escorted the boys to Europe, Floss would stay on in Switzerland to keep an eye on them while Bill returned home to practice medicine and work on new poems. It is reasonable to believe that both Floss and Bill welcomed the separation as a break from marital friction. As for the boys, they would come back to America purged of parochial habits of thought and fluent in French, or so their parents hoped.

One crisis almost immediately tested Floss's mettle: in October, Paul came down with a case of diphtheria that tenaciously resisted treatment. Williams cabled the school doctors, prescribing a heavy dosage of anti-toxins, but his suggestions were spurned. Fearful for her son's life, Floss took him out of school and placed him in the pediatric ward of a Geneva hospital. When he was released from the hospital, she nursed him back to health and the emergency passed. Displeased by the bullying pedagogy and destructive criticism of Paul's work and abilities by the school's head-master, Dr. Schwartz, and by his underhanded, "criminal" ethics—he billed the Williams family for tutoring services promised but not rendered; Floss refused to pay—Floss transferred Paul to the International School in Ouex, where he would get individual attention from the teachers and be helped to acquire disciplined study habits. Not too soon after, she pulled William Eric out, too, and enrolled him at International, where, to her delight, he thrived. Once again Floss had demonstrated cool judgment and decisive action at a critical juncture. Williams saluted her "astounding courage."

The Atlantic crossing back home was somewhat rough, Williams reported to Floss, the "slow old tub" laboring against a strong headwind in choppy seas. Not suffering from seasickness, as many passengers did, Williams enjoyed standing in the stern and staring at "the lash and slash of the waves," letting his thoughts wander. "Part of my trouble was my solitary mind. I am a poor mixer," Williams wrote his wife, but in truth he could not avoid the crowd of Legionnaires who had gone to France to celebrate the tenth anniversary of America's entry into World War I and who continued their noisy partying on the decks and in the salons of the SS *Pennland*, to the annoyance of many passengers. (Eventually, the captain shut down the bar.) Williams was mildly amused by their antics. For socializing, he had Holly Beach, Sylvia's sister, as a genial companion and source of literary gossip, and he could retire to his cabin early to sleep or just read. He was finishing Alfred North Whitehead's *Science and the Modern World*, which he recommended to Floss, and starting Gogol's *Dead Souls* and Joyce's *Dubliners*, a book that helped him sketch his initial ideas about *Paterson*.

Each day, as Floss's absence made his heart grow fonder, Williams wrote a chatty letter to her (twelve in nine days). This shipboard gazette featured items about such colorful personages as the rodeo cowboy "Nevada" and an aviator from Tennessee for whom flying was as all-absorbing as poetry was for Williams, or Holly's story about a beautiful orphan who ran away to join the circus and ended up as a spy in a brothel, which might have inspired the screenplay for a 1930s Marlene Dietrich movie. Williams even looked back, in an impromptu paragraph or two, at his childhood:

> I was really an unhappy, disappointed child—in general—during my early years. It was due to the mood of our home and to my eager desires, which no world, and certainly not the Rutherford of those days, could satisfy. I do not say it was not good for me but I never could do what I really and violently wanted to—either in athletics, studies or amorous friendships—so I was gnawing my insides all day long.
>
> And yet underneath it all there was an enormous faith and solidity. Inside me I was like iron and with a love for the world and a determination to do good in the world that was like the ocean itself. I had a mountainous self pride and a conviction that I could afford to adventure and decide for myself.

None of this psychological profile—the "oceanic" struggle for dominance of his self between two kinds of desire, idealism and amorous fulfillment—would have surprised Floss. In these letters, Williams fervently declared that he was a happy man solely because of her. Indeed, though he mistrusted the word "love," he waxed sentimental, like a gallant beau writing billets doux to his inamorata: she was "the queen of the world" for him; "that feeling went through me like sweetest nectar and . . . I knew it would last forever." Terms of endearment roll trippingly off his tongue: she is his "bunny," "Monkey," "snookie." And he swears eternal fealty to her: "I went direct to you through my own personal hell of doubt and hesitation and I have never changed the millionth part of one inch since that first decision"; "to bring you closer is the only worthwhile thing on earth." What woman could have failed to be disarmed by such extravagant language, not to be heard again until "Asphodel, That Greeny Flower"? The only possible red flag came from a worldly southern bachelor on the ship, who cautioned Williams about the wisdom of leaving his wife in Europe for a year. The man doubted a husband's ability to resist temptation: "a woman doesn't have any difficulty keeping out of trouble unless she goes looking for it, but a man is always billy-goating around one way or another." Floss might have smiled wryly at that cynical bon mot.

Williams did mention to Floss that he was contemplating a new group of poems tentatively called *Sacred and Profane*, and he in fact sketched out three poems dated 9/27, 9/29, and 9/30, which ran parallel to his letters to her. The letters and journal became part of *The Descent of Winter*, which Pound published in 1928 in his magazine *The Exile*. *The Descent of Winter* was the most diffuse of Williams's experiments with long forms in the 1920s. One reads these improvisations with a furrowed brow, puzzled by the poor writing, which verges on self-parody; unlikable, it manages to be at once slapdash and ponderous. There are lovely lines in "My bed is narrow," "that brilliant field," and "In the dead weeds a rubbish heap," but mostly Williams's imagination seems to have deserted him. In "9/30," he levels withering criticism against his poems:

> There are no perfect waves—
> your writings are a sea
> full of misspellings and
> faulty sentences.
> . . .
> waves like words all broken—
> a sameness of lifting and falling mood

And the prose, despite his bold announcement "I will make a big, serious portrait of my time," does not break any new ground. Williams mocks the stolid incompetence of Calvin Coolidge (an easy target), laments the "fragmentary stupidity of modern life," the ruined landscape of rural America, and the empty faces of the citizens going about their business, but the satire is a sort of ranting by numbers; even his praise of Shakespeare merely rehashes points more forcefully made in *Spring and All*. The diary structure for *The Descent of Winter* imposes a superficial unity on the material. One senses that Williams wants to violate the crabbed rules that confine him, but he's frustrated by numerous false starts and incomplete entries.

Back in Rutherford, the optimism of his letters to Floss gradually leaches out as the calendar rushes toward winter. His pledge of fidelity notwithstanding, he barely fights off a young woman who comes to his office and brazenly asks him to fuck her. He tells Floss that only keeping her image in his mind gave him the strength of will to push the hussy out the door. In *The Descent of Winter*, his deepening gloom can be heard in two sardonic Proverbs of Hell: "The perfect type of the man of action is the suicide" and "A cat licking herself solves most of the problems of infection. We wash too much and finally it kills us." Blight is everywhere. America's rivers are as polluted as the Passaic River in "The Wanderer"; poverty abounds, as does gimcrack art, monotonous work, and political chicanery. It is almost as if Williams intuited the Depression waiting in the wings. In *The Descent of Winter*, only in "isolate flecks" do dignity and community survive. Not surprisingly, Williams feels wretched: "And loss, loss, loss. Cut off from my kind—if any exist."

Six years after *The Waste Land*, he had made progress finding his poetic voice—but not readers. To be sure, magazines such as *The Dial* and Pound's *The Exile* offered a home for his work. He was grateful to Marianne Moore and Pound for their backing. In a graceful thank-you note of a poem, "Lines on Receiving the Dial's Award, 1927," Williams likens *The Dial*'s recognition to "a moment shored / against a degradation / ticked off daily round me like the newspapers." Yet he worried that people would think the prize was rigged, that he was accepting handouts from friends. Worst of all, he was embarrassed that at age forty-five he could find no publisher prepared to bring out his poems at regular intervals and stand enthusiastically behind them. Most of his books, brought out in minuscule print runs by small presses, had vanished from bookstores.

In all periods, Williams picked apart the failings of his poetry with unrelenting honesty, vowing to do better on the next go-round; his resiliency had helped him bounce back from disappointments before (and would again), but this time, with Floss and her common sense and soothing balm a continent away, he licked his wounds, brooded, and spat out gobs of bile at an old enemy, T. S. Eliot. Williams's 1927 journal highlights his dyspeptic side. It's not pretty reading. Although he was aware that drinking could erode a doctor's diagnostic skills and ruin his reputation, he consumed more liquor than he normally did. Some worm of dissatisfaction was gnawing at his insides. And while he does not retract the romantic oaths he swore to Floss in his SS *Zeeland* love letters, he reverts to what Reed Whittemore called "the unpredictable mixture of penitence and belligerence that he brought to marriage, brought to it even when he was being happy at it." In a poem to Floss in the journal, Williams confesses he's a lout:

> Christ I have
> lied to you about
> small things
> whoring and
> whatnot
> but never
> did I unknow that your love
> is in me and I
> in it
> Love me
> while I am not disgusting
> like that—
> while I am still warm
> and a liar
> and a poet and a sometimes
> devoted lover
> who
> loves you and will lie
> to you
> always

There's no artifice here, just an odd mixture of chaffing humor, self-hate, and defiance—he repeats three times that he's an unregenerate liar and dismisses whoring as a "small thing." (One of his most admiring comments about Floss is that she never lied to him.) "You have no choice but to take me as I am," he brusquely warns her, "because in my unorthodox fashion, I love you."

Floss was not flustered by this latest saber rattling from her husband. His ultimatums and barbed confessions are familiar marital noise; she blames them on his changeable "moods and torments" and on a boyish immaturity to which he is blind. (If his writing is going badly and he's producing "dabs of foolishness," that, too, can contribute to his tirades.) In her voluminous, mostly loving letters to him from Geneva, Paris, and Munich, she seldom raises her voice. She is confident that despite all the women throwing themselves at him, he will always remain loyal to her. "It's amusing to hear about your sexual trials. I can't say that I am bothered," she begins. "I have more tolerance of your temperament than most women would have." She dissects their different temperaments for him: "I am distant—not easy to make friends with and wanting them. You attract everyone—and like people easily." But she makes sure her husband understands that she's not a patsy or a martyr. Despising Rutherford's boring club and church life, she has taken advantage of her stay in Paris, dining with old friends—the Birds and the Joyces, Lawrence and Clothilde Vail, Sylvia Beach and Adrienne Monnier, and Bob McAlmon—going to the opera, walking in the Luxembourg Gardens, appraising the latest Salon des Indépendants exhibit, or joining in the French equivalent of a pub crawl. She is in fact quite the social dervish. And she is no prim moralist disapproving of the casual promiscuity she observes among her circle of expatriate friends. It piques her considerable interest. With edgy nonchalance she captures Williams's attention by informing him, "It wouldn't have been difficult in Paris to find the opportunity [to conduct an affair]." After that aside on the oboe sunk in, she adds, "But the desire was wholly lacking and so I had just a darn good time, minus all the torments, except wishing for you always." She could doubtless hear his sigh of relief across the ocean.

Paris (and, to a lesser degree, Geneva) was a laboratory in which Floss compiled data on comparative marriages. Both men and women were obsessed with sex. Sally Bird, "sweet and deferent to her husband Bill," whom she considered "a sensitive soul," developed a passion for other men and her obstetrician after her pregnancy ended in a miscarriage. Bill Bird had his share of affairs, too, sanctioned for centuries by the French rules for marital games. When Nancy Cunard seemed poised to go beyond flirting with Bill and threatened to steal him away, Sally's jealousy erupted and she grew hysterical. A drunken Lawrence Vail invited Floss to stay the night when his wife was away, an offer she politely declined. Morality in Paris was far more permissive than in New York; adultery was rarely considered a mortal sin. Libertinism was the (illegitimate?) child of Liberty, not to be fussed over or condemned.

A trickier and more complicated figure in her anecdotal survey of French or expatriate sexual mores was Bob McAlmon, an old friend of both Williamses. With Bill absent, McAlmon played the role of solicitous courtier, escorting Floss to parties and restaurants. This was a harmless way to spend a diverting evening. McAlmon was stimulating company. He sported a saturnine wit, a contrarian's repertoire of unorthodox opinions, and an endless stock of salacious gossip that seemed to have just come out of the oven, so hot and aromatic was it. On and off for eight years, Floss had ample opportunity to study his character carefully. In 1920, during his short but intense collaboration with Bill in putting out five issues of *Contact*, McAlmon came to Rutherford for dinner and to plan the magazine's editorial policy, and choose poems and stories. Twelve years Williams's junior, he became a sort of third son, but one who scorned caution and lived in and for the moment. In his autobiographical short story "Post-Adolescence," McAlmon's fictional stand-in advises the Williams character not to be scared of risks: "You just have to take a leap and if you slip and bang your ass puddle, tra la, c'est la vie." McAlmon lived by that creed. Of course a brash and unattached young man could attack compromise as a betrayal of dreams and ideals. But he did not have to worry about supporting a family.

During their Parisian visit in 1924, McAlmon had been an affable host. Bankrolled by Sir John Ellerman, Bryher's immensely wealthy father, who was very fond of his putative son-in-law, Bob picked up the bill for his friends and the hangers-on for dinners or drinks at La Coupole and other watering holes. McAlmon had uncanny radar for discovering a gamin torch singer in a Montmartre dive before she became the sensation of *tout Paris*. Floss had also observed his darker side when, having drunk to excess, he grew quarrelsome, rowdy, and insulting, which led either to brawls or to a bouncer lifting him into the air like a sack of potatoes and depositing him out on the sidewalk. Fueled by liquor, McAlmon swaggered like a Hemingway tough guy with attitude to spare. Put off by Bob's "stupid, monotonous" addiction to alcohol—he was a binge drinker—Floss laced into him for letting his feckless will and dissolute habits squander his literary talents. Unlike his friends and fellow barflies, she was not used to his vanishing from Paris without warning and holing up in a Provençal hotel room, as in a monk's cell, where like a Spartan he abstained from wine and booze and labored single-mindedly on a novel or story he had left incomplete. Then, as if obeying some invisible prompt, he would slip back to Paris and resume his bouts of all-night carousing, dancing wildly like a maenad, or listening, rapt, to jazz in smoke-filled clubs. In Paris, gratifying the senses was pursued in the open; monitoring a person's sexual preferences was none of the government's business. Prohibition in America struck the French as a ludicrous invasion of privacy and a dangerous curtailing of freedom. Americans came to France in large numbers to breathe the sybaritic air of Paris. McAlmon was Exhibit A.

Floss would have had no reason to suspect that McAlmon harbored any lecherous desires to seduce her. He had always behaved toward her with impeccable manners. Like everybody in their social crowd, she could not help noticing his wiry, hard body, but would that have planted lustful thoughts in her mind? Since he did not hide his homoeroticism and bisexuality, he was fodder for the rumor mills. Sitting in a café, Floss and the Birds, say, would compare notes about McAlmon's nocturnal hunt for sexual partners. Did they or Floss have an inkling that he was the leader of the gay group he cleverly dubbed "The Nightinghouls of Paris"? Unlikely, but they would not have been shocked by anything he did.

Floss's spicy gossip about their friends hopping from bed to bed was meant to titillate her poor husband, stuck in dull Rutherford. What she tells him about McAlmon is intriguing and contradictory. Bob was too much of a "sweet boy" to tempt her into his bed. This is an odd epithet to describe a young man about town who prided himself on his rough masculinity—Edward Dahlberg, a notoriously unreliable judge of human character, praised McAlmon for his "magnificent and lewd nature"—and who often violently acted out emotions and conflicts that agitated him: he's more "post-adolescent" than innocent boy. "Sweet" implies that Bob had behaved chivalrously rather than trying to sweet-talk her into having sex with him. But then Floss hints (it's not quite a boast) that had she signaled her willingness to become his lover, he would have jumped at the chance, never mind his alleged loyalty to her husband. This oblique comment is enough to bring the "green-eyed monster" out of hibernation in New Jersey to check if she was flattering herself or just needling him. About adultery or the brief fling he was not egalitarian, so it's plausible Floss enjoyed his squirming. Her letters make clear that while she doesn't countenance his episodes of infidelity, they will not undermine her love or topple their marriage. Williams concludes that there's no danger of his Desdemona doing the beast with two backs with Cassio and cuckolding him.

What Williams made of Floss's last stab at evaluating McAlmon we can only speculate, as he did not respond to it in his subsequent letters. "Bob gets sullen—to hell with him—yes, say what you will—I think probably you are in love with him—and I understand perfectly how it can be. He has an appeal sexual certainly for both men and women." Her breezy tone notwithstanding, this is obviously a topic that husband and wife had discussed before. Floss concedes Bob's sexual appeal, but his sullenness, she contends, was so annoying that she had to dislodge him from her mind: "to hell with him," depending on the intonation we hear, may express a grievance, such as a rebuff suffered at McAlmon's hands, that still rankled. He is now Bill's problem child. If Floss is right that Williams loved McAlmon, it is not prurient to ask: Did Williams desire to sleep with the virile young man? Or, more likely, did he suppress homosexual feelings for McAlmon, who looked like he'd stepped out of a painting by Thomas Eakins? There is not a shred of evidence to corroborate such a relationship. Given Williams's dossier, crammed with demeaning comments about gays and lesbians, and his obvious discomfort in their company—his friendship with Charles Demuth points up how conventional his revulsion from gay artists was—Williams would deserve to be crowned a world-class hypocrite or a consummate actor if proof emerged that he in fact slept with McAlmon or with other men. What is not disputable is his fascination with, and fantasies about, breaking sexual taboos. But he is no cousin of Angelo, the cruel, legalistic deputy in Shakespeare's *Measure for Measure* who represses his sexual desires but is secretly engrossed by what he most abhors.

One other potential romance comes Floss's way, this time in Geneva, her home away from home. A handsome young Scottish doctor in his early thirties employed by the League of Nations takes a room at the Hotel-Pension des Familles. When Dr. Mackenzie (he is called McFarland in Williams's short story à clef "Hands Across the Sea") and Floss meet, he is smitten with her. Enjoying each other's company, they strike up a friendship, to the disapproval of some elderly American ladies, and spend much time together in cafés or the city gardens. It is ironic that, like Bill, this would-be beau is a doctor poet (he never shows her his verse). A bit lonely, she is enthralled by his lively conversation; he had traveled to Mesopotamia, Egypt, and Africa to supervise projects designed to eliminate malaria and infestations of tsetse flies, and he was an amusing raconteur. Moreover, he had a courtly manner and listened to her ideas and stories, as if she were a charming courtesan like Madame Récamier and the hotel's second-floor parlor her salon. When he vanished for a month, she missed their shared intimacy, but did not feel bereft. In her letters to Williams she notes with asperity that Mackenzie is a specimen of Scottish manhood who seems to be conveying with a touch of complacency, "I'm it." Like the cultivated men in Paris who expect a woman to bow down when they beckon, the Scottish doctor is puzzled why women won't jump through hoops when asked to. These qualities amuse and annoy her.

Dr. Mackenzie confides to Floss that he had been wooing a widow in England, albeit in desultory fashion. Although professing to love her, he is reluctant to commit himself. What makes him cautious and diffident, Floss ferrets out, is his uneasiness with her "advanced ideas." She advises him to grab the lady before some other man proposes to her, and adds, with the pride of an independent American wife, "It's lots more fun to have that sort of wife than a perpetual echo." She herself might be a private woman, and she might hold her fire tactically in an argument with her husband, but she would not padlock her speech. In a letter to Williams, she follows her advice to the diffident Scottish doctor with an interesting linkage of modern writing and modern marriage: "I'm with you absolutely on your desire for only the most loose modern in writing. It's a reflection of our love—yet it is by far the most intense in the end." Then she clinches her analysis with the comment "cut and dried writing is like so many marriages." To enter an affair, however tempting, would be "an insult to me as well as to my ideal of you." Q.E.D. In a passage about Paul's scholastic performance, Floss ventures her opinion that the boy has an imagination like his father, then lays claim to sharing that faculty, even though her parents mishandled hers. Like her husband back in Rutherford, she dreamed of a life free of the unrelenting exigencies of medicine, a quixotic fantasy of leisure time spent writing poems and traveling: in short, escapes from routine, the insidious enemy of a vibrant marriage.

When out of Floss's letters about the Scottish doctor and their mutual platonic infatuation, Williams wrote "Hands Across the Sea," he betrays neither resentment nor skittishness, nor an urge to caricature a phantom rival. Rather, he muses again about the paradoxical mixture of freedom and claustrophobia in a marriage:

Strange, it seemed, that here was a man whom she liked, a doctor too, leading a fascinating life, the very thing Bob [Williams] longed for, a single fellow free to go, to be his own master. And what did he really desire? Naturally what else but to have a wife, a home, a place he could call his own, where he could settle down with children and quit his wandering. Or if not quit it, at least have a retreat waiting for him at the end. He wanted a woman, serious, attractive of course, but intelligent, who would follow him with love and interest. Without that, what is a man's life worth?

Williams is not intent on mocking the conventionality of this yearning, even though he knows from experience it is innocent of reality—the inevitable clashes of egos and ideals, money worries, the tensions of rearing children, the periods of sexual drought, all the incompatibilities flesh is heir to. He was no stranger to the almost irresistible impulse to bolt and escape the daily grind of duty.

He is able to put himself in Floss's mind (in the story, she's called Mrs. Andrews) and mock himself: "Mrs. Andrews would smile to herself thinking of the very opposite expressions she had heard all too often from Bob's almost foaming mouth, when he would want to be quiet, want to relax, and had to go on without respite. To hell with his home, his kids, herself, everything, she had often thought he felt, if he could only get out and away—anywhere." A marriage cannot survive without some entente cordiale in place, which stipulates that neither husband nor wife will try to rule the other. Unlike the fictional Dr. McFarland, Williams did not "want a nice mouse who never thinks a thing but what you tell her to think." The Floss who returned to 9 Ridge Road in July 1928 was more confident and self-directing. The separation had done her much good. Williams was not oblivious to this dramatic sea change, but it would be many years before he came close to satisfactorily resolving his inner struggle between freedom and self-gratification.

In Rome, Williams had compared "the whole colossal record of their [Rome's] oldtime [sic] fullness and our unnecessary subservience to our crippledom [sic]." America's culture, even allowing for the country's youth, was inferior to Europe's. Although this fact disquieted him, he knew that Europe was not for him: "there's little here [in Rome] for me—gravity must drag me down." And of the temptress Paris, he wryly noted, "Paris would be wonderful if I could be French and *Vieux*; it would be still more wonderful if I could only want to forget everything on earth. Since I can't do that, only America remains where at least I was born." This is hardly a ringing endorsement for his returning to America. The decade of long works and the waves of thoughts and feelings set off by his trip to Europe were still unfinished business in his mind. It was time to put the 1920s to bed.

Williams had jotted down impressions of people and places in his 1924 journal, as time allowed and the spirit moved him, and in letters to friends and family. In 1927 he started work on his second novel, *A Voyage to Pagany*, covering the same material. The main problem he had to solve was how to structure the novel in a way that was modern without being fussy, ragged, or self-conscious. The autobiographical material to be turned into fiction dictated to him a simple, elegant design: he would dramatize the odyssey of a doctor writer, who is and is not Williams, in search of an America he could reconcile himself to, the incidents of this belated coming-of-age quest to be framed by a series of "advents and departures" in Pagany (Europe).

The itinerary of his protagonist, Dr. Dev Evans, follows exactly that of Williams's 1924 trip; Evans embarrasses himself at a Paris party, as Williams had done, and spends four weeks in Vienna's hospitals walking the wards with vanguard Austrian doctors, listening to their lectures and, above all, finding in their elucidation of case histories of young children with consumption "this wonder of abandon to the pursuit of knowledge." But these resemblances are superficial; there's a large enough gap between Dr. Evans and Dr. Williams to allow *A Voyage to Pagany* to be safely categorized as fiction.

Floss has been deleted from *A Voyage to Pagany*. In her place are three romantic interests vying for Dev's attentions, each utterly alienated from America and trying to persuade him to set up a ménage with her in Europe. Lou Harris, his lover in Villefranche, plays the role of the pretty but vapid *jeune fille*. She's enough of an adventuress to trade Dev in for a rich, tennis-playing Englishman without a qualm. Because he was not deeply in love with Lou, Dev is merely annoyed, not injured, by her defection.

His romance with Grace Black in Vienna is more involving and layered. She is a cultivated young woman who appreciates the city's musical riches. After a courtship more platonic than erotic, Dev seriously considers marrying her. But their relationship founders on the question of where they should live, Europe or America. In speeches delivered with an almost irrational vehemence Grace vilifies America as a shameful dystopia: "Democracy, she shuddered. It takes away from the top to feed the maggots." America is "fettered to crawling inanities," its idea of education nothing more than the "buffoonery of nitwits." She sounds like Williams at his most truculent. When she relaxes "in the warmth of Dev's devoted attendance," she is happy, but one mention of America and her vicious hatred stirs to life again. Her accusations that he is a coward running away from his aristocratic nature and from European fineness fail to budge Dev. He explains: "I do not run from fineness, but small doses of it suffice. I soon tire. I feel a need for the vulgar. I have been accused before of running away. Well, I want to plant it, IT; to see if it grows. Fineness, too much of it, narcotizes me. It drives me wild. I do not want that." Their relationship ruptures and Dev leaves Vienna for Switzerland and Paris and a rendezvous with his sister, Bess.

The last effort at persuading Dev that Europe is the place for him comes from Bess, the third of the triumvir of anti-American Furies and the queen of his heart. She is not afraid of exploiting his love for her: her appeals that they live together are couched in the coquettish language of emotional, not sexual, incest (they are not blind immoralists like Siegmund and Sieglinde in *Die Walküre*). The nub of Bess's argument, echoing Grace Black's, is that Dev is "no American," that upon returning home he will be "going nowhere." He brushes aside her objections. "Europe is poison to us Americans—delicious—distressing," he tells her, then adds more personally, "I can never be at home here . . . [T]here is a deep loss in me that comes of my inheritance. Years ago I was lost—I am not of this club. That is what I am, a great zero." When she remarks, "Dev, you've never let yourself go. Down inside you—" he immediately cuts her off with a second self-abasing retort: "Down inside me is a small piece of slime full of worm's eggs." She cannot sway him to change his mind about returning to America, even if his prospects of becoming a great writer there are slim. Initially, all he can stammer out is a nebulous hope: "America, said Evans musingly, There are some things there—still some things there I want to gather—." His next formulation, still tentative and general, exposes his sense of vocation as something like the Stations of the Cross: "How to find a way to do it [become a great writer] and not be beaten off, driven off or beaten or dirtied. Yes, that's my life, he replied." Finally, he manages a forthright, if commonplace, reason: "Art is a country by itself—A matter of learning how—." Overpowered by Dev's resolute will, Bess can only sob wildly in his arms and the next day stoically watch his ship sail to the New World and an unknown destiny without her.

Williams sketches the three women with light strokes. They exude charm and are given ample space to articulate their points of view. What's missing in Williams's characterization of them, however, is even an abbreviated sense of their pasts; we never learn how or why they developed their virulent anti-Americanism. It seems to emerge, like multiple sclerosis, after years in hiding, triggered by an obscure genetic or environmental factor. There is no cure for it.

Dev is obsessed with his writing and with his epiphany in front of a marble statue of the Venus Anadyomene, who embodies a perfection that fills him with amazement. No woman in the novel could come close to that ideal of fleshly beauty and sublime tranquillity. Therefore, of course, nothing can possibly come of his exchange of glances with a beautiful German Fräulein, chaperoned by an elderly companion, in the dining room of his Roman *pensione*. (The chapter about Fräulein von J., titled "The Venus," was deleted from the novel at the request of Macaulay, Williams's publisher, who objected to it as an unnecessary digression from the main narrative. Williams published it separately as a short story and it was restored as an appendix in the New Directions edition of the novel.) Ironically, the blue-eyed blonde—who does share thick ankles with the goddess of love—is in Rome to become a nun and enter a convent. The body means nothing to her.

When it comes to the subject of America, unlike the three American Norns, Fräulein J. proves to be an astute questioner: curious, perceptive, and free of preconceptions and animus. Her first question, as they sit in a "pagan grove" near Frascati, is the quintessence of basic: "What is it like, America?" Dev is almost comically hapless in his miscellany of bumbling answers:

It is a world where no man dare learn anything that concerns him intimately—but sorrow—for should we learn pleasure, it is instantly and violently torn from us as by a pack of hungry wolves so starved for it are we and so jealous of each of us is our world.

It is that I may the better hide everything that is secretly valuable in myself, or have it defiled. So safety in crowds—

America seems less encumbered with its dead. I can see nothing else there. It gives less than Europe, far less of everything of value save more paper to write upon—nothing else.

America is a pathetic place where something stupefying must always happen for fear we wake up.

It is a hard, barren life, where I am "alone" and unmolested.

It is hard to know.

It is marvelous, . . . grossly prosperous.

Since Dev cannot solve the riddle of America with words, he produces from his pocket a flint arrowhead found in a Virginia cornfield. Fräulein von J., like a trained anthropologist, turns this totemic object over in her hand, feeling its point, its edge, grasping its symbolic import, and declares it the weapon of a savage. To her dismay, Dev is a pagan with no faith in the Church, but unlike the three American women, she instinctively understands his decision to return to America: "You are brave, she said, to want to find some other way—and one that is American."

In the novel, Williams makes that decision an agonizing one. Like the author, Dev is a serious, divided, intense, brooding man, with a vulnerable side that women find attractive. He bears no relation to the caddish young doctor who trifled with the Baroness Elsa von Freytag-Loringhoven. "He was a good first line doctor," who practices medicine in the same New Jersey town in which he was born. Williams's ode to the romance of his profession is one of his most lyrical, nature and poetry inextricably linked:

But he really loved the irregularity of a suburban practice, rushing out into the weather at any hour; in the spring stopping his car at four a.m. to hear the hylas waken, watching the snow figures on the windswept roadways at night in a blizzard, plunging in his car through impromptu lakes of rainwater with lightning flashing all around him and thunder splitting the sky, dust and mysterious fog banks at sundown, the stars peppering the sky, the new moon coming—and thoughts flinging up words to that accompaniment, words that occasionally would have a bewildering freshness upon them as they rose to his sight, it seemed, from somewhere in the center of his brain.

As aspiring writer, Dev lags far behind Williams at this stage. Paris is not important to him, as it was for the author. How could it be? He's still uncertain about his craft, flailing wildly in an effort to make words sing with "bewildering freshness"; he's not sophisticated enough to take up the challenge of competing with the leading writers of Europe. A *Voyage to Pagany* is not Williams's *Portrait of the Artist in Early Middle Age.* Dev lacks Stephen Dedalus's aesthetic swagger, his joyous vanity in debating and propounding grand theories about tragedy, boldly revising Aristotle, and above all, believing that even if forced into exile, he will storm the heavens and hang his modernist star there for all to admire. A blundering, solitary singer, Dev forges in the smithy of *his* soul self-doubts that he can be any kind of artificer. Williams shines a light on Dev sitting down in his room in the *pensione* to write, "sullen and lonely—beaten by his oppressive thoughts."

It was in Rome, in fact, during these days, that he most made a wife of his writing, his writing—that desire to free himself from his besetting reactions by transcribing them—thus driving off his torment and going quietly to sleep thereafter. But today all day into the night he was especially tormented. He wrote blindly, instinctively for several hours, a steady flow of incomprehensible words and phrases, until he was exhausted and stopped perforce.

All writers report this frustrating slippage of words, this vast disconnect between "riotous emotions" clamoring for "intelligent expression" and the "beautiful thing," the "fleeting presence," that escapes capture in the net of language. Dev frankly admits he's confused, but he wrestles valiantly with his demons and earns a valuable insight from the rich chaos of the city's history. Rome's antiquities teach that the "miraculous modern *must* be built upon a fine run, way ahead," but "it must connect up with the past."

Oppressed by his changeable moods and mental wanderings, Dev arrives in Vienna "to prepare himself for new adventures in his profession," to "enlarge his view," but to his delighted surprise he finds "a high degree of scientific perfection" at the renowned hospital of the Lazarette Gasse.

The stuffy Teutonic mind and method that had suffocated him in Leipzig is replaced at Lazarette by "that sense of beauty in arrangement, that fervor the continental scientific method, built upon their aristocratic thought, had engendered, to go far through the world." Williams often judged science inferior to poetry, but in Vienna the brilliant physicians—Knobloch, Auchmuller, Waldheim, and Kern—were like avant-garde poets opening the world to new discoveries, techniques, even a philosophy of medical ethics. Here at the *Krankenhaus*, Keats's famous adage—fittingly, given Keats's early studies as a medical student—"Truth is beauty, beauty truth," was a reality, not a romantic dream. The Viennese medical geniuses were living proof that "negative capability" was not the exclusive domain of poets. Dev is captivated by the doctors' "fullness of abandon," the same phrase Williams used about Nero and the other debauched Roman emperors, but here abandon is "to the pursuit of knowledge. The beauty of it took [Dev] again and again."

Rapt, he forgets "the sickening recollection of his own morbid youth in America," where the abandon of life was checked and ruin followed in its wake. Indeed, in Auchmuller's lectures on the ear, the topic of Williams's only published medical paper, Dev experiences a hedonist's pleasure that is the natural complement to the clarities displayed in the dissections, surgeries, and public clinical examinations he attended. When Auchmuller operated on a patient's mastoid, he "nonchalantly took up a chisel and a mallet and with one mighty whang was in the middle of the bone soon gnawing away with his rongeur like a beaver." Williams's American vernacular is in full throttle in this passage. Dev, like Williams, had an aversion to pathology, but in Waldheim's course on the diseases of children, this was utterly transformed by "that tall kindly man, curious god of flesh, carefully, carefully taking apart the unhappy bodies of dead children and unwinding out of them the secret stories of rickets, of tuberculosis, of syphilis and the gland deficiencies." In a contiguous passage, Waldheim takes on the godly function of explaining creation, and death, and the models that failed like a flawed poem.

Dev cannot help comparing American medicine to its superior counterpart in Vienna. In America, he concludes, "we save men without too much curiosity. Here they are lustful for knowledge, for completeness of living. These priests of beauty save men, but keep aloof." He despairs that "the washed-out soul of his own country" will ever understand this gold standard. Like Sarastro and the guild of enlightened priests in *The Magic*

Flute, the remarkable, selfless doctors of Vienna initiate Dev into a cult of disinterested service to medicine and poetry, show him that clarity and pleasure can be joined in a fruitful marriage. America might be raw and afraid, but Williams and Dev emerge from Pagany transformed, independent, like the *paganus*, free not to "share the prevailing beliefs" of the land of their birth.

Critic Harry Levin is surely right that after finishing *A Voyage to Pagany*, Williams "remains his unaffected self, that he so manifestly wrote to please himself. He was interested not in making an impression but in registering an impact." An impact indeed. He had produced most of his longest and most important works; confronted Europe and the expatriate artist community; achieved a rough equality with Pound and a stable marriage with Floss; and he was solidly settled into his medical career. The writings and adventures of the 1930s lay ahead.

ELEVEN

Confronting the Great Depression

I.

The Great Depression spread a pall over American life during the 1930s. Few households were spared. Like many of their countrymen, Floss and Bill lost money in the stock market crash, which meant that they had to retrench and he had to work longer hours. They were not so strapped that they couldn't send William Eric to Williams College, but those extra hours left Bill "swamped," "hellishly distraught," and "humpbacked," or, as he had wryly put it two years earlier, "I have done nothing but chase the devil around a bush according to the habits of my profession." As he aged, it got harder and harder, especially in the middle of a frigid night, to stumble out of bed, dress in the dark, start the sputtering engine of his car, and drive to Garfield or Passaic to deliver a "truck driver" or helplessly watch a patient die of heart failure. Williams knew that the Depression most hurt the working classes, his poor patients, who queued up in breadlines and competed for scarce jobs at below-subsistence wages. In his 1938 story "Life Along the Passaic River," he paints a vivid mural of hard times in "the streets of the Dundee section of Passaic": Polish workers stand on corners, idle, smoking, "stunned" by their fate, lacking even the few cents needed to get drunk and court oblivion, while children scavenge for food or coins, fishing in the fetid water for supper. When illness struck the unemployed and elderly, they often could not pay for his medical services. As he had done in the early years of his practice, Williams, who did not have a mercenary bone in his body, often waived his fees.

Everywhere he looked, daily life confirmed his grim diagnosis of democracy in crisis, which had important ramifications for his poetry. For years it had been a recurring lament of his correspondence and his writings that the country's fixation on commerce and materialistic goals accounted for its cultural philistinism, timidity, and shallowness. As he noted in "The Somnambulists," a review of Kay Boyle's *Short Stories*, "There is, in a democracy, a limit beyond which thought is not expected to leap. All men being presumed equal, it becomes an offense if this dead limit is exceeded." In this inert, leveling environment, what was an aspiring leaper like Williams to do? He decided to play the gadfly, while grumbling about the role: "I'm really a stick in the sides of the populace . . . [,] a kind of outpost that is trying to make it safe for ART in the lousy country." (The populace paid no attention, and he continued to labor "under the terrific weight of indifference.") In a letter to Louis Zukofsky, Williams caustically observed: "Pity to waste work on this land of worms on rainy sidewalks. I should say—The delicacy of flavor [that] each one of us possesses to some degree is lost here. It is in us, we use it as it were squirting an atomizer of perfume out the window to stop the stenches of the stock yard."

Williams still careened from euphoria to sullen doubt about the quality of his poems: even though he had purged them of romantic moonshine, they still exposed, he sometimes believed, an insufficient "intellectual control." His faith in the power of imagination had not dimmed; it was still his guide, his Shield of Athena. So if the winds of adversity had blown him off course, the success of his odyssey was not to be determined by the calendar: he was no longer the eternal ephebe, but he'd been disappointed so often, he told Zukofsky, that he might have to postpone his "crys[t]al[l]ization" until he reached seventy!

As the 1930s began, Williams's literary prospects were bleak. No publisher was willing to bring out his books. His morale plummeted as the pile of rejected manuscripts grew higher. After the surge of experimental works of the 1920s, his output dwindled. He tinkered with poems he had written in 1928, most notably a suite called "Della Primavera Trasportata al Morale" ("A Moral Interpretation of Springtime"). This sequence comprises ten poems, all of them loose-limbed and rambling, as if they embodied the motto engraved on the entrance gate to the Abbey of Thélème in Rabelais's *Gargantua and Pantagruel* and echoed in the subtitle of Shakespeare's *Twelfth Night*: "what you will," which happens to be the second line of the first poem, "April." The sources Williams draws on in both poem and sequence make up an untidy democratic miscellany: the bustling street life of Rutherford as its citizens—raffish idlers, shopkeepers, housewives, children, and plumbers—go about their daily business against the backdrop of the rotating seasons; the solidity and contours of physical objects (cars, tools, ramshackle homes and furniture, for example) coexist with discursive thoughts on love, marriage, and domesticity. Although he observes that the rose is "bent into form / upon the iron frame," he only intermittently builds a trellis on which words and the details he's enamored of are bent into shapely forms. The question the sequence raises through its sprawl and high jinks and verbal gymnastics is: Are the poems collage or bricolage? In my opinion, they are sometimes one and sometimes the other.

In "April" and fitfully in the following poems, Williams takes up an old theme: the possibility of achieving release from emotional restraint. "Loose it! / Let it fall (where it will)—again," he exhorts himself. The results are decidedly spotty. Lines and stanzas look at times as if they landed on the page accidentally; transitions are missing in action, or appear rushed. When his train of thought bumps against a barrier—a hectoring sign in bold caps reading "BUY THIS PROPERTY," say—the poem meanders "where it will," switching to a private, abstruse language. The first movement is halted by a sign that offers contradictory advice: STOP : GO. Which should he obey? Unsure, he decides to travel both roads, serially, collecting impressions along the way. Thus the humor of desire, of innocent sexual fantasies, intrudes briefly, lightening his mood. One can imagine him grinning, as

> —she
> opened the door! nearly
> six feet tall, and I . . .
> wanted to found a new country—

This wondrous glimpse passes without Williams planting his flag in that new country; instead, he once more meticulously records the arrival of spring, manifest in a profusion of buds, flowers, trees, bushes, and grass. Suddenly, he issues his first poetic rule—a poem should convey "the clatter and true sound / of verse"—which is curiously fuzzy and general. We can hear clatter in the scraping of a truck on the pavement, but which "true sound" does Williams mean: a ravishing consonance, the howling wind, sassy street talk overheard from his kitchen window? In "April," although sound reinforces meaning, it is wayward syntax and promiscuous diction that rule; sound is of secondary importance. (In "Full Moon," by contrast, Williams experiments with assonance as a kind of rhyme: "curious shapes / awake / to plague me," and fits it neatly into short three-line stanzas.)

What does the sequence tell us about the status of form at this stage of Williams's career? For one, articulated form was still not his goal or specialty. He didn't worry if ragged threads showed, so long as he kept the reader from being lulled into inattention by predictable rhythms. From time to time, he composes lines that might have been drawn with a slide rule and protractor, or composed to a metronome, as in two long, clunky passages of "April" that employ anaphora. The first offers a list of eight "Morals" to a story untold, a sort of monotonous exorcism that ranges from "I can laugh" to "the redhead sat / in bed with her legs / crossed and talked / rough stuff." Then he inserts a ninth, and hackneyed, moral: "—the moral is love, bred of / the mind and eyes and hands—" (the heart is omitted). But love does not guarantee personal satisfaction. On the contrary, he reflects,

> . . . in the cross-current
> between what the hands reach
>
> and the eyes see
> and see starvation, it is
>
> useless to have thought
> that we are full

The section halts at a double sign: "STOP : STOP"

When the poem resumes, Williams shifts to a public rhetoric: a politician sets forth his credo in a stump speech that consists of little more than platitudes. Williams interrupts the recital with catcalls ("taraaaaaa! taraaaaaaa!"), a lyrical cadenza ("reminiscent of the sea / the plumtree flaunts / its blossom-encrusted / branches—"), a town ordinance ("No parking between tree and corner"), and snatches of dialogue redolent of love and abandonment ("The world lost— / in you"). With deadpan humor he next affixes "I believe" to a list of prices and flavors, from expensive spumoni to cheap biscuit tortoni, that might be tacked up on an ice-cream parlor wall. This passage fails to appease the spiritual starvation that earlier the poet speaks of so solemnly.

Williams abruptly returns to the trees, only "seeming dead," and delivers two sexual innuendos with a broad wink:

Maple, I see you have
a squirrel in your crotch—

And you have a woodpecker
in your hole, Sycamore

Glimpsing "a fat blonde, in purple" on the street, he stencils in both the word "POISON!" and the skull and crossbones that drug companies put on bottles to warn users of their lethal contents. Next, hospital arrows direct patients and visitors to the "WOMAN'S WARD" or "PRIVATE" rooms. After a prolonged acquaintance with Williams's poems, one grows accustomed to his casual reversals of direction, as in the coda to "April," where he follows the arrows to an almost hermetic interior. "Having sinned willingly," he undertakes in a tortured syntax to understand the gyrations and "[t]he forms / of the emotions"; however, he cannot decode them.

This kind of randomness, a modernist tic, permeates the sequence: trees, wind, and ghosts "thrash and scream / guffaw and curse," as in a haunted house that doubles as a poem; nonsense words barge in with a chorus of scat singing—"Wheeeeee / clacka tacka / tacka tacka / wha ha ha ha ha / ha ha ha"—all in the service of a battle between the id and the superego over "what you please." The poems fly all over the lot, antic one moment, sarcastic or pensive the next, as if mimicking the wind lashing trees prodigal with bud and leaf. The typography and spacing enact Williams's desire and effort to burst out of constraint. Preferring Dionysian passion to stultifying order, he provisionally defines the poet as

a man
whose words will
bite

> their way
> home—being actual
> having the form
>   of motion

"Motion" is the key word. Sometimes, as in "The Trees," it achieves pleasingly patterned rhythms, and sometimes, as in the quatrains of "The House," it merely moves to a lackluster beat, but however often his words bite, they don't quite find their way home to a convincing free "form / of motion."

The sole exception is "The Sea-Elephant." The sea-elephant is displayed as a freak by an American impresario modeled on P. T. Barnum. (Williams had taken his sons to the Ringling Bros. and Barnum & Bailey Circus.) The elephant seal—like sperm whales, hunted for its oil—derives its name from its curved proboscis, which resembles an elephant's trunk. Williams describes this strange creature with precise, repulsive gusto: "fish after fish into his maw / unswallowing / / to let them glide down / gulching back / half spittle half / brine." Its periodic bellowings—"Blouaugh!"—unnerve some of the paying customers; one indignant woman protests the degrading exploitation of the animal: "it's wonderful but they / ought to / / put it / back into the sea where / it came from." Formally, "The Sea-Elephant" is open and flexible, its quatrains able to accommodate swerves of perspective, rhythms that alternately swing, ride, walk, and catch their breath, tonal shifts from barker's spiel to the seal's grandiose blurt ("But I / am love. I am / from the sea—"), and eerie grunts and cryptic analogies. Lyric moments are conspicuous by their absence, but the poem's sound effects are superbly rendered. As the sea-elephant cavorts amid a pod of females, it is an emblem of libidinous force as enormous and bountiful as the sea from which it emerged with grotesque regality. After an ellipsis, the poem executes a deliberate non sequitur, quoting the thirteenth-century folk song "Spring is icumen in—," in which the woods and meadows spring into new life and the voice of the cuckoo is heard throughout the land. In this wry closure, Williams thumbs his nose at the traditional ending that clicks a poem into place.

In "Rain," a poem he later recycled in his play *A Dream of Love*, Williams reverts to a helter-skelter shower of words. The poem's content is emotionally troubling. Mulling over a woman's love, which seems to "bathe every / open / object of the world," he concludes that "all the whorishness /

of our / delight" leaves no hope; it is impotent to "change the world / to its delight." Because the rain, like "illicit love," is not merciful, the "kind physician" is stymied: "So my life is spent / to keep out love," he confesses. These conflicted feelings lead to lines tumbling in a kind of free fall, clustering for a moment and then further breaking up into scattered downpours of phrases or single words.

Thwarted Eros rouses a surly mood in "Death," the poem that follows. Uncharacteristically, Williams reviles the dead man on the autopsy table in a string of cruel images, calling him an "old bastard," "a godforsaken curio / without / any breath to it," "nothing at all." Why this particular corpse offends, unhinges, and shames Williams is not clear; perhaps it raises in his mind the specter of love beaten and beyond touch. Williams does not worry about the infinite or believe that "Death is the mother of beauty," nor does he, like the rich woman in Stevens's "Sunday Morning," dream nostalgically of "the old catastrophe" or search for an "imperishable bliss"; there is no divinity or metaphysical subtext in Williams's poem. It is not until the aftermath of his strokes in the 1950s that he gingerly takes up questions of death and spiritual belief. Despite occasional biblical cadences and echoes, religion did not for Williams—a professed skeptic throughout his adult years—provide answers or consolation: he had no faith in an afterlife, unless it be the survival of his poems into future generations. "The dream / is in pursuit!"—of artistic accomplishment, that is.

The sequence closes with the graceful lyric "The Botticellian Trees," which won Williams *Poetry*'s 1930 Guarantor's Prize and an honorarium of one hundred dollars. The poem moves felicitously in crisp couplets from measured summation to the music of praise, "quick with desire," of "love's ascendancy." Letters and words, the building blocks of poems, are arranged into sentences, just as Nature's "strict simple / / principles of / straight branches / / are being modified / by pinched-out / / ifs of color, devout / conditions / the smiles of love—." Sound, sight, love, faith, and doubt are interwoven in a comely pattern: this time *summer* has arrived, bringing with it a mood of serene content. The cycle of growth, fading, and renewal, with its Romantic tinge, comes as a relief after the messy bouts of overwrought emotion that preceded it: finally, "The forms / of the emotions are crystalline, / geometric-faceted."

When Louis Zukofsky volunteered to trim the fat off the sequence, Williams cheerfully accepted his offer: "Mark up the script ad lib . . . Delete poems, sections of poems, lines, words, the whole works or nothing as it may happen to suit your fancy or conscience." Such carte blanche bespoke unusual trust in Zukofsky, twenty years Williams's junior, and the young man's editorial skills. As promised, Zukofsky slimmed down "Della Primavera Trasportata" to thirty pages. An abridged version—consisting of the first four poems—appeared in the 1930 *Imagist Anthology* and the entire poem, with a few revisions, in the 1934 *Collected Poems: 1921–1931*.

Williams owed his acquaintanceship with Zukofsky to Pound, who on March 5, 1928, wrote to his latest poetry acolyte, "Re / private life: Do go down an' stir up Bill Willyums, 9 Ridge Rd. Rutherford (W.C. Williams, M.D.) and tell him I tole you. He is still the best human value on my murkn visiting list." Despite repeatedly sneering at America as poor soil for cultivating poetic talent, Pound kept a trained eye on this vast overseas property. He leafed through the little magazines and books for signs of an arresting poetic talent, as a farmer might scan the Burpee catalogue for a seed that, against great odds, will sprout into a hardy fruit-bearing shrub. Or else, as was frequently the case, young poets sought him out, sending a sheaf of poems to the Rapallo guru for approval, advice, or schooling.

The recipient of Pound's letter, Louis Zukofsky, was a skinny, homely, bookish young Jew who had grown up on the Lower East Side in a cramped tenement. His family never escaped from poverty, and Zukofsky himself never earned more than a meager living for much of his adult life. But he did win a scholarship, rare for Jewish students in the 1920s, to Columbia University, where he became part of a literary circle that included Whittaker Chambers. Mark Van Doren took Zukofsky under his wing, as he later would Allen Ginsberg, Richard Howard, and John Hollander. Zukofsky's early poems were often abstruse and arty, but they were also uncommonly ambitious and precocious. After graduation, he rented a small room in East Harlem, toiled at a series of menial jobs, and cranked out the odd piece of literary journalism.

When in the summer of 1927 Zukofsky sent "The" to Pound in Rapallo, hoping it would be published in Pound's latest literary magazine, *The Exile*, Pound replied, "Thanks. First cheering mss. I have recd. In weeks, or months, or something or other." It did not hurt that "The" paid homage to Pound's *Hugh Selwyn Mauberley*, from which it quoted several lines, and was confected, like Pound's, *"out of old bokes, in good feith."* Trying to impress, Zukofsky crammed "The" with references to the Bible,

Socrates, Shakespeare, Marlowe, Bach, Heine, Virginia Woolf, and *The Waste Land*, and sprinkled snippets of Yiddish, German, French, and Italian as garnish. Pound could not have missed Zukofsky's structure, which, shunning the conventional distribution of lines on the page, divided "The" into six movements of unequal lengths and rhythms, each bearing its own subtitle; the poem's 330 lines were numbered, like bar lines in the score of a sonata, and the tonality modulated from the jocose to the lyrical to the prayerful. This young man was without doubt a candidate for Pound's correspondence tutorial in basic poetics.

Heeding his mentor's advice, Zukofsky wrote to Williams. He did not have to wait long for an answer. Williams remarked sarcastically, "By 'human value' I suppose Ezrie means that in his opinion I can't write." But he quickly softened his tone—after all, Zukofsky was not to blame for Pound's provocations—and invited the young man to Rutherford for a "country meal." (In his poem "9 Ridge Road," James Laughlin remarked that for Williams, "A new acquaintance was / At once a friend.") This first meeting did indeed start a friendship that lasted until Williams's death in 1963.

Pleased by Zukofsky's conversation and admiration of *Spring and All*, Williams fired off a letter to Pound:

I like Louis. He has distinction. He knows and is not puffed up, offensive, perverted by what he has absorbed. He puzzles me. His mind is really silky. God knows if he'll ever do anything with it. He has no job, doesn't seem able to get any. They live in a tenement—under trying if not distressing circumstances—yet he is fine. And strong too. I have rarely met a person who can see as clearly, hold as firmly to his point, enjoy excellence and for a clear reason, so gracefully and fault so convincingly—curious.

In judging Zukofsky's poems, Williams was enthusiastic—"Yes, yes. You have the rare gift"—but had his reservations. He complained of the young man's "tripping rhythms," for example, and rapped his knuckles in this passage:

Poems are inventions richer in thought than as image. Your early poems even when the thought has force or freshness have not been objectified to new or fresh observations. But if it is the music[,] even that is not inventive enough to make up for images which give an overwhelming effect of triteness—as it has been said. The language is stilted, "poetic" except in the one piece I marked.

Eyes have always stood first in the poet's equipment. If you are mostly ear—a newer rhythm must come in more strongly than has been the case so far.

Yet I am willing to grant—to listen.

Zukofsky was not resentful of Williams's criticisms, which were neither captious nor dismissive. Williams knew whereof he spoke, since he had labored many years to weed out the poeticisms that overran his own early work. "The" did not impress Williams as it had Pound, perhaps because the images were "clouded with words" and featured too many inversions, taboos that Pound usually inveighed against but had overlooked here. Williams also correctly singled out the parade of abstractions—"all live processes," "orbit-trembling," "our consciousness," "the source of being"—as verbal woolgathering.

Over the decades, Williams became a beloved avuncular figure and sponsor to young poets with often radically different agendas. Although pressed for time, he was ever ready to read and comment on a tyro's poems or launch a first book with an introduction or a blurb; each new generation of poets found the footpath to Rutherford for an afternoon of talk about the latest prodigy the little magazines were touting, racy gossip from bohemia, the pleasures and frustrations of a doctor's life, Charles Sheeler's paintings, and so forth. After a visit to Williams in 1960, James Wright observed to James Dickey, "He looks young men right in the eyes as an equal." So when Zukofsky knocked on his door, Williams construed his admiration as a sign that the rising generation was hammering a nail in the old guard's coffin. (Zukofsky was not keen on Eliot's verse.)

Yet when Marianne Moore, *The Dial*'s poetry editor, accepted some of Louis's poems, Williams surprisingly made light of it: "*The Dial* to me is as dead as last year's birds' nest[s]. One must 'believe in spiders' to spin new webs." To Pound he groused, "I feel so disgusted with The Dial for its half hearted ways that I am almost ready to agree with anyone concerning its worthlessness." But he closely observed Zukofsky's progress, remarking to Pound, "Louis Z. has done good work with his second long poem 'A.' It has a quality of scholarliness and extreme scepticism, combined with a cold certainty of perception in matters of the abstract which flares up icily at times with very unsentimental distinction." What is impressive about this comment is Williams's disinterestedness: he can praise in another poet a set of qualities inimical to his own practice.

Williams's peeve against *The Dial* did not spring from the way Moore imperiously, and notoriously, rewrote other poets' submissions. Like his colleagues, Williams resented her often prudish despotism, complained bitterly to her of censorship, haggled with her to restore words she excised and lines she transposed, and sometimes wrung minor concessions from her, but in the end he seldom took his poems elsewhere. For Williams, Moore was a revered figure and a critical ally; he sometimes felt that she was the only poet of distinction fighting alongside him for an American modernist poetic. He praised her as simultaneous destroyer and creator, a heroic role he wished to play.

Nonetheless, Moore was not a visitor to 9 Ridge Road. One reason is that she didn't travel far from Brooklyn, where, the epitome of a devoted daughter, she lived with her mother. While Williams's letters to Moore over the years are anything but formal, she was never a confidante. Her fastidious sense of propriety ruled out her talking about her family life. Williams's relationship with Zukofsky was different. Even their arguments were enjoyable—"rare as snakes['] feathers," Williams remarked about his conversations with Zukofsky, who respected his elders without muzzling his own opinions. Williams could not hide his pleasure at having found a young poet who "encourages me in my designs" and "[m]akes me anxious to get at my notes." Above all, Williams felt freed from a morose sense of futility: "No matter how we may be ignored, maligned, left unnoticed, yet by doing straightforward work we do somehow reach the right people."

Williams often handed Zukofsky a packet of poems to edit. How to explain this faith in the younger poet? Williams needed no tutoring in filling his lines with "clear or vital particulars," but he was still somewhat insecure about "the resolving of words and their ideation into structure and design," a skill that came more easily to Zukofsky; self-deprecatingly, Williams said of his own work, "Perhaps by my picayune imagistic mannerism I hold together superficially what should by all means fall apart." Perhaps he also believed that Zukofsky could help him train his ear to American speech rhythms, though that was not Zukofsky's forte. Louis listened to jazz and blues and knew enough popular musical comedy to insert a lame joke about it in "The," but his tastes ran mainly to classical music. When he urged Williams to attend a performance of Bach's *St. Matthew Passion*, he did not know that Williams had heard and been moved by the masterpiece in Vienna in 1924. Zukofsky wanted Williams to pay attention to the sacred oratorio's sublime architecture and intricate counterpoint. If counterpoint was not at first Williams's strong suit, by the mid-1930s, as a result of Zukofsky's encouragement and his own growing mastery, he could write poems of complex musical structure: in particular, "The Crimson Cyclamen," his elegy for his old friend Charles Demuth, and "Perpetuum Mobile: The City." For thirty-five years, Williams and Zukofsky read and beneficially influenced each other's poems. Whenever he could, Williams would drive into New York on Fridays to lunch with Zukofsky. Poetry was a communion table at which their friendship was ritualized.

2.

In the fall of 1930, Zukofsky was away teaching at the University of Wisconsin. Williams missed his young friend, as if he were a son who had fled the nest. Despite the Depression and Zukofsky's absence, the literary scene was vibrant: poets, artists, and editors would argue politics and poetics over supper at a trattoria in Greenwich Village and then criticize, even savage, one another in print. Sometimes they launched a new magazine designed to bring about a revolution in taste, to plead the definitive case for or against the long free verse line, to showcase the poems of the next Rimbaud (or the editors' own work), to save American poetry from derivative, self-promoting careerists, or to give a voice to the dispossessed. By pooling their limited resources, they managed to publish an issue or two before the magazine vanished. Sometime in the 1920s, the English poet Keith Preston wrote an amusing quatrain that might serve as an epithet for these little magazines:

> Of all the literary scenes
> Saddest this sight to me:
> The graves of little magazines
> Who died to make verse free

For Williams, though, the little magazines were indispensable for the circulation and survival of his work. They often sported exotic names, such as *Blast, Pagany, Hound and Horn* (*Bitch and Bugle*, Pound renamed it), *Secession*, and *Broom*; while a few were lavishly produced, the majority consisted of stapled-together mimeographed pages or were made from cheap paper stock. Contributors were usually paid nothing. Inevitably, in the 1930s, many of the magazines clashed over questions of which should be uppermost, aesthetics or social action. (Williams had a foot in both camps.) Ideologically driven magazines such as *New Masses*, *The Anvil*, and *Blast* earnestly insisted that individual talent be subservient to "collective" needs. Only hyperrealism and agitprop, like the strokes of the hammer on an anvil, were vivid enough to stir Americans to demand and effect change. To these left-wing magazines, style, nuance, and subtlety were luxury items, the sign of self-indulgent privilege, and thus to be shunned as frivolous and irrelevant. Better to print the authentic voices of proletarians, however clumsy and commonplace their poems and stories were as art, and the writers on the left who addressed the toll the economic collapse was taking on average Americans.

Williams's sympathies were aroused by the misery of the unemployed and the poor, but he remained wary of political cant and artistic edicts that came down from politburos or editorial boards. For him, literary magazines helped, however imperfectly, to keep artists' imaginations unshackled to dogmas of any kind. This meant not dismissing high art and debates about form and style as elitist foppery or libeling the painter experimenting with abstract grids as a solipsist cruelly indifferent to the misery in his neighborhood. *Hound and Horn*, for example, kept close tabs on avant-garde writers such as Gertrude Stein. It took for granted the centrality of modernist writing and art, even at its most obscure and difficult, and so printed Pound, Stevens, and Eliot fairly regularly and praised Henry James's late novels for their plumbing of consciousness and ethical life in a complex, mannered style. Yet it also allowed Lincoln Kirstein to write cogently and sensitively about a James Cagney movie in which the actor plays an Irish gangster from a poor working-class family still tied to his mother's apron strings.* Williams's work was lightly represented in its pages.

Richard Johns's *Pagany* aggressively solicited Williams's poem and stories. The son of an affluent businessman, Johns was a voracious reader

---

Hound and Horn was founded in 1927 by Kirstein and Varian Fry, Harvard undergraduates, and funded by Kirstein's father, the head of Filene's department store. When it moved to New York in 1930, it changed its name from *The Harvard Miscellany* and lost its Harvard accent.

who educated himself in the major texts of modernism. When he realized that his own poetry would never progress beyond the middling, he decided to start a little magazine; his father fostered this ambition by lending him the seed money. Johns, a huge fan of Williams, asked the poet if he could call the magazine *Pagany*, after Bill's novel *A Voyage to Pagany*, and offered him the post of coeditor. A pleased Williams agreed to the first request but declined the second. He would be willing to act as consultant and scout, but he wanted no part of an editor's daily grind and worries.

Although the magazine was called *Pagany*, it did not seek to publish European writers; in fact its subtitle, *A Native Quarterly*, defined its mission. Yet Johns's tastes were eclectic, and on political or artistic questions he was neither chauvinistic nor dogmatic. This is reflected in the diverse roster of poets and fiction writers who appeared in the twelve issues he put out between spring 1930 and February 1933, when he ran out of funds and was forced to shut the magazine down: Gertrude Stein, Kenneth Rexroth, H.D., John Dos Passos, E. E. Cummings, Erskine Caldwell, Parker Tyler, Zukofsky, and Pound. *Pagany* allowed Williams to test out on a small but discerning audience a sheaf of experimental poems, a colloquial short story, and several chapters of his novel in progress, *White Mule*. Johns was a "quiet persistent enthusiast for modern writing," an "odd fish but very likeable, one that can swim," Williams wrote.

The question of audience was a perennial thorn in Williams's side. Nearly all of the literary magazines with which he was associated, from *Others* to *transition*, had puny circulations (*Poetry* was the exception, but even its subscription list was hardly robust). This dismal fact did not scare Williams off from being a founding editor, consultant, fund-raiser, contributor, and judge for several magazines. Succumbing to the romantic dream of discovering a new Emily Dickinson and reshaping American poetry, he solicited manuscripts from friends and strangers, edited poems and stories, wrote rejection letters and reams of splenetic criticism, and saw several issues through the press. The drudgery exhausted him, as did the scramble to scrape together money to pay the printing bills. Floss was not pleased when he dipped into his pocket to keep a magazine's creditors away from its door. And when the submissions betrayed a drought of talent, disenchantment set in: What was the use of all that effort?

Despite having been rubbed raw by all these chores and disappointments, Williams chose to resurrect *Contact*, with the precociously gifted Nathanael West as deputy editor. West had been recommended by Martin Kamin and David Moss, the publishers of West's Dadaist work *The Dream Life of Balso Snell*, and since they had put up the money for this second coming of *Contact*, Williams was in no position to argue. But he soon became an admirer of West's stylistic finesse and vision of the grotesque isolation of so many Americans. Although freed of financial responsibilities, Williams could not throw himself into this venture wholeheartedly; he liked Kamin (Moss less so), but thought the two men were unrealistic in their expectations of what a literary magazine could achieve. Williams did not reckon on the publishers encroaching on his editorial independence, but that was another irritant he had to cope with. Dutifully, he gathered material from a heterogeneous group of writers, many his friends—Cummings, Zukofsky, Burke, poet George Oppen. But his editorial in the first issue betrayed fatigue, echoing the battle cry with which he had rallied the troops in the original *Contact* in the early 1920s: the magazine would "cut a trail through the American jungle without the use of a European compass." Williams managed to slog through the jungle and publish three issues, but the only poem that sparked his enthusiasm was Charles Reznikoff's *My Country 'Tis of Thee* (later retitled *Testimony*), and the only work of fiction that satisfied him was an excerpt from West's novel *Miss Lonelyhearts*. Whenever Williams mentioned *Contact* to Zukofsky, the former's tone was gloomy, weary, and vexed: "I'm next to hopeless about [the magazine]. A dull chore—not enough good work or too much. I can't tell which: a quarterly can't be just amusing, must be weighted—if to be excused." A few months later he griped, "What a monument of ashes buries one when he tries to really do anything." When West left for the greener pastures of Hollywood, and the magazine's backers made clear their discontent with its expense and with Williams, Bill resigned. *Contact* soon folded.

3.

Over the years the Williams family divided its summer vacations between Grandma Wellcome's cottage on Long Island Sound near West Haven and the Herman farm near Monroe, New York, with an occasional excursion to Wilmington, Vermont. In the summer of 1931, with the boys grown and making plans on their own, Bill and Floss were free to travel. Floss proposed a two-week cruise up the St. Lawrence River and across the

Gulf of St. Lawrence, starting in Montreal and ending in Newfoundland, a route that in reverse traced the watery pathway that a few intrepid sailors from Greenland and Iceland took to explore the New World. Floss and Bill enjoyed Montreal's cosmopolitan atmosphere, but he was impatient to set sail for Labrador. In the *Autobiography*, he remarked that "many of the people and places I saw there have deeply influenced my later writing: it was this that I had first desired, to quit the urban life and go out into the wilderness. There facing me, it was, stretching away from the north shore, from Godbou, from Seven Isles, to the North Pole if I wanted to follow." His boyhood dream of being a forester had not died. The wilderness possessed a harsh, magnetic power, even in summertime. The howls of hundreds of huskies, thrown cod livers to subsist on, reminded Williams of a pack of "savage beasts" and led him to conclude, "We live in filth, we eat, drink, and bathe in it; as we can we thrive on it / We are suffocated by the primitive and the pure." "The pure products of America" have multiplied into a vast flock of slatterns. There is no middle ground between the "primitive and the pure." In a memorable coda to this trip, Williams, like an ascetic mortifying the flesh sensuously, strips off his clothes and dives into "the desperately cold" North Atlantic water, gashing his belly on a "shelly rock." "It is strange to bathe alone in an Arctic sea," he concludes. This trip inspired one short poem, "The Cod Head," which is notable for its intricate pattern of natural rhythms: ocean waves that "lift and fall"; "weed / strands, stems, debris" that drift on the surface; fathoms below, fishes that "scud" and "the bottom [that] skids / a mottle of green / sands backward." What most arrests Williams's attention is the decomposing cod heads washed up on the beaches "of red and very coarse sand" or floating on the water. (Cod was the principal catch off Labrador and Newfoundland.)

4.

The first fruits of Williams's increased activity as a short story writer was the 1932 collection *The Knife of the Times*, published in an edition of five hundred copies by Angel Flores, a young professor of Spanish at Cornell who ran the obscure Dragon Press. Flores managed to bring out the book of eleven stories in only two months, but most of the print run went unsold. In the *Autobiography*, Williams recalls that three years later a doctor

friend who was in Atlantic City for a convention spotted a salesman peddling a trove of one hundred copies on the boardwalk for fifteen cents
apiece (a 90 percent markdown). His friend scooped up the books and
shipped them to 9 Ridge Road, where they gathered dust.

In *I Wanted to Write a Poem*, Williams remarks that these stories

> are all about people I knew in the town, portraits of people who
> were my friends. I was impressed by the picture of the times, de-
> pression years, the plight of the poor. I felt it very vividly. I felt furi-
> ous at the country for its lack of progressive ideas. I felt as if I were
> a radical without being a radical. The plight of the poor in a rich
> country, I wrote it down as I saw it. The times—that was the knife
> that was killing them. I was deeply sympathetic and filled with ad-
> miration. How amusing they were in spite of their suffering, how
> gaily they could react to their surroundings. I would have done
> anything for them, anything but treat them for nothing, and I guess
> I did that too.

This passage spotlights Williams's commitment to his destitute patients
in Passaic, Lyndhurst, and neighboring towns. He brings to bear the same
empathic curiosity and indignation that Chekhov brought to the beaten-
down peasants he cared for. In Williams's stories, the shattering impact of
the "depression years" on the poor is explored, but it is not his sole subject; his stories are populated by representatives of all classes—drifters,
grifters, self-satisfied country club types, selfless nurses, unapologetic rac-
ists, possessive mothers and unwanted children, abused wives, lesbians,
farmers, and a patient who ignores Williams's advice and refuses to swallow a pill to combat the symptoms of syphilis. Williams takes most setbacks with a shrug. Like Chekhov, he rarely mounts a high horse to
lecture these mistrustful patients; he tolerates human foibles, though
disgust and irritability do surface. In the course of the story "A Face of
Stone," he expresses hostility toward and stereotypes a Jewish immigrant
couple, "whose looks change the minute cash is mentioned," before breaking out in America-first invective: "People like that belong in clinics, I
thought to myself. I wasn't putting myself out for them, not that day any-
how. Just dumb oxen. Why the hell do they let them into the country? Half
idiots at best. Look at them." By the end of the story Williams has reverted
to his normal benevolent self.

Nevertheless the reader can't help wondering out of what dark recesses such xenophobia and warped language emerged. (The speaker is not a fictional surrogate.) Unfortunately, Williams is guilty of worse linguistic offenses. In his letters to Pound and Kenneth Burke, he casually writes of "kikes" and "niggers," though he did not share Pound's belief that Jewish bankers were engaged in an international conspiracy to control the money supply. Nor did he share T. S. Eliot's more genteel and sanctimonious brand of anti-Semitism. But it is precisely because he treated his patients of all races and religions with dignity, and because he was friends with Jewish poets such as Zukofsky and Reznikoff, that his lapses into the lingua franca of prejudice are so perturbing.

Elsewhere in *The Knife of the Time*, Williams brings a deceptively artless technique to the stories, blending, as Chekhov did, laughter and pain, detachment and intimacy. The pacing is unhurried, the tone relaxed but not slack, as of a yarn spun out at the dinner table. Given his outburst in Natalie Barney's garden and his uneasiness with the lesbians he met in Paris, it is surprising that when he depicts a relationship between two married women, friends from their girlhood years and the mothers of a brood of children, Williams treats the disclosure of ardent Sapphic desire with delicate open-mindedness. He understands the emotional dynamics when what has been hidden and repressed suddenly erupts: Ethel's lust is impatient of limits, intensely physical, whereas Maura is more cautious. Moved by her friend's ardor, she is curious and "fearful," but not emotionally paralyzed: "Ethel had begged her to visit her, to go to her, to spend a week at least with her, to sleep with her. Why not?" And in "The Sailor's Son," Williams's occasional homophobia gives way to a calm, nonjudgmental understanding of a casual gay hookup. Similarly, in "The Colored Girls of Passenack," his admiration for the beauty and eroticism of black women, and for their spunky independence, transcends any parochial racism. There is also no trace of misogyny.

5.

Through his membership in Marxist groups, Zukofsky met George Oppen, the son of a wealthy manufacturer in New Rochelle. Their friendship would lead to the formation of a group—consisting of, besides Zukofsky and Oppen, Charles Reznikoff and Carl Rakosi (and Williams)—

that Harriet Monroe dubbed the objectivists, a label that stuck. Zukofsky disliked it, and Rakosi thought it misrepresented their work, since they did not share fixed ideas about poetics. Too modest to think of themselves as a movement like the Futurists, they issued no manifestos or incendiary declarations of revolutionary intent; if anything, they were reticent to a fault. In the fall of 1930, Monroe invited Zukofsky to edit a selection of poems for an issue of *Poetry*, a task he reluctantly agreed to take on. He began, naturally enough, by compiling the work of friends, including Williams. Nobody could have foreseen that this issue, later republished as *The Objectivist Anthology*, would become a landmark in American poetry.

Objectivism traced its lineage back to Imagism. Pound had championed the economical presentation of the object, and Williams had found Imagistic terseness useful for reining in his romantic prolixity. Traces of Imagism can, in fact, be found in his poems from every decade. As a doctor, he concentrated on the facts and symptoms of an illness. He had to know how muscles atrophied, a heart valve could malfunction, and a tumor could cause blindness. "Clamp down on the object," he wisely advised doctors and poets, but he never made a fetish of scientific fact. Objectivity was important, he argued, but it could not diagnose a perplexing disease or put together a pattern of pleasing speech rhythms. In his estimate, it needed to be balanced by a well-tempered subjectivity, the domain of intuition and imagination. That outlook ("philosophy" would be too pompous a word for it) carried over into the way he scrutinized and wrote about everything. Given his friendship with Zukofsky, Williams naturally forged an alliance with the objectivist poets, though typically he remained on the periphery of the movement.

At its poetic center stood a reluctant Louis Zukofsky; at its financial center stood a modest George Oppen. Although family money had allowed Oppen and his wife, Mary, to live abroad, the expatriate life did not tempt them. Oppen was a man of principle, his political acts at all times springing from his inner core: believing that Hitler was an obscene threat, he fought in World War II and was wounded at the Battle of the Bulge, and during the House Un-American Activities Committee hearings, he courageously refused to divulge the names of fellow Communist Party members. Despite their aversion to the anomie of expatriate communities, the Oppens preferred it to the poisonous atmosphere of the Red Scare in America, so they fled to Mexico, where they lived for many

years, returning in 1958. In 1932, however, Oppen was an important figure in the objectivist constellation, more for his bankrolling of the oddly
named To Press than for his own poems. In its brief but distinguished
existence, To Press published Pound's *ABC of Reading* and *The Spirit of
Romance*, as well as Williams's *A Novelette and Other Prose*, which combined a set of improvisations more agile and seasoned than those of *Kora
in Hell* with a selection of Williams's reviews, articles, and pronouncements, including landmark essays on Gertrude Stein and Marianne
Moore. Williams was not close to Oppen, but their relationship was cordial and professional. To Press rescued *A Novelette* from falling into a
black hole.*

Williams called the method of *A Novelette* automatic writing, but
that is misleading: his typewriter did not take dictation from an unconscious high on drugs, alcohol, or even words. There are nearly as many
leitmotifs in *A Novelette* as there are in Wagner's *Siegfried*. The flu epidemic of 1929 that forced Williams to move rapidly sharpened his powers
of perception: "There is no time not to notice," he remarks. Thoughts and
images flit in and out of his mind, but he cannot stop and record them on
the pad lying on the front seat of his car. He must trust that other ideas
and phrases will take their place. They do, because the need to write is "a
violent acid," a "fierce singleness" that seeks an outlet on the page. He
writes, he tells us, "for relaxation, relief. To have nothing in my head,—
to freshen my eye by that till I see, smell, know and can reason and
be." That is how the physician heals himself. Williams's consecration to
writing is of a piece with his devotion to his patients, but during the flu
epidemic he rushed from one case to another. The telephone rings
throughout *A Novelette*, disrupting the narrative. He cannot ignore it.

Although Williams rightly claimed that *A Novelette* drew on Dadaism
and showed "a tremendous leap ahead of conventional prose," it is not
wildly anarchic. While he sometimes tosses logic and linearity to the
winds, he is not careless about design or structure: rather, he declares,
"Doctrinaire formula-worship—that is our real enemy." Improvisation defeats dullness and triteness by mixing cheeky humor and probing reflection. "Love calls us to the things of this world," Richard Wilbur wrote in
his beautiful poem of that title, and *A Novelette* echoes that enchanting

---

*Williams published three chapters of the book in *transition*. Nancy Cunard refused to publish it
in her Hours Press series.

melody. Williams's prose is honeycombed with details of the "actual," hurried and scattershot though a few of these details may appear. Sometimes the news from "the things of this world" is grim, such as dispatches from the front lines of the epidemic; once, driving to his next patient, Williams is held spellbound by a bare walnut tree, its wintry nakedness permitting a clarification of shapes and textures and essences that the tree in full summer bloom conceals. And the actual includes snatches of conversation between husband and wife. In *A Novelette*, the talks between Floss and Bill reproduce the banter of the comfortably married. Floss, charming and determined, enters the book early, while chasing after a runaway cat and, protecting herself from its sharp claws, triumphantly capturing it. Williams explains himself and his obsession with writing to Floss in easy terms. "You, I, we," he sums up, "cannot you see how in the singleness of these few days marriage and writing have been so fused that the seriousness of my life and common objects about me have made up an actuality of which I am assembling the parts?" Floss in fact does understand and appreciate his "singleness" and is not threatened by it. That awareness and the absence on the scene of other women trying to seduce her husband give their relationship in *A Novelette* an aura of benign intimacy. "Williams's concept of the actual, during a time of stress," Webster Schott sagely observes, "is this frantic, speculative, loving work. It is as rational and irrational as life itself."

Although To Press came to an end, Oppen continued funding new work. With the unexpected success of the objectivist issue of *Poetry*, it was decided that the issue would be reprinted as a book under the aegis of the Objectivist Press. In his *Autobiography*, Williams describes the founding of this new venture in Oppen's apartment in Columbia Heights, Brooklyn. Charles Reznikoff was also present at the birth, and it is significant that Williams tacks on the phrase "lawyer and poet of distinction" to Reznikoff's name while leaving Oppen's without a laudatory epithet. Williams respected the poems of Oppen's first book, *Discrete Series (1932–1934)* for their "technical excellence," "with no loose bolts or beams sticking out unattached at an end or put there to hold up a rococo cupid or a concrete saint." These are apt terms, since Oppen had worked in a factory and, as a carpenter, valued craftsmanship. Reviewing the book in *Poetry*, Williams praised its "sharp restriction to essentials, the seriousness of a new order brought to realization," and added, "It has something of the implications of a work in a laboratory when one is following what he believes to be a profitable lead along some one line of possible investigation." He does not vigorously endorse Oppen's methods or materials; he approves of his "plain words" and "metric taken from speech": minimalist construction is only *possibly* something contemporary poets can build on.

The title of Oppen's book of poems *Discrete Series* refers to stops on the Lexington Avenue subway—14, 28, 32, 42—and to the mathematical concept in which "each term is empirically justified rather than derived from the preceding term," a pattern Oppen applies to New York City life. In theory this is a workable concept, but in practice, because he describes traffic, crowds, geraniums in a window box, and a woman in silk stockings lying on a bed in the same flat tone, the syntax is barely able to gain any rhythmic propulsion, and the speech stammers. Oppen's unrelenting earnestness erects such "a firewall against subjectivity" (to borrow critic Ross Feld's phrase) that the poems seem beaten down, dazed, too modest and detached for their own good. Consider two representative examples:

> This land:
> The hills, round under straw;
> A house
>
> With rigid trees
>
> And flaunts
> A family laundry,
> And the glass of windows
>
> and
>
> No interval of manner
> Your body in the sun.
> You? A solid, this that the dress
>   Insisted,
> Your faith unaccented, your mouth a mouth?
>   Practical knees:
> It is you who truly
> Excel the vegetable,
> The fitting of grasses—more bare than
>   That.

Pointedly bent, your elbow on a car-edge
Incognito as summer
Among mechanics.

The first poem reads like an Imagist exercise, as static and uninviting as a real estate agent's prose about a house for sale. The syntax is as stiff as the tree's trunk, the speaker's voice is remote and disembodied, and the enjambment and white space seem to lead to a dead end. An almost formal primness governs the diction in the second poem. "It is you who truly / Excel the vegetable" is a bizarre compliment to direct to his wife, Mary, the loving partner of Oppen's life. One does not expect a troubadour's extravagance or erotic insinuations—Oppen never loses his head here or elsewhere in *Discrete Series*—but the reader's ear would welcome some inflection of passion amid the overall drabness. One hears the moral probity in the poet's aloof language, but the simile describing the woman's bent elbow as "Incognito as summer / Among mechanics" is far-fetched. In striving to set down accurate perceptions, Oppen sacrifices emotional resonance, and his poems' music is often flat and pallid. In fairness to him, at a later period he defines prosody as "a rigorous music—a music that refuses all trumpets, all sweet harmonies, all lusts and emotions that aren't there, it is a music, quite simply, of image and honest speech." The essayist Eliot Weinberger ably sums up Oppen's point of view:

> Oppen's standard, his obsession, was "honesty" in the poem, Pound's ideogram of a man standing by his word. He insisted on writing only about what he himself had seen, and the act of seeing them: the angels he had mentioned in a poem were the ones in the windows of Chartres. [This insistence also created an obstinate blindness to all forms of surrealism, which he saw as an escape from, and not a way into, current realities.] Uniquely among American poets, there are almost no mythological references and no myth-making, no exotica, no personae, only one or two passing historical references, and almost no similes in his work: in Oppen's world, things are not "like," they are there, right in front of you, and there with an exclamation point.

Oppen remained faithful to this almost self-abnegating view of language; his "sincerity" and "honesty" would compel him to spurn Sir Philip

Sidney's famous definition of poetry as "feigning notable images of virtue," as well as "all trumpets, all sweet harmonies." It is precisely that dogmatic "all" that drastically limits invention. Oppen's "honest speech" is too often an example of aridity, of a monochromatic, prosaic literalism. His late poems are only marginally suppler than the poems of *Discrete Series*.

In 1934, soon after *Discrete Series* was published, Oppen renounced poetry and joined the Communist Party, dedicating his time and money to advancing its agenda. Before the Objectivist Press closed down, however, it published Williams's *Collected Poems, 1921–1931*, the first retrospective of his poetic work, which he called "a lovely gesture from my own gang." It was late in a prolific career—he was fifty-one years old—to offer a sampling of what he'd accomplished, but Williams was in no position to complain. The selection, running to an ample 134 pages, gave the reader a firm idea of his versatility: amiable poems such as "This Is Just to Say" and "As the Cat," which could not stump even a beginning reader of poetry, were presented alongside the Dadaesque sequence "Della Primavera Trasportata al Morale."

Despite blurbs from Pound and Marianne Moore, only a handful of the five hundred printed copies sold—a dismal showing even during the Depression. To make matters worse, the book itself got less attention than Wallace Stevens's introduction, in which, in a phrase that especially nettled Williams, Stevens snipes at him for being "antipoetic." Though Williams had sometimes used this term to distance himself from maundering lyricism, he felt that Stevens gave a misleading impression. The Stevens who shared Williams's belief that reality was an equal partner with the imagination in fashioning a poem was far more of a formalist and fancy aesthete than Williams even at his most playful. No uncle in Williams's poems would peer at the world through a monocle, like a dandy. In "This Florida: 1924," which Williams included in *Collected Poems, 1921–1931*, he spoofs the sybaritic diction of Stevens's *Harmonium*: "orange / of ale and lilies / / orange of topaz, orange of red hair / orange of curaçao / orange of the Tiber / / turbid, orange of the bottom / rocks in Maine rivers." He teasingly calls Stevens's persona in the poem Hibiscus and twits his love of rhyme, iambs, and order, which Williams had schooled himself to escape, he jokes; "by imitation of the senseless / unarrangement of wild things—," he playfully stands, self-accused, as a dangerous bomb-throwing anarchist and "connoisseur of chaos." At the end of the poem, he performs a urine test, "dropping in the acid" of a patient, Peggy Ladd, who "has a little albumen" in her pee. There's no evidence that Stevens took offense at Williams's teasing.

Stevens did have a legitimate gripe about Williams's occasional sentimentality, but it was the miscellaneous nature of the poems that most riled the fastidious Hartford poet. He raises the same objection to Williams's fondness for the piecemeal that he had in the early letter that Williams quoted sardonically in "The Prologue to *Kora in Hell*." Perhaps because of his patrician taste for blank verse and a supple iambic pentameter, and his suave instinct for rich verbal textures, Stevens missed or misread the evidence that in *Collected Poems, 1921–1931* Williams was seriously investigating and trying out new models of syntax, new combinations of rhythm, consonant with American speech timbres—that he wasn't a free-verse outlaw enamored of Whitman's "barbaric yawp," or a Laputan building a poem's structure from the top down, leaving no space for the foundation. (Williams is not averse, now and then, to impersonating a vulgarian who enjoys shocking the reader by violating canons of decorum.) "The Sea-Elephant," "The Young Sycamore," and any of the *Spring and All* poems included in the retrospective should have instructed Stevens that Williams's poems were not slapped together in a gratuitous or uncouth manner but were carefully thought out. Despite the scintillating concreteness of Stevens's imagination, it was more at ease with, and given to, philosophical abstraction than Williams's, as one would expect from an insurance executive who pored over actuarial tables; as a doctor constantly probing the travails of the body, Williams was grounded in the physical. He had imprinted on his brain the interconnectedness of muscles, organs, joints, tissues, nerves, etc. He was not the crusading knight errant of the antipoetic that Stevens sometimes made him out to be.

Only one year separated *Collected Poems, 1921–1931* from *An Early Martyr and Other Poems*, published by the Alcestis Press in 1935. In terms of self-assurance, formal control, and content, the new volume marked a significant advance. With the Depression gripping the country, Williams returned to social subjects, but his portraits of the proletariat (a word he uses ironically) could only dismay the ideologues, for he refused to regard the poor as tragic victims of capitalism. Rather, he captured them in moments of ordinary humanity. In "To a Poor Old Woman," the woman eats a plum on the street, totally absorbed by the pleasure of sucking out its sweetness. The poet's fascination, however, is equally rhythmic: he frames the sentence "They taste good to her" with two irregular breaks in the line—"they taste good / to her. They taste / good to her"—thus imbuing the narrative with subtle syncopations that surprise the ear, as in a slightly fractured round. This repetition functions differently in the poem from a traditional refrain, though it harbors the ghost of that echo. The change is also visual: Williams shoots the scene straight on and from a slightly off-center angle.

"Craft is perfected attention," the poet Robert Kelly's maxim, is apposite to both Williams and the subject of "Proletarian Portrait." Again the setting is the street. "A big young bareheaded woman / in an apron" stops to remove a nail in her shoe that has been hurting her. What could be simpler? Yet in eleven lines Williams evokes the concentration and balance that's required for the successful completion of poem and action. (That she's big adds to the difficulty of her task.) The fact that the young woman is proletarian is incidental to Williams's interest in what she's doing. She is herself, not a symbol of an oppressed working-class girl who cannot afford to repair her shoes.

Williams touches on the plight of the poor twice, in the title poem and in "The Yachts." "An Early Martyr," by far the less satisfactory of the two, is a political parable burdened with indignant editorial comments. It tells of John Coffey, a young Irishman who stole furs from John Wanamaker's Department Store, expecting to be arrested and given a chance to testify in court that his reason for stealing was to put an unjust economic system on trial. Instead he was sent to Matawan, a hospital for the insane in New Jersey. After trying and failing to escape with two other inmates, he was finally released, ostensibly because the asylum was overcrowded. That is the bare bones of the story. In Williams's hands, it becomes a rallying cry for others to keep protesting (blaring like "a factory whistle" is his simile) and not give up the noble fight against a corrupt, failed democracy.

Williams dedicated *An Early Martyr and Other Poems* to Coffey, who was no revolutionary saint who died for the sacred cause, just a well-intentioned, touchingly naive foot soldier in the ranks captured by the police and kept incommunicado. (As a handsome young Irishman, before his arrest, he moved on the fringes of Greenwich Village's bohemia and had a brief affair with poet Louise Bogan.) The poem is prosaic, preachy, a slide into political rhetoric. "The Yachts" is its opposite: a skillful, disturbing political poem that measures, in thirty-three urgent lines, the gap between rich and poor in Depression-era America. The sea, "ungoverned" and "pitiless," tortures and sinks the big hulls. But the sleek yachts, the best wealth can buy, are shielded from the buffetings of wind and ocean. Williams shrewdly depicts the halcyon beauty and arrogance of the yachts: "Mothlike in mist, scintillant in the minute // brilliance of cloudless days, with broad-bellying sails / they glide to the wind tossing green water / from their sharp prows." The easy rhythmic flow conjures the owners' feeling of self-satisfied invulnerability. The crew, like ants, "crawl" over the surface doing an assortment of jobs: "grooming" the prows, releasing and changing the sails, catching the winds. The crew has salable skills in the Depression. In stanza 5, Williams again calls our attention to the preeminence of the yachts. In contrast to the "lesser and greater craft which, sycophant, lumbering / and flittering follow them," the youthful yachts are "rare / as the light of a happy eye, live with the grace / of all that in the mind is fleckless, free and / naturally to be desired." Jockeying for advantage, the yachtsmen master wind and sea, sailing smoothly through life. Then the poem shifts dramatically in the last three stanzas:

> Arms with hands grasping seek to clutch at the prows.
> Bodies thrown recklessly in the way are cast aside.
> It is a sea of faces about them in agony, in despair
>
> until the horror of the race dawns staggering the mind,
> the whole sea become an entanglement of watery bodies
> lost to the world bearing what they cannot hold. Broken,
>
> beaten, desolate, reaching from the dead to be taken up
> they cry out, failing, failing! Their cries rising
> in waves still as skillful yachts pass over.

Abruptly placing the poor in a setting totally alien to them, a regatta, is a clever stroke. This allows Williams to expose the brutal rich who ignore or callously run over the poor, "cut away" as less than flotsam and jetsam. The power of this scene of human wreckage floating and flailing in the sea, clutching to the prow of a yacht, pleading for succor, "to be taken up," staggers the mind; and the cries rising in waves (a fine pun) make the reader, but not the careless rich, blanch. Williams has artfully prepared for this harrowing climax to the race, which doesn't lessen the shock of the carnage. This is not allegory but reality, memorably physical and graphic; those "watery bodies" are not symbols to tug at our heart in order to initiate political action. "The Yachts" indicts not just the rich but indifferent America, unwilling to "take up" the plight of the castaway poor. "The Yachts" is one of a handful of homegrown political poems that succeed artistically.

Three other poems in *An Early Martyr and Other Poems* deserve comment. "An Elegy for D. H. Lawrence" pays tribute to a poet as finely exacting as Williams in writing about flowers, trees, and animals. The poem does not follow the conventions of the elegy, and since Williams knew the eccentric English writer only through his works—Williams was grateful for Lawrence's perceptive review of *In the American Grain*—the tone is impersonal. Williams weaves together favorite Lawrence images: "Blue squills in bloom"; a serpent; the "scorched aridity of / the Mexican plateau," "Mediterranean evenings," and "Ashes / of Cretan fires" (allusions to Lawrence the restless traveler and travel writer); "unfading desire" and sexual friction between men and women; and, obliquely, Lawrence's disaffection from an England that appreciated his novels and poems as little as America did Williams's. The poem ends:

> Sorrow to the young
> that Lawrence has passed
> unwanted from England.
> And in the garden forsythia
> and in the woods
> now the crinkled spice-bush
> in flower.

"The Catholic Bells" is a virtuoso tone poem that shows off Williams's musical ear. Over a sustained ground bass with slight variations, he records the bells ringing in the seasons, or to announce "the new baby of Mr. and Mrs. / Krantz which cannot / for the fat of its cheeks / open well its eyes" (the Krantzes were a Belgian couple having trouble adjusting to Rutherford). On Sunday morning, the bells summon to Mass a cross section of parishioners, from the pious old folk to a "lame / young man in black with / gaunt cheeks and wearing a / Derby hat." (Williams notes an "oil painting of a young priest / on the church wall advertising / last week's Novena to St. / Anthony.") Williams emphasizes that he's not a Catholic, but the ringing of the bells casts a spell that brings him close to the ordinary people of his hometown, particularly an elderly woman friend who cannot hear them but who speaks quietly and with a smile. The quotidian (his conversational tone) and the sacred (the tolling of the bells) mingle in the air of the poem. The final six lines offer a flurry of sound that is self-delighting and prayer-like, commemorating birth and death and the struggles in between:

> O bells
>
>   Ring for the ringing!
>
> The beginning and the end
> Of the ringing! Ring ring
>   Ring ring ring ring ring ring!
> Catholic bells—!

If his attic was his sanctum, where in a state between exhaustion and ecstasy he composed his poems, Williams's office was the nerve center of his medical practice. In "Simplex Sigillum Veri," Williams invites us in for a cheerful tour of this room, which gives off an emanation of a life fully lived. The poem is an affectionate inventory of the clutter on his desk: the paraphernalia of his dual professions, pens, pencils, blotters, a surreal "ink-stand, from whose / imagined top the Prince of Wales / having climbed up, once with all / his might drove a golf ball" (the House of Windsor in Williams's house!), a brochure advertising a three-day conference on an unnamed medical topic, titles for poems (the imagination and the practical are roommates), papers of all sorts stacked in no discernible pattern, which would take a trained archaeologist to retrieve, and "words printed on the backs of / two telephone directories." Translated into English, the Latin title signifies "Keep it simple," or variously "Simplicity is the sign / seal / seat of truth." This is Williams's joke on himself: neither office nor poem is simple.

Williams was a keen amateur painter, and so one can view his poem and the objects strewn in his office as a Cubist still life. What appears to be random is carefully arranged: a blue pencil, for example, is contiguous to a "dullred eraser." Since poet and doctor are never far from the world's business, we glimpse what Williams sees when his eye wanders to what's outside his window: a black bank building, a blue sky, "puffs of white clouds," and "bright green grass." It's no accident that "perspective" is a key word in the poem. The syntax coils and uncoils without benefit of a governing verb, yet clarity and order emerge from the jumble of detail Williams assembles for "Simplex Sigillum Veri."

TWELVE

New Directions in a Tumultuous Decade

I.

Where Williams's sixty-year friendship with Pound mixed melodrama, lectures on poetics, linguistic clowning, and a Niagara of advice and contumely (with plenty of forbearance on Williams's part), his friendship with the painter Charles Demuth was tranquil and intimate. He met Demuth in 1903 "over a dish of prunes" at Mrs. Chain's Philadelphia boardinghouse, where they were both living. Williams was in his first year of medical school, and Demuth was studying art at Drexel. Williams had toyed with the idea of becoming a painter (he had a genuine if minor talent, perhaps inherited from his mother), and Demuth with becoming a writer. Each retained a strong interest in the other's art. Their close friendship, based on deep affection and mutual respect, lasted until Demuth died of diabetes in 1935 at the age of fifty-one.

If Williams was often uneasy in the company of homosexuals, no equivocation disturbed his relations with Demuth, whose homosexuality was out in the open: in his 1916 painting *Turkish Bath with Self-Portrait*, the men standing naked and chatting look comfortable in their skins. Demuth was discreet but neither furtive nor guilty about his preference for men. Usually put off by aesthetes, Williams exempted Demuth from that aversion. Lame at four years old from what Williams diagnosed retroactively as a "tubercular hip," Demuth in his early twenties strolled the streets of New York and Paris, dressed elegantly and flourishing a gold-tipped cane like a Regency dandy. He was a figure of fun and wit and conviviality, his signature whinnying laugh a lot like Pound's. He moved easily in art circles. Unlike Williams, Demuth did not have to work for a living, since his father had left sufficient money in his will for his son to concentrate on his painting, to live like a sybarite, and to travel whenever he wished. Demuth's attachment to his mother, Augusta, a woman almost as difficult as Elena, was genuine, but too much time in the family nest made Demuth identify with the Israelites in bondage in Egypt. (*My Egypt* was the title of a strong 1927 Cubist painting by him.) When Williams grew restless because of the routines of domesticity and of his practice, he drove into the city, where in an hour he could sit and converse with Stieglitz about Matisse or Juan Gris, or flirt, or drink a Gibson at a party. Trips in 1917 and 1921 to Paris had transported Demuth to the modernist hub, where he reveled in the heady, tolerant, and seductive atmosphere. Like Williams, however, Demuth rejected the expatriate life. After 1921, when he was diagnosed with diabetes, he had to curtail his stays abroad. A small studio on the second floor of his mother's house in Lancaster, Pennsylvania, became his cozy atelier; from the window he looked out on silos and a flower garden, which he rendered in beautiful watercolors. When health problems and the nervous tedium of being confined to the Lancaster house oppressed him, he fled to New York, haunted Stieglitz's gallery An American Place, where he could study the latest modernist art hung on the walls, then caroused the night away with sophisticated friends. After a visit to New York, Demuth could return, refreshed in spirit, to Lancaster and *his* "attic of desire."

Williams's and Demuth's meetings became less frequent as the painter grew frailer. One of the first diabetics to be treated with insulin, mainly at a sanatorium in Morristown, New Jersey, Demuth did not stick to the prescribed regimen, with dire consequences: the diabetes attacked his heart and weakened him. Despite gaps in communication—"FORGIVE LONG SILENCE," he wrote to Williams in 1923—their friendship flourished, as each kept close tabs on the poems and watercolors the other was producing. So it was hardly surprising when Demuth produced a painting inspired by Williams's "The Great Figure," the final poem in *Sour Grapes*; it was natural for Demuth to create a painting in 1928 that did not illustrate so much as take off from Williams's poem: "The Figure 5 in Gold." Like Schubert and Schumann's settings of Goethe and Heine poems, the Williams and Demuth pieces are self-standing and symbiotic works of art.

The genesis of Williams's poem was unusual: In 1921, feeling weary after an afternoon spent at a postgraduate clinic, he was walking toward Hartley's apartment on West Fifteenth Street, anticipating the pleasures of a drink, morsels of gossip, and the chance to see Hartley's latest paintings. Williams recounts what happened before he could ring his friend's doorbell: "As I approached his number I heard a great clatter of bells and the roar of a fire engine passing the end of the street down Ninth Avenue. I turned just in time to see a golden figure 5 on a red background flash by. The impression was so sudden and forceful that I took a piece of paper out of my pocket and wrote a short poem about it."

The poem runs as follows:

Among the rain
and lights
I saw the figure 5
in gold
on a red
fire truck
moving
tense
unheeded
to gong clangs
siren howls
and wheels rumbling
through the dark city

Demuth's 1928 poster painting of the poem, though marvelously precise, avoids any hint of literalism. Demuth solves the problem of how to suggest the motion of the truck in two ingenious ways. The truck, a vivid red, occupies the center of the canvas, its shape outlined or accentuated by the headlamps that evoke the "lights" of the poem. Second, a large gilded figure five leaps forward, like a bolt of lightning aimed straight into the viewer's face—it is "tense," but impossible to regard as "unheeded"— while, in the middle, under the wing of the most prominent five, is another five; behind it, in the background, a smaller five in gold recedes, like a setting sun. Curled in the shape of a crescent moon with globes at the end, the numbers link up to the truck's headlights. Words are stenciled on the painting: BILL appears in bold letters next to one headlamp and "carlo" [sic] floats in the shadows behind the ledge of the big five. (Demuth called Williams both Carlo and Carlos.) The initials CD and WCW at the bottom imply that the friends are joint creators.

Demuth had shown Williams the unfinished piece, which Williams called "the most distinguished American painting that I have seen in years" for its "color, composition, clarity, thought, emotional force, ingenuity—and its completeness." Yet he did admit to being bothered by "the blankness of the red." In a letter to Demuth, he wrote:

> Take the hint from the picture itself. That is, to use overlapping of planes, one contour passing partly into the next. If that were used more through the solid red center (as it is used among the figures which surround it) the whole would gain by a unity of treatment that would cast a unity of feeling over it all. You have, in fact, done something of that with the very center of the picture but not enough.

Demuth apparently agreed with Williams, since he implemented many of the proposed changes, especially the "overlapping of planes." The fire truck rests solidly on the grid of the roadbed, and a ray runs diagonally through the red. Curiously, no one seems to be driving the truck.

Three years after painting this iconic masterpiece, Demuth was dead. It was a profound loss for Williams. To honor him he wrote "The Crimson Cyclamen," a long, complex, passionate tribute. (The fact that it was published alongside extended meditations on his father, mother, and Floss in the 1936 volume *Adam & Eve & the City* is a sign of how close Williams felt to Demuth.) Although elegiac in tone, "The Crimson Cyclamen" discards all of the genre's conventions and substitutes an anatomy of the crimson cyclamen (a common houseplant of the primrose family). First, Williams isolates and studies the flower's roots, stalks, stems, leaves, and petals; then he sketches the design of each part of the flower; and finally he reconstructs the process of growth and the gradual emergence of the flower's fully realized form, until decay inevitably withers it. The poem matches the slow rhythm of the cyclamen's unfolding—Williams would have agreed with Blake's wise aphorism "Nature neither hastens nor retards." The plant rises "dark, complex from / subterranean revolutions / and rank odors," the leaves change, and "the first / pink pointed bud" thrusts out into the air.

In each stanza, Williams examines both the surface and what lies beneath, how the crisp young leaves supplant the old ones, whose edge is beginning to "crinkle" and "wrinkle." This image is connected to Williams's aging and to Demuth's physical decline. Like a gardener, Williams digs, layer by layer, toward the center, the vital source, of the flower, in search of the design, yet always cognizant of the nexus between the cyclamen's core and its circumference. The reader feels at times that he is in a medical school laboratory with Williams, dissecting a cadaver and learning the functions of tissue, joints, organs, veins, and arteries. The patterns Williams uncovers he likens to pure thought, which can be apprehended logically yet retain irregularities, edges, quirks, and the "freakish." Counting the streaks of the cyclamen does not annul his sense of wonder, but rather intensifies it:

> It is miraculous
> that flower should rise
> by flower
> alike in loveliness—
> as though mirrors
> of some perfection
> could never be
> too often shown—
> silence holds them
> in that space.

The first six stanzas of "The Crimson Cyclamen" run long: sixteen, thirteen, fifteen, eighteen, twenty, and twenty-seven lines; the lines, by contrast, are kept short. This allows for the dense syntax, an intricately meshed network of clauses and phrases and eccentrically placed dashes, to draw subtle distinctions and to build an "unnicked argument." The sounds, sometimes dissonant and sometimes consonant, drive the poem forward and give it unity. In the middle of the poem, as the subject becomes passion, ecstasy, lust, and the flower's colors, the stanzas are trimmed to quatrains and couplets, as better suited to the highly charged language of erotic excess and release. In the last section, as Williams describes the fading and paling of the cyclamen, as day darkens into night—both harbingers of Demuth's death—Williams lengthens the stanzas again and slows down the tempo.

As a loving homage to Demuth's art, "The Crimson Cyclamen" requires that Williams burrow inside Demuth's imagination and Precisionist method. In this passage, he dons the art critic's hat to explain in detail how Demuth's painting works:

The stem's pink flanges,
strongly marked,
stand to the frail edge,
dividing, thinning
through the pink and downy
mesh—as the round stem
is pink also—cranking
to penciled lines
angularly deft
through all, to link together
the unnicked argument
to the last crinkled edge
where the under and the over
meet and disappear
and the air alone begins
to go from them—
the conclusion left still
blunt, floating
if warped and quaintly flecked
whitened and streaked
resting
upon the tie of the stem

Williams admires Demuth's technique, in particular his playful abstractions, and the passion it serves. And because Demuth excelled as a colorist, Williams takes pains to evoke the painter's subtle shadings—in the first stanza, "White suffused with red / more rose than crimson" and blues and yellows that the light "enfolds and pierces," but that yield to the supremacy of crimson. In the last stanzas, the petals "paling" from violet to white or the red are seen dwindling and "fading through gradations / immeasurable to the eye." Ending on a quietly rhapsodic note, Williams celebrates the wholeness and flowering of Demuth's lovely art, which consoles and reconciles him to his friend's death:

The day passes
in a horizon of colors
of color
all meeting

less severe in loveliness
the petals fallen now well back
till flower touches flower
all round
at the petal tips
merging into one flower—

Italo Calvino was surely right in observing that Williams "describes the leaves of the cyclamen so minutely that we can visualize the flower poised above the leaves he had drawn for us, thereby giving the poem the delicacy of the plant."

2.

Pound—who else?—was instrumental in engineering perhaps the most far-reaching change in Williams's literary fortunes in the 1930s: an alliance with James Laughlin, a twenty-two-year-old neophyte who, on Pound's urging, founded New Directions, which was to become the great twentieth-century publisher of avant-garde poetry. Dudley Fitts at Choate had acquainted Laughlin with *Kora in Hell* and *Spring and All*, and as an editor of *The Harvard Advocate* Laughlin had solicited work from Williams (in 1934 *The Advocate* published his essay "The Element of Time," and in 1935 his story "A Face of Stone"). At first leery of meeting Pound's latest protégé, Williams overcame his reluctance and invited Laughlin to 9 Ridge Road for dinner. In his memoir poem "9 Ridge Road" Laughlin likens himself to a supplicant anxious about entering a sacred shrine, but if he expected a high priest in robes to greet him, Williams quickly disabused the pilgrim of that notion. Stepping out of his office, his face wreathed in a smile, he began telling Laughlin about the patient he'd just left, as if he and the young man were already comfortable old friends. "All doors were / Open. Bill was a non-cutaneous / Man. No skin separated him from others."

Though inexperienced, and smarting from Pound's judgment that he lacked the talent to be a poet himself, Laughlin moved swiftly to carry out his mentor's advice. With money from his father and aunt—the family fortune derived from the Jones and Laughlin Steel Company—and his Scots thrift and business acumen, he launched New Directions, its name a fanfare for the firm's mission: he would not hug the literary shores but would bravely sail into uncharted waters. While he respected his elders—impeccable manners were bred into him in Pittsburgh—Laughlin also trusted his own taste. One of his first moves was to promise Williams that he would bring out *White Mule,* the first novel of what would become a trilogy. Having shopped the book around for several years in vain, an elated Williams wrote to Laughlin a letter filled with whimsy and disbelief:

> DEAR GOD:
> You mention, casually, that you are willing to publish my *White Mule,* that you will pay for it and that we shall then share, if any, the profits! My God! It must be that you are so tall that separate clouds circle around that head giving thoughts of other metal [*sic*] than those the under sides of which we are in the habit of seeing.

Laughlin meant for Williams to be a major star in the New Directions firmament. Like an impresario, he plotted out a schedule of literary performances that would keep Williams in the public eye: the poem "Perpetuum Mobile" in the first *New Directions in Prose and Poetry,* an annual anthology that became an important outlet for experimental writing; *Life Along the Passaic River,* a collection of short stories; a reprint of *In the American Grain,* and, as the crown, *Collected Later Poems.* This seemed to Williams a script dreamed up in Hollywood. When *White Mule* came out, far from "sitting before a severe jury waiting to be decapitated," Williams had the pleasure of savoring almost uniformly favorable reviews. And, miracle of miracles, the novel sold well. The only hitch was that when copies disappeared from the bookstores, Laughlin, an avid skier, was in New Zealand captaining an American team. Five hundred additional copies, printed but not bound, languished in the New Directions office in Norfolk, Connecticut. Williams drove up to see if he could shake those copies free, but Laughlin's father, who was minding the store, though sympathetic to Bill's plight, could do nothing on his own initiative, and so Williams returned to Rutherford miffed and disconsolate at a lost opportunity to increase his readership and earn a modest royalty. When Laughlin returned, he bound three hundred copies, but by then the sales momentum had flagged.

Perhaps this incident led Williams to test Laughlin's loyalty. He mentioned that he was contemplating giving his work in progress, *Yes, Mrs. Williams*, a biography of his mother, to Simon and Schuster, in order to cash in on *White Mule*'s success. Feeling like a jilted lover, the tyro publisher could not brush aside the threat so easily. "You are the cornerstone of New Directions and if you left me I think I wouldn't be able to go on with it. I have built my plans around you. You are my symbol of everything that is good in writing, and if you go over to the enemy I just won't know where the hell I'm at." "You are literature, not merchandise," he scolded Williams. Realizing that he had wounded both Laughlin and his own self-interest, Williams thanked his young champion for carrying the heavy burden of increasing sales of his books: "You're much more likely to break your neck than I am!" he acknowledged. The dust-up was soon forgotten. As for *Yes, Mrs. Williams*, it didn't appear until twenty years later, from Beacon Press.

Floss and Bill had been married twenty-five years when *White Mule* was published. They had mainly overcome the conflicts that earlier caused friction. The boys were grown and well along in pursuing their chosen careers. This did not entirely explain Williams's decision to tell the story of Floss's life, beginning with her birth, as fiction, but he handled the story objectively and with panache. *White Mule* effortlessly weaves together two plotlines: Floss's development from infant to toddler actively exploring the world around her—no American novel studies child development in such depth—and her immigrant family's struggle to negotiate an American society they both dislike and appreciate. The Stecher trilogy (completed by *In the Money*, published in 1945, and *The Build-up*, published in 1952) is closely modeled on the lives and characters of Floss's parents, Pa and Ma Herman. In many ways, despite the tragic death of their beloved son, Paul, in a gun accident, and their bitter consternation that Floss's musically gifted sister, Charlotte, had run off with an older, twice-divorced bohemian painter, Ferdinand Earle, the Hermans were an American success story.

Williams deeply admired and loved his father-in-law, Pa Herman, for his honesty, work ethic, high standards of craftsmanship, kindness, and generosity—it was he who had given Bill and Floss the money to buy the house at 9 Ridge Road. Williams may even have felt closer to Pa Herman than to his own father. In its earthy portrait of Joe, the Pa Herman figure, *In the Money* pays tribute to the man's steadfast ideals. He lives by the traditional view that women rule the hearth and men are the breadwinners:

he will not push the baby carriage in the park. Yet, alone with the baby, he enjoys observing her movements and commenting on them to himself: "That's a funny thing the way a baby tries to spoil everything you do for it. They hate clothes. When they get their clothes off, they're happy. Then they kick like frogs. They kick and if you don't watch yourself they'll kick themselves out of your hands. That's stupid." When he dreams of owning a place in the country with a garden in which the children can play, he worries that they'll pull the plants out of the ground, then cracks a joke: "They want to take things that don't belong to them. That's the Unions. Revolutionists. All the same." But he smiles at Floss, calling her a "little socialist," and approves that impulse: "Take everything you can get. Let somebody else plant it and tend it. Just take it."

His wife, Gurlie, is less appealing: irascible, domineering, sarcastic, bigoted, and materialistic. She nags Joe to start his own business, so that he can bring home more money and she can outshine her neighbors; she carps at American clothes, housekeeping, and parenting, and her avarice sometimes prevents her from understanding Joe's ethic of reciprocity. Williams neither excuses Gurlie's despotic faults—she's a social climber, eager to be noticed and envied—nor caricatures her as a shrew and self-ish busybody. She jumps to Joe's defense when her sister criticizes him, and she retains the Viking spirit of adventure she acquired growing up on a farm in Norway.

In *White Mule*, Williams is a relaxed yet alert storyteller who draws on his rich experience as an obstetrician and pediatrician. Whether describing the cutting of the umbilical cord, the baby's inept attempts to suckle at her mother's breast, her gasps for breath, farts, twisty motions, and crooked smile, or the mother's "disgusted thighs and toppled belly," the prose has perfect pitch; it is remarkably physical and authoritative without trying to impress the reader with bravura linguistic tricks. Williams has not renounced his modernist credentials. The style that changed course frequently in *A Novelette,* mirroring Williams's wayward thinking, would have been forced and inappropriate in *White Mule.* In a review of H. L. Mencken's *The American Language*, Williams wrote, "We're still a colony as far as our badly tutored minds are concerned. We don't quite dare, do we? to say that we have a language that is our own." But his goal of proving that the music of American speech could express an "infinite variety" of moods and meanings was realized in *White Mule.*

In Laurence Sterne's novel, it took Tristram Shandy a few hundred pages to be born. Like a diva, Floss makes her commanding entrance in the very first paragraph. Here is Williams's opening:

> She entered, as Venus from the sea, dripping. The air enclosed her, she felt it all over her, touching, waking her. If Venus did not cry aloud after release from the pleasures of that sea-womb, feeling the new and lighter flood springing in her chest, flinging out her arms—this one did. Screwing up her tiny smeared face, she let out three convulsive yells—and lay still.
>
> Stop that crying, said Mrs. D. [the midwife], you should be glad to get outa that hole.

Williams imbues Floss's birth with a mythic touch: like Venus, she has emerged from the womb into a strange new world, dripping with the fluids of parturition: her tiny scrunched-up face, which the midwife calls ugly, is smeared with blood; the waxy vernix of prebirth that protected her has to be scrubbed clean. The air that Floss breathes is paradoxically both liberating and confining, as if she has moved from one enclosure to another: the reader palpably feels the sensations of air that the newborn feels on her body. The midwife talks to the baby as if she can understand her words of folk wisdom acquired from presiding over hundreds of births; Mrs. D.'s speech is colloquial, bossy, and earthy. The infant, a puny imp with a will of its own and a shrill voice to go with it, and with a kick that's compared to White Mule corn whiskey, irritates Gurlie because she wanted a boy, but the mother waits offstage. It is Floss's star turn.

White Mule is a novel of transformations set within a money-grubbing world. Floss is a plaything and object of curiosity. Vinie, the young black girl who serves briefly as a sort of nanny, scrutinizes Floss's hands and genitals with the thoroughness of a pediatrician and the bemused wonder of a child. "A natural mother," Vinie poses the same question Joe did: What does someone so tiny—by Vinie's measurement the size of "half an arm"—know? "What you seein?" she asks. Ever the empiricist, Williams shuns gaudy psychological explanations; instead he records the baby's vast repertoire of sounds—animal growls, whining, clucks of contentment, a continuous "yell in a high maddening voice"; her need to be held or to repel touch; her learning by imitation, as when she mimics Maggie, her fifteen-year-old babysitter, grinning and showing her teeth. Floss processes sense impressions (birdsong in the park), stimuli (she is constantly being fussed over), and the benign or angry attitudes of those around her. Avoiding clinical or maudlin language, Williams describes the stages of Floss's physical and mental growth with remarkable concreteness: we see the world through her limited but expanding mind. To this consciousness, which moves according to its own inner biological clock, Williams adds the shifting perspectives of family, doctors, total strangers, who can be charming, stiff-necked, ignorant, or impatient. In one chapter, he takes the reader into the home of a poor Irish family to glimpse the narrow choices that the mother has at her disposal because her husband is not a good provider like Joe. All children are the same—and unique. Age and subjective experience color appraisals of Floss: the grandmother touts her old-country remedies to bring down a fever, Gurlie espouses the efficacy of fresh air, five-year-old Charlotte signals her anger at the arrival of an unwanted rival by slapping the baby's face hard, and Joe formulates his opinions in private. Child rearing is not an exact science but an imperfect art, and it is Williams's exceptional achievement that he never simplifies and rarely sentimentalizes the developmental process.

Floss is the cynosure of attention—and of change. By the end of the novel, even her mother acknowledges that the ugly duckling has turned into a good-looking toddler, acquiring language, inspecting the world around her, roaming park and home confidently, throwing a tantrum now and then. The face smeared with the slime of birth, hardly the "stark dignity of / entrance," is smeared at the novel's close with blackberry juice. The tiny idol of mystery and adoration joins the family community as its most junior member.

The disagreements between Joe and Gurlie in *White Mule* consist mostly of what Grace Paley called "the little disturbances of man": family quarrels about money, moving to a larger city apartment or to the suburbs, buying a farm. Although the labor strife that is the social backdrop of the novel takes place in the late nineteenth century, the Depression is also on Williams's mind. Like Joe, he tries to keep from being co-opted by the political absolutists and ideologues of his day and from compromising his moral beliefs; the man in the middle incurs the wrath of those at the poles, bosses and labor. The capitalist owner would rather spend fistfuls of money to break the strike than raise salaries, even "if it costs the works." This obduracy sounds irrational to Joe, but old man Wynnewood grumbles at his manager's honesty as an impediment to doing business, and the typesetter who threw a screwdriver into the press as an act of sabotage is equally put off by Joe's insistence on upright conduct in the printing shop where he works. Joe is sympathetic to the unions' demands, but his punctilious nature is offended by their timing and methods: a strike would mean the company's contract with the government could not be fulfilled. There is a steely backbone to the normally reserved Joe that in a crisis turns him into a formidable opponent: he warns the disgruntled workers accosting him with their demands that they will lose their jobs if they refuse to return to the presses. Violence is averted, the government order completed on time, the shop closed, then reopened on terms that make all content and leave Joe in charge.

This ending is an unusual outcome to a rancorous strike. Capitalists or small businessmen made concessions to workers grudgingly; if they wanted to break a strike, they could call on the police or Pinkerton guards to protect scabs, break up rallies with billy clubs, and even shoot the picketers. Williams's depiction of labor strife in *White Mule* is tame compared to Dreiser's narrative of the Brooklyn trolley strike in *Sister Carrie*, but he did not want the novel to stray for long from its focus on Floss. Joe's code of ethics compels him to cry out, "A pox on both your houses," and he chastises Gurlie for being tempted by America's lax business morality, which sees no wrong in taking or offering a kickback. Williams no doubt romanticizes and identifies with Joe, who has risen to prosperity without tarnishing his conscience. Williams sees his youthful self in Joe's scrupulous morality: Had he not resigned his hospital residency rather than sign a document he knew was falsified?

Williams did not sit on the sidelines while the heated political debates and skirmishes, prompted and intensified by the Depression, swirled around him. He was not particularly gifted at dialectics, but when roused by what he believed to be stupid policy or glib rationalizations or sleazy polemics, he jumped headlong into the fray. His political positions were a crazy quilt of attitudes derived from his experiences as a doctor, his father's socialism, and correspondence with friends on the right (Pound), the left (Fred Miller, the editor of *Blast*), and the center (Kenneth Burke). In 1936, Williams received a questionnaire from the editors of *Partisan Review* asking him and a cross section of writers and intellectuals to comment on the topic "What Is Americanism? Marxism and the American Tradition." Philip Rahv and the rest were not baiting a trap for Williams and probably had no inkling what he would say, but his naive frankness led him into one. Williams often let a feeling of the moment dominate his thought, and sometimes with regrettable consequences. Responding to the questionnaire, he wrote that the American "democracy of feeling . . . will defeat Marxism in America and all other attempts at regimentation of thought and action. It will also defeat Fascism." There is nothing tentative or convoluted in Williams's statement. The Marxist intellectuals and true believers viewed the triumph of Marxism as inevitable; as far as they were concerned, the American democratic spirit meant one thing: subservience to big business and the collusion of capital and government. Did not Williams concede that the American democratic spirit permitted "the brutality of the self-seeker to go its way in the perhaps misguided notion that essential democracy will triumph finally"? Did not the lines of the homeless at soup kitchens and the swelling ranks of the unemployed idling in the streets attest to the failure of capitalism? If he walked around Brownsville in Brooklyn or drove the back roads of Alabama, he could not miss the toll of poverty and despair etched on the faces and stooped bodies of sharecroppers and the vast army of beggars, hoboes, and men selling apples. Walker Evans and Dorothea Lange memorably documented in their photographs the suffering and despair of mothers standing in front of a family hovel in Appalachia, the husbands looking forlorn and defeated in the background and the children staring in mute blankness at the camera, their childhood broken by poverty and hopelessness. Were those images not a sign of the degradation of the democratic dogma and the rottenness of the capitalist system? Surely Williams must admit that the times called for razing the decayed economic structures.

Williams, of course, had sat in the kitchens of the poor and seen hunger and misery stamped on their creased faces. His argument is not speculative, and he was never indifferent to the hardships the poor endured. Two modest poems entitled "The Poor" are instructive. The first in 1921 (*Sour Grapes*) refers to his unglamorous stint as school physician:

> By constantly tormenting them
> with reminders of the lice in
> their children's hair, the
> School Physician first
> brought their hatred down on him.
> But by this familiarity

they grew used to him, and so,
at last,
took him for their friend and advisor.

The tormentor of parents who neglected taking the simplest steps to protect their children and resented his nagging reminders of their responsibility—"hatred" is a strong noun—becomes their trusted friend and advisor. Familiarity breeds mutual respect, but not without a long probationary period. The second poem, in 1938, would have baffled the ideologues, since it begins "It's the anarchy of poverty / delights me." With the affection of a neighborhood preservationist, Williams describes the old wooden houses and cast-iron balconies of the poor, and the anomaly of "fences of / wood and metal in an unfenced / / age and enclosing next to / nothing at all." The lives of the poor reflect "every stage and / custom of necessity," yet the old man sweeping his ten feet of sidewalk has the dignity of Wordsworth's leech gatherer in his effort to keep order despite a wind that "overwhelmed the entire city."

Convinced of their rectitude and their unassailable evidence, *Partisan Review* Marxists could not see their own "regimentation of thought and action" in the mirror Williams held up. In case he hadn't drilled his point deep enough, he next relegated Marxism to obsolescence:

My opinion is that the American tradition is completely opposed to Marxism. America is progressing through difficult mechanistic readjustments which it is confident it can take care of. But Marxism is a static philosophy of a hundred years ago which has not kept up—as the democratic spirit has—through the stresses of an actual trial. Marxism to the American spirit is only another phase of force opposed to liberalism. It takes a tough theory to survive America, and America thinks it has that theory. Therefore it will smile and suffer, quite secure in its convictions that through all the rottenness, all the political corruption, all the cheap self-interest of its avowedly ruling moneyed class—that it can and will take care of itself when the crisis arrives.

Williams was no apologist for the "ruling moneyed class" or its allies at all levels of government; but because as doctor he knew from repeated contact with workers what they believed, he was not seduced by the abstractions put forth by Marxists who knew the "proletariat" mainly through reading *Das Kapital.*

Williams's remarks were published in the April 1936 issue of *Partisan Review.* The retaliation was almost instant. Because he had profaned the Temple of True Doctrine, he deserved, like Kent in *King Lear,* to be put in the stocks and exposed as a churlish fool for challenging sage authority. Since that punishment was not possible, the editors, abandoning any pretense at impartiality, called for "sanctions" against Williams, as if he were a rogue government, ridiculing him as both ignorant and benighted. The magazine also printed a letter from one Charles Forrest that belittled "the whole school of modernist writing of which Mr. Williams is such a shining light." It had "made no dent on the American consciousness," Forrest sneered. Williams was perplexed by the hostility, which only reinforced his mistrust of intellectuals and academics—and of cherished orthodoxies. During World War II and after, *Partisan Review* moderated its dogmatic Marxist stance, and, ironically, championed difficult modernist poetry, even that written by T. S. Eliot, whose social, political, and religious beliefs were reactionary.

As the decade progressed and Europe slid into war, a substantial part of the country sided with the isolationists, who claimed that the collapse of democracies in Europe was none of our business. On this issue, Williams vacillated. He had no reservations about supporting the Republican side in the Spanish Civil War. He chaired the Bergen County Medical Board to Aid Spanish Democracy campaign to raise money for desperately needed medical supplies, and was shocked when not a single colleague responded to his plea. Once again he felt an abyss separating him from his countrymen. The Spanish Civil War was another issue on which he and Pound clashed. When Pound likened Franco's bombing of Republican cities and villages like Guernica to cleaning out an infestation of mosquitoes, Williams excoriated the remark as pathological. Pound's ravings tested the limits of their friendship: it became nearly impossible for Williams to separate Pound the poet, whose verse still showed flashes of exquisite art and "a mastery of language," from the political crank who had lost touch with reality. When Pound visited America in the spring of 1939, he spent an evening at Williams's house sprawled out on the divan like the ambassador from the Pythian oracle, his posture a clue to the "usual indistinct syllables" of his rambling discourse. Afterward Williams wrote to Laughlin:

The man is sunk, in my opinion, unless he can shake the fog of Fascism out of his brain during the next few years[,] which I seriously doubt that he can do. The logicality of fascist rationalizations is soon going to kill him. You can't argue away wanton slaughter of innocent women and children by the neo-scholasticism of a controlled economy program. Shit with a Hitler who lauds the work of his airmen in Spain and so shit with Pound too if he can't stand up and face his questioners on the point.

Williams's prognosis was correct: Pound slipped rapidly into a form of political psychosis from which he did not recover. It could only have pained Laughlin to hear how much his old tutor and literary hero had deteriorated.

In Rutherford, Williams continued to see patients during office hours and to deliver babies day and night. In the hours he waited for a woman to go into labor, he either dozed or jotted down lines for a poem. His "medical badge" had, as he gratefully and humbly admitted in the *Autobiography*, gained him "entrance to the secret gardens of the self," where he could follow "the poor, defeated body into those gulfs and grottos," "foul as they may be with the stinking ischio-rectal abscesses of our comings and goings," and witness "the tormented battles between daughter and diabolic mother, shattered by a gone brain." He did not waste those precious, fleeting revelations. Such encounters make up most of the striking stories of *Life Along the Passaic River*, published by New Directions in 1938.

Williams's one publication in a medical journal was about the ear, the workings of which were crucial for doctor and poet. Acutely sensitive to speech rhythms, broken syntax, and changes of tone, to "black, Italian, and Polack" slang, in *Life Along the Passaic River*, he carefully transcribed the voices of the poor (and others) with the accuracy of a demographic linguist, who could differentiate accents and their origins block by block and even house by house. He was a precursor of Studs Terkel, without benefit of a tape recorder, who could put people from all walks of life at ease and get them talking. The people whose lives he chronicled speak without literary airs or self-censorship: they use epithets such as "wops" and "Polacks," as casually as the educated Williams at moments refers to "kikes" and "niggers." They are ribald and edgy, lazy and platitudinous, and so is their conversation. The plight of the poor obsessed Williams, and he graphically depicts the many casualties of the Depression "up against it." Families are homeless or crowded into two rooms, three kids to a bed, and "slothful" parents are remiss in taking a sick infant to the hospital or even signing a paper granting the school permission to vaccinate their daughter.

But Williams's mural also includes a baker's assistant who prefers wandering the open road to being cooped up in a hot kitchen, even if it means skipping a meal or begging for food at strangers' back doors; young boys building "boats out of barrel hoops and a piece of old duck"; and someone starting a business that ferries people to Coney Island and back. Williams is not a social worker who comes into a poor neighborhood of "dumb Polacks," takes a few notes, and goes home to write a report, certain he knows how the other half lives or should live. He shows us gritty reality as it is. His opposite is a political do-gooder like John Reed, who drops in from Boston and "shoots off his mouth . . . telling us what to do," as a local resident notes with acerbity, and who regards the workers as useful pawns in a political struggle largely taking place elsewhere:

> Who paid for having their kids and women beat up by the police? Did that guy take a room down on Monroe St. and offer his services for the next ten years at fifty cents a throw to help straighten out the messes he helped get us into? He did not. The Polacks paid for it all. Sure. And raised up sons to become cops too. I don't blame them. Somebody's got to take the jobs. Why get excited? But they ain't moved away none; that's what I'm saying. They're still here. Still as dumb as ever. But it's more than that guy ever give up or could think to do to help them.

Most grandees among American Marxists had no contact with workers, except in the most superficial way. A few might have conceded that the fervor for Marx and revolution might burn in the hearts of an unemployed toolmaker like Fred Miller, who scraped together twenty-five dollars to publish an issue of *Blast*—how, Williams could not say. In "The Dawn of a Another Day," Williams employs an American vernacular flavored by whiskey and sex to sketch a debate between a Marxist and a skeptic. In the story, set on a docked boat, a drunken older man and his younger helper have at each other about the likelihood of the revolution succeeding in America. Fred, the owner of the boat, is proud that he has read *Das Kapital* three times, and in the original German; Eddie, an

Irishman, plans to "pull out of this hole on my own." Fred scorns that idea as the discredited panacea of Emersonian scripture: "Self reliant rugged Americanism." Marxism is the New Testament. The crux of their argument is distilled in one exchange:

> I read the lousy book till I damned near knew it by heart. And the old bugger is right. To hell with the Capitalists that enslave the resources of the nation. You know yourself 5% of the people of the United States own 95% of the money. And 95% of the people own only 5% of the money. Now that's not right. We got to have a revolution and take it away from them.
>
> You don't need any fancy theory of a revolution by the proletariat to do that. Be yourself, Fred. We're not back in the last century. Russia was. More power to her then. I'm for Russia. We'd be rotten sports if we didn't help their game. Let 'em work it out. But they're nothing but a lot of monkeys, a lot of thick heads. That sort of thing can never happen in America. We're not that thick. You don't need anything but brains. Looka hear. You want to break up the game of the Capitalists? You want to know how to do it?

Fred's facts do not sway Eddie, one of the good-humored "self-seekers" Williams later wrote about in his response to the *Partisan Review* symposium. Eddie does not get riled up about the inequities in American democracy, believing that problems will eventually work themselves out, more or less to his satisfaction. The pleasure of the story is not in the rigor or sophistication of the argument, but in Williams's handling of the varied cadences of the American idiom—what a reviewer in *The Nation* called his "X-Ray Realism."

Life Along the Passaic River was published in February 1938 in a print run of 1,000 copies. Gone were the days of measly printings of 350 or 500 copies. Laughlin was gradually building Williams's reputation. The reviews, again, were mostly favorable. If the royalties were modest, Williams could at least hope realistically that they would increase. But not from *The Complete Collected Poems, 1906–1938*, which came out in November 1938 in an edition of 1,500 copies. Ronald Latimer, the publisher of Alcestis Press, was eager to take charge of this retrospective, even though he had lost money on *An Early Martyr and Other Poems* and *Adam & Eve & the City*. When Laughlin got wind that Williams might hand over *The Complete Collected* to Latimer, he was unaware that Bill also dreamed of an Oxford University Press imprint, even though it represented the very academic mentality and taste Williams sought to undermine; appearing as an Oxford author would lend the poems cachet, Williams reasoned to himself. Laughlin confronted him in the same distressed tone he had taken when he seemed ready to defect to Simon and Schuster. Williams was not quite the solid rock Laughlin had counted on as the cornerstone of New Directions; he was too flighty, susceptible to the fantasy of riding some Pegasus of a publisher to fame and fortune. The upshot was that Williams backed away again and gave Laughlin the rights to publish *The Complete Collected Poems*. Saving face, he joked, "Weeel James, it's up to you to carry Papa across the river." Laughlin was the hero Aeneas and William his burden Anchises.

In the year or two he spent assembling the poems, Williams was prone to bouts of melancholia and even self-loathing: although many of them wore well, too much of the "old stuff" seemed wan, derivative, choppy, and formally deficient. He had fallen short of his own high aspirations. The reviewers pounced on the book and mostly gave it a drubbing or patronized him. "One cannot feel that he is an important poet, and one knows that he is not an insignificant one." From his lofty seat, Hart Crane's biographer Philip Horton wrote that Williams's style, "stripped" and lacking in genuine feeling and wit, was "aggressively individualistic," skittish, and given to "spiritual hygiene." (This last odd phrase turns Williams into a follower of the mystic Gurdjieff rather than a physician.) Having fallen under the spell of Crane's style, which often sought the rhapsodic, the tessitura of the sublime, Horton could not but judge Williams's style as lukewarm and prosaic. The unkindest cut of all, and it drew blood, was Horton reviving Stevens's old charge that Williams's verse carried a dangerous antipoetic virus and was sentimental to boot. R. P. Blackmur, an admirer of T. S. Eliot, skewered the poems as "a remarkable, but sterile sport"; Williams was incapable of diving below the surface and retrieving magnificent trophies. Blackmur might as well have pinned Williams's phrase "shallow morbidity" on the *Collected Poems*. As a sign of Blackmur's contempt, the work of three decades was herded onto an omnibus review together with four other books of poetry. Blinders on, Blackmur failed to notice the skill with which Williams had transformed the indigenous spoken language into poetic utterance. (Only Horace Gregory appreciated Williams's achievement.) That Williams had heard the tiresome chorus of old tunes from tin-eared reviewers before did not lessen his exasperation. He had no alternative but to start over again. That catechism he could recite by rote.

For Williams, the 1930s ended not in tragedy but in farce. Although he had not seen much of Ford Madox Ford since their cordial meetings in Paris in 1924, they had sporadically kept up an exchange of letters, and Williams greatly admired Ford's trilogy *Parade's End*. In 1937 the bulky, wheezing Ford, who resembled a Dickens character, took a position at Olivet College in Michigan teaching literature. Before sailing back to France, where he was to die only a few months later, Ford spent some amiable days with Williams in New York. In a gust of benevolence, Ford hatched a bizarre plan to form a group called Les Amis de William Carlos Williams. His gesture put Williams in a quandary: he was embarrassed that people would think he was in such desperate straits, yet he did not want to disappoint his friend. So he didn't protest. There were no rules for membership. The Friends would meet each month at a restaurant or a member's house for food, drink, gossip, and poetry readings by the honoree or others. The roster of charter members was impressive: besides Ford, Pound, Marianne Moore, Alfred Stieglitz, Charles Sheeler, and James Laughlin also signed up. Charles Olson sometimes drove to New York for a meeting to show his admiration for Williams, and Zukofsky sometimes attended. After a few years, though, Les Amis disbanded and so did the 1930s.

THIRTEEN

Poetry, the Mistress, and Medicine, the Wife

William Carlos Williams's patients seldom addressed him formally as Dr. Williams; to most he was simply "Doc." Wearing the doctor's white gown, he entered into their feelings and was by all accounts frank, natural, alert, nuanced, testy, resourceful, amused and amusing, modest, and honest. "Where ill kids, or grownups suddenly off kilter with sickness, become teachers," the conflicts that churned in him when the subject was love, sex, or poetry rarely appeared.

Williams's stories and poems about medicine and doctoring offer a remarkable window into his daily comings and goings. The plots are generally based on his cases; their fictional doctors are as a rule Williams himself—often speaking in the first person—and reveal much about the man. Indeed, so difficult is it to distinguish between Williams and the various fictional characters referred to as "doctor" that this chapter will follow the author's own lead and use the terms interchangeably.

In scrutinizing his patients, Williams reflected, the doctor reveals to both patient and reader "the inner secrets of another's private motives," and in these cumulative acts goes to "the base of the matter" to lay them "bare before us in terms which, try as we may, we cannot in the end escape." For Williams, day after day, each encounter with a patient could lead to uncertainty, ennui, friction, and inescapable signs of his own limits; but even the humdrum brought unexpected windfalls of pleasure and insight. The physician plays many roles: spy, skeptic, social worker, novelist, anatomist. With characteristic humility, Williams describes him "observing, weighing, comparing values of which neither he nor his patients may know the significance." To these objective criteria the doctor poet adds a wise passiveness: waiting for the clue when an "inarticulate patient struggles to lay himself bare for you, or with nothing more than a boil on his back is caught off balance, . . . [and] reveals some secret twist of a whole community's pathetic way of thought." Williams speaks reverently of those precious fugitive moments, gifts of the imagination, "when that underground current can be tapped and the secret spring of all our lives will send up its pure water." These *trouvailles*, the fruit of "a lifetime of careful listening," were indispensable for his art, too.

For example, when invited as a medical student to accompany the older doctor on his house calls, the writer Robert Coles reported being deeply affected by the older man's heightened alertness to everything around him in the neighborhood he was summoned to—"where people eat, get home supplies, get some aspirin or bandages and adhesive tape, or maybe a holiday card, or a drink that sizzles"—even before he had knocked on the patient's door and begun listening to a recital of symptoms or delivering a baby. This curiosity about the local is the cornerstone of Williams's poetics and prose.

Williams was acutely aware of the complicated relationship between doctor and patient, as he revealed in this remark to Coles: "They have their say to me, and as they talk they eye my stethoscope, dangling, my [neurological] hammer ready to do a thump or two, get a jerk or two from an arm, a leg—the body answering a pry with its own rejoinder." In "The Practice," one of three chapters of his *Autobiography* in which Williams meditates on his long career as a doctor, he examines that relationship, and its effect on his writing, in a tone no-nonsense and tender:

> They come to me. I care for them and either they become my friends or they don't. That is their business. My business, aside from the mere physical diagnosis, is to make a different sort of diagnosis concerning them as individuals, quite apart from anything for which they seek my advice. That fascinates me. From the very beginning that fascinated me even more than I myself knew. For no matter where I might find myself, every sort of individual that it is possible to imagine in some phase of his development, from the highest to the lowest, at some time exhibited himself to me. I am sure I have seen them all. And all have contributed to my pie. Let the successful carry off their blue ribbons; I have known the

unsuccessful, far better persons than their more lucky brothers. And all have contributed to my pie.

Take his portrait of Ingrid, the garrulous protagonist of the story "Mind and Body." When she arrives at his office to consult the doctor—which is to say, Williams—about her colitis, she brings with her angry scorn for the entire profession, because doctors have offered maddeningly discrepant diagnoses of her condition. At the beginning of her nonstop monologue, as much a recital of her life story as of her medical history, she declares, "I am the only one in my family who has had the courage to live for himself." Appealingly uninhibited, highly intelligent, and opinionated, she tells the doctor's wife how to wear her hair more fashionably, claims that she had a clairvoyant's power to predict that her sick brother would die the day after she visited him, and ridicules the value of book learning. Yet the longer she talks, the more apparent is an underlying disappointment with her life. Restless, she can't stick to good jobs, and her marriage, though happy, requires her to mother her husband, becoming just the kind of martyr she has excoriated as "perverted." When Williams suggests she needs "some woman to love," Ingrid agrees. Mind and body fight each other to a tense standstill.

Throughout the story, the doctor is courteous, attentive, professional but not authoritarian, and even escorts Ingrid to her bus stop. When he examines her—she is self-conscious about her body—he finds nothing wrong with her; he offers possible causes for her condition based on scientific facts and the latest theory, capillaroscopy, most of which she rejects. Williams does not rush her on- and offstage; that she undresses herself so frankly to him is a tribute to the trust he inspires. He does not demand that she cede control of herself to him: as a patient, she is an autonomous person, and this gives her independent life on the page.

In Williams's stories, the patients rule the stage like kings and queens, their natures inexhaustibly varied, expressed in a truculent defiance of authority or meek submission to it, in a haggard look, in an attack of hypochondria, in a husband's stony demeanor as death hovers over his wife's bed, and in small courtesies—for instance, an elderly woman leaving a cup of coffee on the kitchen table for the doctor in gratitude for his good-humored forbearance in the sickroom. Each case is a unique drama played out in real time by a changing cast of characters, sometimes likable and sometimes despicable, and in rapidly shifting scenes.

His most famous story, "The Use of Force," is such a drama, whose cast includes both patient and doctor. With a diphtheria outbreak raging in the town's elementary school, Williams is called to a house to check if the family's nine-year-old daughter has contracted the disease. As if sitting at a chessboard or gazing through binoculars at an enemy army's position, Williams appraises his opponent, Mathilda, admiringly. The girl is pretty, feverish, agitated, distrustful, and mute. His first two ingratiating probes of her defense—in this game, he holds the white pieces—are repulsed. On his third move, as he edges closer to her, the girl employs preemptive force, knocking his glasses off. Embarrassed, the parents alternately reproach their daughter and plead with her to obey the doctor "for her own good," but in "the ensuing struggle they grew more and more abject, crushed, exhausted while she surely rose to magnificent heights of insane fury of effort bred of her terror of me."

Williams adopts a mock-heroic tone, as if he's Achilles matched against the Trojan warrior Hector, not a little girl. The battle escalates in intensity, for the stakes are high: he must pry her mouth open to see if her throat has the telltale redness of diphtheria; if he fails, she could die. Her hysterical shrieks punctuate the room. She wins the first round when she bites the wooden tongue depressor and splinters it, bloodying her tongue. In his fury at her violent resistance, Williams wants to tear the child apart. He recognizes the irrational pleasure of retaliation, which is dictated by his need to protect her and others from contagion. Williams narrates the end of the battle like a war correspondent:

> In a final unreasoning assault I overpowered the child's neck and jaws. I forced the heavy silver spoon back of her teeth and down her throat till she gagged. And there it was—both tonsils covered with membrane. She had fought valiantly to keep me from knowing her secret. She had been hiding that sore throat for three days at least and lying to her parents in order to escape just such an outcome as this.
>
> Now truly she *was* furious. She had been on the defensive before but now she attacked. Tried to get off her father's lap and fly at me while tears blinded her eyes.

Williams does not gloat at his conquest of his adversary, nor does he stop to ask why she kept her sore throat secret. Whatever the reason, it was sheer "idiocy" (his term); she was old enough to grasp the mortal danger, since two children in her school had died from diphtheria. His use of superior force was justified, but he understands the cost to the child's pride. Williams had fallen in love with the "savage brat," he says. He makes clear his usual fondness for rebels—as well as the sexual subtext of masculine power and female vulnerability. Similarly, in "The Girl with a Pimply Face," Williams falls for a fifteen-year-old girl with a severe case of acne. Where other doctors see her as a liar and a slut, Williams admires her spunk and swagger—and prescribes a cream that reduces the acne.

In his dedication, Williams resembled that other famous doctor-author Anton Chekhov, who sacrificed his writing time to care for the local peasants during a cholera epidemic and made house calls in all kinds of weather, not only forgoing a fee but often also dipping into his own purse to pay for medical supplies. (Note, however, that Chekhov earned handsome sums for his literary efforts, whereas Williams could count on a mere pittance.) Williams also shared Chekhov's tough realism: "The peasants [Chekhov] writes about," Iain Bamforth notes, "are drunk, flatly unimprovable, aggressively themselves, and [without] extenuating character traits or dubious *sancta simplicitas.*"

Early on, Williams's practice exposed him to cases of brutality against women that shocked him and stirred in him a tender solicitude. Prostitutes, abused wives, and girlfriends would come to the emergency room badly beaten by pimps or johns or violent husbands: the sight of a woman's breasts livid with welts taught Williams a lesson about cruelty that he never forgot. Hemmed in by poverty, religious beliefs, ironclad gender roles, sanctioned and enforced by a troop of five to ten children to feed, clothe, and educate, and ethnic customs that hardened over the centuries, working-class women in particular had little room or authority to make decisions for themselves, even though they held their families together. During the formative years of his medical training Williams perfected the art of communication with every kind of woman—anxious, maudlin, careless, drunken, doting, sullen, sly, hostile, loving, ignorant, and self-destructive—and developed a special rapport with the immigrant mothers on Guinea Hill, who bore many children and managed at best a halting English. During his examination Williams did not rush them, tactfully interjecting comments and questions, only rarely bullying them. If they spurned his advice and sought out the opinion of another doctor, even one who would recommend needless surgery—the removal of an appendix, for example—he would shrug off their mistrust or rejection.

If a woman wanting an abortion or a rape victim sat in the chair opposite Williams, he listened to her words carefully and studied her body language and gestures, taking in the rhythms, hesitant or torrential, of her thoughts and emotions. Consider the poem "A Cold Front":

> This woman with a dead face
> has seven foster children
> and a new baby of her own in
> spite of that. She wants pills
>
> for an abortion, and says,
> Un hum, in reply to me while
> her blanketed infant makes
> unrelated grunts of salutation.
>
> She looks at me with her mouth
> open and blinks her expressionless
> carved eyes, like a cat
> on a limb too tired to go higher
>
> from its tormentors. And still
> the baby chortles in its spit
> and there is a dull flush
> almost of beauty to the woman's face
>
> as she says, looking at me
> quietly, I won't have no more.
> In a case like this I know
> quick action is the main thing.

Within the confines of the well-groomed quatrains the woman, burdened with eight children, reaches the momentous decision to abort her pregnancy. She is almost inarticulate, as if having to utter her wish requires a superhuman effort. She seems at first unappealing: a "dead face," "open mouth," and "expressionless / carved eyes." But this impression is modified by the "dull flush / almost of beauty" that colors the five irreversible short words she finally spits out, "I won't have no more." The simile that occupies the poem's exact center conveys her feeling of being cornered, at the end of her tether; her choice is as chilling as her inner weather. Even the baby's playful noises, its "grunts of salutation" and the way it "chortles in its spit," cannot alter her resolution to terminate her pregnancy. Williams speaks few words. It's not clear whether he prescribed abortifacient pills, performed the procedure himself—to do so was illegal in New Jersey and could have jeopardized his license to practice medicine—or referred her to a physician who took on clandestine abortions.

If "A Cold Front" unfurls like a silent movie with minimal captions, "The Raper from Passenack" moves in fits and starts, like a fugue of three voices. Williams, a sort of journalist-doctor and case historian, disorients the reader with the opening statement that "The Raper from Passenack was very kind." Crassly, the rapist boasts, "It's all right, Kid, / I took care of you." The ambiguity of American vernacular echoes in his words: deluded, he talks like a concerned friend, while preening that she is *his* sexual conquest and should feel grateful. Williams interjects "what a mess she was in," as if to correct the record and give the victim a chance to recover from her faint. The rapist extends this motif in stanza two: "You'll never forget me now, / And drove her home." Most rapists don't pretend they're gallant swains and Good Samaritans, but this man can't admit that he has criminally violated the victim by breaking into her body.

The fugue passes to the victim, who tells the story in a cascade of raging and puzzled emotions. He overpowered her, despite her biting him, she says, alternating between pride at having fought back and chagrin at having fainted. The woman struggles to regain control of her body and the precious sense of wholeness she has lost. Under the stress of the rape and its aftermath, her thoughts are never linear. She fears infection yet vows not to seek treatment for a venereal disease if she has contracted one from the rapist ("You'll find me dead in bed / first," she exclaims); she wishes she could shoot him, curses him with "every vile name I could / think of," but acknowledges "I was so glad to be taken home." The shame, "the foulness" of the act cannot be cured, just gradually diminish; "hatred, hatred of all men / —and disgust" linger like an ineradicable stench.

Williams's role in the poem is remarkable for its sensitivity. The victim—a nurse he was fond of, as was later disclosed in a comment to John

Thirlwall—has trusted him with her secret. He realizes that as confidant of her revelation, he must restrict his comments to a bare sentence or two, agreeing with her initial statement that "[o]nly a man who is sick . . . / would do a thing like that," or "That's the way she spoke." Nothing is gussied up or prudishly censored, and there are no allusions to famous mythic and literary victims of rape, like Philomela, Lucrece, and Lavinia. What we get is the unvarnished voice of the victim herself, her agitation embodied in the slashing short sentences and questions of the first half of the poem; her effort to restore her dignity and self-possession, without sacrificing her reason, opens up in complexity as the poem unfolds.

Men dominated the medical profession during Williams's long career. Doctors were gods, or at least patriarchal figures whose word carried the authority of scripture. Such was not Williams's way. For him, women were not the weaker or inferior sex, even though few among them, even the college-educated, found the opportunity to exercise their innate powers. Sexist remarks turn up now and then in his letters and poems, but in the examination room, on a house call, in fiction or meditative prose, and in most poems about his patients, he took the plight of women seriously. He was not the kind of obstetrician who is proficient at delivering a baby but indifferent to the woman lying on the gurney. In his poem "The Birth," an account of a particularly difficult delivery, Williams is so stirred by the mother's courage that he declares, "I am a feminist." Recording the baby's weight at an astonishing thirteen and a half pounds, the doctor exclaims, "Madonna!" His tribute to the mother is heartfelt: "Not a man among us / can have equaled / that."

The doctor's unremitting contact and contest with illness elicit in Williams a gamut of emotions. When he saves the life of a premature infant or rushes a man to the hospital in time to prevent a ruptured appendix from developing into peritonitis, he is quietly exhilarated. But when, after struggling to keep a girl alive, he is bested by death, he grows somber and reflective. "Death," he observes in his story "The Accident," "is difficult for the senses to alight on . . . The sense has no footspace." Yet his prose paints the dying girl with the physical immediacy of a Goya etching: "She lies gasping her last: eyes rolled up till only the whites show, lids half open, mouth agape, skin a cold blush white, pasty, hard to the touch—as the body temperature drops the tissues congeal."

In the poem "Dead Baby," there is no denying "the force of the facts"— "the baby is dead." The elegiac stanzas toll the heavy sorrow of the inconsolable mother with "purple bags" under her eyes. Or consider this telephone colloquy between Williams and a desperate mother in "To Close":

Will you please rush down and see
ma baby. You know, the one I talked
to you about last night

What was that?

Is this the baby specialist?

Yes, but perhaps you mean my son,
can't you wait until?

I, I, I, don't think it's brEAthin'

In this movingly terse eight-line poem, we listen along with Williams to the woman's anguished voice, the verb "rush" expressing her panic and the word "specialist" her wish to tap a pediatrician's expertise. Because he believes she is his son's patient, he politely asks if she can wait. That's normally a reasonable request. But the horror is dramatically compressed in her stammering reply and in the spelling of that word essential to life that scrambles lowercase and capital letters: brEAthin'.

Both at home and in the hospitals Williams likened to cities "populated by every human specimen imaginable," patients and doctors provided Williams the writer with rich subject matter. For three decades he had observed, close up, doctors of all stripes, and they made cameo, or longer, appearances in his pages. They included overworked general practitioners like him, whose rapport with patients was warm, folksy, and fatherly; specialists called in to treat a rare blood disease or a neurological anomaly; selfless "humane priests of healing," who gave little thought to Mammon. For these physicians, "the opportunity for the exercise of precise talents," the pursuit of knowledge, and the thrill of discovery sufficed, as they did for the eminent physicians in Vienna.

On the other hand, Williams thoroughly grasped the unsavory side of medicine: from curmudgeonly pathologists to "cads and ignoramuses" (to borrow Chekhov's terms) and mountebanks. Above all, he despised the predatory physicians who would "clean out" patients for twenty-five dollars—a fee that sent the poor into debt—and then discard them like trash. He scorned the mediocre doctors who knew how to market themselves and so became popular with patients, and the "commercial racket carried on by the big pharmaceutical houses," which put pressure on doctors to hand out the latest "popular cure-all," lest their practice suffer a steep decline in revenue. Although he lacked the time or inclination to work up a book-length psychological study of doctors, Williams was gifted with a kind of second sight about their temperaments and skills, as the story "Old Doc Rivers" showcases.

Old Doc Rivers himself is a larger-than-life figure, a doctor of versatile skills and erratic personality. The story traces the arc of Rivers's life over three stages: first, after his brief apprenticeship, he quickly establishes his gold-plated reputation as a brilliant diagnostician of uncanny accuracy, a miracle healer—the preferred medical man, drunk or sober, to call in a crisis. Then, in a middle period, he becomes serially addicted to alcohol, cocaine, gambling, sex, and even high-toned conversation—all temporary releases from what Williams calls the "fevers of overwork"—but remains able to function without compromising his skills. Finally, in the twilight of his career, thanks to those ingrained bad habits, he deteriorates, becoming reckless and "crazy," impairing his judgment though not the dexterity of his hands or his intuition, which remain exceptional to his last suturing in the operating room. So even as he becomes the town scandal for rumored and real vices, he commands loyalty from a core of worshipful patients.

There are similarities between Doc Rivers and Williams: their matter-of-fact, sympathetic treatment of poor patients, their indifference to "the successful scamper for cash," and a streak of sentimentality in their brusque manner. However, the story is not veiled autobiography. In fact, the distinction between personal experience and fiction is clearer here than in most of Williams's stories and poems. Without didacticism, he spells out the casualties of a profession whose prestige does not immunize doctors from the debilitating consequences of stress and disease. It is a cautionary tale of the pitfalls that could do him in, too.

In building up the layers of his portrait, Williams creates a narrator who further distances the story from the author's own life. Far from omniscient, this unnamed narrator is a colleague of Rivers's, and a doctor himself. Like a medical anthropologist, he collects evidence from many sources, sifting hearsay and legend from facts as he contrasts the testimonials of patients who swore by Doc Rivers's curative abilities (he mostly "did the right thing, without delay and of his own initiative") with those who swore at him for being a dope fiend carelessly putting another "decent citizen to death." Graphic and comic particulars save Williams from murky abstractions and psychological stereotyping.

The narrator's research methodology throughout the story is rock-solid. He works from the outside in. For example, he conducts research at St. Michael's Hospital, poring over the registry of cases from the years 1905 and 1908 to discover the kinds of surgery Doc Rivers was in charge of. The catalogue of diseases is impressively long and varied, a "summary of so much misery," from hysterectomies to the repair of a deviated septum. In comparing the two years, the narrator gauges Rivers's effectiveness by measuring it against the successes and failures of other doctors: Rivers's percentage of cures is the highest. (Most of the time, however, Williams was wary of the public's and the profession's obsessions with cures—he likened it to baseball fans' adoration of home runs—because while we may recover from a somatic attack, the war between "battalions of cells laying at this or that lethal maneuver" may end in a systemic "collapse" or in the emergence of "new patterns of knowledge.")

Thus, statistics count, but the narrator is not content to let them carry the burden of proof. As he turns the pages of the heavy registry ledger, his eye roams and his attention lingers on the inks used and the variations in handwriting. He catalogues the occupations of the patients anesthetized on the table: "plumber, nurseryman, farmer, saloonkeeper (with hob-nail liver), painter, printer, housewife, tea merchant." But the registry paragraph that seems at first a digression or a distraction contains a trove of perhaps the most valuable information: the messy domestic lives of physicians. The fates of the doctors who could not heal themselves bear importantly on Doc Rivers's feckless, troubled character—and his practice:

> In the doctor's column, there was Rivers, dead surely of the effects of his addiction, but here another who had shot himself in despair at the outcome, it is said, of an affair with the wife of another physician on the same page, his friend. While this one had divorced his wife and married once again—a younger woman. Another at sixty had quietly laid himself down upon his office couch and said good-bye and died. This one had left town hurriedly, taking himself to the coast, possibly to escape jail—leaving a wife and child

behind him. Some had grown old in the profession and been forgotten though they were still alive. One of these, ninety and more,
totally deaf, still morosely wandered the streets and scarcely anyone
remembered that he had been a doctor. Queer, all that since 1908.

Diligently expanding his investigation and widening the point of
view—like Chekhov on Sakhalin Island meticulously amassing data
about the wasting diseases, malnutrition, and death rates of the prison's
convicts—the narrator interviews doctors who had assisted Doc Rivers
at operations and admired his cool resourcefulness under pressure,
and those so incensed by the man's coked-up behavior that they denounced
him for serious breaches of medical ethics and called for the revocation of
his license. A young woman remembers with gratitude Rivers's kindnesses. A young boy, part mascot, part quasi-indentured servant, and
part companion to the bachelor doctor, describes several examples of
Rivers's whimsical behavior: yanking him out of bed at 2:00 a.m. in sultry
weather—the boy sits in a buggy swatting mosquitoes while the older
man first drinks himself to stupefaction in a saloon, then awakens the
butcher to sell him lamb chops!—or passing the teenager off as a young
doctor to the poor patients occupying every inch of his waiting room during Sunday office hours. Even Floss weighs in with a comment on Rivers's
wandering eye, wistful stoop, and eager smile. The narrator doggedly
compiles contradictory evidence, much of it anecdotal. His subject is an
excellent violinist, a misogynist, a hunter who killed a man in the woods
and caught rattlesnakes for fun (and for their venom). He was twice,
briefly, a resident of the state insane asylum, and a surgeon who before an
operation would inject himself with heroin or morphine to steady himself.
  The narrator refrains from condemning Rivers for his many deranged
acts, not to protect a flawed professional but to salute him as an artist at
his trade, blessed with a laser-like imagination. In a glance, Rivers notices
that a boy's illness is caused by his not having been circumcised, or he
quickly decides that the only way to overcome a huge drunkard's resistance to going under the knife is to make him inhale an entire bottle of
chloroform. Williams is aware how class distinctions and cultural differ-
ences affect our judgment of Doc Rivers's case, so it is only after the narrator finishes presenting the compelling testimonies he has gathered that
he permits himself a tentative conclusion: "It would take a continental
understanding—reinforced as it is by centuries of culture—to compre-

hend and to accept the complexities and contradictions of a nature such as Rivers's. Not in the provincial bottom of the New Jersey of the time had the doctor found such another release." In this coda, he quietly makes his case by citing the difficulty Rivers faced to find release in "the provincial bottom" he inhabited, a problem about which Williams knew a great deal.

In virtually all his writing except "Old Doc Rivers," Williams puts his own character on display for all to see and judge. He was keenly aware that no matter a doctor's treatment, "an explosion can be detonated out of the blue" and the patient will die. If the practice of medicine guaranteed anything, it was that doctors were fallible. In the poem "The Birth," for example, the doctor confesses that he had been lulled by routine into sleepy inattention. The forty-year-old Italian woman's contractions having stalled, it takes her husband's question "Wha's a ma', Doc? / It do'n wanna come," to rouse Williams from his lethargy and induce labor. Wrapping a sheet around the woman's "pendulous belly," he changes the pressure so that the contractions resume and the fetus is "faced downward / toward the exit." This maneuver does the trick. Williams deftly and slowly brings the head and shoulders out of a "tight fit." As this small drama unfolds, Williams reproves himself for being "stupid / not to have thought" of tying the sheet tight earlier.

Worse was the case of wee Jean Beicke, "whose arms and legs seemed loose on her like the arms and legs of some cheap doll." Williams was as crazy about her as the nurses, and labored in vain to save her: "We did everything we knew how to do except the right thing," he laments. An autopsy reveals the medical staff's mistake: the doctors missed "the acute purulent mastoiditis of the left side, going on to involvement of the left lateral sinus and finally the meninges." Williams blames himself for not draining the pus behind Jean's ear: he must resign himself to the unalterable fact of having failed her.

Confronted daily by such responsibility, such failures, and such stakes, it is natural for a doctor to rely on irony and humor, his best defenses against exhaustion from "the fast-paced struggle, again and again, with all sorts of illnesses." Thus, in the midst of an influenza epidemic, Williams jots down this brief dialogue, which might be a bit of byplay in a Laurel and Hardy movie: "Is the doctor in? (It used to ring.) What is it? (Out of the bedroom window.) My child has swallowed a mouse,—Tell him to swallow a cat then. Bam!" If with offhand sarcasm Williams orders the nurses, who are fiercely protective of the emaciated infants in their care, to "[g]ive it [a skeletal infant] an enema, maybe it will grow up into a cheap prostitute or something," he is not being cynical or flip. Detachment is as necessary as empathy for a doctor—and perhaps for a writer, too. Called in the middle of the night to a home where a three-hundred-pound woman was in excruciating labor, Williams is greeted at the door by her burly husband, a policeman brandishing a .45 revolver and warning Williams that if either the woman or the baby dies, he'll get a bullet between his ears. Unruffled, Williams enters the bedroom, where a young attending physician cowers, and examines the woman. Finding her cervix fully dilated, he administers a dose of pitocin, a new drug to induce labor he had prudently stowed in his bag. The delivery proceeds smoothly, but after the baby emerges, he realizes there's a second. The scene verges on comic mayhem, but Williams never loses his self-possession.

Williams felt no dissonance between being a doctor and a writer. His patients, awed by the "superhuman" tasks a doctor faces, asked him how he found the time to write a poem. He explained that "one occupation complements the other, that they are two parts of a whole, that it is not two jobs at all, that one rests the man when the other fatigues him." Here again he resembled Chekhov, who famously said, "I feel more alert and satisfied with myself when I think I have two occupations instead of one. Medicine is my wife, and literature my mistress." (It must be admitted, however, that Chekhov did grumble at the spells of boring routine all doctors endure: "A girl with worms in her ear, diarrhea, vomiting, syphilis—Phui!!! Sweet sounds of poesy, where are you?" Williams occasionally griped even more than Chekhov when forced to spend long hours away from his poetry.)

The conventional wisdom about Williams holds that he was preeminently a poet of the surface for whom the domain of the psychological was alien. Yet his poems and stories about his patients and his reflections about medicine reveal how deeply he thought and felt about the nexus between his two vocations: "There's nothing like a difficult patient to show us to ourselves," he observed. "I would learn so much on my rounds, or making home visits. At times I felt like a thief because I heard words, lines, saw people and places—and used it all in writing. I guess I've told people that, and no one's so surprised! There was something deeper going on, though—the *force* of all those encounters. I was put off guard again and again, and the result was—well, a descent into myself." Those encounters produced a trove of wonderful poems and stories.

FOURTEEN

The Poet in a Time of War

In "Hugh Selwyn Mauberley," a disillusioned Ezra Pound composed a threnody for an entire generation that, believing the lies of politicians, had "walked eye-deep in hell" and died in "the Great War." The vastness of the carnage assaulted reason; this "expense of spirit in a waste of shame" meant swallowing wormwood, and for what cause? "For an old bitch gone in the teeth, / For a botched civilization." Yet twenty years later, the world stood on the brink of another cataclysm. The "botched civilization" had not been repaired. Fascism was in the ascendancy; democracy, in retreat. Savage violence was on a rampage, and another world war looming. This time Pound had switched sides and joined the barbarians.

From Rutherford, aware that Hitler, Stalin, Mussolini, and Franco were madmen and political thugs, and irked by Pound's smug and callous braggadocio, Williams laced into him:

> Your brutal and sufficiently stupid reference to meat lying around on the steppes at this moment is quite an unnecessary flight of fancy, you'll find far more of it encased in your own head. I used to think you had a brain, no more. It looks more like round steak. Every time you try to reveal it . . .
>
> You're just an ignorant infant trying to batter out the sides of his crib . . .
>
> You ask me what I know about doctrines that I do *not* read. What in hell do you know about the doctrines you *do* read? The presumptive effects of them never for one moment dent your

skull—or you wouldn't write such trivial wash. You have, I presume, read all the outpourings of your imbecilic [*sic*] leaders and have swallowed everything they say, spittle and all. Is this or is this not true? Come on, let's have specific statements of just what and whom you are backing. Is it Hitler or Moussie [Mussolini]? Or both. I want facts . . .

But barricaded inside his dogmatic mind, and with "the damndest fund of selfesteem [*sic*]," Pound was impervious to Williams's insults and logic.

Many Americans believed that the four totalitarian regimes did not pose a threat to them, that Hitler's grandiose dreams of conquest were an intramural European problem and therefore none of our business: a false sense of safety, a fortress mentality, emanated from the three thousand miles of ocean separating the East Coast from the Luftwaffe's bombings of London and the Nazi armies overrunning Czechoslovakia and Poland. Williams, though, understood the physiology of convulsions in the body politic as well as in epileptics. The defeat of the Spanish Republican forces had disheartened him and darkened his mood, which is captured in the 1938 poem "These." Hearing and seeing "the flashes and booms of war," he speaks in a craggy, wintry voice:

>   These
> are the desolate, dark weeks
> when nature in its barrenness
> equals the stupidity of man.
>
> The year plunges into night
> and the heart plunges
> lower than night
>
> to an empty windswept place
> without sun, stars or moon
> but a peculiar light as of thought
>
> that spins a dark fire—
> whirling upon itself until
> in the cold, it kindles

to make a man aware of nothing
that he knows, not loneliness
itself—

This global conflagration does not lead to nihilism; Williams refuses to surrender to "emptiness" or despair, because an inner fire keeps the spiritual chill from numbing him. But with death on a destructive spree, nature barren, and man stupid and feeble, what kind of poetry, he asks himself, is adequate to mine such realities? He is equally skeptical that lyricism, "sweetest music," or matter-of-fact poetry "that / seeing the clock stopped, says, / The clock has stopped / that ticked yesterday" affords a viable answer. In this terrible darkness, he clings to a tentative, quixotic hope that stone will become "the sounds of lakewater / splashing."

"These" was published in his 1938 retrospective, *The Complete Collected Poems, 1906–1938*, a collection that generally received tepid or negative reviews. He was understandably disappointed, but twenty years later, in *I Wanted to Write a Poem*, Williams as elder statesman did not challenge the critics' verdict, although he did comment that their dismissive criticisms were too loose, "too conventional, too academic." What struck him most forcibly as he reconsidered the work was that he "didn't know how to divide a poem into what perhaps my lyrical sense wanted." In his own defense, he noted that he had attempted to "get rid of redundancies in the line—and . . . to make it go faster." He did not resemble the "stiff jointed" and "wobble / headed" poets he described in part 2 of "The Poet and His Poems," "who chase / vague images and think— / / because they feel / lovely movements / upon the instruments / of their hearts— / / that they are gifted." In part 1 of this poem, however, he ventured a definition of the poem that, with scathing self-criticism, he rejected as imprecise:

The poem is this:
a nuance of sound
delicately operating
upon a cataract of sense.

Vague. What a stupid
image. Who operates?

And who is operated
on? How can a nuance

operate on anything?
It is all in
the sound. A song.
Seldom a song.

Like Robert Frost, Williams is calculating the nexus of sound and sense. One would expect "a cataract of sound"; it's hard to imagine hearing a nuance of sound through the din of "a cataract of sense," so his inversion is strained. The clunky triad "operating," "operates," "operated" falls on the ear as leaden. So he abandons the lines as hapless. Next he briefly debates how to move from "sound" to "song." More adept at the music of speech than of song, he hesitates to commit himself to a genre of poetry he has used only intermittently. But as he weaves the words and lines of the remainder of the poem, he slips naturally into a troubadour's erotic language:

It should

be a song—made of
particulars, wasps,
a gentian—something
immediate, open

scissors, a lady's
eyes—the particulars
of a song waking
upon a bed of sound.

This lyrical melody is spun out of delicate and sensuous particulars; sense and sound are in harmony. In *Paterson*, he would "make a song" out of particulars drawn from politics and from the words, however unhinged and inadequate, of the common people, "those poor souls [who] had nothing else in the world, save that [massive] church, between them and the eternal, stony, ungrateful and unpromising dirt they lived by . . ." In his last three books, Williams would freely and exquisitely blend speech and song.

Williams's output of poems dwindled over the next few years. He confessed to Harvey Breit, a *New York Times* book columnist, "I'm not writing any poetry now. I can't. I hope I shall be able to surmount present difficulties," and to his friend Charles Abbott he confided that he craved "long periods of silence and loneliness." He was plugging away at *In the Money*, the sequel to *White Mule*, and wrestling with an angel, as Jacob had in Genesis, hoping to obtain a blessing: the secret of a usable form for his long poem *Paterson*. A visitation in which the elusive "Beautiful thing" fluttered on the threshold of 9 Ridge Road and was netted, failed to happen, with the result that Williams's level of frustration rose. In 1941, he managed fifteen scrappy short lyrics he labeled "For the Poem *Paterson*," but his inner censor permitted only the three-line epigraph to enter the finished poem.

In the Money resumes the story of Flossie's development, this time measuring her amazing leap from gangly, frisky baby to more independent two-year-old toddler: Joe is amazed at the end of the novel when she walks down a flight of stairs carefully and steadily. The Stecher girls, Lottie and Flossie, are very different in nature: Lottie is pretty and "high-toned," as if carrying a gene for snobbery she received from her mother, Gurlie. Lottie is outwardly obedient but somewhat hidden. Flossie is stubborn and curious about the world; when she stumbles and falls flat on her face, she picks herself up and again goes after what she desires. She's doted on by all the grown-ups because she is a shy charmer and chatterer with a sense of comic timing. Arrayed against the children is the full spectrum of adult personalities, each with radically different attitudes toward child rearing. The old generation is represented by Gurlie's surly Norwegian mother, whose instinct is to set up rigid rules of behavior and repress children's desires (Mrs. Torlund also plays a female Lear whose daughter, Gurlie, is a selfish ingrate, like Goneril and Regan); Aunt Olga, the loving, generous, overprotective maiden aunt, though literally and figuratively afraid of the children getting their feet wet, chimes in with advice, usually ignored by Gurlie, of staunch common sense; Oswald, Joe's stout bachelor brother, an ex-soldier who works as a butcher in the Chicago stockyards, is a raucous, boozy, free spirit, a hurricane of energy, and an artist with scissors and papers who delights the children at the family Christmas party with cutouts and gifts (his spendthrift way with money is the antithesis of Joe's). Gurlie's sisters, Hilda and Mangna, are permissive parents, whereas Gurlie imposes discipline fitfully and irritably; she is attentive to her children's needs, but snappish, and her mind often drifts off to her fantasy of becoming a rich woman. Joe has an old-fashioned German view of a father's role. (He gives his daughters a bath, but would never change a diaper.) He is amused by their antics and envelops them with loving-kindness: when Flossie, testing limits, bites him for neglecting her, he winces but doesn't spank her. He has the gift of imagination and patience.

When Gurlie takes the children to be vaccinated by a ritzy Fifth Avenue doctor, she comes home with a pamphlet about the behavior of toddlers, which Joe reads. Dr. Talbott's perspective is surprisingly Freudian. He unequivocally asserts that character is formed in the first years of a child's life, before memory or the acquisition of language: "The small prisoner has to be fit into the accidental mould of the life his or her parents find forced upon them in turn by their own more or less accidental economic and hereditary circumstances." This deterministic belief is richly illustrated and modified in the chapters set on a farm in rural Vermont that frame *In the Money*. For the Stecher children it's a kind of pastoral idyll that exposes them to nature and animals (horses, cows, dogs, kittens, sheep). The children, both cousins and the village kids they befriend, learn to resist adult orders, bond with one another, tease, run errands, bully, rough it, improvise games. A farm girl can tell the difference between an edible mushroom and a poisonous nightshade or a timothy leaf that is safe to chew and swallow. There may be no way to intervene and save a young child from dying of tuberculosis, but wise parenting can alleviate the almost irrational fear that grips a child's mind like a tenacious nightmare. The most brilliant piece of writing in the novel is the tour de force chapter in which Williams graphically conveys Flossie's recurrent terror, triggered by a streetlight and angry voices, that keeps awakening her and leads her to cry for help. Gurlie, impatient and unsympathetic, curtly tells Flossie to go back to sleep. These spasms eventually pass, without any evidence that they leave a permanent scar on Flossie's psyche, but Williams has uncannily evoked a toddler's misery and panicky behavior: as a pediatrician he deeply understands the hurdles that all children must negotiate in order to realize their full potential.

As in *White Mule*, much of *In the Money* is devoted to Joe's rise from union foreman to setting up his own printing shop. He is a kind of honest Everyman who outfoxes the corrupt capitalists who try to prevent him from winning a post office contract to print money orders. Vilified by a sensationalist press that, the opposite of muckrakers, prints stories that are often fabricated, and defamed by the grafters whose cushy arrangements for easy profits are being challenged by the upstart immigrant Horatio Alger, Joe fights back with a well-planned strategy that surprises his adversaries. (His start-up business is financed by a better class of capitalists who admire his craftsmanship and granite integrity.) Mr. Wynnewood, Joe's old boss, and his cronies resort to every dirty trick in their playbook and call in every political chit to deprive Joe of the chance to buy printing presses and inks and rent a loft to house the business. In a finely drawn confrontation, they try to intimidate and bully Joe, but he sticks bravely to his principles. He even gets to meet Teddy Roosevelt in the White House. The president at first parrots the slanderous line that Joe is a sly manipulator for whom winning the contract is so crucial he'd resort to underhanded means—"Self-interest is a great benefactor," he observes—but Roosevelt is swayed by Joe's indomitable character and eloquence. When Joe reports to a proud Gurlie that he has beaten back his foes, she calls him "a marvelous little Napoleon" well on the road to success. Although cognizant of what money can buy, Joe deplores the high price that the scramble for money extorts: a tainted conscience and unethical conduct. "Washington is the toughest place in the country to bring a public rascal to justice," he drily observes about the malodorous backroom deals that are standard practice in doing business or the nation's business. The reaction of average citizens to the ethos of greed and bribes is to lust for a share of the profits, however ill-gotten. They whine, "Why ain't I gettin' more?": hardly an inspiring slogan for morality in government and business.

Williams romanticizes Joe (Pa Herman) for his uncompromising probity ("he is not "saleable"), self-discipline, and dedication to the highest standards of excellence: "What works is one man paying attention to what he's doing and understands everything." Practical, ingenious, fair in his dealings with others, Joe is a poet of the printing press—and revered by Williams. Gurlie, by contrast, comes in for criticism from her sisters for her relentless pursuit of money. They argue that money doesn't bring happiness, but she brushes them off like gnats. "He's going to make me a rich woman," she crows. Indeed, she could serve as Exhibit A of the drive for conspicuous consumption that Thorstein Veblen analyzes in *The Theory of the Leisure Class*. Gurlie yearns for status and the "goods" that come in its wake: an elegant home with classy furniture, dining at posh restaurants, sitting in the best seats in a theater, owning a house in the country with a garden, and above all, being "one of the swells" other women will envy and want to emulate. On this subject she holds forth "loud and serious": "What do I want to be rich for? What do you want to live for? Of course I'm not satisfied with what I've got. I want to go places . . . I want to see everything there is to see that I'm interested in." She has already imbibed the American language of sanctioned self-advancement. If "[m]oney is everything in this country," she will scheme and fight to win a handsome share of it. As yet she is a snob with unlimited ambitions and a limited income, but Joe is the gravy train she plans to ride to affluence; she will be the dynamic force pushing "Napoleon" Stecher against his ethical code, to amass a handsome fortune. Other kinds of happiness do not enter into Gurlie's equation. For the sake of domestic peace Joe mostly tolerates and indulges his wife's manic hopes and brusque put-downs; Williams knows better than to portray her simply as a selfish virago with an outsize appetite for material things: she is loyal and ebullient and keen on providing for her children's welfare. Nonetheless, it's clear from the novel that Williams finds Gurlie, the facsimile of his mother-in-law, a strident and exasperating woman. To his relief, Flossie inherited her father's disposition.

In Williams's opinion years later, *In the Money* lacked verve and freshness: "I hoped it would be a good book, but it didn't come up to *White Mule*." The pacing is skillful, the marital conversations colloquially realistic, and the children individualized (no easy task). The indictment of corruption, though heartfelt, is somewhat stale. It would take Williams a dozen years before he completed the Stecher trilogy. *The Build-Up* was published in 1952.

After the Japanese attack on Pearl Harbor and the American declaration of war against the Germans, the country began gearing up for a long struggle on two fronts. Any lingering qualms Williams had about abandoning his previous stance in favor of neutrality dissolved. This war had personal repercussions for him and his family. With most of the young doctors in the central New Jersey area drafted for duty on the battlefields of Anzio and Guadalcanal, it fell on Williams and his older colleagues to take up the slack by covering their practices. Williams accepted this extra service as the fair and patriotic thing to do; it was "military discipline" on the home front. His eldest son, William Eric, newly out of medical school, joined the Navy Reserves and was shipped to a remote island in the South Seas. It was a relatively safe if boring spot to be stationed, since the island was not under siege by the Japanese army, and William Eric had mainly to treat commonplace ailments: no amputations, no emergency brain surgery. Though nearly the same age as the young sailors, he took on the role of paterfamilias and shrink, advising them on how to avoid sexually transmitted diseases. Paul, the younger son, who had studied for an MBA at Harvard and taken a job in Massillon, Ohio, left his new wife, Virginia, and infant son, Paul, Jr., behind and also joined the navy. Paul was assigned to the destroyer *Alden*, which patrolled the shipping lanes of the North Atlantic.

Williams kept up a steady correspondence with both sons, but especially with William Eric. He would share the latest news from home—keeping an eye on the plants in the garden, caulking leaks on the roof—pass on the latest war news (the British cornering Rommel in the desert, the invasion of Algiers), or discuss repairing a ruptured appendix, diagnosing viral pneumonia, examining recruits for the draft, and wondering how he would manage to juggle fourteen maternity cases in twenty-eight days plus the spike in house calls prompted by people's "war jitters." Although separated by a vast distance, Williams felt especially close to his son, whose maturity and independence he saluted. With admirable candor he laid bare his regrets at not always having done the right things for his sons—embarrassing William Eric in front of his friends at summer camp, for example—though he always intended the best for them. Reluctant to send poems to his son, who had literary aspirations and talent, Williams explains why in a letter:

> You say you'd like to see my book of poems. What the hell? Let 'em go. They are things I wrote because to maintain myself in a world much of which I didn't love I had to fight to keep myself as I wanted to be. The poems are me, in much of the faulty perspective in which I have existed in my own sight—and nothing to copy, not even for anyone even to admire. I have wanted to link myself up with a traditional art, to feel that I was developing individually it might be, but along with that, developing still in the true evolving traditions of the art. I wonder how much I have succeeded there. I

haven't been recognized and I doubt that my technical influence is good or even adequate.

Williams is not dining on humble pie. Rather, sensitive to the "benefits to be gained by breaking entirely with the father-son hook-up," he praises William Eric's prose style for being his own, not a copy of his father's, and recognizes that "you are entirely different from me in your approach, and yet we are alike in our interests."

In 1941, in whatever spare time he could snatch for his writing, Williams devoted himself to translating a series of rhymed poems by Yvan Goll about an eponymous sailor named Jean Sans Terre and poems by Nicolas Calas that had a surrealist tinge. The Calas items are weighed down by a ponderous rhetoric, the poet trapped in a labyrinth of agony and despair. Madness and death lurk everywhere; "suffering is without pity." "Sunk in my misery I drown my star," Calas says. The atmosphere is steeped in generic horror, a miasma of passivity; what's missing is a memorable protagonist such as Pentheus, Antigone, or Macbeth to make Calas's tragic world legible and dramatic. Pain stabs the various, undifferentiated speakers (even Narcissus), but the effect is diffuse. Consider this stanza from "Wrested from Mirrors":

> The wind of fear
> A cruel wind all but immutable
> Which tears up the echo buried in sand
> And the smoke imprisoned in fossil bones
> Which robs jackals of their dreams
> And nurslings of the future
> A wind that betrays its furies in its embraces

Calas's lines run long or short or effect a more casual pattern, but the sentiments, though dressed in surrealist robes, are conventional. There's not much Williams can do to breathe life into such inert verse.

Jean Sans Terre, the titular hero of Goll's sequence of ballads, is a mythic figure, like the Wandering Jew and the Flying Dutchman or Bulkington in Melville's *Moby-Dick*, embarked on endless journeys and doomed never to find rest on land. John Landless has circled the earth seven times with his ghostlike crew. Even the prospect of building Westopolis appalls him as futile, pointless; it will be just another "iron city":

Again stores of oblivion factories of ghosts
Again the upright houses down the godless street
And tree of knowledge where friends are hanged

John Landless flees at dawn back toward East alone

Yet there's a cogent subtext to Jean Sans Terre's journey: his lonely, disturbed consciousness mirrors the recurrent nightmare of tyranny and
war, misery and fear, raging in Europe and the Far East. As a Jew in jeopardy from the Nazis, one who fled to America for safety (Williams met
him at Stieglitz's gallery), Goll understood the profound trauma of persecution and exile and did not offer any soporific pieties as consolation. The
tone of the poems is bleakly fatalistic, and the lack of any punctuation at
the ends of lines reinforces the sense of terror recycled without cessation.
Goll's self-contained, orderly rhyme schemes function as an ironic commentary on the failure of "the codes of human reason" in a world in the
throes of disorder on a vast scale. Williams handles the rhymes and quatrains adroitly, though he deprecated his translation to Goll as mediocre.
The French poet thought Williams had succeeded in capturing the spirit
of the sequence's style.

Mesmerized, Williams continued to follow the war in the papers, on
the radio, and in Pathé newsreels. Even in truncated form, the images
projected on the movie screen brought home to him how dreadful the
consequences of war were, especially for ordinary people. The old Futur-
istic belief that violence was purgative and hygienic was a pathological lie.
Hitler represented an ideological madness beyond anything the Futurist
F. T. Marinetti and his swaggering colleagues could have foreseen or
hoped for. Hitler's monstrous racial theories promoted a demented, vengeful form of puritanism; the führer was, to borrow Wallace Stevens's phrase,
"the lunatic of one idea." Williams had probed beneath the ideological
facades of totalitarianism in Stalinist Russia and diagnosed the evil sickness spreading death like a black plague across borders. Hitler was the
carrier of an even more lethal virus, one that seemed as unstoppable as
the flu epidemic in 1918. Williams could not know or guess in 1940–1941
that Hitler had signed off on a blueprint for the Final Solution, whose aim
was genocide: the annihilation of European Jewry. In such a world it was
dangerous but imperative for the artist to speak truth to authoritarianism.
For Williams, this courage to speak out in dissent linked the artist with

the Jews as enemies of the state who would be disposed of brutishly. The alternative was to become, like Pound, a shameless propagandist for depraved mendacities. Pound's arrogance had so occluded his mind that his moral sense was totally eclipsed: he had parted ways with reality. The Hippocratic oath Williams had sworn to, "Do no harm," immunized him from the poisons that blinded Pound.

Williams did not subscribe to the dogma that poetry makes nothing happen; as early as 1908, he had rejected the doctrine of art for art's sake. Retreating into silence was not an option. What to do, then? How could he depict the war in poems? He lacked both the temperament and the luxury of time to compose a meditation on the aesthetics of evil, as Stevens did. "Esthétique du Mal" is Man Thinking, sensuously, articulately, while reaching for the sublime. Yet one feels at times that the pain in Stevens's poem is too metaphysical, too lofty, and thus a bit disembodied. Stevens likens the soldier's hemorrhaging wound to a red rose; Vesuvius groans rather than erupting. Stevens's imagination is fertile in confecting beautiful passages, but the aesthetic elegance keeps the reality of evil and war too distant. This was precisely a subject that might have benefited from including rough elements of the antipoetic that Stevens often claimed marred Williams's poetry, conveying the impression of a straggly and prosaic exercise. When, in 1941, Williams wrote two poems about the war, each in its way was a peculiar specimen. The first, "An Exultation," harkened back to an old grievance: the callous mistreatment Grandmother Wellcome had allegedly suffered at the hands of the English Godwin family. It is so odd it deserves to be quoted in full:

England, confess your sins! Toward the poor,
upon the body of my grandmother. Let the agents
of destruction purify you with bombs, cleanse
you of the profits of your iniquities to the last
agony of relinquishment.
She didn't die! Neither shall you, if
day by day you learn through abnegation
as she did, to send up thanks to those who
rain fire upon you.
Thanks! Thanks to a just and kind heaven
for this light that comes as a blasting fire
destroying the rottenness of your slums as well

as your most noble and historic edifices, never
to be replaced!
If! You will survive if—you accept it with
thanks when, like her, excoriated by devils
you will have preserved in the end, as she did,
a purity—to be that never as yet known
leader and regenerator of nations, even of those
rotten to the core, who by a sovereignty
they cannot comprehend
have worked this cleansing mystery upon you.

Williams impersonates an Old Testament prophet such as Elijah, excoriating Ahab and Jezebel for their sins and iniquities and warning of divine retribution if they don't repent. What precipitated this outburst is unclear; after all, his grandmother had been dead for twenty years. Even more puzzling is why in the midst of a war in which the British, the only country in Western Europe resisting the Nazis, were being bombed every night and enduring numerous casualties, should Williams decide to settle a long-simmering grudge for the alleged mistreatment of his beloved grandmother nearly a century before. There is an unpleasant, vengeful glee in Williams's tone and an illogic in his demands. The British could not avoid learning every day the hardships of abnegation; the blitzkrieg saw to that. Even if the profits of empire derived from robbery on a global scale, and the exploited poor lived in rancid slums—charges that could be leveled against many countries, including America—how could Williams defend his cheering on of the Nazis, peddlers of a despicable bogus theory of racial purity, as cleansing "agents / of destruction"? And did he really believe the British or any country could "be that never as yet known / leader and regenerator of nations, even of those / rotten to the core, who by a sovereignty / they cannot comprehend / have worked this cleansing mystery upon you"? When "An Exultation" was published in *Partisan Review* (July–August 1941), Williams appended a long note explaining that he had inherited Emily's "deep seated resentment against those who had treated her so badly in the country of her birth . . ." Perhaps to give a veneer of plausibility to his strafing attack on the English, he adds, "I have always hated the English ruling class and as a result feel that, in many ways, whatever England gets now is a just retribution." This hatred was fed by his contempt for, and rivalry with, T. S. Eliot, who adopted the

supercilious manners of the ruling class. When Williams declares pride and
love for his English blood, the about-face sounds a bit disingenuous. In its
martial strains, "An Exultation" is a bizarre aria Pound might have sung.

Williams dedicated his other war poem, "War, the Destroyer," to Martha Graham, whom he had met at a party at Charles and Musya Sheeler's
house. An innovative choreographer and charismatic dancer, Graham
was pioneering forms and themes that were both modernist and American. Talking to her and Barbara Morgan, a photographer who had published a book on dance and Graham, Williams on the spot improvised a
project. The women having admired his poems about the Republicans
battling the Fascists during the Spanish Civil War, he asked Morgan if
she would photograph Graham in a pose that illustrated the disasters of
war. The two women devised a composition of a bomb exploding above
Graham's head, the dancer incarnating the victim of terror. Williams sup-
posedly wrote "War, the Destroyer" to illustrate the image, but no bomb
falls in its twenty-seven brief lines.

Instead, the poem lampoons the preachy idea that fighting a war
leaves no time for art. On the contrary, Williams asserts that "when terror
blooms," that is precisely the circumstance that demands letting loose;
dance is his metaphor for the seditious imagination unfettered to "leap
and twist / whirl and prance," defying stasis and death. Poetry, music, and
prayer are ineffectual to stop the bloodbaths of war, but dance is a totemic affirmation of the sensuous life, where body and mind fuse. In
Graham's choreography, she mixed Dionysian and Apollonian elements,
angularity and elegance, and many of her doomed protagonists—Antigone,
for example—bravely confronted the forces of darkness and died as heroic martyrs for their unpopular beliefs. So Graham is, for Williams, an
exemplar of a bold American imagination able to depict "War, the Destroyer" coolheadedly and with passion. Williams's poem moves briskly
and in orderly tercets, but although he shared Graham's nonconformism,
its rhythms, its steps, don't quite match Graham's choreography. Perhaps
it is his slightly hortatory tone that inhibits him. Terror doesn't bloom in
his poem.

In January 1943, while he struggled to assemble and solder together
the jigsaw pieces for *Paterson*, Williams broached to Laughlin the idea of
New Directions bringing out a new collection of poems (Williams called
them "stray ends") drawn from various sources: short lyrics from the sequence "For the Poem *Paterson*" and the chapbook *The Broken Span* that

he'd left on the cutting-room floor, new verse buried in such magazines as *Furioso, Poetry, The New Republic,* and *The New Yorker,* and poems composed for *The Wedge.* Laughlin politely declined Williams's proposal, saying he could not lay hands on enough paper. (The government strictly rationed the allotments to book publishers.) To assuage Williams's disappointment, he promised he'd hoard some, so that he'd be ready to publish *Paterson I* as soon as the manuscript reached his desk.

Perhaps in oblique homage to E. E. Cummings, whose linguistic play in the poetry sandbox he admired and defended but did not wish to imitate, Williams tentatively titled the manuscript *THE (Lang) WEDGE.* Before testing the publishing waters, he sent the bulky manuscript to Zukofsky for vetting, cutting and pasting, and rearranging into linked sections. (Whenever Williams was unsure about the quality of new work, he entrusted it to Zukofsky; this ritual became almost standard practice.) Zukofsky returned the manuscript, heavily edited, with the comment, "Here y'are! Don't accept the detailed criticism unless it verifies your own misgivings," and suggested that the title be simplified to *The Language.* It took Williams only a few days to pore over the meticulous edits and to lop off thirty-three pages. The criticisms, he told Zukofsky, were "excellent," "invaluable," "hard but salutary." Sent out into the world, the manuscript was rejected, in rapid order, by Simon and Schuster and Duell, Sloan and Pearce. Galling as these nos were, they did not compare to the nasty comment of an unidentified Harvard man at Farrar and Rinehart that "it was not good enough."

At this low point Laughlin intervened and steered Williams to Harry Duncan and Paul Wightman Williams, two young men who had founded the Cummington Press on a shoestring, with the mission of publishing poetry books in beautiful handset editions, the print run kept small. Duncan and Williams had the paper and the enthusiasm to take on the project. Before sending them the manuscript, Williams did one last polishing and again asked Zukofsky to read it through (Williams had settled on *The Wedge* as the book's title). Thinking it prudent to meet the small press fledglings, Williams traveled to Cummington, Massachusetts, near the Vermont border—he described the little town to Wallace Stevens as "the birthplace of William Cullen Bryant, completely off the earth"—to meet the proprietors and to discuss business arrangements. Williams put up a hundred dollars for the expense of bookbinding, which a young friend in New York City, aided by "skillful lying," managed to bring off.

The Wedge, in a print run of 380 copies, was published on September 27, 1944. Four and a half years later, Williams gave Pound a brief history of the genesis of the book: "It was gathered together during the war under the incentive provided me by various GIs who wanted a [little] book of my poems, so their letters said, that they could carry in their pockets." With wry and weary humor, he describes *The Wedge*, his most "popular" book, to Pound: "if you haven't seen it [it] is squat, pocket-size, and weighs only an ounce or so. It is very much sought after and nowhere to be found."

With the war raging on two fronts, Williams prepared an introduction to his book, based in part on a lecture he delivered at the New York Public Library, which succinctly covers a number of subjects—in particular, the role of the poet in time of war. He attacks the Freudian idea that "the arts seek to escape from frustration." Like the war, poetry is "the driving forward of desire to a complex end." Action is compatible with frustration. Williams insists that neither the poet nor his work is a "fixed phenomenon"; because he is constantly changing, "Hamlet today, Caesar tomorrow," he cannot be limited in the scope of content or repertoire of forms at his disposal: he is free to address both violence and gentleness, as Williams does in *The Wedge*. If "[t]here is no poetry of distinction without formal invention"—the anthem he sings in *Paterson*—then the poet must shape words, his materials, as the potter kneads clay. "It isn't what he *says* that counts as a work of art, it's what he makes, with such intensity of perception that it lives with an intrinsic movement of its own to verify its authenticity." This pitch of rapturous abstraction is not one Williams often favors, though it reverberates through the prose of *Spring and All*.

Williams's two bald statements—"There's nothing sentimental about a machine" and "A poem is a small (or large) machine made of words"—brought a heap of contumely on his head. To many poets the adages sounded like a robotic definition of a poem, the formula for a mechanistic poetic. Convinced that Williams's poetry was formally slipshod, they refused to credit him with serious thinking about form, and in their indignation they did not follow his explanation to its close: "When I say there's nothing sentimental about a poem I mean that there can be no part, as in any other machine, that is redundant . . . As in all machines its movement is intrinsic, undulant, a physical more than a literary character." Is Williams a modernist heretic? No. By using the machine as his crucial metaphor to illustrate organic form in a rapidly and violently changing world, he is in the mainstream of modernism. In the penultimate paragraph of his brief introduction to *The Wedge*, he cleverly links art to the war: "for it is in the intimate form that works of art achieve their exact meaning, in which they most resemble the machine, to give language its highest dignity, its illumination in the environment to which it is native. Such war, as the arts live and breathe by, is continuous." The poet's imagination, that most local of sites, is the laboratory where change, invention, and clarification of form are generated.

Williams's passionate homily raises the bar so high that it would seem only the greatest poets can vault over it. If we read the poems of *The Wedge* to see if he lives by his own ideals, what do we find? Setting aside a few short love poems that verge on sentimentality ("The Observer," "A Flowing River," "Raleigh Was Right"), there are a few poems, such as "The Semblables" and "The Monstrous Marriage," that demonstrate Williams's powers of invention and his use of language that illuminates "the environment to which it is native." Having argued that the movement of a poem "is distinguished by the character of the speech from which it arises," Williams opens several portals through which a distinctive American idiom may enter and enrich our poetry. One such is "Writer's Prologue to a Play in Verse," which does not follow Shakespeare's practice in *Romeo and Juliet*, for example, in which an actor steps before the audience and requests that they let their imaginations fly off to Verona. Rather, Williams delivers a discourse on what the theatergoers attending his verse play might expect. The first ten or so lines delight in the poet's capacity to dart from image to image, and would not have been out of place at Shakespeare's Globe, where the playwright assumes that all classes, even the groundlings standing in the pit, will follow the action and grasp the meaning of the words and the metaphors:

> In your minds you jump from doors
> to sad departings, pigeons, dreams
> of terror, to cathedrals; bowed,
> repelled, knees quaking, to the-closed-
> without-a-key or through an arch
> an ocean that races full of sound
> and foam to lay a carpet for
> your pleasure or a wood that waves

releasing hawks and crows or
crowds that elbow and fight for
a place or anything.

The rest of this rambling, oratorical poem, however, is an earnest, pre-performance lecture by Williams to an uninformed democratic audience, laying out what they should expect. The speaker works the room hard, like a politician trying to win over skeptical or indifferent voters. He cajoles them, supplicates them, instructs them in the ABCs of poetry and their connection to it: "Would it disturb you if I said / you have no other speech than poetry? / You, yourself, I mean." One imagines blank or incredulous stares from the poet's listeners. He is a doctor prescribing a cure for a moral ailment or deficit: it may seem frightening to swallow the pill, but you must do so for your own good. The language of this poem reflects Williams's grave doubts that they will heed his advice. As he wrote to Horace Gregory, "American culture is crude but at the same time, newer, more dangerous but heavy with rewards for the sensibility that can reap them." That prize dangling before his eyes is worth competing for, but can the crudity be transmuted into cultural gold? He could not abandon hope that change would occur.

Two moderately long poems, "Catastrophic Birth" and "To All Gentleness," debate whether in violence or gentleness we find the core of change. Williams is no staunch pacifist, as the melodramatically titled "Catastrophic Birth" attests to. What is attractive about violence is that "it alone opens the shell of the nut," that is, dislodges entrenched ideas and "known ways" and effects change. Sometimes nature is the cause, as when Mount Pelée erupted in 1902 in Martinique, wiping out the populace of the island. It is human nature "to believe nothing can change": "Life goes on. The orange trees bloom. / The old women talk tirelessly." The jolly "big" woman giving birth to her seventh child and "[s]weating like a volcano" is oblivious to the impending disaster: the "dreadful eruption," despite official reassurance that all is well, cannot be stopped. Violence is cyclical and deceptive. The poem ends:

Rain will fall. The wind and the birds
will bring seeds, the river changes
its channel and fish re-enter it.

The seawind will come in from the east.
The broken cone breathes softly on
the edge of the sky, violence revives and regathers.

"Catastrophic Birth" does not directly address the man-made violence of World War II, its "death-dealing" bombs raining destruction on a vast scale, but it is implied. Peace will be reborn "above the cinders," only to die in a new conflagration. There's no guarantee that change will be for the better.

Nor is gentleness a clear-cut alternative to violence. "A profusion / of pink roses bending ragged in the rain" provokes Williams to meditate on "all gentleness and its / enduring" and to regard it as a sign that "the new and the unlikely" are "bound / indissolubly together in one mastery." The war invades "To All Gentleness" twice. A plane crashes into the sea, the impact ejecting the pilot into the water. An instinct for survival taking over, he swims for fourteen hours, until he is "picked up and returned to life." The waves that drown one man lift another to safety. (Williams's rhythm is wavelike, rising and falling.) The pilot's rescue is construed, rather obscurely, as proof that gentleness can "join our lives together."

Williams's second image of the war is an example of malign violence:

The bomb-sight adjusted destruction hangs
by a hair over the cities. Bombs away!
and the packed word descends—and
rightly so.

The poet's image foreshadows the bombs that dropped on Dresden and Hiroshima. The "packed word" delivers death on an unprecedented scale. Williams understands the "convulsive ecstasy" that unleashes the bomb's hellish path of destruction, blinding and deafening the people in the cities, who are forever shut off from the beauty of the natural world. Williams's phrase "and / rightly so" disturbs because of its cold detachment. (It recalls his casual, twisted approval of the German pinpoint bombing of British cities in "An Exultation.") Before the poem ends he inserts a stanza about another woman and a different birth: the forewoman of a shipyard, as healthy as the Italian peasant in "Catastrophic Birth," has endured three miscarriages (all boys) and is determined to try again. It is as problematic to explain why one birth is easy and another unsuccessful as it is to understand gentleness and violence. Perhaps Williams includes the births to mitigate death's ubiquity in the war. It is not an antidote but, rather, an implacable fact of life he experienced as a doctor every day. Because "gentleness harbors all violence," the two cannot be separated. They are partners in a dance of life and death.

The clarification of form Williams elevated to the necessary first principle for poetry is missing from "Catastrophic Birth" and "To All Gentleness." The language is sometimes felicitous, but the movement is spastic, as if the imagination had forgotten to hand Williams a map to his destination. But two poems in *The Wedge* do achieve a satisfying form: "The Dance" and "Burning the Christmas Greens." The Dance" depicts the famous Brueghel painting *The Kermesse of St. George*, which the Williamses saw in Vienna's Kunsthistorisches Museum in 1924. The poem is short enough to print in its entirety:

> In Brueghel's great picture, The Kermess,
> the dancers go round, they go round and
> around, the squeal and the blare and the
> tweedle of bagpipes, a bugle and fiddles
> tipping their bellies (round as the thick-
> sided glasses whose wash they impound)
> their hips and their bellies off balance
> to turn them. Kicking and rolling about
> the Fair Grounds, swinging their butts, those
> shanks must be sound to bear up under such
> rollicking measures, prance as they dance
> in Brueghel's great picture, The Kermess.

It is nearly impossible to translate the rhythm of a painting into the sounds and movements of a poem, yet Williams captures the boisterous spirit of *The Kermesse* with his words. The symmetry of the identical first and last lines encloses the whirling peasant dance at a fair. "In Brueghel's great picture, The Kermess" is the starter's gun that sets everything and everyone into propulsive motion. Repetition of words ("round," "round," "around"), the joyous ensemble of nouns that name the musical instruments emitting weird noises ("squeal," "blare," and the pungent "tweedle," to characterize the bagpipe's low and exotic rumble), and the gerunds and participles ("kicking," "rolling," "swinging," and the adjective "rollicking") that embody the physical abandon of the dancers—all derive from the bravura agility of the modest "and." Even the parentheses cannot interrupt the flow of the dance or the poem. Williams's comment about the "butts" and "shanks" and "bellies" shuns the jargon and euphemisms of his profession; he is not an outsider looking on from the sidelines; he actively participates in the dance by demonstrating a poet's hedonistic love of vulgar or sensuous words, the "rollicking measures" that with off-balance and swinging feet and internal rhyme reach the finish line in marvelous form: "In my end is my beginning."

The crown jewel of *The Wedge* is "Burning the Christmas Greens." Williams begins with the description of "a landscape of flame": the reader enters a room where a fire crackles and the keepers of the flame are absent. It is not a mystifying or sinister setting, as it would be in a Poe tale, but there are hints that we have stumbled on the vestiges of a puzzling scene. For although he and Floss got married in the Presbyterian church across from 9 Ridge Road, Williams did not believe in any religion's dogmas. Burning the Christmas greens in the Williams household is more a pagan ritual than a Christian one. The emblems of awe he lovingly names and pays homage to are trees—"the coarse / holly, the balsam and / the hemlock for their green"—cut at midnight, "[a]t the thick of the dark / the moment of the cold's / deepest plunge." What satisfies their soul's hunger ("need") is the living green, not a Nativity scene featuring the infant Jesus being adored by the Virgin Mary, the three Magi, saints, angels, and farm animals. The paraphernalia of Christian piety is conspicuously absent. The Williams family decoration is an expression of natural piety: they "stuck" green branches in the window (the verb is a typical Williams locution), and on the mantel "built a green forest and among those hemlock / sprays put a herd of small / white deer as if they were / walking there." Their handiwork pleases husband and wife: like gods, they pronounce it "gentle and good."

But the magic is ephemeral, past; the room must revert to its previous bare state. Then begins a ceremony of great complexity and beauty. Bill and Floss stuff the dead grate with the greens and place them on a "half burnt out / log's smoldering [cyclopean] eye": the pyre for the Christmas greens. As if a minister conducting a burial, Williams delivers a eulogy:

> Green is a solace
> a promise of peace, a fort
> against the cold (though we
>
> did not say so) a challenge
> above the snow's
> hard shell. Green (we might
> have said) that, where
>
> small birds hide and dodge
> and lift their plaintive
> rallying cries, blocks for them
> and knocks down
>
> the unseeing bullets of
> the storm. Green spruce boughs
> pulled down by a weight of
> snow—Transformed!

Green is extolled for its life-giving traits: it is a benison, a solace, a promise of peace, and a shield for little birds and humankind against the "unseeing bullets of the storm" that kill and maim. Williams's language keeps a poised, conversational tone, as the syntax grows as dense as the spruce boughs in which the birds "hide and dodge" and the tree "blocks . . . and knocks down" the dangerous barrage. The strong monosyllabic verbs make the danger audible.

But once lit, the fire, personified as a recreant (a coward), blazes up in violence and roars to life, putting the greens to death. Like a painter with a palette of brilliant colors, Williams portrays the stunning transformation of green to "Black mountains, / black and red," then to ash white. There was no time for him and Floss to mourn the disappearance of green, because what replaces it, "an infant landscape of shimmering / ash and flame" transports them—they are lost in reverie and amazement that the "Beautiful Thing" chose their fireplace for its gorgeous display; theirs is a secular epiphany:

> breathless to be witnesses,
> as if we stood

ourselves refreshed among
the shining fauna of that fire.

This exultant climax of "Burning the Christmas Greens" is masterfully crafted and also a formal triumph, subtly pointing back to the poem's opening stanzas, where, to avoid routine linear narrative, Williams begins in the middle of the anecdote, saving the revelation for last: that change can, unexpectedly, refresh and animate the spirit.

It is no surprise that Williams looked back on *The Wedge* as a milestone in the evolution of his poetry. In typical understatement, he remarked in *I Wanted to Write a Book*, "I have always been proud of this book." This book boosted his confidence that he would gain control of the form of the unruly *Paterson*, which had been giving him conniptions for several years. The wars in Europe and Asia were still not won, but change was afoot in the public sphere: the Germans would surrender in eight months, and the Japanese three months after that. In the continuous war between violence and gentleness, the atomic bomb would tip the balance of terror to violence, and become a powerful symbol in Williams's poems. His hope that his continual frustration with the composition of *Paterson* would soon end was not self-deception: he would finally, after a dicey ordeal, solve the formal problems that had eluded him and, in 1946, rejoice in the birth of Book 1 of his long poem and the acclaim that greeted it.

FIFTEEN

The Magnificent Torso: *Paterson*

I.

Although Williams sometimes expressed skepticism about the long poems he wrote in the 1920s, they were necessary to establish his credentials as a modernist poet. He composed *Spring and All*, his first attempt at a hybrid form mixing poetry and prose, in a burst of creativity, proceeding by instinct and trial and error rather than by an elaborate outline. Driven forward and held together by its dynamic energy, *Spring and All* shows Williams's skill at varying rhythms and integrating a multitude of subjects, and reveals his experiments with the American language, elevated and demotic, into a reasonably coherent whole.

Paterson continues this tradition in epic form. Like most modernist long poems, it has little interest in story or plot. In fact, the narrative spine of the epic poem was broken in the Romantic period. The hero of Wordsworth's 1805 long poem *The Prelude* is himself; the gods have disappeared into the realms of metaphor and myth. The subject is his poetic development from childhood to manhood and the wayward growth of his moral character through exposure to nature, which teaches him beneficence and sets him on the path to virtuous conduct and a poetic vocation. A few episodes, such as the recital of his adventures in France during the tumultuous French Revolution, echo faintly the martial strains of *The Iliad* and *The Aeneid*. But in his invocation of the muse, we can assess the sea change he produced:

> When, as becomes a man who would prepare
> For such a glorious work, I through myself
> Make rigorous inquisition, the report

Is often cheering; for I neither seem
To lack, that first great gift! the vital soul,
Nor general truths which are themselves a sort
Of Elements and Agents, Under-Powers,
Subordinate helpers of the living mind.
Nor am I naked in external things,
Forms, images; nor numerous other aids
Of less regard, though worn perhaps with toil,
And needful to build up a Poet's praise.

Wordsworth sounds here as if he is auditioning for the role of British bard and enumerating his qualifications to write a "glorious work": a long poem. He does not whisper the word "epic," though he makes it clear that he has read Milton and such "Romantic tales" of chivalry as Malory's *Le Morte d'Arthur*. What is most striking, however, despite the poet's modest assurance that he is not "naked in external things," is the centrality of the "I" in *The Prelude*. Story or, more accurately, vignettes are the corollary of introspection, not its motor. This is not to disparage the frequent eloquence of Wordsworth's style, which Keats aptly called "the egotistical sublime," but one feels the world of *The Prelude* shrinking in size and less eventful than that of the great epics.

Across the Atlantic, American poetry offered one model for writing in long forms: Walt Whitman, whose 1855 "Song of Myself" also managed to be a Song of America, celebrating its diverse people and their incomparable energy, its historical triumphs and defeats, and its protean language, by turns lyrical, declamatory, coarse, elevated, and sexually charged. Whitman considered the entire *Leaves of Grass*, and the country itself, an epic poem, and some sections do seem worthy of that honorific title: the narrative of John Paul Jones's naval battle, allowing for a radically different idiom, would not be out of place in Ariosto's *Orlando Furioso* or Byron's *Don Juan*, and the famous heterogeneous catalogue of section 15 harks back to Homer's catalogue in *The Iliad* of the warriors assembled at the gates of Troy. Nonetheless, the democratic heroes scattered throughout *Song of Myself* are mainly satellites orbiting around one sun: Walt Whitman.

Williams sometimes sounded petulant when forced to acknowledge Whitman as a Johnny Appleseed who broke the ground and seeded an American poetry that could rival and even surpass English varieties. Perhaps he occasionally suffered from the anxiety of influence, bristling at the accusation that the torch of Whitman's free verse had been passed on to him. That was a dubious honor he wanted no part of. Whitman's readership was as small as Williams's was. In any case, Williams seems never to have regarded *Leaves of Grass* as a model for his own long poems.

The idea of writing an epic poem was not high on the list for most modern poets, including Williams. They, of course, read and admired the classical epics and sometimes paid them homage by alluding to a scene, a figure, or a line or image in Dante, as Eliot does in *The Waste Land*. In Pound's work, important personages drawn from history—Confucius, Malatesta, John Adams, and Thomas Jefferson—take center stage for several cantos; he quotes selectively from their statements in letters, essays, and books to buttress his theories of statecraft and economics or the proper cultivation of culture and art, but unlike Achilles, Odysseus, and Satan, they are not memorable characters. The epic hero undergoes thrilling adventures and tests, sometimes hanging on to life by a thread: shipwrecks engineered by the enmity of angry gods; sexual rivalry or bondage to Circe and Calypso; single combats demonstrating military prowess and hubris; wily stratagems, such as Odysseus's escape from the one-eyed cannibal Polyphemus. These heroes act out their destinies on the vast stage of history's amphitheater: a civilization is destroyed, and out of its ashes another is born; Aeneas escapes the flames of Troy to found Rome. The reader is enthralled by the epic's richness of experience. In *The Cantos*, except perhaps for the *Pisan Cantos*, not one minor character seizes the reader's attention, as Nestor, Cassandra, Dido, and Penelope do. Narrative has virtually vanished in *The Cantos*. History is reduced to a handful of ideas, all simmering in the mind of Pound the learned scribe. Whatever the merits of *The Cantos*, drama is conspicuously missing.

Williams needed no prodding from Pound to read the great canonical epics as preparation for attempting his long poem. They did not, however, influence him the way they did Pound. He kept up with each installment of *The Cantos* as it came out, reviewed some of them, and exchanged letters with Pound and later James Laughlin about the work in progress Pound hoped would be his magnum opus. Laughlin, who published both men, believed that part of the impetus for writing *Paterson* arose unconsciously from Williams's need to compete with Pound, though obviously he was not interested in cooking up the historico-linguistic bouillabaisse that was the Rapallo chef's specialty. Williams *was* fiercely competitive, whether as a middle-aged man playing a game with his son's friends at a summer camp in Maine or as a poet eager to beat his old friend in the poetry marathon. But Pound's cosmopolitanism and the language it produced existed in a different milieu from Williams's, which staked all on the "local" representing the universal.

For much the same reason, although *The Waste Land* quickly became the emblematic modernist long poem, its grand theme, the decline of Western civilization, could not serve Williams's poetic goals. For Eliot, the cultural unity in the Europe of Dante's time, when "allegory was not a local Italian custom, but a universal European method," was an apogee never to be matched. The twentieth century, hopelessly splintered, morally adrift, and intellectually incoherent, was the disastrous culmination of an inexorable process that had begun in Shakespeare's England.* Williams could not help noticing, and deploring, the fact that the Harvard-educated Eliot—like Pound, multilingual and erudite—bleached out all signs of his American upbringing, and in *The Waste Land* failed to quote a single American text. The poem gave off the musty smell of the Library, which in Book 3 of *Paterson* Williams equated with "desolation, stagnation and death."

Senescence wasn't America's problem; its adolescent immaturity was. The staying power of the country's anti-intellectualism, philistinism, sexual puritanism, and religious intolerance disheartened Williams. Had he not hammered away at, analyzed, dramatized, and exposed, in poems, letters, essays, and *In the American Grain*, the country's moral fault lines? Outward circumstances changed, generations were born and died, but the United States still functioned as a large, slipshod, dysfunctional society. But Williams's resiliency would not let him surrender to despair. After all, he had wrestled successfully with his demons to gain a poetic voice that, however uneven at times, was indisputably his. His faith in the American language as a sonorous and subtle instrument that could produce great art had wavered but not broken. *Paterson*, he hoped, would synthesize and portray all he had learned about the country's degradations and hypocrisies, its cranks and con men, its ordinary people, and its unquenchable ideals. Above all, he would make vocal the "infinite vari-

---

*Henry Adams, in *The Education of Henry Adams* and *Mont-Saint-Michel and Chartres*, also contrasted medieval Europe's unity, incarnated in the widespread worship of the Virgin Mary and the cathedrals, stained-glass windows, and paintings consecrated to her mercy, with the modern world's bewildering multiplicity, symbolized by the Dynamo, which he personified as Chaos.

ety" of its speech—Williams's ambition was never paltry—but *Paterson* is
not really a "personal epic."

The germ of *Paterson* was a modest 1926 poem of that title published
in *The Dial*. What Williams cobbled together resembles the figures
and landscapes that an artist sets down in his sketchbook, trying out ideas
and perspectives for a larger work whose form and conception have not
yet gelled. Mr. Paterson, the protagonist of Williams's poem, is lauded as
a "great philosopher" for his "savage and tender" ideas and music, but
those ideas are still locked in the poet's imagination, even though Mr.
Paterson's thought, we're told, is listed in that most public of documents,
"the Telephone / Directory—"; the rhythm of that thought, the poet admits, is to "alight and scatter." Mr. Paterson as the embodiment of Paterson the city is in an embryonic stage. A few items that were retained in
Paterson appear in the poem, most notably Williams's controversial adage
"Say it, no ideas but in things." Critics have pounced on this catchphrase,
alleging that it proves Williams had a philistine aversion to ideas: this is
very far from the truth. The life of the mind mattered profoundly for him,
but because his sensibility is predominantly empirical, he prefers ideas to
be embedded in facts, in "things," in the plethora of concrete images he
loves as ballast for his poems. James Laughlin thought that "No ideas but
in things" was a paraphrase of the medieval philosophical idea that there's
nothing in the mind that was not first in the senses.

The roar of the Great Falls, which becomes an omnipresent iconic
force in *Paterson*, is audible in the earlier poem once: "the river comes
pouring in above the city / and crashes from the edge of the gorge / in a
recoil of spray and rainbow mists." Here the focus remains chiefly on the
populace of Paterson, who will play major roles in the final work. They are
depicted as a "complex mathematic," defeated yet vitally going about their
daily life: working in a factory, "cranking the car / buying the meat," or
peeling off "for their children's albums" the rare stamps from the pope's
twice-monthly letters addressed to the citizens of Paterson. The "high decorum" of the pope's communiqués is of dubious value in a poem about a
working-class city, where the residents speak colloquially in many tongues
and "are the divisions and imbalances / of his whole concept, made small
by pity / and desire":

They
fall back among cheap pictures, furniture

filled silk, cardboard shoes, bad dentistry
windows that will not open, poisonous gin,
scurvy, toothache—

Williams is aware of his patients' unhealthy habits, the legacy of poverty and its despair—he has treated their root causes in his office—and describes them with clear-eyed dispassion.

The challenges *Paterson* posed proved so difficult to solve that it took Williams nearly two decades for Book 1 to appear. From 1927 through the mid-1930s, he was juggling so many projects and obligations that he lacked the leisure to think about *Paterson* in any depth. He filed it away for future consideration, making sure it did not get lost in a to-do folder. It surfaced again in a letter he wrote to Pound right after Roosevelt's landslide reelection in 1936 (not mentioned in the letter; FDR's name was sure to make Ezra go berserk and slander the president as an economic idiot or worse): "And then there's that magnum opus I've always wanted to do: the poem PATERSON. Jeez how I'd like to get at that. I've been sounding myself out in these years working toward a form of some sort . . ." The sentence trails off with ellipses because Williams still had nothing tangible to report except his intention.

One year later, Williams wrote "Paterson: Episode 17." Although there is no trace of any earlier episodes—the number harks back to the Dada-esque scrambling of chapter titles in *Spring and All*—"episode" does foreshadow the sometimes improvisational, sometimes rambling structure of *Paterson*. Williams is intoxicated with the "Beautiful Thing" he addresses as a stage director might a leading actor, or as Prospero might command Ariel. "The Beautiful Thing" is androgynous, a lyrical female of languid eroticism, who sits "by the ivied / church, one arm / buttressing you / long fingers spread out / among the clear grass prongs," a woman in a "pose of supreme indifference / sacrament / to a summer's day," and a ballerina as Odile/Odette in Tchaikovsky's *Swan Lake* "in your white lace dress / 'the dying swan' / and high heeled slippers—tall / as you already were—till your head / through fruitful exaggeration / was reaching the sky and the / prickles of its ecstasy." But the male counterparts, like Caliban, are violent, unable to restrain their animal appetites, ignorant, "drunk and bedraggled to release / the strictness of beauty / under a sky full of stars." These brutes of Paterson and Newark fought a turf war over boundaries and proprietorship, but there was extreme collateral damage to women, one of whom was socked in the nose—abuse of women was a chronic problem that never ceased to disquiet Williams—but even worse, they gang-raped a black woman, whom Williams probably treated for trauma. Paul Mariani rightly connects "Paterson: Episode 17" to Williams's sketch "The Colored Girls of Passenack" (in *A Knife in the Water*), which is a hymn to the beauty and sexuality of three black women he admired. The first of the trio, Georgie Anderson, worked as a messy housekeeper for Williams's parents. She impressed Ed and Bill, who were eleven and twelve years old, by her prowess throwing a ball much farther than they could, by her entertaining talk (she was "a figure of fun"), but most of all by her femininity. "Wild as a cat," she was the first woman he saw naked, which stoked his sexual curiosity.

The second black goddess, Mable Weeks, came to his office on a ruse, stripping herself naked to offer herself to him. (She was highly successful as a courtesan attracting Rutherford's white men as customers.) Williams remembered her as "built in the style of Goya's *Maja Desnuda*" with African gestures and laugh; he had to summon all his willpower to resist her seductions. Instead, he became her confidant and her doctor, delivering her two children and consoling her through the tragic death of her small daughter, strangled, he believed, by a boarder. The third black beauty who captivated him was "a magnificent bronze figure" he encountered on a house call. When she stood silent in the doorway he feasted on her majestic demeanor: "The force of her—something, her mental alertness coupled with her erectness, muscular power, youth, seriousness—her actuality—made me want to create a new race on the spot. I had never seen anything like it." That humorous vein of exaggeration is typical of Williams in a mood of sexual arousal and phallic fantasy. If Mariani is correct, these women are Kora figures and their violent men and husbands, like heirs of Hades, repeat his abduction and rape of Persephone again and again.

In March 1939, a manuscript titled "Detail and Parody for the Poem Paterson" landed on Laughlin's desk. The poems were predominantly brief lyrics on the subject of love, "a flower / with roots in a parched ground." In love, Williams asserts in "Coda," "the details are all," but the details in the sequence are so uninspired, the words, "once / cadenced melody / full of sweet breath," so enervated that they rise neither to song nor to speech. Lacking invention and a snappy form, they seem utterly unsuitable for *Paterson*. That was obviously Williams's opinion, because he tinkered with

"Detail" three times; disliking all of the versions, he scrapped them or recycled them in other books, such as *The Broken Span* and *The Wedge*, salvaging just four lines for *Paterson*, which he placed prominently in Book 1.

At the beginning of January 1941, in a letter to Laughlin, Williams slips in a reference to *Paterson* that shows it is alive, if still inchoate in his imagination: "I want to bring [it] finally to a focus." Five months later, he elaborates on the challenge that had been "tearing [his] head apart for years": how

> to get at a mode of modern verse suitable for a long poem which would be simple as speech itself and subtle as the subtlest brain could desire on the basis of *measure*. That's been the great problem ever since Whitman. No one has approached it as yet. Almost all long poems are crap to me because they are metrically uninteresting, especially Eliot's work, which is crafty enough, God knows, but not fit otherwise to wipe a good man's bottom.

It will surprise only those lukewarm about Williams's poetry that he is concerned not about the content of *Paterson*, which he will sort out eventually, but about its metrical versatility. (Williams has seldom been given sufficient credit for his contributions to modernist prosody.) "Measure" is a word capable of many meanings, some of which may even contradict one another, but Williams worried the topic in notes and letters, and in drafts of poems that he later discarded. It invaded the italicized words and phrases that serve as an epigraph to the "Preface" of Book 1 and indeed clamored for attention throughout *Paterson*, like a monitory voice he could not quiet.

The false starts and self-recriminations continued unabated. In a letter to Laughlin dated December 27, 1943, he confesses the galling impasse he can't seem to escape: "That God damned and I mean God damned poem *Paterson* has me down. I am burned up to do it but don't quite know how. I write and destroy, write and destroy. It's all shaped up in outline and intent, the body of the thinking is finished but the technique, the manner and the method are unresolvable to date. I flounder and flunk." With the outcome of his struggle to assemble his ideas into a workable shape touch-and-go, Williams feels a desperate urgency: "But it's got to be born; it's got to be pushed out of me somehow and in perfect form. But that form, involving the future and the past is—to my weak powers almost too much. I won't acknowledge I don't have the stuff for it though at times my fears are devastating." The skilled obstetrician finds himself in the position of a woman in the throes of a difficult birth; she can't push the baby out. His fears of inadequacy, that instead of "perfect form," *Paterson* will be stillborn or blemished, threaten to overwhelm him.

As always, when faced with a creative dead end, Williams started over, enunciating a few basic tenets he considered too sound to relinquish: "what is sorely needed is poetic construction, ability in among the words, to invent there, to make, to make well and new." It is hard to imagine poets of any stylistic leanings disagreeing with these truisms. Still, by reviewing the problem once more, as he might scan his notes on a patient's history of chronic anemia or arterial blockage in search of a clue he had overlooked, he hoped to find an ideal balance of freedom and discipline. Too much freedom could lead to sprawl and prolixity:

> (The multiple seed,
> packed tight with detail, soured,
> is lost in the flux and the mind,
> distracted, floats off in the same
> scum)

Too much discipline, however, often leads to an airless, prison-like form, "Minds like beds always made up, / (more stony than a shore) / unwilling or unable." "Order," he contended, "is a servant not a master," adding in earthy terms, "Order is what is discovered after the fact not a little piss pot for us all to urinate in—and call ourselves satisfied." The ideal would be the oxymoron "controlled abandon," a measure flexible enough to include the diverse melodies of American "common speech" inflected with spiky modernist timbres and rhythms, lyrical interludes of rapturous nature description, stichomythia, immigrant dialects, archaic pastoral, scientific terms, political and religious harangue. (Astutely, Robert Lowell called the form interior monologues.) A linguistic melting pot of these ingredients would keep the poem from monotony and convey the amplitude of America, the "widely varying emotions of its people," as Whitman had in *Leaves of Grass*.

One year later, Williams was immersed in the research for *Paterson*— "Thrilling material I'm digging up every day," he reports to Laughlin. In one sentence he issues a wildly optimistic bulletin that he will soon have a section ready for viewing, only to concede sheepishly that with his added medical duties owing to the war and his chronic revisions he needed more time to polish the manuscript. By 1944 he was satisfied he had solved the formal problem that most plagued him: how to unify the disparate parts. In 1945, while feeling confident enough to show Book 1 to Laughlin, Williams still wielded a red pencil on his text, cutting lines and words and moving pieces around. He had devised an efficient adaptive method: by dividing each book into three sections, he could roam freely, within a lightly delimited structure, from stanza to stanza, landing on a theme, like a bee on a flower extracting pollen, unhurriedly meditating on a similar theme in an adjacent section, or veering off to plumb an entirely different topic. Motion, a variant of measure and rhythm, had been assigned an important role in his experimental poems of the 1920s. Now it gained new prominence and saliency. Movement was manifest in the maximum ease with which Williams glided from quatrains to quintains to free verse to tercets; in the artful distribution of line lengths; in his handling of rhythm, alternately stately, staccato, or propulsive, as in this beautiful passage where the water of the Great Falls eddies and drives forward until it plunges to a percussive climax on the rocks below:

> they leap to the conclusion and
> fall, fall in air! As if
> floating, relieved of their weight,
> split apart, ribbons; dazed, drunk
> with the catastrophe of the descent
> floating unsupported
> to hit the rocks: to a thunder;
> as if lightning had struck

Williams could not sustain the verse at this high level throughout *Paterson*. When narrative is a secondary feature, especially in a long poem, it is inevitable for inspiration to flag as the imagination steps out for a breather and stasis sets in. (Even *The Iliad* has its longueurs.) Williams did not pretend otherwise. The guidelines he laid out in the epigraph— "by multiplication a reduction to one; a taking up of slack; a dispersal and a metamorphosis"—had not been easy to execute, as the tolling of the words "roll up" suggests. And although each book has its distinctive character and thematic preoccupations, never severed entirely from the overarching structure, Williams worried that he had not soldered the parts into a satisfactory whole. Some critics felt he had failed at this. Although reviewers were almost unanimous in their praise of Books 1 and 2, negative comments increased as the other books appeared, the vast majority directed against the poem's organization, which was deemed ragged and unruly. Williams always shared these doubts. Searching for the "deathless song," "the radiant gist," "perfect form" or at least its approximation, and a voice that would articulate an "unfaltering language," in Book 3 Williams severely criticizes himself, "Give up the shilly- / shally of art"; you are "a poet (ridded) from Paradise."

In general, two chief reservations were raised about *Paterson*'s fissures. The first has to do with Mr. Paterson, whom Williams conceived as a crucial figure embodying the modern city and the mind of modern man. But the poet forgets about him for long stretches of the poem and never endows him with a recognizable voice: the *Pater* is pushed aside by his *son* William. Mr. Paterson ends up a fanciful stage prop of a concept to raise the curtain on the poem, a statue erected to honor a hometown hero, like the bust of a Roman emperor in the Capitol.

> Eternally asleep,
> His dreams walk about the city where he persists
> Incognito. Butterflies settle on his stone ear.
> Immortal he neither moves nor rouses and is seldom
> Seen, though he breathes and the subtleties of his
> Machinations
> Drawing their substance from the noise of the pouring
> River
> Animate a thousand automatons.

A more profound question raised by skeptical critics of *Paterson*—Marjorie Perloff, for example—is whether Paterson, a New Jersey manufacturing city in steep economic decline and never an important cultural or historical force, could bear the weight Williams put on it as the poem's unifying symbol and backbone. Perloff argues that it does so only spasmodically, and then mainly in the prose extracts. Anticipating this objection, Williams had begged to differ. In 1951, peeved by criticism of his idea that "a man is a city" and Paterson a legitimate proxy to represent it, a defensive Williams twice explained why he chose Paterson as his "reality." In a brief preface to Book 4, he noted that he "knew it [the city] in its most intimate details" and that it had a "definite history associated with the beginnings of the United States." New York's sheer size, its masses of immigrants crowded into tenements, its tumultuous street life, its contrast of ostentatious wealth and dire poverty, its restaurants, theaters, and opera houses, and its financial markets and corporate headquarters were much too vast and complex to sit for a portrait of the local. "It was far out of my perspective," he commented in the last chapter of his *Autobiography*. "I wanted, if I was to write in a larger way than of birds and flowers, to write about the people close about me: to know, in detail, minutely what I was talking about—to the whites of their eyes, to their very smells." Paterson was "large enough to embody the whole knowable world about me." He could trace memories of the city back to boyhood adventures hiking Garret Mountain and swimming in its ponds; to his years as attending physician in nearby Passaic Hospital, where he had taken care of and befriended many of the women who called Paterson home; he had testified in the courthouse and studied Paterson's history from the Dutch founders to the arrival of new ethnic groups. Whitman may have loved the kaleidoscopic variety and accelerated pulse of Manhattan and seen it as the omphalos of American urban life—he began his writing career as a journalist and felt comfortable hobnobbing with bus drivers and bartenders, listening to oratorios in churches, observing parades and politicians, poking his nose into opium dens and brothels in high-crime neighborhoods and dives on the waterfront piers—but to master its full history, Williams knew he would have to spend years rummaging in a vast archive of dog-eared newspapers, books, artworks, police and census reports. He simply lacked the time to invest in such a gargantuan project. Although Paterson's past required study and research, its history was relatively finite and offered a sturdy template of the local.

The Passaic Falls, central to the poem, did in one brief moment incite Alexander Hamilton to envision Paterson as a future industrial hub and an engine of financial growth, in which a young and brash America would become a major player in international trade. Williams had portrayed Hamilton in the Aaron Burr chapter of *In the American Grain* as a calculating scoundrel; in Book 2 of *Paterson*, he inserts several brief paragraphs about Hamilton's maneuverings to get the federal government to assume the debt and create the Federal Reserve System, thereby giving it, rather than the states, monopoly power to issue money and charge high interest rates: a boon for bankers. Again Hamilton is cast as a stock villain who, in addition to being a pioneer of fiscal policy favoring the rich, viewed the people as a "great beast."

During the Civil War, Paterson manufactured uniforms for the Union army, but the city never attracted the cocky entrepreneurs Hamilton envisioned. The engine of growth rushed westward, stranding the small city in a capitalist backwater. In 1913 it was the scene of a long, bloody strike by the Hatters' Union. Veteran radical orators such as Emma Goldman, Elizabeth Gurley Flynn, and Big Bill Haywood spoke at rallies, and a famous pageant was held at Madison Square Garden to drum up support for the workers' cause, but the strike failed. It was Paterson's last major moment in the national limelight. The Depression accelerated the city's downward spiral, and it has now become a symbol of urban decay and intractable poverty.

The prose extracts in *Paterson*, an informal photo-journalistic scrapbook, cover almost two centuries of local social history. Like a reporter with a nose for the unusual, Williams relates anecdotes about Paterson and neighboring towns, unearthed in yellowed newspapers and in antiquarian or public files of local historical societies. Many small towns such as Rutherford harbored sons and daughters who, like Williams, had lived most of their lives in the place where they were born and who turned themselves into experts on local legends, geography, architecture, religious and political preferences, schools. Self-trained historians, they were equally knowledgeable about the picturesque gables of the town millionaire's mansion and the amount of money he spent importing granite from an Italian quarry, the rickety shacks of the poor, the churches, ornate and plain, and the garden of exotic orchids. Encyclopedias of fact, they seemed on a first-name basis with every inhabitant of the town graveyard and privy to their secrets, founts of insight about the strutting swindler, the browbeating husband, and the town drunk. They rattled off the dates the post office and the first movie theater were built, the mayor was indicted for corruption, and two respectable businessmen were caught fleeing their mistresses' bedrooms. (One banker was shot dead by a policeman who mistook the man for a burglar, an ambrosial feast of scandal for gossipers and moralists alike). Sometimes Williams quoted his sources verbatim, editing them lightly or extensively, or fabricated and embellished legends, his skills as a short story writer aiding him to render them colorful and engaging.

The topics of these prose passages vary from the lurid accounts of crimes that readers of tabloid newspapers devour—feuds leading to assault, the sadistic murder of two Native Americans falsely accused of killing three pigs, flimflam schemes, domestic quarrels that take a nasty turn—to human interest stories that are comic (police chasing a mink) or end sadly, such as that of the newly married Sarah Cummings, who, while standing on a platform gazing at the "beautiful, wild, and romantic scenery" of the Falls, mysteriously plunges to her death, her distraught husband restrained from jumping after her by a young man. This grim tale is juxtaposed with the circus atmosphere and holiday spirit of a day when a large throng turns out to watch a "clumsy bridge being pulled into position." When a pin came loose and dropped into the water below, Sam Patch, a local character thought to be crazy, daringly leaps into the water, retrieves the pin, and saves the bridge from collapsing. The episode is a memorable spectacle and "a great day for old Paterson," the narrator says. Patch's jump makes him into an instant celebrity and launches his career as daredevil. A shrewd showman, he tours the West accompanied by a fox and a bear; his exploits always draw crowds and notoriety. (This is Paul Bunyan territory.) Raising the ante, Patch announces he "would leap 125 feet from the falls of the Genesee River on November 13, 1829." (Williams is careful to fix the date of the miscellaneous events he inserts in the prose.) Having survived a practice leap, Patch makes a short speech, then jumps and disappears. The spellbound crowd watches, silent and appalled. Williams completes the tale: the body wasn't recovered until the following spring, when it was "found frozen in an ice-cake." Anecdotes like this anchor the poem and its lyrical flights in the everyday, linking the lives and hopes of the citizens of Paterson in 1746 with those of 1946:

> . . . a mass of detail
> to interrelate on a new ground, difficultly;
> an assonance, a homologue
>
>   triply piled
> pulling the disparate together to clarify
> and compress

The prose takes a variety of other forms in *Paterson*, including extensive quotations from his literary correspondents, both famous (such as Allen Ginsberg and Edward Dahlberg) and obscure (such as Alvin Turner and Marcia Nardi). The letters are usually juxtaposed with passages of verse and, in an odd and somewhat perverse choice, they often attack Williams for personal or poetic offenses. As one example, consider the following analogy:

A man like a city and a woman like a flower

Who are in love. Two women. Three women.
Innumerable women, each like a flower.

　　　　　　　　　　　　　　　　　　But

Only one man—like a city.

Williams follows this stanza with the first of several furious letters from Marcia Nardi, whose poetry he had praised, and persuaded a reluctant Laughlin to publish in the New Directions annual anthology. Many women might take umbrage at Williams for what seems an assertion of male superiority in these lines: the man is singular, the women are plural and alike, even if they resemble a nosegay of flowers. The lavish space accorded the equation man equals city, separated from the first three lines, reinforces this disproportion. Williams himself must have realized the chauvinistic implications of his metaphor, for in a strange act of self-flagellation, most likely connected to remorse over the infidelities that blemished his relationship with Floss, he quotes at length Nardi's outraged condemnation of him for lacking the imagination "to fully understand the maladjustment and impotencies of a woman in my position." She accuses him of being "sheltered from life in the raw by the glass-walled conditions of [his] own safe life," words very close to the Baroness's when she ridiculed him as a timid bourgeois man. A similar charge is echoed in a letter from Dahlberg: "With you the book is one thing, and the man who wrote it another."

While it is true that Williams's inner life and his actions in the world were often in conflict, this discord made him particularly sensitive to Nardi's misery and her sense of herself as an outsider punished for not acting the "standardized" female role. Having himself struggled to find "some ways and means of leading a writer's life," he could certainly empathize with her—he had encouraged her poetic efforts and welcomed her into his home—but her expectations of his help and involvement far exceeded his own. In the grip of an obsessive rage, and disillusioned by what she regrets as a misplaced trust in a surrogate father, Nardi poured out her grievances and reproaches in a torrent of splenetic letters. For a while, Williams absorbed her attacks, but ultimately he cut off the embroiled correspondence: he could not be the hero she wanted to rescue her from her emotional prison, where she was "dying of loneliness."

Elizabeth Bishop, a connoisseur of solitude, took Nardi's side. "People who haven't experienced absolute loneliness for long stretches of time can never sympathize with it at all," she told Robert Lowell. She thought that printing the letters was "mean" of Williams. Lowell had a contrary view of them:

> I think of their effectiveness in two ways 1) so terrifyingly and typically real, and yet I don't think I'd want to read many of them straight—too monotonous, pathological. Yet in the poem they are placed and not pathological, the agony is absorbed. 2) Aren't they really hardest on Williams himself (Paterson)[,] a damning of his insensitivity[?] She's mad, but he, like Aeneas[,] can't handle her and shows up badly. I think that's their purpose in the poem. Paterson has been like water to me, and judgment may be subjective. But doesn't true criticism come that way—the only way to penetrate an author—then after a while intuition becomes objective.

Although Williams's inclusion of the letters may have been dictated by unconscious motives and tinged with guilt and masochism, as a poet, his instincts were shrewd, and James Laughlin is no doubt right that in a poem dominated by masculine voices, Nardi's female voice, strident as it is at times, functions as a necessary counterweight.

In 1948, with the first two books of Paterson out in the world, an exasperated Williams was still fending off Wallace Stevens's old criticism that he "resorts to the antipoetic as a heightening device." In a letter to Parker Tyler, he refutes the charge at length:

> All the prose [in Paterson], including the tail which would have liked to have wagged the dog, has primarily the purpose of giving a metrical meaning to or of emphasizing a metrical continuity be-

tween all word use. It is not an antipoetic device, the repeating of which piece of miscalculation makes me want to puke. It is that prose and verse are both writing, both a matter of the words and an interrelation between words for the purpose of exposition, or other better defined purpose of the art. Please do not stress other "meanings." I want to say that prose and verse are to me the same thing, that verse (as in Chaucer's tales) belongs with prose, as the poet belongs with "Mine-host," who says in so many words to Chaucer, "Namoor, all that rhyming is not worth a toord." Poetry does not have to be kept away from prose as Mr. Eliot might insist, it goes along with prose and, companionably, by itself, without aid or excuse or need for separation or bolstering, shows itself by itself for what it is. It belongs there, in the gutter. Not anywhere else or wherever it is, it is the same: the poem.

Robert Lowell praised the undertaking, calling it "the best poetry by an American, I'd say, after four readings," and Randall Jarrell was similarly enthusiastic: "a reader has to be determinedly insensitive to modern poetry not to see that it [*Paterson*, part 1] has an extraordinary range and reality, a clear rightness that sometimes approaches perfection." Despite such tributes from the literary luminaries of his time, Williams assessed his work gloomily: "I look at what I have done, with Paterson, for instance, and tho at times I am impressed, at other times I find little to praise in my attempts. Laid beside the vigor of some of Pound's cantos, not only the vigor but the sensitiveness to the life in a thousand phases, I feel like a boor, a lout, a synthetic artist." It was a shame that Lowell hadn't forwarded to Williams his astute judgment of "Ezry's" epic: "I've just finished reading all the published *Cantos*—the most self-indulgent long poem in English, and what wasted grace! Someone ought to do a fifty page book of selections." That might have lifted his spirits.

2.

At its best, Williams's poetic language in *Paterson* is resourceful, protean, alternately dense and translucent. In Book 1, he uses typography, white space, and punctuation inventively "to float free, as unrestrained as / The ideas the words were stating." He has at his disposal a repertory of styles. A passage of lyrical description of rocks or "the blue-flowered / pickerel-weed" may be followed by snippets of vulgar slang, dialect, or clever wordplay, such as near-malapropisms: "The how (the howl)," "in our ear (arrears)." Like many poets, Williams went through periods when he loathed his lines as stale as a "whale's breath," grumbling that his meters stuttered, and admitting that his effort "to find one phrase that will / lie married beside another for delight" "seems beyond attainment." But in the first two books of *Paterson* and sporadically in the other three books, because he does not shackle his verse to one meter, one stanzaic form, or one or two syntactic patterns, and the center moves in step with the changing rhythms of his thoughts, the poem is emotionally vibrant, confirming his conviction that structural asymmetry is at least as aesthetically pleasing as neatly engineered design.

At the end of Book 1, he cites a passage from John Addington Symonds's *Studies of the Greek Poets*, in which he found an early prototype of what he was angling for: meters that "communicated a curious crustiness to the style" and where even the iambs, previously banished as "lame or "limping," proved suitable for modernist "prose and common speech." The Greeks, Symonds pointed out, recognized "the harmony which subsists between crabbed verses and the distorted subjects with which they dealt." For those sections of *Paterson* that burlesqued "deformed morality," this ancient Greek prosodic novelty proved a valuable stylistic asset; for lyric moments or an interrupted story, invention and improvisation were the poet's chosen instruments:

> Without invention nothing is well spaced,
> unless the mind change, unless
> the stars are new measured, according
> to their relative positions, the
> line will not change, the necessity
> will not matriculate: unless there is
> a new mind there cannot be a new
> line, the old will go on
> repeating itself with recurring
> deadlines: without invention
> nothing lies under the witch-hazel
> bush, the alder does not grow from among

the hummocks margining the all
but spent channel of the old swale,
The small foot-prints
of the mice under the overhanging
tufts of the bunch-grass will not appear:
without invention the line
will never again take on its ancient
divisions when the word, a supple word,
lived in it, crumbled now to chalk.

The urgency of Williams's warning is underscored by the repetition of the words "without" and "unless," and by his assured handling of line, enjambment, sound, punctuation and cadence (the moving colons), and "supple" words. There are no dead lines in the passage.

While he dwells now and again on his own poetic shortcomings, what most disturbs Williams in Book 1 and in all of *Paterson* is the debasement and insidious corruption of the American language. That theme, so central to his life as a poet, lies at the heart of *Paterson*. Stunned by the evidence he has compiled for his poem, he cannot help shaking his head in dismay and alarm. The citizens walk and die "incommunicado," because the language is "divorced from their minds." ("Divorce" is Williams's code word for impoverished expression—syllables in a poem that do not lie down together amicably—for a serious, perhaps irreparable rift between husband and wife, a kind of sovereign lovelessness, and for the unjust division between classes.) He assigns blame for these cleavages evenhandedly: he wittily puts down his old bugbear, the academic clerisy for being "spitted on fixed concepts like / roasting hogs"; the special interests that make the status quo profitable; the do-nothings, and "Minds beaten thin / by waste—among / the working-classes SOME sort / of breakdown / has occurred." The social pathology of 1923 described in "The pure products of America" has grown worse.

The overall mood of Book 1 is mournful and its rhythms disturbed, mirroring a deep distress in William's mind.

The thought returns: Why have I not
But for imagined beauty where there is none
Or none available, long since
Put myself deliberately in the way of death?

A philosophical despair, rather than a suicidal nihilism, seizes him: "My whole life / has hung too long upon a partial victory." He is not declaring his life or his poetry a failure, though; with a sharp pang two pages later, he admits that he envies the men "who could run off / toward the peripheries—to other centers, direct— / for clarity (if / they found it) / loveliness and / authority in the world—." His competitive spirit has not waned; he half defiantly notes that he is still in training to win the long-distance race, but acutely aware of his age (sixty-three), he grapples with the fact that his mind is more likely to "drink of desire" from the leaves of a tree "streaming with rain" than from his body, that "the magnificence of imagined delights" will be his compensation for the diminishment or loss of sexual pleasure.

The natural history of Paterson, especially the awesome Passaic Falls, offered some consolation and roused Williams's dramatic instincts: the wild scenery was a perfect setting for his poem, serving as stage, back-drop, and symbol. (Romantic poets and painters adored cataracts of water for their grandeur and sign of nature's power.) The park below the falls was a magnet for families; bums; courting couples; oddballs; the elderly sitting on a bench, lost in a daydream or nodding off; and children improvising games—a New Jersey version of Brueghel's famous paint-ing. In Book 2, subtitled *Sunday in the Park*, the poet strolls among the local populace—Williams called it an "incursion"—observing their quirks and gaucheries, eavesdropping on their conversations, their quarrels, their pleasure seeking, their sexual advances spurned or tolerated, their multiple voices and accents coming together, "assaulting the air gaily from all sides," like a polyphonic dissonance in an American chorale. His ears, sensitive antennae, pick up the multitude of voices and snatches of dialogue: harsh, flagrant, inveigling, repellent, "laughter wild, flagellant." His voice, like a soloist's, weaves contrapuntal lines to their speech. Yet in his role as contemplative voyeur, moving among the very people he previously de-picted fondly and with empathy, he has lost some of the ease and humor that governed his relations with them. He even once refers to them in Hamilton's derisive phrase as the "great beast."

The picnickers on this Sunday afternoon, of all ages, are scattered throughout the park, entertaining themselves in diverse ways: they eat and drink, sunbathe, squabble; a tweedy man combs out his collie's long hair; a young man strums the guitar while an old woman lifts her skirts and dances with abandon; one couple engages in bored lovemaking—"their pitiful thoughts do meet / in the flesh," Williams comments—while a second pair reenacts the ancient dance of desire, choreographed by Priapus and Aphrodite. They are not, however, "couriers to the ceremonial of love." That honor is reserved for birds. As the poet climbs the path to the summit, or takes a detour through fields of brambles, his eyes are alert to the nature around him—for instance, "a crow zigzags / with heavy wings before the wasp-thrusts / of smaller birds circling about him / that dive from above stabbing for his eyes" or a "flight of empurpled wings" plunge and disappear, but leave, livening the mind, "a flashing / of wings and a churring song." (This is Williams's homage to Wallace Stevens's "Sunday Morning.")

In section 2 of Book 2, Faitoute, one of Williams's guises and based on his Rutherford friend, the polymath David Lyle—the name suggests "did all," "made all," and possibly a fatuous fop—wanders to the base of the observation tower. The broken benches serve as a pew for a "paltry congregation" of curiosity seekers, women, children, and a dull orchestra of "cornet, clarinet, trombone," and portable organ. The minister, Klaus Ehrens, an old, bald German émigré, is dressed in shirtsleeves, not an ornate robe, but at the beginning of the service he becomes transfigured into an ecstatic or demented evangelist claiming to hear the voice of God; he preaches and gestures to the winds and the void. Williams does not savage Klaus as a religious charlatan; indeed, he likens the man's oratorical skills to "Beethoven getting a crescendo out of an / orchestra." The scene is theatrical and spooky: "The light / fondles" ["his prismed brow"], as if forming a halo above his head. Hypnotized by his own voice, laughing, haranguing, shouting, and whispering, Klaus delivers a rambling sermon on the text "Money is the root of all evil." His is a familiar immigrant story: lured by the myth that America's streets were paved with gold, Klaus amasses a fortune, but money does not make him happy. In a parody of "America the Beautiful," he changes the words to "America the golden! / with trick and money / damned." At first reluctant to heed the Lord's advice to give away all his money, he finally throws Mammon out of the Temple and wins, he says, the happiness that had eluded him. (Klaus is the antithesis of Billy Sunday, the charismatic preacher who drew large crowds and parlayed them into an impressive bank account.) Klaus's rant is both tedious and involving; he doesn't seem to care that few pay attention or that he will fail to convert even one person; he's compelled to speak, like the Ancient Mariner; his words take on the cadences of prayer and a prophet's admonishment of sinners. His sermon mostly stays within the bounds of Christian iconography—the crucified Christ, "the open tomb"—yet he also alludes to Governor John Altgeld of Illinois, who pardoned three of the anarchists charged in the Haymarket Bombing and wrote a book that argued that the poor were not given equal opportunities for a fair trial; Christ the son of Pericles; *femina practa*; and the amphioxus, a marine animal without brain or heart.

As the park shuts down in section 3, Faitoute/Williams grows cantankerous, railing at the debased status of poetry, its language consisting of "words without style," no syllable audible in the uproar of the falls; his "ears are toadstools," his voice "drowning under the Falls." He rejects Klaus as a false poet-Messiah, but "No poet has come," he keeps murmuring to himself. His vision is apocalyptic: "flowers uprooted," "trees dismembered," "women shallow," men inert. "Love is no comforter, rather a nail in the / skull." In this state of sundering, with the language "worn out," how can the poet be reconciled to his world? Curiously, early in the section, Williams inserts "The Descent," which is as close to emulating Eliot's "Ash Wednesday" as he ever got; a meditation on the possibility of renewal in the face of death that ends in muted despair.

3.

In the middle of Book 3, titled "The Library," Williams writes:

> It is dangerous to have written that which is badly written. A chance word, upon paper, may destroy the world. Watch carefully and erase, while the power is still yours, I say to myself, for all that is put down, once it escapes, may rot its way into a thousand minds, the corn become a black smut, and all libraries, of necessity, be burned to the ground as a consequence
>
> Only one answer: write carelessly so that nothing that is not green will survive.

These words come back to haunt him. When he made a similar remark in *Kora in Hell*, "Carelessness is a virtue akin to the stars," the maxim was valuable because, as an apprentice poet, he was attempting to loosen the shackles of derivative verse that held back his progress. At age sixty-six, however, in the middle of an arduous struggle to get his long poem right, "carelessness" sounds like a synonym for losing one's way. In Books 1 and 2, he balances a carefree spirit and a disciplined idiom. But in Book 3, which again uses walking as its primary structural device, his compass frequently fails him.

Faitoute/Williams wanders through the "useless streets" of Paterson, the roar of the nearby falls ringing in his ears. Foraging in "[o]ld / newspaper files," he culls miscellaneous items: a child immolated in a field, unable to crawl to safety; a boy and girl drowned in a canal; a woman lobbyist, a Paterson Cricket Club, and the art gallery of the "Castle," a prominent landmark in a city with a paucity of them, built by Catholina Lambert, an immigrant factory owner, for his wife, which was razed by the city because it allegedly had "no USE." (The autocratic Lambert was a fierce opponent of unions.) And throughout the section, Nature rampages as "cyclone, fire / and flood" turn New Jersey into hell. In 1902, a strong wind fans a fire that destroys the Paterson Library and much of the city; Williams searches for a "redeeming language by which a man's premature death might have been prevented."

Yet Williams's description of the fire that destroyed Paterson is scattershot, far from redemptive or even engrossing. Surprisingly, this dramatic incident is rendered clumsily, almost incoherently, its rhythms blocky and even boring, as in this passage:

> A drunkenness
> of flames. So be it. A bottle, mauled
> by the flames, belly-bent with laughter:
> yellow, green. So be it—of drunkenness
> survived, in guffaw of flame. All fire afire!
> So be it. Swallowing the fire. So be
> it. Torque to laughter by the fire,
> the very fire. So be it. Chortling at flames
> sucked in, a multiformity of laughter, a
> flaming gravity surpassing the sobriety of
> flames, a chastity of annihilation. Recreant,
> calling it good. Calling the fire good.
> So be it.

But the fire is not good and neither is Williams's language, which does not blaze or establish a forceful stylistic authority. The fate of a bottle "mauled" by the flames is of minimal interest; the vocabulary is a mishmash of repetitive or highfalutin words ("multiformity," "recreant," "torque"), and the conflagration seems like a bad joke. The effect is made more grotesque by the clipped, resigned voice that at intervals, like the ticking of doom, cries out, "So be it."

The ill wind that blows through the first part of the poem bears no relation to *ruach*, the Hebrew word for "wind" and "spirit," God's instrument of creation in Genesis. Williams ruminates on the power of books to lead readers' minds away from reality, deluding or enchanting them into believing that the wind they hear rising from the pages is an actual wind: *trompe l'oreille*. The "roar of books / from the wadded library oppresses" him, because the library is the repository of "[d]ead men's dreams" and a "sanctuary to our fears." Sometimes books give a brief respite from the unstoppable cascade of his thoughts, implicitly linked to the roar of the falls; sometimes the riverbed is arid and books "enfeeble the mind's intent." The library itself reeks of "stagnation and death" and, after a "surgery of the wits," something close to castration or lobotomy. For Williams, the only escape from this dilemma is to incorporate the stench into his poems, not to flee it. But if, as he believes,

> The province of the poem is the world.
> When the sun rises, it rises in the poem
> And when it sets darkness comes down
> And the poem is dark

it is too simple merely to repeat the old saw that "nine tenths of the problem / is to live," and that art must be forged out of that mottled experience. The relationship between the world and the poem is distractingly tenuous: language and metaphor obscure as often as they clarify, causing readers to scratch their heads or sneer, as when a man from Rutherford who knew Williams's father asks, "Geeze, Doc, I guess it's all right / but what the hell does it mean?"

In Book 4, Williams's control sags. Take the first section, "The Run to the Sea," subtitled without a pinch of irony, "AN IDYL." The love triangle consists of Corydon and Phyllis—stock figures borrowed from Edmund Spenser's *Shepheardes Calendar*—and Paterson, hospitalized with an unidentified malady. All the same, the old gent is still quite frisky and given to reading poems to his supremely uninterested Phyllis and pursuing her sexually. (The sex scenes are embarrassingly adolescent.) Mr. Paterson, the titular hero of Williams's poem, seems most concerned with whether Phyllis is a virgin: so, inappropriately, is the poet. Williams seems to be reenacting old unresolved fantasies about women, categorizing them as virgins or whores. At a time when we would expect his poems about sex and women to exhibit maturity, he regresses to puerile bantering.

At the opening of section 2, Williams recovers his equilibrium: he takes his young son William Eric to a lecture on atomic fission, hoping to rouse the boy's interest in science. (William Eric is enthralled.) But Williams maintains a peculiar ambivalence: he likens the doctors to "pigs, myself / among them!" and juxtaposes an intellectually probing Madame Curie with the evangelical preacher Billy Sunday inviting his listeners to be saved by Jesus ("splitting the atom of / bitterness") and then going to the counting house to finger his winnings. The fragments of verse devoted to Curie's domestic life and to her discoveries of "the valence of Uranium" are baffling. Williams cannot decide what to make of knowledge, which he terms a "contaminant," or of a man like Pierre Curie, who sacrifices his own scientific investigations to support his wife's, or of the riddle of women's nature:

> Woman is the weaker vessel, but
> The mind is neutral, a head linking
> Continents, brow and toe
>
> And will at best take out
> Its spate in mathematics
> Replacing murder
>
> Sappho vs Elektra!

Yet woman as the weaker sex is certainly not Williams's definitive point of view. In the *Autobiography*, published the same year as *Paterson IV*, it is the husbands, "the technical morons of the tribe," whom he rounds on; women, however enigmatic they remain to him, are the stronger, more integrated, and fascinating sex. But it is typical of Williams's jumbled method in Book 4 that he changes topics on a whim. He drops the matter of women and takes up the question of money at tedious length.

What invigorates this section is the brash, chatty letter from Allen Ginsberg, introducing himself to Williams as another, albeit younger, unknown poet from Paterson and enclosing a sheaf of poems for Williams's comments. In gale-force prose that dispels the surrounding murk, Ginsberg presents himself as a hometown boy "speaking from the inside of the old wracked bum of Paterson" who dreams of becoming a great bard. He is both naive and adept at flattering the "courteous sage," while disavowing any claims to fully understanding Williams's handling of "cadences, line length, sometimes syntax," or "measure." Like Williams, he "envisions for himself some kind of new [poetic] speech," but knows that imitating the master will kill any chance of creating something original. Ginsberg shrewdly sensed that Williams would appreciate the fact that "at least one actual citizen of your community has inherited your experience in his struggle to love and know his own world-city, through your work, which is an accomplishment you almost cannot have hoped to achieve."

Taking his cue from a second Allen Ginsberg letter, in which the younger poet recounts walking the streets of Paterson's seediest neighborhood, near the Passaic River, inhabited by "negroes, gypsies, [and] an incoherent bartender," Williams takes the reader on a tour of historical Paterson, from village to city, with the guide pointing out landmarks—a tavern sign of George Washington, lovely gardens, a bridge General Lafayette crossed over, old houses, churches, and commercial buildings (a nail factory). This history is no idyll. Both verse and prose narrate tales of vicious murders, "inhuman butchery" that leaves corpses strewn on Paterson's mean streets and on the sands of Iwo Jima. Then, in a kind of nod to Whitman's "Out of the Cradle Endlessly Rocking," the poem segues into a sustained rapturous personification of death, *Thalassa*, ending with a squib describing an 1850 public hanging and these lines:

> This is the blast
> The eternal close
> The spiral
> The final somersault
>   The end.

Which read like a premonition of his own death.

4.

In his *Autobiography*, Williams recalls an encounter with a whore in Seville (the year was 1909), who beckoned to him to go with her. Though tempted, he hesitated and then spurned the offer. His comment reveals his fantasy and his conflict: "Had I had the nerve or insanity to follow the little whore who waved her buttocks at me near the plaza that evening, I don't know where I might not have landed in this world or out of it. But I didn't, and so I am a writer." He was susceptible to the perfume the whores dabbed on their skin, finding it erotically intoxicating, but some residue of Puritanism inhibited him from acting on his desire. In Book 5 of *Paterson*, Williams reprints a typescript that the novelist-poet Gilbert Sorrentino sent him called "Bordertown," which tells of the young man mustering the "nerve" to do what Williams had shied away from. Yet in describing the Babel of sounds, the stench, the drunkenness, the crass haggling over price, Sorrentino equates the virgin and the whore: "see a smooth faced girl against a door, all white . . . snow, the virgin, O bride." Here are purity and filth conflated, as Williams had done in his mind and transformed into art, as Toulouse-Lautrec, who lived in a brothel and to whom Book 5 is dedicated, had done in his paintings. It's not surprising that old man Williams, his body deteriorating, would call Sorrentino's story a "knockout" or that, in *Paterson*, he directs his surrogate to "keep your pecker up / whatever the detail [*sic*]?"

Book 5, 1958, is written in a valedictory tone forbidding mourning. By this time, Williams's numerous strokes and his battle with cancer had left him an attenuated shadow of his former self. The poems of *The Desert Music*, *Journey to Love*, and *Pictures from Brueghel*, composed during his last ten to twelve years, were of moderate length and did not require the elaborate counterpoint demanded by *Paterson*. Williams knows that "[t]he eternal close" and "[t]he final somersault" are near, but he does not cower at the prospect of death or rail at the faulty workings of his aging body or at memory, which he likens to the mind of a rebellious eagle; instead, he takes pleasure in all the regal and mundane necessities that gave his life meaning: "the song of the fox sparrow" outside his window, the flowers that grew in his Rutherford garden and blossomed (and withered) in his poems (he never tired of naming them: hepatica, columbine, daisy, "myrtle, dark and light / and calendula"), or those that were sewn into the *Unicorn Tapestries* and countless paintings of the Old Masters.

What is finally most solacing to Williams, and what keeps Book 5 stable amid its many mood swings, is his love of art and of painters who had the supreme gift: an imagination that permitted them to depict reality in its staggering variety, whether Bosch's "congeries of tortured souls and devils / who prey on them / fish / swallowing / their own entrails" or Brueghel the Elder's *Nativity*, a painting that does not feature an idealized, pretty version of the Madonna, Child, and Magi, but "the unkempt straggling / hair of the old man in the / middle, his sagging lips," and "the soldiers' ragged clothes, / mouths open, / their knees and feet / broken from 30 years of / war, hard campaigns, their mouths / watering for the feast which / had been provided." Williams never claimed he belonged in the visionary company of such artists, but often enough, through the magic of his imagination, he transformed what he had seen of human bestiality, hopes crushed and resilient, into descriptions like this one from the Second World War:

> recalling the Jew
>   in the pit
>   among his fellows
> when the indifferent chap
>   with the machine gun
>   was spraying the heap
> he had not yet been hit
>   but smiled
> comforting his companions
>   comforting
>   his companions

The lines exemplify the Manichean split in human consciousness between the evil of the soldier spraying machine gun fire into the "heap" of innocent victims and the smiling Jew, on the verge of annihilation, comforting his companions, just as the line breaks seem to sever life and comfort from his fellow Jews. While the poem bears moral witness to the horrific reality of atrocities, it also preserves man's fragile hope for the ultimate triumph of the beleaguered human spirit. As Williams had written earlier:

> Through this hole
> at the bottom of the cavern

of death, the imagination
escapes intact.

After roaming stylistically far afield, at the end of *Paterson* he brings together the key elements whose interplay gives his long poem a semblance of coherence.

> We know nothing and can know nothing
> but
> the dance, to dance to a measure
> contrapuntally,
>   Satyrically, the tragic foot.

He mocks himself as a satyr, an old lecher, as in a satyr play, which featured buffoonery and lampooning of gods and myths; and since the satyrs were connected to the rites of Dionysus and therefore to Greek festivals at which tragedies were performed, the "tragic foot" accurately calibrated his tempestuous moods and cleverly insinuated the cloven hoof of a goatish temperament. And if, in his great age and affliction, he can no longer literally manage the uninhibited movements of a Dionysian revel, his words and ideas can still sometimes kick up their metaphorical heels. Gazing at Sappho and listening to her quiet, intense voice, he trembles and his tongue feels broken. He has come full circle to his early love of Keats. Sappho is his Grecian urn, and he has earned the right to say "Truth is beauty, beauty truth." Divided though he was throughout his life, like most of us, he remained a poet and a lover of language to his last breath.

In an interview with Mike Wallace, the TV host grills Williams about the meaning of a cryptic Cummings poem, along with a passage of his own work. Williams characteristically and lucidly replies: "I would say that poetry is language charged with emotion. It's words, rhythmically organized . . . A poem is a complete little universe. It exists separately. Any poem that has worth expresses the whole life of the poet. It gives a view of what the poet is." Does *Paterson* succeed in expressing Williams's "whole life"? Robert Lowell told Elizabeth Bishop that "the first two books [of *Paterson*] cry out for the next two, and perhaps the proportion will come out right in the end." Whether the poem found that proportion remains controversial and heatedly debated. Lowell's encomium makes the best case that *"Paterson* is Whitman's America, grown pathetic and tragic, brutalized by inequality, disorganized by industrial chaos, and faced with annihilation. No poet has written of it with such a combination of brilliance, sympathy and experience, with such alertness and energy." One can agree with Lowell's characterization and still withhold full assent, mainly because Williams did not quite solve the problem of unifying the poem. Despite its brave and coruscating pages, it is the parts that lodge in one's mind, while the whole remains a beautiful torso with conspicuous defects.

Am I playing the carping critic too solemnly? If so, let the last word about *Paterson* go to Allen Ginsberg, who in an affectionate, manic letter to Williams brims over with a young man's plans for travel to the North Pole, where he will "write great white polar rhapsodies"; the satyr promises to return to Paterson and "splash in the Passaic again only with a body so naked and happy City Hall will have to call out the Riot Squad." (He's not Whitman's repressed twenty-ninth bather.) Did that image charm Williams and recall his poem "The Wanderer" with his less insouciant, ritual immersion in that same river? One cannot say for sure, but Williams, a satyr metamorphosed by time into a centaur, must have been electrified by Ginsberg's ribald dance, else why would he have placed the letter so prominently in Book 5? In 1958, battered by strokes, Williams did resemble "a big sad poppa," though he could not complain of a dearth of compassion. I suspect that the sentences that would have pleased him the most were these: "In any case Beauty is where I hang my hat. And reality. And America." Williams could not have put the rationale for his poetic career, and *Paterson*, more concisely and eloquently.

SIXTEEN

The Lion in Winter

When news of the armistice reached Rutherford in August 1945, Williams celebrated America's victory along with his countrymen. To his and Floss's relief, William Eric and Paul, both of whom had served in the navy in the Pacific, had returned home safely. Despite the backbreaking days and nights of toil that were the lot of doctors on the home front, Williams had borne his burdens with fortitude and grace, managing as ever to squeeze in time for writing verse. Book 1 of *Paterson* was almost ready for publication (it would appear in 1946). He was buoyed by the prospect of William Eric sharing the office at 9 Ridge Road and taking on half of the patient load, thereby freeing him to surrender himself to his ever-importunate duende. For his part, Paul seemed poised to start a successful business career. Williams was content to bask in the sunny moods of the normal. He had no reason to suspect that his health would soon deteriorate.

In May 1946, Williams entered Passaic General Hospital for a hernia repair operation. It proved a failure. "The bums who sewed up my hernia . . . didn't reckon on my prowess (so they say)," Williams reported to Laughlin, "with the result that the damned thing broke down and I was in a worse situation than before they operated on me. I got disgusted, decided I didn't want to go through the winter that way (with one hand in my right pants pocket holding my guts in)." So on December 13 the operation was redone at New York Hospital, where William Eric was interning and could monitor his father's progress. Thirteen days after his hospital "vacation," Williams was seeing patients again and spitting out his irritation at "dear, asinine ol' Ezra's" latest "guff" and "twaddle." A couple of months later, after reading Pound's *China Cantos*, he remarked to Laughlin that despite Pound's "musical 'intellect,'" "I'm afraid he never really grew up."

In February 1947, Williams was elected to head the medical board at Passaic General Hospital. In spite of doubts that he lacked the stamina to take on such a taxing job, he bowed to his colleagues' pressure and accepted the administrative post. His father had inculcated duty in his son as a supreme virtue, but even more important, Williams was loyal and grateful to the institution he had served with distinction for two decades; the work at the hospital "challenged my abilities and broadened my opportunities for helping the unfortunate and unhappy," he recalled in his *Autobiography*. It was unlikely that the Beautiful Thing would alight and reveal itself in an overheated conference room.

Williams did enjoy a glorious reprieve from these managerial tasks. In July, he, Floss, and her sister, Charlotte set out in his "old faithful 1940 Buick" on a cross-country trip whose itinerary took them to the Rockies and the desert Southwest. For a poet who had taken offense at Pound's gibe that he was ignorant of the real America, the trip was a chance to take in the majestic Rocky Mountains and the "storied rivers." The Southwest in particular—Indian pueblos, Spanish adobe churches, a visit in Taos with Frieda Lawrence—made a lasting imprint on his imagination. To cap off this memorable trip, he met Bob McAlmon in Taos, a reunion that began to repair their long estrangement.

The grand tour rang up other firsts for Williams. He was a featured poet at the Writers' Workshop at the University of Utah in Salt Lake City, along with Allen Tate. Like his ally John Crowe Ransom, Tate was a formalist and classicist whose loyalties lay with T. S. Eliot; Williams feared that, in such company, he'd be judged a Yahoo. Amusingly, before setting out, he armed himself against possible attack by reading George Saintsbury's *A History of English Prosody*, vowing not to be humiliated or viewed as an ignoramus. But at the conference, he got on well with Tate, who was an urbane conversationalist, and with his other colleagues on the summer faculty. Besides meeting with students to discuss their poems or stories, he was required to deliver a lecture. The talk was vintage Williams. He took care not to sound like a modernist vandal bent on defacing the poems of the past. Their perfections, he explained, are "like complex shells upon a shore. Men lived in these poems as surely as fish lived in the shells we find among the fossils of the past but they are not there now." The rules and forms that produced the lyric plenitude of Shakespeare, Donne, and Keats were exquisitely suited to the "social, economic world" of the England of their time. But they would hamper the free expression of realities unique to the America of 1947. So poets must respectfully overthrow venerable traditions: "Everything has to be broken down, not cynically, not without a sense of its old dignity, to get the essential, the formal unit in its purity." The revolution Williams wished to engineer must dismantle the old forms and put in their place "A NEW MEASURE CONSONANT WITH OUR DAY." While praising Whitman for "breaking down the old forms" and "abandoning all the staid usages of writing a poem," Williams distances himself from the idea of free verse: "verse is measure— that is the only permissible term." Since the line is the basic unit of measure, to invent poets have, as the word "radical" intimates, to return to the root, return to the simpler constructive elements of the line—to shake free from the constrictions that have grown into the line and its stanzaic combinations—and to permit freer (thought-governed) association of the elements. Poets, like explorers "nosing along a mysterious coastline" who have not yet broached the continent," are driven by the adventure of "opening new realms of feeling unknown to the [practitioners of] the earlier languages." The prospect of "conceiving the world anew" by redesigning poems to represent contemporary realities was exhilarating. At the same time, Williams made it clear that these were treacherous currents to navigate, that the whole enterprise might end in ignominious failure. Invention was a notoriously fickle demiurge.

The activity and excitements of his poetic life, added to the burdens of his administrative post at the hospital, proved overwhelming for him now at age sixty-five. On a frigid winter night in early January 1948, a frazzled Williams got into his car and drove it straight into a snowbank. After borrowing a shovel from the hospital, he had begun to dig his car out when he felt chest pains and recognized the symptoms of a heart attack. Somehow he managed to drive home safely. The next morning, he called in a cardiac specialist, Dr. Gold, who confirmed Williams's diagnosis and confined him to bed rest for several weeks. Williams teased Floss, who was present at the examination, by asking Dr. Gold if sexual intercourse was allowed during convalescence. The cardiologist replied, deadpan, that he should put a "little nitroglycerin tablet under your tongue and do what you wish."

Williams, however, was sicker than he cared to admit: it was more

than six weeks before he could come downstairs to join the family for dinner. When he wrote about his injured heart, he fell into a jocular tone, as
if ribaldry might deflect the grim warning that death lay ready to strike at
any time. To Robert Lowell he spoke of his "angina (not vagina) pectoris";
to Fred Miller, a friend and collaborator on *Man Orchid*, a novel about
jazz, he mimicked the argot of James Cagney: "They got me, kid, they
got me! Right in the pump! But I fooled 'em, I didn't croak. So what, huh?
Now dey got to do it again. And dis time I'll beat 'em to de punch." For
the pediatric nurses at Passaic General who, worried about "lovable Uncle Billy's" condition, sent him cards, a bathrobe, and a razor (for his "close
shave," he quipped), he played the role of old lecher, confiding that his
bedside reading of Freud's *The Interpretation of Dreams* had stirred up
"such lovely dirty dreams." Once the crisis passed, Floss whisked Williams away at the end of March to Atlantic City for ten days of salt air,
ocean views, and rest.

Williams used his long period of recuperation to read voraciously. Like
his early idol Keats, he was entranced by Chapman's translation of *The
Iliad*, and he dipped into Louis Untermeyer's *Anthology of British and
American Poetry*. Carlo Levi's *Christ Stopped at Eboli*, Santayana's *The
Last Puritan*, and a collection of Frank O'Connor's short stories made up
an eclectic trio of fiction. Edmund Wilson's classic study of modernism,
Axel's Castle, furnished ideas for the talk that Theodore Roethke had invited him to deliver at the University of Washington in July, though Williams could not have enjoyed Wilson's praise of Eliot or his own absence
from Wilson's book. The mention of Eliot's name, for instance with regard
to his lecture on Milton at the Frick Collection in 1947, again brought out
the piss and vinegar in Williams. In a letter to Laughlin, Williams discussed his own diatribe "With Forced Fingers Rude," which appeared in
an obscure little magazine called *Four Pages*:

> What I said about Eliot has nothing to do with his inheritance of
> the King's old underwear but dates from his advice to us in this
> country that we may now read Milton without fear of damage to
> our testicles. Geez what a shit he has turned out to be—to the
> enhancement of his charm, I must confess[,] and drawing power
> among the American snots. Not that he isn't a sort of a good poet
> or a good poet of a sort but from the way they bend down to kiss
> the hem of his metaphorical garments—cerements, I was going to

say—you'd think he possessed the universal genius of a Saint Anthony or . instead [*sic*] of being a very frail sister indeed.

In a less personal vein, Williams found fault with W. H. Auden's *The
Age of Anxiety*. Writing to Babette Deutsch on May 25, he conceded that
the book was "impressive in the ability with which it is thought out and
performed," but he declared Auden's polished lines "dead" because they
lacked "invention." Williams was not glorifying himself at Auden's expense or merely taking potshots, since a rumble of self-deprecation can
be heard in his mixed assessment of his own *Paterson*. He plugged away
at his long poem, jotting down notes for *Paterson III* and the autobiography he contemplated starting; but, too tired to cope with the stress of serious composition, he shelved the projects temporarily.

His recuperation progressed slowly. Alternately fidgety and resigned,
Williams tried to pass the time deciding what to include in *Selected
Poems*. Poems had to be retrieved from periodicals and the Cummington
Press edition of *The Wedge*, and fresh copies had to be typed up. Worrying about a "lump" in his chest and symptoms of new angina attacks, he
nevertheless bantered with Laughlin about royalties, a French translation
of *In the American Grain*, and future publications. (He had written three
"decent" chapters for *The Build-up*, the last installment of the Stecher
trilogy.) The doctors had reassured him that despite his faulty ticker,
he had a future. His appetite for reading, at least, remained promiscuous.
He tackled Zukofsky's "path making" *Bottom: On Shakespeare*—recondite
prose by his old friend was good therapy—and Eric Bentley's study of
Shaw's plays.

By May, Williams was nearly back in full harness, his spirits lifted by
the news that he had been selected to share the Russell Loines Prize with
Allen Tate. This award and the one thousand dollars that went with it was
especially pleasing because in one corner of his mind he still believed
that the Solons who decided reputation viewed him as a minor poet. In
reality, excursions to New York to meet socially with Auden and to conduct business with members of the National Institute of Arts and Letters
proved that the poetry community deemed him one of their own. Robert
Lowell, who was finishing up a term as poetry consultant to the Library
of Congress, managed to get Williams named his successor. On January 29, 1949, an elated Williams wrote to Lowell, provisionally accepting
the position, but he later changed his mind; still frail from his heart attack,

he couldn't muster the enthusiasm or energy to work full-time in Washington at a mostly ceremonial job.

Almost a year later, he was elected, without opposition, to be a fellow of the Library of Congress. What should have been sheer pleasure was spoiled for him by the fact that his old nemesis T. S. Eliot was also made a fellow. So peeved was Williams that he threatened to resign his position. In his eyes, Eliot had renounced his citizenship in American letters and become an Englishman in the mold of John Bull and Colonel Blimp, thus forfeiting his eligibility. Only the tactful intervention of Tate persuaded Williams not to resign.

The autumn of 1949 brought sorrow and joy to the Williams household. On October 7, Williams's remarkable mother died. He tried to sort out his contradictory feelings about her, but her knack for concealment, for mystery, baffled him. What, for example, had been her motive in hiding the medals she had won at the École des Beaux-Arts in 1877–1879? Writing to Helen Russell, a student at the University of Washington, Williams, no stranger to secrets, bursts out in exasperation: "What the devil are we alive for? To hide ourselves? When I think of how little my own mother ever said to me of herself and her ambitions I grind my teeth in fury. There is no sense to it. It is one of the cardinal sins that we do not break bounds one way or another and come out of our prehistoric caves. It's indecent and silly besides . . ." The image of Elena as a willful troglodyte is amusing but not far-fetched, since she successfully kept aspects of her self and her past under lock and key, and passed on some of that "indecent" repression to her oldest son. (As we've seen, the habit of concealment ran in the family: Grandmother Wellcome and William George were adept at it, too.) Still, given his knowledge of Elena's character, it is odd that he would "grind his teeth in fury."

More discoveries followed. Williams thought Elena had died at 93, but in 1956 a friend found a baptismal certificate in Mayaguez that disclosed to her astonished son that his blind and deaf mother had reached the ripe age of 102. Rummaging in her trunk, he found a missal that was earmarked for him. Into that fine, if commonplace, heirloom, Elena had folded a letter that revealed that two years before she married William George, she'd rejected a Frenchman's proposal. Williams could only wonder what other gaps in the biographical record would come to light. He had been his bedridden mother's devoted Boswell, encouraging her to tell stories of her childhood and youth. Her character, however, still eluded and frustrated him.

Mourning was briefly set aside so that the family could celebrate William Eric's marriage to Daphne Spence on November 19, but that joy was soon cut short because Floss's mother died in a nursing home on December 20. Williams had never liked Ma Herman, her grating, bossy manner and her nouveau-riche ostentation especially irking him.

Despite the honors raining on him, Williams was sullen. When *Time* magazine decided to run a feature story about him, they insisted on photographing him in a doctor's white lab coat holding a baby, borrowed on the spot from William Eric's office. Williams griped to Charles Abbott, a librarian at the state university in Buffalo, "I must be thrilled! Smile! Contort myself into favorable attitudes entirely strange to me and act the ass generally—for publicity's stake (which I am forced to treasure tho I despise it) and cash and leisure." Given Williams's hunger for approbation, his response to these honors and the "thuggish" photographer's contrived poses seems excessive. Although he shared Whitman's belief, expressed in the last sentence of the "Preface to the 1855 Edition of *Leaves of Grass*," that "the proof of a poet is that his country absorbs him as affectionately as he has absorbed it," he did not misjudge the likely effects of this wave of publicity. Over four decades, he had battled his compatriots' indifference to poetry, so why should he expect popularity now? He could be excused for regarding the belated prizes and attention as too many too late. In fact, they put him in a foul, belligerent mood, "a small hell." What he needed, he spat out, was enough money to allow him to climb to his attic retreat and finish *Paterson*. Poetry paid no dividends. At most it added a paltry few hundreds of dollars of pocket money to his already reduced income. How would he face the expenses of old age?

Financial worries brought to the surface dormant grievances that led to a near breach of his friendship with James Laughlin. Talking about their falling-out decades afterward still pained Laughlin, whose face grew red with a fury directed less at Williams for a "magnificent kick in the teeth" than at the "venomous snake" David McDowell, who had worked as an editor at New Directions and had stolen the naive poet away by promising lucrative royalties. (They never materialized.) Laughlin took Bill's decision to sign a three-book contract with Random House very hard. It was, he said, a shocking act of disloyalty. Were they not comrades in arms in a war against poetic mediocrity? Hadn't he offered Bill $250 a month for life as an advance against royalties, which in 1950 was a handsome sum? Shortsightedly, Williams had refused the offer. Poets often complained that instead of focusing on sales and finding new outlets for their books, Laughlin ran away like a playboy to the ski slopes in Alta or Gstaad. Pound once sent his publisher a cynical postcard inquiring "ARE YOU DOING ANYTHING? Of course, if you spend 3/4 of your time sliding down ice-cream cones on a tin tea-tray," nobody will be minding the poetry store. Paul Williams further stoked the flames of his father's indignation by mentioning that no salesman from New Directions ever visited Abraham & Straus. (It's hard to imagine the department store's middle-class shoppers buying a Céline novel or a volume of Pound's *Malatesta Cantos*.) Though he felt betrayed by Williams's defection—the strain between them lasted ten years—Laughlin agreed, selflessly, to continue publishing *Paterson* and subsequent books of poetry. Bill, perhaps sheepish at having wronged his old friend, dedicated both *The Pink Church* and the *Collected Later Poems* to the man who had nurtured his poetry and reputation.

In 1951 and 1952, Williams suffered incapacitating strokes, what neurologists call insults to the brain. The first occurred on March 28, 1951, at home. Williams had been caught up in a maelstrom of work: keeping office hours, pushing himself to complete his *Autobiography*, giving a series of readings along the Northeast corridor from the New School to Yale to Wellesley College, including a benefit for the ailing Kenneth Patchen, a New Directions poet too poor to afford insurance. Such a schedule might have fazed a man half his age. The stroke sent Williams, in critical condition, to the intensive care unit at Passaic General Hospital. Floss reported to Laughlin that Bill had to remain in the hospital for three weeks and then take a "long rest"—a regimen he balked at. "The energy that burns in this guy is too much for one human to burn up! He's rarin' to go now—and is anything but a good patient. Thank God he's in the Hospital!—I'd go mad if he were at home. He resents the situation and tries to minimize it out of all proportion!—." After the worst danger passed and he could survey the wreckage that had nearly done him in, he would write Wallace Stevens that it "caught him by complete surprise," though in a telephone call from the hospital to the poet Theodore Weiss at Bard College, where Williams was supposed to preside at a tribute to Stevens, he stammered the word "hemorrhage" as the reason for his absence. Very likely the carotid artery to the brain had become occluded. The apoplectic stroke caused extensive damage. It "disabled my right side and knocked out my speech—for a time," he told Robert Lowell. His heart attack was scary, but a stroke was a dagger aimed at his creative life as a poet. If he could barely peck away at a typewriter or set down a line of verse shakily by hand, he would be condemned to a barren internal exile more terrible than Ovid's.

To his relief, he rapidly regained his mental faculties. He resumed editing his *Autobiography*, a charming, discursive backward glance that he described, imprecisely, as a "history of my books and what brought them on." His original working title, *Root, Branch & Flower*, more accurately captures his intention in composing a memoir. His childhood was a network of roots so important to him that he returned to it at the beginning of part 3, as if his faulty memory had left out key events and people and he needed to fill out the story of his formative years.

During this period of imposed convalescence, he managed to write only one poem of consequence, based upon events in 1950, a year of accolades and turning points: honorary degrees from Rutgers University and Bard College, a cascade of invitations to read his poems or give lectures. He may not have attracted the adulation and celebrity of Dylan Thomas, but he had reached a level of recognition that had eluded him for most of his long career. During that summer, he and Floss flew to Chicago and then boarded a train for Seattle, where, at the invitation of Theodore Roethke and the University of Washington, he was to speak publicly, read poems, and advise students in an informal tutorial. The work was exhausting and the pay hardly munificent, but the response of the students to him and to his poems was gratifying; he saw that he was far from being a fossil. After repeating this success at the University of Oregon, he and Floss journeyed south along the Pacific Coast, stopping over in San Francisco for dinner and stimulating talk with Kenneth Rexroth, another New Directions poet. In Los Angeles, they stayed with Charlotte and her son Eyvind Earle, and Williams read poems before a packed auditorium at UCLA. Then they boarded a train for El Paso and a last meeting with Bob McAlmon. In that drab southwestern city, a quarter of a century and light-years away from Paris, McAlmon worked for his two brothers and puttered with literary projects. To keep from abject poverty, he had been forced to sell first editions of the illustrious modernist books he had published in flush times. When Williams embraced his friend with great warmth at the train station, he saw at once, with a doctor's diagnostic acuity, that Bob was a shell of his former self, a casualty of the literary wars on two continents and of his own taciturn, bellicose personality. Although the mark of weariness was etched in Williams's face, too, by pluck and good fortune he had escaped a scrape with death and what at times seemed a doomed battle of attrition to defeat Pound's and Eliot's poetic practices.

One day during their reunion, the friends crossed into Juárez, Mexico, for a day of sightseeing, a mandatory ritual for gringos eager to sample the tastes and folkways of a somewhat tawdry, unprepossessing Spanish town. Juárez was no exotic or magisterial Tenochtitlán, yet the tourist's standard itinerary and the random impressions it generated imprinted themselves on Williams's imagination. A year later, he drew upon these memories to compose "The Desert Music," a long ruminative cantata with recitatives and snatches of dialogue punctuated by arias and set pieces: he referred to its theme and form as "the music of survival."

The poem rambles and halts, mirroring a mind for whom the rigors of linear narrative are temporarily out of reach. On a holiday from the strain of rebuilding the pathways and synapses in the brain that govern speech, Williams lets his language mutate from elevated diction to vulgar dance music, all transmogrified in the lurid light of a honky-tonk Mexican border town. He plays off the sublime "deep cello tones" of Pablo Casals against "the usual local / jing-ajing," a "lying music" that accompanies a middle-aged whore's striptease. Both leitmotifs affect Williams deeply and are woven into the poem's episodic narrative. Yet the poem is capacious enough to also include scrappy images, wifely gibes, reportage and gossip about the mayor of Juárez, who was reputed to skim off three thousand dollars a week as his share of profits from the town brothel, and cameos of American tourists, mostly Texans, whose vulgarity makes the reader wince. At other times, he seems to be writing a tourist's chatty letter home to his sons and daughters-in-law about picture-postcard scenes: a sandstorm ("Texas rain," it's called); the blur of noisy swallows overhead; the outstretched hands of importunate beggar children; a snapshot of a young Indian couple; colorful serapes; trees and flowers.

Because his stroke precipitated a crisis of confidence about his ability to continue writing poems, Williams inserts a series of urgent maxims, like therapeutic memos to himself, to retrieve from the slippage of memory basic tenets he has enunciated as far back as *Spring and All*: "Only the counted poem, to an exact measure: / to imitate, not to copy nature," "to get said what must be said." The very baldness and familiarity of this stitching together of skeins of thought seems to reassure Williams that, like the cook "working / absorbed, before a chopping block," he has not lost concentration or technique. This premise is immediately put to the test. As he and Floss and his friends (McAlmon and his brothers and their spouses) sit in a restaurant, dining on quail, a stranger accosts him: "So this is William Carlos Williams the poet," adding, "You seem quite normal. Can you tell me? Why / does one want to write a poem?" The man is oblivious that his intrusion is rude and unwelcome. On most occasions, Williams might have been flattered by the attention and, with good humor, tossed off a homey explanation, but wishing to get rid of the pest, he answers curtly, "Because it's there to be written." The stranger persists: "Oh. A matter of inspiration then?" "Of necessity," Williams replies. Dissatisfied with the poet's grudging response, the stranger goes on the attack once more: "Oh. But what sets it off?" Williams cuts off this exchange with a gnomic, and disturbing, utterance: "I am that he whose brains / Are scattered / aimlessly." In the aftermath of the stroke, he clearly feels that his brain—and perhaps his poems—lack coherence.

The first and last images of "The Desert Music" are of a "form / propped motionless" in the middle of the bridge between El Paso and Juárez. Even after close inspection, the party cannot agree on the sex or features of the crumpled figure: Is it a dead body, a drunk sleeping off a tequila binge, or a derelict, whose "inhuman shapelessness / knees hugged up into the belly" in the fetal position is frightening? This "sack of rags" is both real and a projection of Williams's post-stroke collapse. The imagination, however, is not prostrate: it can awaken the effigy to be a partner in an almost otherworldly dance, "following the insensate music." Williams's ear is preternaturally alert to the sounds around him and in his head; "insensate," however, is a curious adjective to modify music, since all its meanings are pejorative: lacking sense, sensibility, and sensation, inanimate, unconscious, foolish. What kind of poem can be composed from "insensate" music? This is the process "The Desert Music" seeks to uncover.

Williams's eye for registering the minutiae of the local did not desert him in Juárez. Like a handheld camera, it tracked and recorded commonplace items on sale in the Old Market ("—paper flowers (*para los santos*), baked, red-clay utensils, daubed / with blue silverware, / dried peppers, onions, print goods, children's clothing": the scrip of souvenir-hunting tourists everywhere. With the keenness of a photojournalist, he zeros in on a six-foot-tall Texas woman wrapped incongruously in a mink cape, a "middle-aged middle western couple on a bargain-hunting spree," Floss's pleasure at "the change of light," and "three half-grown girls, one of them eating / a pomegranate, laughing." A Mexican poet visiting Paterson might have been just as captivated and bemused by the northern city's majestic falls, folkways, tawdry merchandise, "exotic" residents, religiosity, and frenetic pace. Williams makes little effort to edit this material; nervous jump cuts alternate with moments of reflection, and the stop-and-go walking rhythms of the poem subside periodically into a relaxed cadence when the day-trippers stop in a bar to rest or drink an old-fashioned. Kenneth Burke's shrewd comment on Williams's poetic method is germane to this aspect of "The Desert Music": "You talk about one thing, leaving other unmentioned things flitting about the edges, to provide resonance."

The long passage describing the "worn-out trouper's" striptease affords a wonderful tour of Williams's magpie imagination in motion. Why he is fascinated and moved by her gyrations is a question he poses to himself. He is not snookered by the dull show (even the guitarist yawns), the tacky costume, the singer's off-pitch voice, or the "cold eyes" that, barren of passion, "perfunctorily moan." He knows her burlesque routines are ludicrously banal and mechanical—she is "heavy on her feet"—yet he is transfixed by the dancer who shakes her torso lewdly and exposes her breasts to a bald man sitting near the stage. Floss is irked that her husband gapes at the woman like a callow adolescent or old lecher and exclaims, "Wow!" and "Look at those breasts," and grins as if the dancer were Pavlova dancing Odile in *Swan Lake*. He even transforms her into an "Andromeda of the rocks," in whose "mockery of virtue / she becomes unaccountably virtuous." Like a bored critic, McAlmon or somebody else in Williams's group contemptuously dismisses "the expressionless ding dong" and "prattle about their souls and their loves," a judgment that echoes Williams's sarcastic put-down of Latin romance in "Adam." However cheap the scene depicted and Williams's unbuttoned pleasure in it, the experience raises unnerving conflicts in his mind about masculinity and sex in an aging body, and their effect on his sense of himself as a poet.

Out on the street, he interrogates himself, "Am I merely playing the poet? Do I merely invent / it out of whole cloth?" At all periods, Williams might admit or excoriate his flaws and limitations or worry that his imagination would abandon him, but he never debased his calling by adopting the role of poet as fop; indeed, he despised such affectation, whether in Maxwell Bodenheim's smug bohemian mannerisms or in H.D.'s conception of the poet as guardian of spiritual purity, which irked him as too bookish and ethereal, a misguided aesthetic religiosity. From *Kora in Hell* on, he had devised flexible, offbeat forms adapted from Dada and Cubism and given them a local habitation in his poems. Improvisation was theatrical play; it was not self-preening. Still, the paradox that gnawed at him in 1917—can the ersatz produce genuine art?—resurfaced:

> What in the form of an old whore in
> A cheap Mexico joint in Juarez, her bare
> Can wiggling crazily can be
> So refreshing to me, raise to my ear
> So sweet a tune, built of such slime?

Characteristically, he doesn't bother, even perfunctorily, to take a stab at solving the riddle. Instead, the poem segues to the bar area of a family restaurant, where he watches another dance, this time performed by two pairs of drunk Americans, the men dressed up as cowboys and their besotted "gals." Egged on by his "insatiable" partner to the shrill fifing of "Yipee!" one oversize Texan stumbles like a "lil doggie" to keep in step with her.

In the course of the day trip, Williams finds temporary relief from the "changeless, endless / inescapable and insistent music"—and from the burdens of being a poet—that haunts him. Food, drink, and good company were a sort of balm or distraction, but approaching the bridge to El Paso, he is ravished by the plangent melodies of Casals's cello playing a Bach suite, which momentarily renders him speechless. Catching sight of the fetal figure once more, he turns inward, almost hallucinating:

> There it sat
> in the projecting angle of the bridge flange
> as I stood aghast and looked at it—
> in the half-light! Shapeless or rather returned
> to its original shape, armless, legless,
> headless, packed like the pit of a fruit into
> that obscure corner—or
> a fish to swim against the stream—or

a child in the womb prepared to imitate life,
warding its life against
a birth of awful promise. The music
guards it, a mucus, a film that surrounds it,
a benumbing ink that stains the
sea of our minds—to hold us off—shed
of a shape close as it can get to no shape,
a music! a protecting music

In this dense, beautiful passage, the doctor and the poet merge. Williams tries to describe precisely what looks, in the "half-light," like a cadaver or an already dismembered body lying on a slab for an autopsy, or a *nature morte* object in an art sketching class. That the spectral figure, an effigy of death, terrifies Williams is evident in the slow-moving, deliberative syntax and the repetition of four words ending in "-less." In a quiet flurry of notes and images, he contemplates both his mortality and his poetry; the two are indissolubly fused in his mind. He does not panic. His poems have been "packed like the fruit into / [an] obscure corner" (he is not Eliot's Gerontion); he has swum with and against the currents of modernist fashion (the image evokes a salmon fighting to return home, spawn, and die); he has jotted down poems on prescription pads with the "benumbing ink that stains the / sea of our minds"; and as obstetrician and poet he knows that the child in the womb is protected by amniotic fluid, by permeable, filmy membranes, that the birth of an infant or a poem does not come easily. The arresting lines "warding its life against / a birth of awful promise" compress contradictory meanings: "to ward against" is an odd idiom, as if the child is struggling to avert or ward off its own birth, in order to avoid its inevitable journey to death. But "ward" also denotes to guard or protect. Confronting the inescapable destiny looming, that death will return him to the original state of nonbeing, he prays that poetry's "protective music" will comfort him. The oxymoron "awful promise" suggests an event awe-inspiring (potentially marvelous) and terrible (doom). But the shaping hand of imagination kneads shapeless matter into the life of a poem. Williams's crescendo of images in this passage belies any loss of poetic power. Although in "The Desert Music" his ear may succumb here and there to vernacular "jing-ajing," its most authentic idiom, unmistakably American, harks back in theme to the spiritual crises Wordsworth, Coleridge, and Keats explored in their poems.

Williams the doctor poet knows that death and birth march in tandem—he gazed upon both constantly, closing the eyes of a patient who died and gently putting drops into the eyes of a newborn.

All his insecurities, however, did not simply vanish. Hence the two-line outburst that follows, mawkish and defensive, is clumsy verse, however one varies the stress in each repetition: "I am a poet! I / Am. I am. I am a poet, I reaffirmed, ashamed" The lack of a closing period is apt punctuation. But despite the many infirmities and doubts that assailed Williams during his last years, they were a period not of decline but of ripeness.

"The Desert Music" was delivered as the Phi Beta Kappa poem at Harvard's 1951 commencement. According to Williams, it got a mixed reception: "From the faces of some (not all) of the faces on the platform," he joked to Lowell, "I think they must have fumigated Memorial Hall after I left. The student body was, on the other hand, delighted and showed it by their tumultuous applause after I had finished my '15 minute' poem." Thinking about poetry was the best anodyne for the "nervous instability" the stroke brought, which, Williams explained to the publisher David McDowell, "saps your marrow, it really does. It's a terrific drain on the forbearance of a devoted wife and friends."

Floss, too, was concerned by Bill's nervous condition and decided to seek the advice of Dr. Merrill Moore, a Boston psychiatrist and a prolific, if hackneyed, sonneteer. At Floss's urging, Williams consulted with Moore several times. In a terse comment buried in a letter of June 24, 1952, to McDowell, Williams remarked, "He was of considerable help to me, quite a guy." Moore was sympathetic to Bill's plight—he told Floss that Williams was "my favorite American poet"—and wrote to her often in a cordial, gallant tone, evaluating Bill's neurological condition frankly and presciently: "That episode when he lost his speech means another vascular accident. There isn't anything we can do. I see this sort of thing. He is going to have a series of them and he will have one great big one and won't get out of bed after that."

In the postscript to a letter of September 17, 1952, a month after Williams's second stroke, Moore wrote, "And the remarkable thing is that it does not seem to interfere much with the creative art of his mind which I think is deeply in the brain and has a better blood supply." One doubts that Moore would have proposed this theory to a convention of neurologists, but it did reassure Floss and probably Williams as well. The courtly

Moore was sensitive to Floss's anxieties over Bill's medical problems—he addresses her as "my dear Florence" and clearly wants to retain her trust in his judgment. Throughout his involvement with Bill's case he took a commonsensical approach: Williams should hold office hours no more than four hours a day, reduce the emotional strain from seeing too many people and booking too many readings, should not drive by himself, should go off to Florida "far from the madding crowd" and do what his doctors tell him to do "and not overdo"; if he doesn't obey them, "hit him over the head with a baseball bat."

Williams's second stroke smote him in August 1952, at the end of a six-week holiday at Gratwick Farm outside of Buffalo. He and Floss had visited the Abbotts and Gratwicks several summers. This idyllic spot always had a restorative effect on Williams. One evening on his first visit, enthroned on the hood of a tractor Bill Gratwick was driving, Williams was led on a solemn procession to an arbor where Harriet Gratwick, whom he adored, crowned him Poet Laureate of the Tree Peonies. To mark the occasion, he delivered an oration, freely adapted from Valéry's speech to the French Academy, "letting fly" like a Caesar or a "demigod come to earth." The company of old friends warmed him—"absolute friendship," Williams called it. Charles Abbott had confided to Bill and Floss that he wanted to "collect manuscripts of the living poets, material that . . . often was thrown away or lost that could be used later to piece out an understanding of their lives and methods of work." Abbott solicited a donation from Williams, who generously shipped several boxes of poems and manuscripts that formed the nucleus of the extensive Williams archive at the Lockwood Library in Buffalo.

Bliss was it therefore in July 1952 to stroll the sheep paths and gardens of the farm again. Williams remembered everything: the vines climbing the massive walls, the birdsong so loud and chorale-like that "I had never in my life experienced such a luxury of sound and rustic profusion." But near the end of this six-week sojourn in Arcadia, disaster felled him like a bolt of lightning: a stroke damaged the left hemisphere of his brain so severely that he started speaking gibberish and couldn't move his right arm. (It never regained full motion.) Because his vision was "seriously affected," he was prevented from reading. His grave condition did not permit his being moved to Rutherford, so at the insistence of the Abbotts and Gratwicks, the Williamses' apartment over the garage was converted to a sickroom. Doctors shuffled in and out, and Floss shared nursing duties with a local woman whose able care gladdened Williams's spirits. Nurses had always played significant roles in his adult life. In his *Autobiography*, he muses at length on the often unlucky fate of these women who "have caught a glimpse of love, have been offered endless opportunities for its physical fulfillment but, in the end, come away, ignorant, their fine bodies wasted and their minds unsatisfied." Williams diagnoses with sympathetic accuracy the culture of medicine that patronizes these women and is indifferent to their plight, although a few nurses escape by marrying doctors.

Connie, a nurse, is the central character in the last play Williams wrote, *The Cure*, which was prompted by his experience of dependency during his slow recovery. This tepid drama takes a sidelong look at a nurse's desire to exercise her talents. The plot is creaky: a young motorcyclist crashes into a rural upstate home, killing himself and injuring his passenger, a Princeton dropout with the implausible name Prospero— he's a wiseacre and a wastrel and a petty criminal, not a sage (trying to hide his identity from the law, he slyly calls himself John Keats)—who has robbed a bank. Rather than turning him over to the police, Connie hides him. A model of brisk competence, she injects morphine into her captive so his leg can be straightened out. She eventually nurses him back to health. Mildly attracted to her macho patient, she kisses him once, but ultimately remains faithful to her miner husband.

Most germane to Williams's own condition is the opening scene of the play. The stage is crowded with firemen debating how to free the body from the wreckage, ambulance drivers seeking to remove it to the morgue, a flippant state trooper writing up an accident report, curiosity seekers gossiping in low voices, and the bewildered couple whose farmhouse has been wrecked trying to quell their panic and make sense of the confusion. During his career Williams was familiar with similar accidents and crime scenes. He would be rousted out of sleep to sign the death certificates of a man shot in a barroom brawl or killed in a head-on collision. Now he was the patient who could be the corpse in *The Cure*, toted off in a body bag to the autopsy table.

At the end of the play, Prospero's leg heals and he leaves, whether to a life of crime or something more useful the play does not clarify; the ailing poet, however, knows there's no chance of curing his condition, just a hope it won't worsen. In the chapter "The City of the Hospital" in *Autobiography*, he mockingly notes, "Cure to a physician is a pure accident, to the pathologist in his laboratory almost a disappointment." He doesn't deny that medical knowledge has increased a thousandfold during his years as a doctor, but he's skeptical of miracles. Though not impossible, they belong to "the realm of necromancy"; he has no faith that the drugs peddled by the pharmaceutical companies will clear his clogged arteries. Still, there's great comfort in the nurse's hands ministering to his failing body. Eros has become caritas.

When Williams's health improved enough to travel, he took a train from upstate New York to Hoboken, under the watchful eye of William Eric, thence home by ambulance. This trip reenacted the one Williams took as a young doctor forty years earlier when he escorted a rich, terminally ill Mexican back to his village. His task was to keep his patient alive so that he could die in his own bed. Luckily, he succeeded and was paid handsomely in gold. Williams, too, reached home alive, but the second stroke left him a semi-invalid, facing a long, dicey recovery. Feeling dejected, he was unprepared for the agonizing blow from another quarter that soon followed.

To backtrack for a moment: in late April, Williams had met with Conrad Aiken to discuss assuming the duties of poetry consultant to the Library of Congress in September 1952. A week before his second stroke, the newspapers announced his appointment. Almost immediately the harpies roosted outside 9 Ridge Road. The first attack came from Virginia Kent Cummins, a poetaster and editor of *The Lyric* in Roanoke, Virginia, who denounced Williams as a Communist sympathizer. He was too much of a maverick to join political organizations, instinctively shunning all herd dogmas. He knew the working class close-up, not abstractly; for decades, he had entered their homes to treat their illnesses and deliver their babies. He had glanced at the crucifixes nailed to walls or makeshift altars in niches with the Virgin Mary displayed prominently. The Communists, he knew, would never make headway recruiting American workers in such homes.

Still, from time to time, Williams dipped into his pocket and sent small sums to a group set up to aid the unemployed or to protest injustices such as the hangings of Sacco and Vanzetti. A sort of fitful fellow traveler, he had in the late 1930s signed petitions circulated by Popular Front organizations. But he saw that the Communist Party would fail because the American "democracy of feeling" was opposed to "attempts at regimentation of thought and action." If Williams had lacked an FBI dossier, one of Pound's broadcast rants for Mussolini's government in 1939 brought him to the bureau's attention. Pound mentioned that his friend Bill Williams of Rutherford, New Jersey, agreed with his theories about money. Two days later, two agents knocked on Williams's door. How to explain his old friend's flighty, bossy, narcissistic character—it would never have occurred to Pound that his words could land Bill in trouble—and half-lucid, half-harebrained ideas to the agents? He couldn't—nobody could, not even a philosopher who combined the genius of Freud, William James, and Charlie Chaplin. With Pound's arrest for treason in 1945, Williams could only be further tainted by their long association. Hardly renowned for nuanced thinking, government bureaucrats would be inclined to view him as at best a gull and at worst a security risk.

Williams had inherited his left-leaning politics from his father, who had been a Socialist and an adherent of Henry George's single-tax theory. In the poems of the 1920s, Williams's fascination with the new Soviet regime surfaced now and then, probably because anything that promised experiment and change, the overthrow of entrenched ideologies, appealed to the poetic renegade in him. In the early years of Bolshevik rule, Soviet artists—the constructivists, Mayakovsky, Tsvetayeva, Akhmatova, Shostakovich, Prokofiev—were indeed brash, sophisticated pioneers on the frontier of modernism, daringly breaking formal molds, their improvisations more sure-footed than Williams's in *Kora in Hell*. In 1925, Bill met the charismatic Vladimir Mayakovsky at a party in Lola Ridge's apartment in Greenwich Village and was moved by the Russian's declamation of his poem "Willie the Havana Street Cleaner": "A big man, he rested one foot on top of the studio table as he read. It was the perfect gesture. He had a good voice, and though no one understood a word he said, we were all impressed by the rumbling sounds and his intense seriousness . . . For myself it sounded as might The Odyssey from the mouth of some impassioned Greek." When, on Stalin's orders, the Soviet government crushed the spirit of innovation and packed artists off to the gulags, Williams was angry and appalled. When Stalin's reign of terror, the party's brutal machinery cannibalizing its own people, became known and Stalin cynically signed a pact with Hitler, Williams condemned both policies as a horrific betrayal of ideals. Russia had become the behemoth run amok he had foreseen in 1923, in the opening pages of *Spring and All*. He was never an apologist for the Communist regime.

Mrs. Cummins's charge was picked up by Fulton Lewis, Jr., a reactionary journalist and radio commentator. Despite the uproar, Williams continued believing he would be able to take up the Library of Congress consultancy post. But a few days before Bill and Floss were to board the train to Washington, Floss received a stiff, officious letter from Verner Clapp, deputy to the chief librarian, Luther Evans, and chairman of the Library of Congress Loyalty Board. Williams, he wrote, would have to undergo an investigation by the Civil Service Commission and the FBI because a preliminary inquiry had not cleared him of charges of engaging in suspicious activities. Puzzled, Floss phoned Clapp for details. The conversation would have qualified as theater of the absurd if it hadn't been so hurtful. Clapp cited Williams's trips to Germany in 1909 and to Paris and Austria in 1924, as if the poet's real purpose wasn't to study pediatrics or to hobnob with the avant-garde but to hatch clandestine terrorist plots. Clapp's explanations only deepened the mystery. Accustomed to taking action, Floss set up a meeting with him and his staff on December 8. (Bill was there, but Floss spoke for them both.) It did not take her long to see that Clapp presumed Williams guilty. He let slip out some of the other charges: Williams had contributed poems and articles to such "subversive organs" as *Partisan Review* and *New Masses*; he had allegedly called for the abolition of the House Un-American Activities Committee; he had written a disgraceful poem, "Russia," that lauded the Communist government. Clapp, or whoever had leafed through Williams's poems for evidence of Communist sympathies, was obviously out of his depth as a reader of poetry, since that particular poem castigates Russia as "idiot of the world, blind idiot" for persecuting its own citizens. Atheistic Russia was, for Williams, just another hierarchical religion gone wrong: he was definitely anticlerical, but that "heresy" wasn't what disturbed Clapp and those who denounced Williams. It was the belief that he was a "pinko," a shade only slightly less terrible than the color red. (In *I Wanted to Write a Poem*, many years after this sickening battle, Williams eagerly sought to set the record straight, declaring that he always "hated today's version of communism.") At the meeting, Clapp seemed to enjoy his role as middle-echelon inquisitor, shaking his fist repeatedly in Williams's face, as if attempting to cow him into confessing his "guilt." Floss told Conrad Aiken after the meeting, "I came away convinced that the Deputy was either terribly antagonistic to Bill or terribly scared of something."

Why Clapp was so hostile to Williams is hard to say. A career librarian, Clapp rose through the ranks to become in 1947 chief associate director of the Library of Congress. He set up what was to become the Congressional Research Service and, in Nicholson Baker's words, was "the chief apostle of microfilming." (Clapp had friends and contacts in the CIA, which had been in the forefront of those crusading for microfilm as a tool to store information and save space.) Indeed, technology rather than literature mattered to Clapp. After visiting a small public library, he remarked alliteratively and with no irony, "Books are dingy, dreary, dog-eared and dead." Yet after World War II, he established an important library in Japan, where colleagues remembered him as a man with a sense of humor who treated people respectfully. His behavior toward Williams displayed none of that respect. As a venerable institution, the Library of Congress was supposed to be immune from political rancor, but in the violently irrational climate of the McCarthy era, civil servants worried that they could come under attack for even inadvertently aiding and abetting a suspected subversive. Clapp's primary loyalty was to the Library of Congress; his was a company man's dread of upsetting the status quo. Perhaps that was the fear Floss read in his eyes.

Floss enlisted the help of Norman Holmes Pearson, a Yale professor of English and a friend who had served with distinction in wartime counter-intelligence and was well connected in Washington. The FBI had deduced from Bill's poem "The Pink Church" that he was a Communist sympathizer. Clearly the FBI training curriculum omitted a course in the New Criticism, which would have helped them recognize the "pink" in the opening lines as an allusion to Homer's "rosy-fingered dawn." Curiously, in the last lines of the poem, Williams labels John Milton, never one of his favorite poets, as a proto-Communist, presumably because Milton championed Oliver Cromwell, a sort of despotic forerunner of Stalin.

Williams had sat through the highly fraught December 8 meeting with Clapp in silence, but fuming. Both he and Floss worried that the mounting tension would raise his blood pressure to a dangerous level and put him at risk for a fatal stroke. So he tried to restrain himself from boiling over. But his appointment continued to unravel. Although he was not famous enough to be grilled under klieg lights at one of the showcase congressional hearings, he could not escape an appearance before the Library of Congress's own Loyalty Committee, headed by Clapp. When a flustered Williams could not recall having signed petitions or written checks for such causes as the Scottsboro Boys Defense Fund, Clapp construed his answers as proof of stonewalling, if not outright lies. Williams's memory had been affected by his stroke, so it was not surprising he could not recall such details. (He was frequently absentminded about money transactions. Floss, his office manager, kept track of bills and checks.)

Williams decided to hire his lawyer, James Murray, to defend his interests. Murray wrote a blunt letter to Luther Evans, declaring that Williams fully intended to take up the post. Evans took his time to reply, leaving Williams to twist in the wind. Some solace arrived with the announcement that Williams (and Archibald MacLeish) had won the prestigious Bollingen Prize for 1953. The Bollingen had been born into a firestorm of controversy in 1949 when Pound, incarcerated at St. Elizabeths Hospital in Washington, D.C., was named its first winner. Because World War II had ended a short four years before, feelings understandably ran high. Was it possible to separate Pound the poet, with his exquisite ear and undeniable accomplishments, from Pound the anti-Semite and strident propagandist for fascism? Yes, argued his admirers, who included nearly every major poet, including Williams. *The Pisan Cantos* (1948), Pound's latest volume of poems, offered irrefutable proof of his artistry. Although he showed little remorse in the poems, he wrote movingly about his internment in a ramshackle army prison in Pisa, and from that cage roamed the worlds of history, economics, and arts and letters like an indefatigable eagle. In technique and lyric invention he eclipsed the competition. For those rallying behind Pound, it was as if modernism itself were on trial. Led by the conservative Harvard poet Robert Hillyer, Pound's opponents vilified him as both traitor and obscurantist, but they were soon routed from the field.

When Luther Evans unilaterally terminated Williams's appointment as consultant, he denied that it was due to any doubts about the poet's loyalty. Rather, Williams's poor health rendered him unfit to serve. Murray protested that Evans lacked the credentials to pronounce on Williams's health; he also pressed for the FBI to clear Bill's name, but in a catch-22 argument, the FBI countered that since Williams was no longer employed by the government, they could not investigate his loyalty. Apart from what had dribbled out—the charges and innuendos about left-wing causes—Williams and Murray had no idea what information his dossier contained. Given J. Edgar Hoover's appetite for acquiring dirt on people under investigation, some informant might have told stories, made-up or real, about Williams's romantic affairs. Clapp, however, did not dredge up these private matters.

The case dragged on. Leonie Adams and Cleanth Brooks, two fellows at the library, took up the cudgels for Williams and met with Evans to persuade him to restore his appointment. Evans softened a little: if Williams presented a certificate from a doctor saying he was physically able to carry out his duties, he would be allowed to finish out his term until September 14, 1953. But he must first renounce all legal rights to the position. Only if both provisos were followed would the library's Loyalty Board convene and the FBI investigate and decide whether to clear his name. In no condition to fight anymore, Williams consented to Evans's demands, but he never served a day as poetry consultant.

The toll exacted on Williams by the consultancy fiasco was terrible: he fell into a depression so deep that his doctor, Roy Black, advised Floss that Bill would benefit from a stay at a mental asylum. He recommended Hillside Hospital, a private facility in Queens. It was a sign of Floss's alarm at Bill's precarious mental state that she agreed to this momentous step. Husband and wife had been physically separated by an ocean and estranged by periods of marital discord. But after 1948 the two had grown closer. Williams leaned on Floss for support and hope as a child would on his mother; she dutifully supplied both. In his gratitude, he wrote to her about his love with an eloquence and urgency one might expect from a man on his deathbed, and with an unequivocal tenderness that rarely surfaced in his poems:

> I despair of ever again feeling well. But when I think of having another stroke which will leave me bedridden, perhaps blind, it is too much to think of. You, of all people, should know what that means. I might not even be able to communicate as I am doing now. And when I see you growing tired, as you confessed to me that you were already growing tired, desperate,—allow for all exaggeration and false emphasis that you know to be me. Tear this paper up and throw it away as the record of a man who, in spite of everything, loved you and my children to the end . . . I've been a fool for reasons that are not clear to even me, but, believe me, I truly love [you] and believe with all my heart that you love me. Nothing can change that.

This passage exhibits an exceptional concern for Floss's burdens, and a moving honesty about the riddles and defects of Williams's own character.

This is the soul's language; he is too desperate to resort to evasions. How Floss interpreted this ardent avowal of devotion she did not reveal. She concentrated on the crisis at hand. How would Williams adjust to his confinement? Her misgivings, grounded in a deep knowledge of his temperament, told her that he was ill prepared. Williams was not a particularly introspective man. Throughout his adult life, he disdained psychoanalysis and never speculated that the unconscious might be the lair of the imagination. When he had visited Pound at St. Elizabeths, he was disquieted by even the relatively mild restrictions his friend lived with daily. In his *Autobiography*, Williams frankly admits that "the disturbed mind has always been a territory from which I shrank instinctively as before the unknown."

On February 18, 1953, Paul drove his father to Hillside Hospital. When the gates clanged shut, Bill was subject to rules and routines almost as stringent as those at a prison: he was locked up in a ward most of the time, and even when walking the grounds he was kept under close supervision. The city of Hillside Hospital was decidedly not "normal." Its citizens, Williams's fellow inmates, suffered from an array of mental diseases that left them fractured, withdrawn, unable to control aggression, to concentrate, or to relate to other people; they could not fathom what went on in themselves. Williams, too, was subject to rapid mood changes, feeling "on top of the world" in the morning and "crushed" an hour later. His stroke in August 1952 had left his mind disheveled, forgetful, "dizzy and confused"; lassitude gripped him and he fell into "deep depression." Lacking his usual resourceful will or the habit of self-examination, he was helpless to escape the emotional confinement he felt trapped in, like Kora in Hades's desolate kingdom. While his identity had not entirely crumbled, he realized the severity of the crisis that had brought him to Hillside. The causes, he told Floss, have probably "been stewing in my bones since childhood." The questions that molested his peace of mind were: Could he disinter and confront those buried causes, did he face a long incarceration, and would he ever emerge healed and whole?

Williams was almost seventy years old when he entered Hillside, and for a man accustomed to freedom of mobility and contact with people, the environment was scary. Floss had reluctantly agreed to follow the advice of Roy Black, Williams's personal doctor, that Bill's mental instability required immediate attention, lest his nervous breakdown worsen into an irreparable collapse. Alarmed by and intimate with Bill's agitation and despair, she overcame her qualms about psychiatric therapy as a humiliating brand of Cain and consented to putting him in the hands of Hillside's renowned doctors. The first weeks were a difficult adjustment for him. He noted uneasily that most of the staff and patients were Jewish, including his roommate; he felt like an alien landed on a strange planet, wary of the officials (the doctors) and of his fellow lost souls. A feeling of unbearable isolation seized him. But as the hospital's regimen became familiar, some of his former gregariousness slowly returned and his suspicions of the psychiatrists in charge of his case, with whom he met for the "talking cure," relaxed. They were mainly benevolent reality instructors, not jailers, he concluded; so he could safely lower his guard, knowing that they would not stagger him with a blow to his fragile self-esteem. He panicked at the possibility the medical people might choose shock treatment to jolt him out of his tenacious depression, however, and he begged Floss to intercede with the doctors not to administer it; he knew he had no say in the matter. Williams's few statements about the treatment he received are scanty and inconclusive. But from his letters to Floss we can deduce that his conversations with his psychiatrist sometimes reduced his anxiety to more tolerable levels and even gave him some gleams of hope that his future need not be as bleak as he imagined.

The hospital's rules, strict but not excessively so, permitted Williams to write letters to Floss, speak to her on the telephone once a week, and receive one visit from her a week. The portfolio of his correspondence during this period is painful reading. The stroke had so paralyzed his right hand that he had to labor with frustrating slowness to form words and letters. The pencil he used to record his feelings trembled, like a sufferer from palsy. He castigated himself for omitting words or misspelling words—for example, "catastrony" for "catastrophe"—though his syntax was lucid. (Williams was never a good speller; in the past he dismissed such errors as harmless, the result of haste and carelessness.) In the aftermath of his heart attack and strokes, his health deteriorated and his speech sometimes faltered; his family was prone to stammering, he noted in his *Autobiography*. His reliance on Floss increased dramatically. She had always managed the household efficiently, paying bills on time, pushing Bill to ask his patients for payment, leaving supper on the table if he had been called away to deliver a baby. But his fears and insecurities, some neurotic and some rational, made him fuss like a child, so she added skillful nurse and comforting mother to her role as wife. She bore these burdens with grace.

Hillside did not resemble Pound's ramshackle prison cell near Pisa, where he awaited trial for his treasonous broadcasts, but Williams felt trapped and quarantined nonetheless. So the letters he wrote to Floss, sometimes twice a day, served as a sturdy rope he clung to in order to stave off drowning, until Floss, his main hope to escape confinement, rescued him. She punctually took the long trek to Queens and spoke calmly to him over the phone, quelling paroxysms of panic that washed over him. (His emotions were close to the surface.) This could not have been easy for her. Bill had confessed his infidelities to her in such abundant detail that she could not help feeling devastated. In his biography, Paul Mariani argues that she had not known of any of his affairs and so Williams's confession of sins, the return of the repressed in a tidal wave of disclosure, overwhelmed and shocked her. But this interpretation rests on a dubious premise: that Floss, a very bright and perspicacious woman, had willfully averted her eye from the evidence of his philandering left in plain sight in the poems of *Sour Grapes* and in *Kora in Hell*. The first to read nearly everything he wrote, except his *Autobiography*, she treasured that marital benefit. Williams lacked the courage to confess openly to her back then, afraid her wrath would end their marriage. And as the correspondence between them in 1928 proves, she had taken an accurate measure of her husband's flaws and sexual wandering, balancing them against the pleasures of their life together—travel abroad; a fulfilling social whirligig spent in the company of fascinating poets and artists, spellbinding talkers who came to 9 Ridge Road for camaraderie and debates about where modernism was headed; and, not least, their two sons, whom she adored and worried about—and since she knew he loved her and had always returned to her, she chose to tolerate his errant passions, and to keep their marriage intact.

Nonetheless, Williams's letters cruelly tested her self-control. As supplicant for her mercy and forgiveness, he is contrite and self-deprecating: "God how I've messed up my life," he moans. "You don't know how deep I have sunk and I hope you will never know it . . . It is as if the whole top of my head has been taken off, that is the reason for my unreasoning fears" that are "formless but pervasive." In his prolonged dark night of the soul, Williams dreads that he may lose his sanity. Shame for his behavior fuels his apologies and his pledges of mending his ways. He is too shattered emotionally to fabricate lies or excuses. He stakes all on a reconciliation she will embrace: "regardless of what has happened in the past you are the world to me, come what may." Because his faith in her power to save him is so strong, he cannot bear the thought of a future without her. When an attendant comes to his room to "deliver your phone call, [i]t was wonderful!! A weigh[t] was suddenly lifted from my heart. I felt as if I could fly!"

There were days, of course, when he felt isolated from other patients. His life had been one of perpetual motion and activity, so it was hard to accept the limits his anxieties dictated; he fretted that "I cannot read [his eyesight was poor] or play games, or do group exerciseses [*sic*]." "I don't know what to do with myself. I cannot even eat properly." He cherished the infrequent times when he was permitted to walk on the hospital grounds; both the cold weather and the release from confinement invigo-rated him. He was invited to read his poems to an assembly of the pa-tients, which pleased him, though he wondered self-consciously if he was as "nutty" as Coleridge and Rimbaud. He reports hearing a song sparrow and two crows, which reminded him of walks in the meadow as a boy, and he glimpsed cherry tree blossoms "that seemed to glow with subdued light." As far as nature was concerned, his senses were still keenly obser-vant. Williams tells Floss of one adventure that was a harbinger of the release from the hospital he yearned for. He and Stanley Levin received permission to attend Sunday mass on Palm Sunday. (The hospital did not, apparently, find it odd that a Jew, Stanley Levin, and a lapsed Unitar-ian, Williams, should want to celebrate a Christian holiday.) To their sur-prise, the church was packed, and they were forced to stand in the back: a hardship for Williams, who had trouble holding on to the back of a pew with his gimpy hand; he wobbled but did not fall. When an usher came toward them distributing palms, Williams extended his left hand, grabbed a branch, and bolted out the church's back door, with a startled Stanley Levin running after him so as not to be left in the lurch. The episode is a comic lesson in the vagaries of faith.

If Williams originally feared that Hillside would be a hell for the emo-tionally damned, he eventually came to think of it as more like Purgatory, a place where infirm souls went to be redeemed. Spring worked its magic on him once more in the hospital garden, where the strolling poet was alert to the first signs of birds nesting or preparing to "build anew" (always an augury of benign vitality in his poems) and of "early salmon-pink /

clusters of flowers." This rejuvenation prompted him to write, in a style of profound simplicity and empathy, "The Mental Hospital Garden," one of his loveliest poems. Presiding over the garden and its troubled residents is Saint Francis, a figure of ineffable pity and selfless love who helps the afflicted, including Williams, overcome their despair. One sign of Williams's recuperation and his Franciscan discipleship is his gentle, avuncular concern for the young inmates who are sequestered as he is, "divided / from their fellows" outside the hospital walls, and confused and entranced by sexual stirrings and love as he once was. (The hospital allowed the sexes to mingle.) Williams likens them to the young couples in Boccaccio's *Decameron* who took refuge from the plague in a country house and whiled away the days telling mostly licentious tales. The young couples at Hillside lack the confidence of their Tuscan counterparts; they continually struggle to master in themselves the conflict between freedom and repression (symbolized by the walls of the hospital). They wander the lawn and shyly embrace, yet feel they "have nothing." Touched by their plight, Williams prays to Saint Francis to bless the couples, who, despite their darkened, bereft minds, "have seen / a great light, it / springs from their own bawdy foreheads." Eros, he pleads to the celibate saint, is a bountiful version of "the Holy light of love."

Halfway through the poem a stage direction reads, "Time passes." It is spring and the lovers are now "blinded by the light," not sure whether they're cured "and half minded / to escape / into the dark again." The lovers are in fact terrified by the idea of being discharged from Hillside and negotiating the world beyond its gates. Though the sun shines brightly, their imagination falters; they seek a "familiar flower" to warm them; ashamed "before that bounty," "they hide their eyes . . . peering through their fingers timidly." Williams's own emotional shakiness is mirrored in their vacillation between doubt and hope. Saint Francis's unflinching gaze radiates steadfast compassion, but as the season progresses, the mood darkens. The young, Williams observes, "resemble children / roused from a long sleep." When Saint Francis "tactfully" withdraws from the garden, the question that looms, for Williams as well as for the young disordered by "love's first folly," is: How can I safely rejoin the perilous life outside without regressing to the psychic misery that brought me here in the first place? Williams offers no glib answers. Before the curtain lowers on the poem, the reader is left with a poignant image of one patient's anxious wish and reluctance to chance the existential struggle awaiting her. Her look of "wild surmise" speaks volumes:

> One
> emboldened,
>> parting the leaves before her,
>> stands in the full sunlight,
> alone
> shading her eyes
> as her heart
> beats wildly
> and her mind
> . . . drinks up
> the full meaning
>> of it
> all!

When Williams left Hillside on April 18, 1953 (Floss's birthday), he came home in a markedly more hopeful mood, though he harbored no illusions that his troubles were over. He had not regained Paradise. "The crackle / of death's stinking certainty," as he put it synesthetically in the 1942 poem "The Yellow Season," sounded in his ears and assaulted his nostrils. Williams realized he might yet be tested further, might succumb to a worse despair. Nor was there any assurance that his imagination would function in the robust fashion to which he was accustomed. The poems of *The Desert Music* (1954) chart the fluctuations of his mind as he grapples with final questions and the nearness of death. Three themes are braided together in the book: love and sex, death, and—most surprisingly, since Williams professed himself an agnostic—religious faith.

The flurry of bells in the 1935 poem "The Catholic Bells" "ring in Sunday morning / and old age which adds as it / takes away," Williams says rather blithely, but in "For Eleanor and Bill Monahan," old age takes away far more than it adds, as he sinks into a spiritual crisis from which he tries to extricate himself. The Monahans, devout Catholics, were patients of his who became friends. In 1943 a pregnant and worried Eleanor had consulted with Williams. Because her placenta was situated low in the uterus, Williams explained, the fetus might be deprived of nourishment and oxygen; the birth itself could become hazardous to mother and child. (For the Monahans, abortion was not an option.) Williams was impressed by how their faith sustained the couple during the anxious months before Eleanor successfully gave birth. Such unquestioning faith was out of Williams's reach, but in his despondency he sought consolation in Catholicism. In the poem he addresses the Virgin Mary as both her chevalier and a sinner beseeching forgiveness of his offenses. In the early passages—Robert Lowell likened the poem to a psalm—Williams uses the first person plural, as if his suffering qualified him to speak for all who had worn a crown of thorns and could not escape this all-too-human ordeal. Williams's journey to seek the Virgin's blessing and peace of mind is painful, like an ascetic's feet burned by the hot desert sand. Although the poem is a canticle threaded with tenderness for the Mother of God, Williams struggles to close the vast distance between them, conceding that "the heart / is an unruly Master" even as he prays to Mary to "Make us humble and obedient to His rule"; it is hard for him to surrender his will.

In the middle section, Williams confesses to the Virgin that he is "half man and half / woman." How an old man on the verge of death can integrate these two sides of his nature is the conundrum that he again strives to solve. His complicated marital ties, he recognizes, are still a source of friction:

> I have seen the ivy
> > cling
> > to a piece of crumbled
> wall so that
> > you cannot tell
> > by which either
> stands: this is to say
> > if she to whom I cling
> > is loosened both
> of us go down.

Williams can whisper to the Virgin what his heart finds nearly impossible to confide to Floss directly: just how much he needs her and how forlorn he'd be if the "crumbled / wall" collapsed. In the poem's most lyrical passage, Williams depicts Mary stooping to pick a "merest" flower and pressing it to her cheek in a woman's tender gesture, though he declares, despite the evidence of vast numbers of the believers worshipping her, that she has no gallant lovers, although "fit to be loved."

This image also glances at Floss, since many of Williams's most affectionate poems about her are set in a garden where she is gathering flowers. Yet faith in the possibility of healing the rifts in their marriage falters. As P. D. James remarked, "The past [isn't] so easily shaken off. The old sins return, weighted by the years."

> There are men
> who as they live
> fling caution to the
> wind and women praise them
> and love them for it

Williams surely includes himself among that group of men, though in his flings he was careful to protect his marriage. In a cryptic afterthought, grammatically unmoored, he comments, "Cruel as the claws of / a cat . . ." Typically, he expresses his guilty conscience indirectly: because of his tomcatting, he raked his claws across Floss's skin and drew blood. At the end of this broken prayer, he concludes that the ship of his life is sailing toward its final destination: death. For a moment he entertains an alternative ending: if "Their ships / should be directed inward upon." Williams ends the sentence with a period, but lets the thought dangle in the air, unresolved—some revelation may or may not arrive. Too weary to explore this point further, he turns from "they" to himself: "But I / am an old man. I have had enough," which can be parsed two ways: that he is fed up with his life and therefore death is welcome, or that he is satisfied by the banquet his appetites fed on. But almost as if to make sure that he covers all bets, he ends this theologically confused poem with the Latin of the Catholic liturgy: "O Clemens! O pia! O dolcis! Maria!" In his "extremity" of distress he is a petitioner for clemency from three incarnations of the "female principle": Mary, Diana, Floss.

In the Mariolatry of "For Eleanor and Bill Monahan," Williams strikes few "wrong notes." The subject of faith continued to engross him. In "The Host," a more loose-jointed poem, the poet sits at a restaurant table and gazes at fellow diners, representatives of different Christian denominations: "well-fed [black] evangels," "narrow-lipped and bright-eyed nuns," and a "tall, / white-haired Anglican," all sharing in "a common need." "There is nothing to eat, / seek it where you will, / but of the body of the Lord," Williams declares, but he is not literally endorsing a belief in the Communion, since the Lord turns out, in his credo, to be the sovereign imagination, invisible and omnipotent; the appetites fall under its sway. The poem is a half-serious, half-facetious parable whose message is "Only the imagination / is real!" It is sacred but not sectarian.

"Deep Religious Faith" is another hymn to invention, the underlying force from which springs poetry (his own, French poet René Char's, Theocritus's), art (Michelangelo's, El Greco's), and religion. Invention is not the property of a priestly caste, yet Williams worships it as a Catholic would Jesus. As we've seen, Williams preached from this text as early as *Kora in Hell*, and it is still Holy Scripture in *Paterson*. In his late books, he speaks with lyric simplicity:

> It [faith] is what in life drives us
> to praise music
> and the old
> or sit by a friend
> in his last hours.
> All that which makes the pear ripen
> or the poet's line
> come true!
> Invention is the heart of it.
> Without the quirks
> and oddnesses of invention
> the paralytic is confirmed
> in his paralysis, . . .

The last sentence lays bare Williams's dread that his creative life and identity are in jeopardy, that like the poets he scolds for having "quit the job / of invention," his imagination will fall "asleep / in a poppy-cup," an oblivion akin to drinking the waters of Lethe or being numbed by morphine. This fear, like a chronic pain, flares up in nearly every poem of *The Desert Music*.

To his credit, Williams does not fool himself that his "tortured body" and suffering can be healed by willed uplift, though he claims glibly at the end of "To a Dog Injured in the Street" that he shares René Char's belief "in the power of beauty / to right all wrongs." In "The Yellow Flower," he is initially tempted to believe in a miraculous cure, which doesn't require a pilgrimage to Lourdes, just staring at a "crooked," "ungainly," "unnatural" yellow flower, a nod to the "sweet-scented" "daffodils and tulips" that Char put in his poems in an effort to blot out his unbearable memories of World War II. With its "deformed stem" and "twisted petals," the yellow flower serves as an emblem of Williams's body broken by two strokes. Curiously, the flower picks him out and casts a hypnotic spell, under which he meditates on the riddle that obsesses him as man and poet: "why the torture / and the escape through / the flower?" In other words, how does the imagination transform harsh reality into art? By an associative leap, he draws an elaborate analogy between his plight and Michelangelo's monumental slave sculptures, wondering if the flower also inspired Michelangelo to "make the marble bloom." For Michelangelo, the soul is imprisoned in the body, an idea that would not have appealed to Williams when he was young but at this period was an apt metaphor for his ill health. The crux of the poem and a proposed exit from his depression is in its coda:

> Which leaves, to account for,
>> the tortured bodies
>> of
> the slaves themselves
>> and
>> the tortured body of my flower
> which is not a mustard flower at all
>> but some unrecognized
>> and unearthly flower
> for me to naturalize
>> and acclimate
>> and choose it for my own.

Williams realizes that the magnitude of the slaves' suffering far exceeds that of his own. The flower is simply a metaphor for his fragile health and baffled will, which he must find a way to accept, "naturalize / and acclimate." In a subtle reversal of his earlier passivity, he chooses the flower for his own.

In the poems of *The Desert Music*, Williams's tone shifts restlessly every few lines from wry to elevated, from aphorism to prayer, from cacophony to lyric harmony. He takes an old man's liberty to ramble and repeat himself: "it is a principle of music / [and poetry] to repeat its theme," often with variations, he remarks in "The Orchestra." This describes his method in *The Desert Music*: short passages develop over several lines, clash briefly, drop out abruptly, or stall because of maudlin repetitions. Sometimes he shrugs and changes the subject, though he often doesn't notice his lapses or he ignores them. Thus in the passage of "The Orchestra" that commemorates the "dead in their beds," to whom "light / is forever lost," the cello sighs in a triad of "Ah"s "together, unattuned / seeking a common tone": love. His proximity to death heightens the offbeat tribute to Floss that is at the heart of "The Orchestra": by shy, or sly, design Williams strives to integrate the atonal notes he played in his marriage into a composition that will resound with seductive arpeggios of love. But precisely because the sounds are poorly organized he undermines the poem's music and credibility. His imagination stumbles, as so often when expressing bald sentiments:

> Now is the time
> in spite of the "wrong note":
> 　　　　I love you. My heart is
> innocent.
> And this the first
> (and last) day of the world

This inert sequence of lines "stretches / and yawns" and rings false, like the twittering of the birds at the poem's end: platitudes, however deeply felt, cannot hide bad art.

Most of *The Desert Music* is written in the step-down tercets that became Williams's favorite pattern in his late poems through 1955. One might conjecture that they arose out of his need to relearn the fundamentals of speech after his strokes, often with a humbling self-consciousness. He could no longer take verbal fluency for granted: prepositions, those hardworking laborers who glue together the parts of a sentence, got scrambled; nouns and verbs switched places. No wonder he fell silent for more than a year, roughly from March 1952 until October 1953. Tercets, a kind of speech therapy, allowed him to move slowly and tentatively, and to catch his breath before leading the train of thought down another flight of stairs. Lines could consist of one word or several; periods could drift from their normal position at the end of a sentence and extend the cadence a few extra spaces; parentheses could accommodate afterthoughts or sidebars. Williams found that tercets suited his impulse toward statement and away from images and metaphors. As the sands in the hourglass run down, he is seized by an old man's urgent need to sum up what he has learned from life, even if that means occasionally pontificating.

"The Descent," which Williams placed at the head of *The Desert Music*, is a case in point. He explained this positioning as a way of showing how the poem, which first appeared in *Paterson II* six years earlier, laid the groundwork for his experiments with the variable foot, which would, he hoped, break with "the cultured patter of the iambic pentameter, even at the hands of Shakespeare, and look toward wider horizons." To his critics, such statements were tantamount to his swinging the wrecking ball on poetry's landmark mansion and planning to replace it with jerry-built vers libre. But he was no fan of free verse; he considered it prosy, a dead end. Justifiably praised for rethinking and retooling the microdynamics of the poetic line, in particular its heft, speed, cadence, enjambment, and momentum, Williams also devoted himself, as early as 1913, to remaking the macrodynamics of the whole, which for him meant rhythm. His famous (or notorious) offhand maxims—calling a poem a "machine made of words" or saying he got his language from the mouths of Polish women—sprang from his fondness for whimsical remarks that led some critics to dismiss him as a wild man of poetics scattering buckshot all over the lot. But he had a deeper side that thought through aesthetic ideas with the same care in reasoning that he brought to medical diagnosis. Skeptical of received opinions, he argued most persuasively when he argued inductively from facts to conclusions, and he seldom held on to a premise or theory when disinterested analysis and the writing of poems proved it wrong.

Witness his discussion of rhythm and the natural analogy he chose to explain it: "Each piece of work, rhythmic in whole, is . . . in essence an assembly of tides, waves, ripples—in short, of greater and lesser rhythmic particles regularly repeated or destroyed." Williams resorted to repetition and regularity like any poet, but he was quick to discard them when he judged they'd become too predictable. For him, what counts in rhythm "is not sound but motion, of the two kinds: forward and up and down, rapidity of motion and quality of motion." "For this reason," he contends, "the poetic foot—dependent on the number of sounds composing it—cannot, except by chance, embody the rhythm unit." What Williams wishes to circumvent is the "rigid stress and counted syllables" of the old metrical forms. Here is how he defines his "new way": "The same rhythm, swift, may be of three syllables or if two are elided, of one: whereas, slow, it may consist of four or seven or any number that the sense agrees to. This is the flexibility that the modern requires."

Enter the variable foot. Williams's sporadic definitions of his method are not always precise, and can be defensive: "As for my own elliptical approach," he wrote for a *Partisan Review* symposium, "it may be baffling, but it is not unfriendly, and not, I think, entirely empty." It's evident that he intends the variable foot to be a distinctly American "intonation." By the mid-1950s, when he had neither the time nor the patience nor the stamina for testy polemics or lengthy summaries of his prosody, the ghosts of iambic pentameter and rhyme frequently walk the battlements of his poems. Williams is best seen as an old navigator still poring over his charts and maps in order to discover the Northwest Passage to that ever-beckoning linguistic "wider horizon," American speech music. Even if it continues to elude him, he will not abandon his pursuit of it.

On the face of it, "The Descent" is a strange choice as poster poem for American rhythms and words. In its relentlessly abstract vocabulary, it is as remote from the American vernacular as Saturn is from Earth. And it is, astonishingly, the Williams poem that most resembles, in gravity and anguish, T. S. Eliot's religious poems "Ash Wednesday" and *Four Quartets*. For Williams, "The Descent" belongs in this volume because it probes his struggle to make sense of his diminished libido and imperiled poetic powers. With its stately, ceremonious music and bleak eloquence, "The Descent" meditates on what he can salvage from the despair that grips him. Gingerly feeling his way, he opens his inquiry in a hopeful vein: the verb "beckons," with its come-hither connotation, makes the descent to death less frightening, because it is part of the natural cycle whose rhythms he lives by. In the wake of the strokes that damaged his confidence as well as his health, he seeks to rebuild his life. The word "new," always a rallying cry, chimes five times, is tucked into "renewal," and morphs into "now." Unsure if his mental faculties are impaired, he gropes for words: hence the locutions "a kind of" or "a sort of" accomplishment, renewal, and initiation. Once he reaches this last word, what blocks speech begins to break up and his sentence grows complex, manifest in the parallel subordinate clauses that test propositions he's turning over in his mind.

The definitions explain the preponderance of copulative verbs in the poem—and the quest for causal links. What Williams means by "initiation" is a late rite of passage. The spaces it opens are signs that his arteries of thought have not been irreversibly narrowed by his strokes. "Hordes" suggests either a multitude of possibilities or a swarm of undifferentiated material he would be helpless to organize. The movement toward new objectives, previously unrealized or discarded as so many husks of ideas, promises a release from stasis and the resumption of purpose, but a dark cloud hovers overhead, threatening mental eclipse.

In the next stanza, Williams postulates a law of compensations, in which the diminishment of his powers is not absolute. He is not deceiving himself about his loss of energy, confidence, sexual potency, or poetic sharpness. But if "defeat" is not final, there's a small aperture through which he can wiggle to generate new discoveries and poems.

In the third and fourth stanzas, memory speaks in a barely audible voice. As love wakens, his sexual demons no longer roil him; like a child, he falls asleep to words that soothe like a lullaby or like the word "death" that the sea lisps to Whitman in "Out of the Cradle Endlessly Rocking." Because love purged of the physical stirs, he feels no terror at the advance of night, or the blankness of death, just peace. But this serenity begins to dissipate. The last eleven lines of the poem divide into two tributaries, as if Williams is entertaining alternative endings. The first relies on the magical promise of "a new awakening" that transfigures a descent made up of "despairs / and without accomplishment" into a "reversal of despair." This smacks of wishful thinking. The second tallies the disappointments of what might have been and with clear gaze concedes that death is "endless and indestructible." The line extinguishes most of the hope that preceded it.

"The Descent" is a monochromatic poem that reads awkwardly at times because Williams labors to write in an abstract language that is alien to him and bars humor. It is inhabited by "hordes," phantasms, not real people. After the airlessness of "The Descent," the reader is relieved to be taken outdoors in "For Daphne and Virginia" to Gratwick Farm, where the odor of boxwood permeates the grounds, robins build a nest, an old goose waddles in the mud, and even the mind's troubles are blamed on a "worm in the brain." Claiming a privilege of old age, Williams meanders without worrying whether his audience, his daughters-in-law, Daphne and Virginia, and those listening in on the monologue will fidget at his garrulity and fondness for pedestrian maxims. Floss appears briefly as an object of desire and mystery to Williams, as Daphne and Virginia are to their husbands. Williams professes to loving "all women" and being confused by them. Men are irresistibly drawn to women, "snared" by the heat and odor of boxwood (the power of libido), but a barrier keeps the sexes separate and "agonized." When he tries to analyze "a woman's world," Williams summons an image of "crossed sticks," women knitting or snipping off men's lives like the Three Fates. The image also evokes Isis: women as superior beings endowed with the power of divination, and as benevolent figures of consolation. According to legend, Isis resurrected her husband, Osiris, from the dead, but the Williams men have no "easy access" to the goddess or, for that matter, to their wives, who might make them whole.

Williams feels encumbered, but not silenced, by his love. In old age he concedes that because his appetites have dwindled, his love is less than that of his sons, although with a touch of macho swagger he claims it is "infinitely / more penetrant." The love on his mind is of a higher, almost Platonic nature, incomparable for its resources, yet that same mind is tricky, "uncertain," and the "cause of our distresses." Because the mind is in harmony with the poem, sublimation is possible:

> There is, in short,
> a counter stress,
> born of the sexual shock,
>   which survives it
> consonant with the moon,
>   to keep its own mind.

Reaching for conclusive findings about women, Williams turns didactic. But he accepts his weakened physical condition. Happily, he can still write poems that set down affable conversations with his mind. If, against reason, he ventures to "speak of love" and "all women," it's a kind of freedom he's grateful for. The poem, to paraphrase Chekhov, has to pose the right questions, not definitively answer them. Unlike the old goose waddling noisily in the mud and penned in lest he devour the garden, Williams is able to make of his limitations a "new world." His imagination may have slowed down in making connections, but it is not defunct. Used to a busy life, he sits quiet and relaxed, ready to "fly off upon" the mind's wings.

•

In October 1958, Williams suffered a third, crippling stroke that severely circumscribed his activities and plunged him into a black depression and paralysis of the will. He had difficulty speaking, concentrating, walking, and writing; his doctors ordered that he give up poetry readings as too stressful. His reliance on Floss inevitably grew. In "The Loving Dexterity," she sees an intact pink petal fallen off a flower and "deftly / placed it / / on / its stem / again." She may not have been able to restore his health with a sorceress's wave of her wand, but Williams acknowledged in his final poem, aptly titled "The Rewaking," that her love, like a force of nature, sought to extend his time on earth indefinitely "until a whole / spring / rekindle / the violet to the very / / lady's-slipper / / and so by / your love the very sun / itself is revived" The poem, like most of those in *Pictures from Brueghel*, refuses a closing period; four verbs begin with the prefix "re-," as if her faithful love could warm him and revive his dormant belief in new beginnings; the cadence of his last words sounds with subdued gratitude.

Ever the realist on medical questions, however, Williams did not view his illness through rose-tinted lenses. He knew, as he put it in one of the Nahuatl poems he translated, "we vanish once only." The "harsh cry" of a woodpecker in the ruined choir of a bare tree reminds him of a song of death. "Beauty," he remarks in the no-nonsense "Song," "is no more than a sop / when our time / is spent and infirmities / bring us to / eat out of the same bowl!" After a brief hospital stay in August of 1959, Williams wrote a two-quatrain poem titled "The World Contracted to a Recognizable Image." All his injured mind could cling to was an "idiotic" Japanese print. Who would liberate him from this mental prison? Saint Francis was not on the premises.

From 1958 to 1963, Williams was subject to a series of TIAs (transient ischemic attacks), or little strokes, which blurred his vision, slurred his speech, and numbed feeling in his limbs. He mostly endured these infirmities stoically, but his frustration at his body's and mind's betrayals could without warning bring on an unshakable gloom and drive him to self-destructive acts: preparing his last book for publication, he tore the manuscript to pieces and dumped them in the trash. Fortunately, Floss retrieved them and sent them to Laughlin, who put them together like a jigsaw puzzle. A cerebral incident in June 1961 sent Williams to the hospital for an extended stay. "I have poor hopes for his making a good recovery this time, alas," Denise Levertov reported to Robert Duncan. Her foreboding proved correct. Williams could not type even with one finger, and his handwriting was illegible, as that of aphasics commonly is. During this period, the poet Hayden Carruth was organizing James Laughlin's correspondence from 1936 to a few months after Williams's death, prior to their being shipped to Harvard's Houghton Library. Carruth had pledged not to take notes or copy any letters, and he kept his word. When he reached Williams's letters, second only to Pound's in sheer numbers, he could not help noticing the stunning effect of the strokes:

> A characteristic letter from the earlier years of his final illness would contain a few peculiar errors, words repeated or transposed, nothing important, and since he obviously did not reread his letters most of the time he may have been unaware of them. But the letters degenerated more and more quickly in the last years. Sometimes he got no further than:
>
> Dea de de dead ea dea de dead dea dear
>
> Repeated across the page, and the sheet would be rumpled and torn where he had grabbed it out of the typewriter in exasperation. Often the rest of the letter was written by his wife, Flossie, in blue ink, her hand firm and businesslike. I could not understand what was happening in these letters. Aphasia seemed a reasonable symptom of a damaged brain, the tongue and brain being so closely connected, but a typewriter is a machine one can go back and x-out one's mistakes, and this stammering in typescript seemed unaccountable to me. I did not know what even to call it. All I knew was that these letters from the late 50s and early 60s seemed to me among the most woeful things I had ever encountered, and I could not look at them without tears streaming down my face.

People from all classes and walks of life are ignorant about aphasia until somebody close to them is stricken and the world turns topsy-turvy. By a startling coincidence Carruth had met a neurologist at a camping ground who knew Williams and who gave Carruth a kind of abridged explanation of how a stroke impairs the brain. Carruth didn't point out that the halting line he quoted in small type is to the ear a cruel imitation of scanning a poetic line, but his final comment, "In Williams the death of language before the death of the man seems to me—but I have no prose to express it," is heartbreaking, because, like Williams, Carruth cannot locate the missing word and complete his thought.

Williams's last poems were collected in *Pictures from Brueghel*, which would win the Pulitzer Prize for poetry in 1963. An honor that had eluded Williams throughout his career arrived posthumously, when he could not savor the acclaim. (He also was given the Gold Medal for Poetry by the National Institute of Arts and Letters.) In a sense, the Pulitzer was a sort of Lifetime Achievement Award or a belated recognition of his underappreciated late poetry. Laughlin shrewdly decided to add *The Desert Music* and *Journey to Love* to *Pictures from Brueghel* and issue the triptych in paperback.

By the time he was writing and assembling the poems of *Pictures from Brueghel*, Williams plainly lacked the energy, focus, and patience to continue his search for advances in technique; the forms are mostly conventional. But if the wattage was flickering, the titles of poems indicate that Williams still worried about questions of design, whether traditional, as in "Sonnet in Search of an Author," "An Exercise," "Metric Figure," and "Song," or indigenously American, as announced in "Some Simple Measures in the American Idiom and the Variable Foot." This curious composition, a kind of dance suite in nine short movements, is Williams's last attempt to choreograph the variable foot. In his poems from the Armory Show on, he had, like Yeats, associated modernist experiment with dance. A variorum edition of Williams's verse would turn up copious references to and images of dance. He pioneered new poetic steps, dips, jumps, and swerves—the verbal equivalents of Martha Graham's modern dance—in the process liberating the body from the mind's iron control.

At times Williams was so intent on bequeathing to American poets a Promethean gift of fire that would light up a new American prosody that he overestimated the originality of the variable foot. (The slippery nomenclature has confounded even his most devoted admirers.) After all, poets in all periods have searched for ways to avoid a thumping regularity that coarsens or dulls the ear instead of ravishing it. Shakespeare, as Williams had learned in Poetics 101, was not enslaved to the iambic pentameter. When he dropped a trochee or spondee into a line or a soliloquy, were they not variable feet? The contrast between Iago's calculated villainy and Othello's heroic view of himself would be unthinkable without the rhythmic variations in their speech that define their character and motives. All gifted poets from Chaucer to Robert Frost achieved nuanced or startling effects by wedding syntax and sound: by letting punctuation break the meter in the middle of the line, for instance, or by deploying trochees, spondees, dactyls, anapests, and other metrical feet where they were least expected. Rhythm thus escaped the monotony of predictable beats.

In his long career, Williams was no stranger to these practices. Despite its vigorous reforms, modernism had not swept away the prosodic foundations of verse; even the madcap Dadaists, who mocked traditional usage and meaning, could not escape from the skin of language, and the surrealists plumbing the unconscious did not embrace rhythmic anarchy or proclaim that irrationality annulled sentence structure. Williams understood all this. In thinking about American speech rhythms, the poetic frontier he wanted to homestead, he had hit upon the variable foot as a versatile tool. It became, at times, a slogan, a battle cry, and an obsession. Yet if we read "Some Simple Measures in the American Idiom and the Variable Foot" to test his ideas and measures, we can't help being disappointed. The sequence is a set of charming miniatures, but the stage is too small, too cramped, for intricate patterns. As the title of the first poem has it, it is an "Exercise in Timing"; like a ballerina warming up at the bar, Williams flexes his muscles, ventures onstage, takes a few steps, and quickly exits:

> Oh
> the sumac died
> it's
> the first time
> I
> noticed it

This is modernism stripped down to its microcellular elements, barely able to sustain life as a poem; the structure, alternating one syllable with three or four, is simple as an amoeba's. "Histology," the next poem in the sequence, is the shortest anatomical study of a whale on record, as if refuting or lampooning Melville's exhaustive display of cetological knowledge in *Moby-Dick*:

There is
the
microscopic
anatomy

of
the whale
this is
reassuring

Williams doubles the stanza and again hangs utilitarian words such as "the" and "of" on their own lines before adding the wry comment "this is reassuring." But there's no opportunity for the verse feet to kick up their heels and execute variable steps.

After such a sparse beginning, "Perpetuum Mobile" cuts loose in a swinging gait. Serving as ballet master, Williams counts out the beats as his dancers move in rhythms both free and rigorous:

To all the girls
of all the ages
who walk up and down on

the streets of this town
silent or gabbing
putting

their feet down
one before the other
one two

one two they
pause sometimes before
a store window and

reform the line
from here
to China everywhere

back and
forth and back and forth
and back and forth

The dancers move in ranks, sometimes "up and down," "one foot before the other" in a regular "one two" cadence typical of walking. Where the girls put their feet down is as carefully plotted as where the stresses fall in the poem. In crossing the space between stanzas, as the pause between "putting" and "their feet down" wittily shows us, the foot can lose its balance or land gracefully. A line can also be syncopated, a fact that the changing positions of "back and forth" act out visually. In keeping with his oft-stated ambition to "reform the line," Williams cleverly plays with the syntax and admits a modicum of variety. But unlike the development in jazz riffs, the solo in "Perpetuum Mobile" is too brief—an ironic truncation given the poem's title, which refers to a piece of music, like a Paganini caprice, that is marked by "rapid figuration of a uniform and uninterrupted pattern" designed to show off the performer's virtuosity. Williams's poem loosely fits the definition, but the variable foot cannot strut its stuff and surprise us with inventive steps.

"The Blue Jay," the fourth poem in "Some Simple Measures," imitates bird flight and the imagination's love of kinetic movement:

It crouched
just before the take-off

caught
in the cinematograph-

ic motion
of the mind wings

just set to spread a
flash a

blue curse
a memory of you

my friend
shrieked at me

—serving art
as usual

The poem shows off several of Williams's prosodic trademarks. Compact, short lines mimic and control both motion (the syntactic takeoff) and where the sentence, if not the bird, lands. Similarly, Williams places the article "a" at the end of a line instead of at the beginning of the next line, as convention dictates and rhymes them visually, and lets one syllable or two occupy a line by itself. The ear adjusts to these choices, sensing that they are part of musical phrases, not whimsical or aleatory patterns. Yet the variable foot seems to hover between the couplets or at the ends of lines like a too-shy suitor.

In "Chloe," the seventh poem of the sequence, Williams devises a more complicated set of movements and stresses:

The calves of
the young girl's legs
when they are well-made

knees
lithely built
in their summer clothes

show them
predisposed toward flight
or the dance

the magenta flower
of the
moth-mullen balanced

idly
tilting her weight
from one foot

to the other
shifting
to avoid looking at me

on my way to
mail a letter
smiling to a friend

The idiom of this portrait is ingenuously American. Williams gazes at the bodies of the young girls poised between nervousness ("flight") and motion ("dance"). While his flirting makes one nubile ballerina fidget from one foot to the other and avert her eyes, he enjoys miming the role of harmless lecher—after all, he's only an old man mailing a letter—and disconcerting her. The poem's appeal lies in its eccentric playing with balance and weight (the participles in the last three stanzas, for example), but it scans in a traditional fashion; because of the short lines, the variable foot sits out this dance like a wallflower.

Williams begins the last poem, "The Stolen Peonies," tantalizingly: "What I got out of women / was difficult / to assess." But he doesn't make a stab at an answer. Instead, he recalls a commonplace incident, ten years into his marriage, in which thieves stole a "stand of peonies" from the Williamses' garden, which brought husband and wife close together in mourning their shared loss. The poem employs a run-on syntax, but here the variable foot, too, is missing in action.

Poets in their last period are often self-indulgently verbose, as if they've earned the prerogative of not counting words or weeding out repetitions. Others, suspicious of ornament, may prefer an accessible plain style. Williams chose both alternatives. Virtuosity was never his forte, and he was in no condition to walk around Rutherford without help, let alone walk the prosodic high wire without a safety net. The American vernacular would suffice to hold his poems together. There was comfort in choosing familiar subjects: thumbnail sketches of Floss and his grandchildren, old men in town gossiping about "the news from / Russia on a view of / the reverse surface of / the moon . . . ," a theme picked up in the penultimate poem, "Heel and Toe to the End" in *Pictures from Brueghel*, which pays homage to Yuri Gagarin, the Russian cosmonaut. While images of death haunt Williams, he achieves a kind of wintry serenity: "Sooner or later /

we must come to the end of our striving," he notes calmly. The sun sets in the west, and if he is not present to witness its return in the east the next morning, so be it; he will not rage against the dying light.

The book begins with a suite of ten modest poems about Brueghel paintings. These straightforward, sometimes flat descriptions—gone is the Cubist angularity and verve of Williams's anatomy of Juan Gris's collage "Roses" in *Spring and All*—offer a short course in the poet's appreciation, across cultures and centuries, of the Flemish master's art. In 1924, Williams and Floss had spent an enchanted afternoon in the Vienna Kunsthistorisches Museum looking at the Brueghel paintings, but for his poems the reproductions in an art book served his homage well enough; he strove to make his poems imitations, not copies. As Brueghel to his time, so stand I to mine, Williams seems to be saying: because Brueghel passed over a career as a court painter, rooting his art in the local, he illustrates Williams's unshaken conviction that homegrown materials can inspire great art. The paintings Williams selects give a synoptic view of Brueghel's oeuvre: a self-portrait, a mythic subject (*The Fall of Icarus*), two renditions of New Testament themes (*The Adoration of the Kings* and *The Parable of the Blind Leading the Blind*), but mostly scenes drawn from the "workaday world" that depict peasants at hard labor, "with scythes tumbling / the wheat in rows" in "Haymaking," resting indolently after harvesting corn in the heat of day, or celebrating a wedding. Williams loves the teeming life and rough-hewn community in Brueghel's paintings, their humane mixture of humor, grotesquerie, and, above all, inventive detail casually slipped into a corner of the canvas—"an unhinged barn door" used as a trestle for a makeshift table; a waiter "in a red / coat a spoon in his hatband," or an "inn-sign / hanging from a / broken hinge . . . a stag a crucifix / between his antlers." The figures in Brueghel's paintings move in rhythm with the changes in the season, another trait that endears the painter to Williams. And what a crowd Brueghel has effortlessly gathered: hunters with their pack of dogs, women clustering about a "huge bonfire" to ward off the cold, children underfoot or playing, as in the three-part "Children's Games," with any object at hand—they are instinctive improvisers—and ingeniously using it, as an imaginative poet might, for fun or aggression. The sheer physical movement—running and somersaulting, climbing and swinging—is exhilarating to the sedentary poet. The poem is a virtual Whitmanesque catalogue in short lines of children's toys and games—stilts, hoops, pinwheels, even "an empty hogshead into which a boy hollers," an image, as Mariani points out, that encapsulates the end of Williams's life, "his words reduced to a vanishing point."

Elsewhere in these ekphrastic poems, Williams praises Brueghel's compositional technique, his disciplined genius for distributing figures in space, as in "The Parable of the Blind," where the beggars lead "each other diagonally downward / / across the canvas from one side / to stumble finally onto a bog / where the picture / and the composition ends back / of which no seeing man / / is represented." Williams does not set himself up as Brueghel's rival or equal, since he lacks the Flemish artist's superb organizational ability; "there is no detail extraneous / to the composition," he notes apropos of "The Parable." Despite the slowdown of his mind's neural firing, he identifies with Brueghel's "resourceful mind / that governed the whole / / the alert mind dissatisfied with / what it is asked to do / and cannot do." The painter's "covert assertions / for art, art, art," Williams marvels, avoid falling into the trap of the merely aesthetic: in the *Self-Portrait*, Brueghel reveals himself as both coarse (his "bulbous nose") and refined (his "delicate hands"). Williams's diction in *Peasant Wedding* strives to match the unself-conscious particulars that fill this painting with vitality: bagpipers, "a head / of ripe wheat" (a symbol of fertility) affixed to the wall, a hound stretched out under the table, a shy bride "awkwardly silent" while "women in their / starched headgear," who have doubtless attended many such weddings, "are gabbing" next to the "bearded Mayor." (Williams slyly rhymes "gabbing" with "clabber" five lines away.)

Because Williams was not shut off from his own childhood, he could take subdued pleasure in writing affectionate poems about his grandchildren. Occasionally he lapses into the stilted tone of a sage delivering sententious precepts, as in part 2 of "Suzy," a poem about Paul's fifteen-year-old daughter, Williams's favorite grandchild:

life is a flower when it
opens you will
look trembling into it unsure

of what the traditional
mirror may reveal
between hope and despair while

a timorous old man
doubtfully
turns away his foolish head

In the aftermath of the strokes, Williams's emotions rose closer to the surface. In that mirror, he appears to himself as a broken-down, confused, and chastened old man, like Lear after the storm on the heath. Williams was seldom timorous, but he turns away as if ashamed of his condition and his betrayal of feeling. In the third set of three tercets, he momentarily recovers his poise and confesses how much he cherishes Suzy, but his posture—his back is turned to her—tells another story: "he yearns after / [her] protectively / hopelessly wanting nothing." "Hopelessly" almost cancels "protectively," the poem ending poignantly on the word "nothing."

The pall of death permeates "The Children," a solemn memory poem that recalls a moment from Williams's boyhood when he and his friends, while frolicking in the cemetery woods, came across a family plot that included the graves of several children. In an act of respect, the boys lay violets on each headstone. The poem is slight, but the feeling for children and the precariousness of life is not. In "The Gift," Williams revisits the story of the Three Magi. "The pilgrims could not "know / of a mother's needs / or a child's / appetite," as Williams did, but their "wondering eyes" drink in the miracle of an alchemy both physical and spiritual: "Hard gold to love, / a mother's milk!" When Williams, who in so much of his art (and medical practice) grappled with imperfection, asks simply, "What is death, / beside this?" his answer, "Nothing," is purged of any nihilism. But his mood in this period was downcast. Nothingness, he could not deny, was imminent. He was not the kind of person, even in his debilitated state, to whistle in the dark.

The cosmography of the following poem, "The Turtle," which undercuts the Christian one of "The Gift," represents Williams's habitual outlook. Obsessed with his pet turtle, Williams's grandson Paul commissions a poem from his grandfather. The world here is not suffused with love and worship. As if he has read too many comic books, the boy repeatedly attributes "murderous motives" to the turtle, which Williams incorporates into his story and embellishes. Escaping confinement, the turtle

. . . will stride about the world
destroying all

with his sharp beak.
Whatever opposes him
in the streets of the city
shall go down.
Cars will be overturned.

Knowing that children thrill at the proximity to danger, Williams doesn't soft-pedal it: the beaked turtle is a formidable adversary who can maim and terrify, though it can be subdued and controlled. With courtly flourish and syntactic curlicues, he addresses Paul like Merlin speaking to an Arthurian knight:

And upon his back
          shall ride,
          to his conquests,
my Lord,
          you!
          You shall be master!

The poem could end here, but Williams seizes the moment to spin his version of an ancient creation myth:

                    In the beginning
there was a great tortoise
          who supported the world.

Upon him
          all ultimately
          rests.
Without him
          nothing will stand.
He is all wise
and can outrun the hare.
          In the night
          his eyes carry him
to unknown places.
          He is your friend.

Like the turtle, Williams moves haltingly, but sees clearly, and will soon be carried "to unknown places." His simple last line wisely reassures Paul, and offers solace to Williams.

Williams's health had deteriorated steadily over the last fifteen years of his life, so that the final collapse came as no surprise. That he had survived heart disease, a barrage of strokes, and an operation for sigmoid (colorectal) cancer bordered on the miraculous. In his last years, as his primary physician remembered, he could be a whiny, restless, even mutinous patient, and not without cause: despair at the diminished thing he had become held him in its vise. Somehow, though, the creative spark was not extinguished. He might go to the typewriter, bang the keys, and scratch out a line or two, but what mostly came out was often illegible; even Floss could not decipher the scrambled letters. His mind was a black hole with light trapped inside. He had no alternative but to shut down his voluminous correspondence with poets and friends that had served so well as an agora in which he debated poetics and offered a running commentary—inspired, hasty, provocative, charming, generous—on the raucous poetry scene and the fault lines in American culture he had observed for half a century. Showing Williams at his least guarded and self-conscious, these letters are a rich archive of friendships and a gallery of caricatures: Williams might skewer Pound in one letter and thank him for a perceptive review in the next; praise Zukofsky's *The Book of Prosody* for its discerning analysis of modernist forms and harmonic phrasing; narrate a bawdy anecdote about a sixty-five-year-old Englishman, completely sure of himself; and laugh derisively at Oscar Williams's conservative choices for an anthology of modern American verse. Now when his brain functioned sporadically or broke down entirely—he processed information at an excruciatingly lumbering rate—he could not jot down two sentences or even dictate replies to Floss.

Poor eyesight and decreased comprehension made reading impossible. When he slumped in a chair, gazing blankly into space like a dead soul, Floss could not bear the sight, so she spent long hours reading to him. (They had read to each other constantly throughout their marriage.) For brief periods, the eclipse of his mind lifted. One book they shared was the classic young adult novel *The Yearling*. In *Pictures from Brueghel*,

Williams wrote a formally controlled elegy for its author, "To the Ghost of Marjorie Kinnan Rawlings." The writer had been thrown from a horse and broken her neck. "You lived nerves drawn / tense," he addresses her, linking her desperation and valiant struggle to his. "Tapiola," an elegy for Jean Sibelius, dredges up a more personal memory. In paying tribute to the Finnish composer's "placing of sounds together, / edge against edge," Williams might be recalling his own late-night solitary hours in his attic atelier writing poems:

> You stayed up half
> the night in your attic room under the eaves, composing
> secretly, setting it down, period after period,
> as the wind whistled. Lightning flashed! The roof
> creaked about your ears threatening to give
> way! But you had a composition to finish that could
> not wait. The Storm entered your mind where all
> good things are secured, written down, for love's
> sake and to defy the devil of emptiness.

The "devil of emptiness" did not hollow out Williams's memory entirely. The past returned in fragments, and sometimes, as in "Tapiola," surprisingly whole. And the present brought its garland of pleasures: the visits of his children and grandchildren lifted him temporarily out of his morose mood, as did the times young poets knocked on the door of 9 Ridge Road to pay their respects to the veteran general of the poetry wars whom they so admired. Williams would greet them warmly, and Floss set out tea and cookies. Most of the time, however, the atmosphere was poignantly awkward: Williams could barely hold up his end of a conversation.

The literature of aphasia does report cases in which, sometimes, for a few hours a day, the fog that blankets the aphasic's brain clears and he reverts to his former self, able to think and speak clearly. Such a tonic change occurred on June 7, 1960, when the poets A. R. Ammons, John Logan, and Robert Bly paid Williams a visit. Ammons remembers Williams as "kind, genial and spirited as before." Williams suggested an outing to the Paterson Falls, the site of his recently completed long poem. "He knew all the little back roads and short cuts," Ammons notes. Being out in the world once more, Williams threw off his infirmities: the floodgates of memory opened and his speech "had practically no tie-ups, when the words just wouldn't be said." The opinionated, ribald Williams with a roving eye was in rare form: "He noticed lovers particularly. Those parked in cars at the look-out point, those lying in the grass. He got in the words fuck and cock, saying he didn't have any cock anymore. Later he mentioned how with contraceptives it's so much safer for girls than it used to be and how they were more willing to take a chance."

He enjoyed telling the poets about Hamilton and Sam Patch, disparate figures associated with Paterson and the falls. His only concession to his shaky health was to hold on tightly to Ammons's arm as they stood close to the edge of the chasm and its vertiginous drop. He delivered his judgment of Don Allen's *Grove Anthology of New American Poetry* with vulgar relish: "most of it was shit." He was equally interested in seeing the "impressive changes" that were making his town unrecognizable to him, and in pointing out the house at 131 Passaic Avenue in which he was born, and 9 Ridge Road. And he volunteered two facts about his growing up in Rutherford: "He said Indian stories were his nightly provender when he was a boy; that he used to hunt a lot but wasn't a very good shot." This holiday from routine exhilarated Williams, but it was unfortunately only a temporary freedom. The aphasia returned.

A few weeks before Williams's death, Denise Levertov paid him a visit, which she described to Robert Duncan: "He just can't say what he feels or thinks any more & the sad way he gives up in the midst of a stammering sentence now—'O well'—& the slow shake of his head—it's a slow ending to a life so quick & quickening." Floss translated his jumbled thoughts as best she could. Nonetheless, even these nearly wordless communions seemed like sacramental moments.

As a doctor who had stood vigil at the bedside of hundreds of dying patients, Williams knew the myriad ways people coped with their exit from life. Some received extreme unction and shuffled off their mortal coils benignly; some screamed or hallucinated or spoke final gnomic words, while others maintained a stony silence. Some died in isolation, others surrounded by their families. "I'm not sorry for myself," Williams told an interviewer, "for I think I can lie down in my bed and die as uncomplaining as any man," Williams clung to no religious illusions that his soul would migrate to some glorious afterlife.

Williams died in his bed on March 4, 1963, of a coronary thrombosis. Practical to the end, he had discussed with Floss whether he should be buried in the Rutherford cemetery or cremated. After some temporizing, he'd decided on burial. He had purchased a plot in Hillside Cemetery, near where his parents and Floss's mother, father, and brother were interred. The funeral took place on a cold, rainy day in a windowless chapel at Collins Funeral Home, not in a church; Williams had instructed Floss that he didn't want the incensed "religious stuff" perfuming the air. Since he had perhaps written more poems about flowers than any other American poet, sprigs of blossoms appropriately draped his coffin. The chapel was filled with family and friends and a large crowd of townspeople, from a policeman whom Williams had delivered into the world to neighbors, patients, and shopkeepers. By that turnout, his devotion to the local was honored and vindicated. (Few small-town artists die where they were born, as Williams did.) A Unitarian minister presided over the service and read, predictably, "Tract," Williams's harangue against pretentious funerals. The family squelched a suggestion that the cortège walk to the cemetery, as the poem recommended. That would have travestied Williams's profound conviction that life should not copy art.

As the mourners filed out of the funeral parlor the rain stopped, and when everybody reached the cemetery, Levertov remembers, the weather shifted to "incredible bright sunshine & blue sky & the wind blowing in the trees." It was as if the imagination vouchsafed Williams one last glance at the "Beautiful Thing," "The City standing clear to the northeast beyond the swamps, beyond the unseen River—." At the grave site, as the service was winding down, a jalopy drove up carrying Gilbert Sorrentino, Joel Oppenheimer, LeRoi Jones, and other literary disciples; they had come from New York to bid Williams farewell. Dressed in ill-fitting black suits and clutching flowers to toss into the grave (Greenwich Village's deference to suburban customs), they added a touch of comic sentiment to the solemn occasion that Williams would have chuckled over and found touching. "When you're through with sex, with ambition, what can an old man create?" he asked in *I Wanted to Write a Poem*. "Art, of course," he answered, "a piece of art that will go beyond him into the lives of young people . . . The old man meets the young people and lives on." In this goal, Williams had been wholly successful.

Condolence letters and telegrams poured in. Floss, according to Levertov, read Pound's moving words of praise with a crack in her voice, shedding one or two small tears: "He put up a great fight for you & he bore with me for 60 years. I shall never have another poet friend like him." For Floss, donning widow's weeds was probably a relief: the immense burden of caring for Williams, physically and emotionally, for fifteen years had been lifted. In the long nights ahead she would mull over the erratic course of their marriage and evaluate the character and deeds of the man she had lived with for over half a century. Responding to a condolence letter from Marianne Moore, Floss summed up the marriage in her homespun, levelheaded way: discounting the ordeal of the last years when he fell mute, "[they were] years to treasure—full of companionship—partnership—ups & downs—in fact a life." Conspicuously missing, of course, is the word "love," as hard for her to say as it was for her husband. Floss would not compromise her emotional honesty.

Floss was not one of those dragon-like literary widows who guard their husbands' eternal flame. She continued living modestly at 9 Ridge Road until her death on May 19, 1976. Growing royalties from Williams's books ensured that her last years would be comfortable. The storms that punctuated her life with the volatile Williams no longer passed over her. Her days were eventful in commonplace ways. Her sons and grandchildren lived nearby, offering company and filial love; she followed their successes and setbacks with interest, and she didn't lose the pleasurable habit of reading. Then there was the heavy traffic of literary pilgrims, who came hoping for permission to climb the stairs to the attic where Williams wrote so many of his poems, or to glimpse the room where he examined patients, or to stare at the chair Pound sat in when he read a poem to a critical William George while sipping his host's best Goldwasser: the poet's artifacts had quickly become icons. Biographers and readers of poetry who had fallen under Williams's spell, their ranks quickly growing, were curious to meet Floss and to tap her memories.

To most visitors, an hour at 9 Ridge Road was a ticket of entry into a charmed circle, whose magic could be conjured by the courteous, plain woman who doubled as the high priestess of the Rutherford shrine; they believed that she could clear up mysteries—or darken them. Did she? I doubt it. At her core, Floss remained a private woman, capable of keeping a secret or two of her own from the world's prying eyes. She did not confide to the world what she thought his numerous infidelities said about her husband's character. In *The Double Flame*, his elegant study of love and eroticism, Octavio Paz notes that "if practiced by only one partner, it [infidelity] causes the other suffering and humiliation. The unfaithful party is insensitive, cruel, incapable of love." Though in "Asphodel, That Greeny Flower" Williams compared Floss to Helen of Troy, she did not mesmerize him sexually, fire his imagination, and reconcile him to monogamy. It is a mistake, however, to view her, as I did twenty years ago, as a patient Griselda type, colorless, dutiful, and masochistic. We're not privy to her and Bill's pillow talk, but we know from the poems and plays that when he flaunted his affairs and taunted her for her lack of sexual charisma, she did not endure these slights meekly: he felt the lash of her sarcasm and outrage. That his tortuous defense of his inconstancy as necessary to his poetry and to the refreshment of their marriage infuriated her, one cannot doubt. But one suspects that part of her conceded that there were a few grains of truth in his argument. For fifty years she weighed the costs and benefits of remaining in an imperfect marriage. She understood, probably better than her husband, the compulsion that periodically drove him away from and then back to her.

At Floss's funeral service, the Presbyterian minister, at the behest of William Eric and Paul, read the Twenty-third Psalm and "Asphodel." Why on that occasion of grief and remembrance did the sons choose a poem that had touched a chronically inflamed nerve in their mother? To relieve their embarrassment at their father's womanizing: that is the logical answer. Floss's ashes were collected and she was buried next to her husband in Hillside Cemetery on May 19, 1976. No sibyl disclosed what in her heart Floss felt about the handsome poet doctor she had wed—for better and for worse—years before.

Notes

ABBREVIATIONS

The following abbreviations are used in the notes to identify each work by William Carlos Williams:

A	*The Autobiography of William Carlos Williams*. New York: Random House, 1951.
A1	The Autobiography of William Carlos Williams. Unpublished version, in the Collection of American Literature, Yale University.
AQQ	*A Book of Poems: Al Que Quiere!* Boston: Four Seas Company, 1917.
BU	*The Build-Up*. New York: Random House, 1952.
CEP	*The Collected Earlier Poems*. Norfolk, Conn.: New Directions, 1951.
CLP	*The Collected Later Poems*. Norfolk, Conn.: New Directions, 1950.
Diary	WCW's unpublished diary for January–June 1924, in the possession of the Williams family.
EK	*The Embodiment of Knowledge*. Edited by Ron Loewinsohn. New York: New Directions, 1974.
FD	*The Farmer's Daughters: The Collected Stories of William Carlos Williams*. Norfolk, Conn.: New Directions, 1961.
GAN	*The Great American Novel*. Paris: Three Mountains Press, 1923.
I	*Imaginations (Kora in Hell, Spring and All, The Great American Novel, The Descent of Winter, A Novelette and Other Prose)*. Edited by Webster Schott. New York: New Directions, 1970.
IAG	*In the American Grain*. New York: Albert & Charles Boni, 1925.
IM	*In the Money*. Norfolk, Conn.: New Directions, 1940.
Int	*Interviews with William Carlos Williams*. Edited by Linda Welsheimer Wagner. New York: New Directions, 1976.
IWWP	*I Wanted to Write a Poem: The Autobiography of the Works of a Poet*. Reported and edited by Edith Heal. Boston: Beacon Press, 1958.
KH	*Kora in Hell: Improvisations*. Boston: Four Seas, 1920.
ML	*Many Loves and Other Plays: The Collected Plays of Williams Carlos Williams*. Norfolk, Conn.: New Directions, 1961.

P   *Paterson*. Norfolk, Conn.: New Directions, 1963. Books 1 through 5 appeared respectively in 1946, 1948, 1949, 1951, and 1958.

PB   *Pictures from Brueghel and Other Poems*, including *The Desert Music* and *Journey to Love*. Norfolk, Conn.: New Directions, 1962.

RI   *A Recognizable Image: William Carlos Williams on Art and Artists*. Edited by Bram Dijkstra. New York: New Directions, 1978.

Rome   *Rome*. Edited by Steven Ross Loevy, *Iowa Review* 9, no. 3 (Spring 1978), pp. 1–65.

SA   *Spring and All*. Paris: Contact Publishing Company, 1923.

SE   *Selected Essays of William Carlos Williams*. New York: Random House, 1954.

SG   *Sour Grapes: A Book of Poems*. Boston: Four Seas, 1921.

SL   *The Selected Letters of William Carlos Williams*. Edited by John C. Thirlwall. New York: McDowell, Obolensky, 1957.

VP   *A Voyage to Pagany*. New York: Macaulay, 1928.

W   *The Wedge*. Cummington, Mass.: Cummington Press, 1944.

WM   *White Mule*. Norfolk, Conn.: New Directions, 1937.

YMW   *Yes, Mrs. Williams*. New York: McDowell, Obolensky, 1959.

Also the following abbreviations:

Letters EP   *The Letters of Ezra Pound, 1907–1941*. Edited by D. D. Paige. New York: Harcourt, Brace & World, 1950.

Letters JK   *The Letters of John Keats, 1814–1821, Volume 1*. Edited by Hyder Rollins. Cambridge, Mass.: Harvard University Press, 1958.

Letters WS   *Letters of Wallace Stevens*. Selected and edited by Holly Stevens. New York: Knopf, 1966.

ND   *New Directions*.

WCWN   (WCWR as of Fall 1980) *The William Carlos Williams Newsletter* (now *Review*).

OVERTURE TO WILLIAM CARLOS WILLIAMS'S
DANSE AMÉRICAINE

ix **"America of Poets"**: *Selected Poems*, p. ix.

x **"Consistency in the short run"**: R. W. Flint, "America of Poets," *Parnassus: Poetry in Review* 3, no. 2 (1976), p. 164.

xi **"the mysterious late excellence"**: John Berryman, "An Elegy for W.C.W., the Lovely Man," Dream Song 324, in *The Dream Songs* (Farrar, Straus and Giroux, 1969), p. 246.

xi **"hard nervous secular knowingness"**: Robert Lowell, "Dr. Williams," in *Collected Prose*, ed. Robert Giroux (New York: Farrar, Straus and Giroux, 1987), p. 41.

xi **"the most embarrassing poet"**: Donald Davie, "A Demurral," in *Two Ways out of Whitman* (Manchester, U.K.: Carcanet, 2000), p. 64.

xi **"dumb ox"**: Ibid., p. 65.

xi **"anti-intellectual"**: Ibid., p. 66.

xi **"incapable of consecutive thought"**: Ibid., p. 67.

xi **"practice [of poetry]"**: Ibid., p. 69.

xii **"lax and lawless"**: Samuel Johnson, "The Life of Cowley," in *The Lives of the Poets*, ed. John H. Middendorf (New Haven, Conn.: Yale University Press, 2010), vol. 1, p. 63.

xii **"your three-decker"**: Magid and Witemeyer, *Williams and Tomlinson*, p. 2.

xii **"a very delicate ear"**: Seamus Heaney, "'Vowels and History': *Wintering Out*," in *Stepping Stones* (New York: Farrar, Straus and Giroux, 2008), p. 145.

xvi **"just over the back fence"**: *A*, p. 19.

xvii **"In the barnyard"**: Ibid., p. 7.

xix **"This may sound"**: *SL*, p. 7.

xxi **"the infant or"**: Keats to Reynolds, in *Letters JK*, p. 280.

xxi **"Chamber of Maiden-Thought"**: Ibid., p. 281.

xxi **"the fertility of invention"**: Johnson, "Life of Cowley," p. 47.

xxix **"short lines, often in quatrains"**: *SL*, p. 616.

xxix **"Few poets can"**: Robert Lowell, *Collected Prose* (Farrar, Straus and Giroux, 1987), p. 41.

xxix **"He was one"**: *A*, p. 171.

I. POETRY AS BIOGRAPHICAL EVIDENCE

4 **"always recondite sense"**: Adam Phillips, *On Kissing, Tickling, and Being Bored* (Cambridge, Mass.: Harvard University Press, 1993), p. 8.

4 **"with a great deal of guesswork"**: Leslie Stephen, *Studies of a Biographer* (London: Duckworth, 1902), vol. 3, p. 40.

5 **"biography first convinces"**: Dickinson to Higginson, February 1885, in *Letters*, vol. 2, p. 864.

20 **"They don't try"**: WCW, "A New Line IS a New Measure: Louis Zukofsky's *Anew*," *New Quarterly of Poetry* 2, no. 2 (Winter 1947–1948), pp. 8–16.

23 **"You sure would"**: *A*, p. 117.

24 **"an amazing woman"**: Ibid., p. 124.

24 **"That's one thing about sex"**: Ibid., p. 206.

24 **"She [Dotty] was good-looking"**: Ibid., p. 208.

24 **"Suppose you had found me"**: Ibid., p. 209.

2. ROOTS AND BRANCHES OF THE FAMILY TREE

41 **"I was insanely jealous"**: *Int*, p. 47.

42 **"We were mere"**: *A*, p. 29.

42 **"general deviltry"**: Ibid., p. 30.

42 **"He loved to read"**: *YMW*, p. 7.

43 **"bears the marks of Pop's corrections"**: *A*, p. 107.

43 **"I saw him coming"**: Ibid., p. 14.

49 **"A stickler for principles"**: Ibid., p. 103.

49 **"was not one"**: *YMW*, p. 9.

49 **"a dollar"**: *A*, p. 15.

49 **"that the spirits"**: Ibid., p. 17.

52 **"document in madness"**: *Hamlet*, 4.5.173.

53 **"despised women"**: *YMW*, p. 141.

53 **"exhale her fragrance"**: Ibid., p. 33.

54 **"yellow with the juice"**: Ibid., p. 65.

54 **"I don't want"**: Ibid., p. 27.
54 **"How many generations"**: Ibid., p. 53.
55 **"All the races"**: Ibid., p. 35.
55 **"intermarried"**: Ibid., p. 30.
55 **"revolution of sentiment"**: Ibid., p. 35.
55 **"The vortex of her"**: Ibid., p. 59.
55 **"while we were working"**: Ibid., p. 28.
55 *Yes, Mrs. Williams*: Ibid., p. 56.
55 **"In Puerto Rico"**: Ibid., p. 49.
56 **"to relieve the occasional monotony"**: Ibid., p. 17.
56 **"She was almost blind"**: Ibid., p. 18.
56 **She felt, Williams says**: Ibid., p. 94.
56 **"a small woman"**: Ibid., p. 24.
56 **"She is [living in]"**: Ibid., p. 7.
57 **"her romantic ideas"**: Ibid., p. 20.
59 **"She has always been"**: *Kora in Hell* in *I*, pp. 7–8.
59 **"Why am I alive?"**: *YMW*, p. 33.
59 **"That is the defeated romantic"**: Ibid., pp. 33–34.
60 **"Whatever is before"**: Ibid., p. 7.
63 **"bridge between herself"**: Ibid., p. 94.
66 **"We have always been"**: Ibid., p. 16.
66 **"There is an incentive"**: Ibid., pp. 35–36.
67 **"First, that I never"**: *SL*, p. 7.

3. "HALFWAY TO HELL"

69 **"Persephone gone into Hades"**: *A*, p. 158.
77 **"image was to lie"**: Ibid., p. 138.
85 **"Improvisation always requires a plan"**: Octavio Paz, *The Double Flame*, trans. Helen Lane (San Diego: Harcourt Brace, 1996), p. 240.

4. YOUTHFUL FUMBLINGS

93 **"In America"**: Henry Adams, *The Education of Henry Adams*, p. 383.
93 **"materialistic scramble"**: Friedel, Beer, p. xiii.
98 **"nebulous but high-minded"**: *A*, p. 53.
98 **"There would be a bitter"**: Ibid., p. 49.
99 **In a companion poem**: Ibid., p. 53.
101 **"Twenty-three or -four"**: Ibid., p. 77.
101 **"To do what I mean to do"**: *SL*, p. 14.
102 **"her breasts were especially lacerated"**: *A*, p. 81.
107 **"a stickler for his principles"**: Ibid., pp. 102–103.
108 **"I myself am hell"**: Milton's Satan in *Paradise Lost*, p. 259.

5. MANY LOVES

111 **"The real thing is"**: *IWWP*, p. 33.
113 **"My mind was always rebellious"**: *A*, p. 130.

114 **"The whole life"**: *SL*, p. 18.
115 **"how identical is"**: Ibid.
116 **He got no further**: *A*, p. 115.
116 **"sank back once more"**: Ibid., p. 116.
117 **"completely foreign"**: Ibid., p. 117.
117 **"was glad to get away"**: Ibid.
117 **"and my mind was wild"**: Ibid., p. 127.
121 **"violence has begotten peace"**: *KH*, p. 32.
124 **"There is something magical"**: *SL*, p. 20.
128 **"the dark void coaxing him"**: *I*, p. 45.
128 **"misery and brokenness"**: Ibid., p. 57.
128 **"tarantelle that wears"**: Ibid.
128 **"it's hard to tell loss"**: Ibid., p. 55.
129 **"things around me"**: Ibid., p. 23.

6. A RISQUÉ LIAISON WITH THE FABULOUS BARONESS
140 **"I radiated sex attraction"**: *BM*, p. 116.
140 **"a woman of my far-flung"**: Ibid., p. 120.
141 **"was, of course, myself"**: *IWWP*, p. 45.
143 **"City stir——wind on eardrum"**: *Little Review* 7 (September–December 1920).
145 **"gave her two hundred dollars"**: *A*, p. 169.

7. ADVENTURES IN THE SKIN TRADE
152 **"To know the profundities"**: *BU*, p. 301.
155 **"the perfect expression"**: McAlmon and Boyle, *Being Geniuses Together*, p. 6.
155 **"upstart crow"**: Ibid.
155 **"Bill Williams was a soil"**: Ibid., pp. 143–44.
155 **"Williams has often said"**: Ibid., p. 169.
156 **"You and W[atson] are"**: Pound to Thayer and Watson, May 21, 1920, in Sutton, *Pound, Thayer, Watson, and "The Dial,"* p. 37.
157 **"Bob and I thought"**: *SL*, p. 49.
157 **"To tell the truth"**: Ibid., p. 26.
158 **"I wish I had"**: WCW to Lowell, March 6, 1921, in *SL*, p. 51.
158 **"violent appeal"**: Mariani, *William Carlos Williams*, p. 186.
159 **"flow in my smallest capillaries"**: WCW to Moore, March 23, 1921, in *SL*, p. 52.
159 **"no Tennysonianness of speech"**: Pound to Monroe, in Harriet Monroe, *A Poet's Life* (New York: Macmillan, 1938), p. 267.
160 **"My God, have we"**: *SL*, p. 51.
160 **"militant friend"**: Monroe, *Poet's Life*, p. 389.
161 **"Of the few books"**: WCW to Burke, October 21, 1921, in *SL*, pp. 53–54.
161 **"sticking my fingers"**: *IWWP*, p. 32.
165 **"It [means] dissolution"**: WCW, "The Ideal Quarrel," p. 39.
165 **"For to break and begin"**: Ibid.
167 **Elena owned a dress**: *A*, p. 88.
169 **"The Day Nursery had"**: *CP1*, p. 56.

172 **"[T]o deride a wife"**: WCW, "Prose About Love," p. 9.
172 **"Fully roused men"**: Ibid.
173 **The dialogue is**: Ibid.

8. EXPERIMENTAL BREAKTHROUGHS
178 **"Miss Moore, using"**: SL, p. 121.
179 **"Europe is nothing"**: GAN, p. 174.
179 **"a priest, a roisterer"**: Ibid., p. 168.
179 **"America is a mass of pulp"**: Ibid., p. 175.
179 **"What did you say, dear"**: WCW, A Dream of Love, p. 167.
180 **"Words are the flesh"**: GAN, p. 160.
180 **"The imagination will not"**: Ibid., pp. 200–201.
180 **"So as I can hear"**: Ibid., p. 219.
180 **"I wish you could"**: Ibid.
181 **"the essentials of the American situation"**: Ibid., p. 211.
181 **"a new art form"**: A, p. 174.
181 **"the great catastrophe"**: Ibid., p. 146.
182 **"I'm glad you like Eliot's verse"**: WCW & JL, in Witemeyer, *Williams and Laughlin*, pp. 40–41.
183 **"Nobody ever saw it"**: *IWWP*, p. 36.
184 **"Chapter headings"**: Ibid., pp. 36–37.
184 **"It made sense to me"**: Ibid., p. 37.
184 **"positively repellent"**: SA, p. 177.
185 **"[p]oetry that used to go hand in hand"**: Ibid.
185 **"To refine, to clarify"**: Ibid., p. 178.
185 **"to find one phrase"**: P, p. 140.
185 **"The riddle of a man"**: Ibid., p. 107.
185 **"Love is no comforter"**: Ibid., p. 87.
186 **"I speak for the integrity"**: SA, p. 179.
186 **"It is spring"**: Ibid., p. 180.
186 **"In that huge and microscopic career"**: Ibid., p. 182.
189 **"We do not believe"**: Duncan to Levertov, January 12, 1961, in *The Letters of Robert Duncan and Denise Levertov*, ed. Robert J. Bertholf and Albert Gelpi (Stanford, Calif.: Stanford University Press, 2004), p. 272.
189 **"in appreciation for food"**: William Eric Williams, "Life with Father," p. 66.
190 **"had the format of many pages"**: Donald Davie, *Two Ways out of Whitman* (Manchester, U.K.: Carcanet, 2000), p. 68.
190 **Davie fails to see**: SA, p. 189.
191 **"The man of imagination"**: Ibid., p. 188.
191 **"seeking to invent and design"**: Ibid.
192 **"arabesques, skips and jumps"**: Duncan to Levertov, in *Letters of Duncan and Levertov*, p. 272.
195 **"the forms common to experience"**: SA, p. 194.
195 **"familiar, simple things"**: Ibid., p. 197.
198 **"are gaudy in the imaginations"**: GAN, p. 200.
200 **In an effort to free**: SA, pp. 234, 235.
201 **In the poem**: CP1, p. 324.

202 **"rapidity of motion"**: *Int*, p. 67.
203 **"Everything new must be wrong"**: *GAN*, p. 354.
208 **"the wheelbarrow in question"**: *Questia*, p. 60.
209 **"The sight impressed me somehow"**: Richard B. McLanathan and Gene Brown, *The Arts* (New York: Arno, 1978), p. 219.
210 **"civilized"**: ?, p. 193.
211 **"liberated to pirouette"**: *SA*, p. 234.

9. THE "STRANGE PHOSPHORUS" OF AMERICAN HISTORY

213 **"I'd enjoy a trip"**: WCW to Pound, March 29, 1922, p. 57.
214 **"leave his medical practice"**: Ibid.
215 **"The American lives"**: Alexis de Tocqueville, *Democracy in America*, p. 404.
216 **"The motive . . . toward a"**: Alan Trachtenberg, "Mumford in the 1920s," in *Lincoln's Smile and Other Enigmas* (New York: Hill and Wang, 2007), p. 226.
217 **"to find out for myself"**: *A*, p. 178.
217 **"It is the universal nature"**: Ralph Waldo Emerson, "History," in (New York: Library of America, 1983), p. 238.
217 **"we are always coming up"**: Ibid., p. 240.
218 **"Eric loves his friends"**: *IAG*, p. 2.
220 **"a predestined and bitter fruit"**: Ibid., p. 7.
220 **"With its archaic smile"**: Ibid., p. 10.
221 **"upon the foundation"**: Ibid., p. 22.
221 **"the branches growing"**: Ibid., p. 26.
221 **"was neither malicious"**: Ibid., p. 27.
222 **"Scarcely an element"**: Ibid., pp. 32–33.
222 **"The Tenochtitlan chapter"**: *IWWP*, pp. 42–43.
223 **"Decorated with curious imagery"**: *IAG*, pp. 33–34.
223 **"The earth is black"**: Ibid., p. 34.
224 **"laid siege to the intolerable intruders"**: Ibid., p. 37.
225 **"But this time the Yamasses"**: Ibid., p. 44.
225 **"metaphysical subtleties"**: Henry Adams, vol. 1, p. 79.
226 **"Their religious zeal"**: *IAG*, p. 66.
226 **"The result of that brave"**: Ibid., p. 68.
226 **"[America] has become"**: Ibid.
227 **"The future complexion"**: Nathaniel Hawthorne, "The Maypole of Merry Mount," in *Twice-Told Tales*, p. 40.
228 **"Morton's peccadillo with fantastic violence"**: *IAG*, p. 80.
229 **"He is a student"**: Ibid., p. 107.
229 **"there is a source"**: Ibid., p. 109.
229 **"No, no. True they had"**: Ibid., p. 113.
230 **Larbaud was taken aback**: Ibid., p. 115. ("miasma" is spelled "miasm")
230 **"an immorality that IS America"**: Ibid., p. 116.
230 **"the support of history"**: Ibid.
230 **"disentangle the obscurities"**: Ibid.
231 **"blossoming, thriving"**: Ibid., p. 121.
231 **He shared the tribe's privations**: Ibid.
231 **"at the foot of his rude cross"**: Ibid., p. 127.

232 **"sly, covert, almost cringing"**: Ibid., p. 154.
232 **"He is our wise prophet of chicanery"**: Ibid., p. 156.
232 **"as important in founding the nation"**: Ibid., p. 154.
232 **"lived in unconstraint"**: Ibid., p. 203.
233 **"unbeautiful, a scar on her face"**: Ibid., p. 200.
233 **"disrespect for the applause"**: Ibid.
233 **"a yeast in the sap"**: Ibid., p. 193.
233 **"sees the genius of the continent"**: D. H. Lawrence, "American Heroes," *The Nation* 122, no. 3171 (April 1926), p. 414.
234 **"the first great burst through"**: *IAG*, p. 216.
234 **"Either the New World"**: Ibid., p. 219.
234 **"With Poe, words were not"**: Ibid., p. 221.
234 **"*surrounded* by his time"**: Ibid., p. 226.
235 **"The language of his essays"**: Ibid., p. 224.
235 **"It is especially in the poetry"**: Ibid., p. 231.
236 **"with a great bearded face"**: Ibid., p. 234.
236 **"the brutalizing desolation of life"**: Ibid.

10. REVISITING THE SEDUCTIONS OF EUROPE

239 **"home of the wild gods"**: *VP*, p. 3.
240 **"the European virus was injected"**: *SL*, p. 59.
240 **"that release what there is"**: *VP*, p. 13.
240 **"the success story of a young physician"**: *A*, p. 191.
240 **"he knew no limits"**: Ibid.
241 **"Whisky . . . was to the imagination"**: Ibid., p. 194.
241 **"a big hole through the center"**: Ibid., p. 188.
241 **"'Pound writing an opera?'"**: Ibid.
241 **"It must infuriate Ezra"**: Ibid., p. 225.
242 **"unflinching kindness"**: Ibid., p. 193.
242 **"the senses were her meat"**: Ibid., p. 222.
242 **A minor poet, Monnier translated**: Mariani, *William Carlos Williams*, p. 222.
244 **"denied sin by making it hackneyed"**: *A*, p. 222.
245 **"this ripe center of everything"**: *SL*, p. 60.
245 **"the best thing a father"**: *A*, p. 207.
246 **"The monuments of Rome"**: *Rome*, p. 42.
246 **"There is escape"**: Ibid., p. 13.
246 **"other reckless Roman emperors"**: *VP*, p. 115.
246 **"Williams thought of Rome"**: Steven Ross Loevy, *William Carlos Williams's "A Dream of Love"* (Ann Arbor, Mich.: UMI Research Press, 1983), p. 5.
247 **"poor human rose windows"**: *Rome*, p. 23.
247 **"The sum of knowledge"**: Ibid., p. 52.
247 **"is the shallowest"**: *I*, p. 321.
247 **"Intelligence is a motion"**: *Rome*, p. 59.
247 **"clarity is movement"**: Ibid., p. 58.
247 **"Each piece of work"**: Mike Weaver, *William Carlos Williams: The American Background* (Cambridge, U.K.: University Press, 1971), p. 82.
248 **"Williams poured out his radical"**: Ibid., pp. 132–33.

251 **"medieval Place François Ier"**: A, p. 195.
251 **"It was intended as a gesture"**: Ibid., p. 217.
251 **"cupidity," "bitchery"**: Ibid., p. 215.
251 **"a rustic in my own eyes"**: Ibid., p. 216.
252 **"resistant core" . . . "with ardors not released"**: IAG, pp. 105–106.
252 **"about Picasso, his poor beginnings"**: A, p. 213.
253 **"subject to the grievous"**: Philippe Soupault, Last Nights of Paris, pp. 119–20.
254 **"Already the districts"**: Ibid., p. 114.
254 **"a very wonderful little whore"**: IWWP, pp. 47–48.
255 **"Ezra has always been"**: A, p. 228.
255 **"I went out and stood up"**: Ibid., p. 229.
256 **"Roy, the bootlegger"**: William Eric Williams, p. 63.
257 **"Either I must be a tragic ass"**: WCW to Pound, in SL, p. 66.
257 **"You are a foreigner"**: Pound to WCW, in Witemeyer, Pound/Williams, p. 76.
257 **"I need something else"**: WCW to Pound, in ibid., p. 73.
258 **"You talk [like] a crow"**: WCW to Pound, in ibid., p. 78.
259 **"the last and slash"**: SL, p. 86.
259 **"Part of my trouble"**: Ibid., p. 76.
260 **"I was really an unhappy, disappointed child"**: Ibid., p. 80.
260 **"the queen of the world"**: Ibid., p. 81.
260 **"that feeling went through me"**: Ibid.
260 **"I went direct to you"**: Ibid.
263 **"the unpredictable mixture"**: Whittemore, William Carlos Williams, p. 212.
264 **"It's amusing to hear about"**: Floss to WCW, January 25, 1928.
264 **"I am distant"**: Ibid.
264 **"But the desire was wholly lacking"**: Floss to WCW, February 27, 1928.
265 **"You just have to take a leap"**: Robert McAlmon, Post-Adolescence, p. 12.
268 **"I'm with you absolutely"**: Floss to WCW, May 7, 1928.
268 **"Strange, it seemed, that here"**: WCW, "A Knife in the Times," p. 17.
269 **"the whole colossal record"**: SL, pp. 60–61.
269 **"Paris would be wonderful"**: Ibid., p. 64.
270 **"this wonder of abandon"**: VP, p. 155.
271 **"Democracy, she shuddered"**: Ibid., p. 160.
271 **"fettered to crawling inanities"**: Ibid., p. 163.
271 **"I do not run from fineness"**: Ibid., p. 213.
271 **"Europe is poison to us Americans"**: Ibid., p. 240.
271 **"Down inside me"**: Ibid., p. 242.
271 **"How to find a way"**: Ibid., p. 250.
271 **"Art is a country by itself"**: Ibid., p. 251.
272 **"It is a world where"**: Ibid., p. 261.
272 **"It is that I may"**: Ibid., p. 262.
273 **"America seems less encumbered"**: Ibid.
273 **"America is a pathetic place"**: Ibid., p. 261.
273 **"It is a hard, barren life"**: Ibid., p. 263.
273 **"It is hard to know"**: Ibid., p. 265.
273 **"It is marvelous"**: Ibid., p. 267.
273 **"You are brave"**: Ibid.
273 **"He was a good first line doctor"**: Ibid., p. 5.

273 **"But he really loved the irregularity"**: Ibid., pp. 4–5.
274 **"It was in Rome, in fact"**: Ibid., pp. 108–109.
274 **"miraculous modern"**: Ibid., p. 113.
275 **"that sense of beauty"**: Ibid., p. 152.
275 **"to the pursuit of knowledge"**: Ibid., p. 155.
275 **"the sickening recollection"**: Ibid., p. 159.
275 **"nonchalantly took up a chisel"**: Ibid., p. 156.
275 **"that tall kindly man"**: Ibid., p. 157.
275 **"we save men"**: Ibid., p. 156.
275 **"the washed-out soul"**: Ibid., p. 159.
276 **"share the prevailing beliefs"**: Harry Levin, introduction to ibid., p. xiii.
276 **"remains his unaffected self"**: Ibid., p. xx.

II. CONFRONTING THE GREAT DEPRESSION

277 **"swamped"**: WCW to Louis Zukofsky, p. 62.
277 **"hellishly distraught"**: WCW to Zukofsky, p. 64.
277 **"humpbacked"**: WCW to Zukofsky, p. 124.
277 **"I have done nothing"**: WCW to Zukofsky, October 4, 1928.
278 **"there is, in a democracy"**: WCW, "The Somnambulists," p. 338.
278 **"I'm really a stick in the sides"**: WCW to Pound, p. 76.
278 **"Pity to waste work"**: WCW to Zukofsky, February 17, 1931, p. 80.
284 **"Re / private life"**: Pound to Zukofsky, p. 7.
284 **"Thanks. First cheering mss."**: Pound to Zukofsky, August 18, 1927, p. 3.
285 **"By 'human value'"**: WCW to Zukofsky, 1928, p. 93.
285 **"I like Louis"**: WCW to Pound, April 18, 1928, p. 65.
285 **"Poems are inventions richer"**: WCW to Zukofsky, July 5, 1928, in *SL*, p. 101.
286 **"He looks young men"**: *A Wild Perfection: The Selected Letters of James Wright*, ed. Anne Wright and Saundra Rose Maley (New York: Farrar, Straus & Giroux, 2005), pp. 231–32.
286 **"I feel so disgusted"**: WCW to Pound, August 11, 1928, p. 91.
286 **"Louis Z. has done"**: WCW to Pound, October 19, 1929, p. 96.
287 **"No matter how we may be ignored"**: *SL*, p. 96.
287 **"clear or vital particulars"**: WCW to Zukofsky, p. 13.
287 **"Perhaps by my picayune imagistic"**: *SL*, p. 33.
291 **"I'm next to hopeless"**: WCW to Zukofsky, p. 133.
291 **"What a monument of ashes"**: WCW to Zukofsky, p. 146.
292 **"many of the people and places"**: *A*, pp. 274–75.
293 **"are all about people I knew"**: *IWWP*, p. 49.
293 **"whose looks change the minute"**: WCW, "A Face of Stone," in *The Collected Stories of William Carlos Williams* (New York: New Directions, 1996), p. 167.
294 **"Ethel had begged her"**: WCW, "The Knife of the Time," in ibid., p. 6.
296 **"for relaxation, relief"**: WCW, *A Novelette and Other Prose, 1921–1931*, p. 289.
296 **"a tremendous leap ahead"**: *IWWP*, p. 49.
296 **"Doctrinaire formula-worship"**: Max Newburger, *A Novelette and Other Prose, Imaginations*, p. 279.
297 **"You, I, we"**: WCW, *Novelette*, p. 294.

297 **"Williams's concept of the actual"**: Webster Schott, introduction to ibid., in *I*, p. 271.

297 **"sharp restriction to essentials"**: WCW, *Something to Say: William Carlos Williams on Younger Poets*, ed. James E. B. Breslin (New York: New Directions, 1985), p. 57.

299 **"a rigorous music"**: George Oppen, "Statement on Poetics," in *Selected Prose, Daybooks, and Papers*, ed. Stephen Cope (Berkeley: University of California Press, 2007), p. 49.

299 **"Oppen's standard, his obsession"**: Eliot Weinberger, "Oppen Then," in *Oranges and Peanuts for Sale* (New York: New Directions, 2009), p. 5.

300 **"a lovely gesture"**: *IWWP*, p. 5.

12. NEW DIRECTIONS IN A TUMULTUOUS DECADE

309 **"As I approached his number"**: *A*, p. 172.

310 **"the most distinguished American painting"**: *SL*, p. 97.

310 **"Take the hint from the picture"**: Ibid., pp. 97–98.

313 **"describes the leaves of the cyclamen"**: Italo Calvino, *Six Memos for the Next Millennium* (Cambridge, Mass.: Harvard University Press, 1988), p. 75.

313 **"All doors were"**: Laughlin recalled, 9 *Ridge Road*, p. 6.

314 **"You mention, casually, that"**: Laughlin recalled, 9 *Ridge Road*, p. 5.

314 **"sitting before a severe jury"** and **"to float free"**: Laughlin recalled, 9 *Ridge Road*, p. 7.

315 **"You are the cornerstone"**: Laughlin to WCW, in Witemeyer, *Williams and Laughlin*, p. 13.

316 **"That's a funny thing"**: *WM*, p. 47.

316 **"They want to take things"**: Ibid.

320 **"democracy of feeling"**: *SL*, p. 157.

321 **"My opinion is that"**: Ibid., pp. 157–58.

322 **"whole school of modernist writing"**: Mariani, *William Carlos Williams*, p. 389.

323 **"The man is sunk"**: WCW to Laughlin, p. 49.

323 **"entrance to the secret gardens"**: *A*, pp. 288–89.

324 **"Who paid for having"**: *FD*, p. 114.

325 **"I read the lousy book"**: WCW, "The Dawn of Another Day," in *The Collected Stories of William Carlos Williams* (New York: New Directions, 1996), pp. 148–49.

325 **"X-Ray Realism"**: Emma Lou Walton, *Nation*, 1938.

14. THE POET IN A TIME OF WAR

343 **"walked eye-deep in hell"**: "Hugh Selwyn Mauberley," IV, *Selected Poems*, p. 64.

343 **"expense of spirit in a waste of shame"**: Shakespeare, Sonnet 129.

343 **"For an old bitch gone in the teeth"**: "Hugh Selwyn Mauberley," V, op. cit.

343 **"Your brutal"**: Letter from WCW to Pound, November 26, 1941, *Pound Williams*, p. 209.

345 **"that / seeing the clock stopped"**: "Poems 1938," *The Collected Poems*, vol. 1, p. 459.

345 **"too conventional, too academic"**: *IWWP*, p. 65.

345 **"didn't know how to divide"**: Ibid.

346 **"those poor souls"**: *Paterson*, Book 2, section 2, p. 62.
348 **"The small prisoner"**: *In the Money*, p. 156.
349 **"Self-interest is a great benefactor"**: Ibid., p. 174.
349 **"Washington is the toughest place"**: Ibid., p. 170.
349 **"What works is one man paying attention"**: Ibid., p. 180.
350 **"What do I want to be rich for?"**: Ibid., p. 195.
351 **"You say you'd like to see my book of poems"**: WCW to William Eric Williams, September 25, 1942, *Seleted Letters*, p. 202.
352 **"benefits to be gained"**: Ibid.
353 **"the lunatic of one idea"**: Wallace Stevens, "Esthétique du Mal."
355 **"deep seated resentment"**: *Partisan Review*, July–August, 1941.
357 **"Here y'are!"**: LZ to WCW, April 6, 1943, *The Correspondence of William Carlos Williams and Louis Zukofsky*, p. 326.
357 **"hard but salutary"**: WCW to LZ, April, 11, 1943, ibid., p. 328.
358 **"It was gathered"**: Ibid., p. 260.
358 **"the arts seek to escape from frustration"**; poetry is **"the driving forward of desire"**; **"Hamlet today, Caesar tomorrow"**; **"There is no poetry of distinction"**: Author's introduction to *The Wedge*, *The Collected Poems*, vol. 2, p. 53.
358 **"It isn't what he *says*"**; **"There's nothing sentimental"**; **"A poem is a small (or large) machine"**; **"When I say"**: Ibid., p. 54.
359 **"for it is in the intimate form"**: Ibid., p. 55.
359 **"is distinguished"**: Ibid., p. 54.
360 **"American culture"**: Letter from WCW to Horace Gregory, p. 227.
365 **"I have always been proud of this book"**: *IWWB*, p. 70.

15. THE MAGNIFICENT TORSO: *PATERSON*

368 **"the egotistical sublime"**: Keats to Richard Wodehouse, October 27, 1818, in *The Letters of John Keats, 1814–1821*, vol. 1, p. 387.
370 **"allegory was not"**: T. S. Eliot, "Dante," in *Selected Essays, 1917–1932*, p. 205.
370 **"desolation, stagnation"**: *Paterson* (New York: New Directions, 1995), p. 101.
371 **"No ideas but in things"**: *9 Ridge Road*, p. 24.
371 **"the river comes pouring"**: *P*, p. 7.
371 **"high decorum"**: Ibid., p. 27.
372 **"And then there's that magnum opus"**: *SL*, p. 163.
373 **"a figure of fun"**: WCW, "The Colored Girls of Passenack," in *The Collected Stories of William Carlos Williams* (New York: New Directions, 1996), p. 50.
373 **"built in the style"**: Quoted in Mariani, *William Carlos Williams*, p. 315.
374 **"I want to bring"**: WCW to Laughlin, p. 60.
374 **"to get at a mode"**: WCW to Laughlin, p. 64.
374 **"That God damned"**: WCW to Laughlin, p. 95.
374 **"But it's got to be born"**: WCW to Laughlin, p. 96.
375 **"what is sorely needed"**: WCW to Laughlin, p. 97.
375 **"Order . . . is a servant"**: *P*, p. 83.
377 **"unfaltering language"**: Ibid., p. 108.
377 **"Give up the shilly-"**: Ibid., p. 109.
377 **"Eternally asleep"**: Ibid., p. 6.
378 **"definite history associated"**: Ibid., p. xiii.

378 **"I wanted, if I was"**: Ibid.
378 **"large enough"**: Ibid.
378 **Although Paterson's past required**: Ibid.
381 **"to fully understand"**: Ibid., p. 88.
381 **"sheltered from life"**: Ibid., p. 87.
381 **"With you the book"**: Ibid., p. 28.
382 **"People who haven't experienced"**: *Words in Air: The Complete Correspondence Between Elizabeth Bishop and Robert Lowell*, ed. Thomas Travisano with Saskia Hamilton (New York: Farrar, Straus and Giroux, 2008), p. 38.
382 **"I think of their effectiveness"**: Hamilton, *Letters of Robert Lowell*, p. 102.
382 **"resorts to the antipoetic"**: *SL*, p. 265.
382 **"All the prose [in *Paterson*]"**: Ibid., p. 263.
383 **"the best poetry"**: *Words in Air*, p. 16.
383 **"a reader has to be"**: Randall Jarrell, *Poetry and the Age* (New York: Knopf, 1953), p. 28.
383 **"I look at what I have done"**: WCW to Babette Deutsch, May 31, 1948, p. 264.
383 **"I've just finished reading"**: Lowell to Gertrude Buckman, November 30, 1947, in Hamilton, *Letters of Robert Lowell*, p. 75.
383 **"to float free"**: Laughlin, *Remembering William Carlos Williams* (New York: New Directions, 1955), p. 19.
384 **"Without invention nothing"**: *P*, p. 50.
385 **"Minds beaten thin"**: Ibid., pp. 32, 51.
389 **"redeeming language"**: Ibid., p. 279.
392 **"envisions for himself"**: Ibid., p. 173.
392 **"negroes, gypsies"**: Ibid., p. 193.
392 **"This is the blast"**: Ibid., p. 202.
393 **"Had I had the nerve"**: *A*, p. 122.
393 **"see a smooth faced girl"**: *P*, p. 212.
393 **"keep your pecker up"**: Ibid., p. 231.
393 **"the eternal close"**: Ibid., p. 202.
394 **"the unkempt straggling"**: Ibid., p. 220.
395 **"We know nothing"**: Ibid., p. 236.
395 **"I would say that poetry"**: Ibid., p. 216.
395 **"the first two books"**: *Words in Air*, p. 40.
395 **"*Paterson* is Whitman's America"**: Quoted in Christopher MacGowan's appendix in the 1995 edition of *Paterson*, p. 320.

16. THE LION IN WINTER

397 **"The bums who sewed"**: WCW to Laughlin, December 28, 1946, in *SL*, pp. 130–31.
398 **"I'm afraid he never"**: WCW to Laughlin, March 6, 1947, p. 139.
398 **"challenged my abilities"**: *A*, p. 238.
398 **"like complex shells"**: WCW, "An Approach to the Poem," in *English Institute Essays, 1947* (New York: Columbia University Press, 1948), p. 55.
399 **"Everything has to be broken"**: Ibid., p. 75.
399 **"abandoning all the staid usages"**: Ibid., p. 68.
399 **"verse is measure"**: Ibid., p. 64.
399 **"nosing along"**: Ibid., p. 58.

399 **"opening new realms"**: Ibid., p. 57.
400 **"What I said about Eliot"**: WCW to Laughlin, January 18, 1948, pp. 148–49.
401 **"impressive in the ability"**: *SL*, p. 26.
402 **"What the devil"**: WCW to Russell, October 22, 1949, in *SL*, p. 275.
403 **"I must be thrilled!"**: WCW to Abbott, January 29, 1950, in *SL*, p. 279.
403 **"the proof of a poet"**: Walt Whitman, *Leaves of Grass* (1855; New York: Penguin Classics, 1955), p. 24.
403 **"a small hell"**: WCW to Henry Wells, April 12, 1950, in *SL*, p. 287.
404 **"ARE YOU DOING"**: Bartlett, *Rexroth and Laughlin*, p. 3.
404 **"The energy that burns"**: WCW to Laughlin, April 7, 1951, in *SL*, p. 202.
404 **"caught him by complete surprise"**: *SL*, p. 295.
405 **"disabled my right side"**: Ibid., p. 302.
405 **"history of my books"**: *A*, p. 203.
408 **"You talk about one thing"**: Letter from Kenneth Burke to WCW, June 9, 1948, *The Humane Particulars: The Collected Letters of William Carlos Williams and Kenneth Burke*, p. 137.
411 **"From the faces"**: WCW to Lowell, June 1951, *SL*, p. 302.
411 **"nervous instability . . . saps your marrow"**: WCW to McDowell, June 24, 1952, in *SL*, p. 314.
411 **"He was of considerable"**: Ibid.
412 **"hit him over the head"**: May 4, 1953.
412 **"Poet Laureate of the Tree Peonies"**: *A*, p. 326.
412 **"collect manuscripts"**: *A*, pp. 323–24.
412 **"I had never in my life"**: Ibid., p. 325.
413 **"have caught a glimpse"**: Ibid., p. 294.
413 **"Cure to a physician"**: Ibid., p. 292.
414 **"attempts at regimentation"**: *SL*, p. 157.
415 **"A big man, he rested"**: *A*, p. 163.
416 **"hated today's version of communism"**: *IWWP*, p. 78.
417 **"the chief apostle"**: Nicholson Baker, *Double Fold* (New York: Random House, 2001), p. 84.
417 **"Books are dingy"**: Ibid.
420 **"the disturbed mind"**: *A*, p. 335.
420 **"been stewing in my bones"**: WCW to Floss, February 26, 1953.
422 **she had not known**: Mariani, *William Carlos Williams*, pp. 661–62.
422 **"God how I've messed up"**: WCW to Floss, March 27, 1953.
422 **"You don't know how"**: WCW to Floss, May 13, 1953.
423 **"regardless of what has happened"**: WCW to Floss, March 16, 1953.
423 **"deliver your phone call"**: WCW to Floss, February 23, 1953.
423 **"I cannot read"**: WCW to TK, April 10, 1953.
423 **He was invited to read**: WCW to TK, February 25, 1953.
427 **"The past [isn't] so easily"**: P. D. James, *The Murder Room*, p. 263.
431 **"the cultured patter"**: Appendix C of *The Collected Poems of William Carlos Williams*, ed. Christopher MacGowan (New York: New Directions, 1991), p. 511.
432 **"As for my own elliptical approach"**: *Partisan Review*, p. 19.
436 **"I have poor hopes"**: *The Letters of Robert Duncan and Denise Levertov*, ed. Robert J. Bertholf and Albert Gelpi (Stanford, Calif.: Stanford University Press, 2004), p. 294.
436 **"Dea de de dead"**: "The Agony of Dr. Paterson," p. 32.

437 **"In Williams the death of language"**: Ibid., p. 32.
440 **"rapid figuration"**: Eric Blom, ed., *The New Everyman Dictionary of Music* (New York: Weidenfeld and Nicolson, 1991), p. 493.
444 **"his words reduced"**: Mariani, *William Carlos Williams*, p. 748.
449 **"He just can't say"**: *Letters of Duncan and Levertov*, p. 381.
449 **"I'm not sorry for myself"**: AS, pp. 456–57.
450 **"The City standing clear"**: *Letters of Duncan and Levertov*, p. 387.
450 **"When you're through with sex"**: *IWWP*, p. 22.
450 **"He put up a great fight"**: *Letters of Duncan and Levertov*, pp. 388–89.
451 **"If practiced by only one partner"**: Octavio Paz, *The Double Flame*, trans. Helen Lane (San Diego: Harcourt Brace, 1996), p. 144.

Bibliography

LETTERS AND INTERVIEWS

Ahearn, Barry, ed. *The Correspondence of William Carlos Williams and Louis Zukofsky*. Middletown, Conn.: Wesleyan University Press, 2003.

———. *Pound/Cummings: The Correspondence of Ezra Pound and E. E. Cummings*. Ann Arbor: University of Michigan Press, 1996.

———. *Pound/Zukofsky: Selected Letters of Ezra Pound and Louis Zukofsky*. New York: New Directions, 1987.

Bamberger, W. C., ed. *Selected Letters: Guy Davenport and James Laughlin*. New York: Norton, 2007.

Barth, R. L., ed. *The Selected Letters of Yvor Winters*. Athens: Swallow Press/Ohio University Press, 2000.

Bartlett, Lee, ed. *Kenneth Rexroth and James Laughlin: Selected Letters*. New York: Norton, 1991.

Carter, David, ed. *Allen Ginsberg: Spontaneous Mind: Selected Interviews, 1958–1996*. New York: HarperCollins, 2001.

Cooper, David D. *Thomas Merton and James Laughlin: Selected Letters*. New York: Norton, 1997.

East, James H., ed. *The Humane Particulars: The Collected Letters of William Carlos Williams and Kenneth Burke*. Columbia: University of South Carolina Press, 2003.

Gordon, David M., ed. *Ezra Pound and James Laughlin: Selected Letters*. New York: Norton, 1994.

Hamilton, Saskia, ed. *The Letters of Robert Lowell*. New York: Farrar, Straus and Giroux, 2005.

MacGowan, Christopher, ed. *The Letters of Denise Levertov and William Carlos Williams*. New York: New Directions, 1998.

Magid, Barry, and Hugh Witemeyer, eds. *William Carlos Williams and Charles Tomlinson: A Transatlantic Connection*. New York: Peter Lang, 1999.

Morgan, Bill, ed. *The Letters of Allen Ginsberg*. Philadelphia: Da Capo, 2008.

Nadel, Ira B., ed. *The Letters of Ezra Pound to Alice Corbin Henderson*. Austin: University of Texas Press, 1993.

O'Neil, Elizabeth Murrie, ed. *The Last Word: Letters Between Marcia Nardi and William Carlos Williams*. Iowa City: University of Iowa Press, 1994.

Pacernick, Gary, ed. *Talking Together: Letters of David Ignatow, 1946–1990*. Tuscaloosa: University of Alabama Press, 1992.

Paige, D. D., ed. *The Letters of Ezra Pound, 1907–1941*. New York: Harcourt, Brace & World, 1950.

Parisi, Joseph, and Stephen Young, eds. *Dear Editor: A History of Poetry in Letters: The First Fifty Years, 1912–1962*. New York: Norton, 2002.

Phillips, Robert, ed. *Delmore Schwartz and James Laughlin: Selected Letters*. New York: Norton, 1993.

Pound, Omar, and A. Walton Litz, eds. *Ezra Pound and Dorothy Shakespear: Their Letters, 1909–1914*. New York: New Directions, 1984.

Pound, Omar, and Robert Spoo, eds. *Ezra and Dorothy Pound: Letters in Captivity, 1945–1946*. New York: Oxford University Press, 1999.

Rollins, Hyder, ed. *The Letters* of John Keats, 1814–1821, Volume 1. Cambridge, Mass.: Harvard University Press, 1958.

Sutton, Walter, ed. *Pound, Thayer, Watson, and "The Dial": A Story in Letters*. Gainesville: University Press of Florida, 1994.

Witemeyer, Hugh, ed. *Pound/Williams: Selected Letters of Ezra Pound and William Carlos Williams*. New York: New Directions, 1996.

———. *William Carlos Williams and James Laughlin: Selected Letters*. New York: Norton, 1989.

BIOGRAPHIES

Baldwin, Neil. *To All Gentleness: William Carlos Williams, the Doctor-Poet*. New York: Atheneum, 1984.

Berry, Wendell. *The Poetry of William Carlos Williams of Rutherford*. Berkeley: Counterpoint, 2011.

Burke, Carolyn. *Becoming Modern: The Life of Mina Loy*. New York: Farrar, Straus and Giroux, 1996.

Gammell, Irene. *Baroness Elsa*. Cambridge, Mass.: MIT University Press, 2002.

Guest, Barbara. *Herself Defined: H.D. and Her World*. Tucson, Ariz.: Schaffner, 2003.

Koch, Vivienne. *William Carlos Williams*. Norfolk, Conn.: New Directions, 1950.

Mariani, Paul. *William Carlos Williams: A New World Naked*. New York: McGraw-Hill, 1981.

Scroggins, Mark. *The Poem of a Life: A Biography of Louis Zukofsky*. Emeryville, Calif.: Shoemaker & Hoard, 2007.

Whittemore, Reed. *William Carlos Williams: Poet from Jersey*. Boston: Houghton Mifflin, 1975.

MEMOIRS

Carruth, Hayden. *Beside the Shadblow Tree: A Memoir of James Laughlin*. Port Townsend, Wash.: Copper Canyon, 1999.

Epler, Barbara, and Daniel Javitch, eds. *James Laughlin: The Way It Wasn't*. New York: New Directions, 2006.

Laughlin, James. *Byways: A Memoir*. New York: New Directions, 2005.

———. *Remembering William Carlos Williams*. New York: New Directions, 1995.

McAlmon, Robert, and Kay Boyle. *Being Geniuses Together, 1920–1930*. Baltimore: Johns Hopkins University Press, 1984.

Ohannessian, Griselda Jackson. *Once as It Was: A Memoir*. New York: New Directions, 2007.

Sorrentino, Gilbert. *Something Said*. San Francisco: North Point, 1984.

CRITICAL WORKS

Ahearn, Barry. *William Carlos Williams and Alterity: The Early Poetry*. New York: Cambridge University Press, 1994.

Altieri, Charles. *Painterly Abstraction in Modernist American Poetry: The Contemporaneity of Modernism*. University Park: Pennsylvania State University Press, 1989.

Beach, Christopher. *ABC of Influence: Ezra Pound and the Remaking of American Poetic Tradition*. Berkeley: University of California Press, 1992.

The Beinecke Rare Book and Manuscript Library: A Guide to the Collections. New Haven, Conn.: Yale University Library, 1994.

Bremen, Brian A. *William Carlos Williams and the Diagnostics of Culture*. New York: Oxford University Press, 1993.

Bromwich, David. *Skeptical Music: Essays on Modern Poetry*. Chicago: University of Chicago Press, 2001.

Burt, Stephen. *The Forms of Youth: 20th-Century Poetry and Adolescence*. New York: Columbia University Press, 2007.

Conarroe, Joel. *William Carlos Williams' "Paterson": Language and Landscape*. Philadelphia: University of Pennsylvania Press, 1971.

Conrad, Bryce. *Refiguring America: A Study of William Carlos Williams' "In the American Grain."* Urbana: University of Illinois Press, 1990.

Copestake, Ian D., ed. *Rigor of Beauty: Essays in Commemoration of William Carlos Williams*. Bern: Peter Lang, 2004.

Costello, Bonnie. *Planets on Tables: Poetry, Still Life, and the Turning World*. Ithaca, N.Y.: Cornell University Press, 2008.

Cushman, Stephen. *William Carlos Williams and the Meanings of Measure*. Yale Studies in English 193. New Haven, Conn.: Yale University Press, 1985.

Davie, Donald. *Ezra Pound*. New York: Penguin, 1975.

———. *Ezra Pound: Poet as Sculptor*. New York: Oxford University Press, 1964.

Dewey, Anne Day. *Beyond Maximus: The Construction of Public Voice in Black Mountain Poetry*. Palo Alto, Calif.: Stanford University Press, 2007.

Diggory, Terence. *William Carlos Williams and the Ethics of Painting*. Princeton, N.J.: Princeton University Press, 1991.

Dijkstra, Bram. *Cubism, Stieglitz, and the Early Poetry of William Carlos Williams*. Princeton, N.J.: Princeton University Press, 1969.

Duffey, Bernard. *A Poetry of Presence: The Writing of William Carlos Williams*. Madison: University of Wisconsin Press, 1986.

Fisher-Wirth, Ann W. *William Carlos Williams and Autobiography: The Woods of His Own Nature*. University Park: Pennsylvania State University Press, 1989.

Giorcelli, Cristina, and Maria Anita Stefanelli, eds. *The Rhetoric of Love in the Collected Poems of William Carlos Williams*. Rome: Edizioni Associate, 1993.

Golston, Michael. *Rhythm and Race in Modernist Poetry and Science.* New York: Columbia University Press, 2008.

Halter, Peter. *The Revolution in the Visual Arts and the Poetry of William Carlos Williams.* New York: Cambridge University Press, 1994.

Karl, Frederick R., ed. *Biography and Source Studies, Vol. IV.* New York: AMS, 1998.

Kenner, Hugh. *A Homemade World: The American Modernist Writers.* New York: Knopf, 1975.

———. *The Pound Era.* Berkeley: University of California Press, 1971.

Kinnahan, Linda A. *Poetics of the Feminine: Authority and Literary Tradition in William Carlos Williams, Mina Loy, Denise Levertov, and Kathleen Fraser.* New York: Cambridge University Press, 1994.

Koehler, Stanley. *Countries of the Mind: The Poetry of William Carlos Williams.* Lewisburg, Penn.: Bucknell University Press, 1998.

Laughlin, James, ed. *New Directions 47: An International Anthology of Poetry and Prose.* New York: New Directions, 1983.

Leibowitz, Herbert. *Fabricating Lives.* New York: Knopf, 1989; New York: New Directions, 1991.

Lenhart, Gary, ed. *The Teachers and Writers Guide to William Carlos Williams.* New York: Teachers & Writers Collaborative, 1998.

Markos, Donald W. *Ideas in Things: The Poems of William Carlos Williams.* Cranbury, N.J.: Associated University Presses, 1994.

Marling, William. *William Carlos Williams and the Painters, 1909–1923.* Athens: Ohio University Press, 1982.

Marzán, Julio. *The Spanish American Roots of William Carlos Williams.* Austin: University of Texas Press, 1994.

Miller, J. Hillis, ed. *William Carlos Williams: A Collection of Critical Essays.* Englewood Cliffs, N.J.: Prentice-Hall, 1966.

Morris, Daniel. *The Writings of William Carlos Williams: Publicity for the Self.* Columbia: University of Missouri Press, 1995.

Morrow, Bradford, ed. *World Outside the Window: The Selected Essays of Kenneth Rexroth.* New York: New Directions, 1987.

Orvell, Miles. *The Real Thing: Imitation and Authenticity in American Culture, 1880–1940.* Chapel Hill: University of North Carolina Press, 1989.

Paul, Sherman. *Hewing to Experience: Essays and Reviews on Recent American Poetry and Poetics, Nature, and Culture.* Iowa City: University of Iowa Press, 1989.

———. *The Music of Survival: A Biography of a Poem by William Carlos Williams.* Urbana: University of Illinois Press, 1968.

Pound, Ezra. *Literary Essays of Ezra Pound.* Norfolk, Conn.: New Directions, 1935.

Qian, Zhaoming. *Orientalism and Modernism: The Legacy of China in Pound and Williams.* Durham, N.C.: Duke University Press, 1995.

Rapp, Carl. *William Carlos Williams and Romantic Idealism.* Hanover, N.H.: University Press of New England, 1984.

Riddel, Joseph N. *The Inverted Bell: Modernism and the Counterpoetics of William Carlos Williams.* Baton Rouge: Louisiana State University Press, 1991.

Sayre, Henry M. *The Object of Performance: The American Avant-Garde Since 1970.* Chicago: University of Chicago Press, 1989.

Schmidt, Peter. *William Carlos Williams, the Arts, and Literary Tradition.* Baton Rouge: Louisiana State University Press, 1988.

Simpson, Louis. *Three on the Tower: The Lives and Works of Ezra Pound, T. S. Eliot, and William Carlos Williams*. New York: William Morrow, 1975.

Terrell, Carroll F., ed. *William Carlos Williams: Man and Poet*. Orono, Maine: National Poetry Foundation, 1983.

Vendler, Helen, ed. *Voices and Visions: The Poet in America*. New York: Random House, 1987.

Weaver, Mike. *William Carlos Williams: The American Background*. Cambridge, Mass.: Cambridge University Press, 1971.

Zukofsky, Louis. *Prepositions: The Collected Critical Essays of Louis Zukofsky*. Exp. ed. Berkeley: University of California Press, 1967.

Special issue on William Carlos Williams, *The Massachusetts Review*, Volume 12, 1, 1971.

BOOKS ON MEDICINE

Campo, Rafael. *The Poetry of Healing: A Doctor's Education in Empathy, Identity, and Desire*. New York: Norton, 1997.

Carter, Albert Howard, III. *First Cut: A Season in the Human Anatomy Lab*. New York: Picador, 1997.

Cleaveland, Clif. *Sacred Space: Stories from a Life in Medicine*. Philadelphia: American College of Physicians, 1998.

Coles, Robert. *The Call of Service: A Witness to Idealism*. New York: Houghton Mifflin, 1993.

———. *The Mind's Fate: A Psychiatrist Looks at His Profession*. New York: Little, Brown, 1995.

———. *The Secular Mind*. Princeton, N.J.: Princeton University Press, 1999.

Crawford, T. Hugh. *Modernism, Medicine, and William Carlos Williams*. Oklahoma City: University of Oklahoma Press, 1993.

Davis, Robert Leigh. *Whitman and the Romance of Medicine*. Berkeley: University of California Press, 1997.

Flitter, Marc. *Judith's Pavilion: The Haunting Memories of a Neurosurgeon*. South Royalton, Vt.: Steerforth, 1997.

Gawande, Atul. *Complications: A Surgeon's Notes on an Imperfect Science*. New York: Picador, 2002.

Groopman, Jerome. *The Measure of Our Days: New Beginnings at Life's End*. New York: Viking, 1997.

Holub, Miroslav. *Shedding Life: Disease, Politics, and Other Human Conditions*. Minneapolis: Milkweed, 1997.

Konner, Melvin. *Medicine at the Crossroads: The Crisis in Health Care*. New York: Pantheon, 1993.

Lowenstein, Jerome. *The Midnight Meal and Other Essays About Doctors, Patients, and Medicine*. New Haven, Conn.: Yale University Press, 1997.

Loxterkamp, David. *A Measure of My Days: The Journal of a Country Doctor*. Hanover, N.H.: University Press of New England, 1997.

Ludmerer, Kenneth M. *Learning to Heal: The Development of American Medical Education*. New York: Basic Books, 1985.

Mullan, Fitzhugh. *Big Doctoring in America: Profiles in Primary Care*. Berkeley: University of California Press, 2002.

Osler, Sir William. *Osler's "A Way of Life" and Other Addresses, with Commentary and Annotations.* Durham, N.C.: Duke University Press, 2001.

Porter, Roy. *The Greatest Benefit to Mankind: A Medical History of Humanity.* New York: Norton, 1997.

Simmons, John Galbraith. *Doctors and Discoveries: Lives That Created Today's Medicine.* New York: Houghton Mifflin, 2002.

Starr, Paul. *The Social Transformation of American Medicine: The Rise of a Sovereign Profession and the Making of a Vast Industry.* New York: Basic Books, 1982.

POETRY

Doolittle, Hilda. *Collected Poems, 1912–1944.* New York: New Directions, 1983.

Oppen, George. *New Collected Poems.* New York: New Directions, 2008.

Pound, Ezra. *ABC of Reading.* New York: New Directions, 1960.

———. *The Cantos of Ezra Pound.* New York: New Directions, 1993.

———. *Selected Poems of Ezra Pound.* New York: New Directions, 1957.

Wright, C.D., ed., *Spring and All.* New York: New Directions, 2011.

Zukofsky, Louis. *Complete Short Poetry.* Baltimore: Johns Hopkins University Press, 1991.

Acknowledgments

This critical biography of William Carlos Williams grew out of several conversations with James Laughlin, the poet's loyal friend and publisher. I had written an affectionate essay about Williams's *Autobiography* in my book *Fabricating Lives*, which explored the relation of style to character and self-disclosure in American autobiographies, but because I concentrated mostly on autobiography as a genre, I wrote little about Williams's poems, which I had always liked with some reservations. James, who had read the chapter, invited me to his home in Norfolk, Connecticut, to look through his Williams archive, which was a treasure trove of letters, books, and manuscripts. After dinner we would sit and talk about Williams's character, both volatile and generous, and his contributions to American poetry. James had written a charming poem, "9 Ridge Road," about Williams, as well as several prose portraits, and was a rich source of anecdotes about Williams's love life, gift for friendship, and rivalries with other poets. James was not shy of hurling acerbic comments at the poets who failed for so long to appreciate Williams's unique artistry and integrity—a sentiment I shared.

During our talks he broached the possibility of my writing a biography of Williams that paid close attention to the poems and other major works of the prolific doctor poet. In thinking about undertaking a biography, I believed I was aware of all the pitfalls, detours, dead ends, and frustrations I would face in painting a convincing portrait of Williams, but not long into the project, I realized I had underestimated the immense task ahead of me. Williams, who lived to the ripe age of eighty, had produced a huge portfolio of work while simultaneously leading an eventful and taxing life as a doctor and coping with a domestic life that was, in some periods, filled with emotional conflict, not an island of serenity, as his poems make abundantly clear.

Convinced that Williams was a more complicated man and poet than the conventional view of him and his place in American letters put forth by many literary people, I decided that my biography would center on his development as a poet and the fascinating interplay of his life and multitudinous works. James Laughlin gave his blessing to this focus on Williams's poems as integral to grasping his quirky character and both his achievements and setbacks. As I began the project, I periodically did random tests of readers' familiarity with Williams's poems, and discovered that 85 percent identified him with "The Red Wheelbarrow" and "This Is Just to Say," both clever bagatelles, but hardly representative of the experimental and innovative poems Williams had composed during his long, distinguished career. Recently, the University of Iowa Press published an anthology of poems by poets inspired by Williams and his poetry. I was intrigued and dismayed by the number of times poets referred to these two heavily anthologized chestnuts. Why did "so much depend" on these accessible but minor works? Was it part of an unconscious effort to undermine Williams's credentials as a modernist verse master? Was it laziness or envy or superficial readings by those who make and break reputations in the poetry world? Perhaps some or all of these reasons came into play. Yet after living with the bounty of his output for seventeen years, I arrived at a different conclusion. In every period I discovered excellent poems I had overlooked in previous readings.

Anybody who wishes to take the measure of Williams's poems is indebted to the three magisterial collections of the poet's work edited and meticulously annotated by Christopher MacGowan: two volumes of *Collected Poems** and one of *Paterson*. The notes, also a major contribution, allow us to enter Williams's creative laboratory and watch as he strives to make a poem more coherent and expressive, deleting a word here, adding a stanza there, hesitating and then deciding on form or tone or rhythm. The secondary literature on Williams is large and growing. Much of it is valuable. *The William Carlos Williams Review*, for example, is a critical forum for lively discussions of just about everything having to do with Williams. But I want to single out two books for special mention: Mike

---

*Volume 1 was coedited with A. Walton Litz.

Weaver's pioneering study, *William Carlos Williams: The American Background*, is still the most reliable mapping of Williams's themes, sources, and personality; and Paul Mariani's 1981 biography, *William Carlos Williams: A New World Naked*, is an encyclopedia of fact and information I kept on my desk for frequent reference. I may not agree with Mariani's interpretations of Williams's motives and poetic practices, but I have learned a lot from them; they scattered clues I would pursue to confirm or modify my account of a relationship gone sour or of a poem's merit.

The tradition of acknowledging in a book the help of various people and institutions has been derided in some quarters as a tiresome formula. But it is not a perfunctory courtesy or stale ritual. I could not have written this book without the aid of the following: a Guggenheim Fellowship that launched my investigation of Williams's poems; a John D. and Rose H. Jackson Fellowship at the Beinecke Library, Yale University, which afforded me the chance to delve into the immensely important Williams and Pound collections deposited there; a fellowship at the Bellagio Rockefeller Center, where I wrote my chapter on Williams and the Baroness Elsa von Loringhoven, and a fellowship at the Dorothy and Lewis B. Cullman Center for Scholars and Writers, the New York Public Library, during which tenure I read many of the books Williams studied while researching *In the American Grain*. For all these awards, I wish to express my deep gratitude.

Several of the chapters of *"Something Urgent I Have to Say to You"* have appeared in various literary magazines, often in versions I have since substantially changed or lightly revised. I want to thank the following editors for their hospitality and their helpful suggestions for improving prose, pacing, and emphasis: Michael Schmidt of *PN Review* for "William Carlos Williams and Women" (March/April, May/June, July/August, 2003) and "Mistress and Wife: Poetry and Medicine in William Carlos Williams's Career" (January/February 2010); John Matthias of *Notre Dame Review* for "The Lion in Winter" (Winter/Spring 2008); René Steinke and Walter Cummins of *The Literary Review* for "Halfway to Hell": William Carlos Williams's *Kora in Hell* (August 2007), and the late Frederick Karl, editor of *Biography and Source Studies*, for "Strange Bedfellows: Poetry as Biographical Evidence" (1998).

I would like to thank the playwright Mark St. Germain, a Rutherford native, for letting me use the valuable interviews he conducted with people in the poet's hometown who were friends, patients, or acquaintances of Dr. Williams. Their voices and memories provided insights and atmosphere about the place that had informed and fortified Williams's faith in the power of the local to serve as the grounding of his poetry and stories. Andrea Haslanger did superb work as a researcher tracking down information, documents, and rumors in often elusive public records. I am grateful to Jeremy Axelrod, Hilary Dobel, Jeff Greggs, and Alyssa Varner, who trawled the Internet for information relevant to Williams's obsessions and poems, for bibliographical citations, and for tracking down quotations.

Williams's papers are archived in several college and university libraries. I wish to thank Patricia Willis and the staff of the Beinecke Library, Yale University, for their assistance, expertise, and courtesies; the late Robert Bertholf and Michael Basinski of the Lockwood Library, SUNY Buffalo, for furnishing photocopies of Williams's journal and drafts of poems; to David McKnight of Special Collections, the University of Pennsylvania, which houses Williams's voluminous correspondence with his brother, Edgar, and his parents; to the Columbia University Library Special Collections for furnishing the important correspondence of Williams and his wife, Floss; and to the librarians at Indiana University, the University of Maryland, and the University of Virginia for documents and manuscripts pertaining to Williams and his fellow writers. These archives fill out the portrait of Williams by letting us glimpse a friend's canny evaluation of his ambitions, faults, and empathy or an antagonist's shrewd or malicious denigration of those same traits.

Over the years researching this book, I invited many friends to my home for informal discussions of Williams's poems and stories around the dining room table. We analyzed each of the books of *Paterson*, the poems and prose of *Spring and All, Kora in Hell, Adam and Eve and the City, An Early Martyr, Yes, Mrs. Williams*, and *Autobiography*. These evenings offered spirited debates between Williams partisans and poet-critics who took a dim view of his language experiments. I would like to thank the following people who participated in these colloquies: Michael Collins, Ben Downing, Adam Dressler, Robin and Blair Flicker, Jeff Greggs, Susan Lasher, William Meyers, Jill Oddy, Sara Sams, Nahma Sandrow, Alyssa Varner, Susan Yankowitz, and David Yezzi. If I omitted any names, I apologize for my faulty memory. All contributed to my education.

My manuscript was read and vetted and improved, in part and as a whole, by several people. I want especially to thank Nahma Sandrow for her heroic work editing drafts of my chapters about Williams in the

1920s and my chapter on his dual careers as doctor and poet; David Groff for his nuanced suggestions of where to cut portions of my chapters on "Poetry as Biographical Evidence" and "Wife and Mistress," and Nancy Nicholas for her wise, stringent comments on an earlier draft, which encouraged me that I was on the right track and not harshly judgmental about Williams. My old, dear friend Nick Lyons's close reading of the entire manuscript was astute about the centrality of style in poetry analysis, the virtues of clarity, and the special pleasures belles lettres provides the reader. His enthusiasm for my book was tonic. Ben Downing, my friend and the coeditor of *Parnassus: Poetry in Review*, applied his exemplary laser-precise skills to trimming verbal fat and tightening arguments. He played devil's advocate about Williams's poems, forcing me to hone my explications more effectively. The book is the better for his surgeries, painful as they sometimes were. When I was fumbling for a title, my friend and fellow editor, Michael Schmidt, rode to the rescue, proposing *"Something Urgent I Have to Say to You,"* which I embraced immediately. Throughout the writing of the book, my agent, Gloria Loomis, of the Watkins-Loomis Agency, has been a staunch supporter, savvy reader, and reality instructor. My wife, Susan Yankowitz, endured the long gestation of my biography with a combination of loving reassurance, impatience, and sardonic wit, alternately prodding and inspiring me to push ahead, offering practical advice, at the macro level, about the book's organization and, at the micro level, about eliminating lame words and vague sentences and moving paragraphs that were blocking expository flow to a more functional place.

From the beginning of this project, when with trepidation I submitted my prospectus to him, to its finished form, I have been fortunate in having Jonathan Galassi, the publisher and president of Farrar, Straus and Giroux, as my editor and guide. A fine poet-translator himself, he shared with me his profound understanding of the crucial interplay of life and work that marks a poet's career and in particular that influenced Williams's struggles to fashion a style he could be proud of. Jonathan Galassi's trust in my skills as a biographer and fair-minded interpreter of Williams's works has been a constant source of stability. I would also like to thank Jesse Coleman, who has calmed a nervous author's worries, answered a barrage of questions about copyediting, photos, the jacket cover, permissions, and footnotes with kind forbearance, and steered the book through the press with extreme competence. Thanks also go to the production editor, Wah-Ming Chang, as well as to the book's copy editors, Jenna Dolan and Ingrid Sterner.

"Something Urgent I Have to Say to You" is dedicated with love to my son, Gabe, my daughter-in-law, Francesca, and my grandson, Julian— and to James Laughlin, who is the biography's godfather. My chief regret is that he is not around to read it.

Index